Discover Your Spouse's Gifts

Other books by Don and Katie Fortune

Discover Your God-Given Gifts
Discover Your Children's Gifts

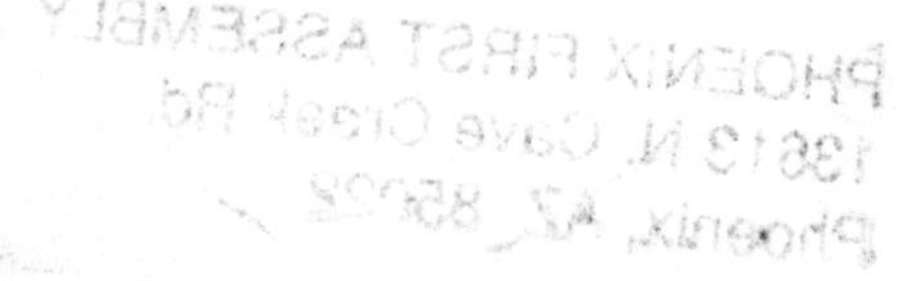

DISCOVER YOUR SPOUSE'S GIFTS

Don & Katie Fortune

Chosen Books
A Division of Baker Book House Co
Grand Rapids, Michigan 49516

Published by Chosen Books
a division of Baker Book House Company
P.O. Box 6287, Grand Rapids, MI 49516-6287

Printed in the United States of America

Library of Congress Cataloging-in-Publication Data

Fortune, Don.
Discover your spouse's gifts / Don and Katie Fortune.
p. cm.
ISBN 0-8007-9239-4 (pbk.)
1. Married people—Religious life. 2. Marriage—Religious aspects—Christianity. 3. Gifts, Spiritual. I. Fortune, Katie. II. Title.
BV4596.M3F675 1996
248.8'44—dc20 96-11815

Unless otherwise noted, Scripture quotations are from The Amplified Bible, Old Testament © 1965, 1987 by The Zondervan Corporation. Used by permission. New Testament © The Lockman Foundation 1954, 1958.

Scripture quotations identified NIV are from the HOLY BIBLE, NEW INTERNATIONAL VERSION®. NIV ©. Copyright © 1973, 1978, 1984 by International Bible Society. Used by permission of Zondervan Publishing House. All rights reserved.

Scripture quotations identified KJV are from the King James Version of the Bible.

Contents

Introduction 7

Part 1 The Gifts That Help Your Marriage Work

1 A Bird's-Eye View of the God-Given Gifts 11
2 Yes, Men and Women Are Different, But . . . 18
3 Test Yourself and Your Mate 25
4 Combination Gifts and Mates 39
5 Your Three-Part Nature and the Gifts 46
6 Introduction to the Seven Spouses 51

Part 2 Living with Another Gift

7 Living with a Perceiver Spouse 59
8 Living with a Server Spouse 96
9 Living with a Teacher Spouse 130
10 Living with an Exhorter Spouse 162
11 Living with a Giver Spouse 194
12 Living with an Administrator Spouse 224
13 Living with a Compassion Spouse 257

Part 3 How to Enrich Your Marriage

14 Dealing with Conflict 295
15 Surveying Your Own Situation 303
16 The ABCs of Christian Marriage 327

Appendix A: Thirteen-Week Study Guide 341
Appendix B: Additional Material Available 346

INTRODUCTION

Over the years we have read many books on marriage. Recently, in preparation for designing a survey to be the basis for this book on marriage, we read or looked at 26 additional books on marriage. We discovered one consistency: Almost every book focused on the differences between men and women as the reason for most difficulties between marriage partners.

We believe there is another major reason that has been overlooked.

While doing a significant amount of marriage counseling over the past 21 years, we have become increasingly aware that the majority of marital problems stem from the couple's lack of knowledge of one another's God-given gifts—the motivational gifts of Romans 12:6–8. We have seen major and minor marital conflicts resolved in a matter of minutes as we have helped couples discover the gifts that have shaped their motivations, interests, modes of operation and personalities. Often it is this discovery that sets a couple free to love and accept one another again, even in a deeper way than when they first fell in love.

It is this knowledge that we will share with you in this book. We believe it will enrich your marriage, help you resolve your conflicts (if you have some) and avoid conflicts in the future.

We wish every young couple planning for marriage knew about their gifts. It would prepare them much better for a life of happiness and equip them to handle differences and potential conflicts with adequate wisdom and understanding. We wish every married couple knew about their gifts. This knowledge is the most useful information we could give to each of them. It is the one consistent thing we give each couple we counsel, and to all the people we teach about the God-given gifts as we travel around the world in ministry. It is the gift we would like to give to you.

We have already written two books on the subject, *Discover Your God-Given Gifts* and *Discover Your Children's Gifts*. The first is about how adults can discover the gifts God has created within them and how they can use that giftedness in every aspect of their lives. The second gives four major age group tests to enable parents to determine their children's gifts; then it provides lots of information on training them up in their gifts. This book, the third in the series, is designed to help couples have even better marriages as well as insights into the problem areas that tend to develop due to differences and similarities of giftedness.

We hope you will have a great adventure as you *Discover Your Spouse's Gifts* and all that means for your relationship.

Don and Katie Fortune
Kingston, Washington

PART

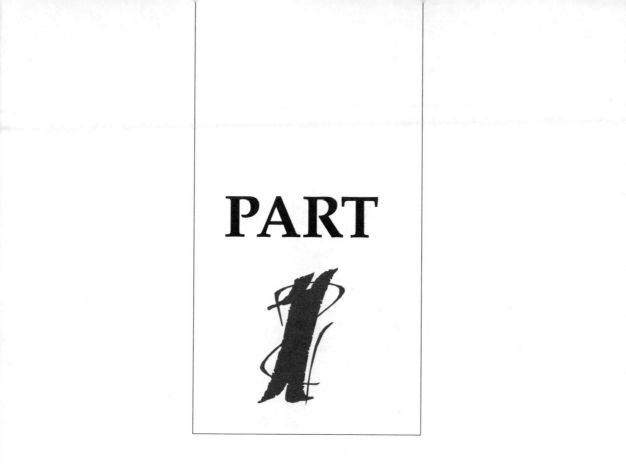

The Gifts That Help Your Marriage Work

A Bird's-Eye View of the God-Given Gifts

Perhaps you have already read our first book, *Discover Your God-Given Gifts*. If so, you probably already know your gifts and can proceed to chapter 2. If not, we recommend that book to you. You will also find the following information helpful.

The Three Categories of Gifts

First it is important to know that the New Testament contains three categories of gifts: the manifestation gifts, the ministry gifts and the motivational gifts. Each category is distinct and should not be mixed with the others as we try to discover our giftedness.

The Manifestation Gifts

The manifestation gifts are found in 1 Corinthians 12:

> To each one is given the manifestation of the (Holy) Spirit—that is, the evidence, the spiritual illumination of the Spirit—for good and profit. To one is given in and through the (Holy) Spirit [the power to speak] a message of wisdom, and to another [the power to express] a word of knowledge and understanding according to the same (Holy) Spirit; To another (wonder-working) faith by the same (Holy) Spirit, to another the extraordinary powers of healing by the one Spirit; To another the working of miracles, to another prophetic insight—that is, the gift of interpreting the divine will and purpose; to another the ability to discern and distinguish between [the utterances of true] spirits [and false ones], to another various kinds of [unknown] tongues, to another the ability to interpret [such] tongues.
>
> verses 7–10

These nine gifts are called manifestation gifts because Paul used the Greek word *phanerosis,* meaning "an exhibition, expression or manifestation." Paul defined these as supernatural manifestations of the Holy Spirit at work through a believer. They are truly spiritual gifts since they operate only through Christians and only by the initiation of the Holy Spirit. They are not gifts a person can "have," since they belong to the Holy Spirit, but a Christian can be like an available water pipe through which these gifts can flow to benefit others.

The Ministry Gifts

The second category of gifts is found in Ephesians 4:11. These five gifts are often called the ministry gifts:

> His gifts were [varied; He Himself appointed and gave men to us,] some to be apostles (special messengers), some prophets (inspired preachers and expounders), some evangelists (preachers of the Gospel, traveling missionaries), some pastors (shepherds of His flock) and teachers.
>
> Ephesians 4:11

The word for *gift* here is the Greek word *doma,* which means "a present or gift." The word *men* is neuter, which means that both men and women can be this kind of gift to the Body of Christ. The five ministry gifts might well be called equipping gifts since their purpose is to equip the saints (all believers) to do the work of ministry:

> To prepare God's people for works of service, so that the body of Christ may be built up until we all reach unity in the faith and in the knowledge of the Son of God and become mature, attaining to the whole measure of the fullness of Christ.
>
> verses 12–13, NIV

Only a small percentage of Christians are called by God to "become" these gifts that carry profound leadership responsibility. From what we have observed, this is less than five percent of all believers (and most of these are committed to full-time service).

The Motivational Gifts

The third category of gifts is found in Romans:

> Having gifts (faculties, talents, qualities) that differ according to the grace given us, let us use them: [He whose gift is] prophecy, [let him prophesy] according to the proportion of his faith; [He whose gift is] practical service, let him give himself to serving; he who teaches, to his teaching; (He who exhorts, encourages), to his exhortation; he who contributes, let him do it in simplicity and liberality; he who gives aid and superintends, with zeal and singleness of mind; he who does acts of mercy, with genuine cheerfulness and joyful eagerness.
>
> Romans 12:6–8

Charismata is the Greek word used here for *gifts,* the same word used (in the singular) in 1 Peter 4:10. Motivational gifts, we believe, are the category of gifts Peter was referring to (echoing the passage in Romans) when he said we were to employ them to benefit one another:

> As each of you has received a gift (particular spiritual talent, a gracious divine endowment), employ it for one another as [befits] good trustees of God's many-sided grace—faithful stewards of the extremely diverse [powers and gifts granted to Christians by] unmerited favor.
>
> 1 Peter 4:10

Charisma is defined in our Greek dictionary as "a divine gratuity . . . a spiritual endowment . . . a free gift." Just as each of us is endowed with certain looks, we are also endowed at our creation with gifting from God. We are commanded not to try to deserve it but to *use* it.

This is the list of gifts that is the focus of this book. These are the gifts we *possess*—

the gifts God has built into us, made part of us, to be used for the benefit of others and for His glory. Since they provide the motivating force for our lives, they have been called motivational gifts. These are the gifts that shape our personalities.

What Are the Motivational Gifts?

Because God has created us with free will, we can choose to use our motivational gifts appropriately, or neglect them, or even abuse them. Everyone in the world is so gifted by God. Thus we like to call them *God-given gifts*. We all tend to use our gifts. But when we give our lives to Jesus Christ, we usually see an enhancement of our gifts and find ourselves using our gifts more and more the way He wants us to.

Here are the seven key words that identify in this book the various recipients of these wonderful God-given gifts:

1. *Perceiver:* One who perceives the will of God clearly. We use this word rather than the word *prophet* to avoid confusion (although there are other subtle differences), since the same root word is used in the other two categories of gifts.
2. *Server:* One who loves to serve others or work with his or her hands; a "doer."
3. *Teacher:* One who loves to discover and communicate truth; an intensive researcher.
4. *Exhorter:* One who loves to encourage others to live a victorious life; an extremely positive person.
5. *Giver:* One who loves to give time, talent, energy and means to benefit others and advance the Gospel.
6. *Administrator:* One who loves to organize, lead, delegate or direct; a natural facilitator.
7. *Compassion person:* One who shows compassion, love, mercy and care—to those who are hurting or in need, or to anyone.

Classic Gift or Combination Gifts?

Everyone has one or more motivational gifts. No one has been left out, as we have seen in 1 Peter 4:10 and Romans 12:6.

Don and I find, after teaching this subject for 21 years in thirty nations, that about one-third of all people have one strong and distinct motivational gift. We call these *classic gifts*. They are easily identified and reflect most of the characteristics of their gift. Our daughter, Linda, is an example. She is a classic compassion gift—loving, caring, tender toward animals (she has seven cats), careful of others' feelings and not fond of rigid schedules.

About two-thirds of all people are what we call *combination gifts*. While they still have a primary gift, they have one or two other gifts significant enough to affect the operation of the primary gift. Sometimes the secondary gift enhances the operation of the other gift; sometimes it modifies it.

Both our sons are combination gifts. Our older son, Dave, is an administrator gift with a strong secondary teacher gift. He has always migrated to leadership in school, job and among his friends. His teacher gift has enabled him to be a top student, seeking truth and enjoying being alone with a good book as much as being with his friends.

Dan, two years younger, is a perceiver/compassion combination. We see many modifying factors in his gifting. He is strong in his beliefs and normally not a compromiser. Yet in some situations his compassion viewpoint enables him to bend in consideration for another person's feelings. Dan is a person of strong convictions who will hit you over the head with a feather duster rather than a baseball bat!

Both his gifts lead him to be a dedicated intercessor.

God Gives Us Gifts at Conception

Isn't it interesting that there are *seven* motivational gifts? Seven is, biblically speaking, the perfect number. It is complete. Whole. A total picture of the human race in regard to gifting.

After teaching about the motivational gifts to tens of thousands of people, we can candidly say that we have never found an eighth gift. Nor has anyone ever said that he or she did not fit at least one of the seven gifts. Many have told us that, looking back on their childhood, they now recognize they were operating in their giftedness long before they even knew God had gifted them.

The Old Testament psalmist recognized God's part in designing each human life:

> You did form my inward parts, You did knit me together in my mother's womb.... Your eyes saw my unformed substance, and in Your book all the days of my life were written, before ever they took shape, when as yet there was none of them.
>
> Psalm 139:13, 16

When a child is conceived, half his DNA inheritance comes from his father and half from his mother. And in that microscopic fertilized egg, the joined DNA forms a helix-shaped genetic ladder more than six feet long, yet marvelously compacted within that tiny egg. How incredible! Everything physical about you is programmed by your DNA—your height, body frame, the shape of your nose, the color of your skin, hair and eyes, and on and on.

It stands to reason that our giftedness is determined at conception, too. Indeed, Don and I have found that sets of identical twins coming to our seminars (who share the same DNA, thus their identical appearance) test out consistently with identical gifting, including the same secondary gifting. Even identical twins separated at birth and raised in different environments are found to have identical gifts.

Our Gifting Can Be Observed in Childhood

We asked a thousand people who took our motivational gift seminar to look back over their childhood and describe their characteristics in twenty different areas. Out of this grew our second book, *Discover Your Children's Gifts*. It is designed to help parents discover their children's gifts and encourage the development of these gifts. Those who work with children or youth also benefit by discovering the giftedness of those they teach or lead. (We developed tests for preschoolers, primaries, juniors and youth. These are listed under the "Additional Materials Available" section in the back of this book.)

In Proverbs the original Hebrew brought out by *The Amplified Bible* gives additional insight to a familiar passage:

> Train up a child in the way he should go [and in keeping with his individual gift or bent], and when he is old he will not depart from it.
>
> Proverbs 22:6

From this we may infer that a child's gifting can be identified and encouraged by the parents, who have the responsibility and privilege to discover each child's gifts and "train him up" in them so that when he comes of age, he will use that giftedness to the glory of God and for his own fulfillment.

Each Gift Is of Equal Value

The following diagram reflects our view that every gift is of equal value in the sight of God and of equal value in the Body of

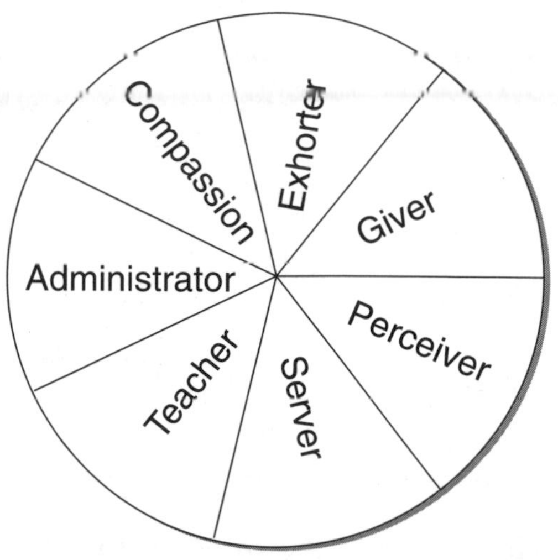

Christ. No gift is better than another gift. Whatever your gifting, it is the best God could have given you for the working out of His purposes in your life and for the benefit of the others whose lives you touch.

We do find that God bestows some of the gifts more frequently than others, but that is because more people are needed in certain functions. From the data we have compiled, here is the percentage of people with each gift:

Perceiver 12%
Server 17%
Teacher 6%
Exhorter 16%
Giver 6%
Administrator 13%
Compassion person 30%

What Do the Motivational Gifts Do?

Just as your sunglasses color everything you see, so your giftedness colors your perception of everything in life. It motivates your likes and dislikes, unfolds your learning style, guides you into specific careers and guides the development of your whole personality.

Each Gift Tends to Meet Specific Needs

The table below is a brief overview of the seven motivational gifts giving a short def-

Gift	Definition	Needs Met	What It Does
Perceiver	Declares the will of God	Spiritual	Keeps us centered on spiritual principles
Server	Renders practical service	Practical	Keeps the work of ministry moving
Teacher	Researches and teaches the Bible	Mental	Keeps us studying and learning
Exhorter	Encourages personal progress	Psychological	Keeps us applying spiritual truths
Giver	Shares material assistance	Material	Keeps specific needs provided for
Administrator	Gives leadership and direction	Functional	Keeps us organized and increases our vision
Compassion Person	Provides personal and emotional support	Emotional	Keeps us in right attitudes and relationships

inition of each, the primary needs that tend to be met and the basic function of each gift. There is, of course, the possibility of overlap and interaction, and secondary gifts will color or modify the operation of a primary gift.

The Gifts Fit into the Body

In beginning to describe the motivational gifts, Paul uses the graphic example of the human body:

> For as in one physical body we have many parts (organs, members) and all of these parts do not have the same function or use, So we, numerous as we are, are one body in Christ, the Messiah, and individually we are parts one of another—mutually dependent on one another.
>
> Romans 12:4–5

It is not happenstance that Paul uses the body example here. He is indicating that

1. the Body of Christ is made up of seven "types" and that it is O.K. to be different;
2. as we each do our part, together we get the job done;
3. we are mutually dependent on one another; no one can be a spiritual Lone Ranger.

It is easy to figure out how each gift represents part of the Body of Christ, as we have indicated in the diagram in the next column.

The *perceiver* is the eye of the Body. Perceivers have special responsibility to keep a clear and sound eye with which to detect God's truth. They are exceptionally insightful.

The *server* is the hands of the Body. Servers have great dexterity and are able to build or fix just about anything.

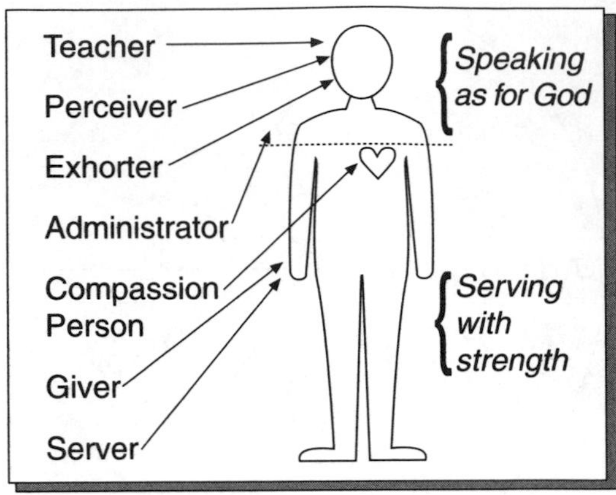

The *teacher* is the mind of the Body. Teachers are gifted with intelligence and will search until the facts convince them that something is true.

The *exhorter* is the mouth of the Body. Their facility of speech enables them to give much encouragement.

The *giver* is the arms of the Body. Givers are great support people, extending the reach of every Christian endeavor.

The *administrator* is the shoulders of the Body. Administrators often carry the load of leadership and shoulder responsibility.

The *compassion person* is the heart of the Body. Compassion people are ruled by the heart rather than the head, showing kindness, care, love and mercy to others.

Peter's statement about the motivational gifts that echoes Romans 12:6 is followed by his identification of two major categories within the seven gifts:

> Whoever speaks, [let him do it as one who utters] oracles of God; whoever renders service, [let him do it] as with the strength which God furnishes abundantly; so that in all things God may be glorified through Jesus Christ, the Messiah.
>
> 1 Peter 4:11

It is easy to see that the four gifts that appear above the dotted line are speaking gifts. The teacher must speak in order to teach. The perceiver must speak in order to proclaim God's will. The exhorter, being the mouth of the Body, obviously has a speaking gift. And the administrator must have good facility of speech in order to lead effectively.

The three gifts that appear below the dotted line are the serving gifts. Compassion people prefer to work behind the scenes serving others through the abundance of love God has given them. The giver is a supportive gift that shuns the limelight, serving in the background. And obviously the server excels in this area.

Peter is urging those with speaking gifts to make sure that what comes out of their mouths is what God wants said. Those with serving gifts are promised that God will give them an abundance of strength and energy for the work they are to do. Peter sums it up by emphasizing that no matter which category our gifts fall into, all must be done so that God is glorified.

We Can Minister in All Areas

Although it is important to define the seven gifts and discover the predominant characteristics that accompany them, it is also necessary to know that we can all operate in all areas to some degree. Each of us is endowed with enough of each gift to be able to function in that area when called on.

There is a difference between *being* (your God-given gifts make you what you are) and *doing* (your service to your mate, family and others). Yet the way you operate in any area is affected by your primary gift. Also, remember that God's grace is sufficient for any circumstance. He will anoint us for any task He calls us to do, and that anointing supersedes our gifting.

Many Scriptures indicate that to some degree we are to function in all seven areas reflected by the seven motivational gifts. We are all to perceive God's will in various situations. We are all to serve the Lord and other people. We are all to teach others in appropriate ways. We are all to exhort, admonish and encourage others. We are all to give of our resources and energies to God and to others. We are all to lead as we are called and enabled to do so. We are all to show love, compassion and mercy. But we will each do these things *from the perspective of our particular gifting.*

Now let's focus on the marriage relationship.

Yes, Men and Women Are Different, But . . .

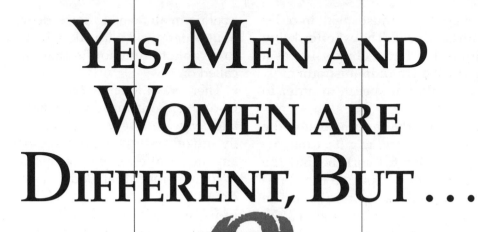

> God created man in His own image, in the image and likeness of God He created him; male and female He created them.
>
> Genesis 1:27

Creating two sexes was God's idea, part of His plan to propagate the earth. It was also His plan to create the special relationship called marriage between man and woman. When God gave Eve to Adam, his response—an interpretative translation of Genesis 2:23 but implied in the original Hebrew—was, "Wow, this is it!"

Then the writer of Genesis proclaims:

> Therefore a man shall leave his father and his mother and shall become united and cleave to his wife, and they shall become one flesh.
>
> Genesis 2:24

Three important aspects of the institution of marriage are given here: leaving, cleaving and intimacy.

Leaving

First of all a man (a woman, too) is to leave the protection and provision of family and set up a new family unit.

While husband and wife come from the culture and experience of a family, together they are to create a new family unit no longer dependent on the previous one. They can continue to benefit from the previous one, but the Genesis mandate implies that the new roles of husband and wife are to supersede the previous roles of son and daughter.

The danger in this step is to assume that the leaving is only physical, and to allow control to continue from either of the previous family units. Problems can develop to the extent that the now-married children allow their mothers or fathers to try to control or unduly influence them. The new couple needs to be free to try their own wings, make their own mistakes and develop a new culture uniquely theirs.

Sometimes a couple needs to address the interference issue firmly. It is usually best if the husband can talk frankly with his parents and the daughter with her parents. (Or they can take a stand together.)

Cleaving

The second important aspect of the institution of marriage is the cleaving of the husband and wife to each other in a new and wonderful way—spiritually, mentally, emotionally and physically.

Spiritually

The husband is to be the spiritual head of the new home unit, an inspiration to his wife in spiritual growth.

From the beginning of our marriage Don has assumed this role. He sets the example for devotional study of the Bible. He starts the day with a predetermined plan, reading five chapters in the Old and New Testaments, a chapter from Proverbs and five psalms. Even when his employment required getting up at six in the morning, he still arose early enough to allow time for devotions.

Don likes to encourage husbands with this admonition: "As a husband you should see that your wife is in the best position she can be in her relationship to the Lord. This could take some sacrifice but it's your responsibility."

Family Times

As our children were growing up, Don set two special times for family devotions. One was immediately after dinner. He read a passage from the Bible (a length suitable to the attention span of the children). We discussed it with them, endeavoring to make it relevant to their lives. Then we worked on a memory verse from the selection, prayed and often sang a song or two. While the time frame was usually about fifteen minutes, I was amazed at how often the children wanted to go longer. It was a fun time and Don made it important, something to look forward to each day.

The second devotional time was "family night" when our boys were growing up—usually Friday night. We allowed almost nothing to take precedence over it except a wedding or important church event. Later, when the boys got involved in sports with some Friday night games, we moved our family night to Thursday or Saturday. Family night lasted from dinner to bedtime. The boys took turns on alternate weeks choosing the dinner menu (within reason!), and after dinner we followed the regular evening devotional time, usually expanded. Then Don read from a Christian book, played a Christian video or led in a discussion of interest to them. The evening was topped off by games (selected by the boy who did not choose the menu) and lots of hugs and affirmations.

The Importance of Prayer

Daily prayer was another part of Don's spiritual leadership—from our first date. As he was driving me home that night he asked matter-of-factly, "May I come in and pray with you?"

Is this guy for real? I wondered. *Is it a ploy or really what he wants to do?*

He came in, sat down, prayed a beautiful prayer of thanksgiving for the nice evening we had had and asked God's blessing on our relationship. Then he said, "Good night," slipped out the door and drove away. I was amazed—and delighted. I had never had a date who did that before. On subsequent dates Don never failed to end the evening with prayer. With this and other evidences of God's leading us together, I could accept his proposal of marriage confidently when it came just two weeks later!

During 34 years of marriage Don has continued to lead us in prayer at the close of each day. I have never had to take the initiative. Even if we are in different locations, he calls and prays with me.

Spiritual Protection

The husband's spiritual headship is also for protection for his wife and children. Whether we are aware of it or not, we are in a spiritual battle. The forces of Satan are looking constantly for opportunities to harass, attack or destroy individuals, marriages and families. The weapons of our warfare are not natural ones but spiritual ones that pull down strongholds and produce victory.

Each morning Don takes spiritual authority, declaring the blood of Jesus over us and our home and property. (When in another location he includes that, too.) He does spiritual warfare for our safety in travel, work, ministry and many other situations. We are aware of many times when trouble and even tragedy have been averted because of Don's prayer coverage.

A woman can take spiritual leadership if she has no husband, or if her husband is unwilling or unable. But there is something special when the husband senses God's nudging to take the lead.

Mentally and Emotionally

Men and women can be very different mentally and emotionally. Most traditional Christian teaching focuses on the man's objectivity and intellect and the woman's subjectivity and emotions. Most books about marriage, in fact, present these male-female differences as the major consideration for understanding how to repair strained or broken relationships.

In general these differences may be valid. They are certainly factors that need to be taken into consideration. But they do not explain why some couples just do not fit the stereotypes. Like the popular song of the '50s:

> Love and marriage, love and marriage,
> go together like a horse and carriage.
> This I tell you, brother,
> you can't have one without the other.

Some factors cannot really be separated. While a man's desire for sexual fulfillment may be stronger than a woman's, and a woman's need for affection going beyond sexual contact may be more crucial for her, both are needed by each partner if the love relationship is to remain healthy. A compassion-gifted wife may actually need *more* sexual contact than her teacher-gifted husband.

The need for meaningful conversation is usually thought of on the female side, yet the ability to communicate effectively is essential to all marriages.

As far as the traditional male expectation that "a woman's place is in the home," server and compassion women fit that scenario more easily, often content to build their lives around home and children. But others, especially administrator wives, need a challenge outside the home—a job, ministry or volunteer task that engages their pioneering spirit.

As far as the traditional female expectation that "the man brings home the bacon," many couples in today's high-cost-of-living society expect the wife to assist in the financial responsibility. We find that the giver wife excels in business so easily that it would be foolish not to let her at least develop a business on the side. She has the highest probability of success. Her compassion husband, on the other hand, may be less successful in the business world and may typically earn less money.

Surveys on marriage that focus only on husband-wife differences usually fall short of explaining all the exceptions to the generializations. No one model fits all men or women. In fact, there are *seven* models for each, based on the seven motivational gifts. We are excited about how the awareness of these models gives a couple insight into their uniqueness and how they can build their relationship into a partnership that really works, whether they fit traditional stereotypes or not.

Scriptural Differences

Scripture points out a major difference between the sexes:

> Let each man of you (without exception) love his wife as [being in a sense] his very own self; and let the wife see that she respects and reverences her husband—that she notices him, regards him, honors him, prefers him, venerates and esteems him; and that she defers to him, praises him, and loves and admires him exceedingly.
>
> Ephesians 5:33

At first glance it looks as though the wife has much more to do than her husband. But Paul points out that a husband should love his wife in every way as he loves himself—a tall order! It implies communicating his love to her in words, thoughtfulness, body language, tenderness, self-sacrifice, preferential treatment and every other action. A wife's security rests in *feeling* loved by her husband. She can put up with almost anything—bad habits, lack of success, financial reverses, even stupidity—if she knows he loves her with his whole heart.

Paul spells out the nourishing effect of love as he directs husbands to love with the depth that Christ loves His bride, the Church:

> Husbands should love their wives as [being in a sense] their own bodies. He who loves his own wife loves himself. For no man ever hated his own flesh, but nourishes and carefully protects and cherishes it, as Christ does the church.
>
> Ephesians 5:28–29

A woman's basic need is *love*. She is a responder to love and blossoms in the midst of it. She is able to love more fully in return if she feels loved. A book by H. Page Williams entitled *Do Yourself a Favor: Love Your Wife* reflects Paul's admonition, showing that the more a man demonstrates his love to his wife, the more he will receive love and respect from her.

A man's basic need is not love but *respect*. If a husband cannot identify that his wife is looking up to him, he is at a loss and may worry that his marriage is insecure. Notice how many ways Ephesians 5:33 in *The Amplified Bible* expresses that respect; love is just one of the ways.

Before my wedding day my mother told me, "Katie, if you're willing to give in to Don what feels like ninety percent of the time, and he feels he's giving in to you ninety percent of the time, you'll have a good fifty-fifty marriage." We have experienced a lot of that and are still learning how to "be subject to one another out of reverence for Christ, the Messiah, the Anointed One" (Ephesians 5:21).

But when two are joined as one, the buck has to stop somewhere. Don has often said to me, "I can handle anything else in life—at work, with other people, with the kids—if I know I have your love and respect." The apostle Paul indicates that as Christ is the head of the Church, so the husband is the head of the wife. Part of the respect a wife can give her husband is to honor him as her head—not being his slave, but honoring his position of responsibility for their well-being as they both serve the Lord:

> Wives, be subject—be submissive and adapt yourselves—to your own husbands as [a service] to the Lord. For the

> husband is head of the wife as Christ is the Head of the church, Himself the Savior of [His] body. As the church is subject to Christ, so let wives also be subject in everything to their husbands.
>
> Ephesians 5:22–24

Although this passage has been used by dominating husbands (and churches) to insist that wives become doormats willing to be manipulated and controlled, this was not Paul's intent. He respected women and welcomed their ministry. He was painting a picture of the godly, submissive wife who looks up to her husband for kind and protective leadership. Such an attitude releases a woman to trust God to work through her husband—which, in turn, enables him to feel respected and not only love and care for his wife more, but take the responsibility that produces godly character in him.

In marriage counseling we often give Ephesians 5:33 as an assignment to study and ponder and put into practice. It brings good results. It amazes us how many couples have never identified this foundational difference.

The two basic needs of wife and husband are like a spiral going either up or down.

The more a husband loves his wife, the more she can respect him. The less a husband loves his wife, the less she is able to respect him. A man can build or tear down his marriage depending on his willingness to demonstrate love. It is not enough for a man to *feel* love for his wife; *it must be put into practice in ways that communicate to her*. She needs to hear it and see it in specific actions. The oft-repeated reply "Of course I love you; I married you, didn't I?" is not adequate.

The more the wife respects her husband, the more he is able to love her. The less a wife respects her husband, the less able he is to demonstrate his love to her. I told one woman who had been biting and devouring her husband verbally, "It's hard for a man to snuggle up to a porcupine." She got the picture and put a guard on her mouth, beginning to focus on things she could respect about him. As she began to share with him how much those positive things meant to her, the things she had not been able to respect began to change.

Either mate can become the positive or negative force moving the relationship closer together or further apart.

Statistical Differences

Other general differences in men and women can be observed. Usually women talk more than men. (Some statistics suggest that women talk *twice* as much!) Even studies of children indicate that little girls carry on intimate, extensive conversations while little boys run around making airplane and truck noises. But when you look at an individual boy or girl, apart from the statistics, you find boys who talk incessantly and girls who are shy and often speechless. Why is this?

Don and I think it has to do with one's gifting from God.

Researchers have discovered the marvelous differences of the left and right hemispheres of the brain. Analytical and reasoning functions tend to originate on the left side, while the artistic and creative functions tend to emerge from the right side. In general we can say that men tend to operate more from the left brain and women from the right. But again, when we examine individual lives, these tendencies do not always hold up. An individual woman can be highly intellectual and rational, with little evidence of creativity, while an individual man can demonstrate great depth of feeling and artistic ability without much interest in the characteristics normally assigned to the male of the species. Why is this?

Don and I think it has to do with one's gifting from God.

We have not seen any books on marriage that focus on the motivational gifts, helping couples understand and accept one another with the characteristics and qualities their gifting produces. This is why the God-given gifting is the theme of *this* book on marriage. We believe it will uniquely help couples to understand themselves and each other, to see why challenges or difficulties have arisen in their relationship and to discover how to build a relationship that can fulfill personal desires as well as God's plan for the marriage. (Section 2 will develop this subject thoroughly.)

Physically

Obviously men and women are different physically. Women's bodies were designed by the Creator to (among other things) procreate, while not one man has been able to take his turn bearing children. Women are created to be nurturers and keepers of the home. For many women this is their greatest fulfillment. Others need a career or ministry outside the home to feel good about themselves. Why is this?

Don and I believe it has to do with a woman's motivational gifts.

Men's bodies equip them for heavier labor (though many women insist that men would never be able to cope with birthing labor), and traditionally they have been the breadwinners. Men are generally thought to be stronger and more muscular than women. Yet individual women athletes can outshine their masculine counterparts who prefer a sedentary office job. Why is this?

Don and I believe it has to do with the God-given gifts that shape a man's interests and abilities.

Intimacy

Sex was God's idea. He created the "one flesh" concept. So the third important aspect of the institution of marriage is sexual intimacy between husband and wife:

> Therefore a man shall leave his father and his mother and shall become united and cleave to his wife, and they shall become one flesh. And the man and his wife were both naked, and were not embarrassed or ashamed in each other's presence.
>
> Genesis 2:24–25

Sexual differences were designed to attract men and women—but not indiscriminately. Marriage was also God's idea. Such a committed union was to become the safe, secure environment within which children could be brought into the world and nurtured, making the family the basic unit of society.

While the propagation of the human race is dependent on sex, that is not its only purpose. It is also to produce pleasure in the most intimate of all relationships—a pleasure without shame, an intimacy shared with no one else. Biblically it is to *know* one another.

Equally important to sexual intimacy is the development of personal intimacy as the husband and wife open up thoughts, ideas, opinions and dreams so completely that love and trust can grow to the deepest level. They can become so one with each other that nothing can split the relationship.

Yet in practice today marriages are breaking up at the most alarming rate in history. Does this have to be so? We do not believe it does. While many divorces reflect the dysfunctional consequences of the fractured homes and culture out of which husband and wife have come, the majority of husbands and wives are unaware that each has a God-given giftedness. That giftedness can explain why problems have arisen in their relationship. It can be the ingredient that brings new understanding to them and binds them together in the pursuit of God's plan for their lives and families.

Yes, men and women are different, but their individual God-given gifting helps husbands and wives understand one another more than anything else can. As you discover your gifts and your spouse's gifts, you can begin to build a better marriage than you ever dreamed possible. We know, because it has happened to us!

Test Yourself and Your Mate

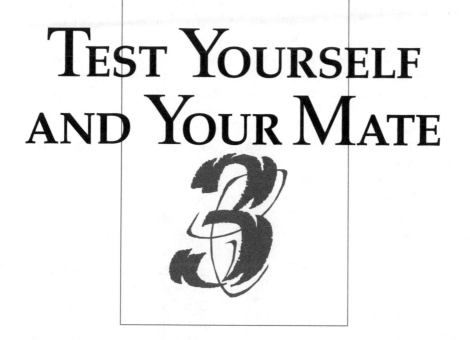

Now it is time to test yourself and your mate. The good news is that this is a test you cannot fail. It is a subjective self-discovery process, as accurate as you are honest and an adventure that will bring positive insights to both of you.

For each of the seven motivational gifts, we have developed a list of twenty characteristics typical of that person's personality and approach to life. They are based on five ingredients:

1. Biblical examples of each gift
2. Some of the initial suggestions of character traits presented by teachers Bill Gothard and Don Pickerel
3. Insights from the input of our brainstorming group on this subject
4. Our own research over 21 years as we have taught tens of thousands of people in 31 countries and benefited from their verbal and written feedback about characteristics consistent in their lives
5. Thousands of letters of confirmation and suggestions

We have tried to include only characteristics unique to each gift. In a few cases the trait of one gift overlaps the trait of another. While each list is reasonably comprehensive, we realize there may be additional characteristics that could be added. But we have attempted to come up with the most indicative qualities in order to develop an effective method of scoring.

The human personality is indeed wonderfully made. Like snowflakes, no two of us are exactly alike. Even though millions share your gift, your expression of it is unique. The differences come from the influence of countless variables in your life.

Maleness or femaleness as a variable is obvious. Health is another variable. For some the event of sickness or injury may thwart giftedness; for others it may be the very thing that challenges them to rise above limitations and use their gifts even more. (Joni Eareckson Tada, utilizing her gifts after a diving accident left her a quadriplegic, is an example.) Other variables are heredity, education, culture, family influence, economics, marital status, location, talents, self-image—well, the list is endless! Each variable has an impact on your life and the way you use *your* gift(s).

This should give you some feeling for the magnitude of God's plan in creating unique individuals—even though, amazingly, we are all influenced primarily by one or more of the seven motivational gifts.

Scoring Your Test

Notice that there are two scoring columns on the test sheets after page 31, one for you and one for your spouse. If you feel you will be influenced in any way by your spouse's answers, cover those before you proceed. We have designed this version of the test to enable you later to compare your scores more precisely.

Here is how the scoring is done. As you go over each characteristic in the following test, ask yourself, "How true is this of me?" Your first response will probably be the most accurate. Do not answer the way you would *like* to be or the way you think you *ought* to be. Be honest! You alone know yourself well enough to be able to score properly.

It is also important to differentiate in scoring between learned behavior and the way you act or think naturally. If you are presently employed, make sure your current duties do not influence your answers unduly. Your job may or may not be utilizing your motivational gifts.

If a characteristic is never true of you, put an *X* (or check mark) in the box under *Never*. Then place a 0 in the points column.

If a characteristic is true of you only on rare occasions, mark under *Seldom* and put a 1 in the points column.

If a characteristic is sometimes true of you (up to 49 percent of the time), score under *Sometimes* and give yourself a 2 in the points column.

If a characteristic is true of you 50 to 75 percent of the time, score under *Usually* and write a 3 in the points column.

If a characteristic is true of you most of the time (more than 75 percent of the time), score under *Mostly* and put a 4 in the points column.

If a characteristic is true of you all of the time, score under *Always* and place a 5 in the points column.

After you have scored yourself on all twenty characteristics, add up your score. It does not matter whether you score high, low or somewhere in the middle. Remember, this is a subjective test. It is the *comparison* of your seven scores that will help you to determine your motivational gifts.

If you were to give yourself a 5 for each of the twenty characteristics of a particular gift, you would receive the maximum score of 100.

Making Your Profile Sheets

Take your total score for each gift and transfer it to one of the profile charts below by shading in the appropriate horizontal column from left (0) to right (100), stopping where your score corresponds to the number at the top of the chart. (See sample profile sheets on pages 28–29.)

After you and your spouse have transferred all seven scores, you will have a composite profile of your motivational gifts. The score that stands out farthest to the right, much like the nose on a person's face, is your primary motivational gift. You will also see at a glance which is your secondary gift, your third and so forth.

It is equally important to identify areas in which you are the *least* gifted. You need to know this so you can:

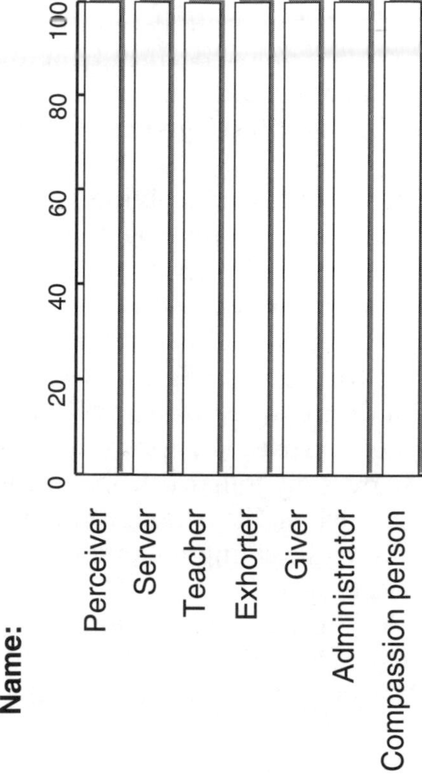

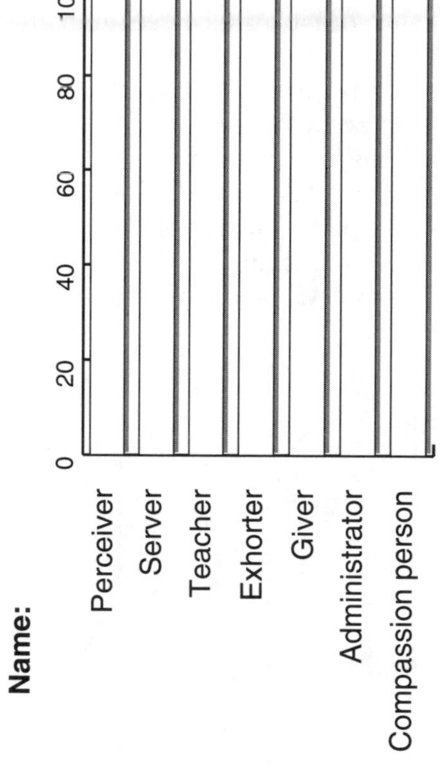

1. Recognize areas where you can be gratefully dependent on your spouse or others whose gifting is different. The apostle Paul wrote that God has made us mutually dependent on one another.
2. Rejoice that your spouse is strong in areas you are not. Variety is the spice of life in your God-given gifting.
3. Avoid trying to be what you are not. There is no such thing as super-husband or super-wife. Free your spouse to be what God created him or her to be.
4. Realize that you do not necessarily do everything well or like everything your spouse likes. It is O.K. to say, "I hate painting fences," or "Opera is just not my cup of tea."
5. Discover how beautifully your spouse's strengths can complement or balance your weaknesses. If your giver wife wants to handle the family finances and your giver score is 6 or 7, let her do it.

Checking Your Scores

If you and your spouse have questions about the other's accuracy of scoring, here are a couple of options:

1. Go over your mate's scores visually and identify any areas that have not been scored realistically. See if he or she understood the characteristic correctly. Make adjustments accordingly.
2. Using a different colored pen or pencil, score for your mate on the same column he or she used. Then compare the scores and examine the ones that are considerably different. Talk it over. Sometimes we can be so close to the trees that we cannot see the forest. Possibly a mate can give the perspective needed.

Evaluating Your Profile Sheets

Now that your profile sheets are completed, they will look something like the following samples. What does all this mean? How can you evaluate it? What if you have a tie for first and second place? What if your scores seem too high or too low? We offer our own profile sheets to try to answer these questions.

Here is what we see from my profile sheet:

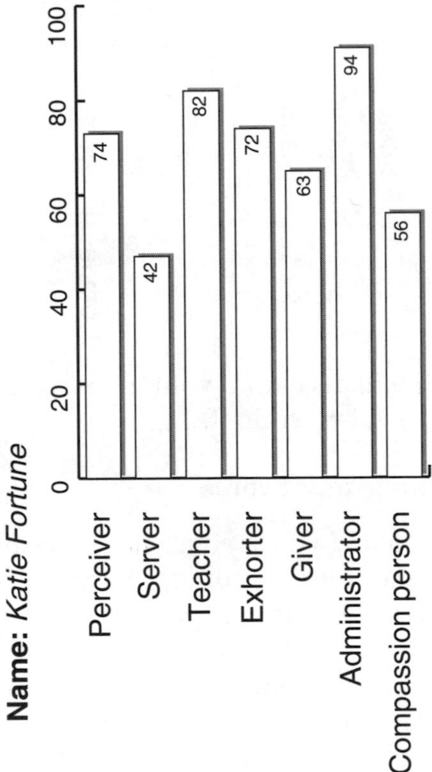

1. My primary gift is administration, the high score (94) indicating that I function in it nearly all the time. It means I am comfortable in leadership and that I organize easily.
2. My secondary gift of teaching (82) is high, too, indicating that I am also operating in that gift a lot of the time. It shows that my teaching gift is constantly modifying my primary gift of administration. It also indicates that I can operate specifically in my secondary gift, although the way it functions is still colored by my primary gift.
3. My third gift of perceiving (74) is medium-high, indicating that this gift has some influence in my life, but not nearly so much as the first two. It is strong enough to provide me with a keen sense of right and wrong and a desire to see God's will done through the use of my primary gifts.
4. Close by is my fourth gift, exhorting (72), which is, like the first three, a speaking gift giving me fluent communication skills.
5. My three lowest gifts are the serving gifts—giving (63), compassion (56) and serving (42)—that do not affect my life much.
6. My lowest score is server, indicating that I am least capable in this area. My viewpoint, of course, is that I serve when I give myself to leadership and teaching for the benefit of others.
7. The fact that Don and I both score low on server indicates that our home and yard sometimes get neglected in favor of involvement with people in areas where we can both use our speaking gifts.

Now about Don's profile sheet:

1. Don's primary gift is exhortation. His high score of 89 reveals that he functions in it most of the time. Don naturally encourages people in every situation. This is also a speaking and leadership gift; he does a lot of both.
2. His secondary gift of giving (73) is strong, too. This has given him a keen interest in missions and evangelism, and it is why he especially likes min-

istering on the mission field and supporting missionaries and outreach projects financially.

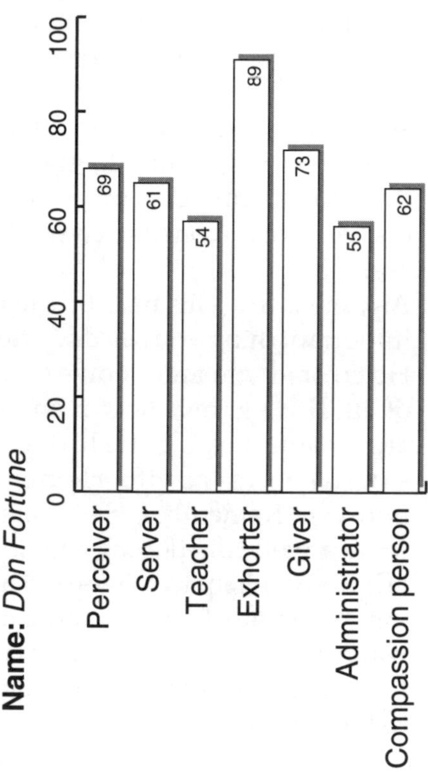

3. Perceiving (69), his third gift, is close to his giver gift. From this combination comes his call to prayer and intercession. He finds his participation in the prayer meetings at church fruitful and essential.
4. Compassion (62) and serving (61) are almost a tie, while Don's two lowest scores, administration (55) and teaching (54), are also only a point apart. Don's teaching ability stems from his exhortation gift and not his teaching gift.
5. Notice that his last two gifts are my first two. This means we complement one another in our approach. This makes for some interesting challenges from time to time in our marriage, but one thing is for sure—we are never bored!

Don exercises his primary gifts as a home fellowship leader and church elder, in teaching seminars, heading up missions outreach at our church and in counseling.

This is the kind of evaluation *you* can make from your profile sheet. Remember, there is only one of you in all the world, and God has designed you to be a vital part of the Body of Christ and a special blessing to your mate.

When the Score Is Close

You may be one of the people who have such close primary and secondary scores that it is difficult to determine the main one. There may be a number of reasons for this:

1. It may be that your motivational gifts have been squelched in childhood or are being hindered by some present circumstance. Another gift may be rivaling or taking precedence over the primary one.
2. A self-image problem may be keeping you from getting in touch with your real personality and actual giftedness.
3. You may be involved in activities or employment that make use of some secondary gift, causing your scoring to be influenced more by your present involvement than by your innate giftedness.
4. You may be trying to be someone you are not, or trying not to be someone you are.
5. You may indeed have two motivational gifts that are equally strong because God gifted you in just that way. The two gifts modify each other in order to bring the balance needed

for who that person is destined to be. We will share more about combination gifts in the next chapter.

Tie-Breakers

If you find you have nearly identical scores on your first two gifts, how do you determine whether they are equally strong or whether one belongs ahead of the other? We have developed tie-breakers to help with this. These are available in chapter 28 of our first book, *Discover Your God-Given Gifts*, and in the adult, objective and secular testing sets.

Clarifying Close Scores

Here are some other suggestions that can help you make sure of your primary motivational gift:

1. Set your test aside for a few days or weeks, even a few months. Become more observant of your behavior, interests and motivations. Now that you are familiar with the seven gifts, you will be more aware of their operation in your life. Then take the test again. This time it may be more decisive.
2. If you tended to avoid giving yourself fives and zeroes, take the test again willing to record the extreme scores where appropriate. Remember, it is not prideful to score a five. If you always do something, it is just a fact.
3. Look for patterns. Go over the scoring sheets for consistency within a major gift. You may have had a similar score on two gifts, for instance, but scored from two to five on one gift and mostly fours on the other. The latter is most likely your primary gift.
4. Look at the problem characteristics. Some people have told us, "The problem area shouted the loudest, 'That's you!'" This is especially true if you are a fairly new Christian or one who still has a lot of problems to resolve.
5. Ask your spouse or close friend or relative to help you take the test or even score it for you. Sometimes others see things about us that we do not see.
6. Ask the Lord. This may be the most important thing you can do. After all, He created you and knows you best of all. If He knows how many hairs are on your head (and He does), He surely knows the gifts He has built into you. Remember, He wants you to be a well-functioning member of His Body, a help to others and a loving helpmate to your spouse. He wants you to have the joy that comes from using your motivational gift(s) to the fullest.

Combination Gifts

Suppose, after you have done all the above, that two or more gifts are still tied for first place. Some people are what we described in chapter 1: combination gifts. God has created them with two motivational gifts of equal strength; they apparently need both to be who they are and fulfill His purpose in their lives. More on this in the next chapter.

Scoring the Problem Areas

Each of the seven motivational gifts has its own set of problems. We have found it helpful for people to know that along with their gifts come specific challenges and negative tendencies. One woman told us, "It's a relief to know that my problems are typical for my gift! I thought I was the only one in the world wrestling with these things. Now I have hope and direction."

The problem areas give opportunity for spiritual growth. As you take an honest look at them:

1. You will be relieved that you are not alone.
2. Your identification of the problems will assist you in discovering solutions.
3. You will know better how to pray for God's help and grace in overcoming the problems.
4. You will see how the problems have affected your marriage and be able to ask your spouse's forgiveness.
5. You can ask your spouse to assist you in overcoming the problems.

The scoring is the same as it was for the twenty positive characteristics, but you will not fill out a negative profile on yourself! Simply use the negative scores as an indicator of the problems you need to work on. Also, they can help you see how your maturity level is coming along.

In the next chapter we'll look at combination gifts.

The Gift of Perception

Characteristics

1. Quickly and accurately identifies good and evil and hates evil.
2. Sees everything as either black or white; no gray or indefinite areas.
3. Easily perceives the character of individuals and groups.
4. Encourages repentance that produces good fruit.
5. Believes the acceptance of difficulties will produce positive personal brokenness.
6. Has only a few or no close friendships.
7. Views the Bible as the basis for truth, belief, action, and authority.
8. Boldy operates on spiritual principles.
9. Is frank, outspoken, and doesn't mince words.
10. Is very persuasive in method of speaking.
11. Grieves deeply over the sins of others.
12. Is eager to see his own blind spots and to help others see theirs too.
13. Desires above all else to see God's plan worked out in all situations.
14. Strongly promotes the spiritual growth of groups and individuals.
15. Is called to intercession.
16. Feels the need to verbalize or dramatize what he "sees."
17. Tends to be introspective.
18. Has strong opinions and convictions.
19. Has strict personal standards.
20. Desires to be obedient to God at all costs.

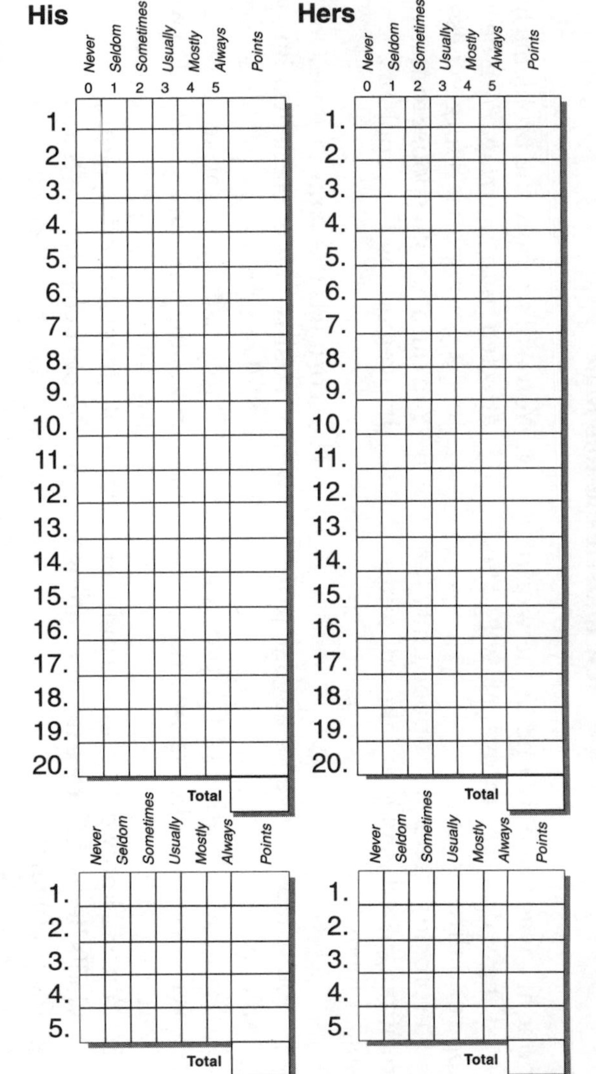

His

	Never 0	Seldom 1	Sometimes 2	Usually 3	Mostly 4	Always 5	Points
1.							
2.							
3.							
4.							
5.							
6.							
7.							
8.							
9.							
10.							
11.							
12.							
13.							
14.							
15.							
16.							
17.							
18.							
19.							
20.							
						Total	

Hers

	Never 0	Seldom 1	Sometimes 2	Usually 3	Mostly 4	Always 5	Points
1.							
2.							
3.							
4.							
5.							
6.							
7.							
8.							
9.							
10.							
11.							
12.							
13.							
14.							
15.							
16.							
17.							
18.							
19.							
20.							
						Total	

Typical problem areas of the gift of perception

1. Tends to be judgmental and blunt.
2. Forgets to praise partial progress due to goal consciousness.
3. Is pushy in trying to get others and groups to mature spiritually.
4. Is intolerant of opinions and views that differ from his own.
5. Struggles with self-image problems.

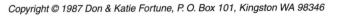

	Never	Seldom	Sometimes	Usually	Mostly	Always	Points
1.							
2.							
3.							
4.							
5.							
						Total	

	Never	Seldom	Sometimes	Usually	Mostly	Always	Points
1.							
2.							
3.							
4.							
5.							
						Total	

The Gift of Serving

Characteristics

1. Easily recognizes practical needs and is quick to meet them.
2. Especially enjoys manual projects, jobs and functions.
3. Keeps everything in meticulous order.
4. Is a detail person with a good memory.
5. Enjoys showing hospitality.
6. Will stay with something until it is completed.
7. Has a hard time saying no to requests for help.
8. Is more interested in meeting the needs of others than own needs.
9. Enjoys working on immediate goals rather than long-range goals.
10. Shows love for others in deeds and actions more than words.
11. Needs to feel appreciated.
12. Tends to do more than asked to do.
13. Feels greatest joy in doing something that is helpful.
14. Does not want to lead others or projects.
15. Has a high energy level.
16. Cannot stand to be around clutter.
17. Tends to be a perfectionist.
18. Views serving to be of primary importance in life.
19. Prefers doing a job to delegating it.
20. Supports others who are in leadership.

Typical problem areas of the gift of serving

1. Is critical of others who do not help out with obvious needs.
2. May neglect own family's needs by being too busy helping others.
3. May become pushy or interfering in eagerness to help.
4. Finds it hard to accept being served by others.
5. Is easily hurt when unappreciated.

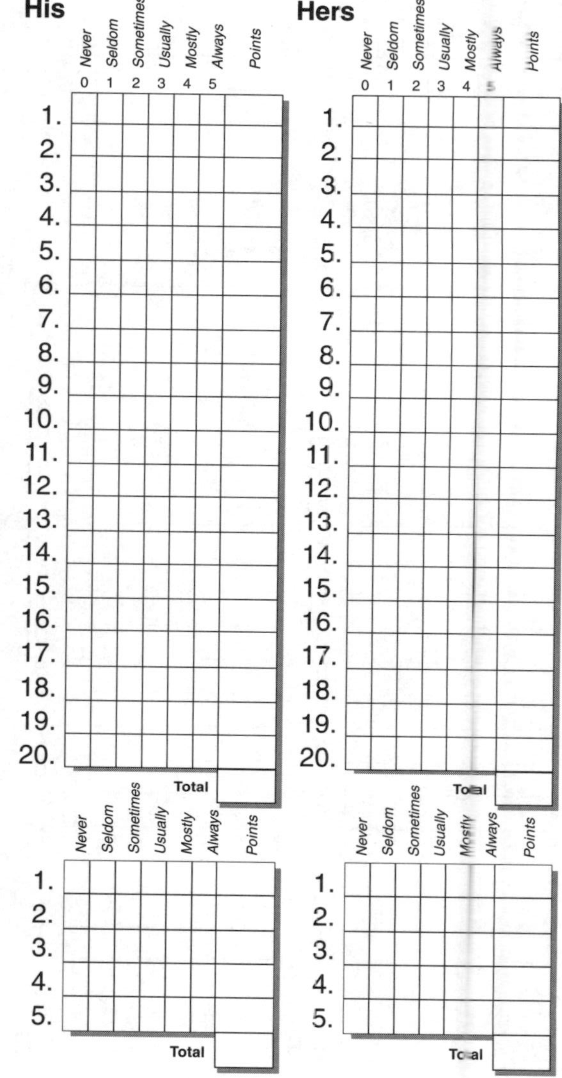

The Gift of Teaching

Characteristics

1. Presents truth in a logical, systematic way.
2. Validates truth by checking out the facts.
3. Loves to study and do research.
4. Enjoys word studies.
5. Prefers to use biblical illustrations rather than life illustrations.
6. Gets upset when Scripture is used out of context.
7. Feels concerned that truth be established in every situation.
8. Is more objective than subjective.
9. Easily develops and uses a large vocabulary.
10. Emphasizes facts and the accuracy of words.
11. Checks out the source of knowledge of others who teach.
12. Prefers teaching believers to engaging in evangelism.
13. Feels Bible study is foundational to the operation of all the gifts.
14. Solves problems by starting with scriptural principles.
15. Is intellectually sharp.
16. Is self-disciplined.
17. Is emotionally self-controlled.
18. Has only a select circle of friends.
19. Has strong convictions and opinions based on investigation of facts.
20. Believes truth has the intrinsic power to produce change.

Typical problem areas of the gift of teaching

1. Tends to neglect the practical application of truth.
2. Is slow to accept viewpoints of others.
3. Tends to develop pride in intellectual ability.
4. Tends to be legalistic and dogmatic.
5. Is easily sidetracked by new interests.

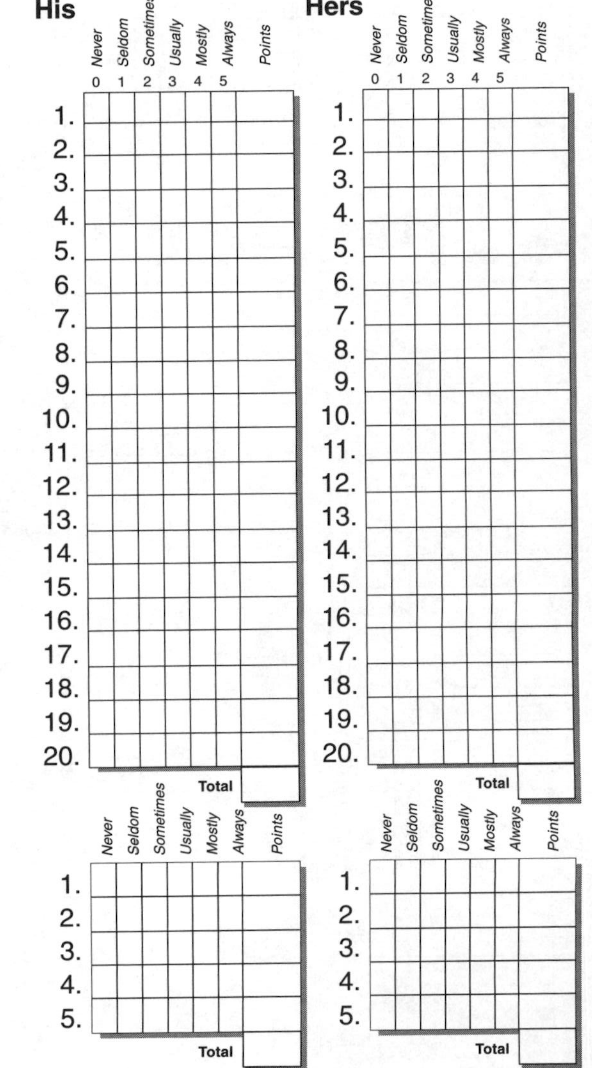

The Gift of Exhortation

Characteristics

1. Loves to encourage others to live victoriously.
2. Wants a visible response when teaching or speaking.
3. Prefers to apply truth rather than research it.
4. Prefers systems of information that have practical application.
5. Loves to prescribe precise steps of action to aid personal growth.
6. Focuses on working with people.
7. Encourages others to develop in their personal ministries.
8. Finds truth in experience and then validates it with Scripture.
9. Loves to do personal counseling.
10. Will discontinue personal counseling if no effort to change is seen.
11. Is fluent in communication.
12. Views trials as opportunities to produce personal growth.
13. Accepts people as they are without judging them.
14. Is greatly loved because of his positive attitude.
15. Prefers to witness with life rather than verbal witnessing.
16. Makes decisions easily.
17. Always completes what is started.
18. Wants to clear up problems with others quickly.
19. Expects a lot of self and others.
20. Needs a "sounding board" for bouncing off ideas and thoughts.

Typical problem areas of the gift of exhortation

1. Tends to interrupt others in eagerness to give opinions or advice.
2. Will use Scriptures out of context in order to make a point.
3. May be "cut and dried" in prescribing steps of action.
4. Is outspokenly opinionated.
5. Can become overly self-confident.

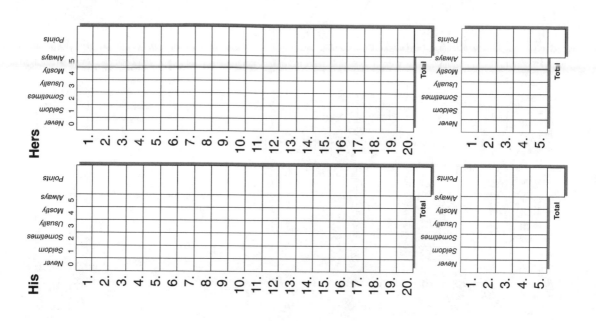

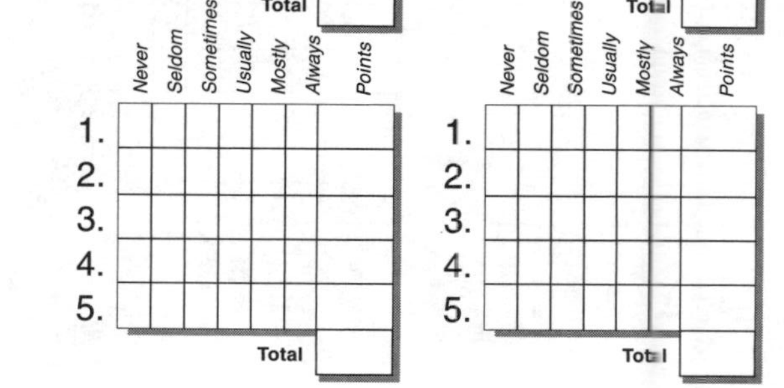

His

	Never 0	Seldom 1	Sometimes 2	Usually 3	Mostly 4	Always 5	Points
1.							
2.							
3.							
4.							
5.							
6.							
7.							
8.							
9.							
10.							
11.							
12.							
13.							
14.							
15.							
16.							
17.							
18.							
19.							
20.							
						Total	

	Never	Seldom	Sometimes	Usually	Mostly	Always	Points
1.							
2.							
3.							
4.							
5.							
						Total	

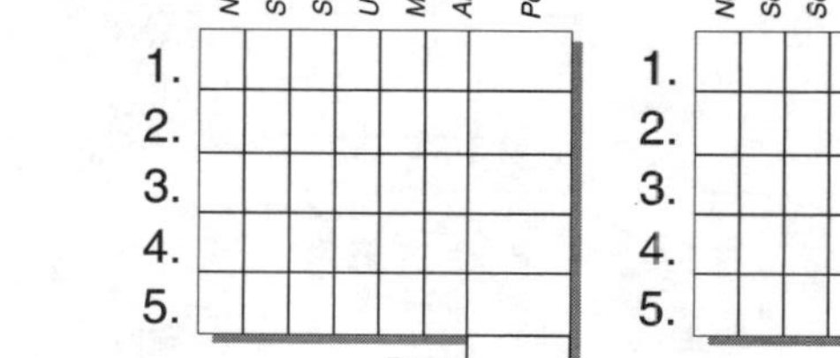

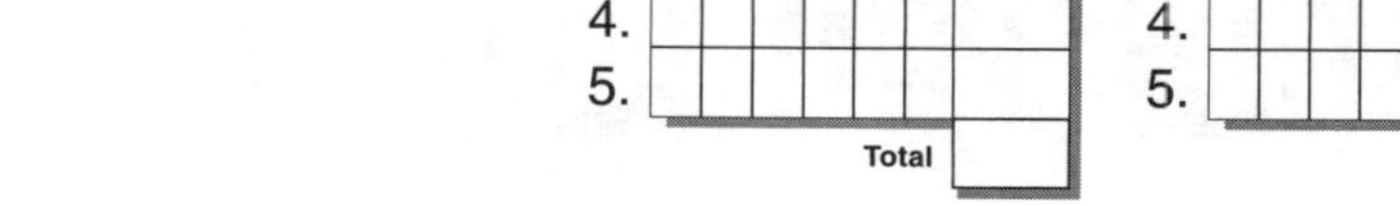

Hers

	Never 0	Seldom 1	Sometimes 2	Usually 3	Mostly 4	Always 5	Points
1.							
2.							
3.							
4.							
5.							
6.							
7.							
8.							
9.							
10.							
11.							
12.							
13.							
14.							
15.							
16.							
17.							
18.							
19.							
20.							
						Total	

	Never	Seldom	Sometimes	Usually	Mostly	Always	Points
1.							
2.							
3.							
4.							
5.							
						Total	

The Gift of Giving

Characteristics

1. Gives freely of money, possessions, time, energy and love.
2. Loves to give without others knowing about it.
3. Wants to feel a part of the ministries to which he contributes.
4. Intercedes for needs and the salvation of souls.
5. Feels delighted when his gift is an answer to specific prayer.
6. Wants gifts to be of high quality or craftsmanship.
7. Gives only by the leading of the Holy Spirit.
8. Gives to support and bless others or to advance a ministry.
9. Views hospitality as an opportunity to give.
10. Handles finances with wisdom and frugality.
11. Quickly volunteers to help where a need is seen.
12. Seeks confirmation on the amount to give.
13. Has strong belief in tithing and in giving in addition to tithing.
14. Focuses on sharing the Gospel.
15. Believes God is the Source of his support.
16. Is very industrious with a tendency toward success.
17. Has natural and effective business ability.
18. Likes to get the best value for the money spent.
19. Is definitely not gullible.
20. Possesses both natural and God-given wisdom.

Typical problem areas of the gift of giving

1. May try to control how contributions are used.
2. Tends to pressure others to give.
3. May upset family and friends with unpredictable patterns of giving.
4. Tends to spoil own children or other relatives.
5. May use financial giving to get out of other responsibilities.

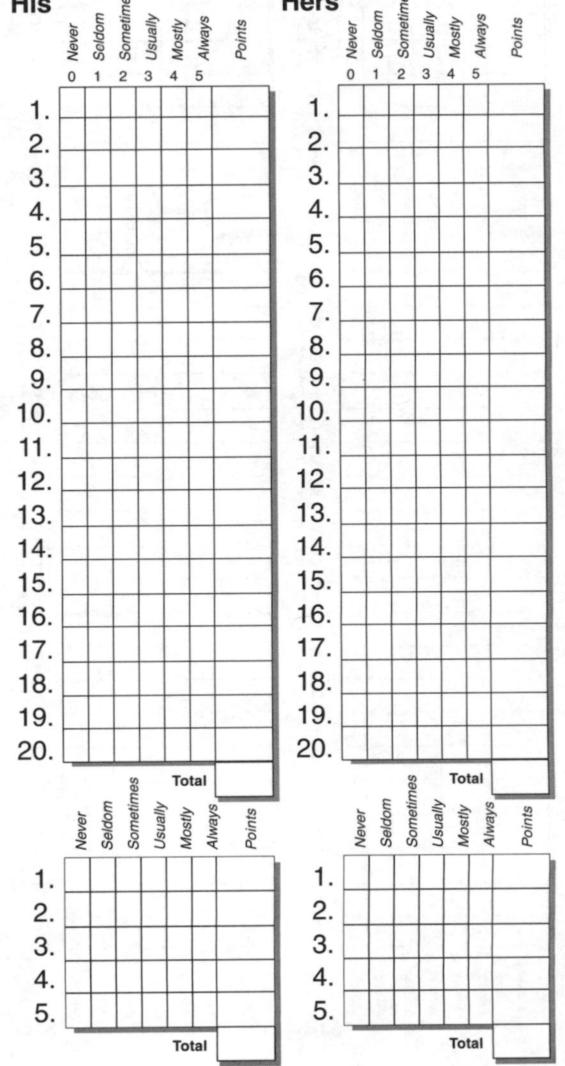

The Gift of Administration

Characteristics

1. Is highly motivated to organize that for which he's responsible.
2. Expresses ideas and organization in ways that communicate clearly.
3. Prefers to be under authority in order to have authority.
4. Will not take responsibility unless delegated by those in authority.
5. Will assume responsibilities if no specific leadership exists.
6. Especially enjoys working on long-range goals and projects.
7. Is a visionary person with a broad perspective.
8. Easily facilitates resources and people to accomplish tasks or goals.
9. Enjoys delegating tasks and supervising people.
10. Will endure criticism in order to accomplish the ultimate task.
11. Has great zeal and enthusiasm for whatever he is involved in.
12. Finds greatest fulfillment and joy in working to accomplish goals.
13. Is willing to let others get the credit in order to get a job done.
14. Prefers to move on to a new challenge once something is completed.
15. Constantly writes notes to self.
16. Is a natural and capable leader.
17. Knows when to keep old methods going and when to introduce new ones.
18. Enjoys working with and being around people.
19. Wants to see things completed as quickly as possible.
20. Does not enjoy doing routine tasks.

Typical problem areas of the gift of administration

1. Becomes upset when others do not share the same vision or goals.
2. Develops outer callousness due to being a target for criticism.
3. Can regress into "using" people to accomplish own goals.
4. Tends to drive self and neglect personal and family needs.
5. Neglects routine home responsibilities due to intense interest in "job."

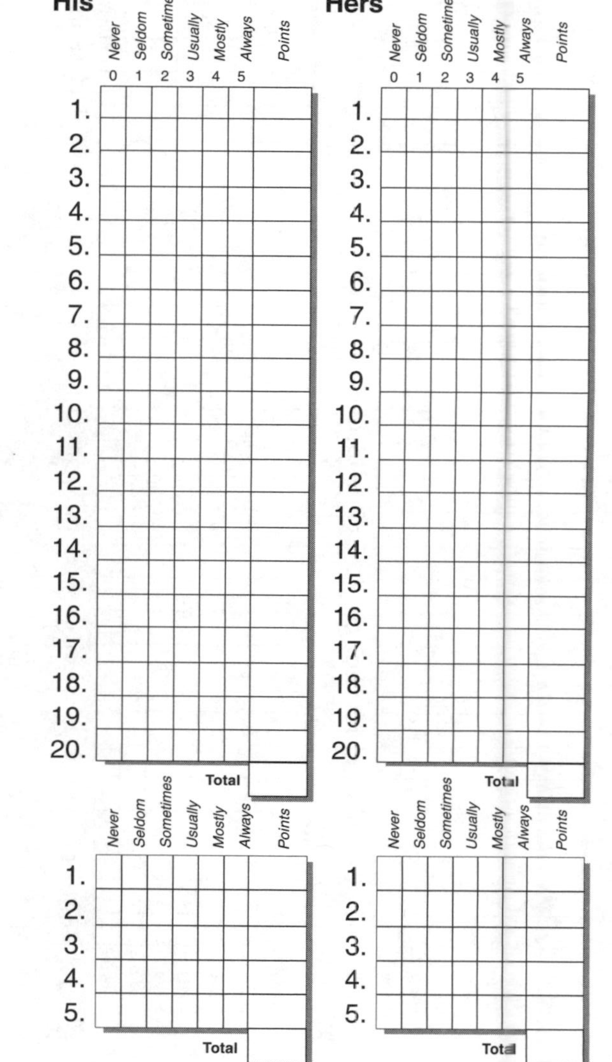

His

	Never 0	Seldom 1	Sometimes 2	Usually 3	Mostly 4	Always 5	Points
1.							
2.							
3.							
4.							
5.							
6.							
7.							
8.							
9.							
10.							
11.							
12.							
13.							
14.							
15.							
16.							
17.							
18.							
19.							
20.							
						Total	

	Never	Seldom	Sometimes	Usually	Mostly	Always	Points
1.							
2.							
3.							
4.							
5.							
						Total	

Hers

	Never 0	Seldom 1	Sometimes 2	Usually 3	Mostly 4	Always 5	Points
1.							
2.							
3.							
4.							
5.							
6.							
7.							
8.							
9.							
10.							
11.							
12.							
13.							
14.							
15.							
16.							
17.							
18.							
19.							
20.							
						Total	

	Never	Seldom	Sometimes	Usually	Mostly	Always	Points
1.							
2.							
3.							
4.							
5.							
						Total	

The Gift of Compassion

Characteristics

1. Has tremendous capacity to show love.
2. Always looks for good in people.
3. Senses the spiritual and emotional atmosphere of a group or individual.
4. Is attracted to people who are hurting or in distress.
5. Takes action to remove hurts and relieve distress in others.
6. Is more concerned for mental and emotional distress than physical distress.
7. Is motivated to help people have right relationships with one another.
8. Loves opportunities to give preference or place to others.
9. Takes care with words and actions to avoid hurting others.
10. Easily detects insincerity or wrong motives.
11. Is drawn to others with the gift of compassion.
12. Loves to do thoughtful things for others.
13. Is trusting and trustworthy.
14. Avoids conflicts and confrontations.
15. Doesn't like to be rushed in a job or activity.
16. Is typically cheerful and joyful.
17. Is ruled by the heart rather than head.
18. Rejoices to see others blessed and grieves to see others hurt.
19. Is a crusader for good causes.
20. Intercedes for the hurts and problems of others.

Typical problem areas of the gift of compassion

1. Tends to be indecisive.
2. Is often prone to take up another person's offense.
3. Is easily hurt by others.
4. Empathizes too much with the suffering of others.
5. Affectionate nature is often misinterpreted by opposite sex.

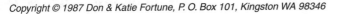

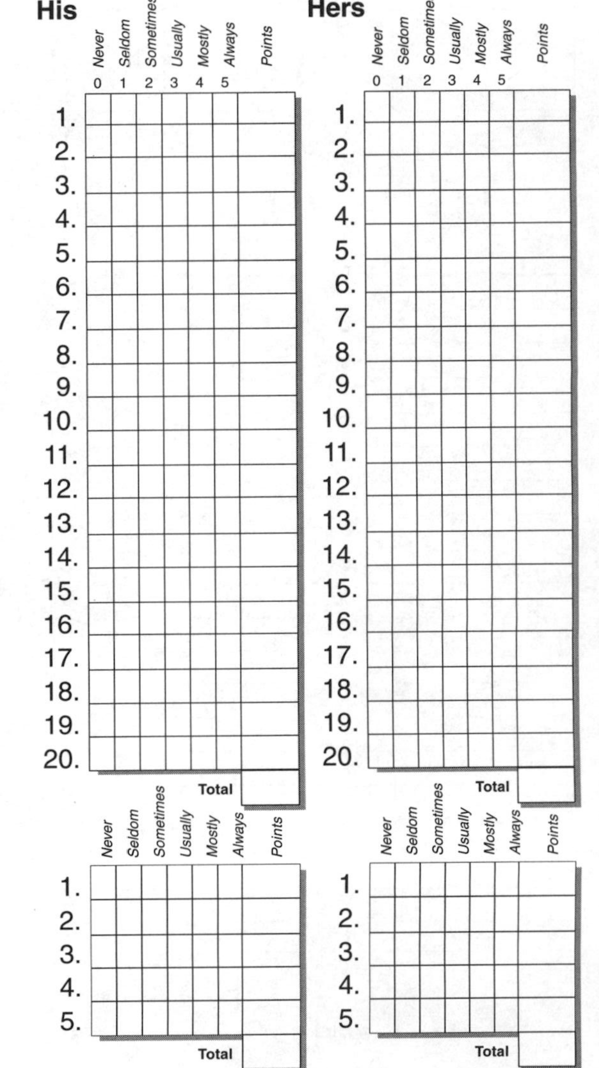

His

	Never 0	Seldom 1	Sometimes 2	Usually 3	Mostly 4	Always 5	Points
1.							
2.							
3.							
4.							
5.							
6.							
7.							
8.							
9.							
10.							
11.							
12.							
13.							
14.							
15.							
16.							
17.							
18.							
19.							
20.							
						Total	

Hers

	Never 0	Seldom 1	Sometimes 2	Usually 3	Mostly 4	Always 5	Points
1.							
2.							
3.							
4.							
5.							
6.							
7.							
8.							
9.							
10.							
11.							
12.							
13.							
14.							
15.							
16.							
17.							
18.							
19.							
20.							
						Total	

	Never	Seldom	Sometimes	Usually	Mostly	Always	Points
1.							
2.							
3.							
4.							
5.							
						Total	

	Never	Seldom	Sometimes	Usually	Mostly	Always	Points
1.							
2.							
3.							
4.							
5.							
						Total	

Combination Gifts and Mates

Only about a third of us have classic gifts—primary gifts so strong compared to secondary gifts that their operation is influenced little by the secondary gifts or not at all. A person with a classic gift typically exhibits most or all of the characteristics of this gift clearly.

About two-thirds of us have combination gifts, meaning we have one or more strong secondary gifts to some extent modifying the operation of our primary gifts.

My primary gift of administration (94 points) is modified somewhat by my strong secondary gift of teaching (82 points). Both gifts constantly influence my life, interests, actions, relationship to my husband and approach to situations. The two gifts work together; sometimes they blend and sometimes a characteristic of one or the other takes precedence. Throughout our marriage my administrative gregariousness has dominated my teacher's tendency to have fewer friends. Yet I also enjoy quiet times alone with a good book.

Don's gift of exhortation (89 points) is colored to some extent by his gift of giving (73 points). His desire to help people with a financial need manifests itself in encouraging them to earn what they need, rather than in gifts of money. Yet he gives generously to missions.

Multiple Gifting for a Purpose

Please understand that neither a classic gift nor a combination of gifts is better. God has endowed people the way they are for His own purposes. A person with two motivational gifts of equal or similar strength can be assured he will need both to fulfill God's plans for his life's work or ministry. A person with one strong gift will need that focus of characteristics that will enable him to fulfill God's plans for his life.

Each combination produces interesting modifications. Often these enable the person to have a broader range of operation, from the gift mode of one to the gift mode of the other with a variety of possible modifications in between. A relationship or circumstance may draw out of the person the mode that fits the situation. A combination-gifted spouse may be more challenging to figure out since sometimes one gift may be primarily in operation and sometimes the other. Also, the modified mode may show up at any time.

A spouse gifted in both perception and compassion finds that the latter gives him special sensitivity to his mate, causing him to be less blunt and judgmental than a classic perceiver. His gift of perception also modifies his gift of compassion, enabling him to be more decisive and punctual (much to his mate's delight!). The tendency of his compassion gift to compromise is balanced by the refusal of his perceiver gift to compromise, which means he will compromise only when there is valid reason and after seeking valued input from his spouse on the matter.

A spouse with a teacher/exhorter combination is more adaptable and able to "hang loose" than a classic teacher. Communication is important to him but his teacher gifting may spare his mate from a barrage of words at every turn.

A giver/server spouse loves serving others, including his spouse. He does a little better relating to his mate's extended family since his giver gift makes him more social than his server's stay-at-home social inclination.

The list goes on and on. If you or your mate have a combination gifting, thank God for its unique blend in your life. Do everything possible to understand what it means for you and your marital relationship. Remember to ask the Lord what He has in mind for your life.

Here's How to Score

With what you have now learned about the seven motivational gifts, you should be able to recognize and understand some of the modifying effects that a combination of gifts may have in your life or your spouse's life. In order to help, we have prepared comparison scales, one or more for each of the thirty categories we have designated, plotting the seven gifts in relationship to each other. We have used abbreviations for the gifts: *P* for perceiver, *S* for server, *T* for teacher, *E* for exhorter, *G* for giver, *A* for administrator and *C* for compassion.

Here is how it works. Suppose you are an administrator with a close secondary gift of serving. In many ways these are opposite gifts, but the resulting modifications will enable you to do both meticulous work and overall organization. You will be less gregarious than a classic administrator but more outgoing than a classic server.

Look at the first scale under *Emotions* (page 41). Circle the *A* and the *S*. The *A* is three sections to the right of *Unemotional*, and the *S* is four sections to the left of *Emotional*. Your combination gift, therefore, would place you just to the left of the *Balanced* position. You are neither extremely unemotional nor extremely emotional. This near-center position makes you an easy person to live with.

The second scale under *Emotions* will show similar balanced results: You are neither too social nor too shy. You may find that while your administrator gift enables you to socialize well in an especially compatible group, your server gift keeps you from feeling as comfortable in a large group.

Proceed to the next scale, *Verbal Expression*. Circle the *A* and *S* again. The administrator verbalizes easily; the server does not. Again the gifts balance each other, producing about average verbal skills. Yet in some situations, such as with your mate, you may be very verbal, and in large groups, less so.

Making the same three comparisons for a person who is an administrator/teacher, we see the scores falling on the extreme left. These characteristics have been further enhanced, therefore, by the "doubling-up" process. Expect this person to be cool, calm and collected, quite social and exceptionally skilled in speech.

Should a person have three strong gifts, circle all three on each comparison scale and observe how they modify each other.

A giver/server/compassion combination compared on the first scale lands the person definitely on the emotional side. This person remains on the shy side and finds verbal expression somewhat difficult.

Proceed through all the comparison scales if you have combination gifts and you will gain a more comprehensive picture of your personality. Have your spouse do the same, using a different colored ink. Remember, these scales are general; individuals may vary from the norm.

1. Emotions:

| T | - | A | - | E | G | S | P | - | C |
Unemotional — *Balanced* — *Emotional*

| E | A | - | T | G | - | P | C | S | - |
Outgoing — *Balanced* — *Shy*

| T | S | A | E | G | - | C | - | - | P |
Not easily angered — *Average* — *Easily angered*

| C | - | E | G | A | - | P | T | S | - |
Very loving — *Average* — *Hard to express love*

| C | - | - | S | G | E | A | T | P | - |
Easily wounded — *Average* — *Not easily wounded*

| C | S | G | E | A | T | - | P | - | - |
Forgiving — *Average* — *Slow to forgive*

2. Verbal Expression:

| E | A | T | P | - | G | C | - | S | |
Easy — *Average* — *Difficult*

| E | - | A | T | P | G | - | C | - | S |
Interrupter — *Average* — *Noninterrupter*

| A | E | T | P | G | - | - | C | - | S |
Comfortable speaking in front of groups — *Average* — *Not comfortable*

3. Self-Image:

| A | E | T | G | - | S | - | C | P | - |
Good — *Average* — *Poor*

| E | A | T | - | G | S | - | C | - | P |
Self-accepting — *Average* — *Introspective*

4. Approach to Life:

| P | C | - | E | G | A | - | T | - | S |
Idealistic — *Balanced* — *Practical*

| E | T | A | P | - | - | C | G | - | S |
Speaker — *Balanced* — *Doer*

| E | G | S | C | - | A | - | P | T | - |
Adaptable — *Balanced* — *Inflexible*

| T | A | P | - | E | G | S | - | - | C |
Systematic — *Balanced* — *Spontaneous*

| T | - | A | E | P | S | - | G | - | C |
Realistic — *Balanced* — *Imaginative*

| C | E | - | G | A | S | - | P | T | - |
Fun loving — *Balanced* — *Too serious*

5. Behavior:

| S | E | C | G | T | A | - | - | P | - |
Most obedient Average Most rebellious

| T | - | A | S | G | E | - | P | - | C |
Predictable Balanced Impulsive

| C | E | G | S | A | - | T | - | P | - |
Tolerant Balanced Judgmental

| C | - | S | - | G | E | - | A | P | T |
Cries easily Balanced Seldom cries

6. Personal Habits:

| S | E | G | T | P | - | C | A | - | - |
Neat Average Untidy

| T | P | S | E | G | - | A | - | - | C |
Punctual Average Late

| S | G | C | - | E | - | P | A | - | T |
Voluntarily helpful Average Has to be asked

7. Intellect:

| T | A | E | P | G | - | S | C | - | - |
Very intellectual Average Nonintellectual

| T | P | A | - | E | G | - | S | - | C |
Questioning Average Accepting

| P | T | A | E | - | G | S | - | C | - |
Highly opinionated Balanced Unopinionated

| T | A | P | E | - | G | - | S | - | C |
Very analytical Balanced Nonanalytical

| T | - | A | P | E | - | G | S | - | C |
Likes to correct Average Does not correct

| T | A | P | E | G | - | S | - | C | - |
Very studious Balanced Seldom studious

8. Reading Interests:

| T | A | P | E | G | - | C | - | S | - |
Prolific Average Minimal

| T | A | P | - | E | G | - | S | - | C |
Nonfiction Both Fiction

9. Relationships:

| A | E | - | C | G | - | S | T | - | P |
Broadest relationships Average Narrowest relationships

| E | A | - | C | G | - | - | T | S | P |
Many friends needed Balanced Few friends needed

10. Authority:

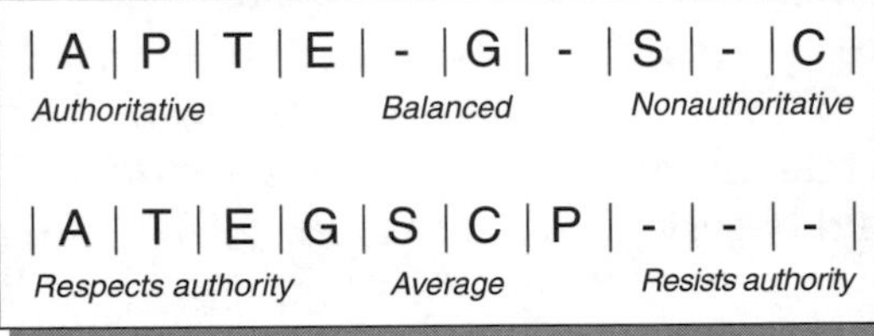

| A | P | T | E | - | G | - | S | - | C |
Authoritative Balanced Nonauthoritative

| A | T | E | G | S | C | P | - | - | - |
Respects authority Average Resists authority

11. Leadership:

| A | E | P | T | - | G | - | C | - | S |
Leader Average Follower

| A | P | E | - | T | - | G | - | C | S |
Bold Balanced Bashful

12. Interests:

| A | E | T | - | C | G | S | - | P | - |
Great variety Average Narrow focus

| C | P | - | T | A | E | - | - | G | S |
Artistic Balanced Practical

| S | - | C | - | G | E | - | P | T | A |
Domestic Both Nondomestic

| T | A | P | E | - | G | - | C | - | S |
Academic Balanced Nonacademic

13. Source of Joy:

| A | T | - | P | E | G | - | S | - | C |
Accomplishments Balanced Relationships

| E | A | T | P | - | - | C | G | - | S |
Approval/Accolades Both Helping/Serving

14. Qualities:

| E | A | - | G | C | T | - | S | P | - |
Extroverted · *Balanced* · *Introverted*

| T | P | A | E | - | G | - | S | - | C |
Objective · *Balanced* · *Subjective*

| P | T | A | - | G | E | S | - | - | C |
Uncompromising · *Balanced* · *Compromising*

| T | A | - | E | G | - | S | - | P | C |
Matter-of-factual · *Balanced* · *Sensitive*

15. Spirituality:

| P | G | - | C | A | E | T | - | - | S |
Spiritual focus · *Balanced* · *Practical focus*

| P | C | G | - | E | A | - | T | S | - |
Intercessor · *Average* · *Prays occasionally*

16. Expectations:

| E | P | A | T | - | G | - | S | - | C |
Expects a lot of mate · *Balanced* · *Accepts mate as is*

| E | A | T | G | C | S | - | P | - | - |
Encourager · *Average* · *Discourager*

17. Marital Cohesion:

| E | A | C | G | T | S | - | P | - | - |
Natural cohesion · *Average* · *Difficult cohesion*

| E | A | T | G | S | - | C | P | - | - |
Feels secure · *Average* · *Feels insecure*

| C | E | - | A | G | S | P | T | - | - |
Attentive · *Average* · *Inattentive*

| C | E | A | G | S | T | P | - | - | - |
Quality time together · *Average* · *Lack of time together*

| C | E | A | G | - | S | T | - | P | - |
Feels close · *Average* · *Feels lonely*

| C | E | G | A | P | S | T | - | - | - |
Very affectionate · *Average* · *Shows little affection*

18. Roles and Responsibilities:

| A | P | T | E | - | G | - | S | - | C |
Authoritative · *Balanced* · *Nonauthoritative*

| A | T | P | E | G | S | C | - | - | - |
Responsible · *Average* · *Irresponsible*

| A | P | T | E | G | - | - | S | - | C |
Fits traditional roles (husbands) · *Balanced* · *Nontraditional*

| S | C | - | G | E | - | T | P | A | - |
Fits traditional roles (wives) · *Balanced* · *Nontraditional*

| P | A | T | E | - | G | - | S | - | C |
Dominant · *Balanced* · *Submissive*

19. Conflict Resolution:

| E | A | T | P | G | - | S | - | - | C |
Resolves conflicts well · *Average* · *Avoids conflicts*

| T | A | E | - | G | S | - | C | - | P |
Manages anger well · *Average* · *Difficulty handling anger*

| P | - | A | T | E | - | G | S | - | C |
Argumentative · *Average* · *Nonargumentative*

| A | E | T | G | - | S | C | - | - | P |
Accepts responsibility for actions · *Average* · *Tends to blame*

| C | S | G | E | A | T | - | - | - | P |
Apologetic · *Average* · *Stubborn*

| E | A | P | T | - | G | - | S | - | C |
Addresses issues · *Average* · *Clams up*

20. Personality Issues:

| P | - | T | - | A | E | - | G | S | C |
Prideful *Balanced* *Humble*

| E | T | A | G | - | S | - | C | P | - |
Good self-esteem *Average* *Poor self-esteem*

| E | C | G | A | T | S | - | P | - | - |
Complimenter *Average* *Complainer*

| C | S | G | E | A | T | - | P | - | - |
Considerate *Average* *Inconsiderate*

| P | C | - | E | A | - | S | G | T | - |
Bothersome habits *Average* *No bothersome habits*

| E | A | C | G | S | T | - | P | - | - |
Good attitudes *Average* *Bad attitudes*

21. Volitional Issues:

| A | E | P | T | G | - | S | - | - | C |
Decisive *Average* *Indecisive*

| P | T | A | E | G | - | S | - | C | - |
Strong willed *Balanced* *Weak willed*

| G | S | C | E | A | T | - | P | - | - |
Cooperative *Average* *Independent*

| - | P | - | T | A | E | G | S | - | C |
Judgmental *Average* *Nonjudgmental*

| P | T | A | E | - | G | - | S | - | C |
Persuasive *Balanced* *Timid*

| P | - | T | A | E | G | - | S | - | C |
Uncompromising *Balanced* *Compromising*

| P | A | T | E | G | - | S | - | C | - |
Strong convictions *Balanced* *Deferring to others*

22. Priorities:

| A | T | P | - | E | G | - | S | - | C |
Likes priorities *Average* *Not priority minded*

23. Work and Accomplishments:

| G | A | S | E | T | P | - | - | C | - |
Industrious *Average* *Unmotivated*

| A | T | E | G | P | S | - | - | - | C |
Organized *Average* *Disorganized*

| A | T | G | P | E | S | - | - | - | C |
Career centered *Average* *Relationship centered*

| A | T | P | E | G | - | S | - | - | C |
Goal oriented *Average* *Non-goal oriented*

| G | A | E | P | T | - | S | - | - | C |
Best business ability *Average* *Least business ability*

| - | S | A | G | E | P | - | C | T | - |
Workaholic *Balanced* *Knows when to quit*

24. Financial Management:

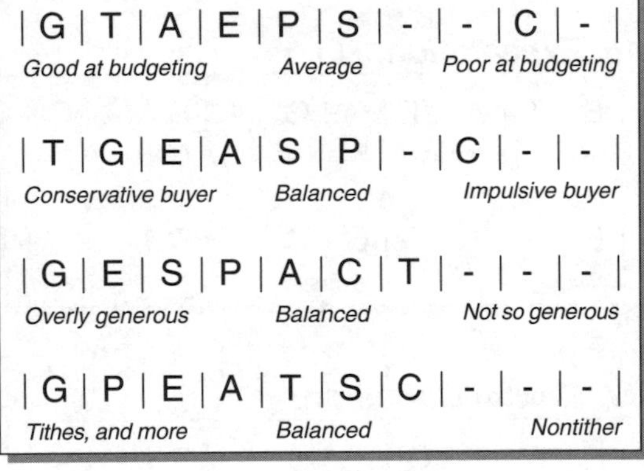

| G | T | A | E | P | S | - | - | C | - |
Good at budgeting *Average* *Poor at budgeting*

| T | G | E | A | S | P | - | C | - | - |
Conservative buyer *Balanced* *Impulsive buyer*

| G | E | S | P | A | C | T | - | - | - |
Overly generous *Balanced* *Not so generous*

| G | P | E | A | T | S | C | - | - | - |
Tithes, and more *Balanced* *Nontither*

25. Leisure Activities:

| A | E | - | P | G | S | - | C | - | T |
Athletic *Balanced* *Nonathletic*

| E | A | C | G | - | T | S | P | - | - |
Loves to go out *Average* *A stay-at-home*

| C | E | A | T | G | P | S | - | - | - |
Uses leisure time well *Average* *Neglects leisure time*

| C | S | G | - | E | - | T | A | - | P |
Watches too much TV *Balanced* *Seldom watches TV*

| S | C | G | - | E | A | - | T | P | - |
Loves hobbies *Average* *No hobbies*

26. Sports Interest:

| A | E | - | G | P | - | S | - | C | T |
Most — Average — Least

| E | A | - | G | - | S | - | C | P | T |
Active group sports — Balanced — Individual sports

| A | E | - | G | P | T | - | S | - | C |
Competitive — Balanced — Noncompetitive

27. Parenting:

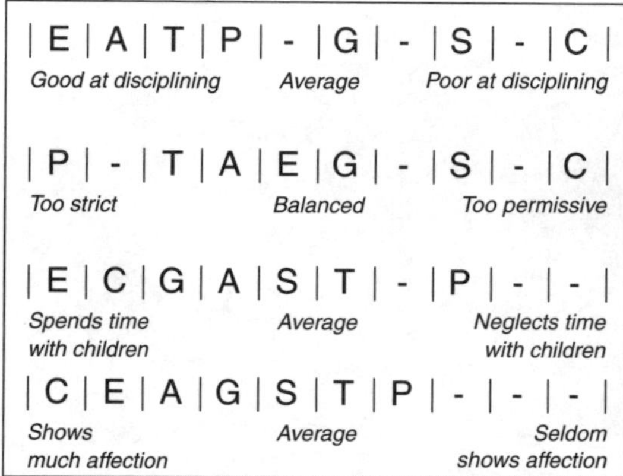

| E | A | T | P | - | G | - | S | - | C |
Good at disciplining — Average — Poor at disciplining

| P | - | T | A | E | G | - | S | - | C |
Too strict — Balanced — Too permissive

| E | C | G | A | S | T | - | P | - | - |
Spends time with children — Average — Neglects time with children

| C | E | A | G | S | T | P | - | - | - |
Shows much affection — Average — Seldom shows affection

28. Extended Family:

| A | E | P | T | G | - | S | - | C | - |
Leaves and cleaves well — Average — Tends to cling

| G | E | S | A | C | - | P | T | - | - |
Relates well to in-laws — Average — Relates poorly to in-laws

29. Social Relationships:

| E | A | C | - | G | S | T | - | P | - |
Very social — Balanced — Unsocial

| S | G | C | E | A | T | - | P | - | - |
Loves to entertain — Average — Seldom entertains

| A | E | - | C | G | T | S | - | P | - |
Enjoys large groups — Balanced — Prefers small groups

| A | E | S | - | C | G | T | - | P | - |
Over-involvement in groups — Balanced — No involvement in groups

| C | E | A | G | S | T | - | P | - | - |
Lots of time with friends — Average — Little time with friends

30. Maturity:

| T | A | E | - | P | G | S | - | C | - |
Very mature — Average — Less mature

| T | E | A | P | G | - | S | - | C | - |
Copes well with stress — Average — Copes poorly with stress

| E | A | T | G | S | - | P | C | - | - |
Normal behavior — Average — Some dysfunctional behavior

| - | P | T | A | E | G | S | C | - | - |
Too prideful — Balanced — Too humble

| E | A | T | G | S | C | - | P | - | - |
Good attitudes — Average — Poor attitudes

| C | E | A | T | G | S | - | P | - | - |
Forgiving — Average — Unforgiving

Your Three-Part Nature and the Gifts

One of the most marvelous concepts in the Christian faith is that human beings are created in the image of God. God (Himself triune—Father, Son and Holy Spirit) has made us tripartite in nature—spirit, soul and body.

> God said, Let Us [Father, Son, and Holy Spirit] make mankind in Our image, after Our likeness.
>
> Genesis 1:26

> May the God of peace Himself sanctify you through and through—that is, separate you from profane things, make you pure and wholly consecrated to God—and may your spirit and soul and body be preserved sound and complete [and found] blameless at the coming of our Lord Jesus Christ, the Messiah.
>
> 1 Thessalonians 5:23

The three parts of the human being can be diagrammed like this:

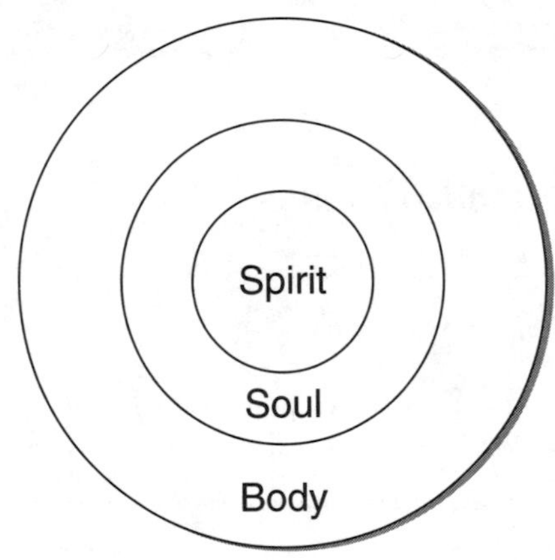

It is the *spirit* that is saved when a person receives Jesus Christ as Savior. This new birth is the guarantee of eternal life.

> Jesus answered, I assure you, most solemnly I tell you, except a man be born of water and (even) the Spirit, he cannot [ever] enter the kingdom of God.
>
> John 3:5

It is the *soul* that is involved in the process described by the apostle Paul:

> . . . work out—cultivate, carry out to the goal and fully complete—your own salvation with reverence and awe and trembling. . . .
>
> Philippians 2:12

Salvation is worked out in the soul in the process called sanctification. Much like a woman kneading the separate ingredients of flour and yeast and liquid into bread dough, we can allow Christ's life to permeate all areas of our soul in a lifelong process of practical application of the spiritual inheritance we have already received.

It is the *body* that will be saved in the future, transformed into a resurrection body suitable to live in forever.

> We shall all be changed (transformed) in a moment, in the twinkling of an eye, at the (sound of the) last trumpet call. For a trumpet will sound, and the dead [in Christ] will be raised imperishable—free and immune from decay—and we shall be changed (transformed).
>
> 1 Corinthians 15:51–52

Our Soul Is Triune, Too

In the same way that the human being is made of three parts—body, soul and spirit—so the soul is triune in nature. Jesus pointed out the three areas of the soul when He said:

> You shall love the Lord your God out of and with your whole heart, and out of and with all your soul (your life) and out of and with all your mind—[that is] with your faculty of thought and your moral understanding—and out of and with all your strength. This is the first and principal commandment.
>
> Mark 12:30

The three parts of the soul are the *mind*, the *will* and the *emotions*. The "heart" in Jesus' statement refers to the seat of the emotions, the "mind" refers to thought, and "strength" refers to the will. The soul comprises all three areas.

Each is also identified in the following passage:

> All that is in the world, the lust of the flesh [craving for sensual gratification], and the lust of the eyes [greedy longings of the mind] and the pride of life [assurance in one's own resources or in the stability of earthly things]—these do not come from the Father but are from the world [itself].
>
> 1 John 2:16

John is describing the negative things that come from the three areas of the soul—the lust of the flesh from the emotions, the lust of the eyes from the mind and the pride of life from the will. Jesus was tempted in these three areas of the soul and passed all tests.

And many good things come from these areas. With the mind we think and reason. With the will we make decisions. From the emotions come our feelings. We need all three areas operating in balance in order to function normally. But sometimes we are motivated by one area more than the others. Sometimes two of the three areas seem to have greater influence.

We have discovered that the seven God-given gifts come primarily from one or more of the three areas of the soul. Of necessity we function in all areas. But the way we think, feel and act is colored greatly by our motivational gifting, which is influenced in turn by the area or areas of the soul that predominate. This helps to explain why God has gifted us in seven specific ways and why there is no eighth category. Each gift relates to the mind, will and emotions in a specific way.

The following diagram helps to explain this:

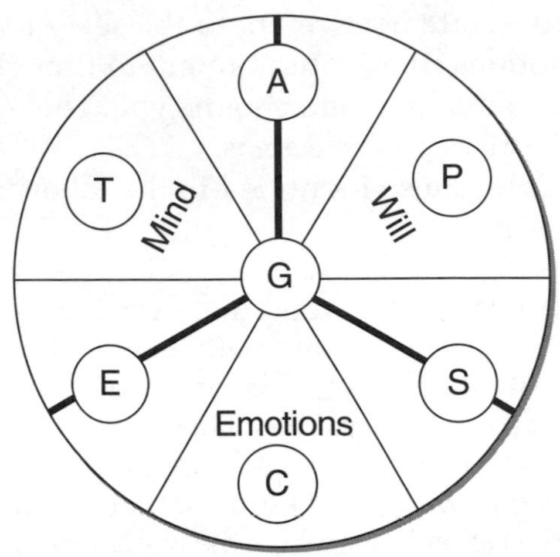

Note that three of the gifts correspond directly to the mind, the will or the emotions:

The teacher gift operates primarily out of the *mind* area of the soul.
The perceiver gift operates primarily out of the *will* area of the soul.
The compassion gift operates primarily out of the *emotions* area of the soul.

Three more of the gifts are influenced by two of the three areas of the soul:

The administrator gift operates out of the *mind* and *will* areas of the soul.
The exhorter gift operates out of the *mind* and the *emotions* areas of the soul.
The server gift operates out of the *will* and *emotions* area of the soul.

The seventh gift, the giver gift, operates about equally in all three areas of the soul.

How Do Gifts Relate to Each Other?

Because the characteristics of a particular gift extend naturally from the area(s) of the soul that influence it, each gift finds it easier to relate to related gifts and more challenging to relate to "opposite" gifts.

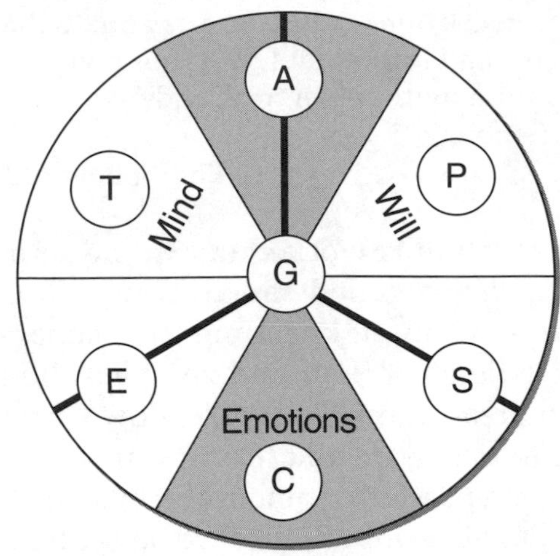

In general we find it is most difficult to relate to a gift directly opposite our own. A compassion gift, for instance, finds it hard to cope with an administrator gift (and visa-versa), the latter operating from the mind and will and the former from the emotions. More effort needs to be put into such a marriage relationship, especially in allowing for the other's differences in interests and mode of operation.

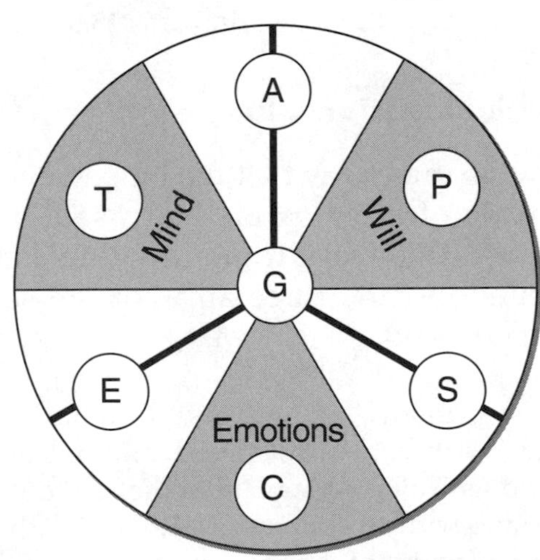

The gifts that fall into the triangular arrangement also have some relationship challenges since they are still somewhat "opposite." The compassion gift, for instance, operating primarily from the emotions, finds it hard to understand a teacher mate who operates from the mind or a perceiver mate who operates from the will.

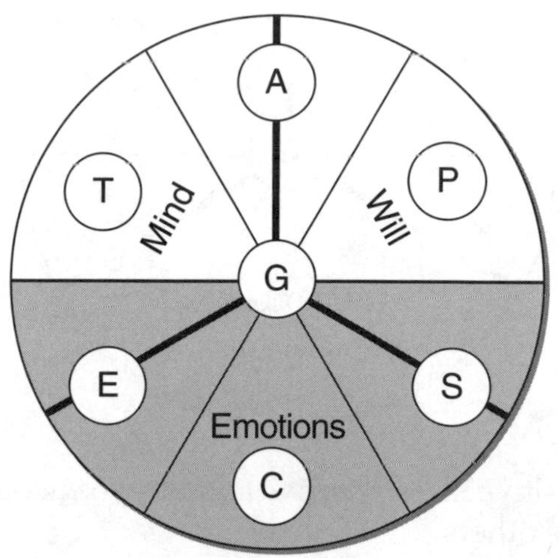

The easiest relationship for the compassion gift is with a mate who is "next door" and shares some of the same influence from the emotions area. An exhorter (mind/emotions) mate or a server (will/emotions) mate, therefore, has more in common with the compassion person.

The giver gift is unique in that all three areas of the soul are of about equal influence. Thus the giver can relate well to the other six gifts. In fact, we find that giver gifts are often the most difficult to identify at first since they share some characteristics with all the gifts:

Like the server, they enjoy working behind the scenes and also with their hands.
Like the compassion person, they are very loyal to their friends.
Like the teacher, they love studying and sharing the Word of God.
Like the exhorter, they love working with and encouraging people.
Like the perceiver, they love sharing the Good News of Jesus Christ.
Like the administrator, they can take leadership when necessary.

Where Do You Fit?

Apply the relationship between your gifting and your spouse's gifting to these diagrams to see how you fit together.

When I look at Don's gift of exhorting and my gift of administering, I can see they are in the triangular relationship. Both gifts share the mind part of the soul. Don benefits more from the emotions area and I benefit more from the will area. Since we both have strong secondary gifts, however, we see that they help us to be more cohesive.

Don also has a giver gift and I also have a teacher gift. Both of us have perceiver as our third gift, so we both operate most strongly from the mind and the will. Our gifting keeps us on the left side of the diagram. The server and compassion gifts are low for both of us, so we are weakest in these areas in the emotion area of the soul.

Remember that if you have the same gifts, you can be very understanding of each other in some aspects of your relationship, while in other areas you can be very competitive or even stubborn or conflicting. If you and your spouse have complementary gifting, you may find that you work together well, supporting one another's gifting. Or you may find that you approach some situations so differently that certain areas require patience and work.

The diagrams on page 50 are for you to fill in so you can see the areas of the soul that influence your gifting, perspective and mode of operation. Where you are strong, pray for wisdom and guidance in functioning in your marital relationship. Where you are weak, seek understanding and the ability to accept that you cannot be all things to all people. God has a special plan for your lives together and has gifted you both to enable you to accomplish that plan.

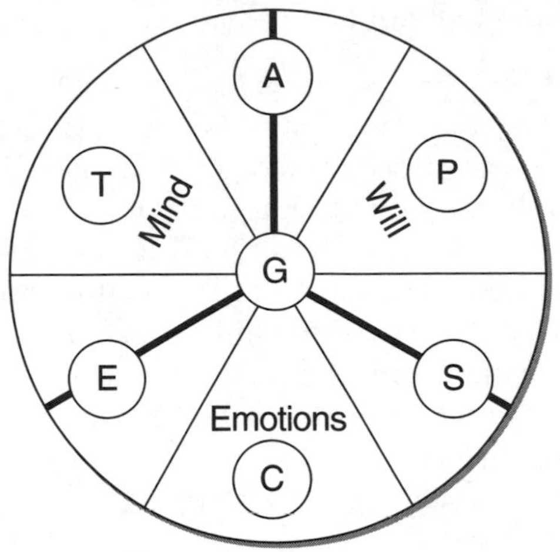

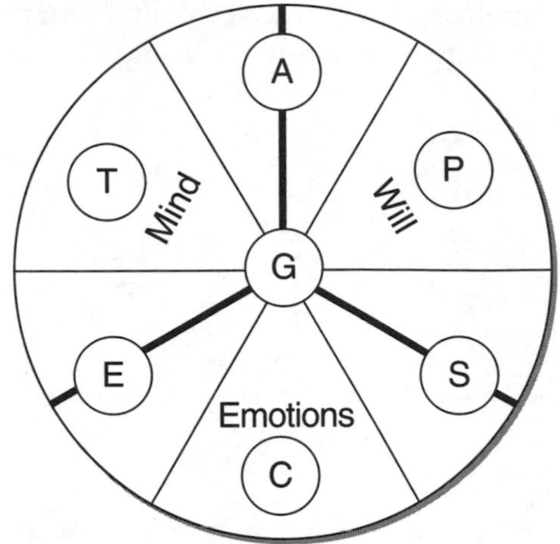

All Needs Can Be Met

Notice on the main diagram on p. 15 that each person's gifting enables him to meet the needs of others, including his mate's, in a special way. This ability is not limited to a particular gift, but the focus of each gift is distinct.

Perceiver-gifted people are exceptional at meeting spiritual needs. They are strong in faith and good at building faith in others, capable in giving spiritual insight and direction.

Server-gifted people are exceptional at meeting practical needs. They are highly motivated and skilled to do and serve and are great accomplishers.

Teacher-gifted people are exceptional at meeting mental needs. They are the natural intellectuals who love to study and research and provide education for others.

Exhorter-gifted people are exceptional at meeting psychological needs. They are positive in perspective and love to encourage others.

Giver-gifted people are exceptional at meeting material needs. They are spontaneously generous, loving the opportunity to bless others and promote evangelism.

Administrator-gifted people are exceptional at meeting functional needs. They are natural organizers and leaders who function with diligence and zeal.

Compassion-gifted people are exceptional at meeting emotional needs. They are caring and cheerful expressers of mercy and love to everyone who needs it.

In a marital relationship these gifts can bless the other. Needs will be met; love will flow. Spouses in a marriage blessed in this way will continue to meet needs and bless people wherever they go. The love of Christ will truly be shed abroad in the hearts (or souls) of people throughout the world.

Now let's meet seven spouses, each of whom is gifted differently.

Introduction to the Seven Spouses

Bob walked into our counseling office with a swagger that announced he was in charge. Alice slipped in timidly, a few reluctant steps behind him. He told her to sit in the seat nearest the window and he took the seat by the door.

"Here's my wife," he announced as if we had not noticed her. "I want you to fix her!"

"What do you mean?" Don asked.

"Fix her!" he repeated, irritated that we had to ask what he meant. "Make her obey me!"

"Would you explain a little further?" I said.

"We were at a small get-together at a friend's house last weekend," he said, "and when I told her it was time to go home, she wouldn't leave. She wouldn't obey me. I told her again and she still wouldn't go. I was so mad. A wife is supposed to obey her husband and she wouldn't do it. I want you to fix her so she'll obey me!"

I turned to Alice, sensing there was more to the situation than Bob's obviously one-sided account.

"Tell me what happened from your perspective," I encouraged her.

She glanced at Bob as if to see if it was safe to speak. Then she said gently, "Bob has strong ideas. He doesn't always agree with others, and, well—" She paused, seemingly afraid to go on. "He said some unkind things to several of our friends and I felt so ashamed. I could see they were hurt. I wanted Bob to apologize and make things right but he wouldn't. He just wanted to leave. I couldn't bear to leave the situation unresolved. I thought if we just stayed a little longer, maybe Bob would tell them he was sorry that he came on so strong."

"I don't care what she thought," Bob interrupted. "When I tell her to do something, she's supposed to do it! Besides, they deserved what I said. They needed to be straightened out."

"But they were really hurting," Alice insisted. "You could have done something to make the situation better."

"No way! If they were hurt by what I said, that's their problem. I was right. I'm always right."

"I don't think you are. You're always hurting people."

"That's their problem. God shows me how to straighten people out. I just tell them what's wrong with them and if they can't handle it, tough."

"Maybe Alice has a valid viewpoint," I suggested. "She seems to have a compassion gift and they always want relationships to be right."

"Who cares about relationships? If people don't think right, I don't want to be around them anyhow."

"Don't you think there can be more than one opinion about something?" Don asked.

"Nope. Right is right and wrong is wrong. Anything else is compromise. That's a sin, and I never sin."

Don was taken aback. "You never sin?"

"Never."

"I thought Jesus was the only one who never sinned," Don offered.

"Well, I don't sin either," Bob said emphatically.

We were amazed at his presumption and even more amazed at how completely Bob seemed to believe this deception as truth.

"Now I want you to start counseling Alice and get her straightened out," he continued. "I'll sit in on the sessions so I can be sure you're doing it right."

I could not believe my ears. "Do you think it's possible *you* are the one with a problem, not Alice?"

"Are you kidding? I don't have any problems. If Alice will just obey me, everything will be fine."

"I don't think so," Don said. "You are obviously a perceiver gift, but your pride has allowed your gifting to become distorted and polluted. You are blind to your own sins and imperfections. Your wife's compassion gift causes her to place great importance on relationships. You could learn from her."

Bob stood up quickly, his shoulders stiff.

"I won't listen to this," he said angrily. "I came to get help for my wife, and if you won't do the job, I'll take her to somebody who will!"

Grabbing Alice's arm, he pulled her out of the chair toward the door.

"I'm sorry," she said meekly. "I'm terribly sorry. Maybe I *am* the problem. Please don't be mad at us. I'll try to do better." Her voice trailed off to a whisper as he pulled her through the door.

We were not surprised not to hear from Bob again. But three days later I got a call from Alice, her timid voice betraying Bob's domination over her life.

"Bob was right, you know. I'm trying very hard to be more obedient to him. Please don't worry about me. I'll be all right."

When I tried to suggest that Bob had unhealthy control over her life and needed help, she only protested more insistently that she alone was the problem.

How sad!—a polluted perceiver lording his deceived beliefs over a hurt and frightened compassion wife. Locked into an intolerable relationship, neither was willing to seek the kind of help they needed desperately.

Since that day ten years ago I have often wondered what has become of Bob and Alice. I would not be surprised to hear that Alice is in a mental institution or that she took her own life with an overdose of sleeping pills, and that Bob is on his fourth or fifth wife.

While this is obviously an extreme case of dysfunctional motivational gifts in a marriage relationship, Don and I are amazed at how many couples demonstrate various degrees of this kind of marriage quagmire. Most of them do not have a clue about the basis of their conflicts or what to do about it.

How We Could Have Helped Bob and Alice

Had Bob allowed it, we would have shared with him the nature of his perceiver's gift and prayed for him for deliverance from his deception, arrogance and pride. Then we would have dealt with him about repentance until his mind could grasp the truth of the Word of God that says we deceive ourselves when we say we have no sin (1 John 1:8). We would have tried to teach him the absolute necessity of his becoming a humble intercessor, slow to speak and quick to pray.

We would have taught Bob what it means to be married to a compassion wife, how her giftedness motivates her naturally to care that relationships be harmonious, and how she hurts when she sees others hurt. He could learn from her how to be more sensitive to others and to be more careful about what he said.

We would have dealt with Bob on his tyrannical treatment of Alice as a possession to be ordered around, a pawn to be manipulated, a person without the right to feelings and opinions. We would have tried to get him to see that pollutions in his own gifting and the consequent squelching and dysfunctioning of her gifting, and not the difference in their giftings or sexual roles, were the primary sources of their marital problems.

But Bob's pride and hardness of heart prevented him from receiving help. His domination of his wife prevented her from seeing the truth that would have set her free to be the loving, caring and joyful person God created her to be.

Of all the seven gifts, the perceiver gift is fraught with the most dangers. Yet perceivers dedicated to following the Lord wholeheartedly are the most godly people of all. Because perceivers tend to be a people of extremes, it is easier for them to be either incredibly rebellious and self-centered or completely dedicated and God-centered. They can make the most difficult mate or the most wonderful.

How This Book Is Organized

Don and I have identified twenty major categories in which couples have problems. The first nine, along with the sex and financial categories, are the most significant.

Category 1: Communication
Category 2: Expectations
Category 3: Marital Cohesion
Category 4: Roles and Responsibilities
Category 5: Conflict Resolution
Category 6: Personality Issues
Category 7: Emotional Responses
Category 8: Intellectual Capacity
Category 9: Volitional Issues
Category 10: Physical Conditions
Category 11: Sexual Relationship
Category 12: Work and Accomplishments
Category 13: Financial Management
Category 14: Leisure Activities
Category 15: Parenting
Category 16: In-Laws and Family
Category 17: Social Relationships
Category 18: Religious Orientation
Category 19: Maturity
Category 20: Dysfunction

In the next seven chapters (one for each of the seven gifts), we will take a careful look at each of these twenty categories, as well as the five most significant problem areas for a couple with that gifting. (A problem may fit under more than one category.) Some of the problems were identified by our survey. Some have emerged from our many years of counseling. Some we have discovered through our 21 years of research and teaching about the motivational gifts around the world. Some have come from feedback via letters, phone calls and personal reports from our seminars and books. In many cases the problem areas have been confirmed through all these sources.

We have divided each of the twenty categories into three sections.

For each "A" section we will show the computer-generated statistics from our survey that show the percentage of women (She) and men (He) indicating a problem in this category. Whether the problem is minor or major, it affects the marriage relationship. At times we will also refer to the norm—the general charts for men and women—to show how much the response of a particular gifting differs from the computer-averaged responses from all men and women.

In some cases the responses reflect the situation of a particular gift and his or her mate. In other cases the responses indicate that the person responding and the spouse see things differently. In a few cases it is evident that the respondent is pinpointing the problem as the spouse's.

For each "B" section we will show the computer-generated statistics from the survey that indicate the average response for men (right side) and women (left side) based on a scale of 1 to 7, with 4 as the mean (or average) position.

This does not mean that a score of 4 is necessarily the average score for people in general. Since more people consider themselves on the "good communicator" side of the scale than the "poor communicator" side, for instance, an average score might be closer to 5. So a 5.5 score of a particular gift, even though it exceeds the average score of 4 by 1.5 points, indicates only slightly higher than the average score in light of all the gifts.

Each combination must be viewed in the light of the range it expresses. In some cases the mean score of 4 between two opposites is a balanced, desirable position, as it would be on an idealist/realist scale. In other cases a score of 4 is not desirable, such as on a scale of abuser/non-abuser (indicating that the person is an abuser about half the time).

For each "C" section we will present the computer-generated statistics that show the percentage of spouses with this gifting—first of men, then of women—who indicate they consider the statement true. Remember, it is the respondent's opinion and may not be the opinion of the mate. In fact, the mate may have exactly the opposite opinion from the perspective of his or her own gifting. An exhorter wife, for instance, may answer *true* to the statement "I need more conversation with my mate," while her server husband thinks their conversation time is more than adequate.

Looking at these scores is valuable because it enables spouses whose opinion of their situation differs from their mates' to examine the differences in light of their giftings and understand why these differences exist. Then they can decide to accept the status quo, modify it or change it drastically, if necessary.

Each section A, B and C has seven responses. Sometimes we will see that a particular problem is more likely to occur in the husband or wife. Occasionally we will see that typical problems tend to develop in specific relationships (like a male or female perceiver spouse married to another motivational gift).

The Possible Gift Combinations

There are seven *general* marriage combinations between one gift and the seven mate possibilities, but since the spouse having that gift can be either male or female, there are thirteen *actual* marriage combinations.

When we look at how the perceiver gift affects a marriage relationship with an otherwise-gifted spouse, here are the seven general combinations possible:

1. Perceiver married to a perceiver
2. Perceiver married to a server
3. Perceiver married to a teacher
4. Perceiver married to an exhorter
5. Perceiver married to a giver
6. Perceiver married to an administrator
7. Perceiver married to a compassion person

Here are all the actual combinations possible:

1. Perceiver husband married to a perceiver wife
2. Perceiver husband married to a server wife
3. Perceiver wife married to a server husband
4. Perceiver husband married to a teacher wife
5. Perceiver wife married to a teacher husband
6. Perceiver husband married to an exhorter wife
7. Perceiver wife married to an exhorter husband
8. Perceiver husband married to a giver wife
9. Perceiver wife married to a giver husband
10. Perceiver husband married to an administrator wife
11. Perceiver wife married to an administrator husband
12. Perceiver husband married to a compassion wife
13. Perceiver wife married to a compassion husband

So in the seven chapters that follow, we will cover all 49 possible marriage relationships. Don and I have included many personal illustrations in order to show how practical and life-related the knowledge of the gifts is.

Now let's move to part 2 and the first motivational gift.

PART 2

Living with Another Gift

Living with a Perceiver Spouse

Perceivers are called by God, without exception, to be intercessors. While some may not hear the call and others (like Jonah) may be running from it, intercession is an essential part of their lives and well-being. A perceiver not actively involved in intercessory prayer is likely to be critical and judgmental, causing serious problems in the marriage relationship. Criticism damages the partner's self-esteem. Bit by bit the perceiver can chip away at the love that once formed the foundation for the marriage. Like the woman in Proverbs 14:1 who is destroying her own home, the perceiver can eventually ruin the most basic relationship of life.

Terry was married to such a perceiver wife. He had first been attracted to Amy because she expressed her faith precisely and confidently. With his compassion gifting he was shy and quiet, but in her company he found an inner boldness being stirred up. During their courtship she was positive about her feelings and had encouraging words for him. But after they were married she began to find fault with little things she had never mentioned before. If he did not comply with her corrections, she became more critical. To cope, he clammed up. Communication became one-sided, which motivated Amy to harangue him even more.

After several years Terry felt so judged that he decided to end the relationship. Under the threat of divorce, Amy came to me for counseling.

It did not take long to discover the primary cause of their breakdown in communication and the erosion of their relationship.

"Have you ever realized," I asked Amy, "that God has called you to be an intercessor?"

"No," she replied. "I'm too busy for that. Besides, it takes so long for God to answer prayers. When I see something wrong, I prefer to take action."

"Like with Terry?"

"Well, yes," she replied, perturbed with my direct question. "He's got so many faults it makes me upset. So I tell it like it is, but he's not man enough to change. It's not *my* fault he has so many faults! What am I supposed to do?"

"Pray," I replied simply. "With your perceiver gifting it is essential if you are to do God's will, and especially if you want a good marriage."

I explained to her how becoming an intercessor would enable her to commit to God those things she felt were wrong with Terry (or anyone else), allowing God to deal with his heart and change his behavior from the inside out.

"Your tongue has become an instrument of hurtfulness," I continued, "destroying your husband and your marriage. But you can turn it around through intercession, letting God do indirectly what you have tried to do confrontationally. Stop judging your husband. That's God's job. Your job is to love and pray for him. Stop criticizing him. Encourage him. Respect him according to Ephesians 5:33."

I read it to her from *The Amplified Bible*:

> Let each man of you (without exception) love his wife as [being in a sense] his very own self; and let the wife see that she respects and reverences her husband—that she notices him, regards him, honors him, prefers him, venerates and esteems him; and that she defers to him, praises him, and loves and admires him exceedingly.

"Let your mouth do just that," I said. "You'll be amazed at what will happen as you take your complaints to God and communicate with your husband in harmony with Paul's directive."

Amy was quiet for a moment. Then she said, "I had no idea how unscriptural I've been with my mouth. It's my fault my marriage is falling apart. I feel awful. Do you think Terry will ever forgive me?"

"Ask him," I replied. "Tell him what you've learned about this negative tendency of your gift and demonstrate genuine repentance. I think he'll give you a chance to prove your sincere desire to change."

Terry did welcome her repentant heart. Hope blossomed in both of them. When Amy queried the Lord about intercession, she found He *had* called her to it, but she had been too busy correcting others to listen. She changed literally overnight. And the more she interceded, the more her communication with Terry improved. Their marriage is on the mend and she has since encouraged several other perceiver wives with similar problems.

Five Major Problem Areas

First we will look at the five most significant problem areas of the perceiver gift—problems that influence each of the twenty subject categories of our survey.

1. The I-Am-Right-and-Everyone-Else-Is-Wrong Mentality

Perceivers think they are always right. Many times they are. God has planted in their hearts a desire to be right, a desire to do what is right and pleasing to Him. But without a humble spirit and a heart dedicated to God, the positive can turn into the negative. They can be totally wrong and have a bulldozing effect on their spouses.

Of all the gifts, perceivers need most to know about the seven motivational gifts and about the validity of each perspective.

2. Pride

While everyone is subject to some degree to pride, perceivers are by far the most vulnerable. Believing (as Amy did) that they are always right, they can easily think of themselves more highly than they ought to think, as the apostle Paul warned:

> By the grace (unmerited favor of God) given to me I warn every one among you not to estimate and think of himself more highly than he ought—not to have an exaggerated opinion of his own importance; but to rate his ability with sober judgment, each according to the degree of faith apportioned by God to him.
>
> Romans 12:3

Pride stinks. But perceivers are often unaware of its presence in their lives. And when pride is identified by others, they often deny it.

3. Criticism and Judgmentalism

The ability of perceivers to see easily what is wrong (or what appears to be wrong) often causes them to be quick to criticize. This can be devastating in a marriage relationship, to the point that the spouse believes he or she can do nothing acceptable to the critical mate. This can lead to discouragement, depression, a poor self-image, hopelessness, constant fights, loss of love and divorce. God's plan is for the perceiver to be quick to pray and slow to criticize. Commitment to pray for concerns is the antidote for a critical attitude.

4. Bluntness and Tactlessness

Perceivers often employ the bull-in-the-china-shop approach to interpersonal relationships or suffer from foot-in-mouth disease. Due to the intensity of their personalities, as well as their tendency to see and feel things in the extreme, they often speak before they think, leaving their spouse offended or even crushed. They need to learn to think first and weigh the consequences of the intended words. They often need to pray first or pay later. Tact does not come naturally to perceivers; it must be learned.

5. Poor Self-Image

Because of their focus on rightness, tendency toward perfectionism and keen awareness that their own attitudes and behavior often fall short of the ideal, perceivers tend to be upset by their imperfections and failures. They can be harder on themselves than on anyone else, leading to a sense of frustration, failure and some measure of depression. To the degree that perceivers do not resolve these matters, their self-image diminishes. This can result in withdrawal and moodiness or be covered up with fits of anger, deprecation of others or attempts to control them. This can also be harmful to the mate involved, who may not know how to cope with the effects of the self-image problem.

The Twenty Problem Categories of the Perceiver Gift

Let's take a look at the twenty categories of problem areas for perceiver spouses indicated by our marriage survey.

Category 1: Communication

A. I FEEL WE HAVE SOME PROBLEMS IN COMMUNICATION IN THESE AREAS:

	He	She
1. Misunderstandings	37%	32%
2. Free to share	33%	46%
3. Listening	74%	54%
4. Conversation	33%	46%
5. Correction	44%	56%
6. Body language	33%	44%
7. Ridicule	37%	44%

Thirty to forty percent of the perceivers we surveyed indicate that they have frequent major or minor misunderstandings.

This puts a lot of pressure on the marriage relationship. Because perceivers are forthright in what they think, and because they like to have their way, their spouses may recoil from their pushiness, understanding only what they find palatable.

The perceiver, being candid, can find it difficult to follow the imprecise meaning of the words of the more gentle and tactful spouse.

While perceiver husbands and wives indicate they do not always feel free to share their feelings honestly, it is definitely a bigger problem for the wives. Feelings are necessarily neither good nor bad; they just are. Often a husband will dismiss his wife's honest feeling because it does not seem logical to him. But it is important to her. Couples benefit by allowing one another to express true feelings without being judged. Accept that feelings are. Then explore the feelings gently to see *why* they are and what can be done about them (if anything).

In any relationship, stomped-on feelings result in "turtling," the process by which a person opens up, is hurt by another person's disregard for or judgment of those feelings, and retreats to a safe place, declining to share feelings in the future.

Notice in the chart above that not listening well to the other spouse is the major communication problem, especially for the perceiver husband. Feeling ignored feels like rejection. It hurts! More than half of the perceiver women respondents saw not listening as a problem in their marriages. About 75 percent of the men said it was a problem. Communication is not simply speaking; it is knowing that the other person has received what is said.

Perceivers believe that what they say is important. In their eyes it is truth or they would not bother to say it. Perhaps that is why listening is so important to them.

If you are married to a perceiver gift, try to be more attentive. You may not always agree with your partner, but indicate that you have heard what he or she has said.

Sometimes talk takes place without much content. Women tend to agree that meaningful conversation means opening up on the feeling as well as factual level. And perceiver wives have a special need (as the statistics indicate) for substantive conversation over and above an exposé of the day's stresses or what the kids did today. They especially want conversation to include openness and honesty, even if it hurts. They are not afraid to hit issues head-on.

Men in general (except compassion men) find it more difficult to communicate on the feeling level. Perceiver men do this to some degree, but they are more likely to communicate convictions and opinions based on what they believe or think rather than what they feel.

Perceiver husbands and wives have such strong opinions about how things should be said and done that they tend to correct their spouses more than they need to. They are quick to say what they think, often hurting the spouses' feelings. But the perceiver married to a teacher gift can run into a brick wall, since typically the teacher also thinks, "I am right," defending a strong viewpoint with great logic. And if the mate is a perceiver gift, too, watch out—sparks can fly! They may never resolve who is right.

While the male perceiver is good at negative nonverbal communication, the female perceiver is significantly more explicit. Her eyes can flash with wrath, her set mouth proclaim stubbornness and her folded arms signal "You won't get me to budge one inch!" Since some reports indicate that as much as 75 or even 85 percent of communication can be nonverbal—especially in the marriage relationship in which even tiny signals can easily be identified—perceivers should watch how they hold their arms, cock their heads or sigh. A frown or pout or deep sigh can cancel out positive-sounding words or set up a confusing double message.

The innate bluntness of immature perceivers enables them to use every weapon they can think of to manipulate their mates. The tongue can be their weapon of choice to cut down their spouses' confidence or defenses quickly. One perceiver ridiculed her husband so much that he felt increasingly drawn to his exhorter secretary who had only encouraging words to say to him each day. The shock of discovering their affair finally caused the perceiver wife to seek counseling. As she turned her cutting words to caring words, the marriage was restored.

Men and women perceivers (see chart B below) consider themselves reasonably good communicators. Since perceiving, along with teaching, exhorting and administrating, is one of the speaking-type gifts of 1 Peter 4:11 (the gifts above the dotted line in the body diagram in chapter 1), it stands to reason that speaking comes naturally to perceiver spouses.

Perceiver husbands see themselves as balanced, not talking too much or too little. But perceiver wives admit they tend to talk too much. Those married to exhorter husbands find themselves regularly outtalked and often interrupted. An administrator spouse can also at least match the perceiver in talkativeness.

Perceiver husbands consider themselves slightly better than average in paying good attention to what their partners say. Perceiver wives view themselves as even more attentive. Perhaps it is because women in general enjoy chit-chat more than men that the perceiver women responded more positively here. Even so, the score is only moderately above the mean of 4, indicating that while the perceiver wife can enjoyably engage in a measure of chit-chat, she usually prefers more serious subjects.

Regarding criticism, the location of both scores slightly on the "critical" side reflects one of the five major problem areas of the

B. To what degree, from 1 to 7, are you one way or the other:

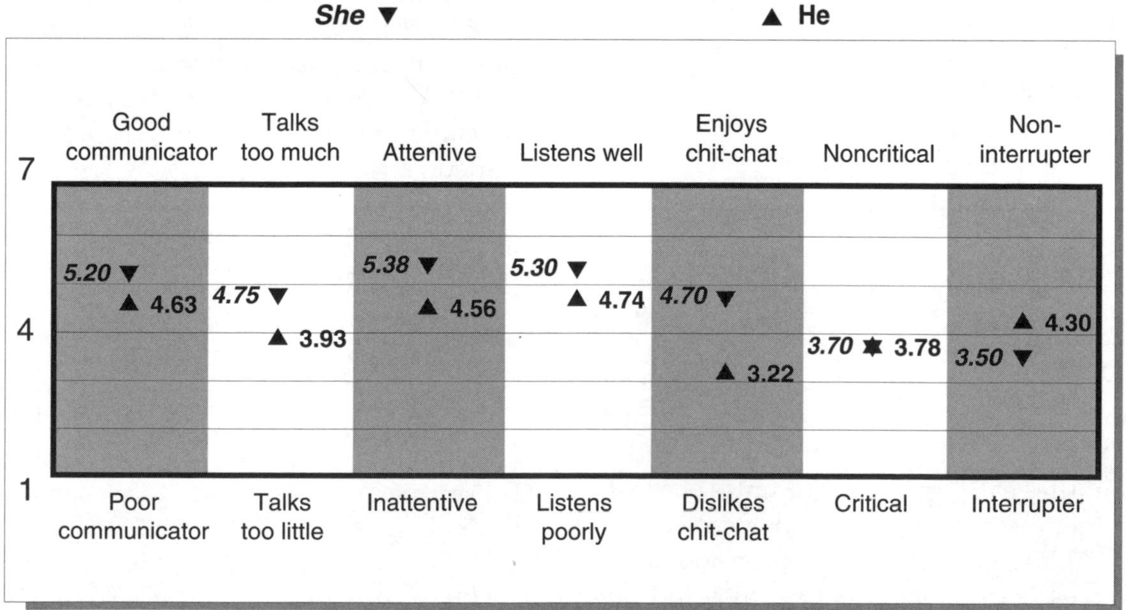

perceiver and the importance of the perceiver's becoming an intercessor.

Mel, a perceiver husband married to a server wife, Melaine, has embraced intercession so seriously that he has become exceptionally mature. His consistent desire to please God and do His will has overcome his former critical spirit. Melaine shares that she never hears criticism from him toward her or others. Surely this is God's plan for perceivers.

C. My genuine needs, views or beliefs are:

	He	She
1. I need more conversation with my mate.	52%	46%
2. I need my partner to listen to me more attentively.	33%	54%
3. I need more quiet time without conversation.	19%	22%
4. I feel we need to share more intimately our thoughts and feelings.	33%	51%
5. I get hurt easily by my mate's unkind remarks.	41%	49%
6. I need more of my partner's undivided attention.	22%	49%
7. I am satisfied with our communication and conversation.	52%	29%

About half of all perceiver respondents said they needed more communication in their marriages—not just casual talk but meaningful conversation. Take time for this; schedule it if necessary. Turn off the TV, take a walk, put the kids to bed fifteen minutes early, get up ten minutes earlier to linger over that second cup of coffee.

Although most perceivers consider themselves reasonably attentive, they indicate here that they need more attentiveness from their spouses.

While perceivers like conversation, they also value quiet time. This reflects the loner aspect of their gifting. They need space to ponder, reflect, pray or read.

Notice that perceiver wives need more intimate communication. Women in general need this more than men, many of whom are satisfied with more surface conversation.

The perceiver's dislike of insensitive or unkind talk is significant. The irony is that perceivers are the most likely to be blunt and unkind to their mates. They can dish it out but cannot always take it themselves, especially if they perceive something to be untrue. Food for thought and a good place for perceivers to practice the Golden Rule.

The lack of undivided attention, while not a major problem for most perceiver husbands, *is* a problem for most perceiver wives. Don and I recommend that they let their mates know when they are not getting it. Husbands of any gifting are not mindreaders.

Half of the perceiver husbands we surveyed and two-thirds of the perceiver wives were dissatisfied with the level and quality of communication in the marriages. (And perceivers can easily turn to criticism and blaming when they are dissatisfied.)

Category 2: Expectations

A. I feel we have some problems in what we expect of each other in these areas:

	He	She
1. Lifestyle	26%	22%
2. Priorities	33%	56%
3. Ideals/goals	22%	24%
4. Holidays	26%	5%
5. Hopes/dreams	26%	29%

	He	She
6. Conduct	15%	29%
7. Homework	15%	22%

Perceivers tend to be perfectionists, wanting everything to be right, correct and in order. While they are often hardest on themselves, they can be just as hard, or harder, on their mates. A perceiver husband like Bob (whom we met in the last chapter) may use his strong sense of authority to demand his wife's compliance. If she is a server, giver or compassion gift (like Alice), she may comply. But if she is a perceiver, too, she may resent being told what to do; and her tendency to stubbornness may cause her to dig in her heels and resist his verbalized expectations, even if inwardly she agrees with them.

A perceiver husband married to a teacher, exhorter or administrator wife may find that she has strong enough opinions of her own that she will not yield to his heavy-handed tactics.

More than half of the women perceivers and a third of the men perceivers reported conflict over the establishment of priorities. This is probably because perceivers have strong opinions and expect their mates to comply. Taking time to sit down and list mutual priorities helps defuse this problem.

The expectations of perceivers in the area of ideals, goals and values seem reasonable. (Perceivers need to be careful not to be pushy here.) Perceivers are also good at articulating hopes and dreams.

We were surprised that perceiver husbands consider how the holidays are celebrated to be of more importance than perceiver wives do. Expectations of conduct are of greater importance to perceiver wives. Men perceivers hang looser.

Typically women are concerned that work at home (traditionally their responsibility) be shared to some degree by their husbands. But only a small percentage of the perceivers identified this as a problem. Working wives expect more help, and in

B. To what degree, from 1 to 7, are you one way or the other:

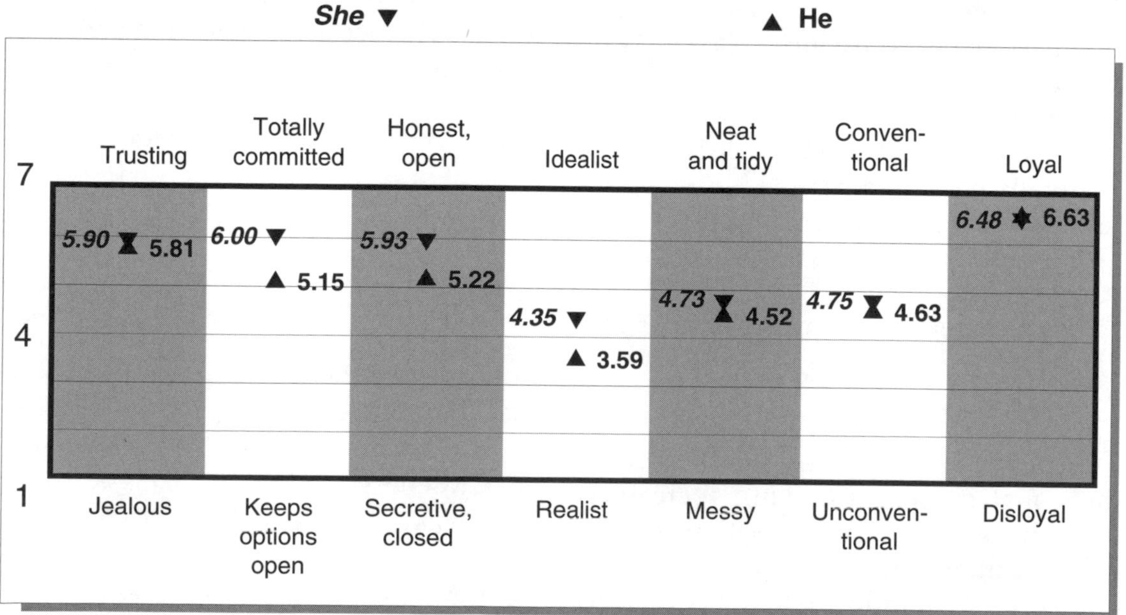

today's culture of double incomes, men have increasingly risen to the task.

The commitment level here (see chart B on page 65) shows that perceiver wives are very committed to their mates and expect them to be committed, too. Perceiver husbands leaned in that direction, although not quite as strongly. Perceivers are trusting of their mates and high in loyalty.

Perceivers also value open and honest relationships. While they would like everything in life to be ideal, and may work toward that end, they are also empirical realists, dealing with life as it is.

It is safe to conclude that perceivers, leaning only slightly to the "neat and tidy" side, can go either way. No "Mr. Cleans" or "Mrs. Messys" here!

C. My genuine needs, views or beliefs are:

	He	She
1. I need to be more sure of my partner's motives.	11%	39%
2. I need a mate who is dependable.	48%	51%
3. I feel we need to work more at setting joint priorities.	41%	49%
4. I need to be more confident in how my mate handles stress.	44%	34%
5. I need my spouse to be totally honest with me.	48%	61%
6. I need to have former family customs a part of my life.	11%	12%
7. I feel our expectations are realistic and workable.	78%	66%

Perceiver husbands seem fairly sure of their mates' motives, while perceiver wives have some difficulty with this. This may be because they are more discerning of motives, wanting their nonperceiver mates to place significant value on their own motives.

Half of the respondents held dependability in a mate to be of great value. Perceivers themselves, unless rebellious or dysfunctional, are usually very dependable.

Close to half indicated they needed more effort in setting joint priorities. But imagine the frustration of a perceiver spouse married to a compassion spouse who, by nature, lives for the "now" and sees no point in planning ahead! Administrators married to perceivers, by contrast, have a great time prioritizing.

Perceiver responses on stress are typical of all gifts except exhorters, who are gloriously flexible and adaptable. Perceiver mates feel confident about their own ability to handle stress and may expect their mates to be less capable.

Perceivers are honest to a fault. Sometimes their honesty pours out so candidly that they leave their spouses burned. They expect their spouses to be honest, too, and can take the truth even if it hurts—at least so long as they perceive it to be the truth.

A high percentage of perceivers seem to feel their expectation level in marriage is reasonable.

Category 3: Marital Cohesion

A. I feel we have some problems in getting along with each other in these areas:

	He	She
1. Time together	41%	37%
2. Give and take	22%	32%
3. Feeling one	19%	37%
4. Closeness	30%	41%
5. Goals/priorities	41%	41%
6. Loneliness	7%	24%
7. Love/affection	44%	44%

More than a third of the perceivers we surveyed feel they need more time with their mates. While this may be typical of every couple in our age of two-bread-winner families, it may point to the need to prioritize how time is used. The evening time-robber, TV, may have to be turned off or limited. Social time with others may also need to be whittled down to ensure more quality time together. It may be wise to schedule time alone or even make dates to get away without phone interruptions or the kids. When we do not plan, time has a way of filling itself up.

Perceiver women had more difficulty with the "give and take" item. Women tend to do more giving and feel resentment because of it. It is important for them to speak up more.

Almost twice as many perceiver women as men admit some difficulty in feeling truly one with their mates. Not only is the "one flesh" experience part of marriage; it is essential that partners feel one in spirit, purpose and relationship. Perceivers must be careful not to let their loner tendencies build too much space between them and their mates.

Perceiver wives who see feeling close as more of a problem need to share their feelings more with their mates. Granted, they can be so frank that the mate pulls back. But when perceivers pray for guidance in how to share, and when they endeavor to be gentle in approach and words, they help open their mates to a more intimate relationship.

About forty percent of perceiver husbands and wives confessed problems with goals and priorities. Perceivers have such strong opinions that they tend to overwhelm their mates, often squelching them or causing them to shrink from saying what they really think.

Loneliness is not a problem, especially for perceiver husbands, who scored only seven percent. This is because perceivers see time alone—to think, pray or remain quiet and undisturbed—as an asset and at times a necessity.

The major problem in this category is the lack of romantic love and affection. It is unlikely that perceivers married to compassion people feel this, since compassion mates are exceptionally loving, communicating love in both words and actions. Givers, exhorters and servers are generally demonstrative, too. Teacher and administrator mates, although feeling loving, tend to be less demonstrative.

Perceiver wives (see chart B on page 68) show more supersensitivity. A wise husband of any gifting recognizes this, making allowances and extending greater kindness.

Perceiver mates are independent by nature, the husbands slightly more so. While agreeability scores prevail, the tendency of perceivers to extremes produces some yo-yoing, especially among immature perceiver spouses.

Consistency scores are high, reflecting perceivers' strong convictions. Perceivers see themselves as exceptionally reliable. They are true to their word. They follow through. They are dependable. (Dysfunctional or rebellious perceiver spouses are an exception to this.)

Peace at any price is not the mode of operation of perceiver spouses; rather, peace growing out of a foundation of what is right. Our server friend Melaine is so confident of her perceiver husband Mel's ability to hear from God that peace reigns in their home.

The high scores on encouraging are based on the fact that perceivers like to encourage righteous living. A less mature perceiver mate can flip to the *dis*courager mode.

B. To what degree, from 1 to 7, are you one way or the other:

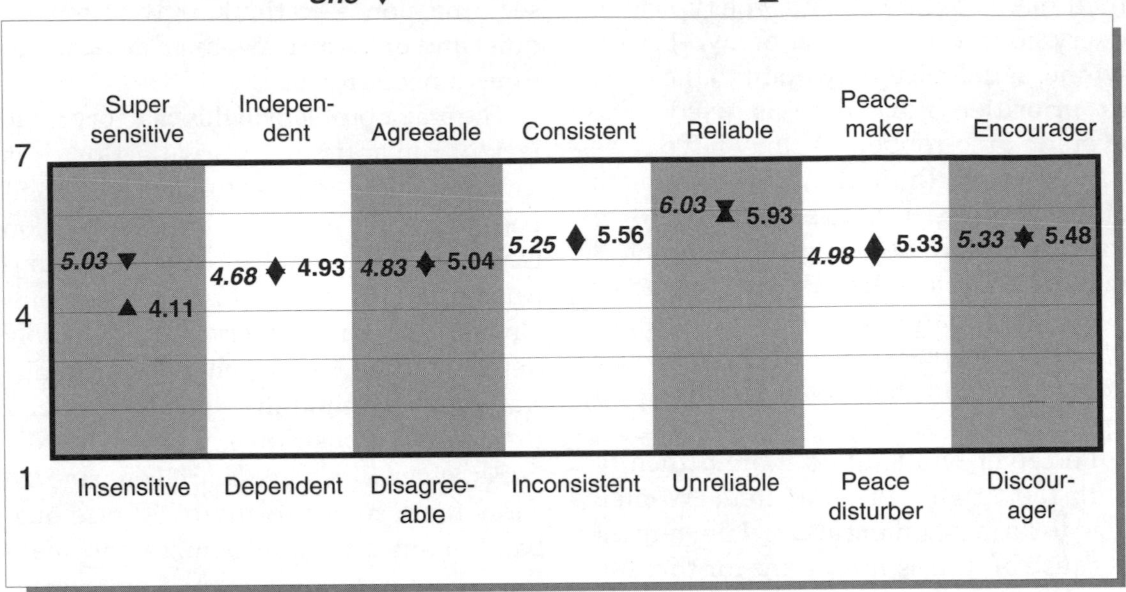

C. My genuine needs, views or beliefs are:

	He	She
1. I need to be able to confide more in my mate.	30%	24%
2. I feel there needs to be more unity in our relationship.	22%	34%
3. I need to feel more secure in our marriage.	4%	17%
4. I am afraid to share some of my feelings with my partner.	37%	32%
5. I need my mate to be more sensitive to my needs.	26%	41%
6. I do not consider divorce ever to be an option.	81%	83%
7. I am satisfied with our marital interaction and closeness.	70%	51%

Between 24 and 30 percent of perceivers want more opportunity to confide in their marital partner. To be sure, some thoughts and feelings are best left confided to God, especially since prayer and intercession are such an important part of the perceiver's lifestyle. But the more mates confide in each other, the more intimacy blossoms.

Most perceiver husbands are reasonably satisfied with their marital unity. A third of the perceiver wives feel more unity is needed, reflecting the tendency of non-perceiver husbands to be threatened by the strong personality of their perceiver wives. They may withdraw, causing their wives to wonder why there is increasing space between them.

Perceiver husbands are amazingly secure in their marriages. Some perceiver wives are less so, but it may depend on their spouses' gifting. About a third of perceivers confess to some fear in sharing their feelings honestly. Sometimes their mates cannot handle such candor, causing the perceivers to hold in feelings more often.

A higher percentage of perceiver wives desire their mates to be more sensitive to their needs. Women in general want this. Both husband and wives do well to practice it.

Perceivers feel strongly about the durability of marriage. Normally they do everything in their power to hold the marriage together no matter what problems come along.

More men than women are satisfied with their marital cohesion. Strong marital leadership on the part of perceiver husbands could account for this, while the lack of leadership by more passive husbands can leave perceiver wives dissatisfied.

Category 4: Roles and Responsibilities

A. I feel we have some problems in our marriage roles and responsibilities in these areas:

	He	She
1. Authority	30%	7%
2. Submission	19%	15%
3. Responsibilities	26%	22%
4. Decision making	30%	27%
5. Roles	11%	5%
6. Feeling overworked	26%	27%
7. Home management	30%	39%

Perceiver husbands have far fewer problems with authority because they want and easily take the authoritative role themselves. Perceiver women scored near the norm. They can feel comfortable either taking authority themselves or being married to someone who in their estimation handles authority well.

Because perceivers understand authority, they also understand submission. Most perceivers agree heartily with the apostle Paul that they should "submit to one another out of reverence for Christ" (Ephesians 5:21, NIV).

Role definition comes easily to perceivers They are willing to define areas of responsibility for themselves and their mates and to operate in those responsibilities faithfully.

Perceivers score below the norm in decision-making and try to work well with their mates, articulating their ideas and opinions clearly. They also tend to accept traditional roles.

In terms of feeling overworked, perceiver husbands reflect the norm for all men, while perceiver women score less than the norm for all women. For them, not having enough to do is boredomsville!

Perceiver wives tend to feel that more home management falls on their shoulders than on their husbands'. This is especially so if these wives have outside jobs.

While perceiver husbands (see chart B on page 70) tend to be slightly more authoritarian than perceiver wives, both are fairly close to a balanced position. Bossiness can from time to time be a problem. Both tend to cooperate, unless they perceive something to be unreasonable or contrary to their understanding of God's will.

Decisiveness for perceiver mates is no problem. They are good at it, sometimes to the point that their spouses may feel dominated or left out of the decision-making process.

Perceivers are straightforward in what they think or say. This often creates the bluntness problem. Any attempts at manipulation are not hidden.

The responsibility level for perceiver spouses is high. They take life seriously and try hard to fulfill their responsibilities.

C. My genuine needs, views or beliefs are:

	He	She
1. I need my role clarified more.	11%	10%

B. To what degree, from 1 to 7, are you one way or the other:

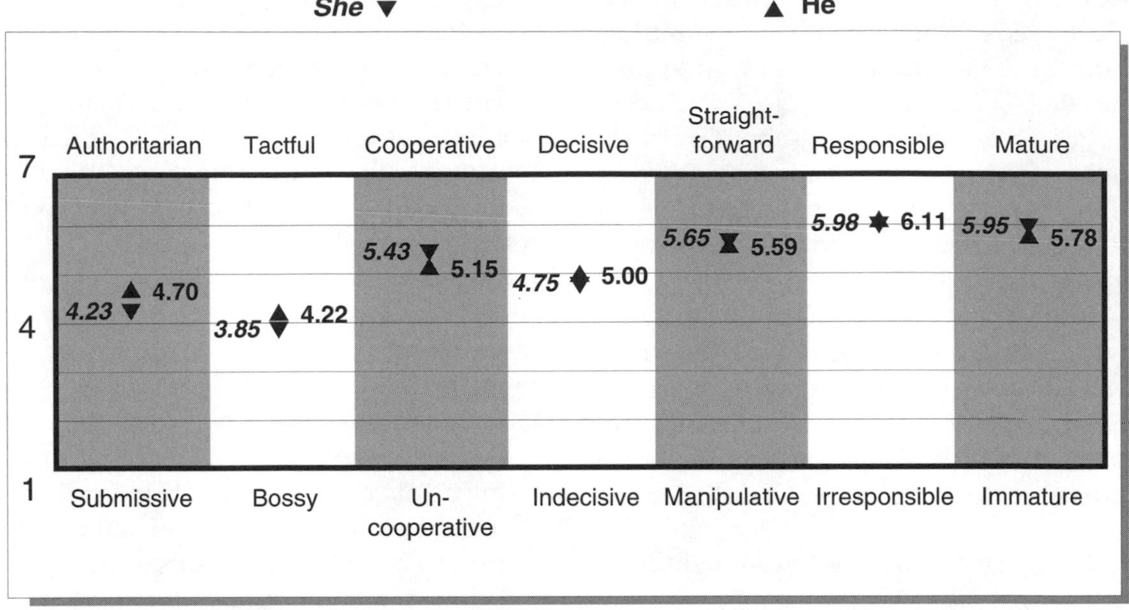

	He	She
2. I need more freedom to discuss ideas and options.	11%	20%
3. I need to use some of my capabilities more.	41%	32%
4. I need to receive more respect from my partner.	26%	27%
5. I need more domestic help and support from my spouse.	7%	24%
6. I would like to help more in planning together.	22%	24%
7. I am satisfied with the roles and responsibilities we have established.	67%	56%

Role and responsibility clarification does not seem to be a felt need for perceivers. But both husbands and wives express some need to utilize more of their capabilities. Only a quarter indicate the need for more respect from their spouses. For perceiver wives the need for more domestic help is significant. Such a feeling of overload can lead to resentment and conflict.

Category 5: Conflict Resolution

A. I feel we have some problems in how we deal with conflicts in these areas:

	He	She
1. Anger management	44%	59%
2. Who's right	33%	32%
3. Final decisions	33%	10%
4. Silent treatment	30%	46%
5. Ultimatums	15%	7%
6. Personal attacks	22%	49%
7. Blame game	30%	37%

Perceivers are honest in admitting they have problems managing anger. It is because they feel so deeply and believe so strongly that they react so intensely. It is normal to feel anger, at least from time to time. What is done with the anger becomes the problem. Anger must be resolved properly or it will not go away. Anger expressed will likely hurt others; anger stuffed will hurt the stuffer.

Jesus gave the only pattern that deals successfully with anger: forgiveness (see Matthew 5:21–26 and 18:21–35). (Refer to "Additional Material Available" at the back of the book for material on proper anger management.)

At least a third of the perceiver respondents indicate a problem with arguments over who is right. This is to be expected, given their propensity to feel they are always right.

Final decision-making is not an issue with perceiver wives but is of significant concern for perceiver husbands. They like being the ultimate decision-makers.

Mum's the word. Or is it? Perceivers do not usually resort to the silent treatment themselves but see it as a spousal problem, not only in communication but as a barrier to conflict resolution. Being verbally motivated, they see clamming up as escapism that solves nothing. Perceiver women in particular dislike the male tendency to turtle.

Ultimatums are not identified as a particular problem, yet immature perceivers may resort to these occasionally as a means of attempted control.

Personal attacks are considered a problem by half of the perceiver women but only a quarter of the men. Perhaps this is because women feel more hurt by a verbal diatribe while men can objectify the situation more readily. One author on marriage describes each partner as having an emotional bank account enabling him or her to love the other. When positive input is given, marital love grows. But personal attacks deplete the account. Spouses can thus build or destroy their marriage.

The blame game started with Adam blaming Eve: "The woman you put here with me—she gave me some fruit from the tree, and I ate it" (Genesis 3:12, NIV). Our Adamic nature gives every human being the tendency to blame others instead of facing responsibility. This is a particular temptation for perceiver spouses. Blaming causes reactions and the cycle of finger-pointing continues. Self-centeredness increases it. Maturity diminishes it. Genuine humility can stamp it out.

Perceiver spouses (see chart B on page 72) lean slightly to the calm, cool and collected side; but we have found that they can rebound into the anger mode easily when their wills are crossed.

Agreeability and adaptability seem to be more the norm, but perceivers have a greater tendency than the other gifts to be stubborn. Their desire to be right enables them to dig in their heels.

Perceivers generally are forgiving. Strong differences can last for a while but grudges are uncommon. Most perceivers are well aware of the biblical admonitions to forgive, the benefits of forgiving and the dangerous consequences of not forgiving.

It would be logical to conclude that, with all their strengths and strong beliefs, perceivers are not easily wounded. (The most common wounder in a marriage relationship, we have found, is the perceiver spouse.) Yet they are vulnerable, too. Don and I were surprised at the high scores perceivers give themselves in being easily wounded.

We have also found that perceivers tend to handle stress overtly. Their marriage partners, therefore, are aware of the process but do not always define the perceivers' handling as good. Sometimes the partners become the targets of the reaction and not the beneficiaries.

While we do not necessarily expect to see strongly opinionated perceivers apologize, their responses show that they feel their tendency is to do so. They definitely do so when they realize they have been

B. To what degree, from 1 to 7, are you one way or the other:

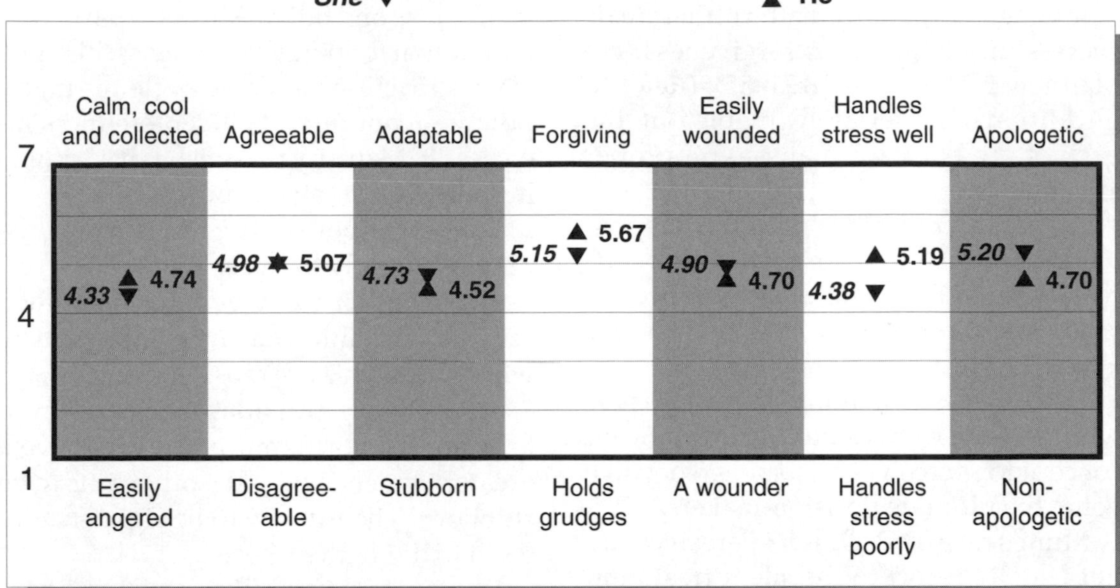

wrong. Being willing to say, "I'm sorry" is an asset to any marriage.

C. My genuine needs, views or beliefs are:

	He	She
1. I need to gain control over my temper.	37%	41%
2. I need my spouse to gain control over his/her temper.	30%	39%
3. I need to have my point of view heard more often.	11%	20%
4. I feel a strong need to avoid arguments and conflicts.	33%	27%
5. I need my mate to forgive me more quickly.	22%	12%
6. I think we need better ground rules for resolving conflicts.	30%	34%
7. I am satisfied with the way we resolve conflicts.	59%	44%

Not only do perceivers tend to have a temper, but they usually recognize the need for control over it. They are apt to blow first and be sorry for it later. Meanwhile, of course, damage has been done. Relationship repair needs to be applied.

Many perceivers see conflicts as the normal and healthy process of working through marital differences. Some see the need for better ground rules for the resolution of conflicts. About half are satisfied with their present methodology.

Category 6: Personality Issues

A. I feel we have some problems in personality conflicts and issues in these areas:

	He	She
1. Being right	26%	44%
2. Pride	30%	37%
3. Understanding	30%	49%
4. Change attempts	22%	20%
5. Methodologies	30%	39%
6. Habits	41%	34%
7. Forgetfulness	48%	49%

While the perceiver always wants to be right, some of the other gifts do, too. So if a perceiver gift is married to a teacher gift who bases rightness on researched truth, heated arguments may develop. An administrator gift may also champion a position, accusing the perceiver spouse of narrow-mindedness in not looking at the whole picture. An exhorter mate may also expound a strong opinion, but is likely to be more flexible.

Pride is a major problem with perceivers. It must be dealt with or it will be the source of personality conflicts with the spouse and others. The perceiver who chooses the path of humility will bless a spouse of any gifting.

The high score in misunderstandings for perceiver women reflects their tendency to come on too strong. They may think, *Why doesn't he understand me?* or *Why can't he accept me as I am?* Understanding requires the ability to stand outside one's own frame of reference to see the other person's viewpoint. Perceivers cannot always do this.

Reasonably low scores in the area of one mate trying to change the other indicate that perceivers believe they have already been successful in making the changes in their spouses that they would like, or else they have given up trying. Their mates may tell another story, revealing changes they would like to see in their rather rigid partners.

About a third of perceiver spouses report conflicts in marital methodologies. This is not surprising. They are unique in their modes of operation in relationship to the other six gifts.

Jim, a wise perceiver, has said, "It's better if my wife and I can see that my way or her way is not necessarily the best and be willing to lay it down and seek God's way for the two of us."

All partners find some of the habits of their spouses irritating. Perceiver spouses scored about average on this. But they are a bit more resistant to changing their own habits.

Half of the perceiver mates indicate that forgetfulness is a problem. This is higher than the norm of forty percent. One perceiver said he tended to forget more insignificant things because his mind was on more important things. Hmm! Do we detect a bit of pride here?

Perceiver spouses (see chart B on page 74) see themselves (surprisingly) slightly more on the adaptable side. This may be a blind spot. Our experience indicates they are slightly more on the rigid side, and in some situations very much so.

Respect comes out high. Perceivers tend to show respect to others in general and to their mates in particular, except when a mate has proven untrustworthy.

Perceiver husbands score higher than perceiver wives on self-esteem, although both are on the plus side. The more mature a perceiver is, the higher his or her self-esteem. Those who are more immature can vacillate drastically, causing problems in the marriage relationship. Moodiness, self-pity and depression can be unwelcome companions.

Being a complimenter rather than a complainer seems to be the bent, but perceivers can flip into the negative without warning. One perceiver wife I counseled complained about her husband constantly in front of him during our sessions. Only occasionally did she heed my efforts to get her to see how she was "biting and devouring" him.

C. My genuine needs, views or beliefs are:

	He	She
1. I wish my partner complimented me more.	30%	37%
2. I need more encouragement from my mate.	41%	34%

B. To what degree, from 1 to 7, are you one way or the other:

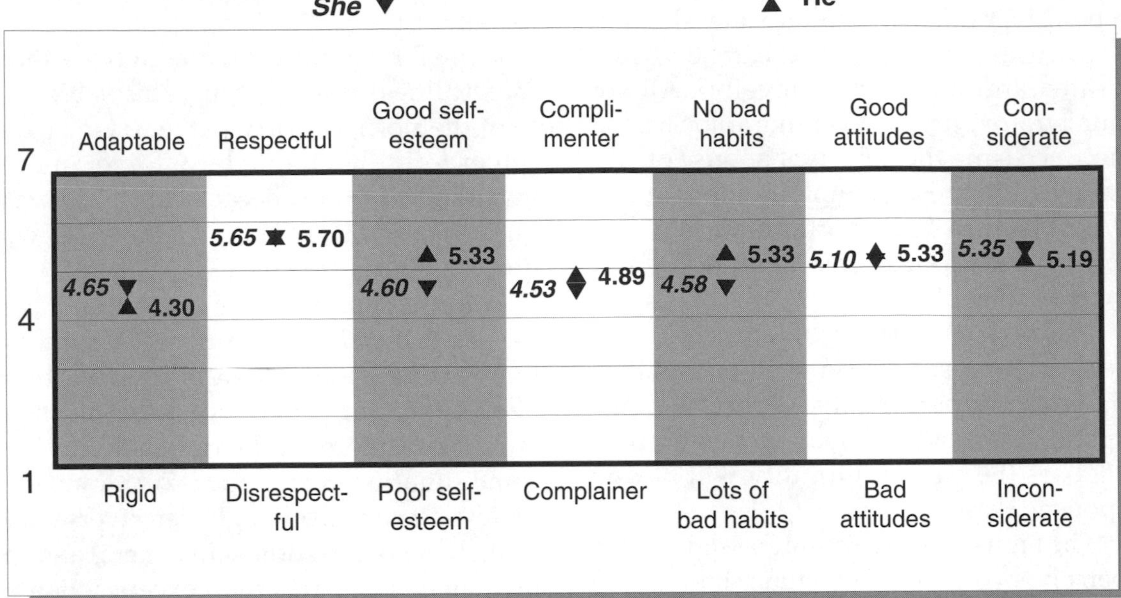

	He	She
3. I need to be accepted and appreciated for who I am.	41%	37%
4. I need to retain my unique identity.	22%	29%
5. My partner needs to understand my gifts.	30%	44%
6. I need more admiration and respect from my partner.	26%	20%
7. We do not seem to have any personality conflicts.	44%	34%

The first three items show that about a third of all perceivers need more compliments, encouragement and appreciation from their mates. (Don't we all?) Since perceivers usually seem self-confident, their mates do not always realize their need for positive input.

Perceiver wives especially need to have their mates understand their giftedness. Of all the seven gifts, perceivers are the most often misunderstood. Their strong beliefs and opinions, their uncompromising stance and their intensity of feelings make for uniqueness of character. Anyone married to a perceiver needs to work at understanding this gift.

Category 7: Emotional Responses

A. I feel we have some problems in the ways we respond to each other emotionally in these areas:

	He	She
1. Hurt feelings	48%	56%
2. Carrying offenses	22%	29%
3. Unforgiveness	11%	15%
4. Insensitiveness	30%	32%
5. Feeling unloved	22%	32%
6. Moodiness	44%	49%
7. Anger	33%	51%

With their notorious bull-in-the-china-shop approach, it is amazing that about half of the perceiver spouses report problems with their own hurt feelings. In reality they are more likely to hurt their mates emotionally than be hurt. But the scores reflect hurt feelings on both sides.

Carrying offenses too long is only a moderate problem. Perceivers are willing to move to speedy resolution of offenses. (Compassion mates may not be so willing.)

Perceivers are quick to forgive unless pride keeps them from it.

About a third of the perceiver respondents admitted that they or their spouses can be insensitive. This can be an even larger problem, we find, for perceivers who are blind to it.

About 32 percent of perceiver women, as opposed to 22 percent of perceiver men, feel unloved by their spouses. This is close to the norm for all gifts. Almost every marriage can benefit from increased expressions of love as well as demonstrations of it.

When perceivers cannot get their way, they may revert to pouting, withdrawal, mood swings, even full-fledged depression. This solves nothing, of course, and the mate is left to endure the situation. Perceivers need to face up to why they are moody and do something about it. Repentance is often a requirement, getting right with God as well as the spouse.

If there are two classifications of angry people, expressers and stuffers (with some flipping between the two, depending on the situation), perceivers tend to be the expressers. They let it all hang out, and it is the mate who has to be scraped off the floor. Learning to put a guard over the mouth is a wise lesson for perceiver spouses.

All too often perceivers can be physically as well as verbally abusive to the ones they are supposed to love the most. God never meant for a spouse to live with abuse. Mates of perceiver abusers need to draw the line and not be enablers. Unresolved anger usually indicates unresolved hurtful experiences in the past. Healing can come through prayer counseling. (See our book *Dealing with Anger* for details.)

Perceivers, especially women perceivers, tend to be sympathetic (see figure below). The more mature the perceiver spouse, the more he or she will express spontaneous sympathy.

B. To what degree, from 1 to 7, are you one way or the other:

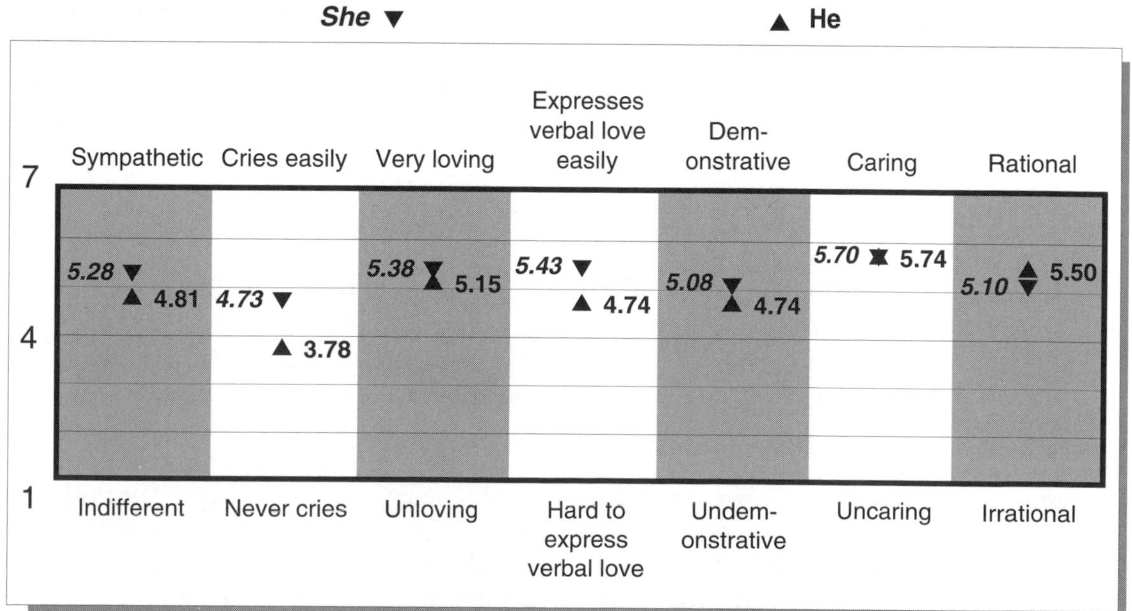

Perceiver wives cry more easily than their male counterparts. But both are close to the norm, indicating a good deal of self-control over their emotions.

Their ability to love is strong, even intense. They tend to love wholeheartedly and devote themselves totally to the objects of their affection. The verbal expression of love comes more easily to women perceivers, but the men can be good at it, too.

Both are demonstrative, which helps a lot. Hugs and kisses build up the bank account of love. Perceivers are usually caring, feeling love deeply and seldom blocking its flow.

While able to operate on the emotional level, they are also rational—a good balance.

C. My genuine needs, views or beliefs are:

	He	She
1. My feelings tend to rule my life.	15%	12%
2. My mate needs to understand my moods more.	26%	24%
3. I need to hear more "I love you's" from my partner.	22%	37%
4. I need to be able to express both positive and negative feelings.	37%	49%
5. I feel my spouse takes everything too personally.	30%	29%
6. I often feel put down by my partner.	22%	34%
7. I am satisfied with our emotional responses to each other.	52%	41%

The scores are low until the need for hearing "I love you." Perceiver wives need more of this. Gentlemen, pay attention! It costs you little and the rewards are great.

Both wives and husbands need the freedom to express negative as well as positive feelings, especially perceiver wives. Perceivers tend to feel ashamed of their negative feelings. But since emotions are neither right nor wrong, they need to be expressed. It is a wise mate who allows their expression and simply listens, neither threatened by them nor trying to talk the spouse out of them. Being a sounding board is a most useful role in marriage.

Fewer than a third of the perceivers we surveyed feel that their spouses take everything too personally, but the perceiver woman finds being put down by her partner hard to take. The putdown is best understood as the teeter-totter effect: Anyone who puts his or her spouse down feels elevated by contrast. Thus, the reason for the unkindness can usually be determined as insecurity.

Category 8: Intellectual Capacity

A. I feel we have some problems regarding intellectual interests and capacities in these areas:

	He	She
1. Different interests	41%	34%
2. Reading	30%	22%
3. Continuing education	19%	2%
4. Know-it-all attitude	11%	20%
5. Correcting grammar	19%	12%
6. Children's education	7%	5%
7. Being accurate	33%	24%

A perceiver for whom the Christian faith is vital has an intense interest in Bible study and growing in righteousness. He or she may deem a mate less motivated as unspiritual, even if that spirituality is expressed in a different but no less valid way.

"My server spouse directs her faith into practical works," says Alan, "like Meals on Wheels to shut-ins. I realize I must be careful not to judge her spirituality."

B. To what degree, from 1 to 7, are you one way or the other:

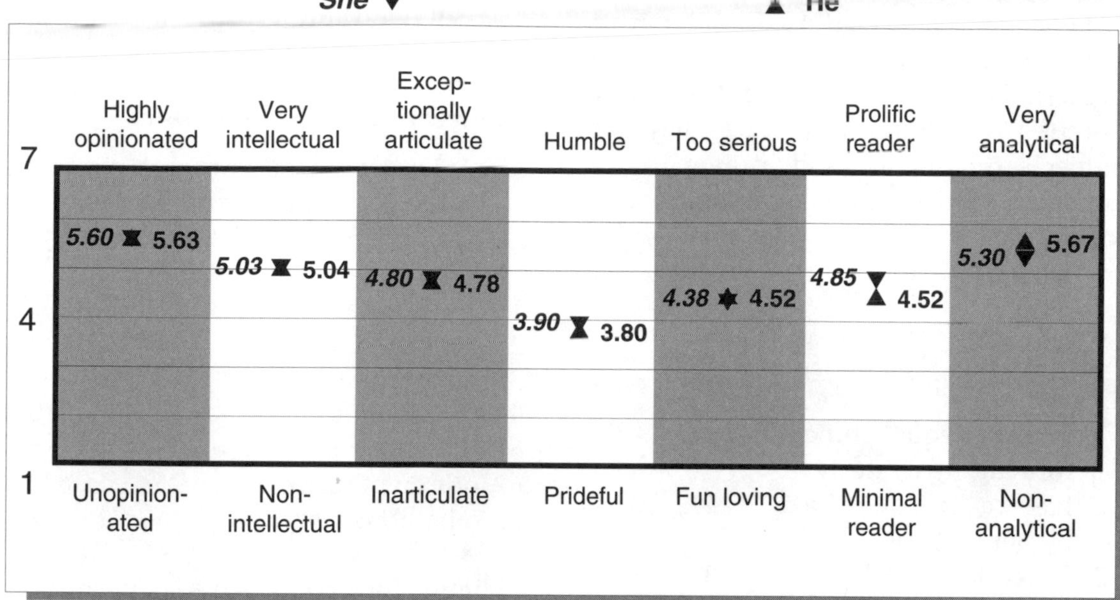

Perceivers especially enjoy biographies, adventures and mysteries, relishing the challenge of figuring out who did it. They also pursue Christian material on theology, spirituality and prayer. What perceivers read is not usually a problem, but how much they read can be, especially when it comes to the Bible. Some perceivers have been heard to say proudly, "I study *only* the Bible."

Continuing education is virtually no problem for perceiver wives; only sometimes for perceiver husbands.

We were surprised at the low scores on know-it-all attitudes—perhaps another blind spot, since perceivers are notorious know-it-alls. Would their spouses stand up, please, and comment on this?

Correction of grammar is a minor problem, but perceivers will correct improper facts.

Most perceivers agree with their spouses on the education of their children. They place high value on Christian education.

At least a quarter of the perceivers see being accurate and factual as a problem area, probably because they are precise and factual themselves and expect their mates to be so, too.

Perceivers (see chart B above) are the most opinionated of all the giftings. If their spouses accept this characteristic, it can be lived with. To the degree that their spouses resist or challenge it, relational problems emerge.

Perceivers lean to the intellectual side, close to the most intellectual gift, the teacher. When a perceiver is married to a teacher, their pursuits utilize this intellectual propensity. Both spouses are exceptionally articulate and accurate and apt to correct the mate who is not.

Perceivers admit a tendency toward pride. It is a lifelong struggle until they successfully humble themselves before God in a process of brokenness. Pride in a perceiver pollutes his relationship with God as well as with his spouse.

Tending toward a more serious approach to life, perceivers handle reality well. They are highly analytical, sometimes to the distress of their mates! They do need to learn to hang loose once in a while and just have fun with their spouses.

Perceivers enjoy reading. Their interests tend toward nonfiction, unless the fiction has a strong spiritual emphasis (like Frank Peretti's *This Present Darkness*). They like subjects relating to God, prayer, righteousness, justice and biblical topics of all kinds.

C. MY GENUINE NEEDS, VIEWS OR BELIEFS ARE:

	He	She
1. I need adequate time for reading or study.	63%	73%
2. I am easily sidetracked by new interests.	44%	39%
3. I need to question things before I can accept them.	70%	78%
4. I need my mate to listen to my opinions more.	33%	29%
5. I realize I need to be less dogmatic.	26%	24%
6. I find I constantly analyze what my partner says and does.	33%	37%
7. I am satisfied with how we handle intellectual matters.	67%	61%

A high percentage of perceivers indicate a need for more time for reading and study. They want to learn more. Perceiver spouses need time alone to pray and study.

Like the teacher gifts, perceivers can get sidetracked since their interests are so broad. But eventually they get back on course. They tend to question everything that does not fit their frame of reference immediately, which often irritates their spouses.

Although about a third said they needed their mates to listen to their opinions more, we must remember that perceivers are quick to express their opinions whether they are invited to or not.

About two-thirds are satisfied with how they handle intellectual matters.

Category 9: Volitional Issues

A. I FEEL WE HAVE SOME PROBLEMS IN THE USE OF THE WILL IN THESE AREAS:

	He	She
1. Decisions and choices	19%	32%
2. Practical decisions	15%	29%
3. Stubbornness	33%	32%
4. Agreements	11%	10%
5. Right actions	4%	5%
6. Judgmentalism	41%	32%
7. Rebelliousness	15%	7%

Slightly fewer than a third of the respondents mentioned problems with making decisions or choices. Since perceivers believe they are always right, they make decisions accordingly. Perceiver wives more than perceiver husbands report some problems with practical decisions, accounted for by the fact that the wives may not speak up as much.

About a third reported that stubbornness is a problem in their marital relationships. Their mates would probably complain even more. It is difficult, especially for a spouse, to persuade a perceiver about something. But in spite of stubbornness, perceivers are eventually able to reach agreements.

Doing what they perceive is right comes easily for perceivers.

Judgmentalism in volitional issues in marriage is the main problem. Since their analytical function is always "on," they slip easily into a critical attitude, especially with their spouses. They must take seriously Jesus' admonition to "judge not."

Since most perceivers who responded to our survey are on the mature side, their rebelliousness scores were low. But immature or self-centered perceivers can be the

B. To what degree, from 1 to 7, are you one way or the other:

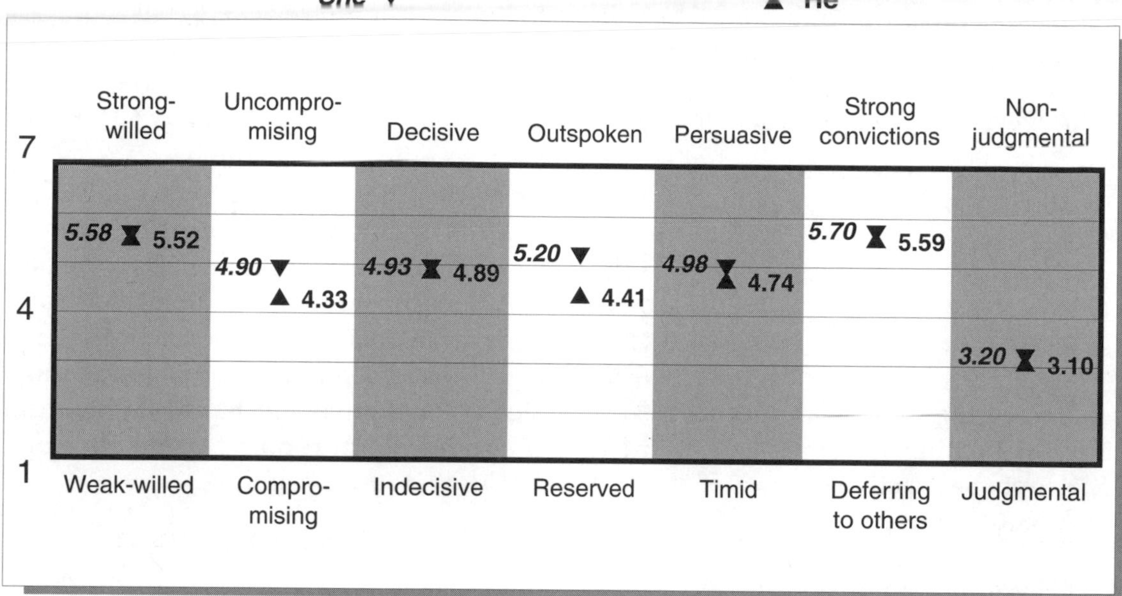

most rebellious and obnoxious of all the motivational gifts.

The reasonably high scores on the first six items (see chart B above) reflect the strength of the perceiver's personality and will. We seldom think of perceivers as wishy-washy! But although these traits can produce strong Christian character, they can also produce a dominating, controlling personality in a self-centered perceiver spouse. It is essential that he or she develop an active prayer life and seek God's will above all else.

Perceivers admit their tendency to be on the judgmental side. We suggest great doses of prayer to balance this out. Those who become intercessors will not stay judgmental.

C. My genuine needs, views or beliefs are:

	He	She
1. I have a definite inner need to be right.	41%	49%
2. I have a strong need to be a decision-maker.	52%	17%
3. I need my mate to make most of the decisions.	4%	24%
4. I will do what is right even if it hurts.	78%	76%
5. I need to operate by definite principles.	74%	68%
6. I need my mate to be more tolerant of my opinions.	26%	15%
7. I am satisfied with how we make decisions.	63%	63%

The need to be right is obvious here for both perceiver husbands and wives. One perceiver wife says, "I've recognized my tendency to make decisions but wish my compassion husband would do more of it because it feels like our roles are reversed."

Note the extremely high scores on items four and five. Perceiver mates want to do what is right in all circumstances and operate by godly principles.

Matching percentages of 63 percent show that perceivers are satisfied with their decision-making processes, indicating that even with differences, resolutions work out well.

Category 10: Physical Conditions

A. I FEEL WE HAVE SOME PROBLEMS IN THE PHYSICAL REALM IN THESE AREAS:

	He	She
1. Being fit	59%	73%
2. Enough exercise	74%	73%
3. Fatigue	48%	56%
4. Overeating	48%	39%
5. Proper eating	48%	54%
6. Keeping attractive	15%	29%
7. Adequate sleep	56%	54%

The overall responses are close to the average responses for all seven gifts. Being fit and getting enough exercise are of major concern. Coping with fatigue and getting adequate sleep are next, with overeating and eating healthfully close behind.

Perceiver Arnold comments, "I feel guilty about not keeping fit. My desk job doesn't help. I've got to get on a good program of regular exercise or I won't be able to live with myself."

June's problem is overeating: "Now that I'm back to work at an office job, I'm not so tempted to snack as much as I did when I was at home and feeling bored."

While the perceiver husband (see chart B below) is slightly on the athletic side and above average in energy, the perceiver wife is decidedly nonathletic and average in energy. Most perceivers are not at a proper weight and need a little more sleep than the average. Eating habits are at the mean; both report reasonably good health and few disabilities.

C. MY GENUINE NEEDS, VIEWS OR BELIEFS ARE:

	He	She
1. I desire to see my mate at the proper weight.	59%	59%
2. I need to overcome my own weight problem.	59%	51%

B. TO WHAT DEGREE, FROM 1 TO 7, ARE YOU ONE WAY OR THE OTHER:

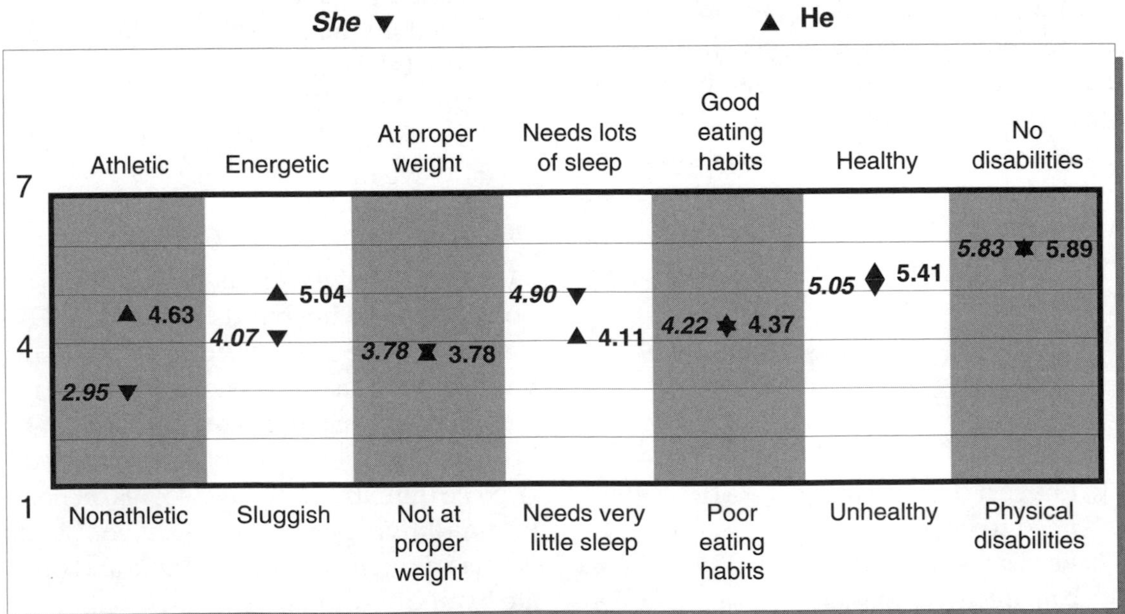

	He	She
3. I need to get adequate exercise on a regular basis.	81%	80%
4. I would like to see my spouse get more exercise.	56%	54%
5. I need my mate to be as attractive as possible.	37%	34%
6. I need to improve my eating habits.	67%	59%
7. I am satisfied with how we keep fit, healthy and attractive.	22%	20%

More than half want to see their mates at the proper weight as well as work on their own weight problems. Exercise is an even greater priority. Eating habits need to be improved. Only a fifth of the perceivers are satisfied with how they and their mates keep fit and healthy. Health and fitness programs would be of great assistance, not only for their physical benefits but also to help the respondents feel better about themselves.

Carolyn, a lanky perceiver who teaches aerobics classes, saw a need she could meet: "I was amazed to see so many overweight and out-of-shape people in our church. So I organized classes for women three days a week and evening classes for both men and women the same days. The turnout was great and I felt good about being able to help increase fitness."

Category 11: Sexual Relationship

A. I feel we have some problems in our sexual relationship in these areas:

	He	She
1. Frequency	52%	34%
2. Quality	41%	22%
3. Prior affection	30%	44%
4. Nonsexual affection	41%	51%
5. Sexual dissatisfaction	19%	17%
6. Incompatibility	7%	2%
7. Infidelity	4%	2%

The quality of sexual relations was double the concern for perceiver husbands as for perceiver wives. This difference is typical.

Husbands tend to be satisfied with sex with or without prior affection. More wives report the need for more affection prior to sex, enabling them to enjoy the sex that follows. A wise husband will take time to make his wife feel loved for who she is, not just for the sexual pleasure her body brings him.

Most perceiver spouses express a decided need for adequate affection in nonsexual times.

All the responses (see chart B on page 82) for perceiver husbands and wives are on the positive side.

C. My genuine needs, views or beliefs are:

	He	She
1. I need more nonsexual affection from my mate.	44%	51%
2. I need more sexual relations with my mate.	41%	20%
3. I feel I need more hugs and kisses from my spouse.	37%	41%
4. I need to hear more "I love you's" from my partner.	22%	37%
5. I need my husband to better understand my monthly cycle.	0%	7%
6. I feel dissatisfied with our current sexual relationship.	19%	22%
7. I feel satisfied with our current sexual relationship.	74%	61%

B. To what degree, from 1 to 7, are you one way or the other:

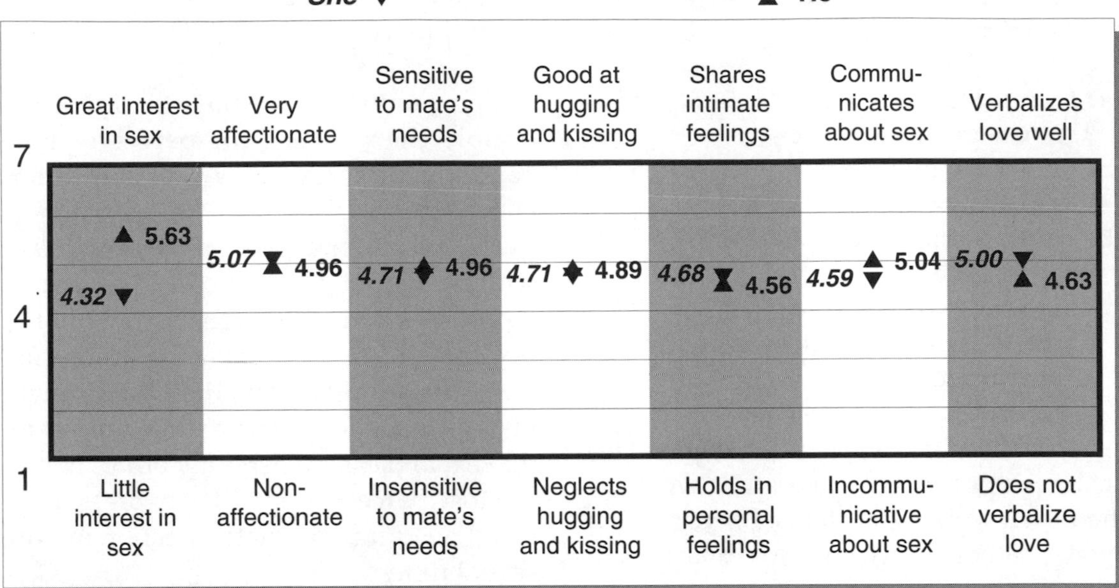

Once again nonsexual affection represents a genuine need of both men and women. More hugs and kisses and "I love you's" will help. Perceiver husbands express a need for more sexual relations than perceiver wives, but overall both are more often than not satisfied with their current marital sexual relationship.

"My perceiver husband read a good book on improving marital relationships," one wife reported, "and he discovered how much women need affection. He put what he learned into action and our sex life has improved more than either of us could have imagined."

Category 12: Work and Accomplishments

A. I feel we have some problems regarding work and accomplishments in these areas:

	He	She
1. Too busy	56%	59%
2. Career conflicts	30%	15%
3. Overtime work	22%	22%
4. Inadequate income	37%	39%
5. Volunteer work	26%	15%
6. Wife working	7%	12%
7. Priorities	30%	27%

Over half of the respondents reported being too busy. Sometimes it takes a crisis to focus the priorities of life. But a choice can be made to "un-busy" life before pressures get unbearable or damage the marriage. If necessary, make a written list of priorities and lop off the least important.

Career conflicts are less frequent for perceiver wives than perceiver husbands. Overtime work is a problem for some. John's perceiver gifting made him aware that the amount of overtime he was being required to work was costly to his marital relationship as well as his family. "I told my boss that even if it cost me my job, I had to cut out the extra hours. I was grateful he understood. I had to draw the line somewhere."

B. To what degree, from 1 to 7, are you one way or the other:

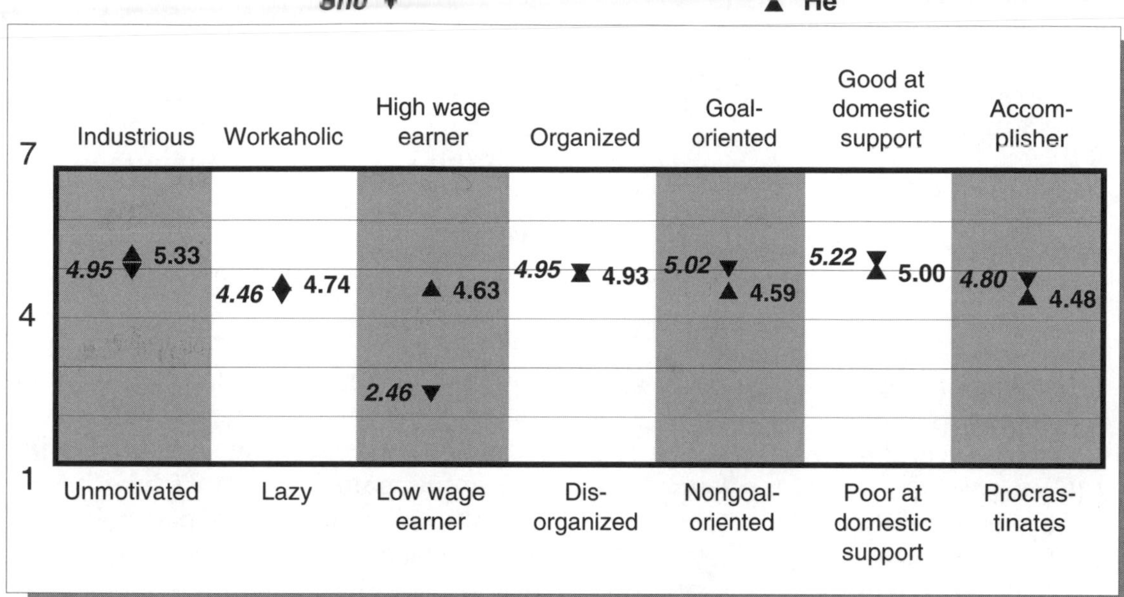

Inadequate income is a problem for more than a third of the perceiver spouses. We must weigh this in view of the pressure in our society for more material possessions, which are wants and not actual needs. A helpful trend in many Christian circles is to simplify life and get by with less, not more.

Perceivers (see figure above) for the most part have excellent work ethics. They are industrious without overdoing it in the workaholic department. They set goals well and accomplish more than the average. While male perceivers do reasonably well in wage-earning, female perceivers do not, on the average, unless they are following a full-time career. Both are good at domestic support.

"My perceiver husband works hard on his job," Madeline says. "Then when he comes home and sees me doing house chores, he usually steps right in to help me. I really appreciate it, but sometimes I can tell how tired he is and insist that he relax and read the paper."

C. My genuine needs, views or beliefs are:

	He	She
1. I need my husband to provide our basic expenses.	0%	71%
2. I need my wife to be a full-time homemaker.	33%	0%
3. I need to be the sole provider for my family.	15%	0%
4. I need a fulfilling career.	44%	20%
5. I need a challenge to work toward.	52%	41%
6. I get great joy out of my accomplishments.	81%	63%
7. I am satisfied with the way we handle work and accomplishments.	63%	63%

Most perceiver spouses are satisfied with the way they handle work and accomplishments, and get great joy from them. More than two-thirds of perceiver wives look to their husbands to provide the basic financial support. Only a third of perceiver husbands prefer their wives to be full-time homemakers. The responses toward work or career indicate that most perceivers find it fulfilling or challenging.

Category 13: Financial Management

A. I feel we have some problems in financial matters in these areas:

	He	She
1. Establishing budget	48%	63%
2. Keeping to budget	52%	73%
3. Living beyond means	37%	39%
4. Credit cards	26%	39%
5. Impulsive buying	41%	34%
6. Money arguments	22%	27%
7. Wife's work role	4%	0%

Half or more of all perceivers acknowledge some problems in establishing a budget. Since the handling or mishandling of money can become a major marriage problem, it is important for a couple to design a budget they can live with. Many do not have a clue about how to set up a realistic budget. One church that arranged for a seminar on the subject followed up by offering appointments for couples who wanted specific help. Older couples with successful life experience in the area were paired with those in need. Everyone benefited.

Keeping to a budget—a problem for half of the perceiver husbands—was an even larger problem for perceiver wives. When one wife overspends her clothes allowance, her husband (according to a prior agreement) cuts something out of the budget that month that she enjoys, like the $80 going-out-to-dinner item.

Nearly forty percent of perceiver spouses admitted to living beyond their means. In a culture so focused on material possessions and overwhelmed with the proliferation of easy credit, a couple must be aggressive to overcome the societal momentum. Paul's admonition to owe no man anything but love (see Romans 13:8) applies today. Many perceivers are cutting up their credit cards and paying cash for what they can afford.

A third of perceivers admit to impulsive buying—surprisingly more men than women.

But money arguments are only a moderate problem for perceivers. Sometimes the gifting of each partner shapes his or her viewpoint. A giver spouse may want not only to tithe but to give generously to additional missions or evangelism, while a perceiver spouse may not want to give beyond the tithe apart from God's particular leading. A teacher spouse tends to be systematic about giving, while a compassion spouse, moved by a stirring missionary message, may write a check for more than is in the bank. Counsel may be needed.

Perceivers (see chart B on page 85) see themselves on the conservative side when it comes to spending money and keeping within a budget, yet previous answers show problems in these areas. The maturity level of the individual perceiver determines the actual situation.

Perceivers are good bargain-hunters, generous and definitely committed to tithing. Most tend to save for what they need. Median scores indicate that most perceivers feel they are in a balanced position in regard to financial security.

C. My genuine needs, views or beliefs are:

	He	She
1. I feel we need to reduce our debts more effectively.	44%	68%
2. I feel the need to be in charge of our family finances.	52%	24%

B. To what degree, from 1 to 7, are you one way or the other:

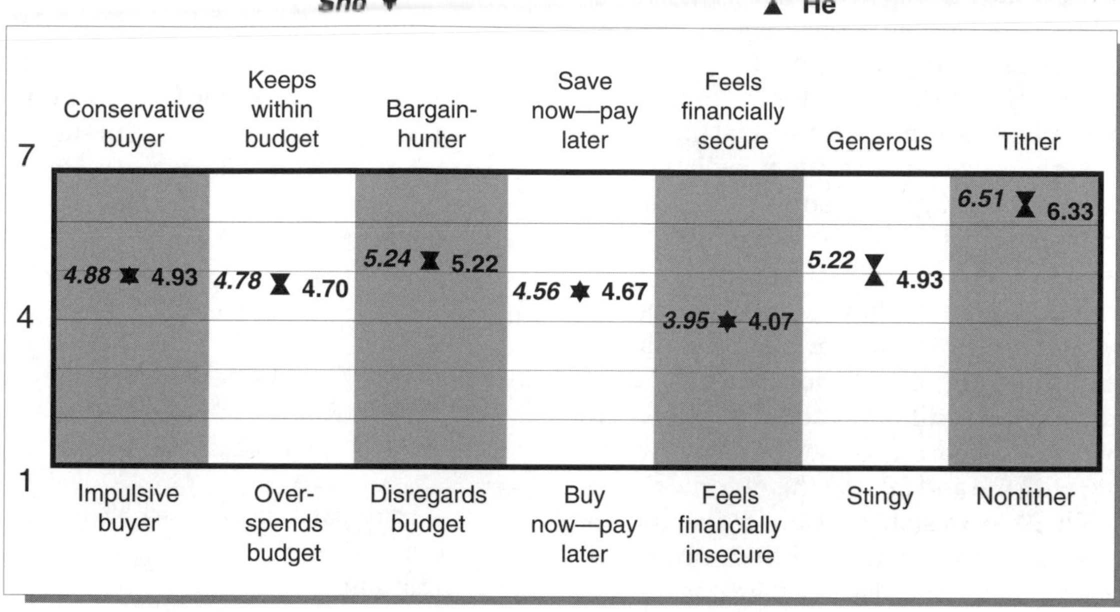

	He	She
3. I believe the husband should handle the family finances.	11%	32%
4. I think the most capable partner should handle the family finances.	78%	61%
5. I need to learn how to handle money more responsibly.	37%	34%
6. I would like to give more to church, missionaries, charity, etc.	70%	59%
7. I am satisfied with how we handle finances.	41%	37%

More women perceivers than men feel the need for more effective debt reduction. A perceiver wife told us her giver husband kept giving to those in need to the point that they were in financial trouble themselves. "Pastoral counseling helped him see that he did not have to help everyone in need," she reported. "He also agreed that I should be consulted."

A vast majority of perceivers think the most capable partner should handle the family finances. Half of the perceiver husbands, however, feel they should be in charge. One-third admit the need to learn how to handle money better, while about one-third are satisfied with how they presently handle finances. A majority indicate the desire to give more charitably.

Category 14: Leisure Activities

A. I feel we have some problems in how we spend our free time in these areas:

	He	She
1. Interests	26%	27%
2. Recreational preferences	22%	15%
3. Hobbies	26%	22%
4. Entertainment	19%	17%
5. Vacation preferences	15%	10%
6. Sports	30%	17%
7. TV-watching	37%	37%

One Christian counselor, Willard Harley, the author of *His Needs, Her Needs* (Fleming H. Revell), considers the sharing of interests and recreational experiences so important that he often recommends one spouse's giving up a special interest if the other spouse does not enjoy it, too.

Don and I agree to some extent, especially if the activity causes significant time separations. But we also believe it is good for each spouse to have something special to excel in or enjoy. For instance, I am a shell collector; Don is not. I love to swim and Don is indifferent about it. But when we are at a beach together, he enjoys walking with me and talking (his favorite thing) while I keep a sharp eye out for shells. He enjoys a short swim and does not mind waiting while I finish my long one.

For couples who have few or no shared recreational interests, it is a good idea to explore new ones and find something both can enjoy.

TV-watching causes the highest percentage of problems, not just because of different program interests but because of the time-robbing effect of watching too much TV.

The scores (see chart B below) for perceiver husbands and wives are close to the norm for all gifts, except the wives are once again on the nonathletic side. Interest in travel stands out and reflects a perceiver's interest in the world. The women indicate more sociability while the men are more prone to stay at home, characteristic of the loner tendency of perceivers.

C. My genuine needs, views or beliefs are:

	He	She
1. I need my partner to be a recreational companion.	63%	34%
2. I need to do more fun things with my spouse.	70%	59%
3. I need more meaningful vacations.	59%	39%
4. I need to be involved in nonathletic leisure activities.	37%	37%

B. To what degree, from 1 to 7, are you one way or the other:

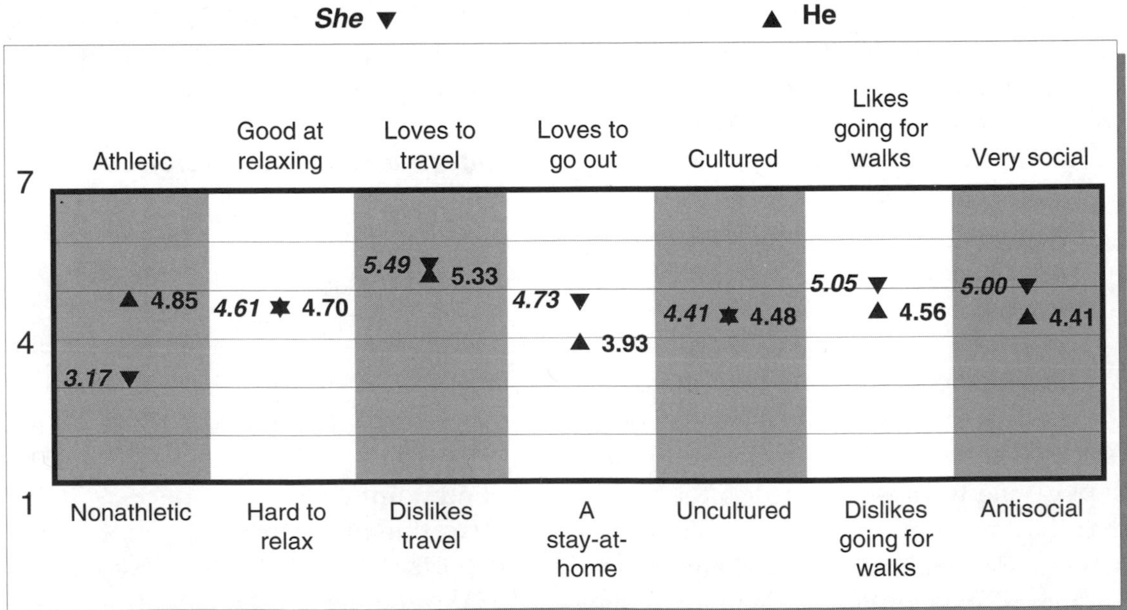

	He	She
5. I prefer active group or competitive sports.	26%	12%
6. I prefer individual noncompetitive sports.	30%	32%
7. I am satisfied with how we spend our leisure time.	44%	41%

Nearly twice as many perceiver husbands as wives expressed the need to have their partners as recreational companions. Their scores were also higher on needing more fun activities together. Perceivers can forget that having fun is part of life.

Vacations—times for refreshing, relaxing and renewing—should meet the needs of both partners. Julie, an exhorter married to perceiver Ted, loves to visit as many friends and relatives as possible during their vacation time. Ted loves to rent a cabin in the woods, fish in the lake and relax with Julie and the kids. Once Julie and Ted understood their gifts, they could compromise and schedule a vacation that met the needs of each—time at the cabin with some of that time designated for drop-in friends.

Category 15: Parenting

A. I FEEL WE HAVE (HAD) SOME PROBLEMS IN THE CHILD-REARING PROCESS IN THESE AREAS:

	He	She
1. Type of discipline	48%	41%
2. Amount of discipline	33%	32%
3. Who disciplines	19%	20%
4. Misconduct determination	33%	27%
5. Love expression	19%	29%
6. Time spent	33%	34%
7. Money given	15%	27%

Perceivers' responses on parenting are normative except for the kinds of discipline and training that the husbands felt were proper. Because perceivers themselves are the most challenging children to rear, requiring more stringent discipline, they often discipline their own children the same way whether they need it or not. This can lead to conflict with their non-perceiver mates. Spouses need to agree so that their discipline is consistent. Our book *Discover Your Children's Gifts* offers a detailed explanation of the discipline and training effective for a child of each gifting.

Perceiver husbands, like all husbands, need to spend more time with their children (see chart B on page 88). Perceiver wives do better in the "time spent" department and also in affectionate touching.

A study indicated that children determine love not by a nice home or lots of toys or special advantages, but by affectionate touch and time spent with them.

C. MY GENUINE NEEDS, VIEWS OR BELIEFS ARE:

	He	She
1. We need to provide better spiritual guidance for our children.	44%	44%
2. We need to give our children more love and affection.	37%	37%
3. I would like my spouse to help more with the children.	15%	20%
4. I need to be more affirming of our children.	22%	29%
5. I feel we need to agree more on discipline.	22%	22%
6. I feel we need more quality family time and activities.	56%	49%
7. I am satisfied with our parenting styles and skills.	41%	46%

B. To what degree, from 1 to 7, are you one way or the other:

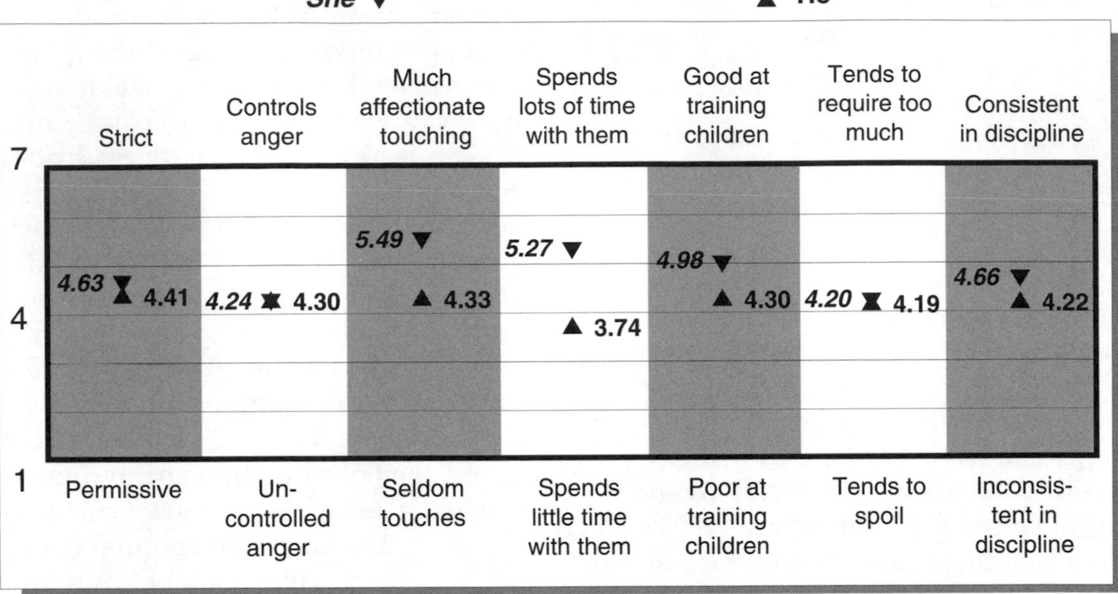

Although almost half are satisfied with their parenting, 44 percent express the need to provide better spiritual guidance, and even more for better quality family time. See chapter 17 of *Discover Your Children's Gifts* on "How to Enhance Your Parenting Style."

Category 16: In-Laws and Family

A. I feel we have some problems with our families and in-laws in these areas:

	He	She
1. Interference	19%	41%
2. Their expectations	15%	41%
3. Their visits	4%	12%
4. Comparisons	4%	5%
5. Borrowing money	7%	10%
6. Former abuse	22%	22%
7. Dysfunction affect	26%	46%

Perceiver husbands do not have much difficulty for the most part with their in-laws, but perceiver wives do, in the areas of interference and expectations. This may be because traditionally the wife is expected to fit into the husband's family's mode of operation and because the perceiver wife has stronger-than-average opinions about how things should be done.

The perceiver wife is more perceptive in recognizing dysfunction. She is more likely to define it and complain about it than wives of other gifting. Her husband would do well to take an objective-as-possible look at her discernment and take prayerful, positive action to overcome the negative behavior.

Perceiver responses (see figure on page 89) on the first three items show a healthy marital relationship in light of relationships to former families. The high degree of honoring mother and father yields the biblical harvest of emotional and spiritual health.

Even though women perceivers tend to come from slightly more dysfunctional families, they and their male counterparts report that they presently relate better than the average to their in-laws.

"My family was a little dysfunctional in

B. To what degree, from 1 to 7, are you one way or the other:

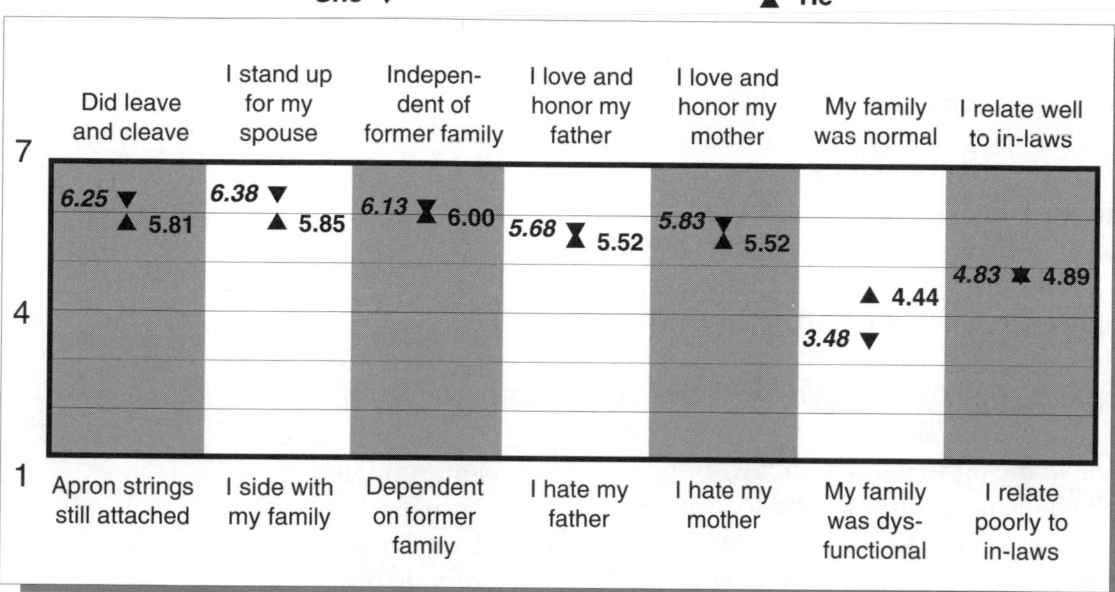

a few areas," Sabrina says, "but there was still lots of love and there is today, too. I also love my husband's family. They give me a chance to see what really normal family relations are like."

C. My genuine needs, views or beliefs are:

	He	She
1. I need my spouse to put me before his or her family.	33%	41%
2. I need to see or talk to my parent(s) regularly.	22%	29%
3. I need to include my family in holiday celebrations.	37%	39%
4. I need help in overcoming in-law problems.	15%	24%
5. I need to be accepted by my in-laws.	7%	22%
6. I need to be financially free from my family and my in-laws.	33%	32%
7. I am satisfied with our family and in-law relationships.	56%	49%

Overall perceivers are satisfied with their in-law relationships, although women need more help in overcoming in-law problems and being accepted by them. Both have a reasonable need to include their families in holiday celebrations and to be free financially.

Category 17: Social Relationships

A. I feel we have some problems in social relationships in these areas:

	He	She
1. Friends' demands	4%	5%
2. Time for friends	41%	54%
3. Unsocial partner	7%	15%
4. Too social partner	7%	10%
5. Wrong friendships	0%	2%
6. Negative influence	0%	2%
7. Over involvement	0%	7%

In social relationships perceivers seem to have few problems except having enough time for friends. This is a major problem for all the gifts, showing that time pressures and limitations are felt by almost everyone.

One busy dual career couple came up with a solution that worked for them. "We decided to make Sunday after church," Jean said, "a time we have to eat anyway, as a scheduled time for friends. Using our planning calendar we invite friends for dinner at our house or arrange to meet them at a restaurant, filling about two or three Sundays a month. This way we get to see friends we've meant to get together with but usually have not gotten around to it before."

Although perceivers (see figure below) tend more than any of the gifts to be loners, they are not entirely antisocial. They are more comfortable having a few close friends rather than many, and relating to small groups rather than large ones. They can relate reasonably well in social relationships, but may not seek such relationships as readily as their mates.

Jenny, an extroverted compassion gift, shared how her perceiver husband always grumbled about prospective social engagements but always wound up enjoying them. "Had I listened to his complaints," she said, "we would never do anything with our friends."

C. My genuine needs, views or beliefs are:

	He	She
1. I need to have many friends.	7%	12%
2. I especially love to entertain in our home.	22%	32%
3. I need a good deal of private time.	44%	44%
4. I need our home to be a haven of rest.	78%	59%
5. I need to be involved in social groups.	11%	32%
6. I think we need to change some friendships.	7%	15%

B. To what degree, from 1 to 7, are you one way or the other:

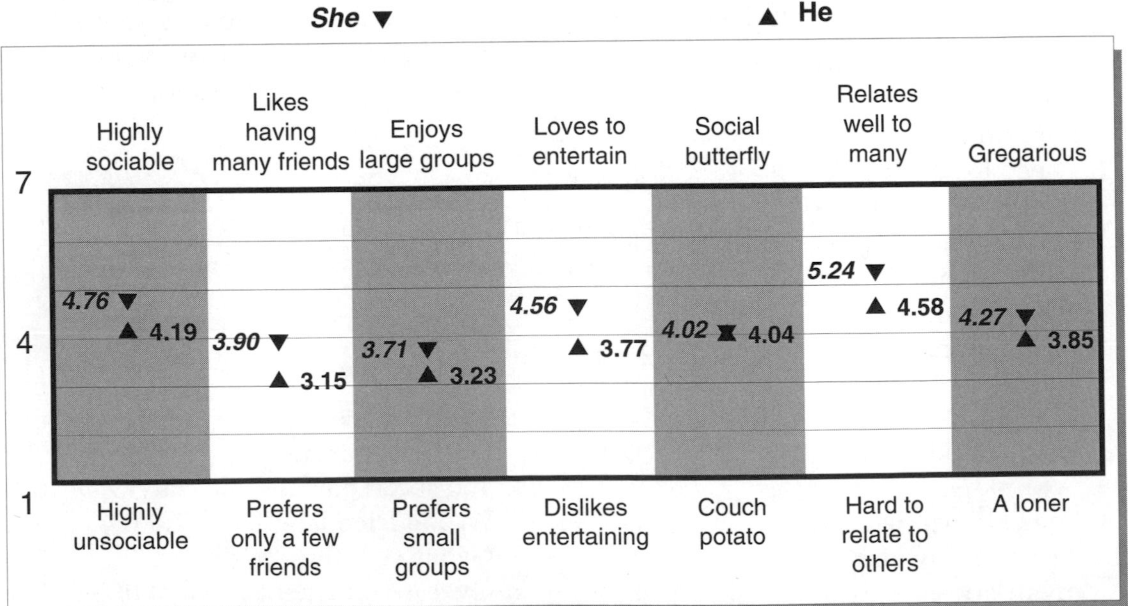

	He	She
7. I am satisfied with our social life.	67%	46%

Perceivers enjoy a high degree of satisfaction with their limited social lives. Their need for friends is low, their interest in entertaining is moderate, but their need to have home as a haven of rest is high. Perceiver husbands and wives indicate a need for a significant amount of private time, especially in between social relationships.

Category 18: Religious Orientation

A. I FEEL WE HAVE SOME PROBLEMS IN OUR SPIRITUAL LIVES AND ORIENTATION IN THESE AREAS:

	He	She
1. Affiliation disagreement	4%	0%
2. Church attendance	0%	5%
3. Different backgrounds	0%	7%
4. Theological differences	7%	2%
5. Commitment level	19%	29%
6. Irregular attendance	4%	12%
7. Hypocritical behavior	7%	15%

Most problems for perceivers in the area of spiritual life and orientation are relatively insignificant except for commitment level. Perceiver wives, whose commitment to God tends to be high, are concerned about the lesser commitment or hypocritical behavior of a mate of another gifting. Perceiver Alice said, "It really bothers me that my husband talks the talk but doesn't consistently walk the walk."

These scores (see chart B below) suggest that perceivers see themselves as very spiritual, people of prayer and regular readers of the Bible. They have strong faith, spiritual commitment and regular church attendance. But they need to be careful to allow their spouses to express their spirituality in a way that is natural for them.

Darlene was critical of Jim's seemingly inferior spirituality. His server gifting caused him to spend more time in practi-

B. TO WHAT DEGREE, FROM 1 TO 7, ARE YOU ONE WAY OR THE OTHER:

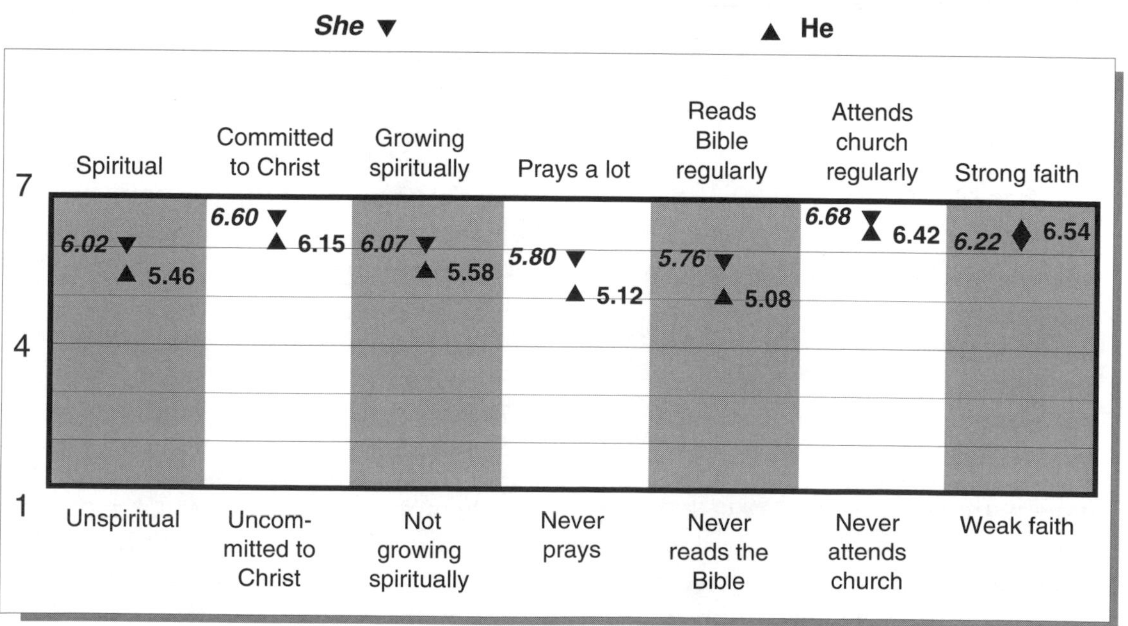

cal service to others than in prayer. "But when I realized he was geared to brief prayers and much loving action," she said, "I quit criticizing him and began to be grateful for a godly server husband."

Prayer is the safety valve for the perceiver. This is especially true in marriage, when closeness enables a perceiver to observe areas for potential criticism or judgment. If the perceiver mate does not take such matters to prayer, a critical attitude will result.

C. My genuine needs, views or beliefs are:

	He	She
1. I need to attend church regularly.	85%	78%
2. I need my partner to pray with me daily.	59%	66%
3. I greatly desire to see my spouse grow spiritually.	81%	76%
4. I believe we need to have regular family devotions.	63%	73%
5. I need my spouse to give spiritual leadership.	15%	78%
6. I need to be able to live my faith, not just talk about it.	78%	73%
7. I am satisfied with our religious orientation and practice.	85%	71%

A high percentage of perceivers show satisfaction with the way they practice their faith. They want to see their spouses grow spiritually and they put great importance on family devotions. Since all perceivers without exception are called to be intercessors, those who have not entered this ministry are the ones who have not yet listened to the call of God.

Perceiver husbands take spiritual leadership naturally. Perceiver wives, even though they can (and sometimes have to) take spiritual leadership, long to have their spouses take it. When Karen complained to me that her husband never exercised spiritual leadership for their family, I asked her, "How can he when you keep filling the void? Why don't you step back and see what he does?" She later reported, much to her surprise and delight, that he had stepped in.

Category 19: Maturity

A. I feel we have some problems in maturity in these areas:

	He	She
1. Inexperience	0%	5%
2. Irresponsibility	11%	10%
3. Blame game	19%	15%
4. Stress coping	44%	49%
5. Criticism	22%	20%
6. Infidelity	0%	2%
7. Dishonesty	0%	7%

Four of the seven items here have insignificant responses. One was greatly significant: coping with life's stresses. As the environment of the world in general and Western culture in particular becomes increasingly stressful, coping is a skill to be mastered. Perceivers' stress is enhanced since they hold such intense opinions and beliefs. In addition to simplifying life as much as possible, prayer is the key to effective coping.

The other two items, continuous criticism and the "blame game," would be expected in those who are less mature. While blame originated (as we have observed) with Adam and Eve, and since the whole human race is prone to it, maturing perceivers will grow in their ability to own up to their responsibilities and be less likely to blame their spouses.

Responses here (see chart B below) are all on the positive side. Since perceivers do tend to take life seriously, they mature well. The highest score is their trustworthiness. They do what they say they will do. Their word is their word. They handle responsibility well.

Their forgiving score is also high—a good thing since unforgiveness is dangerous to one's spiritual health. Forgiveness is a choice, not a feeling, although feelings may follow. Perceivers forgive *because it is the right thing to do*, not necessarily because they feel like it.

C. My genuine needs, views or beliefs are:

	He	She
1. I need to be able to trust my mate.	67%	73%
2. I need my spouse to be dependable.	67%	71%
3. I need to be quick to forgive and, I hope, be forgiving quickly.	74%	68%
4. We need to learn from and grow through every experience.	74%	78%
5. I need my mate to be able to handle responsibility well.	63%	71%
6. I need my mate to love me unconditionally.	67%	66%
7. I feel that we are a reasonably mature couple.	93%	88%

Not only do perceivers rate their needs in regard to the first six items as extremely high, but almost all feel that they and their spouses are reasonably mature. Most perceivers believe that they can learn and grow through every life experience and that even negative experiences can work together for good for those who love the Lord (Romans 8:28). They try to be mature in their attitudes and actions, and want their mates to be equally so.

B. To what degree, from 1 to 7, are you one way or the other:

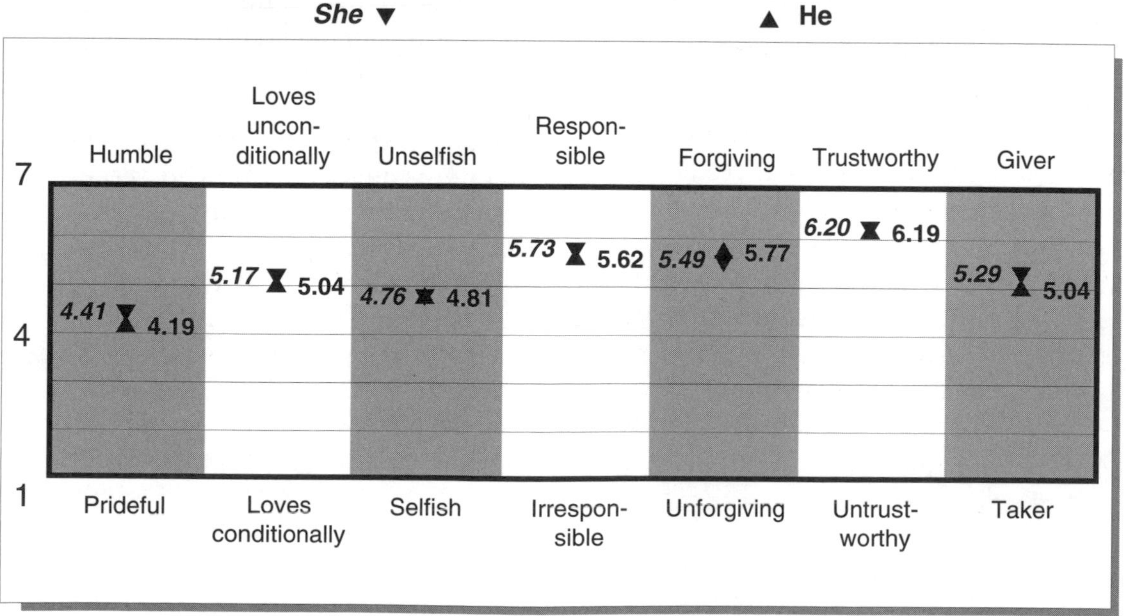

Category 20: Dysfunctionality

A. I FEEL WE HAVE SOME PROBLEMS IN THE FOLLOWING AREAS THAT PRODUCE DYSFUNCTION:

	He	She
1. Alcohol abuse	0%	7%
2. Drug abuse	0%	2%
3. Physical abuse	0%	2%
4. Sexual abuse	4%	5%
5. Verbal abuse	15%	20%
6. Emotional abuse	0%	17%
7. Unresolved abuse	22%	29%

Alcohol, drugs and physical and sexual abuse are minor problems for perceivers. Verbal or emotional abuse is apparent in about ten to twenty percent of the marriages in which a perceiver is involved. Most of that abuse is likely to come from the perceiver's mouth—that part of the body most difficult to control. Perceivers often speak before they think, then regret what they have said. "Pray before you speak" is a helpful admonition to them. Once the hurtful words have come out, the damage has been done, even if an apology follows. For women the hurt lingers longer, as evidenced by their higher scores.

Unresolved abuse from the past is the highest score for both. This can often be traced to childhood experiences of abuse that have never been defused and healed. The pattern of the abused becoming the abuser is well-known. The wise person seeks help rather than let the experience continue to fester and cause ongoing marital problems. Women are more likely to recognize the need for help and go for it. The pride of men, especially perceivers, often blinds them to their need and prevents them from seeking help.

These scores (see chart B on page 95) reflect the previous scores in part A. It is obvious that perceivers do not want to abuse anything or anyone.

C. MY GENUINE NEEDS, VIEWS OR BELIEFS ARE:

	He	She
1. I need our marriage to be free of alcohol use and abuse.	59%	49%
2. I need our marriage to be free of drug use and abuse.	59%	59%
3. I need my spouse to treat me more kindly.	4%	29%
4. I need my mate to give me positive emotional support.	48%	51%
5. One or both of us need to get help for abuse in childhood.	11%	22%
6. One or both of us need to get help for dysfunctional behavior.	7%	27%
7. I believe there is no dysfunctional behavior in our marriage.	70%	56%

Many respondents answered the first two items as a general need rather than something they wanted and did not have. Some answered the latter way—that freedom from alcohol or drugs *is* something they want and do not have.

Most perceivers believe there is no dysfunctional behavior in their marriage; the rest recognize some degree of it. Both could use more positive emotional support.

B. To what degree, from 1 to 7, are you one way or the other:

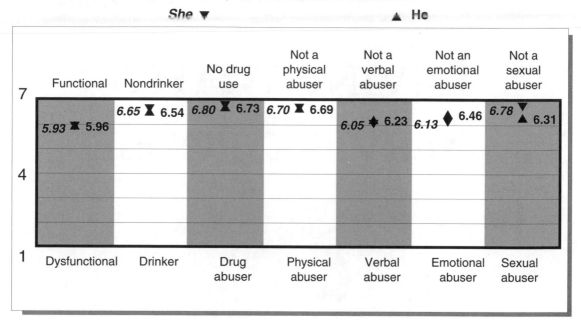

	Functional / Dysfunctional	Nondrinker / Drinker	No drug use / Drug abuser	Not a physical abuser / Physical abuser	Not a verbal abuser / Verbal abuser	Not an emotional abuser / Emotional abuser	Not a sexual abuser / Sexual abuser
She ▼	5.93	6.65	6.80	6.70	6.05	6.13	6.78
He ▲	5.96	6.54	6.73	6.69	6.23	6.46	6.31

Scale: 7 (top) – 4 – 1 (bottom)

Living with a Server Spouse

Servers are called by God to serve, work with their hands and come alongside others to help. Paul's exhortation to servers in Romans 12:7 is, "Let him give himself to serving." For servers this is spiritual service. It is God's love through them in action, accomplishing His will.

Often we hear servers say, "I'm not very spiritual. I'm no preacher. I don't get any big revelations from God. All I can do is help people." Then we explain to them that they are doing what God created them to do—to serve. And the more they serve, the more spiritual they are. This does not mean they should not pray, read the Bible, attend church or grow in grace. It means that practical service is the primary sphere within which they function in doing God's will for their lives.

The byproduct of such service is joy.

I walked over to Paul and Candy's campsite on Lake Chelan, Washington, to interview them while their children napped. They had both come out highest in the server gift at our marriage seminar. Having known them for several years, I had observed that they were gentle of spirit, supportive of each other and pleasant to those around them. Aware that server gifts usually have kind and considerate natures, I wondered if they had any conflicts.

Perhaps I'll find the idyllic marriage, I thought, *perfect peace between two supportive people.*

So it was interesting to see some hidden feelings come out (gently, of course) during our conversation. While Paul and Candy, typical of server gifts, love to practice hospitality, they had never really discussed with each other how much hospitality was appropriate.

"How do you feel, Candy," I asked, "when Paul invites people over to the house?"

"Usually fine," she replied, "if I'm feeling up to it. But there are days I wish he'd check with me first. Sometimes I've had such a busy day with the kids that I'd love a quiet evening to get refreshed. While we both love to show hospitality, the fact is that the workload falls on me—the meal preparation, the extra housecleaning, trying to coordinate getting ready with the persistent requirements of three children. All he has to do is issue the invitation."

"So you'd like more help from Paul?" I asked.

"Not only then," she replied. I could tell she was glad to open up some of her feelings. "I need more help with the kids in general. He always has so many projects going that he feels he's too busy to help. If I ask, I sense he feels imposed upon, and then I feel bad for asking.

"Then there's his perfectionism. It takes him forever to do something. It drives me nuts sometimes. His projects always turn out great. But I hold my feelings of frustration inside and then forget to thank him for what he does."

"I'm guilty of that, too," Paul admitted. "Candy is such a hard worker—a great wife and dedicated mother. I forget to show her appreciation for all she does."

The more we talked, the more problems came out. But I was glad to see that their server gift tendency to keep feelings in and not communicate enough was overcome by their joy in talking more honestly with each other.

A few days later I visited Paul and Candy again to see how they were doing.

"Thanks for helping us see some things about our relationship," Paul said. "Candy and I realize now that we've both been neglecting to show appreciation to each other verbally, and it's something we both need. We're already learning to express it more."

"Paul has agreed to cut down on his projects and help with the kids more," Candy reported with enthusiasm, "especially on weekends. He's decided the lawn doesn't have to be trimmed *every* week, and that some of his construction projects can be put off till next fall. This will give us more time to do family things this summer."

Five Major Problem Areas

First let's look at the five most significant problem areas of the server gift, which in turn influence the problems experienced in each of the twenty categories of our survey.

1. Hurt When Unappreciated

Servers thrive on appreciation. They will work endlessly if someone says occasionally, "Well done!" or "Thank you very much!" How can this be a problem area, you ask? Simple. The lack of appreciation is like pulling the rug out from under their feet. Suddenly they feel unnoticed, resentful, even angry.

Steve, a jack-of-all-trades server husband, says, "If my wife doesn't notice something I've done, I feel hurt. *She doesn't appreciate me,* I think. Or, *I've worked hard at this and she doesn't even seem to care. How thoughtless of her!* I go into my own little internal pity party with *Just see if I do anything else for her!* I know my attitude is wrong and I'm trying to overcome it. One thing that has helped me is knowing that even if my wife fails to appreciate what I've done, Jesus sees it and appreciates me."

Servers identify what they do with who they are. So when their doing goes unappreciated, they transfer the lack of appreciation to themselves personally and feel hurt. Mates may not realize this and wonder why they are upset or moody. Our suggestion to those married to servers is, be more observant and express appreciation. Our suggestion to servers, if something goes unnoticed, is to point it out to your spouse, giving him or her the opportunity to express appreciation. Or talk it over with the Lord. He appreciates you!

2. *Criticism of Others Who Do Not Help Out with Obvious Needs*

Servers see easily what needs to be done and are highly motivated to do it. It comes so naturally to them that if they are unaware of the seven motivational gifts and how some people can be oblivious to obvious needs, they tend to get critical. They may also feel that their non-server spouses are lazy, indifferent or unwilling to do their share.

3. *Perfectionism*

Servers aim to do everything as perfectly as possible. There is no place, as far as they are concerned, for projects done halfheartedly. If you do something, do it well, is their motto. If their mates do something imperfectly, they wish they had done it themselves so it would have been done right. They may even offend their mates by doing the job over.

Whatever servers start, they finish. They see unfinished projects as inexcusable. They cannot understand administrator mates who get sidetracked and leave things unfinished.

Servers are detail people who file things away immediately where they can easily find them. They believe strongly that there should be a place for everything and everything should be in its place. They may get upset if a spouse uses something and does not put it back. They do not mind the nicknames of *Mr. Neat* or *Mrs. Clean*, wearing them as badges of honor. Many of the other gifts find these server standards annoying and hard to live up to.

4. *Lack of Leadership Ability*

Servers have the least leadership ability of any of the seven motivational gifts. They are followers by nature and happy in that mode. They are glad to let their spouses take the leadership role in the marriage or family.

This is not usually a problem for server wives since they fit easily into the traditional wife role. But the server husband finds it difficult to take on responsibilities as head of the household. If his wife assumes the role, he may resent it but remain unwilling to remedy the situation. If he does not assume the role, his wife may be frustrated that by default she finds herself in charge. Server husbands are wise to seek training or counsel in fulfilling at least some marital leadership responsibility.

5. *Doing Too Much*

Because servers are doers, they do not know when to stop and often wind up doing too much. This is not as much of a problem when they focus their efforts on the marriage and home, but when they do too much for people outside the family, problems can emerge. Servers can be so busy doing things for others that they neglect home and family responsibilities. One cause: lack of appreciation, with the server seeking to serve where appreciation is expressed.

Doing too much for children can be another problem, leading to spoiling and the indirect teaching of irresponsibility.

One server wife admits now that she did too much for her kids. "I'd pick up after them instead of making them keep their rooms tidy," she says. "I'd start to teach my daughter how to cook a meal, and when she was slow at it, I'd take over and do it myself. I'd give my son the job of weeding a flowerbed, and when I saw him pulling out some flowers by mistake, I'd send him off to play while I finished the job myself. I thought I was being loving and helpful but I realize I spoiled them. Now their spouses have to put up with it."

The Twenty Problem Categories of the Server Gift

Let's take a look at the twenty categories of problem areas for server spouses indicated by our marriage survey.

Category 1: Communication

A. I FEEL WE HAVE SOME PROBLEMS IN COMMUNICATION IN THESE AREAS:

	He	She
1. Misunderstanding	40%	42%
2. Free to share	38%	53%
3. Listening	62%	66%
4. Conversation	53%	47%
5. Correction	27%	29%
6. Body language	24%	18%
7. Ridicule	31%	26%

Misunderstandings for server mates occur more often than usual, probably because servers' communication skills are fewer than for most gifts. Sometimes servers believe they have said enough to have communicated what they wanted, while the recipients have insufficient information for clear understanding.

Not sharing what they really feel is a problem for about half of the servers, partly because they have some difficulty expressing their feelings and partly because they do not feel their mates would be receptive. Rather than risk rejection, they clam up.

Not listening to what their spouses say is the major problem area in communication for all gifts, and even more so for servers. Feeling somewhat inarticulate anyway, more than sixty percent feel that their mates often do not really listen to them. One server wife confided, "I feel my husband always has better things to do than listen to me. He often seems distracted when I'm telling him something. Later when I refer to it, he acts like he's never heard about it before. It makes me feel very insecure about our relationship, like I'm not important to him."

Interestingly (since women usually put greater stock in conversation), server husbands even more than wives complain of not having enough meaningful conversation. Perhaps part of the problem is that server men are usually not good conversationalists and therefore neglect engaging their mates in it.

Servers are not likely to correct their mates, so most of their responses to the "correcting your mate" item on our survey likely reflect how servers feel about their spouses. Ginger, a server gift married to teacher-gifted Thomas, spoke of this problem: "Sometimes he drives me up the wall! He's always correcting my grammar. If I give my opinion about something and it's different from his, he gives me five reasons why I'm wrong."

Negative nonverbal communication is definitely less of a problem for servers, but they may resort to it, especially when they feel their mates are not listening.

Ridicule, sarcasm or unkind words are mentioned by about a quarter of the server respondents. Servers tend to be kind and easygoing, not prone to use words to hurt their mates. It is likely once again that many of the responses here reflect servers on the receiving rather than the giving end of ridicule and sarcasm.

Women servers (see chart B on page 100) see themselves as slightly better than average communicators, men as slightly poorer than average. Neither is likely to win oratory contests. Of all the gifts, servers are normally the least comfortable with the art of communication; many would definitely be considered the silent type. Server husbands agree they talk too little. Server wives admit they sometimes talk too much, due in part to the measure of talkativeness that graces the female

B. To what degree, from 1 to 7, are you one way or the other:

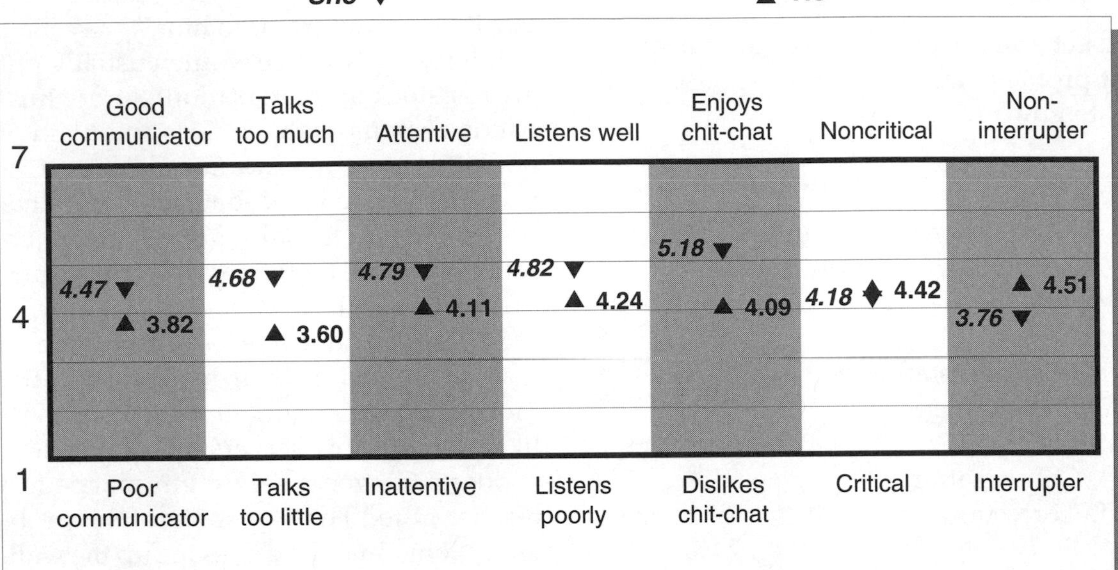

species. (We saw in chapter 2 that girls in studies of pre-schoolers talked far more than boys, who ran around making airplane and truck noises.)

Both husbands and wives see themselves on the positive side of attentiveness and listening well to their spouses. Because they have less need to talk, they become good listeners.

Server wives do enjoy chit-chat, while their male counterparts prefer talk that is practical and to the point. Only the women admit they sometimes have a tendency to interrupt.

C. My genuine needs, views or beliefs are:

	He	She
1. I need more conversation with my mate.	44%	71%
2. I need my partner to listen to me more attentively.	22%	63%
3. I need more quiet time without conversation.	18%	8%
4. I feel we need to share more intimately our thoughts and feelings.	60%	53%
5. I get hurt easily by my mate's unkind remarks.	40%	42%
6. I need more of my partner's undivided attention.	29%	34%
7. I am satisfied with our communication and conversation.	38%	26%

Only one-quarter to one-third of servers are satisfied with their marital communication and conversation. While both admit the need for more conversation, server wives see it as a major need, along with the need for more attentive listening from their mates.

Sufficient quiet time is not a problem, but the need for more intimate sharing is. Unfortunately, many marriages get by with adequate physical intimacy but inadequate sharing of intimate thoughts and feelings.

While deep sharing does not come easily for servers, they can grow in this ability with even a little encouragement from their mates.

Unkind remarks are a problem for about forty percent of servers—an area that can easily be reduced through a commitment to practice the Golden Rule and be more loving. The tongue, Paul says, is the most unruly member of the body. It can tear down a relationship or build it up. One psychological study showed that it takes four positive statements to overcome one negative one. If spouses really grasped this, they would spend far more time building one another up than undermining the most precious relationship with thoughtless and hurtful words.

Category 2: Expectations

A. I FEEL WE HAVE SOME PROBLEMS IN WHAT WE EXPECT OF EACH OTHER IN THESE AREAS:

	He	She
1. Lifestyle	20%	26%
2. Priorities	53%	53%
3. Ideals/goals	22%	34%
4. Holidays	13%	16%
5. Hopes/dreams	9%	16%
6. Conduct	9%	13%
7. Homework	40%	34%

Servers are practical people. Their expectations are likewise: a good job, a comfortable home, well-behaved children, someone to love. Servers seldom reach for the stars; their expectations are reasonable and their lifestyles simple.

More than half indicate problems with priorities (a problem for most couples). Marlene, a conscientious server, felt that a neat and clean house was her first priority. When her husband wanted to sit and talk about the events of the day, she walked around the room dusting. "At first I resented his complaints about it," she admitted. "But he helped me see that special time with him was more important."

Normally servers are not interested in long-range goal-setting, but short-term goals *are* important to them. They are comfortable with planning a week or even a month ahead, but next year is almost out of the question. A server married to an administrator hot on two- to five-year plans is bound to face problems, especially if the administrator expects the server to project ahead, too. But ideals and values are important to all servers who tend to be realistic rather than idealistic, with the emphasis on the practical outworking of those ideals and values. Since servers fit in easily with another's plans, they are quick to adapt to their spouses' hopes and dreams.

At holiday times servers are prolific decorators. My server hairdresser, Kathy, makes her home come alive on holidays. One Halloween I arrived to find orange streamers and rows of tiny cut-out pumpkins everywhere, to the delight of her two small boys. The dining room table was graced with freshly carved pumpkins that matched the jovial ones that had greeted me at the front door. "We celebrate the positive aspects of each holiday," Kathy explained. "No witches or goblins around here!"

Being glad to follow instructions and willing to adjust their conduct to please their mates, servers have few problems in the area of what is proper and acceptable conduct.

Server women are naturally the most domestic of all the gifts. They are happy to do all that wives have traditionally been expected to do, and more. Yet in the '90s server women are increasingly happy to have some assistance from their husbands, as our survey reflects. Server husbands are the most likely of all men to chip in and help with domestic chores at home, and

B. To what degree, from 1 to 7, are you one way or the other:

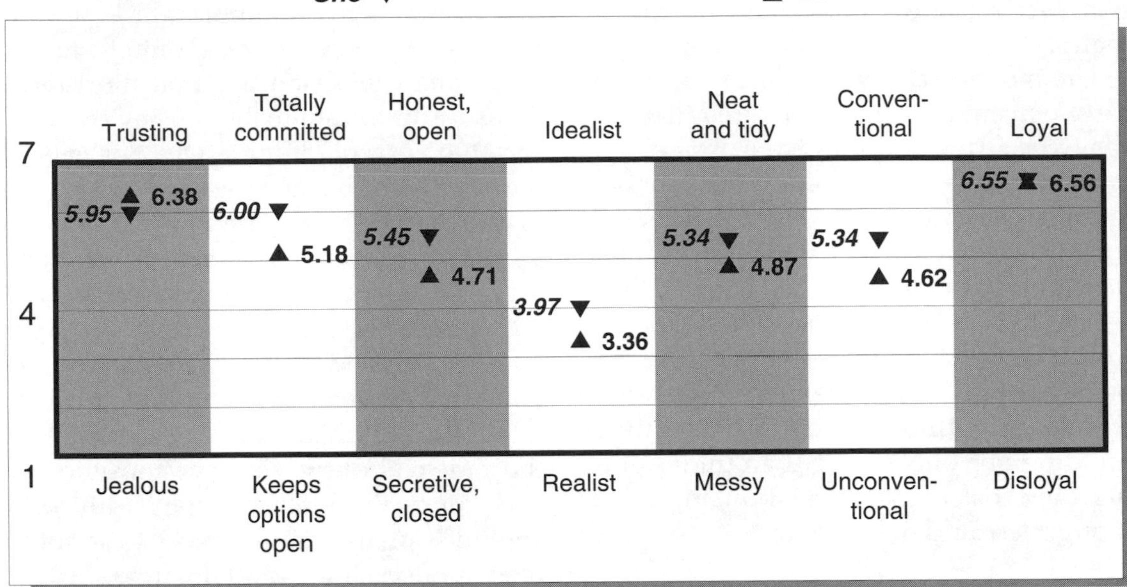

also the most likely to do a superior job on the work a man is traditionally expected to do.

Very high scores are expressed here (see chart B above) on trust, commitment and loyalty. Servers make good spouses for these qualities as well as many others.

Server wives are more open than their male counterparts, who are less communicative. Both are realists rather than idealists. A server married to a compassion mate, who can be idealistic to the point of being unrealistic, will face special challenges. One compassion wife who repeatedly brought home hurting people needing a place to stay was blowing the budget until her server husband brought her back to reality.

Servers are neat and tidy. In fact, Don and I expected their scores to be close to 7! Barbara, a compassion gift married to Larry, a server gift, expressed frustration about this aspect of his gifting. "He used to fuss at me if the kids or I left even a scrap of paper around somewhere or didn't put something back in its place," she said. "Fortunately we learned about the motivational gifts and he was willing to adjust his expectations of us."

Servers tend to be more conventional than unconventional. They like to fit in.

C. My genuine needs, views or beliefs are:

	He	She
1. I need to be more sure of my partner's motives.	4%	11%
2. I need a mate who is dependable.	31%	37%
3. I feel we need to work more at setting joint priorities.	53%	55%
4. I need to be more confident in how my mate handles stress.	27%	24%
5. I need my spouse to be totally honest with me.	31%	45%
6. I need to have former family customs a part of my life.	11%	26%
7. I feel our expectations are realistic and workable.	76%	84%

Once again we see in these responses that setting priorities is important to more than half of all server respondents. Expectations include honesty and dependability. Handling stress is a minor issue. Incorporating former family customs into present family life is important to a quarter of the server wives but not very important to server husbands. A vast majority feel that their expectations are both realistic and workable.

Category 3: Marital Cohesion

A. I FEEL WE HAVE SOME PROBLEMS IN GETTING ALONG WITH EACH OTHER IN THESE AREAS:

	He	She
1. Time together	58%	42%
2. Give and take	18%	32%
3. Feeling one	13%	16%
4. Closeness	29%	21%
5. Goals/priorities	51%	50%
6. Loneliness	11%	24%
7. Love/affection	38%	42%

While having enough quality time together is a significant problem area for server wives, it is even more so for server husbands, who tend to be homebodies. They love to have their wives around, not necessarily for conversation but just for being together—watching TV, reading books or the newspaper, watching the sun set.

Servers are givers more than takers. They often are willing to do more of the adjusting necessary in marriage. As one server wife put it, "I just love to fit into my husband's plans. I love being supportive of whatever he wants."

The feeling of oneness is easy for servers. Their scores for problems in this area are significantly lower. Denny, a server husband for twenty years, says, "My perceiver wife has strong ideas and opinions, but I've come to recognize that she hears from the Lord a lot. I trust her leadings, and through them we feel a oneness with each other and God's purposes for our lives."

Only twenty to thirty percent of servers have problems with closeness. Most find they can identify easily with their mates and experience intimacy at every level. Women servers are especially good at this. Server Nancy says, "Ben and I do everything together. After thirty years of marriage, we've always felt very close to each other."

About fifty percent of all servers have problems setting goals and priorities, reflecting their focus on short-term rather than long-term goals. Working together on goals and priorities is especially difficult with spouses who love more intensive, long-range planning.

Loneliness is not a major problem, and the servers' tendency to reach out and do things for others helps them to make or enhance relationships. "To have a friend, be a friend" applies to the servers' style. Servers often say their mate is their best friend.

About forty percent of servers admit some problems in the romantic love and affection department, partly because of their more limited ability to communicate their affection verbally. Tom, a shy server, told us, "I have all kinds of wonderful feelings for my wife, but I feel so inadequate in my ability to express them that often I don't. I'm working on it because I know my wife needs to hear what I'm feeling. She's not a mind-reader."

The sensitivity rating (see chart B on page 104) for servers is reasonably good, especially for the wives. Melaine, a mature server, said, "I can often sense Mel's needs and reach out to meet them. I count it a privilege to do so. I'm grateful God has given me good sensitivity."

Server men tend to be more independent than server women. Both tend to be agreeable, consistent, reliable and encour-

B. To what degree, from 1 to 7, are you one way or the other:

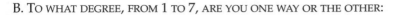

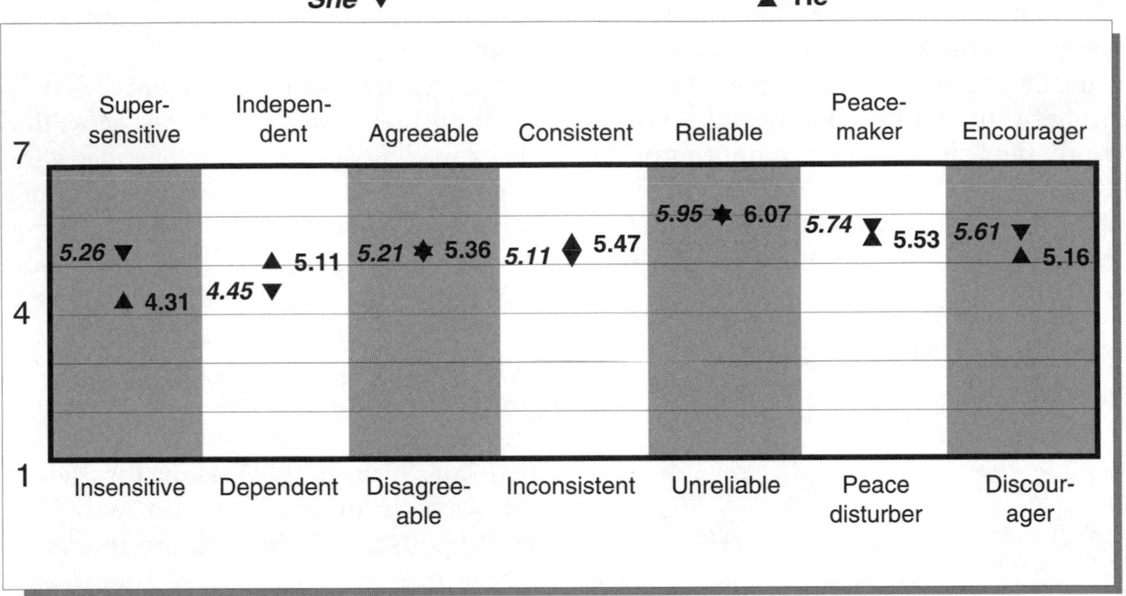

aging. All these qualities, along with servers' propensity to be peacemakers, contribute to marital cohesion.

C. My genuine needs, views or beliefs are:

	He	She
1. I need to be able to confide more in my mate.	22%	39%
2. I feel there needs to be more unity in our relationship.	31%	18%
3. I need to feel more secure in our marriage.	2%	5%
4. I am afraid to share some of my feelings with my partner.	22%	34%
5. I need my mate to be more sensitive to my needs.	36%	42%
6. I do not consider divorce ever to be an option.	89%	87%
7. I am satisfied with our marital interaction and closeness.	53%	63%

Almost twice as many server wives as husbands report the need to confide more in their mates. More wives also say they are afraid to share some of their feelings. But more husbands indicate the need for greater marital unity. Insecurity is virtually not an issue.

More than a third want their mates to be more sensitive to their needs, but this is typical of most relationships. A vast majority say they do not consider divorce ever to be an option—a good indication of the stability of server mates. More than half indicate satisfaction with their marital interaction and closeness.

Category 4: Roles and Responsibilities

A. I feel we have some problems in our marriage roles and responsibilities in these areas:

	He	She
1. Authority	22%	24%
2. Submission	11%	11%
3. Responsibilities	31%	34%
4. Decision making	29%	29%

	He	She
5. Roles	11%	11%
6. Feeling overworked	29%	34%
7. Home management	38%	39%

Since servers are followers more than leaders, they do not strive to take authority in their marital relationships. Server wives especially are comfortable under their husbands' authority. Server husbands, while able to take marital leadership in a nondominating mode, often find shared authority more to their liking. Joe, an easygoing server with a flair for business and accounting, found he enjoyed the routine responsibilities and financial management of their small clothing store. "I let my creative administrator wife handle the planning, projections and purchases," he says. "At home I take more of a leadership role, but with lots of input from her."

Servers understand marital submission and comply readily. Some server husbands need help from men with more natural leadership ability in order to move from the role of follower to the role of head of the household. "I was so grateful to my pastor," Scott told us, "that in his premarital counseling he taught me principles of godly leadership. With my classic server gifting, I knew I was not strong in this. It has helped me tremendously."

Servers are naturally responsible people who tend to do more than their fair share in marriage. They can be taken advantage of and find resentment building inside. It is best if they can share their feelings with their spouses before the pressure builds up. Donna told us that when she and Darryl were first married, he never picked up after himself. "At first I didn't mind carting his dirty dishes to the kitchen," she recounts, "and picking up and putting away his clothes. But after a few months I began to feel like his maid. I went on strike until I got his attention. We worked out a more amicable arrangement."

Problems in decision-making are minor due to the practical approach to life of server mates. They prefer making decisions jointly with their spouses.

Servers have few problems with traditional male/female roles in marriage, especially server wives, who are compliant. Some server husbands, however (unless they have a strong secondary gift enabling them to assume leadership easily), may find themselves feeling awkward in areas of marital leadership. Teaching on the role of the husband is particularly helpful.

While the responses regarding overwork are close to thirty percent, they are below the average. Servers enjoy work and often find things to do while others relax. Our pastor, Mike, is such a case. When we had his family over to our cabin for a day of rest at the beach, he was soon looking for something to do. When he discovered we had an outboard motor in questionable condition, he spent three hours getting it working while the rest of us relaxed on the deck.

While servers express discontent about domestic management, we suspect it comes from the server spouses who feel their mates do not take their fair share of domestic duties.

Server spouses (see chart B on page 106) are balanced at the midpoint between submission and authoritarianism. They are reasonably tactful, not bossy. They are highly cooperative, probably giving in more than they should.

Their decisiveness is close to average; they are honest and straightforward and highly responsible. They do what they say they will do and even more. They can be counted on.

They see themselves as mature. "My server husband is very mature and responsible," Dixie says, "and not just because

B. To what degree, from 1 to 7, are you one way or the other:

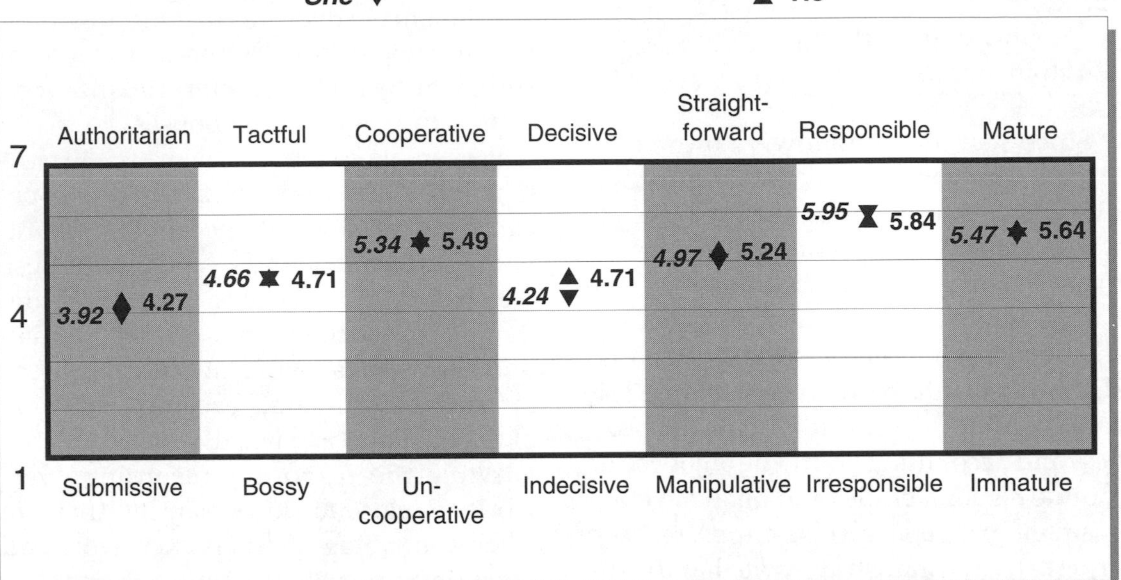

he's in the golden years. I observed this even in the first years of our marriage."

C. My genuine needs, views or beliefs are:

	He	She
1. I need my role clarified more.	11%	5%
2. I need more freedom to discuss ideas and options.	11%	11%
3. I need to use some of my capabilities more.	29%	29%
4. I need to receive more respect from my partner.	18%	21%
5. I need more domestic help and support from my spouse.	9%	32%
6. I would like to help more in planning together.	13%	24%
7. I am satisfied with the roles and responsibilities we have established.	64%	66%

Both husbands and wives would like to use some of their capabilities more often. As doers, servers need opportunities to use their gifting. The wise spouse of a server will allow broad possibilities for these abilities to be expressed.

Server wives report a need for more domestic help from their spouses, who probably take advantage of their wives' tendency to overdo in that department. Almost two-thirds of the server respondents are basically satisfied with their roles and responsibilities.

Category 5: Conflict Resolution

A. I feel we have some problems in how we deal with conflicts in these areas:

	He	She
1. Anger management	36%	37%
2. Who's right	40%	45%
3. Final decisions	16%	18%
4. Silent treatment	38%	58%
5. Ultimatums	9%	13%
6. Personal attacks	16%	32%
7. Blame game	18%	18%

While one-third of the respondents report problems with anger, the scores are decidedly lower that the average scores for all the gifts. We can say that servers are easygoing, more mellow than most and prone to work through angry feelings rather than stuffing them. Some of the scoring most likely represents the anger problem of the spouses.

The scores on arguments over who is right are higher than we would expect and higher than some of the other gifts. While the initiation for some of the arguments may come from the spouses of servers, the scores indicate that servers can have strong feelings of being right and defend that position.

Mark, a server-gifted auto mechanic, says, "I seldom argue with my wife. I even let her think I'm in agreement with her by not saying anything, if it's about something insignificant. But when it's a matter of great importance, I speak up and stand my ground."

Final decision-making is not much of an issue with servers. They are usually happy to have their spouses make decisions or do it together. This works well with most relationships except when the spouse is a compassion person—a gift often characterized as indecisive.

Clamming up is a major problem for servers, especially for wives of this gifting. Servers usually feel the least capable of winning a verbal battle. Thus they will retreat into silence and hope the problem goes away. Sally, married to an exhorter gift, explained, "Harold is so verbose that he easily overwhelms me. When we argue, I feel he's beating me over the head with words, so I clam up or walk away. He's finally learned to listen to my silence, to realize he needs to back off, give me some hugs and let me express what I feel."

Threats and ultimatums are not usually in a server's arsenal. Server husbands do not see verbal assault as much of a problem, but server wives do. "My administrator husband has a way of making me feel under attack sometimes," Edna says. "He sees problems where I don't. He analyzes my motives and declares them wrong when I know they aren't. I wish I had better verbal skills so I wouldn't feel so overwhelmed."

The blame game is not much of a problem for servers. But they can become the target of the blame more easily than some gifts and are not so prone to resist it.

Servers (see chart B on page 108) see themselves as calm, agreeable, adaptable and able to handle stress well. They seldom wound others but may get wounded themselves. Yet they are reasonably quick to forgive or apologize. No wonder servers usually make good spouses!

C. My genuine needs, views or beliefs are:

	He	She
1. I need to gain control over my temper.	22%	29%
2. I need my spouse to gain control over his or her temper.	18%	26%
3. I need to have my point of view heard more often.	16%	18%
4. I feel a strong need to avoid arguments and conflicts.	49%	45%
5. I need my mate to forgive me more quickly.	22%	21%
6. I think we need better ground rules for resolving conflicts.	29%	29%
7. I am satisfied with the way we resolve conflicts.	47%	47%

Half of the server respondents are satisfied with the way their marital conflicts are resolved and about half feel a strong need

B. To what degree, from 1 to 7, are you one way or the other:

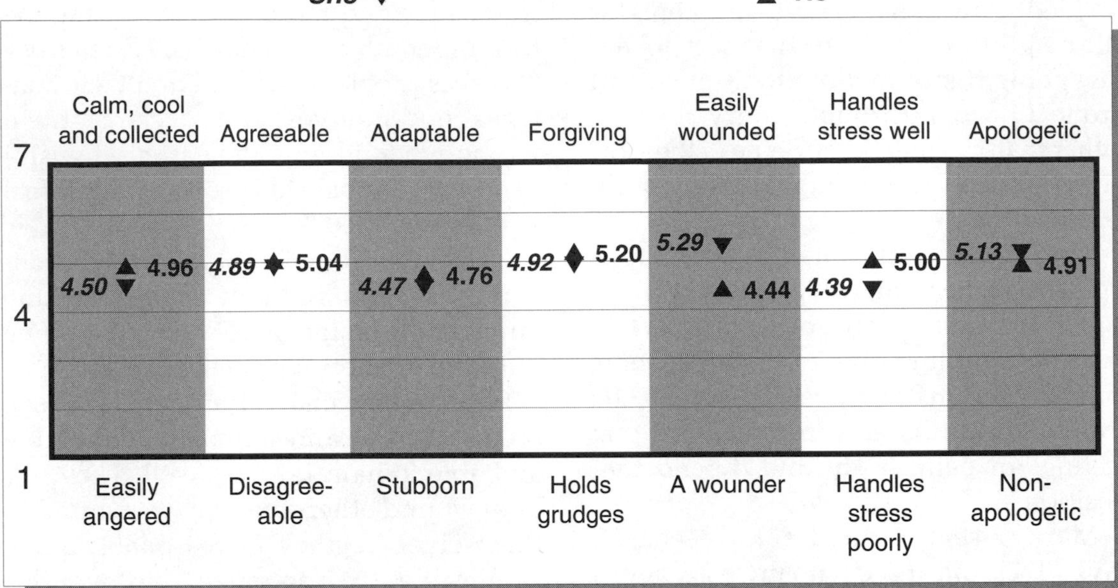

to avoid arguments and conflicts. As one server stated it, "We're lovers, not fighters." The need for temper control for servers or their spouses was not major, but 29 percent expressed the need for better ground rules for resolving conflicts.

"I'm not a volatile person," Louann says, "but I get upset with my husband once in a while. Ross is a hit-and-run person with a strong perceiver gift. His temper can flare, and by the time I've figured out why he's angry, he's got his nose back in the newspaper. I wish we could work out a way to deal with conflicts that's workable for both of us."

Category 6: Personality Issues

A. I feel we have some problems in personality conflicts and issues in these areas:

	He	She
1. Being right	20%	37%
2. Pride	13%	37%
3. Understanding	44%	50%
4. Change attempts	13%	37%
5. Methodologies	42%	42%
6. Habits	29%	37%
7. Forgetfulness	31%	45%

Being right is only moderately important to servers in general and even less so for server husbands—about half the average for all men.

Malcolm explains it this way: "If Abby tries to argue with me about being right about something, I usually just defer to her. It's usually not worth the time or effort to argue." Pride is not a major problem for server spouses, who seem to have a sincerely humble estimation of themselves.

The scores for misunderstanding each other are higher than the average. This reflects the limited communication skills of this gifting. It may also reflect the tendency of servers to expect others to be as simple and practical in their approach to life as they are. Susie told us, "I don't know why

B. To what degree, from 1 to 7, are you one way or the other:

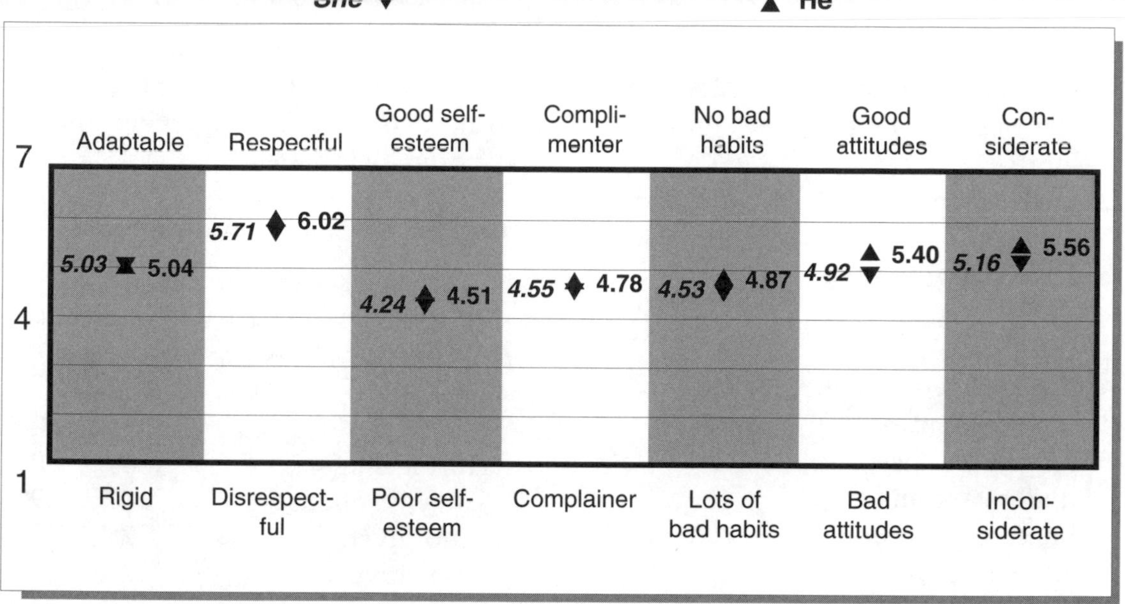

my husband has to analyze everything so much before he makes a decision. I figure if there's an opportunity to do something, just do it."

Server women were average in reporting problems of one mate trying to change the other. Men servers had very low scores in this, showing how accepting they are of their spouses.

About forty percent of the servers report problems in methods of doing things (not surprising, given their perfectionism). Whatever they do, they do well. Mates who do not line up with the same standards may be urged to do so or even be criticized for not doing so. Servers need to give their spouses the opportunity to do things their own way.

Around thirty percent of the servers observe bothersome habits in themselves or their mates. Extreme neatness can be one of these. While servers put everything back in its place, other gifts find that is not always necessarily needful. Beth, a compassion gift married to Doug, a classic server gift, told us she felt it was more important for a house to look lived in and be comfortable to relax in than for it to be neat and orderly. "I keep the house clean," she says, "but he's always on our case to put stuff away. I wish he'd loosen up a bit."

Between 30 and 45 percent of the servers admit they are forgetful. One server wife said, "If my husband gives me too long a list of things to do, I'm bound to forget some of them. The only way I've learned to cope is to make a list and check it off as I go."

Servers (see chart B above) have reasonably high scores on adaptability, respect and consideration toward others. They seem sensitive to others and tend to be complimenters rather than complainers. They see their self-esteem as slightly better than average and rate even higher in good attitudes.

If servers compare themselves to exhorters or administrator mates, and if they do not understand the uniqueness and value of each gift, they can rate themselves lower than they ought.

C. My genuine needs, views or beliefs are:

	He	She
1. I wish my partner complimented me more.	22%	29%
2. I need more encouragement from my mate.	22%	39%
3. I need to be accepted and appreciated for who I am.	20%	53%
4. I need to retain my unique identity.	11%	29%
5. My partner needs to understand my gifts.	18%	16%
6. I need more admiration and respect from my partner.	11%	24%
7. We do not seem to have any personality conflicts.	40%	34%

While more than a third of the servers said they have no personality conflicts, server wives expressed a significant need to be accepted and appreciated for who they are. Being laid back and noncompetitive, they are content to *be* and hope their spouses will accept them accordingly. They also need more encouragement and respect from their mates.

Category 7: Emotional Responses

A. I feel we have some problems in the ways we respond to each other emotionally in these areas:

	He	She
1. Hurt feelings	38%	50%
2. Carrying offenses	18%	29%
3. Unforgiveness	7%	18%
4. Insensitiveness	22%	37%
5. Feeling unloved	16%	26%
6. Moodiness	29%	50%
7. Anger	31%	45%

Although problems with hurt feelings rate fairly high for servers, especially server wives, the scores are slightly below the

B. To what degree, from 1 to 7, are you one way or the other:

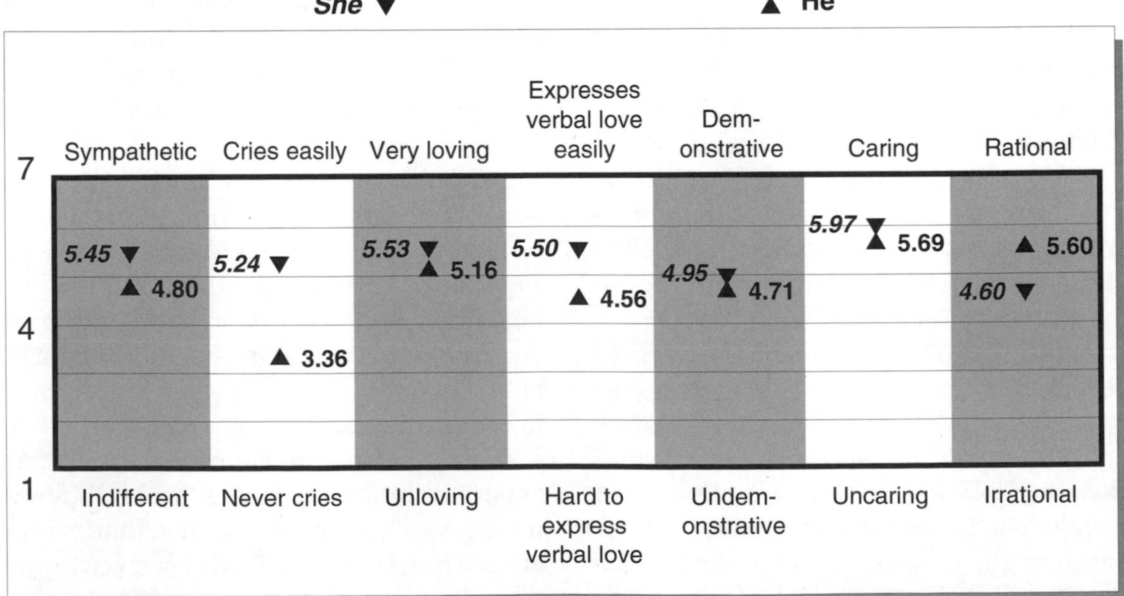

average for all the gifts. Server spouses have a good measure of control over their emotions, yet their feelings (like everyone's) can be hurt.

Being practical and sensitive, server spouses do not carry offenses long. Their willingness to forgive is high. Charlene, a server married for thirty years, says, "Stan's perceiver gift makes me angry at times, but I've learned to keep short accounts. I forgive him before the sun goes down, as the apostle Paul recommends in Ephesians 4:26. It keeps me emotionally sound and our marriage healthy."

More server wives than husbands see insensitivity as a problem. Those married to perceivers, teachers and administrators have greater problems here.

Not feeling loved is less of a problem area for server spouses, who are good at reading body language as well as responding to verbal expressions of love. If servers know they are loved, it is enough. They do not need an abundance of verbal affirmation.

Moodiness is more than an average problem for server wives and less so for server husbands. Most of that comes from stuffing feelings. Expressing anger inappropriately is a universal problem, but the servers scored lower than average here. They are good forgivers and tend to resolve their anger well.

Servers (see chart B on page 110) tend to be on the sympathetic rather than indifferent side. They are caring people, especially to their mates. They believe they are very loving, reasonably demonstrative and good at expressing love verbally. The latter is more true of wives, but husbands and wives are *less* able than most of the other gifts to communicate love verbally. "I kept thinking I was expressing verbal love well to my wife," Isaac said, "until I found out most men say it every day. I thought once a week was enough."

C. My genuine needs, views or beliefs are:

	He	She
1. My feelings tend to rule my life.	20%	39%
2. My mate needs to understand my moods more.	11%	37%
3. I need to hear more "I love you's" from my partner.	13%	24%
4. I need to be able to express both positive and negative feelings.	40%	61%
5. I feel that my spouse takes everything too personally.	20%	18%
6. I often feel put down by my partner.	20%	26%
7. I am satisfied with our emotional responses to each other.	44%	45%

Close to half of the server respondents are satisfied with the emotional responses in their marriage relationship. But what about the other half? We see their expressions of emotional need in their other responses—for example, their need to be able to express negative as well as positive emotions. Perhaps servers hold in their negative feelings for fear of disturbing the marital peace, even though feelings (as we have seen) are usually neither right nor wrong. Acceptance of emotions, whatever they are, gives the mate the opportunity to resolve negative feelings appropriately.

Server women are moodier and more emotional than server men (as you might expect) and have deeper feelings. They need to hear more "I love you's." This is the gift that costs little to give and reaps enormous benefits in *any* marriage relationship!

Category 8: Intellectual Capacity

A. I FEEL WE HAVE SOME PROBLEMS REGARDING INTELLECTUAL INTERESTS AND CAPACITIES IN THESE AREAS:

	He	She
1. Different interests	36%	47%
2. Reading	20%	24%
3. Continuing education	4%	11%
4. Know-it-all attitude	13%	26%
5. Correcting grammar	9%	29%
6. Children's education	4%	8%
7. Being accurate	27%	18%

Servers do not usually take a keen interest in intellectual pursuits. Being oriented toward the practical, servers would rather *do* something than read something. A server gift married to a teacher gift would probably not get excited about signing up for a lecture series or reading *War and Peace*.

In most cases servers read less than their spouses, and they enjoy adventures or mysteries. This surprises Don and me since servers are conservative rather than adventuresome, but these books apparently provide them with vicarious enjoyment. They also enjoy historical novels. Nonfiction is not usually their cup of tea—except, of course, how-to books on building a cupboard for those teacups!

Most servers prefer work that requires excellence in manual skills. Many are not interested in higher education but do not mind if their spouses pursue it. Servers continue to learn as they go—from observation, trial-and-error or practical extension courses.

Know-it-all attitudes are not normally found in server spouses, but servers may get frustrated at this attitude in their mates. Servers themselves are unlikely to correct anyone's grammar, unless perhaps that of their children. Servers agree that the education of their children is not a problem area.

Being accurate or factual is only a nominal problem, with server mates always looking on the practical side. As one server puts it, "If it's workable, it's probably true."

Servers' scores here (see chart B on page 113) are close to the mean, which, if compared to perceivers, teachers, exhorters and administrators, would be considered low. They see themselves as nonintellectual, but that does not mean they are not smart. Their opinions are flexible and their articulation skills nominal. Pride is usually not a problem unless it is in the quality of their work. They are not highly analytical. And server husbands especially are minimal readers.

Rex, a carpenter, says, "I didn't do too well in school and reading was particularly hard for me. But now I'm taking an adult reading improvement program to enhance my ability to read contracts, blueprint data and practical things like that."

Note that servers are definitely on the fun-loving side. They enjoy life and do not take themselves overly seriously. They make easy-to-get-along-with mates.

C. MY GENUINE NEEDS, VIEWS OR BELIEFS ARE:

	He	She
1. I need adequate time for reading or study.	42%	55%
2. I am easily sidetracked by new interests.	31%	34%
3. I need to question things before I can accept them.	49%	47%
4. I need my mate to listen to my opinions more.	11%	32%
5. I realize I need to be less dogmatic.	13%	18%
6. I find I constantly analyze what my partner says and does.	13%	11%

B. To what degree, from 1 to 7, are you one way or the other:

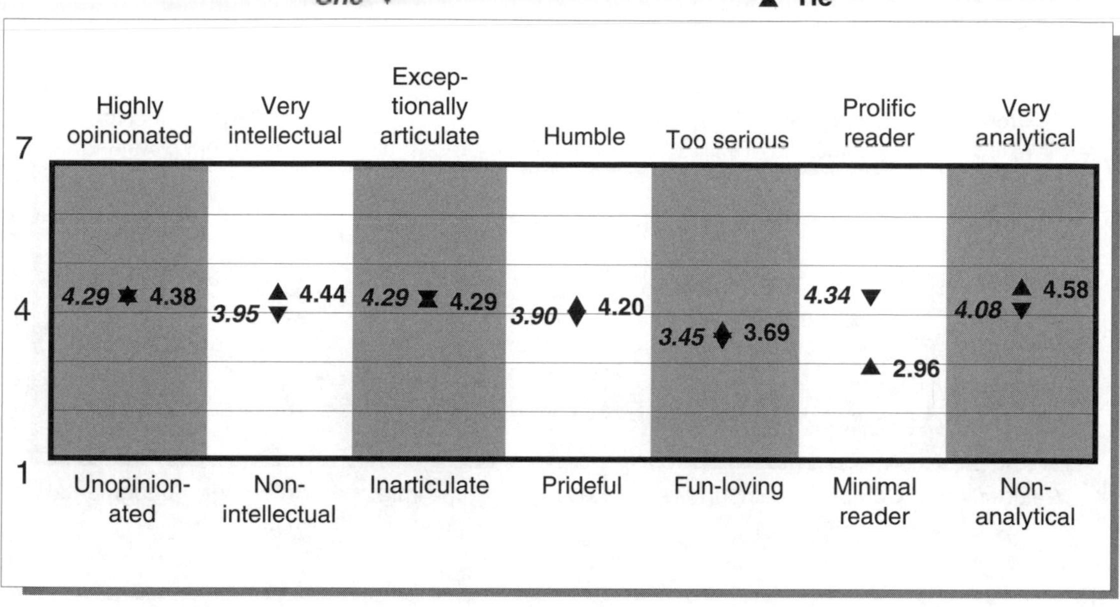

	He	She
7. I am satisfied with how we handle intellectual matters.	51%	58%

Server wives express more of a need than server husbands for adequate time for reading or study. Not easily sidetracked, servers try to finish what they start. The fact that almost half of the respondents said they need to question things before accepting them indicates more internal intellectual activity than is evidenced by their outward expression. More than half are satisfied with how intellectual matters are handled within their marital arrangement.

Category 9: Volitional Issues

A. I feel we have some problems in the use of the will in these areas:

	He	She
1. Decisions and choices	33%	45%
2. Practical decisions	11%	21%
3. Stubbornness	20%	34%
4. Agreements	13%	18%
5. Right actions	7%	11%
6. Judgmentalism	13%	26%
7. Rebelliousness	7%	21%

Servers are not particularly good decision-makers, often preferring that their mates carry that load or that they work together at it. Their decisions are based on their practical outlook on life. Joan, a classic server wife, said, "When Wes and I have to make a decision about going somewhere, I usually do not have strong feelings one way or the other. My main concern is that I am caught up on the work I need to do before going."

The adaptability of server spouses enables them to make decisions they can live with. As Mike puts it, "If my wife and I cannot come up with a really workable decision that fits both of us, we just put it on hold until it can be practical."

The stubbornness level of server wives is about average, while server husbands

B. To what degree, from 1 to 7, are you one way or the other:

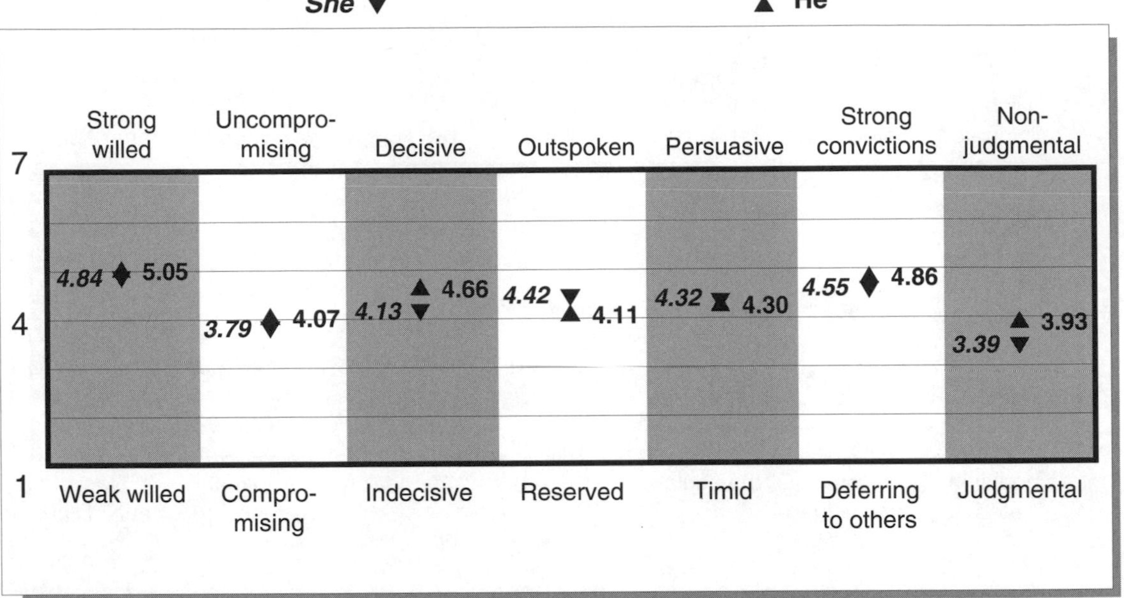

scored significantly lower, indicating their eagerness to please. Bob, in his practical server perspective, says, "Why should I be stubborn about anything? It doesn't do anyone any good."

Servers' low scores show their good skills in reaching agreements. Doing what is right is not a problem in the eyes of servers. They tend to equate it with doing what is practical and therefore logical. Low scores show servers as basically nonjudgmental.

Server wives show a bit of rebelliousness; for server husbands it is practically nil.

Most of the scores here (see chart B above) show the tendency of the server toward the average. In comparison with the other gifts, particularly the speaking gifts, servers tend to be more shy or timid, definitely more likely to be reserved than outspoken.

"A lot of times I don't say what I really think," Becca says. "I'm a bit on the shy side, even with my husband. I appreciate the fact that he encourages me to speak up more. His genuine interest in what I have to say has helped me overcome really painful childhood shyness."

C. My genuine needs, views or beliefs are:

	He	She
1. I have a definite inner need to be right.	33%	34%
2. I have a strong need to be a decision-maker.	22%	18%
3. I need my mate to make most of the decisions.	9%	37%
4. I will do what is right even if it hurts.	49%	50%
5. I need to operate by definite principles.	44%	53%
6. I need my mate to be more tolerant of my opinions.	11%	39%
7. I am satisfied with how we make decisions.	49%	55%

Servers show only a moderate need to be right. Scores are much stronger in willingness to do what is right even if it hurts. Around half of the servers operate by definite principles and are satisfied with how they, along with their mates, make decisions.

Many server wives admit they prefer to have their mates make most of the decisions.

Category 10: Physical Conditions

A. I FEEL WE HAVE SOME PROBLEMS IN THE PHYSICAL REALM IN THESE AREAS:

	He	She
1. Being fit	60%	58%
2. Enough exercise	73%	79%
3. Fatigue	42%	66%
4. Overeating	42%	37%
5. Proper eating	42%	42%
6. Keeping attractive	11%	32%
7. Adequate sleep	49%	53%

Being physically fit seems to be a major problem with all the gifts, and with fully sixty percent of the servers. Exercise is the major problem. Granted, our culture is permeated with temptations to overeat or ride rather than walk. Nevertheless, choices can and must be made.

Bertha explains that in rainy weather she usually drives to work, a distance of seven blocks. "The problem is, I wind up driving instead of walking on most good days as well, when I should be getting the exercise. I sit all day at work, too, and just don't burn off enough calories."

Servers who work at strenuous jobs have no problem keeping fit, but many others complain that they do not get enough exercise. They would do well to plan for it.

More women servers than men have problems with fatigue, which may be due in part to a more sedentary lifestyle or improper diet. One server wife reported that due to low energy levels, she was advised to eat more fresh fruit and vegetables, less red meat and starches and to exercise twenty minutes a day. Within two weeks all her fatigue was gone.

Overeating problems are typical for all the gifts; about forty percent of servers report it. Part of Ken's problem was that his server wife was such a good cook that he ate more than he knew he should. When he talked his wife into making smaller portions for every meal, they both lost weight slowly and healthfully.

B. TO WHAT DEGREE, FROM 1 TO 7, ARE YOU ONE WAY OR THE OTHER:

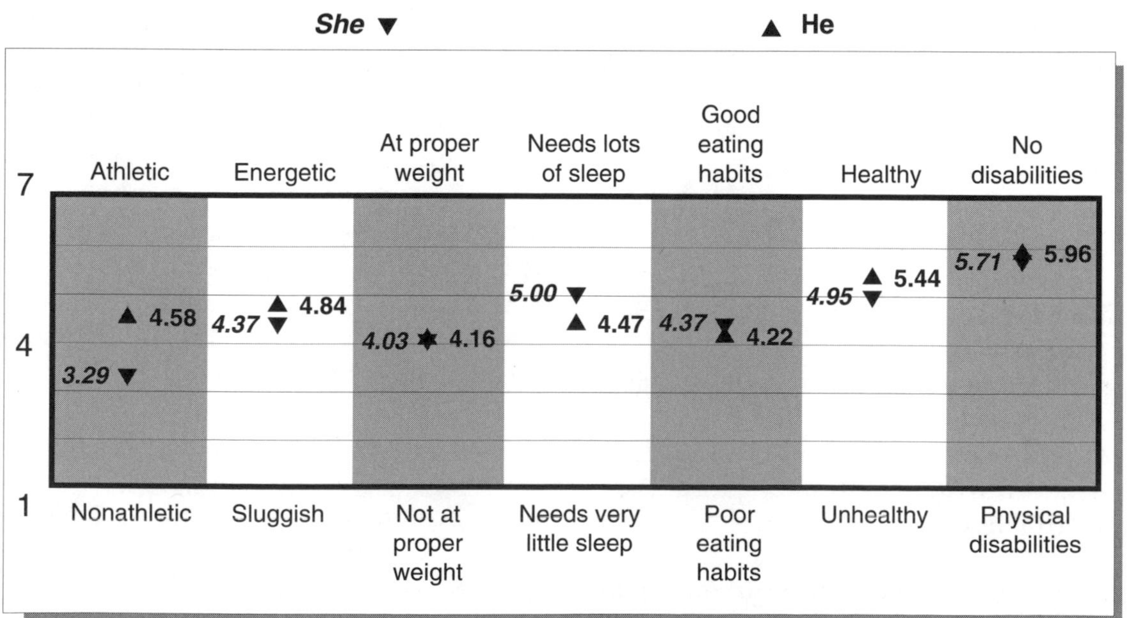

Since servers are doers and have a high energy level, they tend to burn the candle at both ends. They can often get by with less sleep at night. But this can be frustrating to a mate who needs eight hours. One server husband says he does fine with six hours of sleep but that his compassion-gifted wife needs nine. "For years we had difficulty determining sleeping hours that worked for both of us," he says. "I liked to stay up late and she conked out at nine o'clock and felt slighted because I wouldn't come to bed. We finally compromised at ten and I just get up earlier. It works for us."

Although server husbands and wives are energetic, the women see themselves as nonathletic (see chart B on page 115). They also report a greater need for sleep. Both report a midpoint situation regarding weight and slightly better-than-average eating habits.

C. My genuine needs, views or beliefs are:

	He	She
1. I desire to see my mate at the proper weight.	49%	42%
2. I need to overcome my own weight problem.	42%	68%
3. I need to get adequate exercise on a regular basis.	71%	87%
4. I would like to see my spouse get more exercise.	73%	50%
5. I need my mate to be as attractive as possible.	33%	32%
6. I need to improve my eating habits.	49%	66%
7. I am satisfied with how we keep fit, healthy and attractive.	18%	18%

Only eighteen percent of server respondents are satisfied with how they keep fit, healthy and attractive. Many server wives confess to weight problems, and most admit the need to improve eating habits. The need for regular exercise is extremely high. Server husbands scored a bit lower but have similar problems. Many report a desire to see their mates exercise more and be as attractive as possible.

Category 11: Sexual Relationship

A. I feel we have some problems in our sexual relationship in these areas:

	He	She
1. Frequency	60%	47%
2. Quality	13%	18%
3. Prior affection	29%	53%
4. Nonsexual affection	27%	47%
5. Sexual dissatisfaction	11%	13%
6. Incompatibility	2%	3%
7. Infidelity	0%	5%

Server husbands have more difficulty with the frequency of sexual relations than server wives; both score a little higher than the average for all gifts. And, typically, the women indicated a greater need for more nonsexual and prior affection than the men.

Server respondents (see chart B on page 117) scored reasonably high in affection and hugging and kissing. Interest in sex is in the average range, with server husbands scoring higher than server wives. Both are reasonably sensitive to their mates' needs. While communication about love, feelings and sex is just slightly higher than the mean, it shows that servers need to work at developing greater facility here.

"I'm very good at showing affection to my husband," Jocelyn says, "but I need to learn how to verbalize it more. He's so good at it that my efforts seem pale by comparison. But he loves it that I'm trying and encourages me constantly."

B. To what degree, from 1 to 7, are you one way or the other:

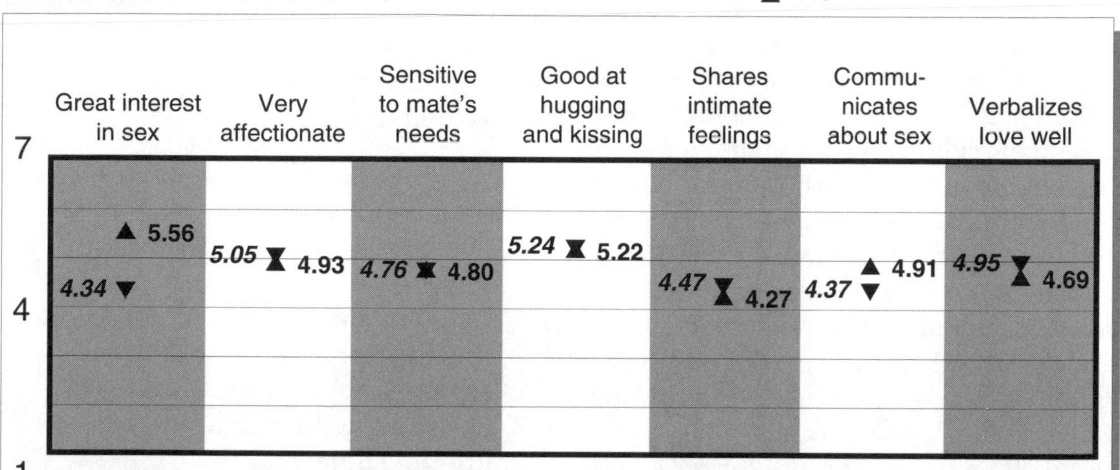

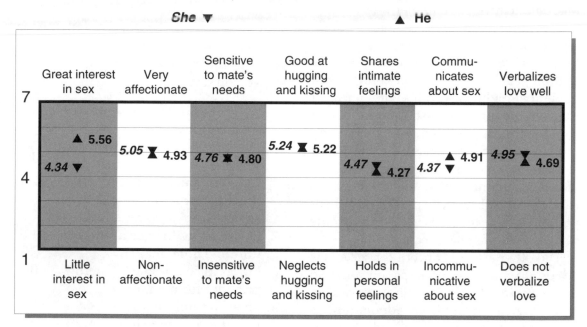

C. My genuine needs, views or beliefs are:

	He	She
1. I need more nonsexual affection from my mate.	24%	45%
2. I need more sexual relations with my mate.	33%	21%
3. I feel I need more hugs and kisses from my spouse.	29%	39%
4. I need to hear more "I love you's" from my partner.	13%	24%
5. I need my husband to better understand my monthly cycle.	0%	26%
6. I feel dissatisfied with our current sexual relationship.	24%	24%
7. I feel satisfied with our current sexual relationship.	53%	58%

No surprises here. More than half of the server respondents are happy with their current sexual relationship; only 24 percent are not.

Category 12: Work and Accomplishments

A. I feel we have some problems regarding work and accomplishments in these areas:

	He	She
1. Too busy	51%	39%
2. Career conflicts	20%	13%
3. Overtime work	22%	8%
4. Inadequate income	33%	26%
5. Volunteer work	16%	24%
6. Wife working	7%	11%
7. Priorities	22%	24%

Server women scored a little lower than average for being too busy; server men, by contrast, are busier than the average. Answers regarding overtime work were similar proportionally, indicating that server men tend to overdo more. This can be a problem for their non-server wives who may feel neglected or resentful over inadequate time for togetherness.

Our builder friend Steve, with a strong server gift, finds himself often working overtime in order to "get the job done right." He seldom gets home for dinner before seven or eight at night. I asked his wife, Teresa, if this was a source of frustration for her. "I could let it be," she admitted. "But my mother gave me some wise advice—that if my husband was working overtime to provide for our family, be grateful and adjust to it. So I go ahead and feed the kids on schedule, and when Steve gets home I have some time with him while he eats."

The other area of concern for servers is adequate income, perhaps because so many are involved with hands-on careers that may not provide as adequately as careers that are considered white-collar professional. But most servers maintain a high level of satisfaction in their work and accomplishments.

Servers (see figure below) get high marks for being motivated accomplishers. They are industrious, organized and short-term-goal-oriented. They are the best doers of all the gifts. They are also the best at domestic support. The only drawback mentioned is the level of wages, often unfairly low compared to the energy expended, especially for women servers.

C. My genuine needs, views or beliefs are:

	He	She
1. I need my husband to provide our basic expenses.	4%	42%
2. I need my wife to be a full-time homemaker.	27%	11%
3. I need to be the sole provider for my family.	16%	0%
4. I need a fulfilling career.	38%	8%
5. I need a challenge to work toward.	42%	37%
6. I get great joy out of my accomplishments.	67%	74%
7. I am satisfied with the way we handle work and accomplishments.	62%	61%

B. To what degree, from 1 to 7, are you one way or the other:

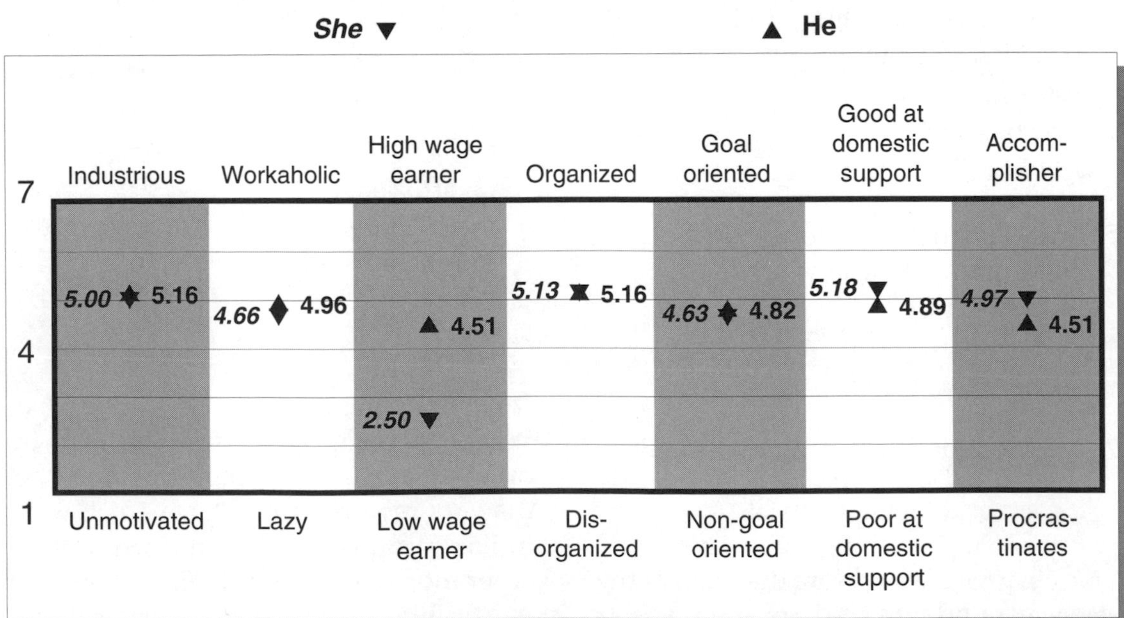

More than sixty percent of all servers are satisfied with the way they and their mates handle work and accomplishments. They enjoy a challenge and get great joy out of their accomplishments. Seldom does the wife of a server have cause to complain that he is not an adequate provider or hard worker. Similarly, the husband of a server wife is blessed with her superior skills in homemaking or work outside the home.

Category 13: Financial Management

A. I FEEL WE HAVE SOME PROBLEMS IN FINANCIAL MATTERS IN THESE AREAS:

	He	She
1. Establishing budget	56%	58%
2. Keeping to budget	58%	63%
3. Living beyond means	31%	42%
4. Credit cards	40%	34%
5. Impulsive buying	29%	42%
6. Money arguments	18%	32%
7. Wife's work role	2%	8%

More than half of all servers have some problems in budgeting. The best advice for the server and spouse unable to establish a budget by themselves is to get help.

Keeping to a budget is another major problem where help may be necessary. Server wives have an even greater problem than their male counterparts living within their means. This is a tendency of women in general more than men, and also reflects the cultural influence to buy now and pay later. It is important for husbands and wives to be realistic about spending and set goals they can handle.

Surprisingly, server husbands have more of a problem than wives with buying too much on credit, although the problem of both is greater than the norm. If credit-buying is out of control, it may be necessary to cut up the cards and make some major lifestyle changes.

Over forty percent of server wives and about thirty percent of server husbands admitted that impulsive buying is a problem. One woman reported, "Agreeing with my husband to a modest limit for on-the-spot spending helped curb this problem for me."

Server Jim said, "Money arguments were becoming a serious deterrent to our marital harmony. As we developed a workable budget and followed it, the arguments disappeared."

While some servers (see chart B on page 120) are impulsive buyers and have difficulty staying within a budget, many are conservative buyers who keep well to a budget. They tend to save before buying and feel on the secure side financially.

Interestingly, servers tend to be bargain-hunters who like to stretch their dollars. Server mates are definitely generous and score very high in tithing.

C. MY GENUINE NEEDS, VIEWS OR BELIEFS ARE:

	He	She
1. I feel we need to reduce our debts more effectively.	58%	50%
2. I feel the need to be in charge of our family finances.	27%	13%
3. I believe the husband should handle the family finances.	13%	24%
4. I think the most capable partner should handle the family finances.	62%	68%
5. I need to learn how to handle money more responsibly.	29%	26%
6. I would like to give more to church, missionaries, charity, etc.	44%	58%

B. To what degree, from 1 to 7, are you one way or the other:

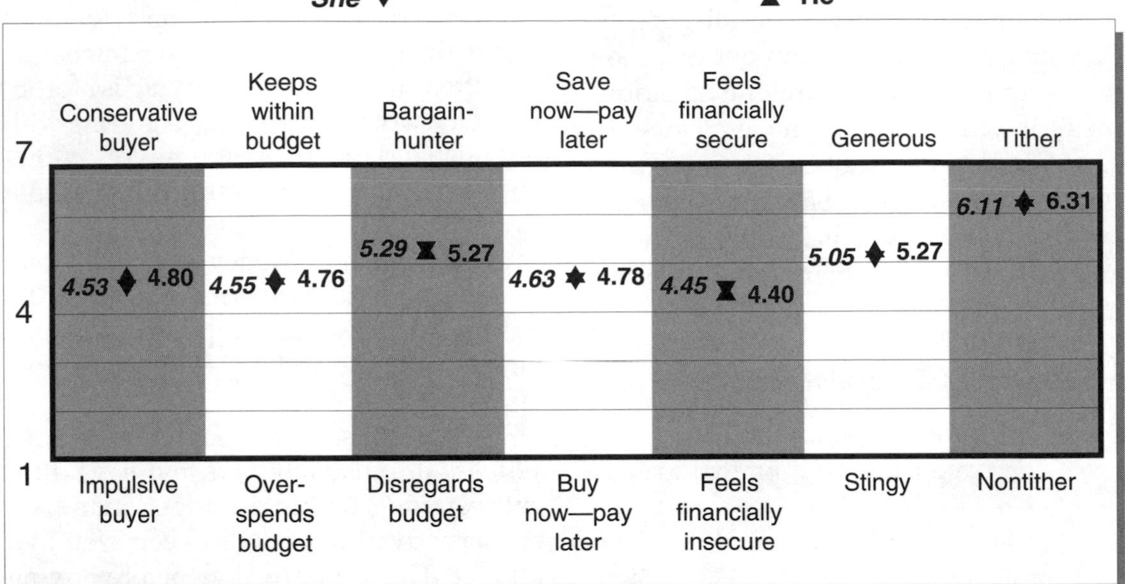

	He	She
7. I am satisfied with how we handle finances.	44%	53%

While close to fifty percent are satisfied with how they, with their mates, handle finances, the other half express a need to reduce indebtedness. Some two-thirds agree that the most capable partner should handle the family finances. "My compassion husband realized I was more detailed in handling finances," Renata explained, "so he delegated the responsibility to me. I don't mind. I actually enjoy it."

Close to half say they would like to give more to church, missionaries or charities.

Category 14: Leisure Activities

A. I feel we have some problems in how we spend our free time in these areas:

	He	She
1. Interests	27%	29%
2. Recreational preferences	11%	13%
3. Hobbies	20%	24%
4. Entertainment	7%	18%
5. Vacation preferences	2%	13%
6. Sports	11%	26%
7. TV-watching	51%	50%

Scores on the first three items are typical of all the gifts. But on the next three items, server husbands scored significantly lower than the other gifts; server wives did not. Perhaps server husbands are so adaptable in regard to entertainment, vacations and sports that they adjust easily to the plans and preferences of their mates.

The one major problem (as for all the gifts) is TV-watching. Television can be a blessing or a time-robber, depending on how it is used or misused. It can be low-cost entertainment that enhances marital cohesion or it can cause the polarization of relationships. It is important for couples to evaluate how they use TV, how each feels about it and how mutual adjustments can be made to prevent its negative influence in the marriage.

Server spouses (see chart B below) see themselves primarily in the mid range in most of these opposites. They like to travel but prefer short vacation times rather than long ones. Too much time away from productive work makes them feel they are wasting time. They also enjoy walks and other types of exercise. Servers consider themselves fairly social, but they are not as social as exhorters, administrators and compassion gifts.

C. My genuine needs, views or beliefs are:

	He	She
1. I need my partner to be a recreational companion.	40%	32%
2. I need to do more fun things with my spouse.	58%	68%
3. I need more meaningful vacations.	24%	21%
4. I need to be involved in nonathletic leisure activities.	18%	29%
5. I prefer active group or competitive sports.	29%	13%
6. I prefer individual non-competitive sports.	27%	45%
7. I am satisfied with how we spend our leisure time.	36%	37%

Only a third of the respondents claimed to be satisfied with how they spend leisure time. More server men than women enjoy active and competitive sports. Women tend to enjoy individual or noncompetitive sports. Both indicate a need for more recreational companionship from their partners and to do more fun things together.

Beth, a server married to Glenn, a giver, found they were always too busy to engage in special activities like hiking, swimming or tennis. "So we started scheduling fun times," she said, "and our relationship improved along with our attitudes and actions."

B. To what degree, from 1 to 7, are you one way or the other:

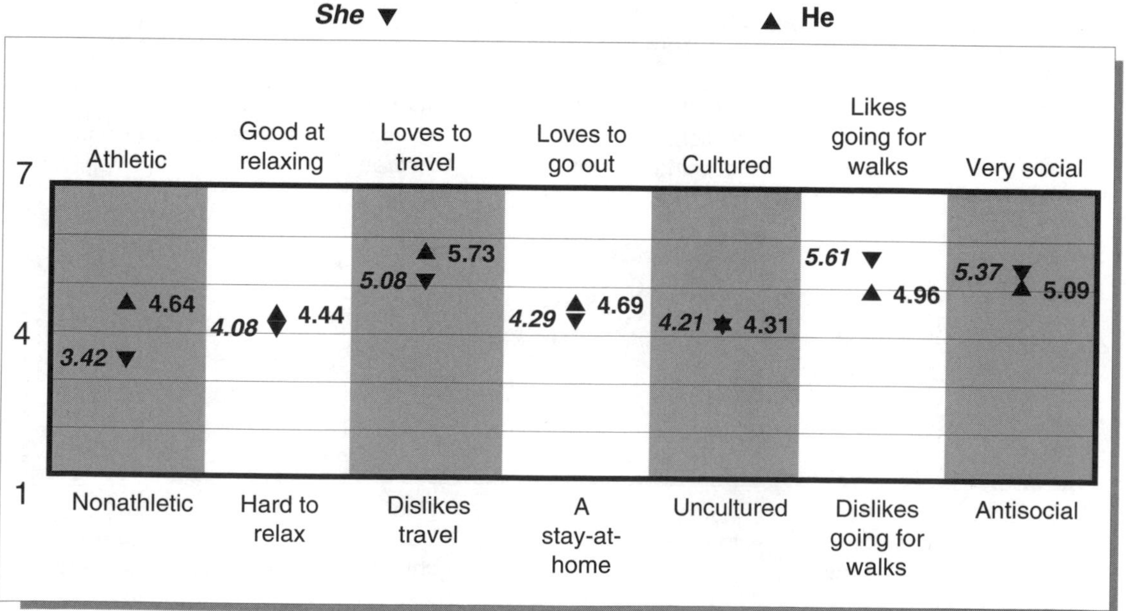

Category 15: Parenting

A. I feel we have (had) some problems in the child-rearing process in these areas:

	He	She
1. Type of discipline	44%	37%
2. Amount of discipline	22%	24%
3. Who disciplines	22%	26%
4. Misconduct determination	22%	18%
5. Love expression	18%	21%
6. Time spent	38%	32%
7. Money given	11%	24%

The servers' responses to these items are typical, for the most part, of all the gifts. Server husbands, however, indicated they have more problems with the kind of discipline and training they give in relationship with their spouses. Sometimes they overdo the discipline.

Jim, a server gift married to a teacher gift, told us, "Julie and I are both strong disciplinarians and found we were doing so much of it that our kids began to think they couldn't do anything right. We adjusted our style, set priorities for what had to be disciplined and loosened up on other things. It worked much better and the kids have all turned out fine."

The other significant difference between servers and the other gifts regards the money given to or spent on the children. In general servers are good, consistent parents. They tend to have a balanced perspective and are open to positive suggestions that will enhance their parenting skills. They can err in doing too much for their children and prevent the development of positive self-care habits.

Server wives (see chart B below) seem to spend more time with their children than server husbands. Wives also do slightly more affectionate touching, but they have more of a tendency to spoil their children. While servers are about average in training their children, they can wind up doing too much for them. Don admits he took advantage of his server mother, who

B. To what degree, from 1 to 7, are you one way or the other:

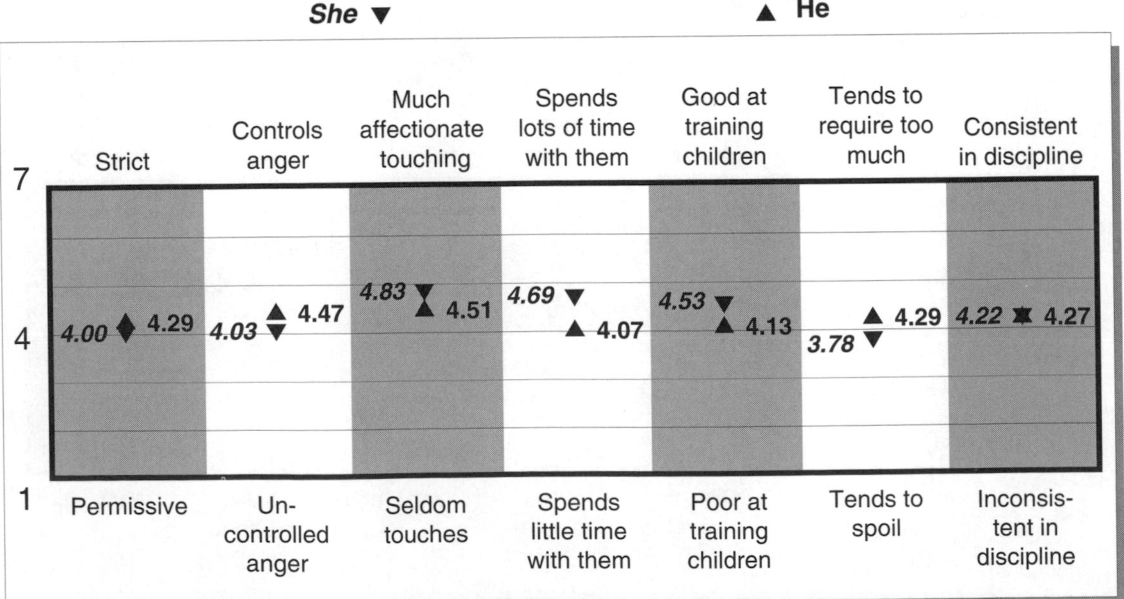

was a perfectionist. "She would give me a job to do," he says, "and if I was slow at it, she would take over and do it herself to get it done sooner. Thus I missed out learning some of the things I should have."

C. My genuine needs, views or beliefs are:

	He	She
1. We need to provide better spiritual guidance for our children.	49%	50%
2. We need to give our children more love and affection.	31%	24%
3. I would like my spouse to help more with the children.	2%	21%
4. I need to be more affirming of our children.	33%	45%
5. I feel we need to agree more on discipline.	13%	21%
6. I feel we need more quality family time and activities.	51%	47%
7. I am satisfied with our parenting styles and skills.	29%	39%

Servers are less satisfied than you might expect with their parenting styles and skills. They recognize the need to provide better spiritual guidance, give more love and affection, be more affirming and spend more quality time in family activities.

Server wives say they need more help with the children. One server wife admitted that because she enjoyed motherhood and domestic roles so much, she had enabled her husband to get by with little involvement in the care of their children. "When I finally spoke up and let him know of my need for help," she recounted, "he was glad to pitch in and do more."

Category 16: In-Laws and Family

A. I feel we have some problems with our families and in-laws in these areas:

	He	She
1. Interference	13%	16%
2. Their expectations	16%	16%
3. Their visits	0%	3%
4. Comparisons	4%	8%
5. Borrowing money	4%	11%
6. Former abuse	9%	13%
7. Dysfunction affect	16%	18%

The servers' answers are typical of all the gifts except for the seventh item, in which they scored half the average. This indicates that either these servers did not come from dysfunctional families, or they do not perceive them as dysfunctional, or they do not think the former dysfunction is affecting them negatively now. With the adaptability of servers, all these things can be true in a given relationship.

Very high scores (see chart B on page 124) reflect a server spouse's potential for a healthy marital relationship. They cut the apron strings easily and move on to building a good home situation. Scores on loving and honoring parents are high and release the biblical promise that things will go well with them (Ephesians 6:1–3). Their relationships with in-laws are also better than average, showing the server's ability to get along well with others.

C. My genuine needs, views or beliefs are:

	He	She
1. I need my spouse to put me before his or her family.	24%	32%
2. I need to see or talk to my parent(s) regularly.	11%	34%

B. To what degree, from 1 to 7, are you one way or the other:

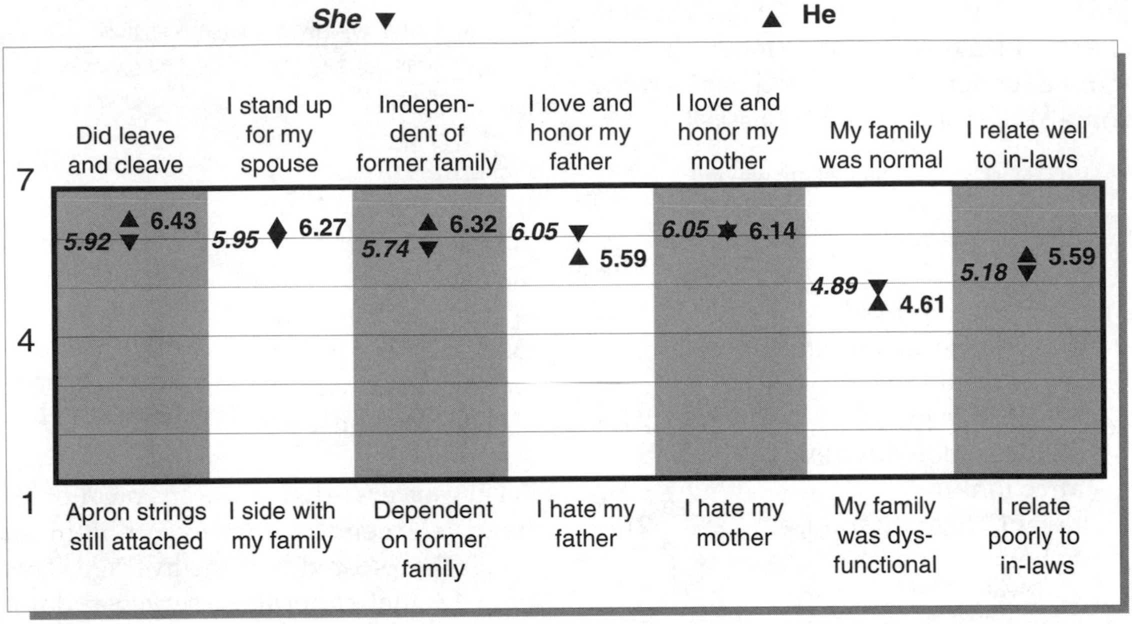

	Did leave and cleave / Apron strings still attached	I stand up for my spouse / I side with my family	Independent of former family / Dependent on former family	I love and honor my father / I hate my father	I love and honor my mother / I hate my mother	My family was normal / My family was dysfunctional	I relate well to in-laws / I relate poorly to in-laws
She ▼	5.92	5.95	5.74	6.05	6.05	4.89	5.18
▲ He	6.43	6.27	6.32	5.59	6.14	4.61	5.59

	He	She
3. I need to include my family in holiday celebrations.	31%	50%
4. I need help in overcoming in-law problems.	7%	8%
5. I need to be accepted by my in-laws.	11%	26%
6. I need to be financially free from my family and in-laws.	18%	16%
7. I am satisfied with our family and in-law relationships.	71%	63%

Servers express a high degree of satisfaction over relationships with family and in-laws. Server wives report more need for relationships with their parents and for family to be included in holiday celebrations. Their gifting in hospitality fits them well to host such events. At times some servers feel their spouses put former family first—a situation that can produce marital insecurity.

Category 17: Social Relationships

A. I feel we have some problems in social relationships in these areas:

	He	She
1. Friends' demands	16%	18%
2. Time for friends	56%	53%
3. Unsocial partner	11%	21%
4. Too social partner	4%	3%
5. Wrong friendships	0%	3%
6. Negative influence	2%	5%
7. Over involvement	9%	8%

The major problem for server spouses in social relationships is having enough time for their friends. The scores were even higher than the norm for all the gifts, indicating that servers may not take the initiative as readily to schedule time to be with friends.

Dennis, an electrical contractor, said, "I work hard at my job and do a little moonlighting on the side. I'm usually just too tired to be social. Bev and I miss seeing our friends as much as we'd like to, but we are trying harder to find time for them."

Servers' preference (see chart B below) for small groups suggests their comfort zone—one-to-one relationships or just a few at a time. Servers often feel overwhelmed with large groups. They like to entertain people in their homes, and if someone needs a temporary place to stay, servers are the first to offer to take them in.

C. My genuine needs, views or beliefs are:

	He	She
1. I need to have many friends.	13%	21%
2. I especially love to entertain in our home.	36%	50%
3. I need a good deal of private time.	20%	42%
4. I need our home to be a haven of rest.	58%	61%
5. I need to be involved in social groups.	11%	39%
6. I think we need to change some friendships.	0%	5%
7. I am satisfied with our social life.	56%	55%

While a little more than half are satisfied with their social lives, even more say they need to have their homes as a haven of rest. Server wives especially need a good deal of private time. Half of them love to entertain in their homes. As Don and I travel and teach, we primarily stay in homes, and have found that in the majority of cases our hostess is a server gift. We can confirm that each one is truly "the hostess with the mostest!"

Category 18: Religious Orientation

A. I feel we have some problems in our spiritual life and orientation in these areas:

	He	She
1. Affiliation disagreement	0%	3%
2. Church attendance	0%	3%
3. Different backgrounds	0%	11%

B. To what degree, from 1 to 7, are you one way or the other:

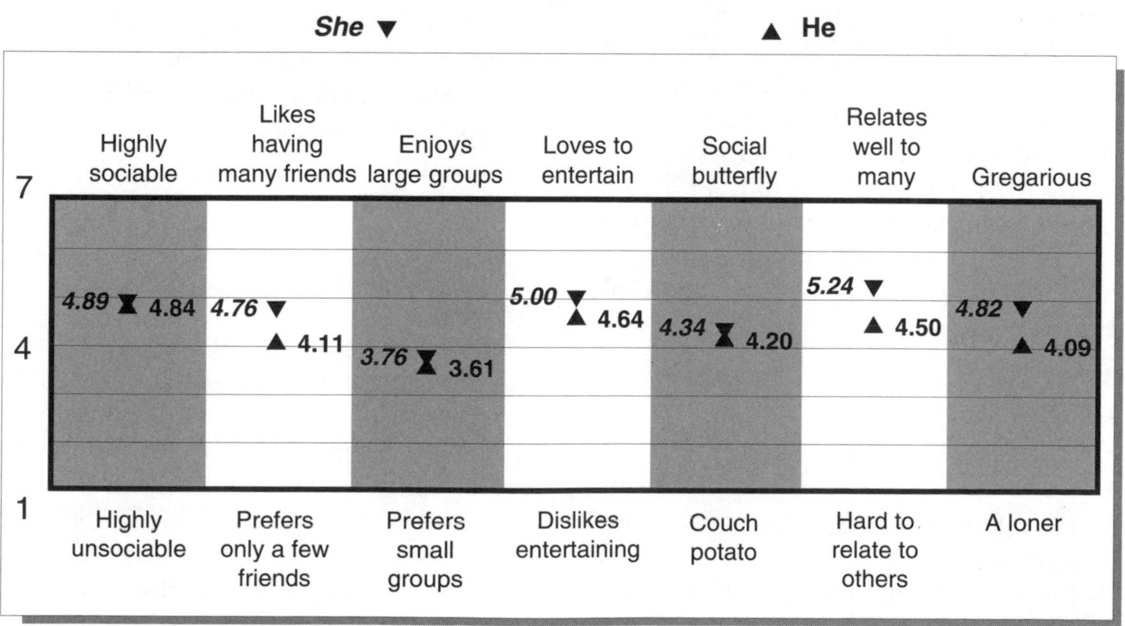

B. To what degree, from 1 to 7, are you one way or the other:

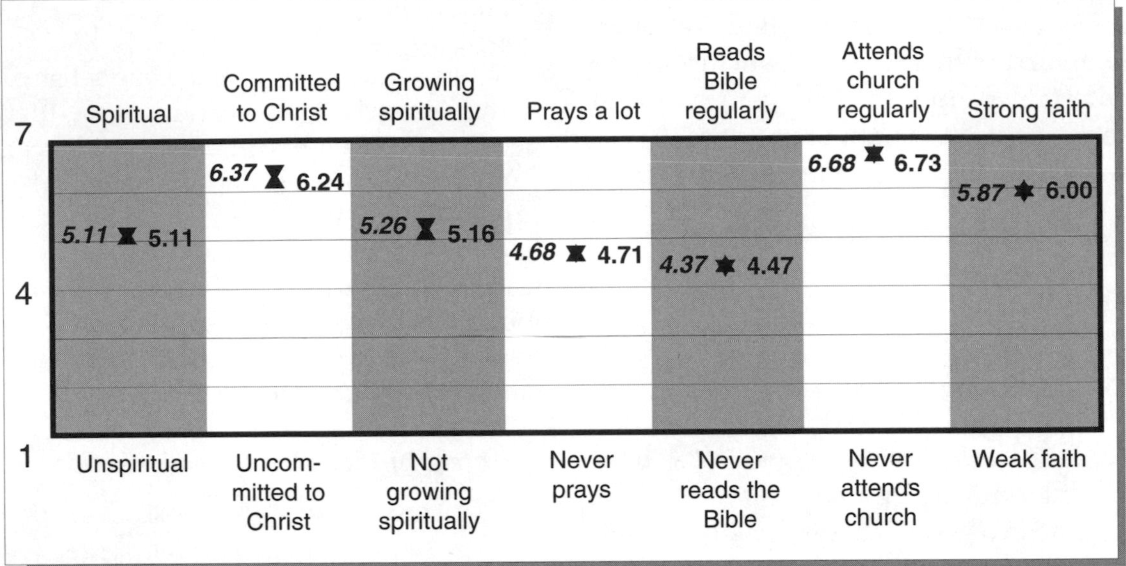

	He	She
4. Theological differences	2%	8%
5. Commitment level	20%	21%
6. Irregular attendance	0%	11%
7. Hypocritical behavior	9%	5%

Servers express few problems here, except in the area of commitment to God. Even then only about twenty percent see this issue as a significant challenge.

Scores (see chart B above) are definitely on the positive side here. Church attendance is close to a perfect 7, and faith and commitment are both near 6 or more. Servers see themselves as spiritual and growing spiritually. Even the scores for prayer and Bible reading are good.

C. My genuine needs, views or beliefs are:

	He	She
1. I need to attend church regularly.	58%	74%
2. I need my partner to pray with me daily.	42%	58%
3. I greatly desire to see my spouse grow spiritually.	62%	71%
4. I believe we need to have regular family devotions.	73%	76%
5. I need my spouse to give spiritual leadership.	4%	61%
6. I need to be able to live my faith, not just talk about it.	69%	68%
7. I am satisfied with our religious orientation and practice.	47%	47%

Exactly 47 percent of both men and women servers express satisfaction with their marital spiritual orientation and practice. They are practical in living their faith day by day, often doing something for someone as an expression of God's love. They believe a truly spiritual person should walk their talk, and they try to do just that.

Server spouses greatly desire to see their mates grow spiritually, to have prayer together and regular family devotions. Server wives love to have their husbands take spiritual leadership, and gladly take a subordinate role in order to encourage them to do so.

Category 19: Maturity

A. I FEEL WE HAVE SOME PROBLEMS IN MATURITY IN THESE AREAS:

	He	She
1. Inexperience	7%	11%
2. Irresponsibility	16%	11%
3. Blame game	11%	16%
4. Stress coping	31%	45%
5. Criticism	9%	21%
6. Infidelity	0%	3%
7. Dishonesty	4%	3%

Answers here are typical of all the gifts. Server men have a bit less trouble coping with stress than most other men, which reflects their adaptability and hang-loose mentality. They are also prone to be less critical than the other gifts and less likely to blame. In general servers tend to take responsibility well and develop mature attitudes and actions more quickly than most.

These responses (see chart B below) reflect good maturity. Their ability to be loving and forgiving is a good foundation for living. Their trustworthiness is high. You can count on servers to do what they promise. They are givers rather than takers and are able to handle responsibility well. Humility comes easily. If they are proud, it is usually in the quality of their work.

C. MY GENUINE NEEDS, VIEWS OR BELIEFS ARE:

	He	She
1. I need to be able to trust my mate.	38%	50%
2. I need my spouse to be dependable.	38%	50%
3. I need to be quick to forgive and, I hope, be forgiving quickly.	60%	68%

B. TO WHAT DEGREE, FROM 1 TO 7, ARE YOU ONE WAY OR THE OTHER:

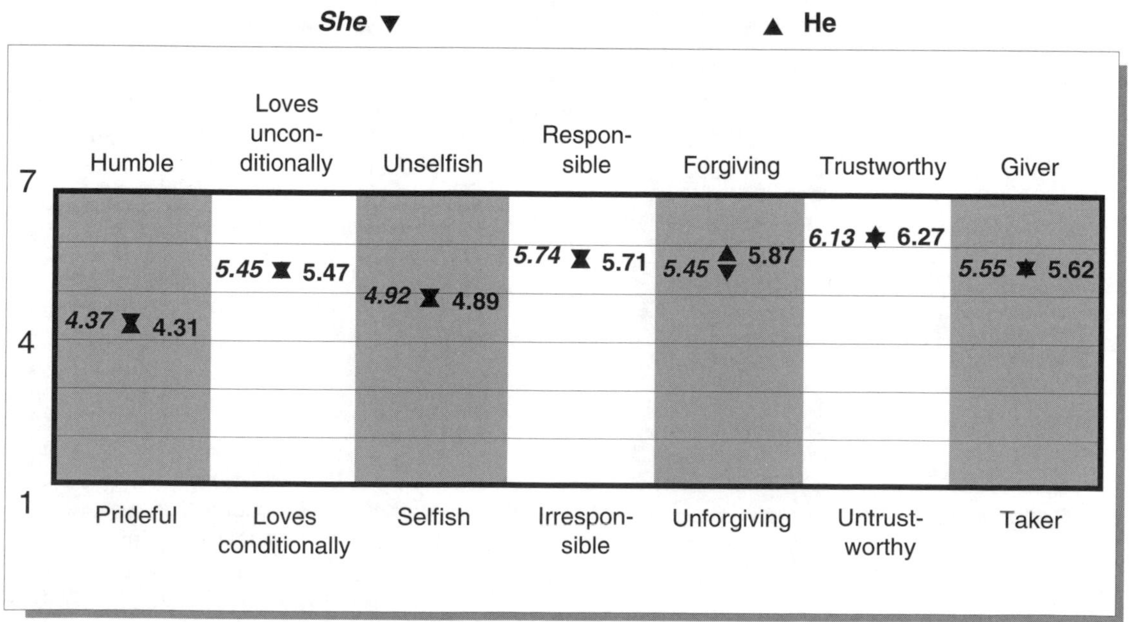

	He	She
4. We need to learn from and grow through every experience.	56%	74%
5. I need my mate to be able to handle responsibility well.	36%	53%
6. I need my mate to love me unconditionally.	42%	61%
7. I feel that we are a reasonably mature couple.	89%	89%

Server respondents give themselves amazingly high scores on being part of a reasonably mature couple. They also tend to *be* so. Note their high expectations of their mates—dependability, trustworthiness and the ability to handle responsibility well. Because these are natural server qualities, they want to see their spouses exemplify them, too. Learning through every experience is part of the practical life application viewpoint of servers.

Category 20: Dysfunctionality

A. I FEEL WE HAVE SOME PROBLEMS IN THE FOLLOWING AREAS THAT PRODUCE DYSFUNCTION:

	He	She
1. Alcohol abuse	2%	3%
2. Drug abuse	0%	3%
3. Physical abuse	0%	3%
4. Sexual abuse	2%	3%
5. Verbal abuse	4%	8%
6. Emotional abuse	2%	5%
7. Unresolved abuse	13%	8%

The first four items are virtually not a problem for our server respondents. And they scored much lower in the last three items than the average for all the gifts. Perhaps it is the servers' accommodating lifestyle that eliminates some of the potential for verbal or emotional abuse. Their lower facility in verbal communication may also be a factor: They tend neither to speak abusively nor stay around to hear it. If servers have suffered abuse in the past,

B. TO WHAT DEGREE, FROM 1 TO 7, ARE YOU ONE WAY OR THE OTHER:

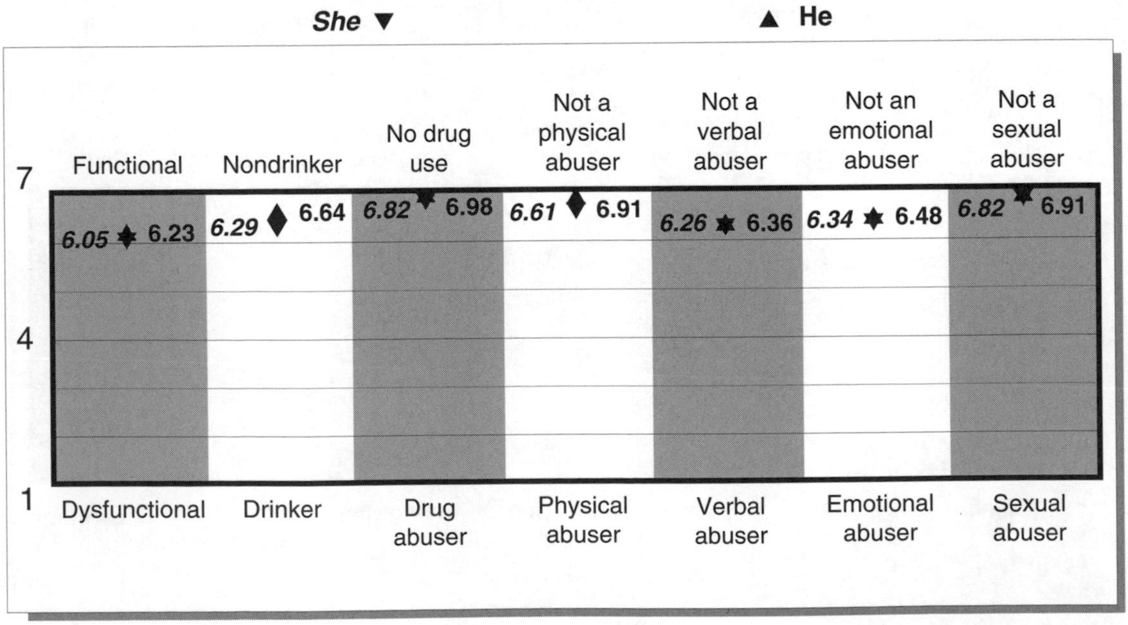

7 (high)	1 (low)	She	He
Functional	Dysfunctional	6.05	6.23
Nondrinker	Drinker	6.29	6.64
No drug use	Drug abuser	6.82	6.98
Not a physical abuser	Physical abuser	6.61	6.91
Not a verbal abuser	Verbal abuser	6.26	6.36
Not an emotional abuser	Emotional abuser	6.34	6.48
Not a sexual abuser	Sexual abuser	6.82	6.91

they try to work through it, forgive and get on with their lives.

The fact that all scores (see chart B on page 128) are above 6 here, and many are almost 7, indicates little if any dysfunction in servers' lives. Our respondents are seldom substance abusers and hardly ever abusive to others, including their mates.

C. My genuine needs, views or beliefs are:

	He	She
1. I need our marriage to be free of alcohol use and abuse.	36%	34%
2. I need our marriage to be free of drug use and abuse.	38%	39%
3. I need my spouse to treat me more kindly.	4%	13%
4. I need my mate to give me positive emotional support.	29%	45%
5. One or both of us need to get help for abuse in childhood.	9%	0%
6. One or both of us need to get help for dysfunctional behavior.	9%	3%
7. I believe there is no dysfunctional behavior in our marriage.	76%	82%

A significant majority of server mates believe there is no dysfunctional behavior in their marriages. The only specific need seems to be in the area of more positive emotional support. The reward for giving such positive input to one's spouse is so beneficial that we wonder why all marriage partners do not do more of it!

Living with a Teacher Spouse

Von, a teacher gift who taught at the university, was married to Peg, a vivacious compassion-and-exhorter combination who was very romantic and determined to prod her emotionally reserved spouse into at least a measure of amorous marital expression. He ignored her once-a-year comments about how wonderful it would be if he brought her flowers, since he was convinced that the short lives of cut flowers made them a waste of money. His gifts were of a practical sort—a can-opener, a new pair of walking shoes, tickets to the latest lecture series.

But when their tenth anniversary drew near, Von recognized it as a special milestone in their lives and decided to heed the patient hints that had been piling up. He visited the local florist and was shocked to find out the price of a dozen long-stemmed red roses.

Good grief! he said to himself. *All that money, and in a week the roses will be dead and gone!*

Not to be deterred from his newfound effort to be romantic, he went across the street to K Mart and bought Peg a dozen long-stemmed red *plastic* roses.

No, teacher spouses do not win any Most-Romantic-Mate-of-the-Year awards. They tend to be the *least* romantic husbands and wives. Their tremendous objectivity makes them overtly practical and calculatingly careful, especially when it comes to spending money, being spontaneous or acting with abandon. They can learn in these areas, especially from compassion gifts, who are the most romantic and impulsive of all.

Five Major Problem Areas

First let's look at the five most significant problem areas of the teacher gift, which in turn influence the problems experienced in each of the twenty categories of our survey.

1. Pride in Intellectual Ability

Teachers are usually the most intellectual of the gifts, often scoring the highest on IQ tests. When we place the seven motivational gifts in a diagram of a body, they represent the mind. God has given them superior intellects because that is the part they utilize the most in all they do. Many go into teaching, science, math, engineering, computer programming or other areas that require good mental facility.

They read profusely and learn constantly, gaining much knowledge. But they can also develop pride in their intellectual capacity. John and Debbie, both teacher gifts, admit they enjoy sparring with each other intellectually. "It's almost the way physical exercise is for others," John explains. "It keeps us sharp intellectually. However, I think we overdo it sometimes and get into ridiculous debates just to win a point."

Nonteacher spouses can be made to feel inferior, even though they may excel in other areas. A wise teacher spouse will pray for humility and avoid pride like the plague.

2. Questioning Everything

Teacher gifts need to know there is a solid foundation for what they believe. It is almost impossible for them to accept what someone else says is true until they are able to verify it for themselves. They may question their spouses persistently to make sure what they say is factual. Such a beleaguered spouse may feel he or she is being put through an inquisition.

Sometimes I realize I am bombarding Don with too many questions. "Can't you just accept that what I'm saying is true?" he will ask me. I try. But it is hard not to press to know what his statement is based on. It is part of the research function of my teacher gifting.

3. Legalism and Dogmatism

Since teachers base what they believe on the facts they have researched, and since they consider their beliefs absolutely true, they may come across as legalistic or dogmatic to their spouses, who feel the door has been closed to further discussion. They need to realize there may be more than one valid viewpoint on a subject and be willing to hear what their spouses have to say.

4. Correcting Others

Teacher gifts come with a built-in editing function. When I was the editor of *Aglow* magazine, my best copy editor was Agnes, a classic teacher gift. She went over every manuscript with a fine-toothed comb, catching every jot and tittle that was incorrect or out-of-place. She shared with me that reading the evening paper was a challenge because her editing function would not turn off. If she shared a mistake she found with her husband, he would say, "Just ignore it, honey. You're not at work."

Another teacher wife said, "I married a man who says things like 'he don't' and 'they was.' At first I corrected him, but he didn't really appreciate it. So I decided our relationship was more important than having him speak correctly. But it still bothers me."

5. Getting Easily Sidetracked

Getting sidetracked easily is another characteristic of teacher gifts. They are interested in many things, always wanting to learn and moving on to new subjects before a previous one is completed. Often a spouse will complain that his or her teacher partner has left several books around not completed. "I tell my wife I mean to finish all those books eventually," Evan says, "so please don't put them away."

Another teacher researcher, Dick, loves books so much that at one point he had filled all his bookcases to overflowing. "He had books stacked on the dresser, the nightstands, our desks, in the corners of his study," his wife Betty reported. "But when he started stacking them on the kitchen counter I said, 'Enough! Either these books go or I go.'" Not wanting to lose either his books or his wife, Dick did the next best thing: He built another room onto the house.

The Twenty Problem Categories of the Teacher Gift

Let's take a look at the twenty categories of problem areas for teacher spouses indicated by our marriage survey.

Category 1: Communication

A. I FEEL WE HAVE SOME PROBLEMS IN COMMUNICATION IN THESE AREAS:

	He	She
1. Misunderstandings	32%	28%
2. Free to share	44%	36%
3. Listening	59%	48%
4. Conversation	41%	56%
5. Correction	49%	44%
6. Body language	34%	36%
7. Ridicule	34%	24%

Teacher gifts are articulate. Misunderstandings that develop in the marriage relationship are more likely to originate not from the teacher-spouses but from their less articulate mates. Teacher husbands and wives do not easily read between the lines. They are specific and expect clear communication from their mates. They tend to be literalists and are apt to say something like, "You just told me to bring home bread; you didn't say whole-grain bread."

Sharing inner feelings does not come easily to teacher mates. They are good at communicating facts and information but can be awkward in letting their spouses know about personal desires and inclinations. It is not unusual for a teacher husband to go a long time without whispering sweet nothings into his wife's ear. When she complains, he may respond, "Well, of *course* I love you; you know that!"

A major problem in all marriages is not paying attention to what the other says. Teacher husbands see this as their own problem. "When I'm reading a book or the newspaper," John confesses, "my mind is totally engrossed. When Marilyn says something to me, I don't mean to ignore her; I usually just don't hear her. I seem to have a one-track mind." We counseled Marilyn to call his name first and then proceed when he responded. It works well.

Teacher wives have more complaints about not enough meaningful conversation. While they enjoy intellectual conversation, they also need conversation of a more personal or intimate nature. Scheduling time for this may be helpful—after work or after dinner or after the kids are in bed.

The teacher is the gift most likely to correct others. While this is an asset for the teacher who works as a teacher or editor or speech therapist, it can be very annoying to the spouse.

I find I have a hard time turning off my editing mode. Often before I even think about it, I find myself correcting or "improving" something my exhorter husband has said. I am trying hard to listen more and correct less, remembering that God has given me *two* ears and *one* mouth!

The problem of negative nonverbal communication is reported by more than one-third of the teacher respondents. While they are good at verbal communication, they are also good at body language, which constitutes the largest portion of marital communication. Teachers can register disapproval in a glance, dis-

B. TO WHAT DEGREE, FROM 1 TO 7, ARE YOU ONE WAY OR THE OTHER:

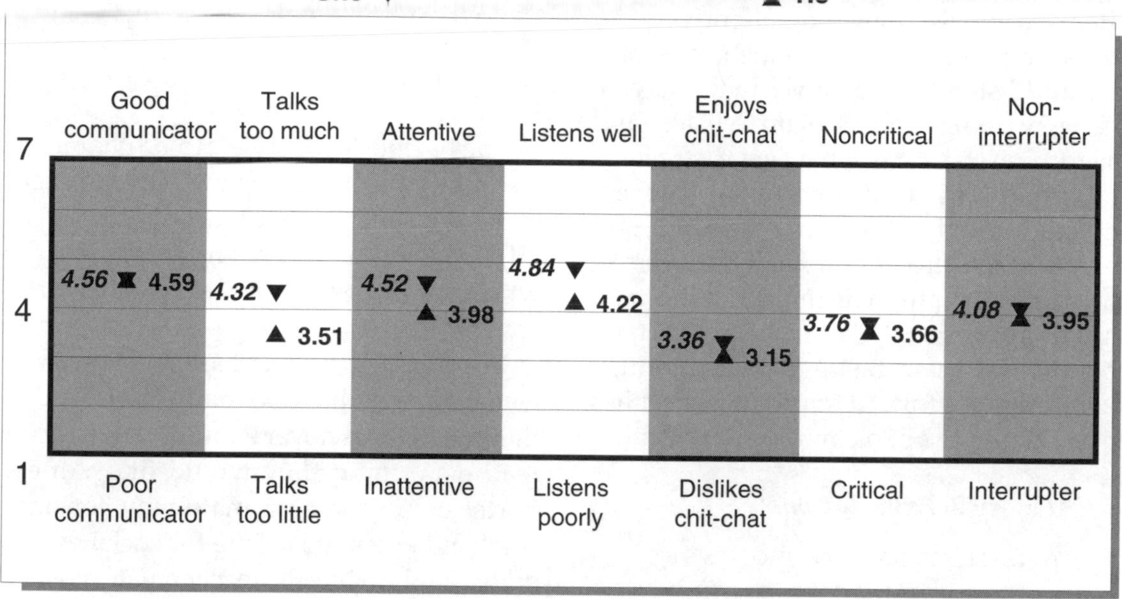

agreement in the set of the mouth, anger in the hands on the hips.

While ridicule is not a major problem, it is a problem. Teacher spouses can utilize language as a way of deprecating or controlling their mates. No spouse deserves verbal abuse, nor should he or she put up with it.

Teachers (see chart B above) probably rate higher than the modest scores they give themselves on communication, especially in light of their exceptional intellects, excellent vocabularies and ability to articulate. Teachers can be on the shy side, however, especially socially, and so may hold back in conversation. My reserved teacher father told my extroverted exhorter mother, "I married you to do my talking for me." This was true in social situations and their marital relationship, although in his role as university professor he spoke fluently.

Teachers dislike chit-chat. When they talk they want it to be about something worthwhile. They are reasonably attentive and do not often interrupt. They do admit their tendency at times to be critical.

C. MY GENUINE NEEDS, VIEWS OR BELIEFS ARE:

	He	She
1. I need more conversation with my mate.	37%	52%
2. I need my partner to listen to me more attentively.	29%	52%
3. I need more quiet time without conversation.	22%	16%
4. I feel we need to share more intimately our thoughts and feelings.	46%	56%
5. I get hurt easily by my mate's unkind remarks.	27%	36%
6. I need more of my partner's undivided attention.	20%	44%
7. I am satisfied with our communication and conversation.	44%	32%

Most teacher spouses show room for improvement in the area of personal communication. Wives see up to twice as many needs for improvement as their husbands—needs like more of the partner's undivided attention and listening more attentively. An exhorter mate may talk too much, for example, and listen little; a server mate may be too busy doing things to stop to listen; and an administrator mate may get distracted.

More than half of the women teachers indicate a need for more conversation, and men teachers are not far behind. Both feel the need to share their thoughts and feelings more intimately. Because teachers tend to hold in their feelings, sharing may require some effort. At times the teacher has to put down the book and communicate.

Category 2: Expectations

A. I FEEL WE HAVE SOME PROBLEMS IN WHAT WE EXPECT OF EACH OTHER IN THESE AREAS:

	He	She
1. Lifestyle	17%	20%
2. Priorities	51%	48%
3. Ideals/goals	32%	20%
4. Holidays	10%	20%
5. Hopes/dreams	20%	32%
6. Conduct	15%	16%
7. Homework	24%	56%

The teacher's lifestyle can be characterized like this: "Learning and always eager to learn more." As one teacher wife put it, "If I had the time, I'd enjoy reading the whole set of encyclopedias from cover to cover!"

Priorities for teachers are a major problem area. They have so many interests that they feel there is never enough time to do or read everything they would like. An exhorter or compassion mate may consider weekend evenings a time for social events with friends, while the teacher mate may see these as times to catch up on study or reading or just having a quiet evening together.

Teacher husbands are more definite in their goals and values, which may conflict with those of their spouses. It is important for a couple to take a serious look at one another's viewpoint and aim for that which

B. TO WHAT DEGREE, FROM 1 TO 7, ARE YOU ONE WAY OR THE OTHER:

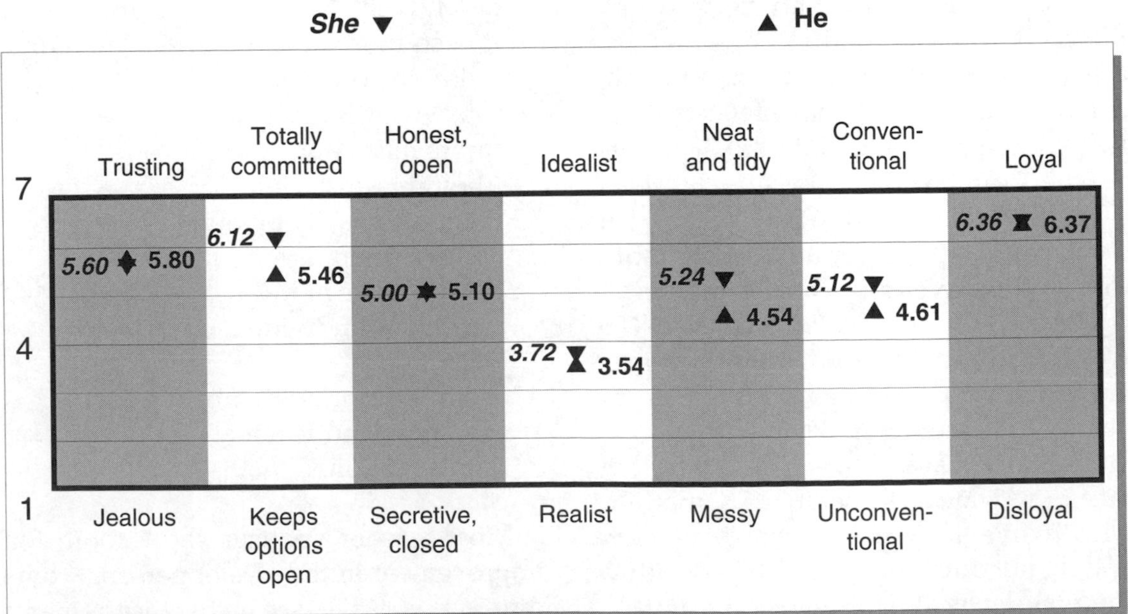

is workable for both. Teachers are adaptable in hopes and dreams.

Teachers tend to have strong opinions about proper conduct but not about how holidays are celebrated.

More than half of the teacher wives indicate that shared work at home is a problem; only 25 percent of the teacher husbands believe it is. A high percentage of teacher wives work outside the home, often in professional fields. They do not excel in domestic skills, doing housework because it has to be done and not because they love it. It is natural for them to expect their husbands' help at home and to be displeased if the help is not given.

Teachers (see chart B on page 134) score high in trust, loyalty and commitment, basing these qualities not on feelings but on what they deem right. They are honest, open, conventional and tidy. But note the scores on realist rather than idealist. They deal with life the way it is, not the way they would like it to be.

C. My genuine needs, views or beliefs are:

	He	She
1. I need to be more sure of my partner's motives.	7%	16%
2. I need a mate who is dependable.	54%	56%
3. I feel we need to work more at setting joint priorities.	56%	56%
4. I need to be more confident in how my mate handles stress.	39%	32%
5. I need my spouse to be totally honest with me.	41%	36%
6. I need to have former family customs a part of my life.	15%	4%
7. I feel our expectations are realistic and workable.	76%	64%

Most teacher respondents feel their expectations are realistic and practical. They are logical, systematic and rational. When an expectation proves unrealistic, they will change it, provided they receive new information enabling them to do so.

More than half list dependability in their mates to be of major importance, and they admit more work needs to be done with their mates in setting joint priorities. Honesty is also important; they consider lying inexcusable.

They express some concern about how mates handle stress. Teachers tend to be cool and calm and do not understand why their mates (especially compassion mates) are not the same.

Category 3: Marital Cohesion

A. I feel we have some problems in getting along with each other in these areas:

	He	She
1. Time together	37%	56%
2. Give and take	27%	24%
3. Feeling one	27%	24%
4. Closeness	29%	44%
5. Goals/priorities	51%	56%
6. Loneliness	15%	28%
7. Love/affection	29%	60%

As with the other gifts, teachers indicate that, regarding marital cohesion, time together, priorities and love and affection are the major areas of concern. Teacher wives in particular want more time with their spouses, probably because their busy lifestyles create time restraints.

Teachers feel reasonably close to their mates, but their tendency at times to be aloof can unsettle that closeness. Still, the feeling of unity is a reality for about three-fourths of them.

More than half of the teachers we surveyed would like to spend more time with their mates setting goals and priorities. Andy, a teacher gift doing research for a university, said, "I've always been a strong goal-setter, but my work is so demanding that my wife and I hardly have time to work on it together. So we are setting aside one day a month for our own private 'planning retreat.' It's working for us."

Feeling lonely is not often a problem since teachers enjoy alone times.

Lack of romantic love and affection is a major problem for many teacher wives. While they are not themselves prone to be very romantic, they still desire romance from their husbands. Fewer than thirty percent of teacher men, notorious as the least romantic of all the gifts, see this as a problem. They would do well to take a lesson from their compassion brothers, who are the most naturally romantic of all men.

Teacher sensitivity (see chart B below) is not high. Teachers do not easily read between the lines. What you say is what they get. But their scores on the other items are good. Their consistency can be counted on. They are reliable, sometime so much so that there are seldom any spontaneous surprises. "My husband is so consistent and predictable," Georgia complained, "that sometimes it drives me crazy! I wish he'd do something unusual like whisking me off to a romantic dinner."

Teacher spouses try to get along. They are natural peacemakers. While they enjoy a lively debate, they are also quick to allow their spouses to have independent opinions. Teacher husbands are a little better at being encouragers than teacher wives.

C. My genuine needs, views or beliefs are:

	He	She
1. I need to be able to confide more in my mate.	32%	28%
2. I feel there needs to be more unity in our relationship.	27%	24%
3. I need to feel more secure in our marriage.	7%	16%

B. To what degree, from 1 to 7, are you one way or the other:

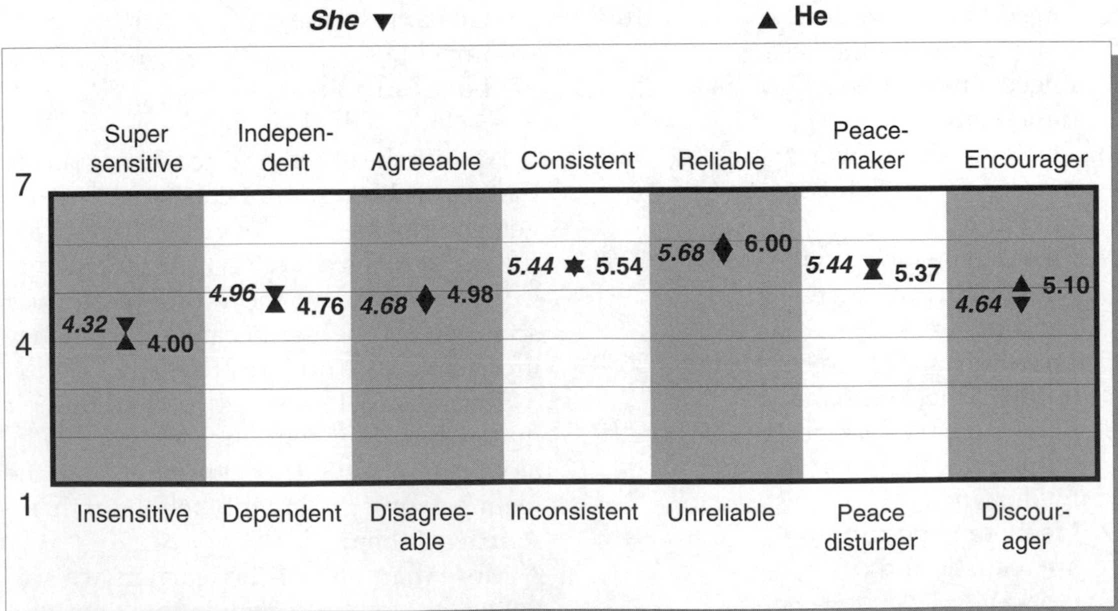

	He	She
4. I am afraid to share some of my feelings with my partner.	29%	52%
5. I need my mate to be more sensitive to my needs.	27%	48%
6. I do not consider divorce ever to be an option.	80%	84%
7. I am satisfied with our marital interaction and closeness.	56%	44%

Close to half of the teacher respondents are satisfied with their marital cohesion. Teacher wives' scores indicate that about half are afraid to share some of their feelings with their spouses. They also feel their spouses need to be more sensitive to their needs.

Note the scores regarding divorce. Teachers, like perceivers, feel strongly about the durability of marriage. They marry not only because they are in love but because it is a logical decision accompanied by strong commitment. As one teacher husband put it, "Before I decided to propose to my wife, I made a long list of pros and cons. The pro list was so much stronger that I knew she was the right one for me."

Category 4: Roles and Responsibilities

A. I FEEL WE HAVE SOME PROBLEMS IN OUR MARRIAGE ROLES AND RESPONSIBILITIES IN THESE AREAS:

	He	She
1. Authority	22%	28%
2. Submission	27%	24%
3. Responsibilities	27%	52%
4. Decision making	46%	32%
5. Roles	12%	28%
6. Feeling overworked	24%	40%
7. Home management	32%	52%

Not many problems with authority are reported. Teachers are more likely to define lines of authority early on in marriage and also to make corrections if the lines get confused or out of order.

Submission does not come easily for teacher spouses since they like to be in control. If married to a server, giver or compassion person, the teacher takes the leadership position and the spouse complies happily. But if married to a speaking gift like a teacher, perceiver, exhorter or administrator, the teacher may vie for authority.

Teacher wives scored much higher than the norm in role definition, and higher than teacher husbands, indicating they have strong ideas about how responsibilities should be shared. They like to do their part, but they also like to have a say in almost all matters.

Teacher husbands consider themselves excellent decision-makers. They look at a matter logically and systematically, believing that once all the facts are considered, their decisions will be fair and right.

Teacher husbands seem to accept the traditional roles easily; teacher wives do not. A teacher wife may see herself as a co-breadwinner with her husband and co-disciplinarian of their children. She needs to feel that her gifts are used and appreciated. She does not want to be a competitor with her husband so much as a teammate with equal status.

Once again it is the teacher wife who sees household responsibility as more of a problem. She likes to have home responsibilities defined clearly and arranged fairly. Especially if she has a full-time job outside the home, she expects help with domestic chores.

Teachers (see chart B on page 138) see themselves as mature, and for the most part they tend to be. They tend to be highly

B. To what degree, from 1 to 7, are you one way or the other:

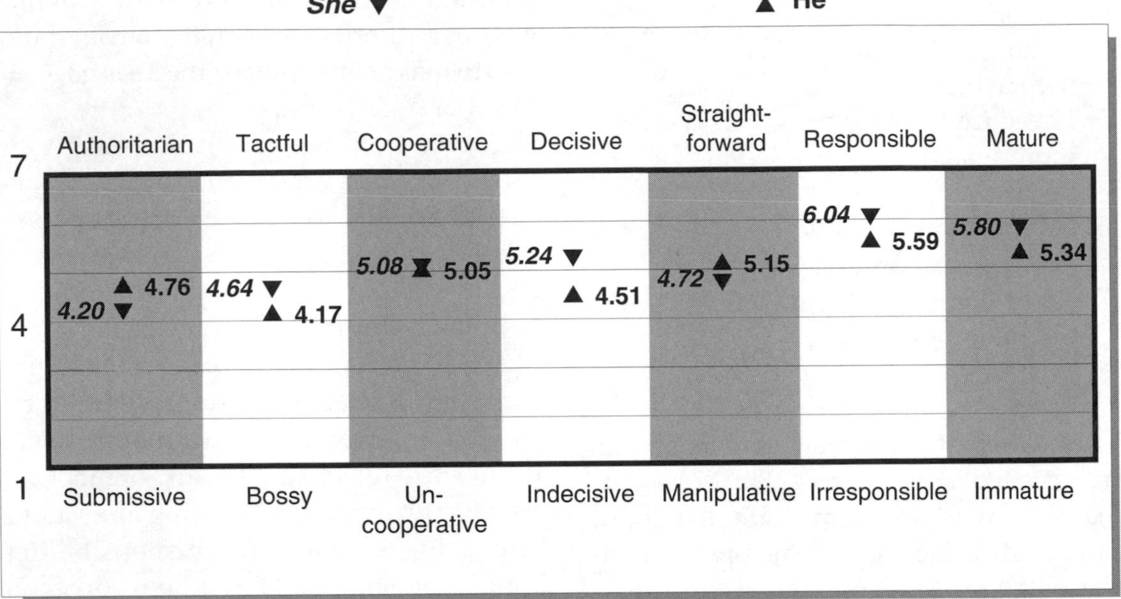

responsible, decisive, cooperative and straightforward in what they say and do.

While their scores in tact are higher than the mean, they can also be bossy and know-it-all. They score barely above the mean on the submissive/authoritarian scale, which is probably realistic. They may think they are not more authoritarian in their marriages, but their spouses would say otherwise.

C. My genuine needs, views or beliefs are:

	He	She
1. I need my role clarified more.	5%	20%
2. I need more freedom to discuss ideas and options.	15%	16%
3. I need to use some of my capabilities more.	44%	16%
4. I need to receive more respect from my partner.	20%	8%
5. I need more domestic help and support from my spouse.	5%	52%
6. I would like to help more in planning together.	17%	12%
7. I am satisfied with the roles and responsibilities we have established.	68%	44%

Teacher husbands are satisfied with the roles and responsibilities they have established with their spouses. Teacher wives are less so. That, coupled with their significantly higher score on the need for domestic help, highlights again the fact that teacher wives do not necessarily fit the traditional wife's role. Their expression of the need to use some of their capabilities more also shows their need for fulfillment outside the home.

Category 5: Conflict Resolution

A. I FEEL WE HAVE SOME PROBLEMS IN HOW WE DEAL WITH CONFLICTS IN THESE AREAS:

	He	She
1. Anger management	41%	36%
2. Who's right	32%	32%
3. Final decisions	20%	16%
4. Silent treatment	56%	52%
5. Ultimatums	15%	8%
6. Personal attacks	29%	24%
7. Blame game	17%	24%

Teachers are better than average at anger management. Their strongly rational approach to life enables them to be more objective and emotionally detached than most. There are problems in this area, however, for about a third of the teachers.

Arguments over who is right can be a problem, especially when the teacher's mate insists on being illogical or going by feelings rather than facts. I cannot help but think of the professor in *My Fair Lady* who is obviously a teacher gift trying to cope with the emotionally charged behavior of the young woman under his tutelage!

Teachers seem to find a way—logically, of course—to get final decision-making into their own hands. But occasionally they are content to share the decision-making process.

The silent treatment seems to be a common weapon of marital warfare for more than half of the teacher respondents. They will battle with words as much as possible, but when they hit a brick wall they may switch to silence. Threats or ultimatums are not usual weapons; teachers prefer logic. They seldom resort to personal attacks or blame. But they can get the upper hand quite nicely with logic or rationalization.

Teacher spouses (see chart B below) may rate even higher on the cool, calm and collected side than they rate themselves. They are more that way than any of the other gifts. We also give them higher scores on handling stress well.

B. TO WHAT DEGREE, FROM 1 TO 7, ARE YOU ONE WAY OR THE OTHER:

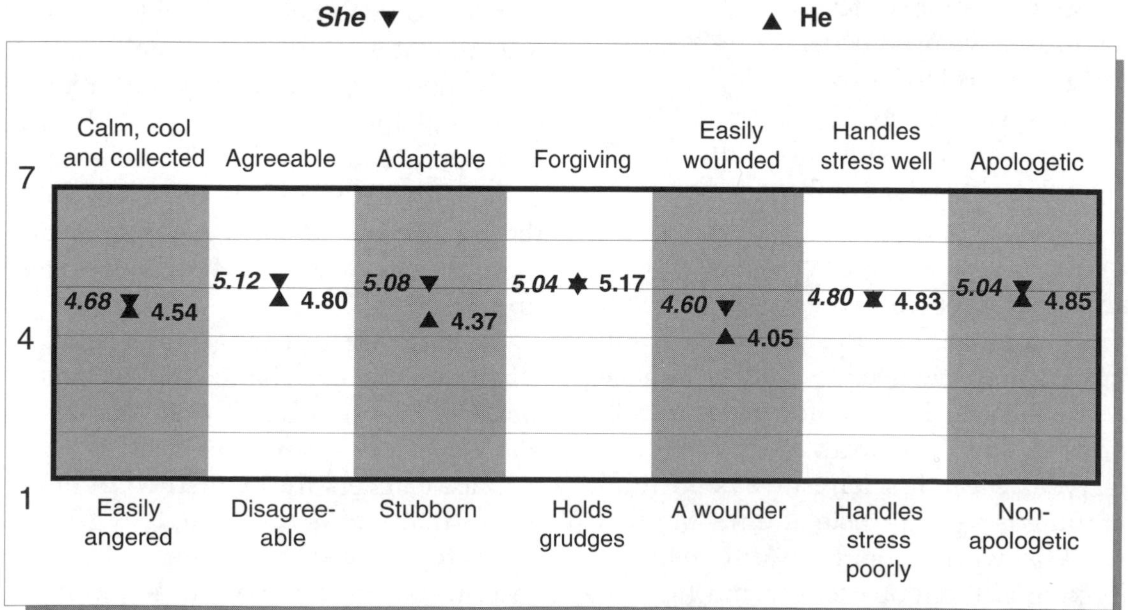

Had the opposite trait on number 5 been *not easily wounded,* we believe the scores would be less than 4. Next to the exhorter gift, the teacher is the least woundable of all the gifts. Teachers are able to forgive easily, often rationalizing the reason for the wounding and excusing their mates for it. They also tend to be agreeable, adaptable and reasonably apologetic.

C. My genuine needs, views or beliefs are:

	He	She
1. I need to gain control over my temper.	27%	20%
2. I need my spouse to gain control over his or her temper.	20%	24%
3. I need to have my point of view heard more often.	17%	12%
4. I feel a strong need to avoid arguments and conflicts.	49%	52%
5. I need my mate to forgive me more quickly.	17%	12%
6. I think we need better ground rules for resolving conflicts.	24%	24%
7. I am satisfied with the way we resolve conflicts.	49%	56%

About half of the teacher respondents are satisfied with the way they resolve conflicts with their spouses. Almost as many indicate a strong need to avoid arguments and conflicts. They prefer peace in relationships and will work toward that end. Jerry, a research scientist, says, "I think arguing is such a waste of time. My wife and I can work through any differences by looking at them objectively and figuring out what is best for both of us."

Category 6: Personality Issues

A. I feel we have some problems in personality conflicts and issues in these areas:

	He	She
1. Being right	34%	24%
2. Pride	29%	24%
3. Understanding	41%	40%
4. Change attempts	34%	32%
5. Methodologies	32%	48%
6. Habits	32%	40%
7. Forgetfulness	34%	28%

Teachers do want to be right. But they do not defend their beliefs just because they believe them. If they can be proven wrong, they will change their ideas or opinions.

Teacher men have a greater problem with pride than teacher women. It is true that teachers tend to do the best academically, have the highest IQs and that they can be walking encyclopedias of knowledge. If they recognize this giftedness as being from God and maintain a humble spirit, pride will not be a problem. If not, teacher mates can become obnoxious.

Teachers have a tendency to think that others, including spouses, should think and operate just as they do. So when a spouse does not understand something, the teacher is surprised. As a good communicator he or she will endeavor to clear up the matter.

Teachers try to change their spouses when they believe change will be beneficial. On the other hand, they are able to enjoy the God-given differences.

Once teachers find a method of doing things that works for them, they tend to follow that procedure repeatedly. They can become inflexible. If the mate is, too, problems arise.

Thirty to forty percent of teachers report bothersome habits—not surprising since teachers can get into ruts. Becky, married to a teacher gift for twenty years, complains about her husband's homecoming habit. "He gives me a quick hug and peck on the cheek when he comes in the door," she says. "Then he grabs the evening paper, turns on the TV, plops into his recliner and disappears for thirty minutes. Only a major crisis pries him out of this rut."

Forgetfulness is much less of a problem for teachers than the other gifts. Teachers usually have good memories, especially for facts. They may lack patience with spouses who do not have as good a memory, and they may deride them for it. Understanding and humility are needed.

Teacher spouses (see chart B below) are adaptable if they understand why something is necessary. A teacher's self-esteem is better than average, and he or she must try to follow Paul's admonition in Romans 12:3 "not to estimate and think of himself more highly than he ought."

Attitudes are usually good; respect and consideration come easily. Teachers see themselves as having what they consider only a few bad habits, but their spouses may disagree. The teacher's tendency to correct the grammar of the mate, for instance, can be a major source of irritation unless the mate has invited such correction.

C. My genuine needs, views or beliefs are:

	He	She
1. I wish my partner complimented me more.	22%	20%
2. I need more encouragement from my mate.	22%	32%
3. I need to be accepted and appreciated for who I am.	20%	56%
4. I need to retain my unique identity.	24%	40%

B. To what degree, from 1 to 7, are you one way or the other:

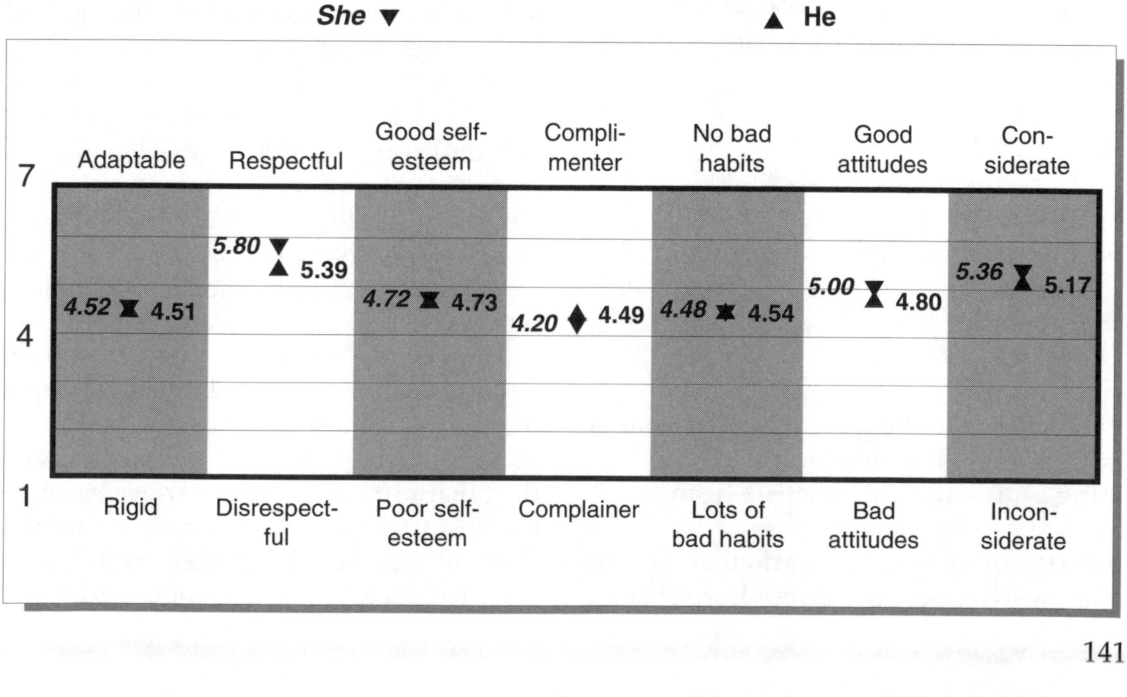

(7)	Adaptable	Respectful	Good self-esteem	Complimenter	No bad habits	Good attitudes	Considerate
She ▼	4.52	5.80	4.72	4.20	4.48	5.00	5.36
▲ He	4.51	5.39	4.73	4.49	4.54	4.80	5.17
(1)	Rigid	Disrespectful	Poor self-esteem	Complainer	Lots of bad habits	Bad attitudes	Inconsiderate

	He	She
5. My partner needs to understand my gifts.	20%	28%
6. I need more admiration and respect from my partner.	20%	16%
7. We do not seem to have any personality conflicts.	39%	44%

Around forty percent of teacher respondents feel they have no personality conflicts with their spouses. Teacher wives feel they need to be accepted and appreciated more for who they are and to retain their unique identity. It is usually not enough for a teacher wife to get her identity from her wife role; she probably wants a career, position or accomplishments that help establish who she is. Often that is in the field of education, science or theology. Julie enjoyed being a missionary wife but got additional satisfaction from writing a book about their adventures. She has also developed and written Bible studies for women.

Category 7: Emotional Responses

A. I FEEL WE HAVE SOME PROBLEMS IN THE WAYS WE RESPOND TO EACH OTHER EMOTIONALLY IN THESE AREAS:

	He	She
1. Hurt feelings	41%	44%
2. Carrying offenses	20%	24%
3. Unforgiveness	12%	4%
4. Insensitiveness	41%	32%
5. Feeling unloved	15%	36%
6. Moodiness	44%	36%
7. Anger	37%	36%

Teachers are the least prone to sustain hurt feelings. They tend to objectify everything and detach themselves from situations that would hurt most of us. They have the most control over their emotions, tending to think things through well before acting or reacting. In spite of all this, however, they can still have their feelings hurt, as indicated by their scores.

Teacher spouses are better than average in letting go of offenses and forgiving.

Teacher husbands take what their wives say at such face value that they may not pick up on body language or subtle innuendo. They see little that is not obvious. They do not mean to be insensitive; it is just the way they are.

Teacher wives can know intellectually that they are loved but still not feel it unless that love is demonstrated physically or emotionally. Teacher husbands are better able to handle the knowing without necessarily requiring the demonstration.

Teacher wives are far less moody than the average, yet their scores are still significant, indicating that many do not always express what they really feel to their spouses. Teacher husbands are a bit moodier than their female counterparts, possibly because they are less communicative, especially regarding negative feelings.

Generally teachers are better than average in handling anger. Still, about a third find that they and their spouses have a problem with it. Most classic teachers are not easily angered, but when they do find themselves angry at something, they are most likely able to work it out logically. "My teacher husband is amazing in how he handles anger," Ellen says. "It's not that Tom even gets angry very often, but when he does he apologizes almost immediately and declares, 'Now I know there's a better way to work this out.' Then his logic kicks into action and we see good results."

Most of the responses (see chart B on page 143) on the first five items suggest a midpoint position, but they are on the low end when compared to the responses of all the other gifts. Note also that teacher husbands say they almost never cry. If they do, they are usually embarrassed by it. Teachers are the least emotional of the gifts, but

B. To what degree, from 1 to 7, are you one way or the other:

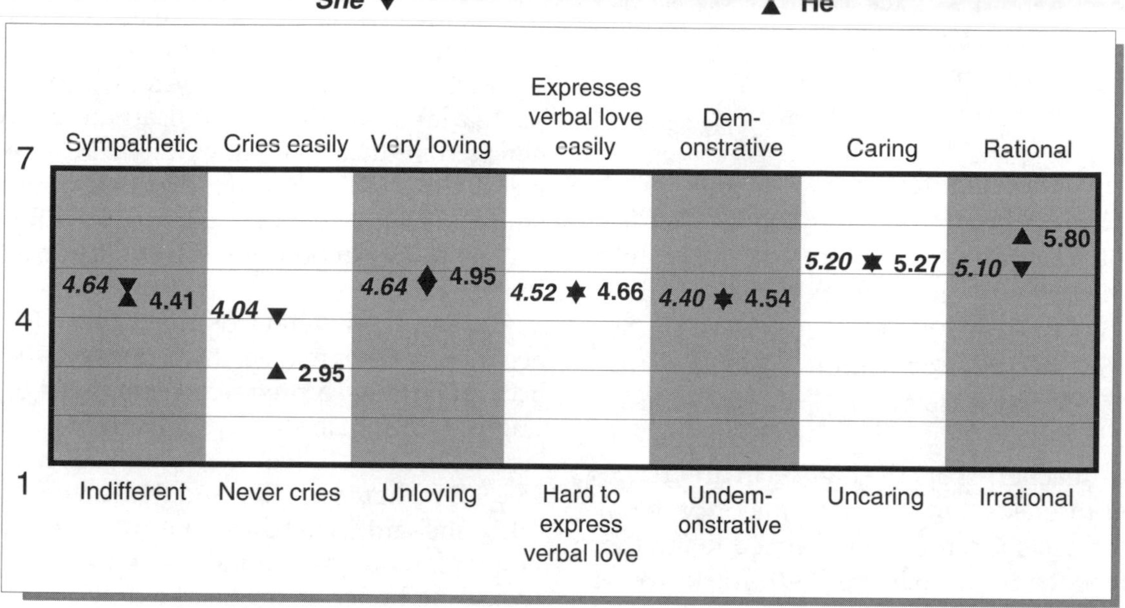

that does not mean they are without feelings. They just keep them well under control and often find it difficult to express them. This reserve makes it difficult for mates with other gifts who are more effervescent and desire emotional reciprocation.

Much higher scores are found in the caring department. The high rational score is to be expected of teacher spouses.

C. My genuine needs, views or beliefs are:

	He	She
1. My feelings tend to rule my life.	7%	4%
2. My mate needs to understand my moods more.	15%	24%
3. I need to hear more "I love you's" from my partner.	17%	32%
4. I need to be able to express both positive and negative feelings.	39%	36%
5. I feel my spouse takes everything too personally.	44%	16%
6. I often feel put down by my partner.	15%	20%
7. I am satisfied with our emotional responses to each other.	29%	44%

Teacher spouses without question are not ruled by their feelings. Yet their satisfaction level in regard to their marital emotional responses is not very high. Perhaps that shows they are unhappy to some degree with their emotional inhibitions. Many teachers would, in fact, like to be more expressive emotionally but find doing so uncomfortable or difficult to accomplish. Teacher Bill married to compassion gift Mary says, "I can share my positive feelings with her fairly well, but when I'm upset I tend to keep it in. She encourages me to open up more and sometimes I'm able to do so. But then sometimes she takes things so personally I back off."

Category 8: Intellectual Capacity

A. I feel we have some problems relating to intellectual interests and capacities in these areas:

	He	She
1. Different interests	41%	28%
2. Reading	27%	20%
3. Continuing education	7%	16%
4. Know-it-all attitude	20%	16%
5. Correcting grammar	20%	8%
6. Children's education	10%	16%
7. Being accurate	20%	16%

Teachers score the highest in differences of interests, but it is not a major problem. Interests for a teacher married to another teacher or an exhorter, administrator or perceiver are likely to be more similar than interests for a teacher married to a server, giver or compassion gift.

Reading and studying are so important to teacher spouses that they will continue to pursue them whether or not their spouses are interested. Books are often their best friends. They love nonfiction, always wanting to learn more. They also enjoy historical novels, mysteries and biographies. They may consider a new book the best gift they can receive.

Teacher spouses are always in the process of learning. Many enjoy taking college-level courses from time to time. A spouse may or may not understand this need and may object to it for the extra financial commitment or the time it takes away from the family.

Know-it-all attitudes come easily to teacher spouses. They like to share what they know, even when the spouse prefers not to know it. A good policy is for teachers to answer only the questions their spouses have asked. Don often says teacher gifts talk almost as though they have swallowed a computer!

Correction of grammar can be especially irritating to a teacher's spouse. This function comes so naturally to teachers that they believe it is being helpful.

Teacher spouses tend to be a little more particular than the average about their children's education. They want to be sure it is of high quality. Because they enjoy pursuing higher education personally, they can get pushy in pointing their children in that direction.

Having high standards themselves for accuracy, teachers expect their spouses to be accurate. Jenny, a precise teacher, used to bug her administrator husband about his estimated arrival time. "He would call and say, 'I'll be home at 6:30,' and then arrive at 7:15," she said. "That drove me nuts. I could never plan anything for sure. I told him it would be better to tell me he'd be home sometime *after* 6:30 or *between* 6:30 and 7:30."

High scores (see chart B on page 145) on five of the seven items show the nature of the teacher spouse—intellectual, articulate, analytical, opinionated and a prolific reader. Teachers' opinions can be so strong that they intimidate their spouses. Many a relationship would benefit if the teacher partner gave more opportunity to the nonteacher mate to express an opinion.

Teachers, along with perceiver mates, tend to have a pride problem. Exercising humility produces not only good character but better marital relationships.

That teacher spouses often take life so seriously can weigh down their spouses, robbing both of the spontaneous joy that should be part of life. Teachers sometimes have to learn how to have fun. An exhorter or compassion spouse can teach this easily.

C. My genuine needs, views or beliefs are:

	He	She
1. I need adequate time for reading or study.	68%	72%

B. To what degree, from 1 to 7, are you one way or the other:

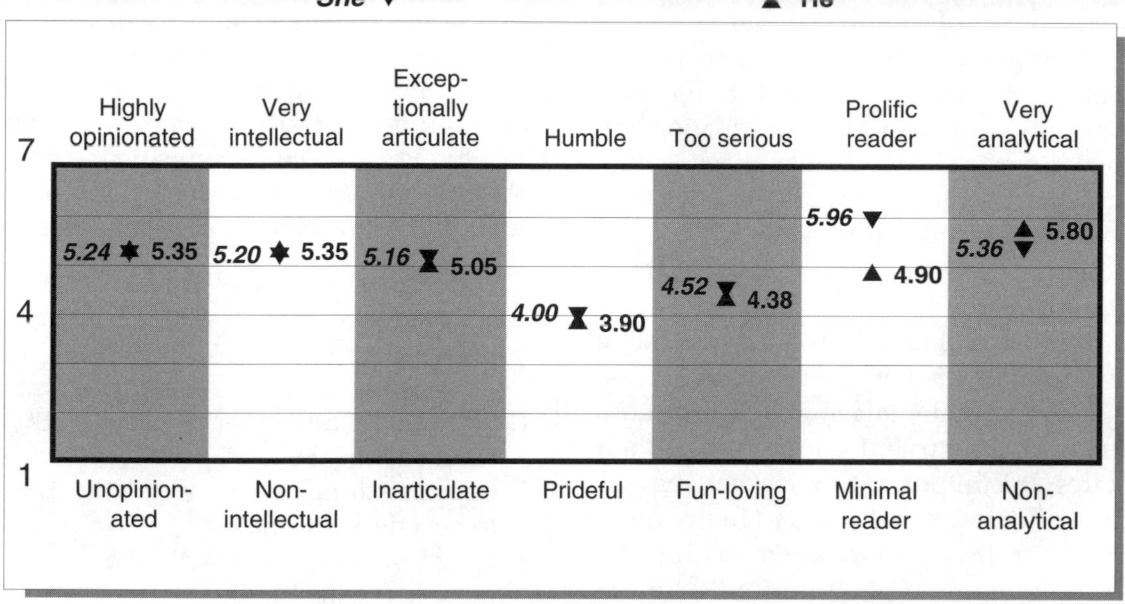

	He	She
2. I am easily sidetracked by new interests.	39%	20%
3. I need to question things before I can accept them.	73%	72%
4. I need my mate to listen to my opinions more.	20%	32%
5. I realize I need to be less dogmatic.	29%	24%
6. I find I constantly analyze what my partner says and does.	20%	24%
7. I am satisfied with how we handle intellectual matters.	54%	68%

Teachers are fairly satisfied with how intellectual matters are handled within their marital relationships. Two important areas of need stand out: adequate time for reading and the right to question before accepting things. Mates of other giftings may not always understand these needs and may find them irritating. My own mode of life is to examine, analyze and question—traits that led me into the field of journalism. I always want to know who, what, when, where and why.

Teacher husbands admit to more sidetracking than teacher wives, but both are prone to it. One teacher husband admitted, "It's hard for me to look up anything in an encyclopedia. I keep seeing subjects I'd like to know more about and I stop to read a little. Sometimes it takes me half an hour to get to the subject I'm aiming for!"

Category 9: Volitional Issues

A. I feel we have some problems in the use of the will in these areas:

	He	She
1. Decisions and choices	27%	28%
2. Practical decisions	12%	12%
3. Stubbornness	34%	36%
4. Agreements	17%	12%
5. Right actions	7%	12%
6. Judgmentalism	29%	24%
7. Rebelliousness	17%	12%

Teachers enjoy making decisions and do so systematically and objectively. They also welcome input from their spouses.

Their stubbornness rating increases on matters on which they have a strong opinion. Only convincing new information will cause them to change their opinions. Agreement can usually be reached if enough time is allowed to talk it through.

Teacher spouses nearly always want to do what is right.

Because of their highly analytical mode of thinking, teacher spouses can slip easily into a judgmental mode. This can cause stress or resentment on the part of their mates. It is important for teacher spouses to say, "It *seems* that . . ." or "In my opinion . . ." rather than make emphatic statements that allow no opportunity for another viewpoint.

Teachers (see chart B below) are strong-willed, decisive and opinionated. They may not understand why a partner does not have as much control in the area of the will, and may put him or her down because of it. If married to a compassion person who is by nature not strong-willed, the teacher spouse may become critical, viewing this trait as a character flaw.

Teacher mates are outspoken and persuasive, often talking their mates into things they would otherwise not agree to. The close-to-average "compromising" scores hold true only when the teacher spouse sees reasonable justification for such adjustment.

C. My genuine needs, views or beliefs are:

	He	She
1. I have a definite inner need to be right.	32%	36%
2. I have a strong need to be a decision-maker.	27%	32%
3. I need my mate to make most of the decisions.	2%	8%
4. I will do what is right even if it hurts.	56%	64%
5. I need to operate by definite principles.	68%	68%
6. I need my mate to be more tolerant of my opinions.	15%	16%

B. To what degree, from 1 to 7, are you one way or the other:

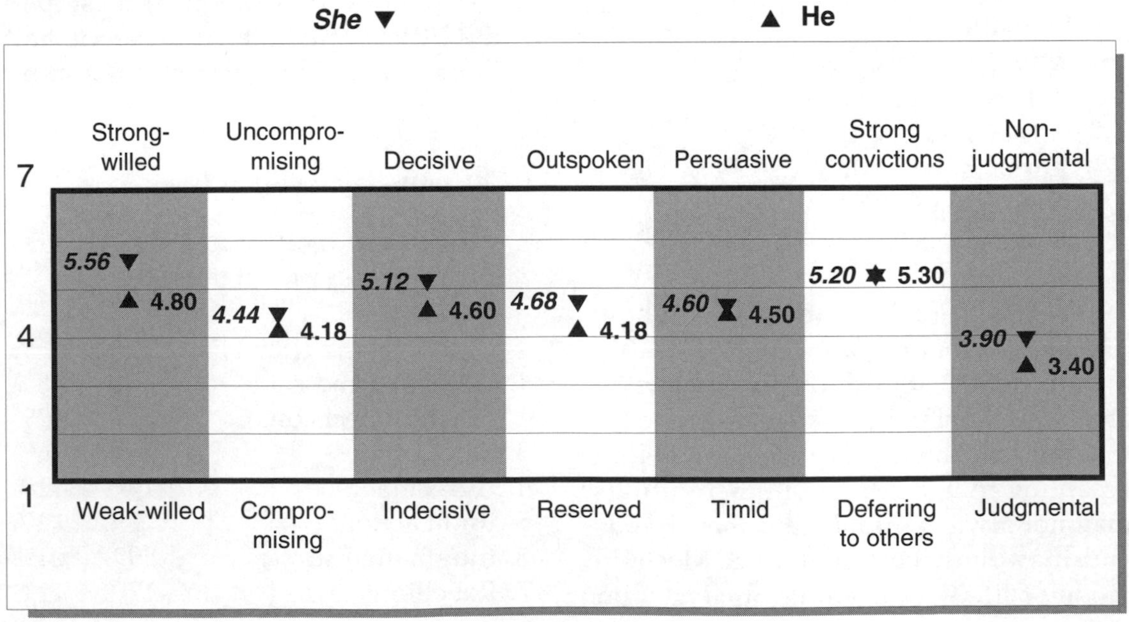

She ▼ ▲ He

7	1	She ▼	He ▲
Strong-willed	Weak-willed	5.56	4.80
Uncompromising	Compromising	4.44	4.18
Decisive	Indecisive	5.12	4.60
Outspoken	Reserved	4.68	4.18
Persuasive	Timid	4.60	4.50
Strong convictions	Deferring to others	5.20	5.30
Non-judgmental	Judgmental	3.90	3.40

B. To what degree, from 1 to 7, are you one way or the other:

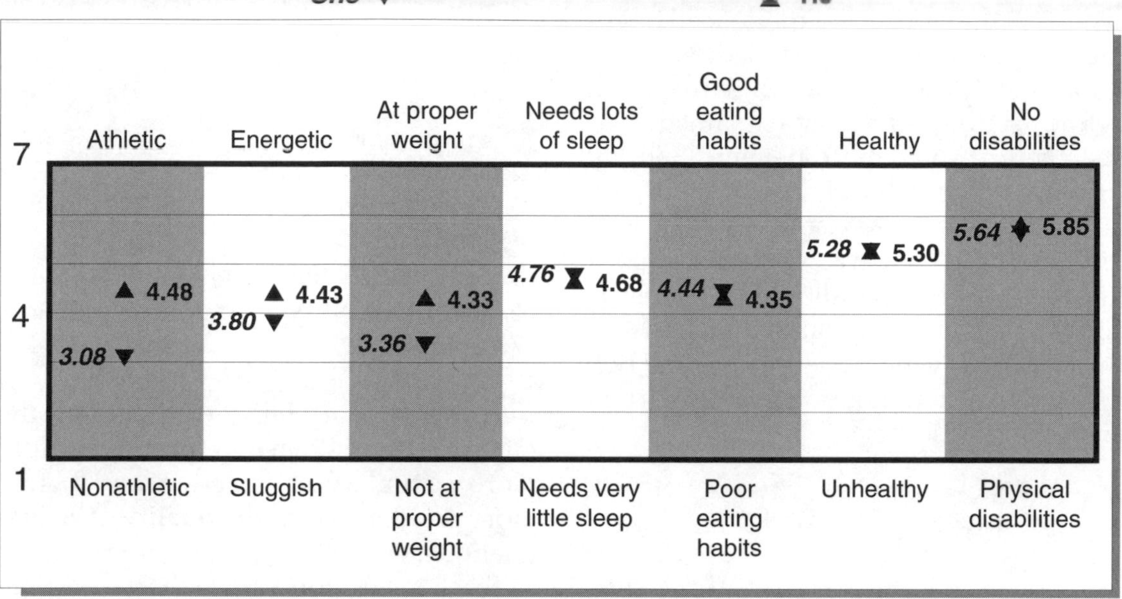

	He	She
7. I am satisfied with how we make decisions.	56%	64%

More than half of the teachers say they are satisfied with how they make decisions. About two-thirds say they operate by definite principles. For those who are Christians, these principles will be biblically based. More than half agree they will do what is right even if it hurts or puts them at a disadvantage.

Teachers do not push decision-making off on their spouses, nor do they always want the full responsibility themselves. Rather, they want to be a part of the process.

Category 10: Physical Conditions

A. I feel we have some problems in the physical realm, in these areas:

	He	She
1. Being fit	68%	68%
2. Enough exercise	76%	80%
3. Fatigue	44%	60%
4. Overeating	29%	60%
5. Proper eating	49%	60%
6. Keeping attractive	17%	32%
7. Adequate sleep	56%	44%

Teachers are greatly concerned, as are all the gifts, with being fit and getting enough exercise. Because they often work in more sedentary jobs, and many would just as soon read a book as jog, they tend not to get enough exercise.

Teacher wives have more of a problem with overeating than teacher men, who are actually much below the norm.

Getting adequate sleep is a problem for about half of the teacher respondents, as it is for almost all the gifts.

While the scores (see chart B above) show that most teachers are healthy, note that teacher wives view themselves as nonathletic, more sluggish than energetic and not at their proper weight. If married to athletic spouses, problems can arise.

Karen, an accomplished high school teacher married to exhorter Bob, the school's athletic coach, experienced ongoing frustration in this area. "After school Bob likes to jog laps around the track before heading home," she explained. "For years he pressured me to join him. One day I finally realized that I was allowing my lack of interest in exercise to get in the way of something that was special to Bob. I knew I couldn't handle all the laps he could, so I began joining him halfway through. I have more energy now and Bob loves the fact that I've become part of something he loves."

C. MY GENUINE NEEDS, VIEWS OR BELIEFS ARE:

	He	She
1. I desire to see my mate at the proper weight.	56%	56%
2. I need to overcome my own weight problem.	27%	64%
3. I need to get adequate exercise on a regular basis.	83%	88%
4. I would like to see my spouse get more exercise.	59%	32%
5. I need my mate to be as attractive as possible.	44%	24%
6. I need to improve my eating habits.	49%	60%
7. I am satisfied with how we keep fit, healthy and attractive.	17%	20%

The satisfaction level regarding health and fitness is very low for teacher spouses. More than eighty percent recognize the need to get regular, adequate exercise. They also admit the need to improve eating habits. While teacher husbands and wives desire to see their mates at the proper weight, it is the teacher wives who admit the need to overcome their own weight problems.

Category 11: Sexual Relationship

A. I FEEL WE HAVE SOME PROBLEMS IN OUR SEXUAL RELATIONSHIP IN THESE AREAS:

	He	She
1. Frequency	54%	48%
2. Quality	22%	32%
3. Prior affection	29%	48%
4. Nonsexual affection	29%	40%
5. Sexual dissatisfaction	17%	24%
6. Incompatibility	5%	12%
7. Infidelity	2%	4%

Scores here are fairly typical of all the gifts, with teacher wives reporting slightly more sexual dissatisfaction and a few more problems with the quality of sexual relations.

Teachers' responses (see chart B on page 149) seem to be on the positive side of the average, but not particularly high compared with some of the more emotionally responsive gifts. Most teacher mates would do well to work at being more expressive and affectionate. Teacher wives show less interest in sex than most women, but understanding husbands can help modify the situation by increasing nonsexual affection.

C. MY GENUINE NEEDS, VIEWS OR BELIEFS ARE:

	He	She
1. I need more nonsexual affection from my mate.	20%	60%
2. I need more sexual relations with my mate.	39%	20%
3. I feel I need more hugs and kisses from my spouse.	20%	32%
4. I need to hear more "I love you's" from my partner.	12%	32%
5. I need my husband to better understand my monthly cycle.	0%	20%

B. TO WHAT DEGREE, FROM 1 TO 7, ARE YOU ONE WAY OR THE OTHER:

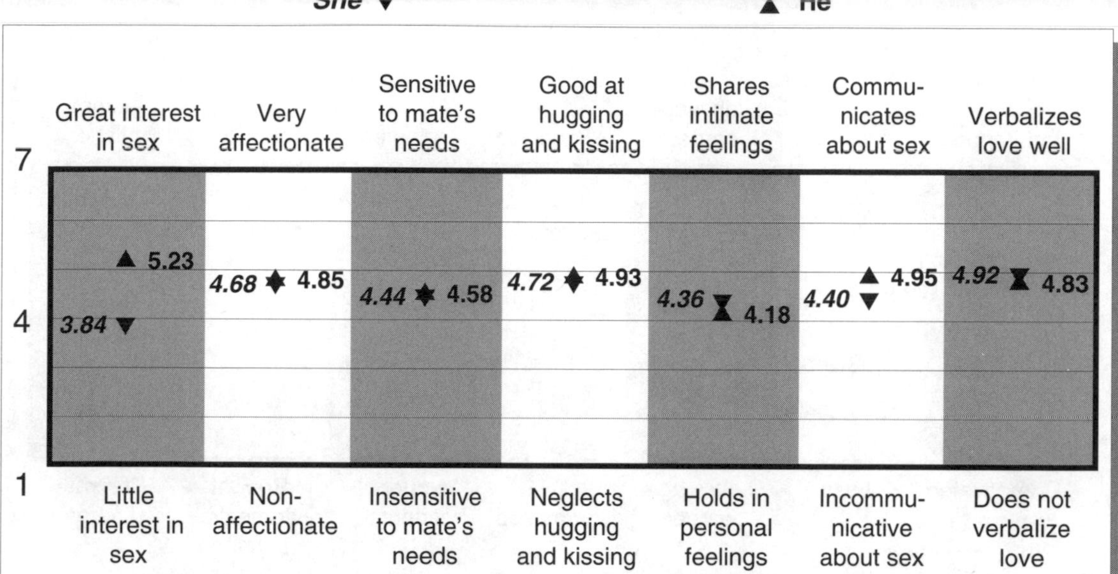

	He	She
6. I feel dissatisfied with our current sexual relationship.	29%	44%
7. I feel satisfied with our current sexual relationship.	54%	44%

The same percentage of teacher wives is dissatisfied and satisfied with their sexual relationship. Other factors, like their mates' genuine love and tenderness, may determine which way a relationship goes.

Category 12: Work and Accomplishments

A. I FEEL WE HAVE SOME PROBLEMS ABOUT WORK AND ACCOMPLISHMENTS IN THESE AREAS:

	He	She
1. Too busy	37%	40%
2. Career conflicts	10%	28%
3. Overtime work	20%	16%
4. Inadequate income	32%	28%
5. Volunteer work	17%	16%
6. Wife working	7%	0%
7. Priorities	22%	36%

About one-third of the teachers say they have problems being too busy, although the scores are less than average. About the same number say priorities are a problem. The two are linked. Teachers are good at analyzing such situations and coming up with a workable plan.

Teacher wives, who are more likely to desire their own careers, report less conflict with the careers of their husbands. Inadequate income was the next-rated problem area, even though it ranked about ten percent less than the average for all the gifts. This problem may be more perceived than real, since teacher gifts tend to have higher than average incomes.

Note that there are virtually no problems, from the viewpoint of the women, with the wife working, and problems for only seven percent of the men. "I've al-

B. To what degree, from 1 to 7, are you one way or the other:

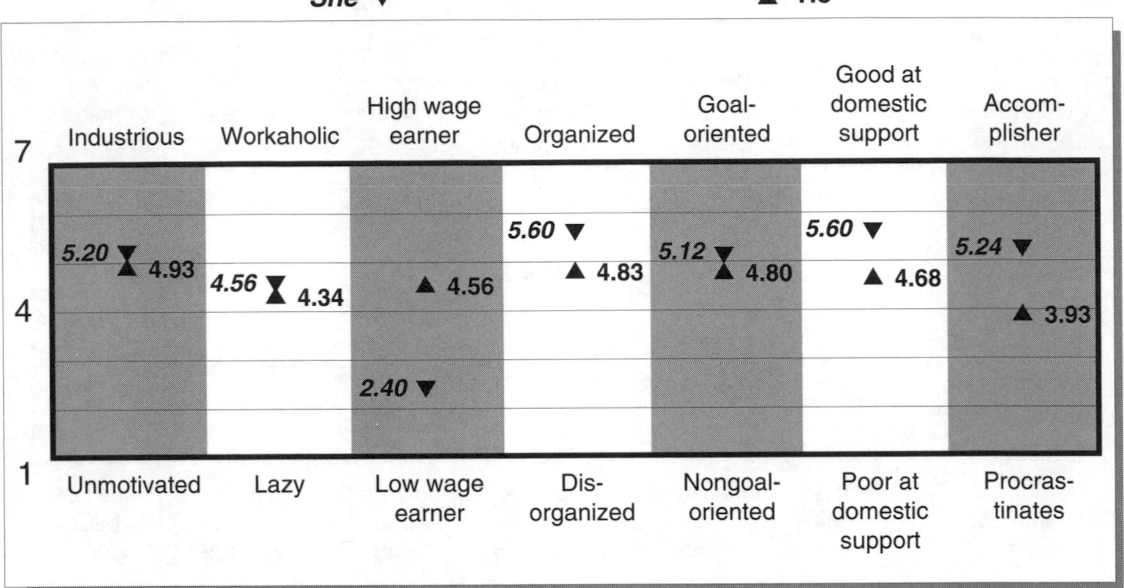

ways loved my job teaching at our local junior college," Rosemary says. "Even after I married Robert, we both agreed I could juggle job and family well. Our children are all grown and have turned out fine."

In general teachers (see chart B above) are industrious, organized and goal-oriented. Their work ethic is balanced; they do not usually become workaholics. Men usually get reasonably good wages while women reported low wages. This may be because some teacher wives are content with part-time work and some work in jobs that give them personal satisfaction in preference to jobs with higher wages. They are capable of earning higher wages if they want.

C. My genuine needs, views or beliefs are:

	He	She
1. I need my husband to provide our basic expenses.	0%	72%
2. I need my wife to be a full-time homemaker.	20%	0%
3. I need to be the sole provider for my family.	17%	0%
4. I need a fulfilling career.	59%	24%
5. I need a challenge to work toward.	49%	40%
6. I get great joy out of my accomplishments.	61%	68%
7. I am satisfied with the way we handle work and accomplishments.	54%	56%

A surprisingly high number of teacher wives said they wanted their husbands to provide their basic expenses, indicating that most teacher wives who work outside the home see themselves as supplementing an already adequate income.

Many teachers report that they like to have a challenge to work toward and that they get great joy out of accomplishments. Work for a teacher must be meaningful and will most likely utilize their intellects. A little more than half report satisfaction with the way they and their spouses handle work and accomplishments.

Category 13: Financial Management

A. I FEEL WE HAVE SOME PROBLEMS IN FINANCIAL MATTERS IN THESE AREAS:

	He	She
1. Establishing budget	44%	44%
2. Keeping to budget	51%	52%
3. Living beyond means	32%	24%
4. Credit cards	24%	32%
5. Impulsive buying	24%	20%
6. Money arguments	17%	24%
7. Wife's work role	0%	8%

In general teachers report fewer financial problems than the norm for all gifts. Still, the challenge of establishing and keeping a budget stands out as the greatest problem. Teachers, being systematic, can easily develop and keep a budget. They like to live within their means.

Impulsive buying is not usually a problem for teachers; most handle credit cards wisely.

Not only are most teachers (see chart B below) conservative buyers and prone to save; they also like to stretch the available dollars. Bertha admits she is an avid bargain-hunter. "I'm always checking out the sales to see how far I can make the money go," she says. "I also love garage sales, and when I find something we really need at an incredibly low price, I'm ecstatic!"

Teachers tend to be generous but must have sound reasons to do so. They will not fund irresponsible people or ill-governed causes. They are faithful tithers and give beyond the tithe when they recognize a genuine need. One teacher told us, "I love the philosophy that if you give a man a fish, you've fed him for a day, but if you teach him how to fish, you've fed him for life. I'd rather invest in scholarships or fund special training to help people get on their feet financially than give money directly to them."

C. MY GENUINE NEEDS, VIEWS OR BELIEFS ARE:

	He	She
1. I feel we need to reduce our debts more effectively.	46%	40%

B. TO WHAT DEGREE, FROM 1 TO 7, ARE YOU ONE WAY OR THE OTHER:

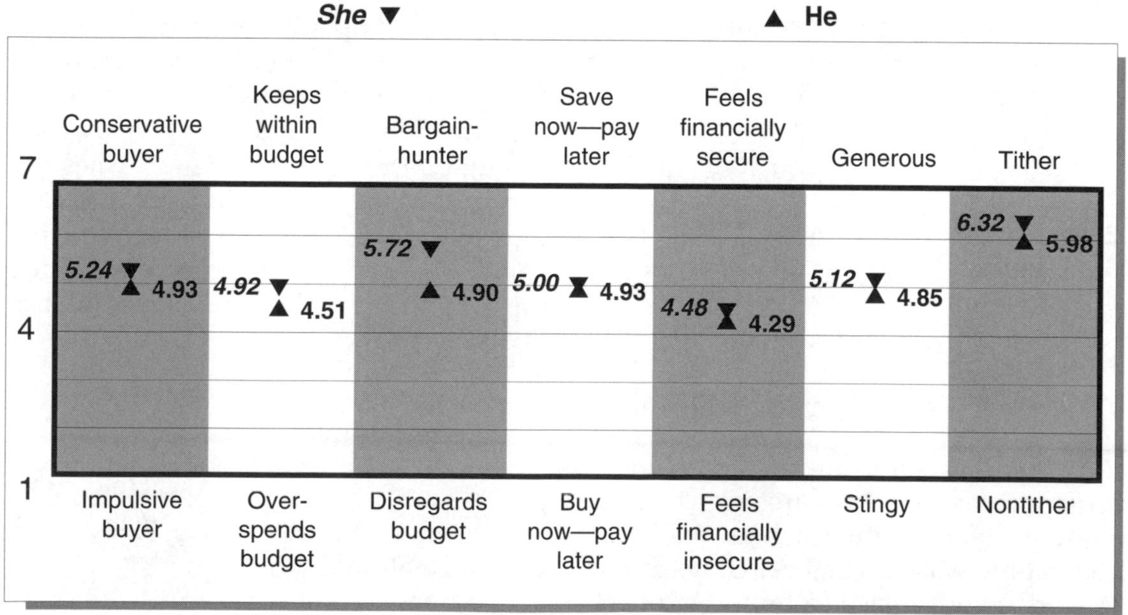

	He	She
2. I feel the need to be in charge of our family finances.	29%	28%
3. I believe the husband should handle the family finances.	15%	16%
4. I think the most capable partner should handle the family finances.	51%	72%
5. I need to learn how to handle money more responsibly.	22%	16%
6. I would like to give more to church, missionaries, charity, etc.	56%	60%
7. I am satisfied with how we handle finances.	46%	48%

Almost half of the teacher respondents say they are satisfied with how they and their mates handle family finances. Most think the more capable partner should do it. Debt reduction is a concern for more than forty percent. More than half would like to give more to charity.

Category 14: Leisure Activities

A. I FEEL WE HAVE SOME PROBLEMS IN HOW WE SPEND OUR FREE TIME IN THESE AREAS:

	He	She
1. Interests	15%	24%
2. Recreational preferences	17%	24%
3. Hobbies	24%	24%
4. Entertainment	12%	20%
5. Vacation preferences	12%	16%
6. Sports	29%	16%
7. TV-watching	41%	48%

Teachers' responses are close to the norm in most cases. But TV-watching is still a major problem, with teachers realizing what a time-waster it can be. "It helps me unwind at night," Jason admits, "but I get really mad at myself when I realize I've wasted my time watching a program that has little redeemable value."

Teacher husbands, who do not particularly like to participate in sports (although they do enjoy being spectators at times, live or via TV), have more of a problem with sports than teacher wives, who are not for the most part interested. Spousal differences in recreational interests and entertainment cause more problems for teacher wives than teacher husbands.

Many teachers view as the best vacations those in which seclusion allows them to read several books they have been meaning to read. More action-oriented spouses may not enjoy such inactivity. Teacher spouses may want to consider vacations that allow for multiple interests to be satisfied.

Teachers (see chart B on page 153) are not highly social and often would just as soon stay home as go out. They do love to travel, taking any opportunity to see the world, often studying about a place before going there. They love going to places of historical interest, even archeological digs. But unless their mates share the latter interest, they may go on their own.

Their cultural interests are varied—fine arts, music, opera, symphony, drama, sometimes all of these. Teachers are likely to support cultural activities in their communities—financially, promotionally, even through patronage. "My wife wishes she had developed her musical talent more," John explains, referring to his teacher wife. "Now she spends a lot of her leisure time raising funds for the symphony. She has my blessing."

C. MY GENUINE NEEDS, VIEWS OR BELIEFS ARE:

	He	She
1. I need my partner to be a recreational companion.	37%	28%

D. To what degree, from 1 to 7, are you one way or the other:

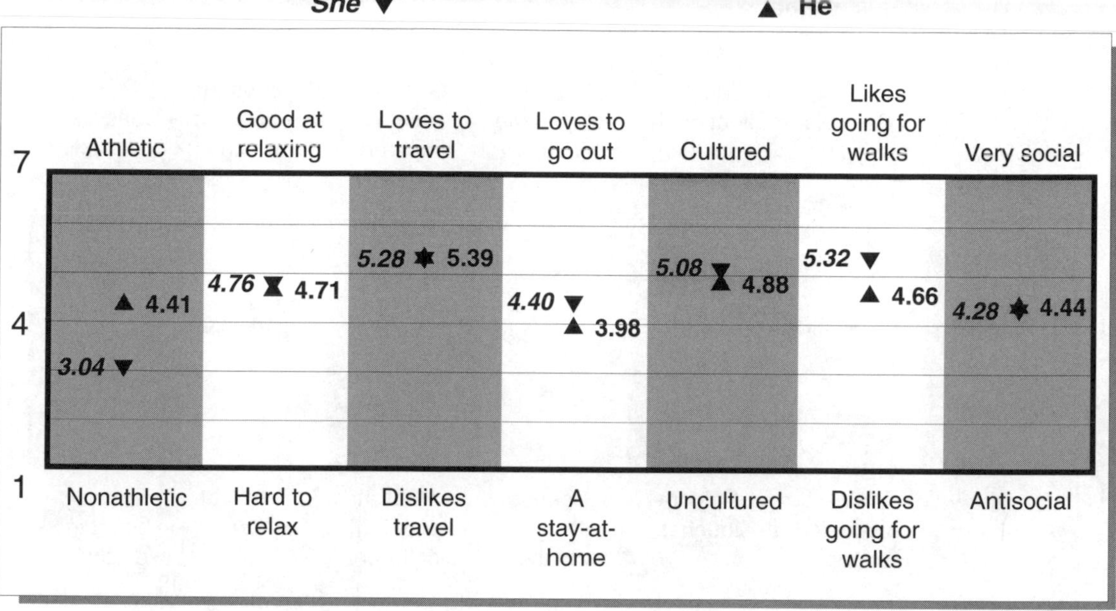

	He	She
2. I need to do more fun things with my spouse.	46%	52%
3. I need more meaningful vacations.	20%	20%
4. I need to be involved in nonathletic leisure activities.	24%	32%
5. I prefer active group or competitive sports.	29%	4%
6. I prefer individual noncompetitive sports.	27%	48%
7. I am satisfied with how we spend our leisure time.	41%	48%

Many teachers report satisfaction with their leisure time activities. Only about a third feel the need to have their partners as recreational companions, indicating that teachers can enjoy their recreation individually as well as with their mates. Yet close to half want to do more "fun things" with their spouses—evidence that teachers take life seriously, often neglecting fun. They can benefit from spouses who "hang looser."

Category 15: Parenting

A. I feel we have (had) some problems in the child-rearing process in these areas:

	He	She
1. Type of discipline	17%	20%
2. Amount of discipline	22%	20%
3. Who disciplines	12%	24%
4. Misconduct determination	20%	32%
5. Love expression	17%	16%
6. Time spent	27%	32%
7. Money given	24%	28%

Teachers are firm and fair disciplinarians. Even if their spouses are not particularly good at training, teachers will naturally take the lead. In the process they may even teach their spouses to handle discipline better.

Because teachers are less expressive emo-

B. To what degree, from 1 to 7, are you one way or the other:

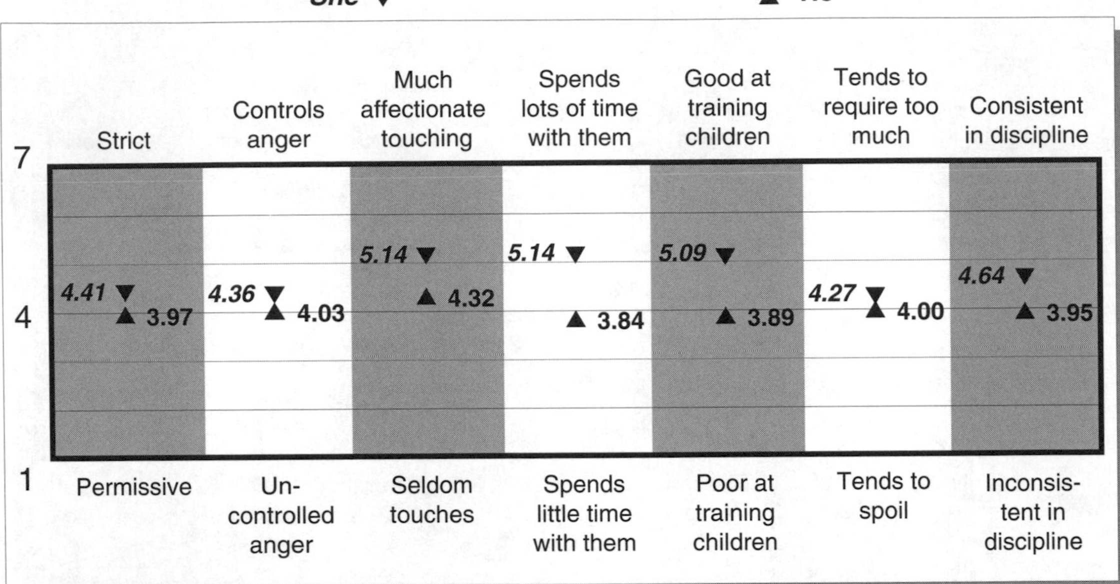

tionally, they may not be naturally fluent in hugs and kisses; but they can learn to be. Once convinced of the value of expressive love, teacher gifts can determine to be more expressive to their children.

We think the men teachers (see chart B above) score themselves too low here. While most of their scores are in the average range, we find teacher dads more strict than permissive, good at training and consistent in discipline. Yet if anything they tend to be balanced, avoiding extremes. They do need to learn how to invest more time in their children's lives. Women teachers seem to be more realistic about themselves and usually do well at parenting.

C. My genuine needs, views or beliefs are:

	He	She
1. We need to provide better spiritual guidance for our children.	41%	48%
2. We need to give our children more love and affection.	15%	16%
3. I would like my spouse to help more with the children.	0%	28%
4. I need to be more affirming of our children.	34%	16%
5. I feel we need to agree more on discipline.	15%	20%
6. I feel we need more quality family time and activities.	32%	56%
7. I am satisfied with our parenting styles and skills.	27%	36%

Teachers tend to agree with their spouses and believe they give adequate love and affection to their children. Their level of satisfaction with their parenting skills, however, is surprisingly low. The area in which they feel they need the most improvement: giving better spiritual guidance and having more quality family time and activities.

Category 16: In-Laws and Family

A. I FEEL WE HAVE SOME PROBLEMS WITH OUR FAMILIES AND IN-LAWS IN THESE AREAS:

	He	She
1. Interference	10%	24%
2. Their expectations	22%	24%
3. Their visits	0%	8%
4. Comparisons	5%	4%
5. Borrowing money	10%	16%
6. Former abuse	17%	12%
7. Dysfunction affect	27%	32%

Scores in this category are typical of the scores averaged for all gifts. Teachers are take-charge people who are not likely to allow interference in their lives by family or in-laws. They will be firm but nice as they set boundaries.

While about thirty percent recognize some negative effects from former family dysfunction, teachers are generally more able to handle and overcome it than most gifts.

Strong scores here (see chart B below) indicate how healthy teachers' attitudes and actions are in handling leaving and cleaving and in-law relationships. Also, their honoring of mother and father facilitates their marital relationships. Even when teacher wives scored slightly on the dysfunctional side in their former families, they are better than average in coping with dysfunction.

"My home was very dysfunctional," one teacher gift told us. "My father was an alcoholic with all the typical problems. I resented him and judged him a lot in my heart. But when I came to Christ after I was married, I learned how important it was to forgive my father and cancel my judgments of him. He's still an alcoholic but it no longer has a negative effect on me."

C. MY GENUINE NEEDS, VIEWS OR BELIEFS ARE:

	He	She
1. I need my spouse to put me before his or her family.	39%	36%

B. TO WHAT DEGREE, FROM 1 TO 7, ARE YOU ONE WAY OR THE OTHER:

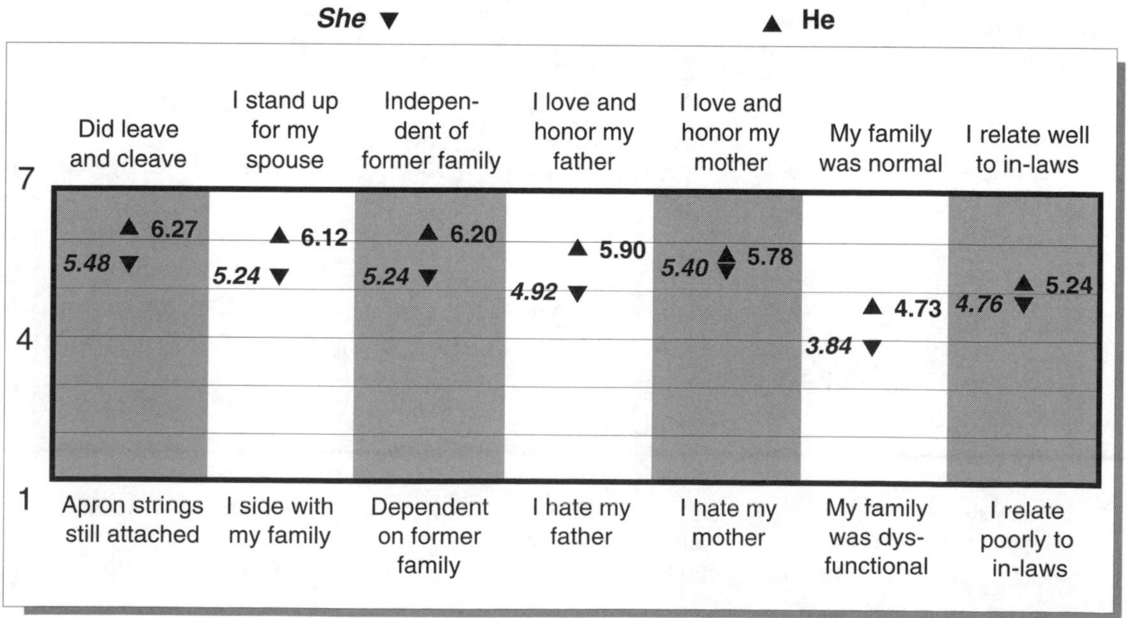

	He	She
2. I need to see or talk to my parent(s) regularly.	22%	36%
3. I need to include my family in holiday celebrations.	24%	40%
4. I need help in overcoming in-law problems.	7%	8%
5. I need to be accepted by my in-laws.	12%	28%
6. I need to be financially free from my family and my in-laws.	22%	36%
7. I am satisfied with our family and in-law relationships.	73%	60%

A high percentage of the teacher respondents indicate satisfaction in family and in-law relationships. This is also reflected in their very low scores in needing help to overcome in-law problems. But teacher wives have a greater need than their male counterparts to include their families in holiday celebrations and to be financially free from them and in-laws.

Category 17: Social Relationships

A. I FEEL WE HAVE SOME PROBLEMS IN SOCIAL RELATIONSHIPS IN THESE AREAS:

	He	She
1. Friends' demands	7%	12%
2. Time for friends	46%	52%
3. Unsocial partner	2%	12%
4. Too social partner	2%	8%
5. Wrong friendships	2%	4%
6. Negative influence	0%	4%
7. Over involvement	7%	4%

As with all the other gifts, teachers' main complaint in social relationships is not having enough time for friends. Scheduling is the best way to overcome this. Martha, a busy college teacher, made a New Year's resolution to increase time for friends by scheduling one extra social engagement each month. "It worked for us," she said. "We plan to do it again next year."

B. TO WHAT DEGREE, FROM 1 TO 7, ARE YOU ONE WAY OR THE OTHER:

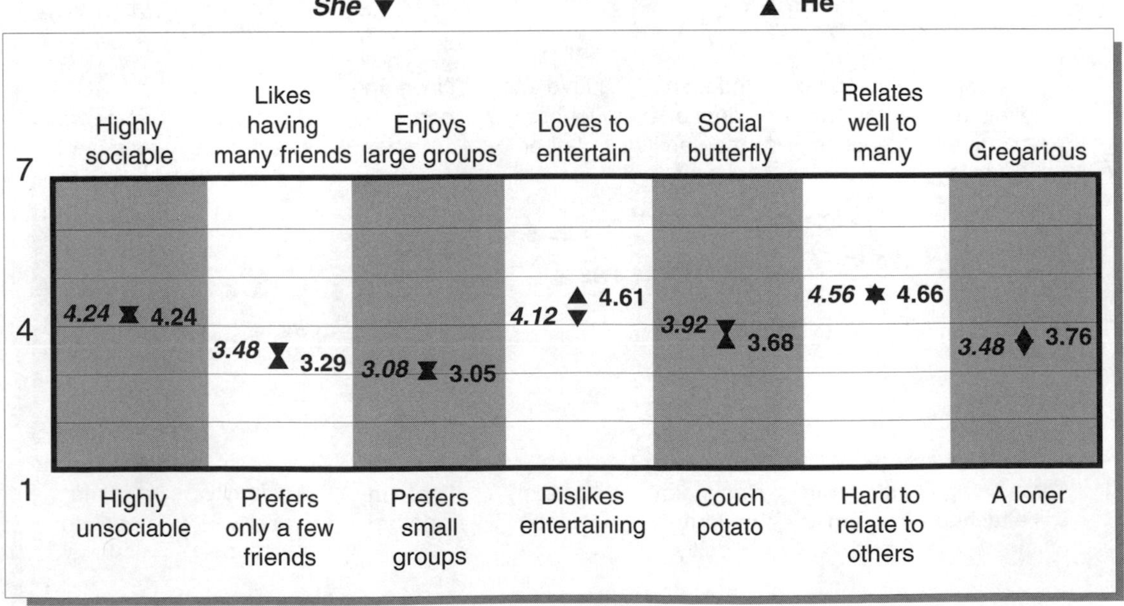

Teachers (see chart B on page 156) prefer smaller groups and having only a few close friends. While their loner tendency causes them to score on the side of couch potato rather than social butterfly, they can and do relate well to many people, enjoy entertaining (smaller groups or just another couple) and view themselves as slightly higher than of average sociability.

C. My genuine needs, views or beliefs are:

	He	She
1. I need to have many friends.	5%	12%
2. I especially love to entertain in our home.	34%	24%
3. I need a good deal of private time.	56%	60%
4. I need our home to be a haven of rest.	83%	96%
5. I need to be involved in social groups.	22%	32%
6. I think we need to change some friendships.	5%	4%
7. I am satisfied with our social life.	51%	60%

More than half are satisfied with their present social lives and also express a need for a good deal of private time. Note the extremely high scores on needing the home to be a haven of rest. Surprisingly, even more teacher men than women love to entertain at home.

Category 18: Religious Orientation

A. I feel we have some problems in our spiritual life and orientation in these areas:

	He	She
1. Affiliation disagreement	0%	8%
2. Church attendance	0%	4%
3. Different backgrounds	0%	4%
4. Theological differences	7%	0%
5. Commitment level	17%	12%
6. Irregular attendance	0%	0%
7. Hypocritical behavior	10%	12%

Teacher wives find they are more prone to disagree with their husbands on the choice of a church, probably because they have strong opinions about such an affiliation. Surprisingly, teacher husbands reported no perceived problems in this matter.

Theological differences are of more than usual importance to teacher spouses. Where some gifts feel that spiritual beliefs are not crucial to marital harmony, teachers put great stock in the correctness of their theological positions. They may even become argumentative with their spouses, badgering them into accepting a particular doctrine.

My exhorter husband says, "What does it matter whether you are pre-trib, mid-trib, post-trib or no trib?"

My teacher response is, "Your belief can affect how you live and plan for the future. And besides, only one of those positions can be correct."

Commitment level and hypocritical behavior is of concern, and teachers are interested in integrity and would like to see their partners live up to what is true.

Scores here (see chart B on page 158) are high. Teachers see themselves as spiritual, committed and having strong faith. Searchers after the truth, they will follow it as they find it. Teacher spouses will never be accused of being wishy-washy in their faith, but it must be faith they have discovered for themselves, not faith passed on by parents or early church training. They are most likely of all the gifts to question their childhood faith in light of increased knowledge. A teacher spouse may become a doubting Thomas on a particular belief, putting that belief on hold

B. To what degree, from 1 to 7, are you one way or the other:

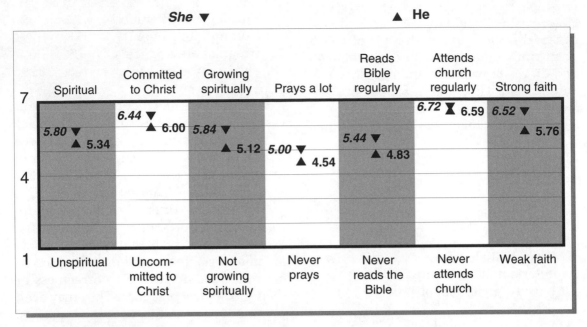

She ▼ ▲ He

7	She ▼	He ▲	1
Spiritual	5.80	5.34	Unspiritual
Committed to Christ	6.44	6.00	Uncommitted to Christ
Growing spiritually	5.84	5.12	Not growing spiritually
Prays a lot	5.00	4.54	Never prays
Reads Bible regularly	5.44	4.83	Never reads the Bible
Attends church regularly	6.72	6.59	Never attends church
Strong faith	6.52	5.76	Weak faith

until more facts are in or even becoming agnostic on it for a while, saying, "I honestly don't know what I believe on that matter right now." Be patient with such a spouse. The truth will prevail.

Teachers tend to learn constantly and continue to grow spiritually. They have a strong desire to attend church regularly, pray a lot and read the Bible consistently. They are not afraid to question what they read and discuss it openly with their spouses. They often receive insights on the Word through this questioning process.

They are likely to build a personal library of reference and study books. Give them a handbook on the Bible, a new concordance or the latest book by their favorite Christian author (nonfiction, of course) and they will thank you profusely.

C. My genuine needs, views or beliefs are:

	He	She
1. I need to attend church regularly.	63%	64%
2. I need my partner to pray with me daily.	37%	56%
3. I greatly desire to see my spouse grow spiritually.	68%	64%
4. I believe we need to have regular family devotions.	68%	64%
5. I need my spouse to give spiritual leadership.	7%	60%
6. I need to be able to live my faith, not just talk about it.	63%	72%
7. I am satisfied with our religious orientation and practice.	49%	72%

Along with regular church attendance and prayer, teacher spouses need to live and practice their faith lest they judge themselves hypocritical. They will be diligent to see that their spouses grow spiritually, too. When Jack, a classic teacher gift, married Patricia, they were both involved with a Christian campus ministry.

B. To what degree, from 1 to 7, are you one way or the other:

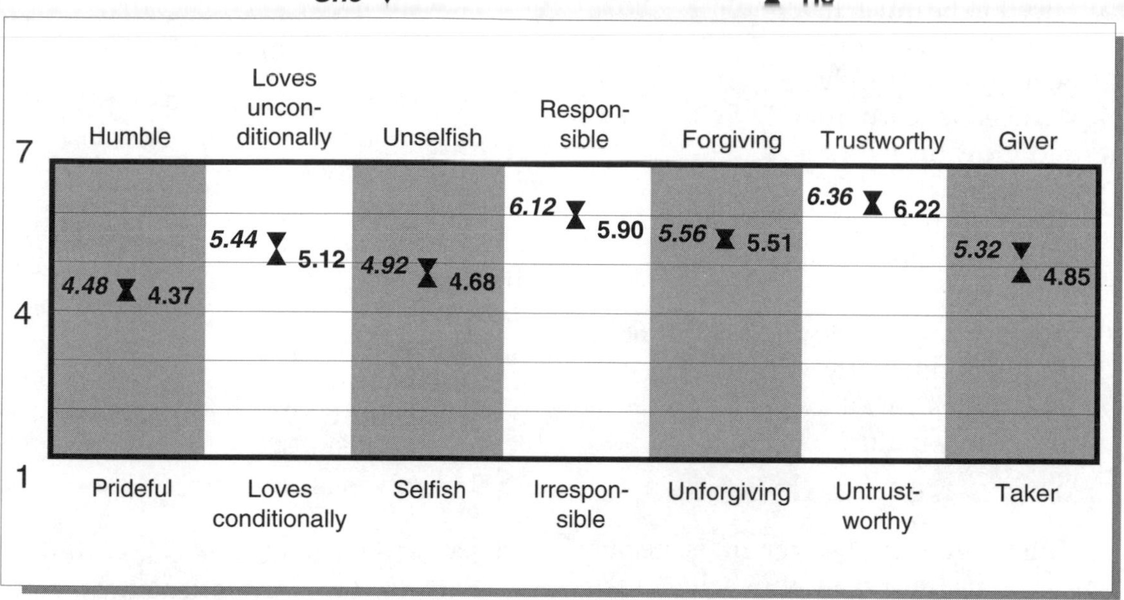

"When the kids came along," Jack recounted, "Patricia's spiritual life seemed to go downhill. Then one day the Lord showed me I could do something about that, like take care of the kids a while each day so Patricia would have time for prayer and Bible study. It made a huge difference."

Teacher spouses do well at encouraging or leading family devotions. They tend to be consistent and promote Scripture memorization.

Category 19: Maturity

A. I feel we have some problems in maturity in these areas:

	He	She
1. Inexperience	0%	4%
2. Irresponsibility	7%	8%
3. Blame game	15%	16%
4. Stress coping	49%	52%
5. Criticism	10%	12%
6. Infidelity	0%	4%
7. Dishonesty	2%	12%

Most of the answers here are significantly under the norm. Our teacher respondents have few maturity problems. They do tend to think about and mull over stressful situations, however, sometimes dwelling on them more than necessary.

Our teacher spouses (see chart B above) see themselves on the mature side, and for the most part they are. Responsible and trustworthy, they tend to conduct themselves well in marriage, as well as in other relationships. Although they are not known for effervescence in their expressions of love, they love deeply, unconditionally, unselfishly. Quick to give and forgive, they also do fairly well in humility. Pride in their amassed knowledge, however, can be a pitfall.

C. My genuine needs, views or beliefs are:

	He	She
1. I need to be able to trust my mate.	54%	60%
2. I need my spouse to be dependable.	49%	68%

	He	She
3. I need to be quick to forgive and, I hope, be forgiving quickly.	66%	56%
4. We need to learn from and grow through every experience.	59%	64%
5. I need my mate to be able to handle responsibility well.	46%	52%
6. I need my mate to love me unconditionally.	46%	68%
7. I feel that we are a reasonably mature couple.	93%	88%

Of all the gifts, the teacher gift is the one that matures most readily. Teachers take life seriously, sometimes too seriously. They often have to learn how to relax and have fun. This can be frustrating to the exhorter or compassion mate who is more spontaneous and vivacious.

Note that all the things teacher mates tend to be—dependable, responsible, loving, trustworthy, forgiving—are exactly what they expect their mates to be.

Category 20: Dysfunctionality

A. I FEEL WE HAVE SOME PROBLEMS IN THE FOLLOWING AREAS THAT PRODUCE DYSFUNCTION:

	He	She
1. Alcohol abuse	0%	8%
2. Drug abuse	0%	4%
3. Physical abuse	2%	0%
4. Sexual abuse	0%	4%
5. Verbal abuse	10%	4%
6. Emotional abuse	15%	12%
7. Unresolved abuse	17%	8%

Teacher gifts scored very low in dysfunctionality. Our respondents who grew up in dysfunctional or abusive homes believe they have overcome the problems and are able to establish good relationships within their marriages. Their incredible objectivity seems to be the key. They can detach themselves from situations that tend to impact other gifts more negatively.

B. TO WHAT DEGREE, FROM 1 TO 7, ARE YOU ONE WAY OR THE OTHER:

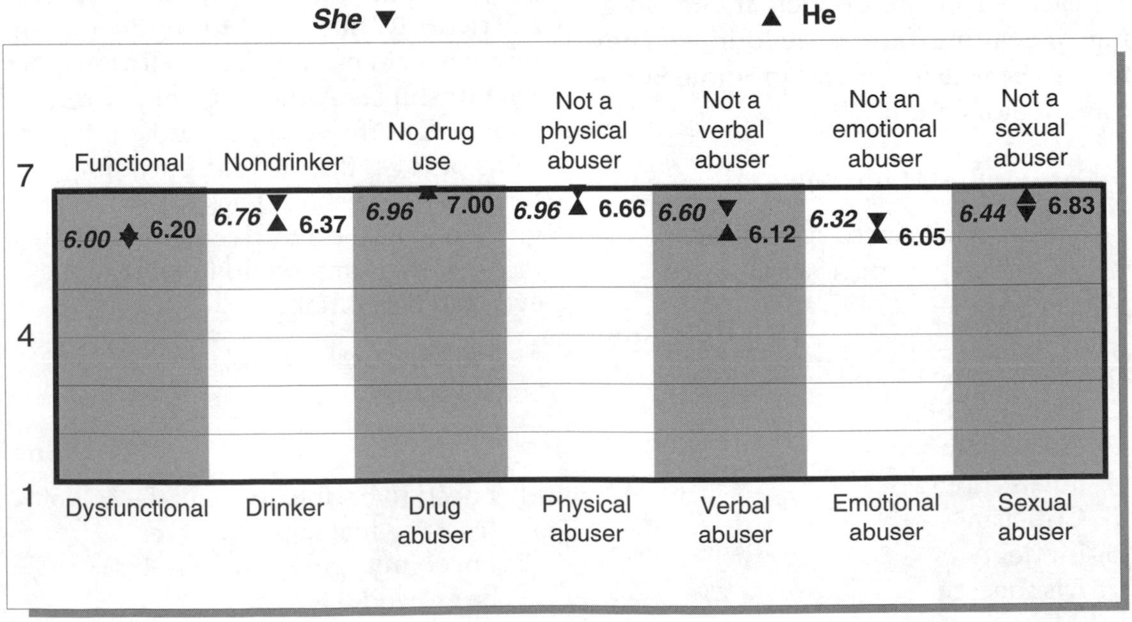

She ▼ ▲ He

7	Functional	Nondrinker	No drug use	Not a physical abuser	Not a verbal abuser	Not an emotional abuser	Not a sexual abuser
She	6.00	6.76	6.96	6.96	6.60	6.32	6.44
He	6.20	6.37	7.00	6.66	6.12	6.05	6.83
1	Dysfunctional	Drinker	Drug abuser	Physical abuser	Verbal abuser	Emotional abuser	Sexual abuser

With scores from 6 to 7, it is easy to see that teacher mates (see chart B on page 160) seldom become abusers of people or substances. Their propensity to maturity and objectivity serves them well.

C. MY GENUINE NEEDS, VIEWS OR BELIEFS ARE:

	He	She
1. I need our marriage to be free of alcohol use and abuse.	29%	36%
2. I need our marriage to be free of drug use and abuse.	41%	40%
3. I need my spouse to treat me more kindly.	7%	12%
4. I need my mate to give me positive emotional support.	41%	56%
5. One or both of us need to get help for abuse in childhood.	5%	0%
6. One or both of us need to get help for dysfunctional behavior.	7%	8%
7. I believe there is no dysfunctional behavior in our marriage.	61%	72%

The majority of teacher spouses believe their marriages are free of dysfunction. But many of the teacher respondents express the need for more positive emotional support.

Living with an Exhorter Spouse

10

Exhorters love to talk. They are the most verbal of all the gifts and cannot understand why everyone is not as fluent and expressive as they are.

Bob and Judy had come in for marriage counseling. I had given them the motivational gift test so I could see where they were coming from gift-wise. Judy scored 93 in exhorter and Bob's highest score was 79 in server. His exhorter score was 27.

"Can you tell me what your problem is?" I asked.

"The problem is, he never tells me he loves me," Judy answered quickly.

Bob looked at her in astonishment. "What do you mean?"

"You don't!" Judy responded accusingly.

"I do, too."

"No, you don't!"

"Why, just yesterday I fixed the toaster you said didn't work," Bob declared. "Last night I gave you a great backrub when you told me your back hurt. Last week I repaired the back stairs, and I'm building the sewing room in the basement that you wanted."

Bob was ready to describe more, but I turned to him and said, "Hold it. Is this the way you tell Judy you love her? By the things you do for her?"

"Of course," Bob replied. "I wouldn't do them if I didn't love her."

"I hope you're hearing him, Judy," I said, turning back to her. "You are married to a server gift, and they express their love primarily by what they do, not by what they say. They are the least verbal of all the gifts."

"I never thought of it that way," Judy said. "But I long to hear the words *I love you.*"

"I can understand that, Judy," I said. "Being an exhorter, you need to hear those words, since words are your primary mode of communicating love. Bob needs to learn how to verbalize his love for you more. But you need to learn to hear Bob's way as well. You also need to realize that thanking Bob for what he does for you is what *he* needs to hear. Servers thrive on appreciation."

"I know I neglect to do that," Judy said. "I think I just take all he does for me for granted." She turned to her husband. "I do appreciate what you do for me, Bob. Please forgive me for not telling you more."

"I forgive you, Judy," Bob replied. "Would you forgive me for not understanding how you need to *hear* how much I love you?"

"I do forgive you, Bob," Judy said. "I can see why you didn't realize my need."

I could see healing was underway. All they needed to know was how the other expressed and received love. It opened up a whole new world of communication for them.

After a week's assignment to practice what they had learned, their need for counseling was over.

Five Major Problem Areas

First we will look at the five most significant problem areas of the exhorter gift, which in turn influence the problems experienced in each of the twenty categories of our survey.

1. Interruptiveness

The number-one problem of the exhorter is interrupting. My husband admits he is guilty of this. You would think that after 34 years of marriage, with the last 21 of them teaching about motivational gifts around the world, the situation would have improved. But Don and I have an ongoing competition because we both like to talk, he from the exhorter gifting and me from the administrator/teacher gifting. We do a lot of it. We especially love talking to our three grown children. We are both so eager to catch them up on what is going on in our lives that we tend to jump in whenever the other one takes a breath. But I think (and Don might agree) that his jumps outnumber mine three to one!

Because we understand the interrupting characteristic of the exhorter, we can talk about it openly without offense. I am free to say, "Wait a minute, honey, let me finish what I'm saying. Then it's your turn."

2. Overtalkativeness

We have often said that exhorters have the best-oiled jaws of anyone! Their mouths move fluently and easily. They love to talk, sometimes nonstop. Yet it is through the mouth that the exhorters exhort. God has blessed them with fluency of speech. At times the spouse of the exhorter may not be sure it is a blessing, especially if he or she enjoys some quiet time.

Often when I hear Don talking, I am not sure if he is talking to me or to himself. I have to ask. Sometimes his response is, "Oh, I'm just thinking out loud." But if I think that is what he is doing and it is not, I may get, "Why aren't you paying attention to me?"

Exhorter spouses like their mates to be sounding boards. They need someone to hear what they are saying and respond to it. But I have learned that Don does not want my evaluation of what he has said so much as he wants an approving nod or "Yes, that's interesting."

3. Stretching the Truth

Exhorters can sometimes speak evang-e-l-a-s-t-i-c-ally, as Don calls it. "After all," he says, "it's the point I'm trying to get across that's important. Who cares if the facts aren't exactly perfect?"

We go 'round and 'round on this because my teacher gift wants the facts to be accurate. But I have found that exhorters do not like to be corrected, especially in public, so I remind myself how well Don gets the point across.

Exhorters are notorious for using Scripture out of context. Don and I imagine it was an exhorter who started a Christian diet class and used as her motto "He must increase, but I must decrease" (John 3:30, KJV) and an exhorter dentist who posted in his waiting room "Open wide your mouth and I will fill it" (Psalm 81:10, NIV)!

4. Being Outspokenly Opinionated

Exhorters are always glad to tell you what they think. They are not as opinionated as perceivers or teachers, but on matters of life application they have strong ideas. That, coupled with their well-oiled jaws, makes their opinions spill out readily. They usually believe that their opinions are the most practical and workable of all.

Exhorters can also be gossipy, bossy and feisty. Actually, as one exhorter put it, "My mouth often runs ahead of my mind. It can easily get me in trouble with my spouse."

Perhaps the most effective prayer for the overly talkative exhorter spouse is this: "Lord, put a guard over my mouth. Help me to think first and speak carefully."

5. Giving Advice

Exhorters are natural counselors. They are good at it. They love to give advice, and others are often drawn to them for it. But their propensity to advise their mates may backfire.

"My husband can be really irritating sometimes," Jane says. "Just because he's an exhorter, he thinks he's supposed to give me advice on everything. Sometimes he tells me what to wear, as if I'm not capable of making that decision. When he tells me how to clean the house a 'better' way, I feel like giving the job to him. When he tells me how I should change an aspect of my personality, I'm ready to wring his neck!"

Someone once said, "Don't answer questions that haven't been asked and don't give advice that hasn't been asked for." Exhorters can benefit from that wisdom.

The Twenty Problem Categories of the Exhorter Gift

Let's take a look at the twenty categories of problem areas for exhorter spouses indicated by our marriage survey.

Category 1: Communication

A. I FEEL WE HAVE SOME PROBLEMS IN COMMUNICATION IN THESE AREAS:

	He	She
1. Misunderstandings	35%	29%
2. Free to share	41%	46%
3. Listening	71%	63%
4. Conversation	47%	37%
5. Correction	35%	40%
6. Body language	47%	31%
7. Ridicule	12%	37%

Because the exhorter spouse is so verbal, misunderstandings are no more frequent than normal in a relationship. When there is misunderstanding, the exhorter tends to talk about it and resolve it rather than stuff it and let it simmer.

Most exhorters feel free to say what they feel. They are candid, articulate and transparent, sometimes saying more than they should. They like to get things out in the open. They want their spouses to do that, too. But when an exhorter is married to a compassion gift, this process is not always smooth.

When exhorter Jeremy asked his new bride, "What's wrong, honey?" he expected her to be honest with him.

But she replied, "Nothing."

"Something's wrong," he prodded.

"No, it's not."

But her sadness and silence spoke volumes.

"Look, sweetheart," he said, determined to clear the air, "I know something's wrong and I feel bad that I've done something to upset you. I want to apologize but I need to know what you're feeling." He pulled her into his arms. "I love you, you know."

It worked. She felt safe and free to share her feelings.

Because exhorters love to do the talking, they can have a major problem with listening. If there is a void, they want to fill it. Worse is the exhorter tendency to think of what to say next instead of hearing what the spouse is saying. More than seventy percent of the men and more than sixty percent of the women admit this is a problem area.

"It's so frustrating," Betty explained, "to be sharing something with Jack and know that he's tuned me out in preference to thinking about what he wants to say. I find myself sometimes saying, 'Hello, earth to Jack, are you there?' It usually brings him back."

Exhorters love lots of meaningful conversation, especially with their mates. Don admits he looks forward to our times of travel by car so we can have uninterrupted conversation. With my gifting I see the time as opportunity to catch up on my reading, so I slip a book into my purse. But I have seen his disappointment and learned that he needs my attention, so we talk most of the way. He also allows me quiet time to read. It is a compromise that works for us.

About forty percent of exhorters see overcorrecting—either their own or their mates'—as a problem. If married to a perceiver, teacher or administrator, an exhorter may feel overcorrected. If married to a server, giver or compassion person, an exhorter is more likely to *be* the overcorrector. If married to another exhorter, it is likely to be a draw.

Exhorters see the correction they give as a benefit to help the mate improve. It may not always be taken that way, however, and they may need to learn how to give correction as a suggestion only.

While the response of exhorter wives on negative nonverbal communication was average, exhorter husbands scored very high. They are, in contrast to exhorter women, more analytical and therefore more aware of negative nonverbal communication. They read between the lines more easily and pick up negative spousal "vibes." They may also contribute more readily to the problem through their own body language or vocal intonation.

Most of the time exhorters want to be positive in marital relationships, but they may resort to ridicule, sarcasm or unkind words. Women exhorters see this as more of a problem than men, although their responses may reflect that they are the recipients, not the expressers, of the ridicule.

Exhorters (see chart B on page 166) are the best communicators. We rate them more highly than they rate themselves. Interestingly, exhorter wives admit they talk too much, while exhorter husbands do not. Our experience shows us that both are verbose. One reason exhorter husbands may not see themselves as overly talkative is their dislike of chit-chat, while exhorter wives admit enjoying it.

The slightly negative scores about being on the critical side reflect the exhorter characteristic of being highly opinionated. They further admit their tendency to interrupt. That they consider themselves attentive and good listeners shows they try hard in this area, but there are exceptions.

C. My genuine needs, views or beliefs are:

	He	She
1. I need more conversation with my mate.	35%	57%
2. I need my partner to listen to me more attentively.	29%	60%

B. To what degree, from 1 to 7, are you one way or the other:

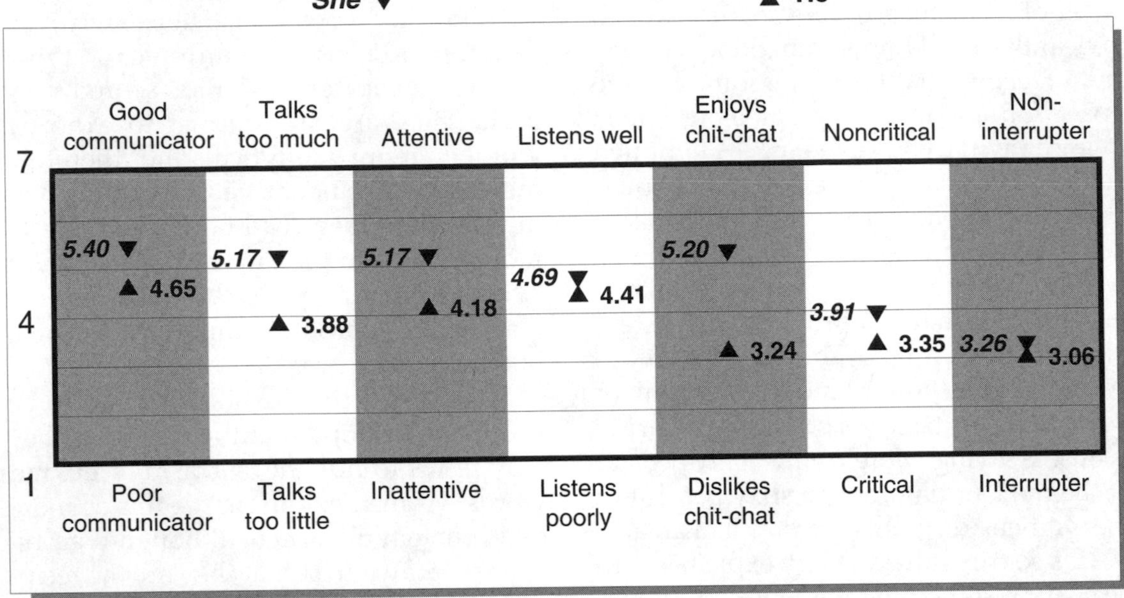

	He	She
3. I need more quiet time without conversation.	18%	14%
4. I feel we need to share more intimately our thoughts and feelings.	41%	51%
5. I get hurt easily by my mate's unkind remarks.	18%	29%
6. I need more of my partner's undivided attention.	18%	37%
7. I am satisfied with our communication and conversation.	29%	40%

The exhorter's satisfaction level with communication suggests room for improvement in most cases, especially in the area of more intimate sharing of thoughts and feelings. Exhorters are easily transparent people who love it when their mates are transparent, too. Barbara told me, "I was amazed at how Jeff opened up his life to me even before we were married. It was as if he were saying, 'This is who I am, with all my mistakes and faults. Can you accept me?' I loved him for it and was able to open up my life to him, too."

Category 2: Expectations

A. I feel we have some problems in what we expect of each other in these areas:

	He	She
1. Lifestyle	24%	20%
2. Priorities	53%	60%
3. Ideals/goals	29%	26%
4. Holidays	12%	14%
5. Hopes/dreams	24%	17%
6. Conduct	12%	17%
7. Homework	29%	49%

Exhorters expect the best from their mates and encourage it, too. More than half of the exhorter respondents view priorities as a problem in their marital relationship. Among the top priorities: good relationships with mates and others, living their faith in practical ways and having opportunities to talk—a lot.

B. To what degree, from 1 to 7, are you one way or the other:

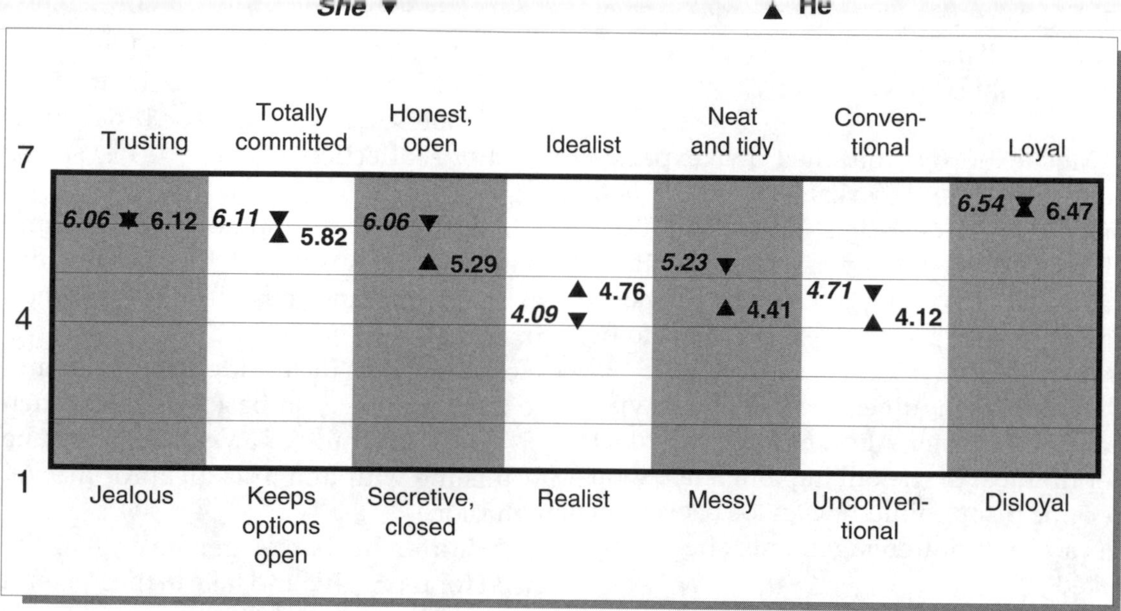

Exhorters tend to have solid ideals and practical values and do well setting goals with their spouses. Because they communicate their hopes and dreams and yet are adaptable, they seldom have problems here. They enjoy being with family on holidays.

Exhorter mates want to do what is right and be reasonable and adaptable. Exhorter wives, especially those who work outside the home, expect their husbands to help out with domestic chores.

Sarah took an outside job when she and her administrator husband, Todd, decided it was time to save money to buy a home. "I had been a full-time homemaker and did all the domestic chores. It was hard for Todd to see he needed to help with these now. I found resentment boiling up inside of me when he'd disappear into the evening newspaper while I cleaned up the kitchen, did the laundry and got the baby ready for bed. My exhorter gifting prompted me to share my feelings honestly, and we were able to come up with a fair plan."

Exhorters (see chart B above) see themselves as trusting, committed, honest, open and loyal. They work earnestly at building a good marital relationship and try to live up to their own expectations and those of others. In most areas they are balanced.

C. My genuine needs, views or beliefs are:

	He	She
1. I need to be more sure of my partner's motives.	6%	26%
2. I need a mate who is dependable.	41%	37%
3. I feel we need to work more at setting joint priorities.	41%	63%
4. I need to be more confident in how my mate handles stress.	18%	17%
5. I need my spouse to be totally honest with me.	35%	49%
6. I need to have former family customs a part of my life.	24%	9%

	He	She
7. I feel our expectations are realistic and workable.	59%	77%

Most exhorters find their own expectations realistic and workable. If they do not, they will work at adjusting the situation. They expect a lot of themselves and of their mates. It helps if they know their partners' gifting and adjust their expectations to fit that reality.

When Joe, the quiet, compassionate type, married exhorter Alice, he was glad to let her do most of the talking. But Alice soon became disappointed when Joe backed off from the social engagements she dearly loved.

"I have to drag him out of the house," she complained to me. "And when he gets there, he just sits like a bump on a log."

"Was he that way before you married him?" I asked.

"Well, yes," she replied, "but I thought he'd change."

"Your expectations are unrealistic," I told her. Then I explained the motivational gifts to her and that Joe would probably never be a great conversationalist.

Later, when Alice took the pressure off, Joe was more willing to attend social events as long as she did not expect him to do a lot of talking.

Setting joint priorities seems to be a major need for exhorter mates, as is the need for mutual openness and honesty.

Category 3: Marital Cohesion

A. I FEEL WE HAVE SOME PROBLEMS IN GETTING ALONG WITH EACH OTHER IN THESE AREAS:

	He	She
1. Time together	35%	40%
2. Give and take	35%	26%
3. Feeling one	29%	20%
4. Closeness	41%	23%
5. Goals/priorities	59%	57%
6. Loneliness	18%	9%
7. Love/affection	41%	37%

Exhorters long for more quality time with their spouses just to talk. But my exhorter husband tells me it is more than that. "I just like being with you," Don says. He often wants me to ride along with him to the post office, sit beside him to watch TV or go with him for a walk. I am glad he wants me with him. It is great for marital cohesion.

Exhorter husbands generally feel the need for more give and take in marriage. "I constantly want to be sure everything is O.K. between Kim and me," says exhorter Bart. "Our feeling of oneness is very important to me. It gives me a sense of security and well-being." Exhorter husbands indicate a much greater need for closeness than men of all other types.

Mutual goals and priorities are important to exhorter spouses and their scores are significantly higher. They like working with their mates. Relationship is of utmost importance.

Exhorter wives scored very low on loneliness. If they experience loneliness in marriage, they compensate to some degree by building close relationships with others. Marsha, whose emotionally and physically handicapped husband could not fill the void in her life, found that her volunteer work at church and in a children's hospital made her feel needed, loved and no longer lonely.

About forty percent of all gift respondents indicate a lack of romantic love and affection in their lives. Exhorters are no exception.

After two years of marriage, exhorter

Bud and his server wife, Annette, decided it would be wise to program some romance. On alternate weekends each is responsible for surprising the other with something spontaneous or amorous. Sometimes one prepares a candlelight dinner or reservations for a window table at the restaurant by the lake. Occasionally they do something special with another couple. Once they read love poems to each other. Now and then they buy tickets to the ice follies, the symphony or a romantic movie. "We love surprising each other," Bud says.

Exhorter spouses, living up to the definition of their gifting, are great encouragers (see chart B below). They like to build up their mates' self-esteem. Whenever I am discouraged, Don comes alongside me to affirm me. When I have had hurt feelings, he is right there to help me see the larger perspective and forgive. As I step out in public ministry, he prays for me and assures me of the Lord's help. I am grateful for his constant encouragement.

Exhorter mates are peacemakers. They are also reliable, agreeable and consistent. Their sensitivity is balanced with an edge of positive caring.

C. MY GENUINE NEEDS, VIEWS OR BELIEFS ARE:

	He	She
1. I need to be able to confide more in my mate.	18%	26%
2. I feel there needs to be more unity in our relationship.	29%	23%
3. I need to feel more secure in our marriage.	0%	0%
4. I am afraid to share some of my feelings with my partner.	24%	31%
5. I need my mate to be more sensitive to my needs.	18%	34%
6. I do not consider divorce ever to be an option.	76%	89%
7. I am satisfied with our marital interaction and closeness.	59%	54%

B. TO WHAT DEGREE, FROM 1 TO 7, ARE YOU ONE WAY OR THE OTHER:

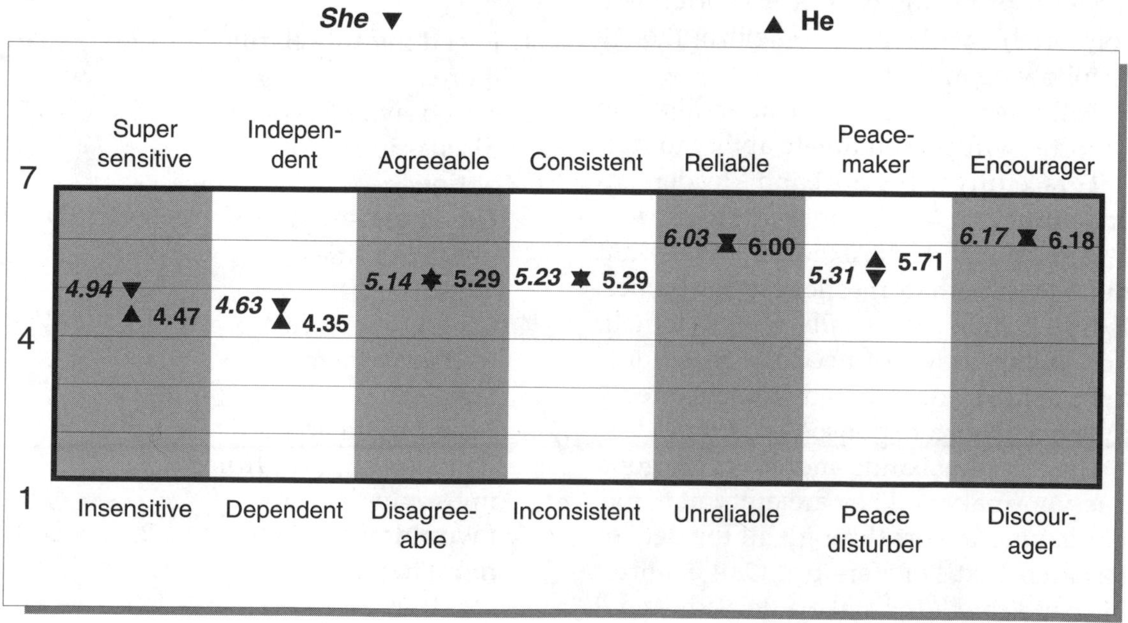

More than half of our exhorters expressed satisfaction with their marital interaction and closeness. Most of the rest indicated not dissatisfaction but the recognition that there is room for improvement. All reported feeling secure in their marriages. Exhorters always look for a way to repair or improve a relationship rather than abandon it.

Category 4: Roles and Responsibilities

A. I FEEL WE HAVE SOME PROBLEMS IN OUR MARRIAGE ROLES AND RESPONSIBILITIES IN THESE AREAS:

	He	She
1. Authority	29%	26%
2. Submission	12%	17%
3. Responsibilities	24%	46%
4. Decision making	35%	23%
5. Roles	12%	6%
6. Feeling overworked	29%	49%
7. Home management	24%	46%

Only a quarter of the respondents identify some problems with the authority structure in their marriages. Three-quarters have no problems with it. Exhorters are comfortable with either being in authority or following authority.

Although capable of leadership, the exhorter wife has an innate ability to submit gracefully to her husband's leadership and authority. Most want him to take it.

Almost half of the exhorter wives want more help with domestic responsibilities. Exhorter men are usually willing to help out where they are needed. Traditional marital roles are accepted wholeheartedly by most exhorter spouses.

Exhorter husbands and wives are good decision-makers. They are quick at it, too, not having to sort through all the data or research that teachers do. One exhorter husband said, "If I make a decision and it turns out to be not so good, I don't worry about it. I figure God will get my attention and help me straighten things out."

Almost half of the exhorter wives report they feel overworked. This is especially true when they are employed outside the home. But they often do more than is necessary for their husbands and families, or they may neglect to delegate tasks that would be fair for others to do. "When Sue and I made a list of everything that needed to be done and who was doing it," Bill admitted, "I realized she was carrying most of the load. Without realizing it, I had been taking advantage of her pleasant and adaptable personality. When I took my share of responsibility, our relationship improved tremendously."

Exhorters (see chart B on page 171) give themselves high marks for being mature, responsible, cooperative and straightforward rather than manipulative. I have seen and admired these qualities consistently in Don over the years.

C. MY GENUINE NEEDS, VIEWS OR BELIEFS ARE:

	He	She
1. I need my role clarified more.	12%	3%
2. I need more freedom to discuss ideas and options.	18%	20%
3. I need to use some of my capabilities more.	35%	20%
4. I need to receive more respect from my partner.	18%	17%
5. I need more domestic help and support from my spouse.	0%	34%
6. I would like to help more in planning together.	29%	26%

B. TO WHAT DEGREE, FROM 1 TO 7, ARE YOU ONE WAY OR THE OTHER:

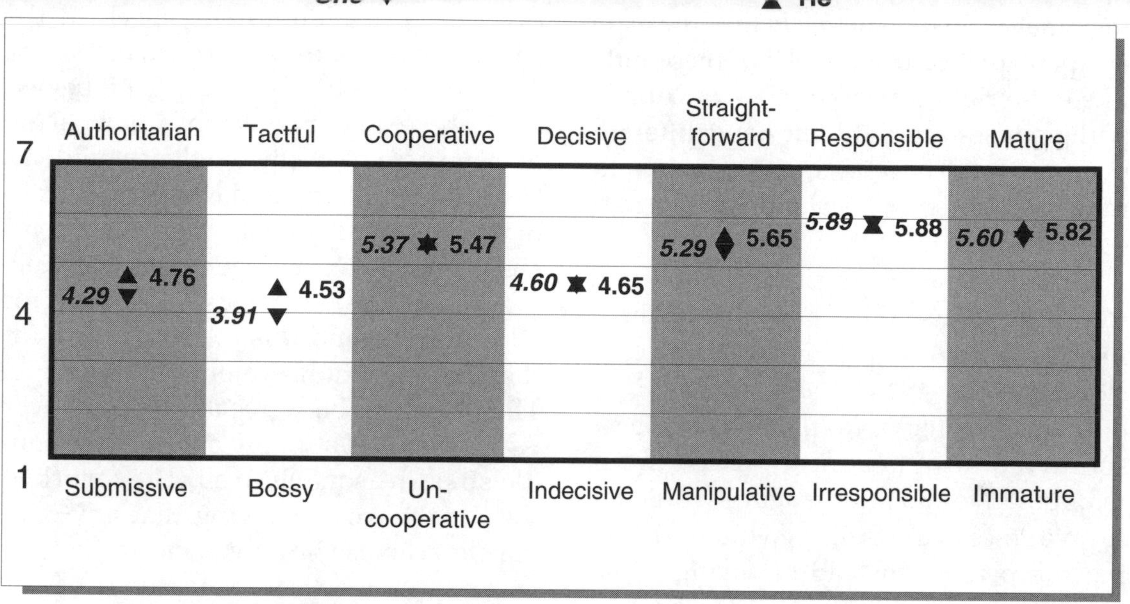

	He	She
7. I am satisfied with the roles and responsibilities we have established.	53%	57%

More than half of all exhorter spouses affirm their satisfaction with their roles and responsibilities. The rest likely have only a measure of dissatisfaction. More planning together would help, and many exhorter wives would dearly love more domestic help.

Category 5: Conflict Resolution

A. I FEEL WE HAVE SOME PROBLEMS IN HOW WE DEAL WITH CONFLICTS IN THESE AREAS:

	He	She
1. Anger management	76%	37%
2. Who's right	41%	40%
3. Final decisions	24%	9%
4. Silent treatment	29%	43%
5. Ultimatums	12%	9%
6. Personal attacks	29%	34%
7. Blame game	18%	31%

Anger is a major problem for fully 76 percent of exhorter husbands, compared to 37 percent for men of all gifts. I was shocked by this statistic, yet relieved. The number-one problem in my relationship to Don has been his occasional explosive outbursts of anger for (to me) unjustifiable reasons. Until the survey I had not believed it was typical of exhorter men. But Don is not alone.

When he and I looked at this graph and I asked him if he could explain the anger problem, he said, "An exhorter man wants everything to go right, and when it doesn't, and especially when he has no control over it, he gets angry. But once he lets off the steam, he gets over the anger quickly." Exhorter husbands need to work at this since the wife is left hurt, often in a puddle of tears. He may be over it in twenty minutes but it may take twenty hours for her to recover.

Arguing over who is right is a problem for about forty percent of all exhorters and their mates. Sparks can really fly if the mate is a perceiver or teacher. All of these gifts like to be right. In some cases, of course, both spouses are right but have different perspectives. The wise spouse seeks common ground rather than hold out for a personal position.

Final decision making is more important to exhorter husbands, but most of them like to take their wives' opinions into consideration.

More exhorter wives than husbands resort to the silent treatment. At best this is manipulative and not very effective. Better to give voice to the feelings without attacking the person. Instead of saying, "You make me so mad!" try, "What you said caused me to feel hurt and unloved. I'm having a hard time controlling my emotions." This gives the husband the freedom to say, "I'm sorry, I didn't mean to hurt you. Will you forgive me?"

Exhorters seldom use threats or ultimatums or resort to personal attack or blame. But they can identify the speck in the spouse's eye and miss the log in their own.

Exhorter husbands' (see chart B below) scores here do not reflect the full measure of their anger problem. But they would say, "I'm not *easily* angered. It takes a lot to make me blow my cool." Note that scores are high for being apologetic and forgiving.

Adaptability is a strong characteristic for all exhorters, and it is relatively easy for them to make adjustments in marriage. They tend to be agreeable except over issues they feel strongly about. They handle stress reasonably well. They work at their marriages, believing that any relationship can use improvement.

C. My genuine needs, views or beliefs are:

	He	She
1. I need to gain control over my temper.	41%	34%

B. To what degree, from 1 to 7, are you one way or the other:

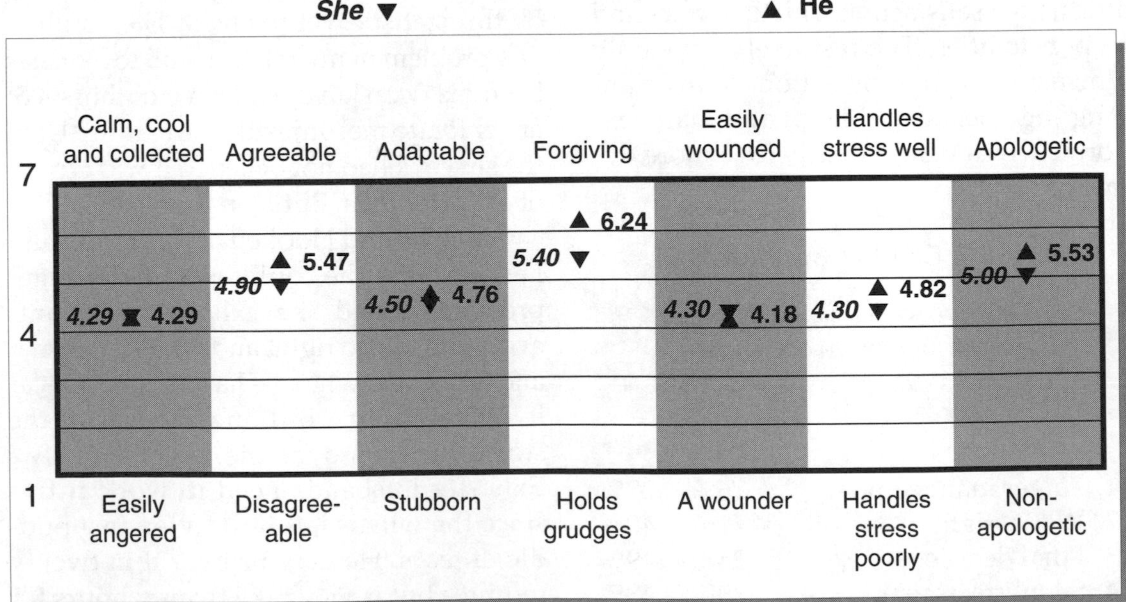

	He	She
2. I need my spouse to gain control over his or her temper.	29%	14%
3. I need to have my point of view heard more often.	6%	20%
4. I feel a strong need to avoid arguments and conflicts.	29%	20%
5. I need my mate to forgive me more quickly.	18%	11%
6. I think we need better ground rules for resolving conflicts.	24%	29%
7. I am satisfied with the way we resolve conflicts.	47%	43%

About half of those who said anger management was a problem admit their need to gain control over their tempers. Perhaps the rest see themselves as not having a temper, but rather just getting angry sometimes.

Exhorters view conflict as a part of life that helps them grow and become stronger spiritually. They see working through problems with their mates as opportunities to learn something they can use later in life for themselves, their marriages or for the benefit of others.

Category 6: Personality Issues

A. I FEEL WE HAVE SOME PROBLEMS IN PERSONALITY CONFLICTS AND ISSUES IN THESE AREAS:

	He	She
1. Being right	41%	40%
2. Pride	24%	31%
3. Understanding	53%	43%
4. Change attempts	41%	43%
5. Methodologies	47%	43%
6. Habits	35%	29%
7. Forgetfulness	24%	37%

Exhorters like being right, although not as much as perceivers and teachers. If an exhorter is married to a perceiver or teacher, there is likely to be more than average conflict. While all human beings are subject to a measure of pride, exhorters are more likely than most to humble themselves. If there is pride in exhorters, it is most likely to be over the advice they like to give.

Exhorters are especially determined to make their mates into what they perceive to be ideal partners. Knowing the motivational gifts can do wonders to take the pressure off.

Wanda was frustrated with her husband's long work hours and yearned for him to spend more time with her—talking. She had concluded that he did not love her enough to come home earlier. I showed her that he was a server gift who worked hard to provide for the family and that this was one way he expressed his love for her. She needed to appreciate him more and tell him so. When she did, he was so thrilled that he began coming home earlier more often, just to be with her.

While exhorters can become irritated at their mates' methods, they can also adapt to them well. Exhorter wives are even better at this than their male counterparts. An exhorter husband may spend two hours telling his wife how to do something better when she can do the task her way in an hour!

Exhorters can change their own habits easily. Their philosophy: If you want to change a habit, just do it. Not all gifts can do that so matter-of-factly.

Some exhorter wives have more trouble than exhorter husbands with forgetfulness.

One told us, "I don't seem to have any problems remembering things having to do with relationships, but if my husband asks me to do five tasks for him and I don't write them down, I'm likely to forget one or two of them. I get sidetracked easily by people interruptions."

Adaptability is a strong endowment of the exhorter (see chart B below). One Air Force wife said she moved nine times in twenty years. "I could have resented it," she explained, "but I decided to make the best of it. Instead of bemoaning the inevitable loss of friendships, I looked at it this way: Really close friends keep in touch, and a new town means new opportunities and the development of new friends."

Exhorters are known for good self-esteem. When Don and I analyzed the percentage of each gifting we have counseled over the years, we found that exhorters are the gifting we have counseled the *least*. They seldom need counseling because they tend to accept themselves as they are, adjust well to most situations and try hard to work out their problems.

They also usually have good attitudes, are considerate, respectful and quick to compliment their spouses.

C. My genuine needs, views or beliefs are:

	He	She
1. I wish my partner complimented me more.	12%	34%
2. I need more encouragement from my mate.	35%	40%
3. I need to be accepted and appreciated for who I am.	24%	34%
4. I need to retain my unique identity.	6%	29%
5. My partner needs to understand my gifts.	18%	23%
6. I need more admiration and respect from my partner.	12%	9%
7. We do not seem to have any personality conflicts.	47%	37%

B. To what degree, from 1 to 7, are you one way or the other:

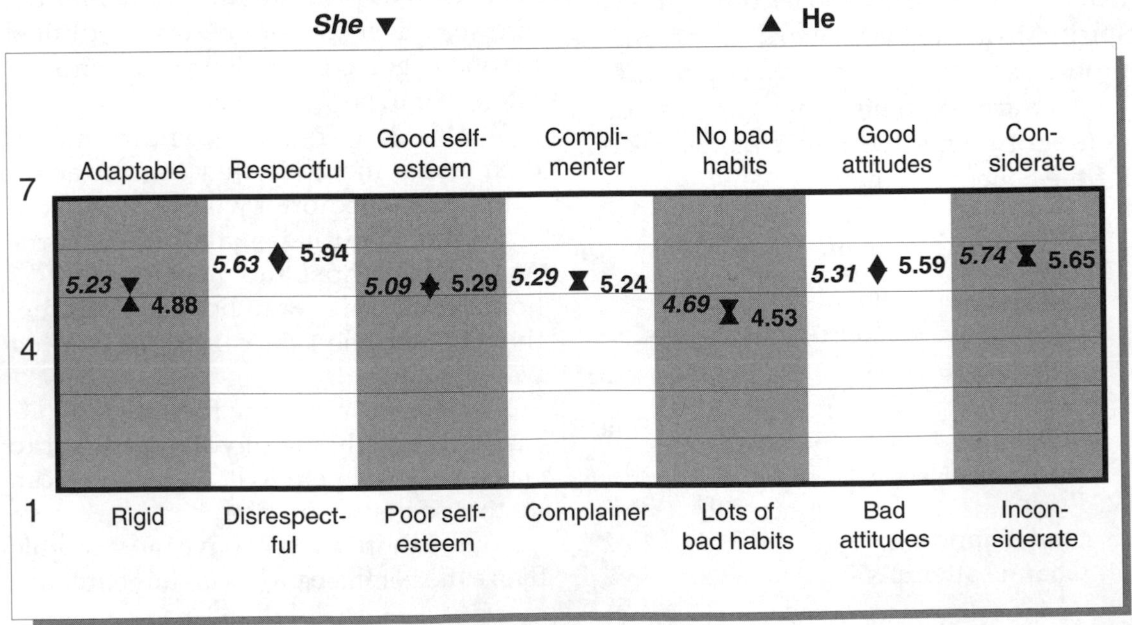

While exhorter wives feel the need for more compliments, all exhorters would like more spousal encouragement. This is especially true when the mate is one of the less verbal gifts—the server, giver or compassion gift.

One-third to one-half of the exhorter respondents feel they have no personality conflicts in their marriages. The ones who report conflicts feel that most relationships have some measure of clash simply because of personality or motivational gift differences. "If we did not have some things to work through now and then," says Don, "then one of us is probably not being honest. I believe we grow, build character and learn from the process. It's helpful and healthy."

Category 7: Emotional Responses

A. I FEEL WE HAVE SOME PROBLEMS IN THE WAYS WE RESPOND TO EACH OTHER EMOTIONALLY IN THESE AREAS:

	He	She
1. Hurt feelings	53%	51%
2. Carrying offenses	18%	14%
3. Unforgiveness	6%	14%
4. Insensitiveness	24%	29%
5. Feeling unloved	18%	20%
6. Moodiness	59%	37%
7. Anger	47%	46%

Feelings may be based on right or wrong perceptions, but they are real and must be dealt with for a healthy marital relationship. About half of the exhorters indicate problems with hurt feelings but make sincere efforts to eliminate the hurt once it happens. Talking it through is one of their favorite methods.

Usually exhorters do not hang onto offenses but are quick to forgive, forget and work through problems. "One of my favorite Scriptures," Larry told us, "is about the man who was forgiven much but then was unwilling to forgive a little. If I want to live in a forgiven state in relationship to God, I must be a constant forgiver."

Most exhorter mates give love easily and feel it in return. When they do not feel loved, they pursue the issue in a positive way until it is resolved.

Some exhorters have a problem with moodiness. Loren admitted to us that when things do not go the way he wants, he tends to pout or withdraw from his wife. "I've improved, though," he wrote, "and am still working on it."

Again, anger can be a problem for exhorters, especially husbands. Many admit that their impatience causes them to blow. George told us he used to express exactly what he felt when Mary did something he did not like. "The old adage *Think before you speak* has done wonders for our marriage," he reported, "when I've utilized it."

While exhorters (see chart B on page 176) put a premium on reasoning, they are also able to express their feelings well. They score high on being loving, able to express that love verbally and doing it often and well—which pleases their mates and makes them more responsive. Women exhorters are a bit more demonstrative. Both are high in the caring department and tend to be sympathetic. They cry on occasion but usually not out of control.

"I'm always telling my teacher husband I love him," Judith, a classic exhorter, said. "He likes to hear it, but frankly, I wish he would tell *me* that more. When I complain, he comes back with, 'You should know I love you. I married you, didn't I?'"

C. MY GENUINE NEEDS, VIEWS OR BELIEFS ARE:

	He	She
1. My feelings tend to rule my life.	24%	26%

B. TO WHAT DEGREE, FROM 1 TO 7, ARE YOU ONE WAY OR THE OTHER:

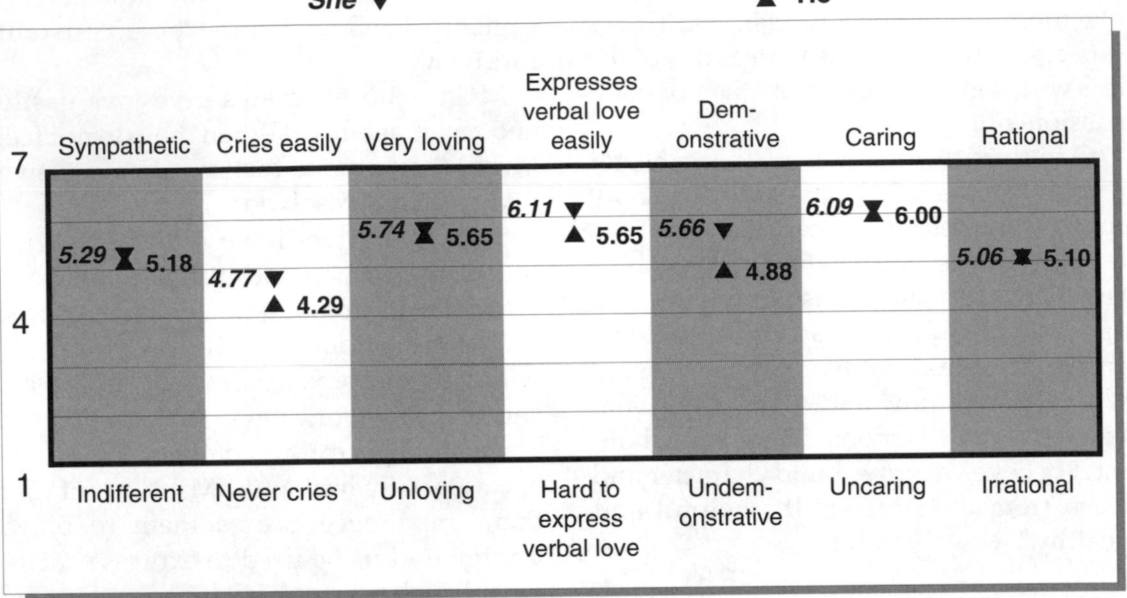

	He	She
2. My mate needs to understand my moods more.	24%	20%
3. I need to hear more "I love you's" from my partner.	24%	34%
4. I need to be able to express both positive and negative feelings.	41%	46%
5. I feel my spouse takes everything too personally.	41%	26%
6. I often feel "put down" by my partner.	6%	29%
7. I am satisfied with our emotional responses to each other.	47%	46%

About half of the exhorter respondents say they are happy with the emotional responses in their marriages. Others are working on areas that need improvement. Exhorters married to each other have few, if any, problems in the area of emotional expression.

Exhorters need to express negative feelings as well as positive ones. "Once I get my feelings out," Rene said, "I can deal with them. I have a hard time trying to keep them inside. I need to verbalize and then resolve them."

Category 8: Intellectual Capacity

A. I FEEL WE HAVE SOME PROBLEMS RELATING TO INTELLECTUAL INTERESTS AND CAPACITIES IN THESE AREAS:

	He	She
1. Different interests	35%	29%
2. Reading	18%	20%
3. Continuing education	6%	11%
4. Know-it-all attitude	29%	17%
5. Correcting grammar	6%	9%
6. Children's education	12%	6%
7. Being accurate	35%	29%

In general exhorters welcome their mates' intellectual interests. More than some gifts, they like variety and new horizons in their lives. Exhorters enjoy historical novels, biographies, autobiographies and fiction. Exhorters are always learning from life, whether through formal education or not.

Exhorter husbands seem to have a greater problem with know-it-all attitudes. Estelle told us that when she first married her exhorter husband, he drove her crazy in the kitchen. "For some reason Al thought he had great expertise in culinary arts," she wrote. "He would wander in, tell me what I should do and how to do it, and what I should have done if I hadn't done it his way. To save my sanity and our marriage, I had to draw the line. 'Out,' I said, 'and stay out, unless you want to prepare the meal!' Actually, he's cooked some really good ones now and then."

Correction of grammar is not a problem. Exhorters give great leeway in the use of the king's English. They are adaptable in working with their mates to give their children the best education possible. Quite a number like to home-school.

Exhorter spouses are casual in how they handle facts. Sometimes when I question a statement, Don replies, "Well, you know what I mean." No, I usually don't, since my teacher gifting gears me to specifics while Don's exhorter gifting gears him to generalities. We often have to back up and look at what has been said so I know for sure I have gotten the message right.

Exhorters do have opinions!—often based on their life experience (see chart B below). When an exhorter is married to a perceiver, opinions sometimes clash over "revelation" and rightness (as opposed to practical experience). When an exhorter is married to a teacher, the issue is hard facts. When an exhorter is married to an administrator, the problem may be the overall view. In any case, a healthy discussion of the viewpoints can usually bring understanding and resolution.

Exhorters see themselves a bit on the intellectual side, but always with a practical, life-related perspective. They are analytical but not overly so. They enjoy read-

B. To what degree, from 1 to 7, are you one way or the other:

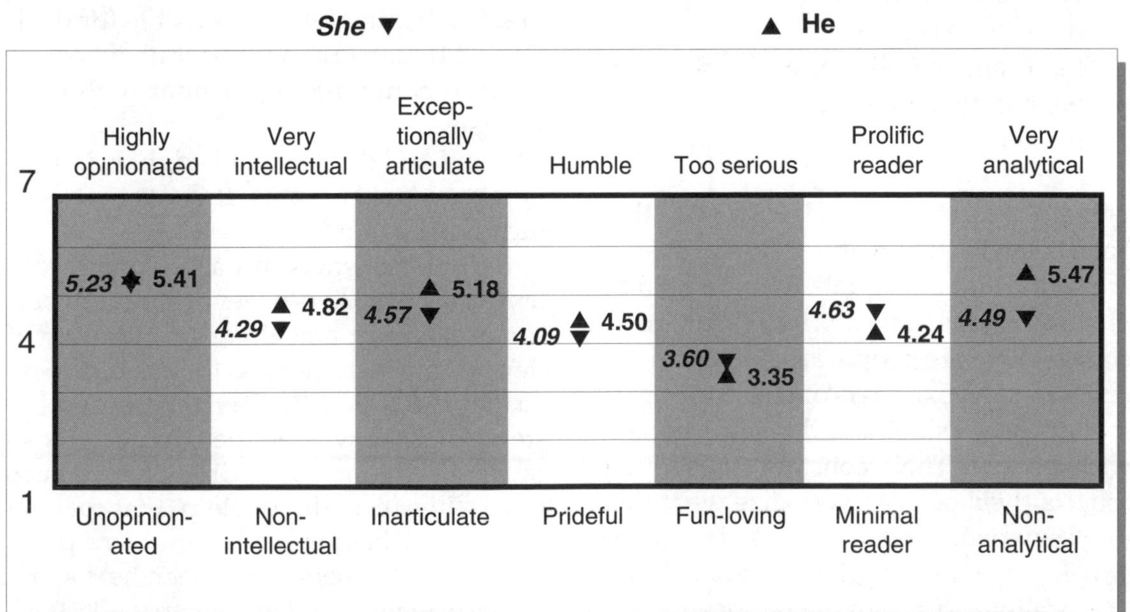

ing but can bypass it in preference to interacting with others. They talk all the time, sometimes to their mates' distress.

They are fun-loving and do not overdo it in the serious department. One of the things that attracted me to Don was his spontaneous sense of humor. It was good for me because I tend to take life too seriously. He has helped me to hang loose and have more fun.

C. My genuine needs, views or beliefs are:

	He	She
1. I need adequate time for reading or study.	47%	60%
2. I am easily sidetracked by new interests.	47%	37%
3. I need to question things before I can accept them.	41%	51%
4. I need my mate to listen to my opinions more.	6%	17%
5. I realize I need to be less dogmatic.	24%	20%
6. I find I constantly analyze what my partner says and does.	18%	23%
7. I am satisfied with how we handle intellectual matters.	71%	69%

Exhorters are satisfied with how they handle intellectual matters. But three areas are significant. Adequate time for reading or study seems to be a priority—unless, of course, there are people around to relate to or encourage. Exhorters' interests are broad so they can get sidetracked easily, especially with people. Their constant questioning reflects their need to verbalize what they think or wonder about. They need to process new ideas or information, examine it as to practicality and accept it if reasonable.

Category 9: Volitional Issues

A. I feel we have some problems in the use of the will in these areas:

	He	She
1. Decisions and choices	35%	17%
2. Practical decisions	35%	14%
3. Stubbornness	47%	29%
4. Agreements	18%	11%
5. Right actions	6%	9%
6. Judgmentalism	18%	26%
7. Rebelliousness	12%	9%

Exhorters are decisive. They size up the situation quickly and draw a conclusion that is pragmatic. One husband said of his exhorter wife, "If she discovers that her decision is not the best, she adjusts it accordingly." Twice as many exhorter husbands as wives have trouble making joint decisions they can live with.

Stubbornness is the greatest problem area of this section. Exhorter men especially can dig in their heels when they believe they are right. True, an exhorter husband usually gives his wife the opportunity to have her say, but as one exhorter said, "I feel the buck stops with me. I am ultimately responsible for decisions." It may take a while, but exhorters want to come into agreement with their spouses.

Being and doing what is right is important to exhorter mates. If proven wrong, they will change.

Judgmentalism is only a moderate problem. Most exhorters believe that every person is at some point along a continuum of development. Their task, they feel, is to do all they can to help that person take another step along the way. So they do not look so much at what is wrong in that person as what they can do to help that person improve. Rebellion is not normally a problem unless the person has been hurt a lot.

Once again (see chart B on page 179) we

B. To what degree, from 1 to 7, are you one way or the other:

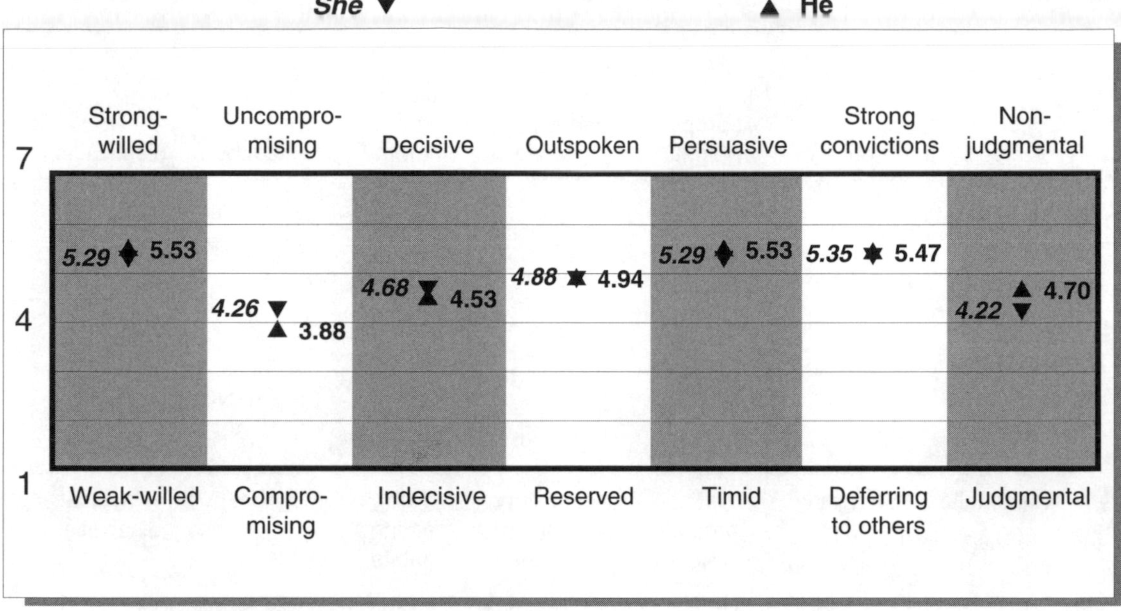

see the nonjudgmental stance of the exhorter, along with the willingness to compromise—a status justified by exhorter mates because they want a good working relationship with their partners.

Exhorters are strong-willed, outspoken, persuasive with strong convictions. All this can be modified for the purpose of working out a marital relationship.

C. My genuine needs, views or beliefs are:

	He	She
1. I have a definite inner need to be right.	47%	37%
2. I have a strong need to be a decision-maker.	65%	37%
3. I need my mate to make most of the decisions.	6%	6%
4. I will do what is right even if it hurts.	65%	63%
5. I need to operate by definite principles.	59%	60%
6. I need my mate to be more tolerant of my opinions.	24%	23%
7. I am satisfied with how we make decisions.	35%	57%

Exhorter wives are more satisfied than exhorter husbands with how they make decisions. The husbands' strong need to be the decision-maker may account for this, indicating that many may not have been involved adequately in marital decision-making.

Most exhorters want to do what is right even if it hurts. They try to operate by definite principles and are faithful to those they have established. Again and again I have heard Don say, "I am operating on principle!" He is usually immovable on the matter unless new information is added that makes a difference.

Category 10: Physical Conditions

A. I feel we have some problems in the physical realm in these areas:

	He	She
1. Being fit	65%	66%

B. To what degree, from 1 to 7, are you one way or the other:

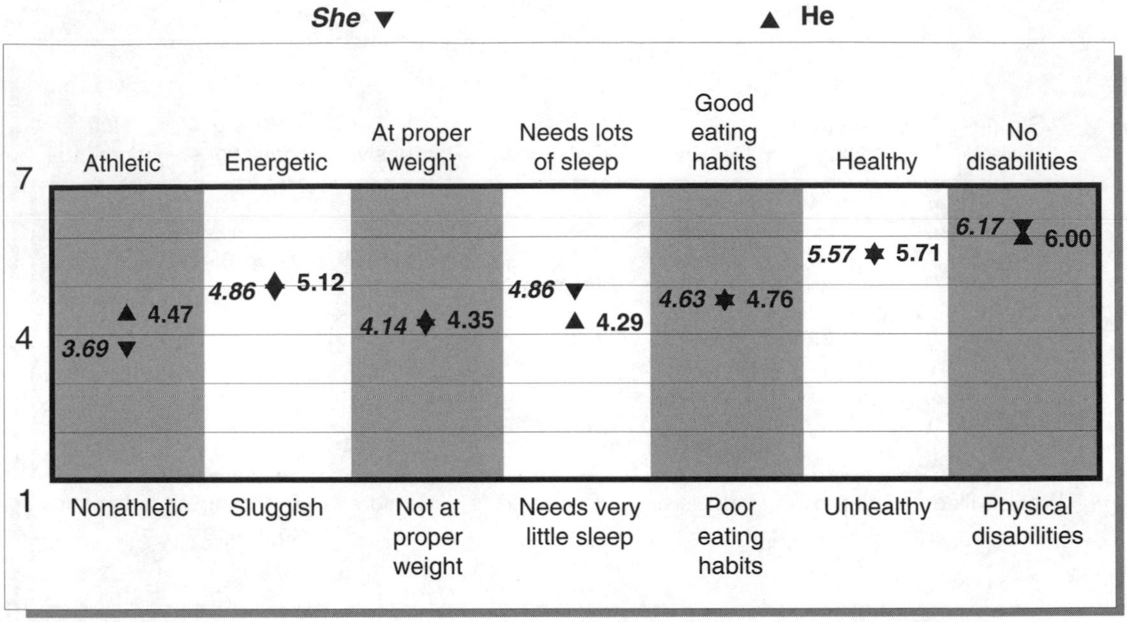

	She ▼	He ▲	
Athletic / Nonathletic	3.69	4.47	
Energetic / Sluggish	4.86	5.12	
At proper weight / Not at proper weight	4.14	4.35	
Needs lots of sleep / Needs very little sleep	4.86	4.29	
Good eating habits / Poor eating habits	4.63	4.76	
Healthy / Unhealthy	5.57	5.71	
No disabilities / Physical disabilities	6.17	6.00	

	He	She
2. Enough exercise	65%	83%
3. Fatigue	47%	49%
4. Overeating	29%	37%
5. Proper eating	29%	23%
6. Keeping attractive	18%	11%
7. Adequate sleep	35%	49%

Exhorters are fairly good at keeping fit and getting enough exercise, yet a majority said they have problems in this area. Because of their people-relatedness, exhorters are more consistent in planned exercise programs with others. Walking or exercising with their mates may prove more successful than attempting to keep it up alone.

Being practical and conscious of the consequences of poor eating habits, exhorters tend to eat the foods that promote good health. Getting adequate sleep is a problem for about half of all people, no matter what their gifting.

Exhorter husbands (see chart B above) say they are slightly higher than average athletically, while exhorter wives admit they are less than average. The "energetic" rating reflects this as well. Most are average regarding proper weight and see themselves as healthy with fairly good eating habits.

C. My genuine needs, views or beliefs are:

	He	She
1. I desire to see my mate at the proper weight.	59%	43%
2. I need to overcome my own weight problem.	35%	54%
3. I need to get adequate exercise on a regular basis.	71%	83%
4. I would like to see my spouse get more exercise.	65%	57%
5. I need my mate to be as attractive as possible.	41%	26%
6. I need to improve my eating habits.	53%	63%
7. I am satisfied with how we keep fit, healthy and attractive.	41%	14%

While 41 percent of exhorter husbands report satisfaction with how they keep fit, healthy and attractive, only 14 percent of exhorter wives did so. Melody, an enthusiastic exhorter, says that she and her giver husband, Lance, have a reasonable exercise program since both of them have desk jobs. "But we don't always follow it perfectly," she admits. "And even when we do, I still feel we are not doing enough." She also revealed they had both checked boxes 1 and 2 of this section, even though neither is more than ten pounds above their ideal weight.

So it is possible that exhorters are harder on themselves than they need to be. Even though exhorters have the best scores on proper eating in part A, more than half indicate the need to improve eating habits even more.

Category 11: Sexual Relationship

A. I FEEL WE HAVE SOME PROBLEMS IN OUR SEXUAL RELATIONSHIP IN THESE AREAS:

	He	She
1. Frequency	47%	43%
2. Quality	24%	11%
3. Prior affection	24%	31%
4. Nonsexual affection	41%	34%
5. Sexual dissatisfaction	24%	9%
6. Incompatibility	6%	3%
7. Infidelity	6%	3%

Exhorter women are significantly more satisfied than the average of women in general with the quality of their marital sex, affection prior to sex and affection apart from sex; and they scored lower on general sexual dissatisfaction. This indicates that they are good sexual partners and that they have mates who understand a woman's need for affection, not just sex.

At a Christian women's conference, the wise speaker on positive marital relations asked the women, "How many of you have husbands who are mindreaders?" When no hands were raised she continued, "Then tell your husbands what you enjoy in your lovemaking." Since exhorter women are good communicators, perhaps they have already done this.

Exhorter wives (see chart B on page 182) communicate with their husbands about sex. They verbalize love well and share intimate feelings. They see themselves as affectionate, good at hugging and kissing and sensitive to their mates' needs. While exhorter husbands' scores were fair, there is room for improvement.

C. MY GENUINE NEEDS, VIEWS OR BELIEFS ARE:

	He	She
1. I need more nonsexual affection from my mate.	29%	46%
2. I need more sexual relations with my mate.	47%	17%
3. I feel I need more hugs and kisses from my spouse.	18%	40%
4. I need to hear more "I love you's" from my partner.	18%	34%
5. I need my husband to better understand my monthly cycle.	0%	9%
6. I feel dissatisfied with our current sexual relationship.	41%	20%
7. I feel satisfied with our current sexual relationship.	59%	60%

About sixty percent feel satisfied with their sexual relationship. Many exhorter husbands want more sex and would probably get more if they understood a woman's

B. To what degree, from 1 to 7, are you one way or the other:

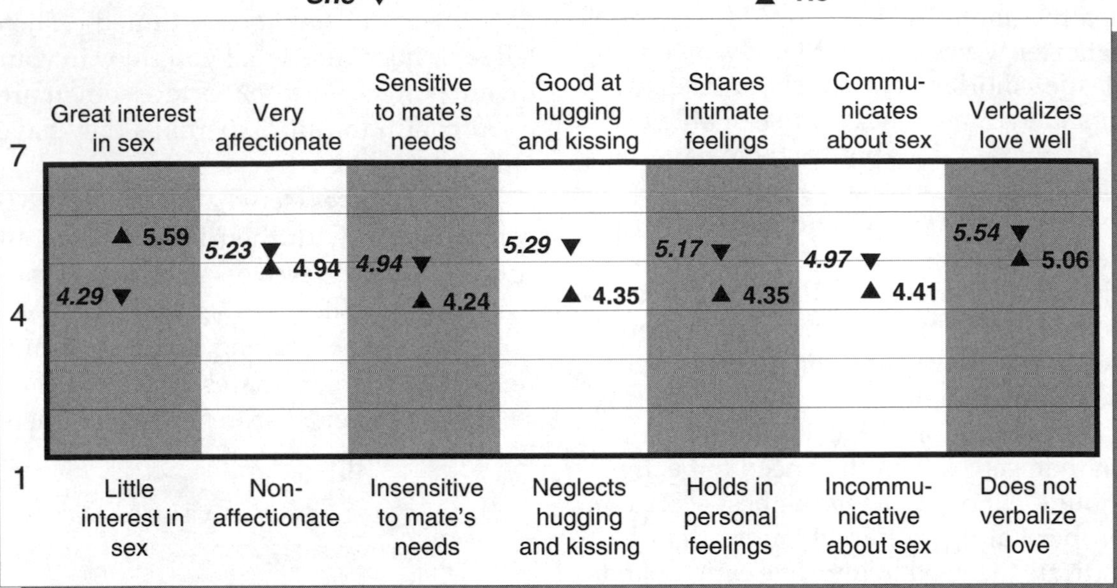

need for more affection, hugs, kisses and verbal affirmations of love.

Category 12: Work and Accomplishments

A. I feel we have some problems about work and accomplishments in these areas:

	He	She
1. Too busy	53%	43%
2. Career conflicts	24%	11%
3. Overtime work	24%	23%
4. Inadequate income	29%	26%
5. Volunteer work	18%	23%
6. Wife working	12%	9%
7. Priorities	24%	11%

Like all respondents, exhorters feel the problem of being too busy. By talking over what is really necessary in their schedules, couples can trim the superfluous and get more quality time together. Vacuum once a week instead of twice. Cook twice as much for dinner and put the rest in the freezer for another meal. Take the bus instead of driving to gain a ride in the fast lane and more time for office work, devotional time or writing letters.

Career conflicts are fewer than average for exhorter women, as are problems of misplaced priorities. Exhorters report fewer problems with inadequate income.

Exhorters (see chart B on page 183) are good achievers; their scores are positive on being industrious, goal-oriented, organized and good accomplishers. Unfortunately, exhorter women often are not paid adequately for their work skills, although they are great assets to any workplace that requires good people relationships. Once the owner of a large accounting firm called me to ask what gifting would make the best secretary-receptionist. Without hesitation I said, "A server-exhorter combination. She will handle details superbly and make everyone feel loved and accepted." Two months after testing applicants and hiring that combination, he called to say

B. To what degree, from 1 to 7, are you one way or the other:

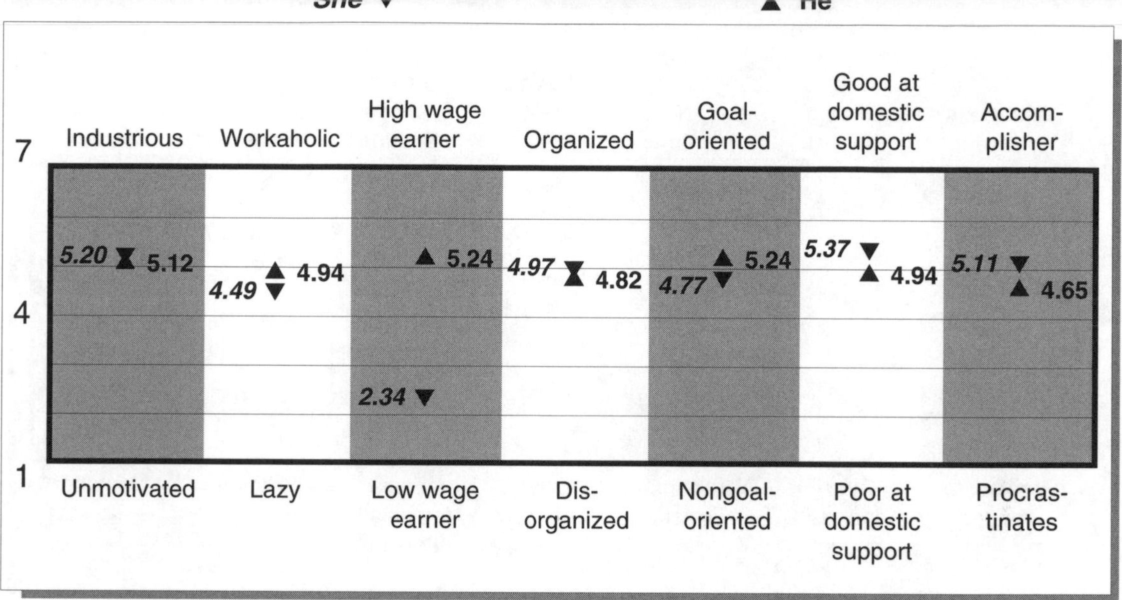

she was the best secretary-receptionist the company had ever had.

C. My genuine needs, views or beliefs are:

	He	She
1. I need my husband to provide our basic expenses.	0%	60%
2. I need my wife to be a full-time homemaker.	35%	0%
3. I need to be the sole provider for my family.	6%	0%
4. I need a fulfilling career.	53%	14%
5. I need a challenge to work toward.	47%	29%
6. I get great joy out of my accomplishments.	59%	71%
7. I am satisfied with the way we handle work and accomplishments.	59%	71%

Exhorters get great joy out of their accomplishments. An equal number express satisfaction with the way they handle work and accomplishments. The men need a challenge and a career that is deemed fulfilling, definitely with a people-orientation. They make good bosses, encouraging the development of people's talents and abilities and expecting wholehearted effort and accomplishment.

Category 13: Financial Management

A. I feel we have some problems in financial matters in these areas:

	He	She
1. Establishing budget	59%	46%
2. Keeping to budget	59%	63%
3. Living beyond means	53%	23%
4. Credit cards	29%	29%
5. Impulsive buying	47%	29%
6. Money arguments	29%	20%
7. Wife's work role	6%	3%

About half of the exhorter respondents say they have some problems establishing and keeping a budget. But so did the other gifts.

B. To what degree, from 1 to 7, are you one way or the other:

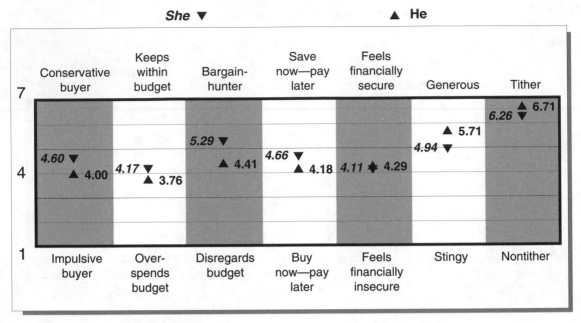

7 (top)	She ▼	He ▲	1 (bottom)
Conservative buyer	4.60	4.00	Impulsive buyer
Keeps within budget	4.17	3.76	Over-spends budget
Bargain-hunter	5.29	4.41	Disregards budget
Save now—pay later	4.66	4.18	Buy now—pay later
Feels financially secure	4.11	4.29	Feels financially insecure
Generous	4.94	5.71	Stingy
Tither	6.26	6.71	Nontither

Two areas in which exhorter husbands report fewer problems than average are living beyond their means and impulsive buying (either their own or their spouses'). Being practical and outspoken, they are able to diminish these problems.

Commitment to tithing (see chart B above) stands out for exhorter spouses, which means they have not only a firm grasp of the biblical principle but good control over family finances. They feel reasonably secure financially, balanced in buying habits and budget concerns. As exhorter Andrew says, "If we don't have it, we don't spend it. It's just that simple."

C. My genuine needs, views or beliefs are:

	He	She
1. I feel we need to reduce our debts more effectively.	59%	51%
2. I feel the need to be in charge of our family finances.	24%	9%
3. I believe the husband should handle the family finances.	29%	23%
4. I think the most capable partner should handle the family finances.	41%	69%
5. I need to learn how to handle money more responsibly.	35%	40%
6. I would like to give more to church, missionaries, charity, etc.	71%	63%
7. I am satisfied with how we handle finances.	41%	43%

Around forty percent are satisfied with how they handle finances; the rest see room for improvement. Some admit the need to reduce indebtedness and learn how to handle money more responsibly. A majority, already tithers, would like to give even more to church, charities and missionaries. Don's exhorter gift, coupled with his secondary gift of giving, has focused him along these lines. Being in charge of the missions department of our church has been a joy to him. He is always looking for ways to encourage others to give more to missionaries through the "adopt-a-missionary" plan that has doubled giving.

Category 14: Leisure Activities

A. I FEEL WE HAVE SOME PROBLEMS IN HOW WE SPEND OUR FREE TIME IN THESE AREAS:

	He	She
1. Interests	35%	14%
2. Recreational preferences	24%	9%
3. Hobbies	29%	17%
4. Entertainment	18%	14%
5. Vacation preferences	18%	11%
6. Sports	41%	14%
7. TV-watching	35%	31%

Exhorter wives score lower than the norm in all of these—evidence once again of their adaptability. But exhorter husbands feel more strongly than the average about what they like to do and are less willing to adjust to their wives' preferences. Both scored lower than the norm on too much TV-watching. As exhorter Oliver puts it, "I've got lots of better things to do than be a couch potato!"

Exhorter mates (see figure below) are highly social and will encourage even the least social mate to spend time with others. They also like to be on the go, whether traveling or going for walks or just going out to dinner together. At first Norm was overwhelmed with his exhorter wife's yen for social interaction. "I'd just as soon stay home and read a book," he admitted. "If we didn't have a social engagement, she'd develop one. It took us several years to work out a system that worked for both of us. But I'm glad she persisted, for we have wonderful friends as a result of it."

C. MY GENUINE NEEDS, VIEWS OR BELIEFS ARE:

	He	She
1. I need my partner to be a recreational companion.	41%	31%

B. TO WHAT DEGREE, FROM 1 TO 7, ARE YOU ONE WAY OR THE OTHER:

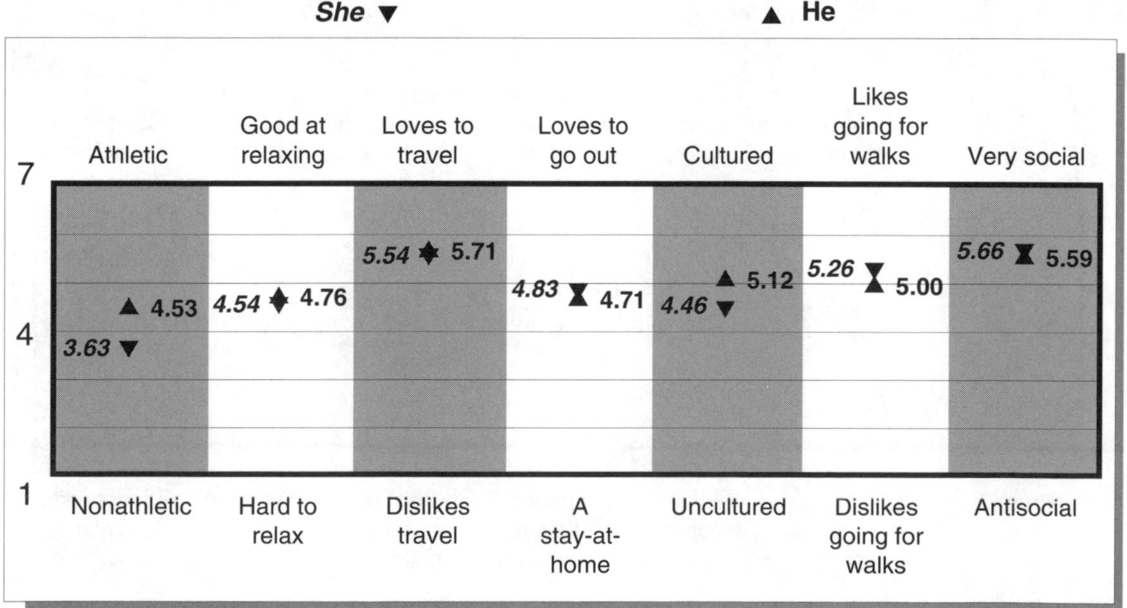

	He	She
2. I need to do more fun things with my spouse.	53%	66%
3. I need more meaningful vacations.	41%	40%
4. I need to be involved in nonathletic leisure activities.	24%	14%
5. I prefer active group or competitive sports.	18%	14%
6. I prefer individual noncompetitive sports.	59%	37%
7. I am satisfied with how we spend our leisure time.	53%	46%

While about half of the exhorters are satisfied with how they spend their leisure time, half are not. They especially feel the need to do more fun things with their spouses. Not only is there truth in the saying "Couples that pray together stay together," but it can be said that "couples that *play* together stay together." Meaningful time together builds a good relationship.

I do not think Don will ever share my love for painting. He claims that he cannot even draw a straight line and says that I should paint the house instead of pictures! I do not have much time for painting, but when I do, it is *with* Don on the deck of our cabin—while he reads another one of the *Zion Chronicles*.

Category 15: Parenting

A. I feel we have (had) some problems in the child-rearing process in these areas:

	He	She
1. Type of discipline	24%	40%
2. Amount of discipline	24%	46%
3. Who disciplines	24%	34%
4. Misconduct determination	24%	43%
5. Love expression	12%	23%
6. Time spent	41%	46%
7. Money given	29%	20%

Exhorter wives report more problems with how misconduct is determined, with

B. To what degree, from 1 to 7, are you one way or the other:

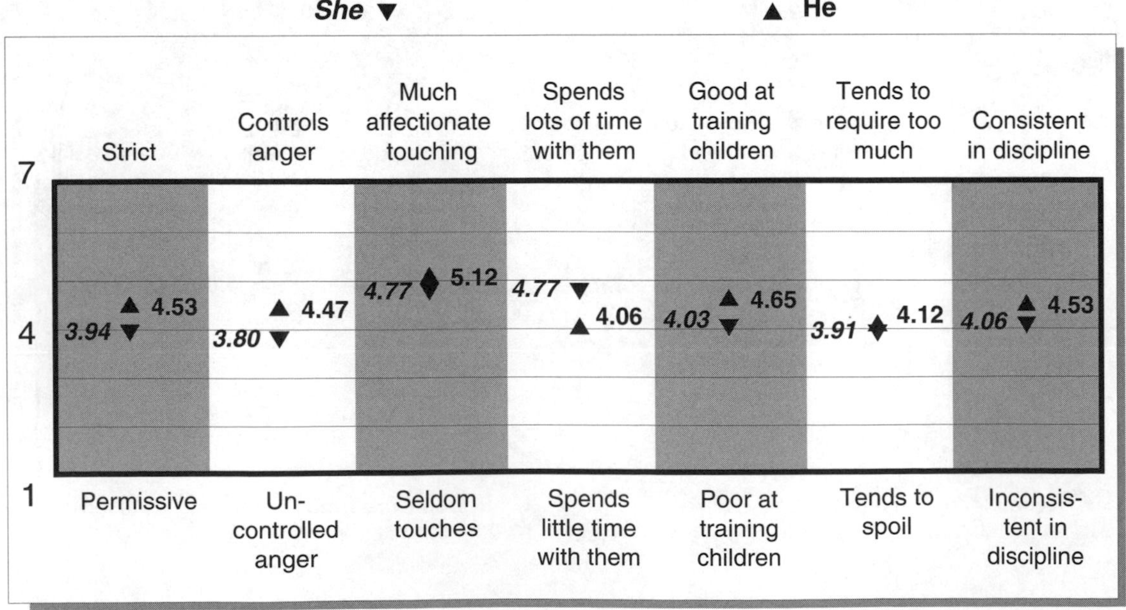

the type and amount of discipline and who does it. They tend to be a little more flexible and less strict.

The amount of time spent with the children is less of a problem for exhorters than the norm for all the gifts. Since exhorters value relationships so much, they build good relationships with their children by investing quality time in them.

Scores here (see chart B on page 186) are balanced. Exhorter parents, for example, are neither too permissive nor too strict, and they believe they neither spoil their children nor expect too much of them.

C. My genuine needs, views or beliefs are:

	He	She
1. We need to provide better spiritual guidance for our children.	24%	40%
2. We need to give our children more love and affection.	29%	26%
3. I would like my spouse to help more with the children.	0%	23%
4. I need to be more affirming of our children.	24%	29%
5. I feel we need to agree more on discipline.	6%	23%
6. I feel we need more quality family time and activities.	47%	60%
7. I am satisfied with our parenting styles and skills.	41%	31%

Exhorters are good at parenting, giving lots of love and affection. Some exhorter wives see the need for providing better spiritual guidance, and both see the need for more quality family time and activities. Nancy, the mother of seven children, says, "Parenting is my favorite thing. I love nurturing and encouraging my kids. I love home-schooling them. I guess it enables me to use my exhorter gifting a lot."

Category 16: In-Laws and Family

A. I feel we have some problems with our families and in-laws in these areas:

	He	She
1. Interference	24%	14%
2. Their expectations	12%	11%
3. Their visits	6%	3%
4. Comparisons	12%	3%
5. Borrowing money	6%	20%
6. Former abuse	6%	17%
7. Dysfunction affect	18%	26%

Because of their skill in relationships, exhorters do not have major in-law problems. Exhorter husbands do report a few more problems than the norm with in-law interference and with their wives' comparing them to their own parents.

With most of the scores (see chart B on page 188) in the high 5s or 6s, it is evident that exhorters leave and cleave properly, defend their spouses adequately, are realistically independent, yet show healthy love and honor to their parents.

C. My genuine needs, views or beliefs are:

	He	She
1. I need my spouse to put me before his or her family.	35%	20%
2. I need to see or talk to my parent(s) regularly.	41%	37%
3. I need to include my family in holiday celebrations.	47%	31%
4. I need help in overcoming in-law problems.	6%	14%

B. To what degree, from 1 to 7, are you one way or the other:

She ▼ ▲ He

	Did leave and cleave	I stand up for my spouse	Independent of former family	I love and honor my father	I love and honor my mother	My family was normal	I relate well to in-laws
She ▼	6.03	6.29	6.06	6.12	5.97	4.38	4.97
He ▲	6.06	6.12	6.12	6.82	6.71	5.59	5.94
	Apron strings still attached	I side with my family	Dependent on former family	I hate my father	I hate my mother	My family was dysfunctional	I relate poorly to in-laws

	He	She
5. I need to be accepted by my in-laws.	6%	17%
6. I need to be financially free from my family and my in-laws.	12%	14%
7. I am satisfied with our family and in-law relationships.	76%	74%

Three-fourths of the exhorter respondents are satisfied with their extended family relationships. Their need to relate to parents regularly and include them in birthday and holiday celebrations is expected and will likely be handled well.

Category 17: Social Relationships

A. I feel we have some problems in social relationships in these areas:

	He	She
1. Friends' demands	18%	9%
2. Time for friends	29%	49%
3. Unsocial partner	12%	17%
4. Too social partner	6%	3%
5. Wrong friendships	6%	3%
6. Negative influence	6%	3%
7. Over involvement	6%	11%

Social relationships come naturally to exhorters, who love relating to all kinds of people. The only major problem area (shared by all other gifts) is having enough time for friends. Exhorters are more likely than most to work at making time. If married to a less sociable gift, like a perceiver, teacher or server, the exhorter's effort will not necessarily be shared. Still, the exhorter is likely to prevail.

The highly sociable nature of exhorters is evident here (see chart B on page 189). They like having many friends and relate well to all kinds of people. They love to entertain, often having friends over for dinner or opening their homes for church activities. The exhorter husband prefers smaller groups; the exhorter wife feels the more the merrier.

B. To what degree, from 1 to 7, are you one way or the other:

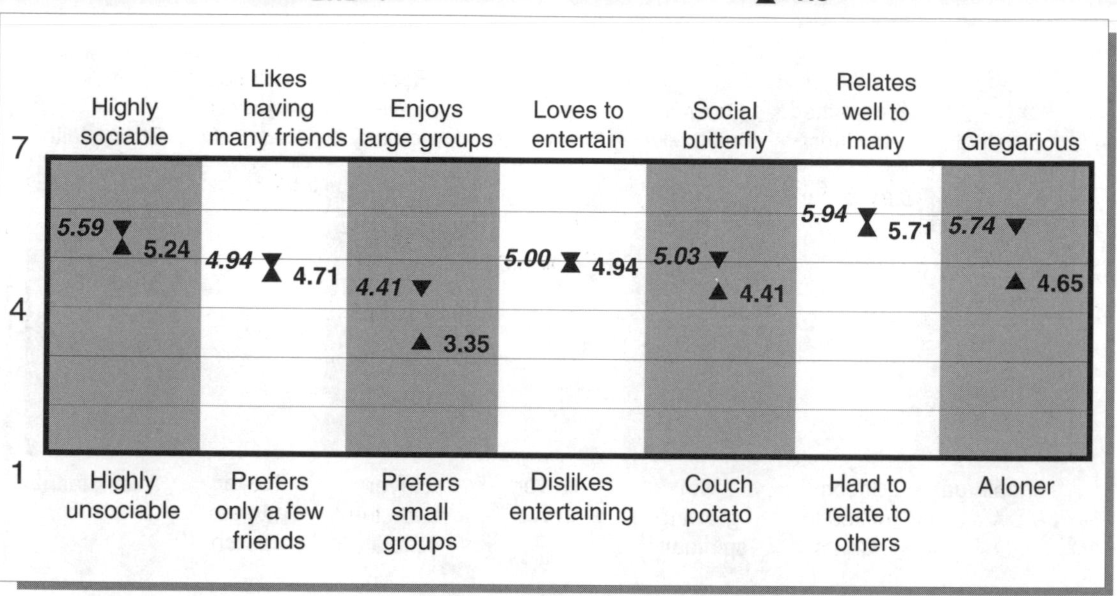

C. My genuine needs, views or beliefs are:

	He	She
1. I need to have many friends.	35%	34%
2. I especially love to entertain in our home.	29%	43%
3. I need a good deal of private time.	29%	43%
4. I need our home to be a haven of rest.	53%	51%
5. I need to be involved in social groups.	24%	37%
6. I think we need to change some friendships.	18%	0%
7. I am satisfied with our social life.	76%	66%

It is interesting that even though exhorter spouses have great social lives and love to entertain in their homes, they also need to have homes that are havens of rest. They need spaces between social times for rest and refreshing.

Category 18: Religious Orientation

A. I feel we have some problems in our spiritual life and orientation in these areas:

	He	She
1. Affiliation disagreement	6%	6%
2. Church attendance	6%	3%
3. Different backgrounds	6%	6%
4. Theological differences	18%	6%
5. Commitment level	24%	20%
6. Irregular attendance	18%	3%
7. Hypocritical behavior	6%	9%

While scores here are not so different from the norm, exhorter husbands note more than twice as much concern as the norm for men—and twice as much concern as exhorter wives—regarding irregular church attendance and theological differences with their spouses. Exhorters believe that what is accepted theologically should not be just theory but should translate into lifestyle. Belief to them is practical. They put great stock in practicing what they preach. Church attendance, to them, reflects spiritual beliefs.

B. To what degree, from 1 to 7, are you one way or the other:

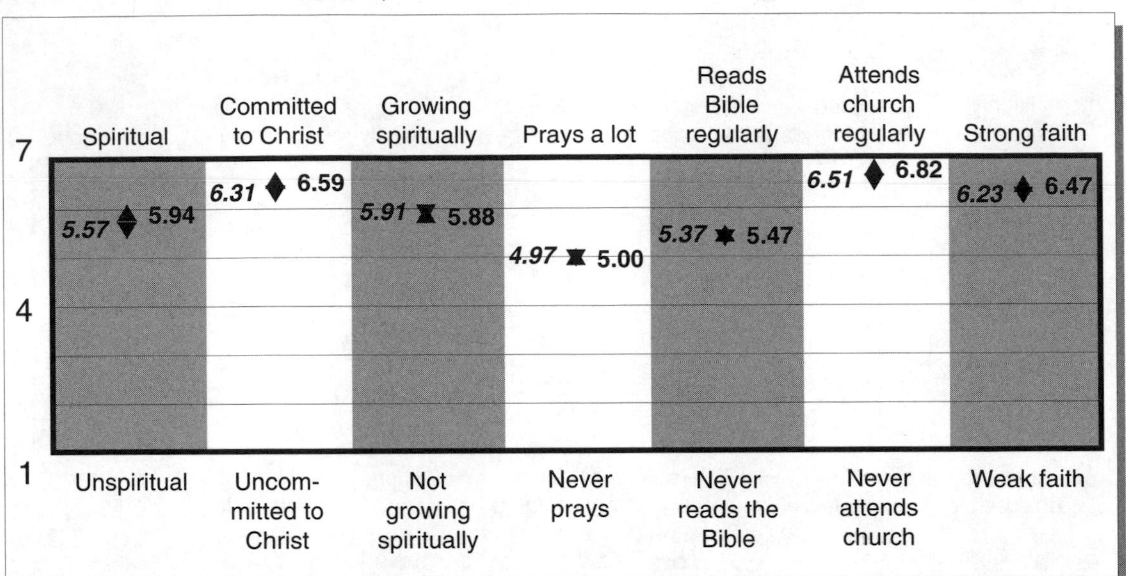

Exhorters (see chart B above) see themselves as strong in their faith, committed, growing spiritually and involved regularly in the life of their churches. Their involvement in prayer and Bible study is on the positive side.

C. My genuine needs, views or beliefs are:

	He	She
1. I need to attend church regularly.	76%	63%
2. I need my partner to pray with me daily.	53%	74%
3. I greatly desire to see my spouse grow spiritually.	76%	83%
4. I believe we need to have regular family devotions.	82%	83%
5. I need my spouse to give spiritual leadership.	18%	77%
6. I need to be able to live my faith, not just talk about it.	65%	71%
7. I am satisfied with our religious orientation and practice.	65%	57%

High scores here indicate that exhorters take their spiritual lives seriously and practically. I have watched my husband live his faith faithfully over the years and set an example for me and our family. He prayed with me not only on our first date but on 99 percent of the 12,410 days we have (at this writing) been married. He has always given me spiritual leadership, inspiration and encouragement.

Category 19: Maturity

A. I feel we have some problems with maturity in these areas:

	He	She
1. Inexperience	6%	9%
2. Irresponsibility	6%	9%
3. Blame game	24%	31%
4. Stress coping	24%	31%

	He	She
5. Criticism	18%	23%
6. Infidelity	6%	3%
7. Dishonesty	6%	6%

Like Adam and Eve, exhorters can lapse into the blame game, but for the most part they take responsibility for their own actions. They indicate few problems, in comparison to the norm for all gifts, in coping with life's stresses. They tend to mature well.

Good qualities come through strongly in these exhorter responses (see chart B below). Their ability to love is extensive, they are givers rather than takers and they are trustworthy, responsible and quick to forgive. Note their humility with their answers regarding humility!

C. My genuine needs, views or beliefs are:

	He	She
1. I need to be able to trust my mate.	59%	40%
2. I need my spouse to be dependable.	59%	43%
3. I need to be quick to forgive and, hopefully, be forgiving quickly.	76%	60%
4. We need to learn from and grow through every experience.	88%	63%
5. I need my mate to be able to handle responsibility well.	65%	43%
6. I need my mate to love me unconditionally.	59%	49%
7. I feel that we are a reasonably mature couple.	94%	94%

Exhorters love to see the same qualities they have developed demonstrated in their spouses' lives as well. Many encourage their mates to that end. Server Sue married to exhorter Ben found that trait a challenge sometimes: "He would occasionally get really pushy about my spiritual growth

B. To what degree, from 1 to 7, are you one way or the other:

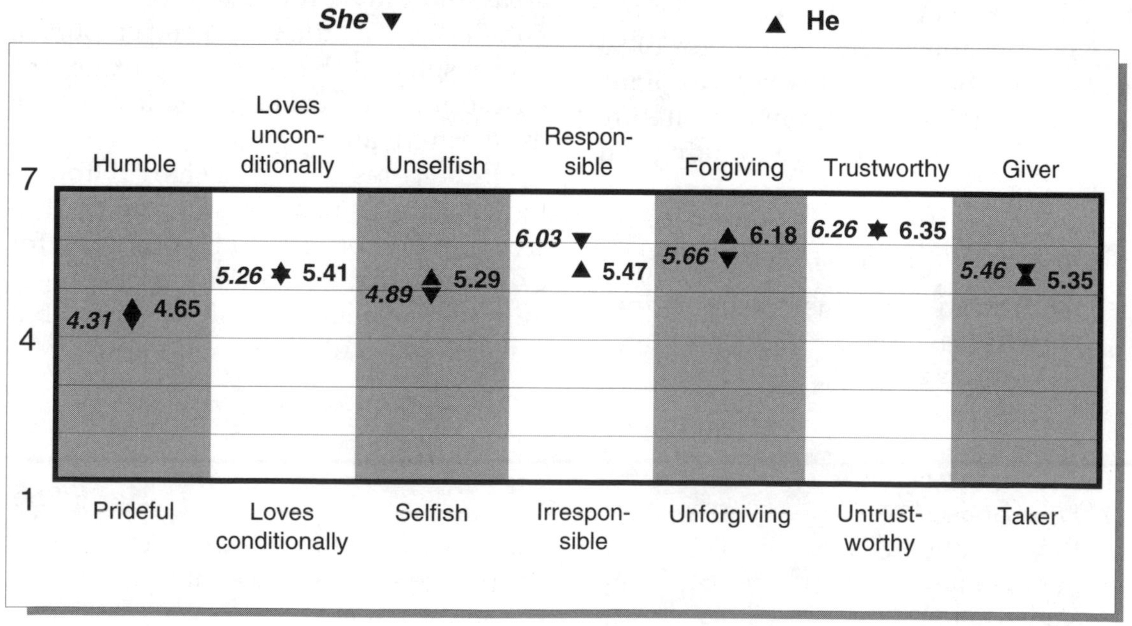

B. To what degree, from 1 to 7, are you one way or the other:

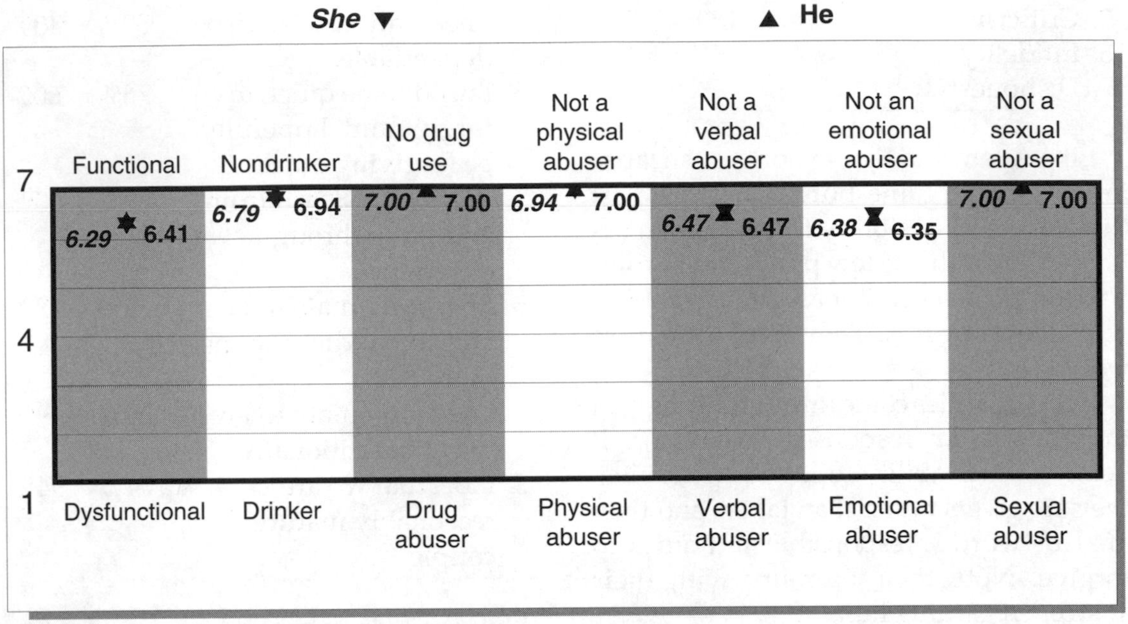

She ▼ ▲ He

	Functional / Dysfunctional	Nondrinker / Drinker	No drug use / Drug abuser	Not a physical abuser / Physical abuser	Not a verbal abuser / Verbal abuser	Not an emotional abuser / Emotional abuser	Not a sexual abuser / Sexual abuser
She	6.29	6.79	7.00	6.94	6.47	6.38	7.00
He	6.41	6.94	7.00	7.00	6.47	6.35	7.00

and I'd have to tell him to back off a bit. The nice thing is he would back off and let me grow at my own pace."

Exhorters believe that every experience in life, good or bad, provides the possibility for learning and growing, especially if approached with a good attitude. They can turn just about anything around to "work together for good."

Note the amazingly high scores of 94 percent for considering themselves, along with their wives, a reasonably mature couple. Talk about positive thinking and believing!

Category 20: Dysfunctionality

A. I feel we have some problems in the following areas that produce dysfunction:

	He	She
1. Alcohol abuse	0%	3%
2. Drug abuse	0%	3%
3. Physical abuse	0%	3%
4. Sexual abuse	0%	6%
5. Verbal abuse	6%	9%
6. Emotional abuse	12%	9%
7. Unresolved abuse	12%	17%

Abuse scores from our respondents are very low, with no reports by exhorter husbands of abuse problems in the first four areas and only a few by exhorter wives. Both indicate a little verbal and emotional abuse, some of that unresolved from the past; but the percentages are lower than the norm for all the gifts.

High scores here (see chart B above) indicate that substance abuse and abusiveness do not tend to be problems for exhorters. The exception may be anger outbursts, which can wound a mate, but resolution usually follows quickly.

C. My genuine needs, views or beliefs are:

	He	She
1. I need our marriage to be free of alcohol use and abuse.	41%	40%

	He	She
2. I need our marriage to be free of drug use and abuse.	47%	37%
3. I need my spouse to treat me more kindly.	6%	3%
4. I need my mate to give me positive emotional support.	53%	43%
5. One or both of us need to get help for abuse in childhood.	0%	11%
6. One or both of us need to get help for dysfunctional behavior.	0%	11%
7. I believe there is no dysfunctional behavior in our marriage.	76%	66%

Of all the gifts, exhorters normally have the least amount of dysfunction in their lives.

Living with a Giver Spouse

11

When Jean learned that her husband, Leonard, was a giver, it helped her understand why he did certain things that drove her up the wall.

One day she was cleaning out some kitchen cupboards and placed a nice set of tumblers on the counter. Then she was distracted by a call from her daughter, who needed an immediate babysitter for an hour. When Jean got home, meaning to finish the cleaning project and put the glasses back, they were gone.

"What happened to my glasses?" she asked her husband.

"Oh, I gave them away," Leonard replied nonchalantly.

"What? Those are my best tumblers!"

"I thought you wanted to get rid of them," he said. "They were just sitting there, and the Vietnamese woman who moved in up the street came by, and we were talking, and I asked her if she could use them. She was delighted! So I gave them to her."

Jean was not delighted.

Another time Leonard gave away two easy chairs without checking with Jean first. Later, when the church announced a need for the nursery workers to get the sermon over closed-circuit TV, he waited until she was out of town speaking to a women's group, then donated their TV.

"Why did you do that?" Jean demanded. "Why didn't you wait and ask me about it?"

"I knew you'd say no," he replied sheepishly, "and I felt they really needed it."

The only saving grace was that he bought a new TV.

Then Jean learned about the motivational gifts and realized that Leonard was practicing one of the negative characteristics of his giver gifting. And Leonard agreed that in the future he would ask Jean first before giving things away.

Five Major Problem Areas

Let's look first at the five most significant problem areas of the giver gift, which in turn influence the problems experienced in each of the twenty categories of our survey.

1. *Overgenerosity*

Giver spouses need to check with their mates before giving away anything of value. They love being generous, but their spouses may not share this propensity. Each couple must work out what fits their joint needs.

Ben and Mary used to argue over his tendency to give too much to their children.

"It seemed that whatever they asked for, Ben gave them," Mary recounts. "I could see that the kids began to manipulate their father into more and more expensive items. They weren't just getting spoiled; they *were* spoiled."

"I hadn't realized how spoiled they were getting," Ben admits. "I was just enjoying the joy of giving and all the *thank you's* I was getting. We heard a lot of complaints when I cut back, but the kids appreciate more what they get now."

2. *Focus on Money*

God gives givers an interest in and focus on money. He gives them wonderful business ability so they can earn money well and have plenty to give to others as He directs. A non-Christian giver, or a Christian giver who does not stay in contact with the Lord, can so focus on making money that his or her priorities get out of whack. In extreme cases givers become compulsive gamblers or white-collar thieves. More often they simply neglect their spouses and families in preference to pursuing the almighty dollar.

Givers are called by God to be intercessors. This alone will keep their priorities straight. They need to give as God leads and pray for others as He directs. Then God can bless them and give them financial success that will not ruin them.

3. *Frugality*

Givers can flip-flop from overgenerosity to extreme frugality. While they naturally handle money well, they can handle it too tightly or become authoritarian over the family budget, vetoing their spouses' suggestions that do not fit their own ideas.

"I've read about people dying in poverty, only to have someone to discover $200,000 sewed inside a tattered mattress," Marie said. "I was truly afraid Grant was becoming one of those. He makes good money in his business, but it was ten years before he'd let me trade in our hand-me-down couch for a new one. It was only after he took a financial seminar at church that he realized that his frugality was extreme. He's still improving, and it's good to see the balance in his giver gifting."

4. *Workaholism*

Givers have the greatest success rate of all the gifts in developing and running businesses. They are naturally good at making money. But they get a certain "buzz" out of it and sometimes do not know when enough is enough. They may work long hours to start a business but continue doing overtime when it is no longer needed. As the wife of one giver said, "I don't want a successful husband with a heart attack at forty. I'd rather have fewer material things and a husband who takes time to be with me and the kids."

5. *Unpredictable Giving*

Givers give a number of ways: systematically (such as tithing), impulsively and "as the Lord leads." This makes sense to the giver but not necessarily to the spouse, who may deem it illogical or unfair. Since finances are such an important part of marriage, it is important for givers to talk over methods of giving with their spouses and come up with procedures that satisfy both.

"My giver wife had been used to earning, spending and giving her own money for many years before we were married," Thurman said. "We had a real challenge to find a new pattern that would work for us together. She spends lots of time in prayer before she gives and nearly always I find the Lord confirms it to me. If He doesn't, we just pray more. We both want to give according to His will, not hers or mine or ours."

The Twenty Problem Categories of the Giver Gift

Let's take a look at the twenty categories of problem areas for giver spouses indicated by our marriage survey.

Category 1: Communication

A. I FEEL WE HAVE SOME PROBLEMS IN COMMUNICATION IN THESE AREAS:

	He	She
1. Misunderstandings	11%	33%
2. Free to share	39%	33%
3. Listening	39%	47%
4. Conversation	33%	20%
5. Correction	33%	27%
6. Body language	33%	27%
7. Ridicule	28%	40%

Women givers report three times as many misunderstandings with their spouses as men, who report few. This may be due in part to a woman's greater ability to identify misunderstandings.

About a third report hindrances in sharing feelings. Givers tend to hold things in more than most, other than server gifts. Not usually high in communication skills, they are better than most in listening skills; but even so, many report communication a problem.

Givers are honest and forthright in what they say and engage in meaningful conversation reasonably well. They tend to accept how their partners think and speak. Most do not see overcorrection as a problem, and those who do may be indicating correction given by their spouses. Any gift can resort to unkind words, but givers are more likely to build up or encourage their mates.

Givers, whose scores (see chart B on page 197) are close to the midpoint, tend to be balanced and middle-of-the-road. Giver wives are a little better at communication than their male counterparts, who, like them, dislike chit-chat. Their caring nature enables them to listen well. Joyce told us that her giver husband gives her one hundred percent attention when she tells him something. "I really appreciate it," she said. "Todd makes me feel that what I am saying is tremendously important, whether it is or not. It makes me feel good."

C. MY GENUINE NEEDS, VIEWS OR BELIEFS ARE:

	He	She
1. I need more conversation with my mate.	61%	40%
2. I need my partner to listen to me more attentively.	28%	47%
3. I need more quiet time without conversation.	17%	0%
4. I feel we need to share more intimately our thoughts and feelings.	50%	40%
5. I get hurt easily by my mate's unkind remarks.	33%	27%
6. I need more of my partner's undivided attention.	28%	27%

B. To what degree, from 1 to 7, are you one way or the other:

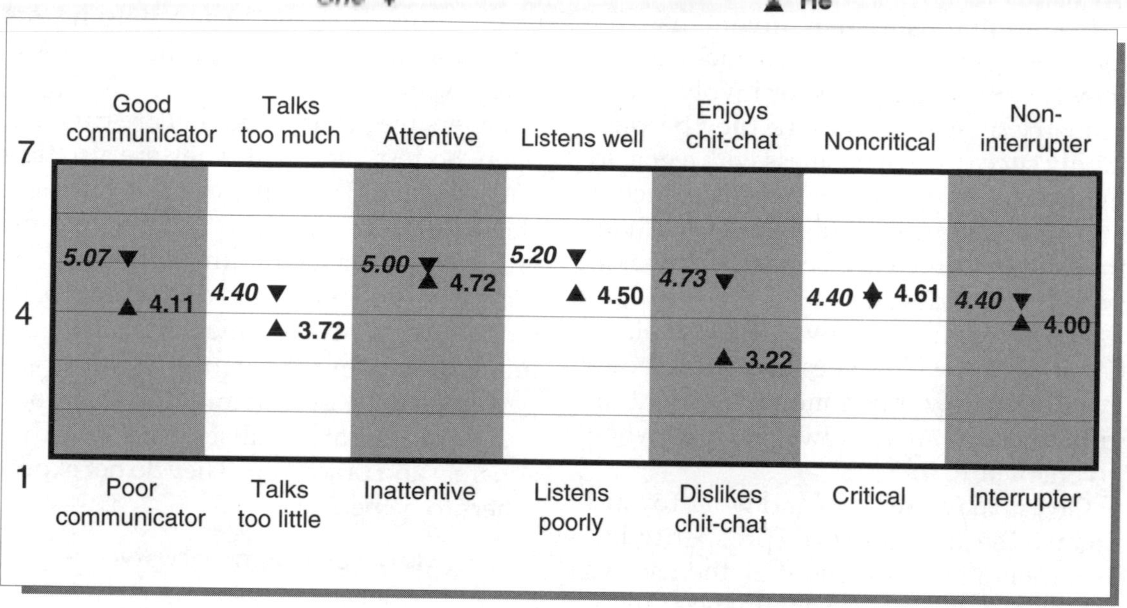

	He	She
7. I am satisfied with our communication and conversation.	39%	60%

Giver wives seem more satisfied with marital communication than giver husbands. Both feel the need to share their thoughts and feelings more intimately.

Trena, an administrator gift married to a giver evangelist, said, "Rod does pretty well in conversation with me, but where he really shines is when God's anointing comes on him in a crusade. I think he could speak all night, and sometimes it looks like he might!"

Category 2: Expectations

A. I feel we have some problems in what we expect of each other in these areas:

	He	She
1. Lifestyle	17%	7%
2. Priorities	44%	33%
3. Ideals/goals	28%	13%
4. Holidays	11%	13%
5. Hopes/dreams	17%	20%
6. Conduct	11%	20%
7. Homework	22%	20%

Givers are positive, affirming and hardworking. They view priorities as the major problem area in terms of expectations, yet their scores fall a bit below the norm. Making money, one of the most important priorities of giver spouses, can easily get out of hand in the eyes of their mates.

Leslie married Wesley when he first started his own business. "I was so proud of him and his success," she admitted, "but he put in such long hours. I knew his giver gift gave him a love for business. He'd promise to cut back, but there was always a reason he had to go back to work even at night. I felt neglected, and when the children came along they felt it, too. Family life was not his priority. We came to a crisis and he learned from it. We have quality family life now, and business is in balance."

Committed Christian givers usually focus along one or both of two tracks. Either they become evangelists (or involved in a ministry of evangelism), or they become highly successful in business with a goal to financially support and advance such a ministry. If married to a fellow Christian, their goals can easily be meshed. If not, problems can develop.

Holidays are usually not a problem. Givers adapt well. Issues may arise, however, over how much money is spent on gifts. Spouses are not always happy when givers overdo it.

Givers may dream of and work toward financial security and even prosperity, but usually not just to spend it on themselves or their families. They want financial abundance so they can help generously to advance the Gospel.

Givers, like servers, like to help out around the home. Retired carpenter Ed, a hard-working giver, often wished there were more he could do around the house. Everything was constantly polished and spotless, including the yard. Determined to do something, he began helping his neighbors and even swept the cul-de-sac every week.

Givers (see chart B below) are trusting, open, honest and loyal. They are also tidy and organized. "Dan's cabinet business started in our basement," Evelyn told us. "It was no problem unless one of us borrowed something and didn't put it back in the same place, or unless the kids left a mess after using his equipment. He expected us to be as neat and tidy as he is."

But givers are realists who face life squarely and practically. They do not expect others to be perfect.

C. My genuine needs, views or beliefs are:

	He	She
1. I need to be more sure of my partner's motives.	39%	20%
2. I need a mate who is dependable.	44%	33%

B. To what degree, from 1 to 7, are you one way or the other:

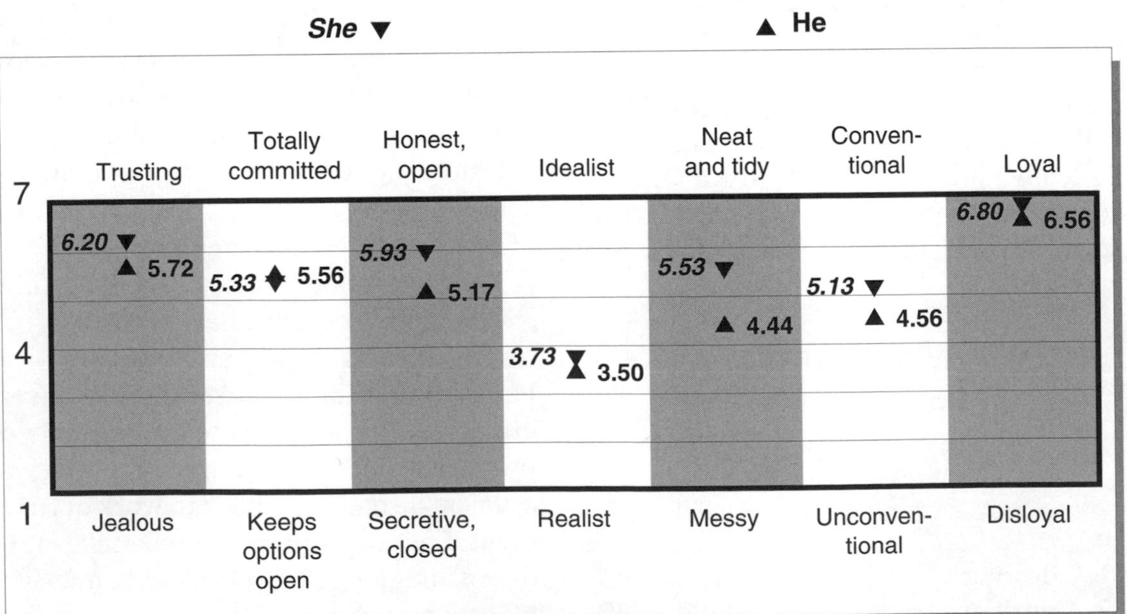

	He	She
3. I feel we need to work more at setting joint priorities.	50%	27%
4. I need to be more confident in how my mate handles stress.	39%	33%
5. I need my spouse to be totally honest with me.	28%	40%
6. I need to have former family customs a part of my life.	11%	20%
7. I feel our expectations are realistic and workable.	61%	93%

Almost all giver wives and the majority of giver husbands feel that their expectations of one another are realistic and workable. Givers are good team players, including in their marriages. Giver husbands mention the need for setting joint priorities and for their mates to be dependable, with good motives and an ability to handle stress well. The main concern of giver wives is for their mates' total honesty.

Category 3: Marital Cohesion

A. I FEEL WE HAVE SOME PROBLEMS IN GETTING ALONG WITH EACH OTHER IN THESE AREAS:

	He	She
1. Time together	67%	13%
2. Give and take	11%	13%
3. Feeling one	22%	7%
4. Closeness	33%	27%
5. Goals/priorities	17%	20%
6. Loneliness	33%	13%
7. Love/affection	50%	47%

Giver wives report few problems spending enough time together, while giver husbands report it to be a serious problem. Could it be that the wives focus more than the husbands on initiating more time together?

Both scored only half of the norm on the need for more give and take in marriage, indicating they are good at this process. Givers also do well setting goals and priorities.

Wives had few problems and husbands scored at the norm in feeling one. Both feel the need for more closeness. As Sarah says, "No matter how close Paul and I feel to each other, it seems that we even desire more."

Giver wives score much lower than the norm on loneliness, while giver husbands scored much higher. It is possible that these women tend to work more on their relationships than their male counterparts.

About half of the giver respondents feel a lack of romantic love and affection. Are they among those who work at romance in a relationship until they catch the one they love, then relax and put the romance on simmer?

Crystal complained about such a situation so much that her parents gave her and her giver husband, Steven, a weekend at Marriage Encounter. "It was the best investment my folks could have made in our marriage," she reports. "Ever since, we've both seen to it that the old spark is back in our marriage!"

Excellent scores for everything here (see chart B on page 200)! Givers have many qualities with which to build a cohesive marriage relationship. They build up and encourage their spouses, try to be agreeable and are eager to make peace when tension arises. They are regularly reliable, consistently consistent and independent without being aloof.

C. MY GENUINE NEEDS, VIEWS OR BELIEFS ARE:

	He	She
1. I need to be able to confide more in my mate.	28%	7%

B. To what degree, from 1 to 7, are you one way or the other:

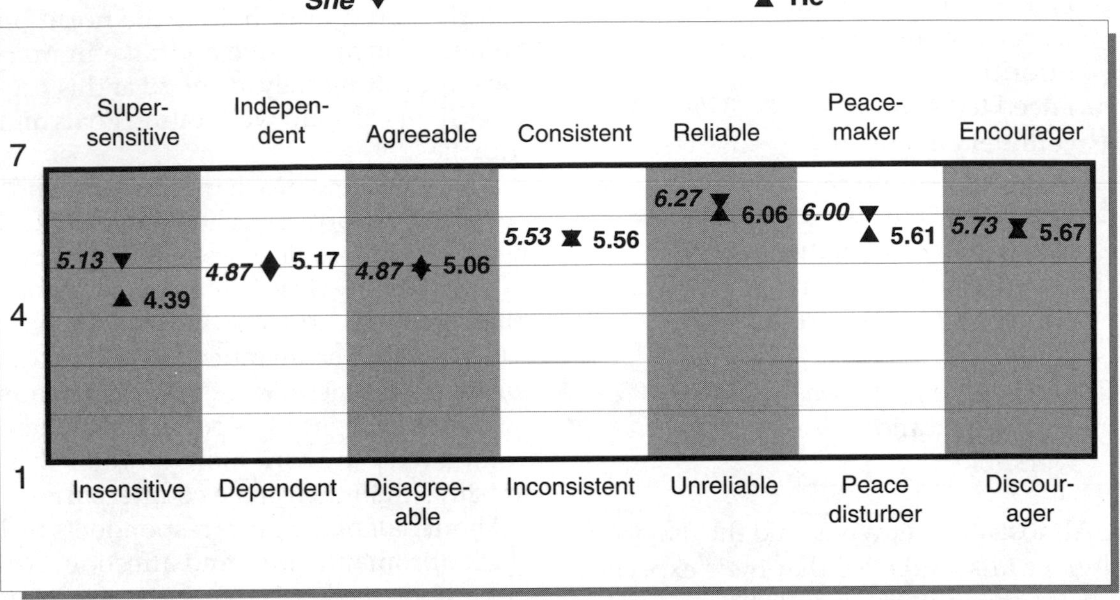

	He	She
2. I feel there needs to be more unity in our relationship.	50%	20%
3. I need to feel more secure in our marriage.	0%	7%
4. I am afraid to share some of my feelings with my partner.	44%	20%
5. I need my mate to be more sensitive to my needs.	39%	47%
6. I do not consider divorce ever to be an option.	89%	80%
7. I am satisfied with our marital interaction and closeness.	61%	67%

A good percentage are satisfied with their marital cohesion, and a vast majority do not consider divorce an option. Many would like their mates to be more sensitive to needs, and giver husbands would like more unity and opportunity to share their feelings. Giver Gary affirms, "My relationship with Barbara is wonderful, and God has helped us build a lot of love and unity. But I'd love to have even more."

Category 4: Roles and Responsibilities

A. I feel we have some problems in our marriage roles and responsibilities in these areas:

	He	She
1. Authority	50%	7%
2. Submission	0%	0%
3. Responsibilities	28%	20%
4. Decision-making	22%	20%
5. Roles	0%	0%
6. Feeling overworked	17%	20%
7. Home management	17%	27%

Few giver wives but half of the giver husbands report authority problems in their marriages. A giver wife is content to be under her husband's authority no matter what his gifting may be. Giver husbands have to work hard to fit into the head-of-household role and may yield it to a wife who is a perceiver, teacher, exhorter or administrator. Even if they do so voluntarily, they may secretly resent it.

Most givers are pleased to work together with their mates in decision-making. They are flexible and do not have a strong desire to control. Givers Bart and Virginia told us they look at decision-making somewhat as they run their business. "We weigh the pros and cons," Bart said, "and sometimes we make check-off lists to see the whole picture more clearly. We try to see what is best for both. It works for us."

Givers enjoy working. In fact, they thrive on it. Only when the workload is overwhelming do they complain.

Not only do givers do their domestic parts gladly, but often they do more than their fair share. "I don't mind at all giving my wife a hand with the housework," Ned explained. "It's a refreshing break from the kind of desk work I do on my job."

Note that giver husbands (see chart B below) are a bit on the authoritarian side and giver wives on the submissive side. Both are cooperative, straightforward and responsible and see themselves as mature. "I love working with my husband," explains Marvel, a classic giver. "It gives me such a sense of fulfilling my destiny! I know that sounds corny, but it's true."

C. My genuine needs, views or beliefs are:

	He	She
1. I need my role clarified more.	22%	13%
2. I need more freedom to discuss ideas and options.	17%	7%
3. I need to use some of my capabilities more.	17%	20%
4. I need to receive more respect from my partner.	22%	13%
5. I need more domestic help and support from my spouse.	17%	7%
6. I would like to help more in planning together.	6%	7%

B. To what degree, from 1 to 7, are you one way or the other:

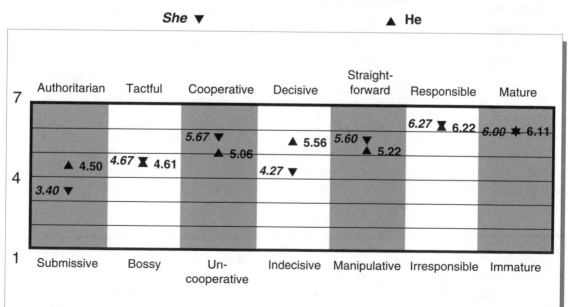

She ▼ ▲ He

7	Authoritarian	Tactful	Cooperative	Decisive	Straight-forward	Responsible	Mature
She ▼	3.40	4.67	5.67	4.27	5.60	6.27	6.00
He ▲	4.50	4.61	5.06	5.56	5.22	6.22	6.11
1	Submissive	Bossy	Un-cooperative	Indecisive	Manipulative	Irresponsible	Immature

	He	She
7. I am satisfied with the roles and responsibilities we have established.	61%	87%

High satisfaction is reported by givers in roles and responsibilities they have established. Heidi, a capable administrator who runs a productive home business, says she is delighted with her giver husband's involvement in it: "He handles the orders and all the bookwork and taxes. Those things drive me crazy. He loves it and does it so well. I wouldn't possibly be able to do all the P.R. work that I love if he weren't there to help me so much."

Category 5: Conflict Resolution

A. I FEEL WE HAVE SOME PROBLEMS IN HOW WE DEAL WITH CONFLICTS IN THESE AREAS:

	He	She
1. Anger management	56%	40%
2. Who's right	39%	20%
3. Final decisions	17%	7%
4. Silent treatment	39%	27%
5. Ultimatums	17%	13%
6. Personal attacks	33%	13%
7. Blame game	33%	27%

Scores on anger management are close to the norm. Still, anger is a problem for close to half of the respondents and must be dealt with appropriately. Stuffed or ignored anger does not go away; it has to be resolved. Givers need to learn how to express their anger verbally in ways that do not damage their mates but vent what is going on inside.

Giver husbands are more prone to defend their rightness. Giver wives are more likely to think, "Who cares? It's not worth arguing over."

Some givers use silence as a way to make a point, but they do not prefer it as a method of manipulation. Carla, a giver in her forties, says, "I used the silent treatment on Ted when we were first married. It seldom did any good. He would just ignore me, too, and the problem lingered. Soon I learned it was better to talk it out with him and pray about it. We'd find solutions."

Ultimatums, personal attacks and blame are seldom problems except with immature givers. Givers are usually willing to own up to their part of a problem.

The nature of givers to want to resolve marital conflicts is evidenced in their responses here (see chart B on page 203). They are agreeable, adaptable, apologetic and forgiving. They are not easily angered, but their feelings can easily be hurt.

C. MY GENUINE NEEDS, VIEWS OR BELIEFS ARE:

	He	She
1. I need to gain control over my temper.	22%	13%
2. I need my spouse to gain control over his or her temper.	22%	33%
3. I need to have my point of view heard more often.	28%	13%
4. I feel a strong need to avoid arguments and conflicts.	50%	40%
5. I need my mate to forgive me more quickly.	39%	13%
6. I think we need better ground rules for resolving conflicts.	11%	27%
7. I am satisfied with the way we resolve conflicts.	50%	67%

Half or more are satisfied with the way they resolve conflicts. Note the major felt

B. TO WHAT DEGREE, FROM 1 TO 7, ARE YOU ONE WAY OR THE OTHER:

She ▼ ▲ He

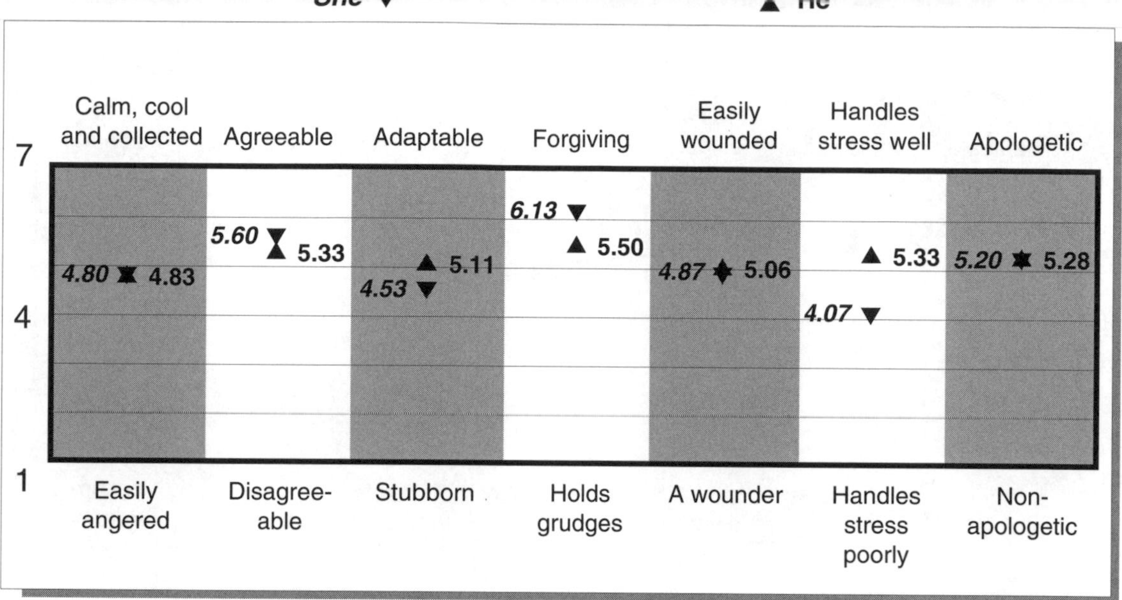

need is to avoid arguments and conflicts. Givers want to get along with their mates. They are not likely to start arguments and they are quick to try to resolve them if they develop.

Kim admits she dislikes conflict and avoids it like the plague: "When Stan and I were newlyweds, I'd give in to him on everything just to keep the peace. I still do sometimes, but I've learned to express myself more when something is important to me. I'm never pushy or argumentative. Actually, he's glad I speak up more these days."

Category 6: Personality Issues

A. I FEEL WE HAVE SOME PROBLEMS IN PERSONALITY CONFLICTS AND ISSUES IN THESE AREAS:

	He	She
1. Being right	39%	27%
2. Pride	17%	20%
3. Understanding	33%	20%
4. Change attempts	28%	13%
5. Methodologies	22%	33%
6. Habits	22%	27%
7. Forgetfulness	33%	47%

Scores on personality issues for givers are lower than the norm for all gifts. As one giver said, "Being right is not so important as being in right relationship." Giver spouses seldom try to change their mates; they accept them as they are.

Pride is not a major problem for givers because their gifting carries a certain degree of natural humility. A wife of a successful evangelist with a strong giving gift noted, "The Lord uses my husband in amazing ways. Sometimes thousands of people come to the Lord under his ministry night after night. But when people compliment him, he always gives all the glory to the Lord. He keeps a true servant attitude in his heart."

A third of giver husbands but few wives report problems in understanding. One told us that whenever she does not under-

B. To what degree, from 1 to 7, are you one way or the other:

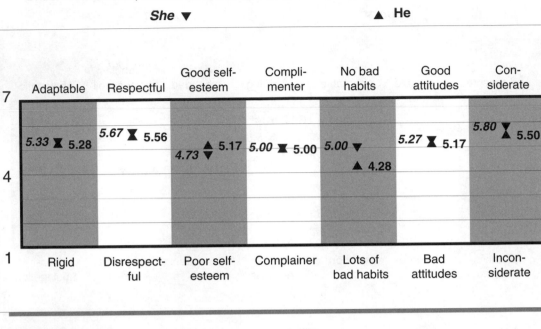

She ▼ ▲ He

	Adaptable / Rigid	Respectful / Disrespectful	Good self-esteem / Poor self-esteem	Complimenter / Complainer	No bad habits / Lots of bad habits	Good attitudes / Bad attitudes	Considerate / Inconsiderate
She ▼	5.33	5.67	4.73	5.00	5.00	5.27	5.80
He ▲	5.28	5.56	5.17	5.00	4.28	5.17	5.50

Scale: 7 (top) – 4 – 1 (bottom)

stand her husband, she prays a lot. "The Lord helps me to see why he is the way he is," she explains, "and how I can love him more."

We may consider someone else's habits bothersome simply because they are different from our own. One giver bride used to complain because her husband rinsed his hair with his head forward, while she held her head back with her face to the shower spray. After a few months of fussing at him about it, she realized, "Who cares? I shouldn't. He should be able to do it as he pleases." She repented of her pettiness and asked his forgiveness.

Good scores here (see chart B above) give evidence of well-rounded, pleasant personalities. "Attitudes are really important in a marriage relationship," one giver told us. "Whenever Ed or I display a poor attitude, the other says, 'Attitude check. One, two, three, four.' It's our signal to adjust."

Most givers do not believe they have any serious bad habits. Being considerate, respectful and adaptable, they are easy to live with. Their reasonably good self-esteem makes them compatible and complimentary.

C. My genuine needs, views or beliefs are:

	He	She
1. I wish my partner complimented me more.	50%	33%
2. I need more encouragement from my mate.	22%	27%
3. I need to be accepted and appreciated for who I am.	39%	33%
4. I need to retain my unique identity.	22%	13%
5. My partner needs to understand my gifts.	33%	20%
6. I need more admiration and respect from my partner.	28%	20%
7. We do not seem to have any personality conflicts.	50%	53%

Half report no personality conflicts. About a third would like to feel more accepted and appreciated, and giver husbands wish their partners would be more generous with compliments.

We believe that the giver, of all the gifts, has the most well-rounded personality.

Category 7: Emotional Responses

A. I FEEL WE HAVE SOME PROBLEMS IN THE WAYS WE RESPOND TO EACH OTHER EMOTIONALLY IN THESE AREAS:

	He	She
1. Hurt feelings	39%	40%
2. Carrying offenses	28%	20%
3. Unforgiveness	11%	13%
4. Insensitiveness	11%	27%
5. Feeling unloved	22%	13%
6. Moodiness	56%	13%
7. Anger	50%	40%

About forty percent of the giver respondents report some problems with hurt feelings. Because givers like to resolve relational problems, they tend to let go of offenses quickly. Like exhorters, they know everything can work together for good if they do not hold onto the negative. Peter, a classic giver, says, "I've learned that most offenses are not as bad as they seem at first. If I talk an offense over with my wife, I usually find it was not really intended."

Givers are good forgivers. They try to be sensitive to their mates. They are careful to guard their relationships and identify their mates' feelings about the relationship. Most givers say they feel secure in their marriages, not only knowing their mates' love but feeling it, too.

Giver wives have few problems with moodiness, while giver husbands have a surprisingly significant problem with it. Perhaps their intense interest in business success causes them to bring their concerns home.

Givers do not usually express anger inappropriately but tend to feel guilty about angry outbursts and try to mend the situation as quickly as possible.

Givers' general sensitivity is reflected in these high scores (see chart B below). Al-

B. TO WHAT DEGREE, FROM 1 TO 7, ARE YOU ONE WAY OR THE OTHER:

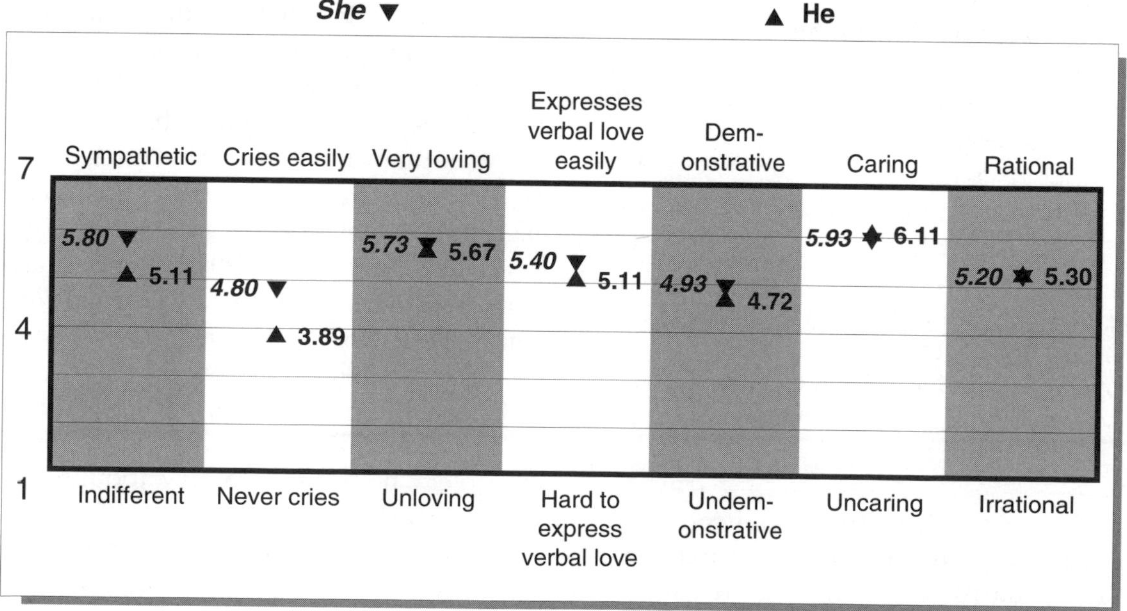

though on the rational side of the scale, they are nevertheless sympathetic, caring and demonstrative. They allow their emotions to operate well. They are not ashamed to cry, yet are not prone to do so. They see themselves as loving and able to express their love easily.

Gary is a good example of a giver capable in his own business. He is dedicated and works hard, yet will drop everything to be with his wife when she needs him. He loves to surprise her by whisking her off to lunch in a romantic café or taking her shopping when he hears there is a fifty-percent-off sale. He affirms his love to her often, even publicly, and points out her good qualities and "how wonderful she is."

C. My genuine needs, views or beliefs are:

	He	She
1. My feelings tend to rule my life.	11%	13%
2. My mate needs to understand my moods more.	33%	27%
3. I need to hear more "I love you's" from my partner.	22%	20%
4. I need to be able to express both positive and negative feelings.	44%	27%
5. I feel my spouse takes everything too personally.	33%	13%
6. I often feel put down by my partner.	28%	20%
7. I am satisfied with our emotional responses to each other.	50%	60%

Givers fall into the "balanced" category. They are not people of extremes. Emotionally they are stable and in control. Half or more are satisfied with their emotional responses. Problems in this area are not serious, and most giver spouses are working on improvements where needed.

Category 8: Intellectual Capacity

A. I feel we have some problems relating to intellectual interests and capacities in these areas:

	He	She
1. Different interests	33%	13%
2. Reading	17%	7%
3. Continuing education	28%	0%
4. Know-it-all attitude	17%	13%
5. Correcting grammar	28%	7%
6. Children's education	11%	7%
7. Being accurate	17%	13%

Only a few giver wives but a third of giver husbands identify different intellectual interests and capacities as a problem. Academics are not of major interest to givers, although they tend to do reasonably well in school.

Givers enjoy a wide variety of reading material, especially adventure fiction. A giver married to a teacher or administrator gift who prefers nonfiction may not read the same books, but abide happily by a read-and-let-read philosophy.

While many have chosen business school or on-the-job training in preference to college, some want to go back to school or get specialized training to further their business careers. Givers are not usually plagued with know-it-all attitudes, but in the area of business they are likely to know the most.

Correction of grammar and the education of their children are not major issues for givers, nor do they worry about being accurate or factual.

These scores (see chart B on page 207) show giver balance. They tend to score in

D. To what degree, from 1 to 7, are you one way or the other:

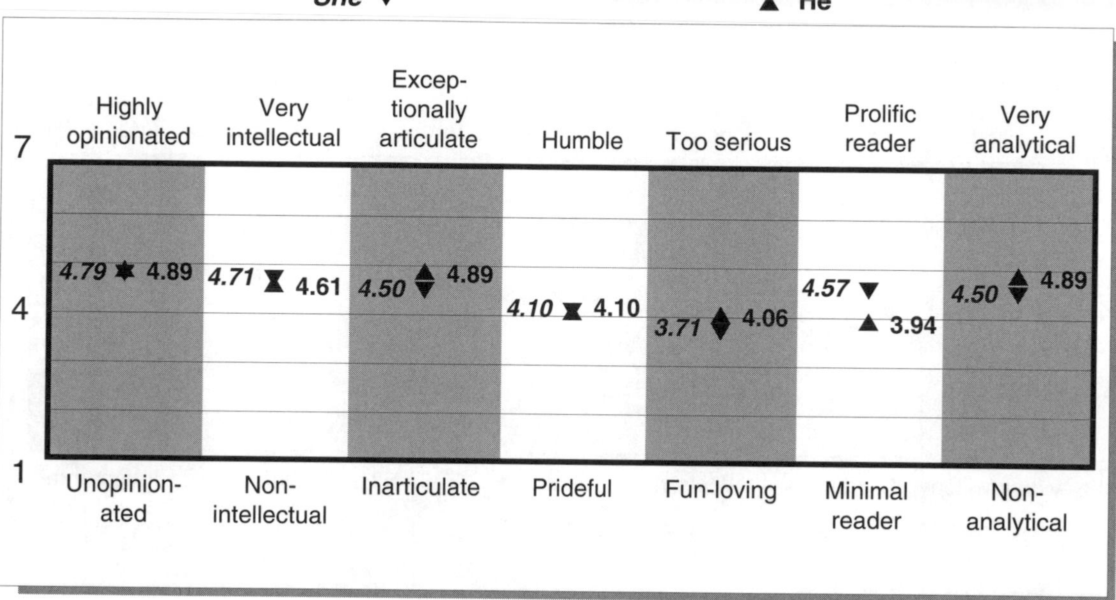

the middle on almost everything except in areas of business, evangelism and intercessory prayer.

C. My genuine needs, views or beliefs are:

	He	She
1. I need adequate time for reading or study.	50%	40%
2. I am easily sidetracked by new interests.	11%	13%
3. I need to question things before I can accept them.	67%	40%
4. I need my mate to listen to my opinions more.	39%	13%
5. I realize I need to be less dogmatic.	11%	13%
6. I find I constantly analyze what my partner says and does.	33%	13%
7. I am satisfied with how we handle intellectual matters.	56%	67%

More than half of the givers are satisfied with how they and their mates handle intellectual matters. They need adequate time for reading or study and the freedom to question things before they accept them. John and Beth are givers who run their own business together. "We feel we are kind of like the Berean Christians who searched the Scriptures to be sure what Paul told them was so," John says. "We are always checking something out, whether it has to do with our business, our church or our personal faith. It's not that we don't believe people; we just want to be sure of something before we accept it."

Category 9: Volitional Issues

A. I feel we have some problems in the use of the will in these areas:

	He	She
1. Decisions and choices	33%	13%
2. Practical decisions	11%	7%
3. Stubbornness	50%	47%

B. To what degree, from 1 to 7, are you one way or the other:

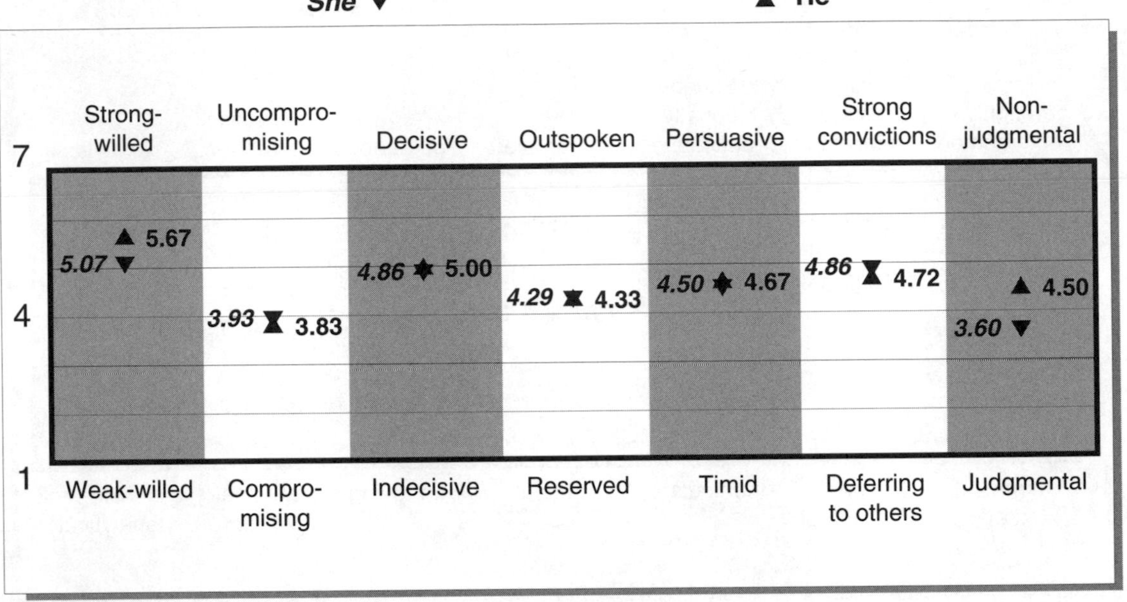

	He	She
4. Agreements	17%	13%
5. Right actions	0%	0%
6. Judgmentalism	33%	27%
7. Rebelliousness	28%	20%

Few wives but a third of giver husbands indicate problems with marital decisions and choices. The giver has a fairly strong will. While wives try to be adaptable, husbands are more likely to want their own way. They like being involved in the decision-making process and work toward decisions that are practical and workable. Those married to speaking gifts find more competition for that role.

Stubbornness is the big problem. When givers think they are right, they dig in their heels and hold out for their position. "When Belinda gets stubborn about something, I get even more so," Glenn admits. "It's a constant challenge in our relationship." Even with their stubborn streak, however, giver spouses want to work out their problems as quickly as possible. They tend to try to negotiate until agreement can be reached.

Most givers are not judgmental and may get after themselves when they fall into that mode. Neither are they normally rebellious. They try to get along with their mates. Those who do become rebellious will probably feel guilty about it and try to change.

Most answers (see chart B above) are in the average range, except that givers tend to be strong-willed and decisive with strong convictions. These characteristics enable them to do well in the business world, where they shine. For those called to full-time ministry, especially in the field of evangelism, these traits are essential to strong faith and action.

Our evangelist friend Rod felt God called him to hold crusades throughout the Philippines, and he did so for seven years. As he became convinced through much prayer that he was to hold a crusade in a certain part of the country, he set his course of action to do it, no matter what the dangers or difficulties, and was tremendously successful.

C. My genuine needs, views or beliefs are:

	He	She
1. I have a definite inner need to be right.	33%	33%
2. I have a strong need to be a decision-maker.	0%	7%
3. I need my mate to make most of the decisions.	17%	13%
4. I will do what is right even if it hurts.	72%	47%
5. I need to operate by definite principles.	61%	40%
6. I need my mate to be more tolerant of my opinions.	28%	20%
7. I am satisfied with how we make decisions.	67%	73%

Two-thirds or more of the giver respondents are satisfied with how they and their mates make decisions. As one told us, "We work at it till it works!"

Givers make decisions based on principles, especially biblical ones. "The Bible teaches us to honor those in authority," Rod told us. "So when I am led to do a crusade in a town, the first thing I do is go see the mayor. I explain what I'd like to do, encourage his involvement and invite him to sit on stage and bring greetings to the people. I get great cooperation this way."

Givers not only want to be right; they will do what is right even when it hurts. Warren gets kidded in his used car business, but he is known throughout his town for his integrity. "Sometimes a car I sell turns out to have something wrong with it I did not know about," he says. "But if the customer brings it back, I'll make it right, even if I lose money on it."

Category 10: Physical Conditions

A. I feel we have some problems in the physical realm in these areas:

	He	She
1. Being fit	50%	33%
2. Enough exercise	61%	53%

B. To what degree, from 1 to 7, are you one way or the other:

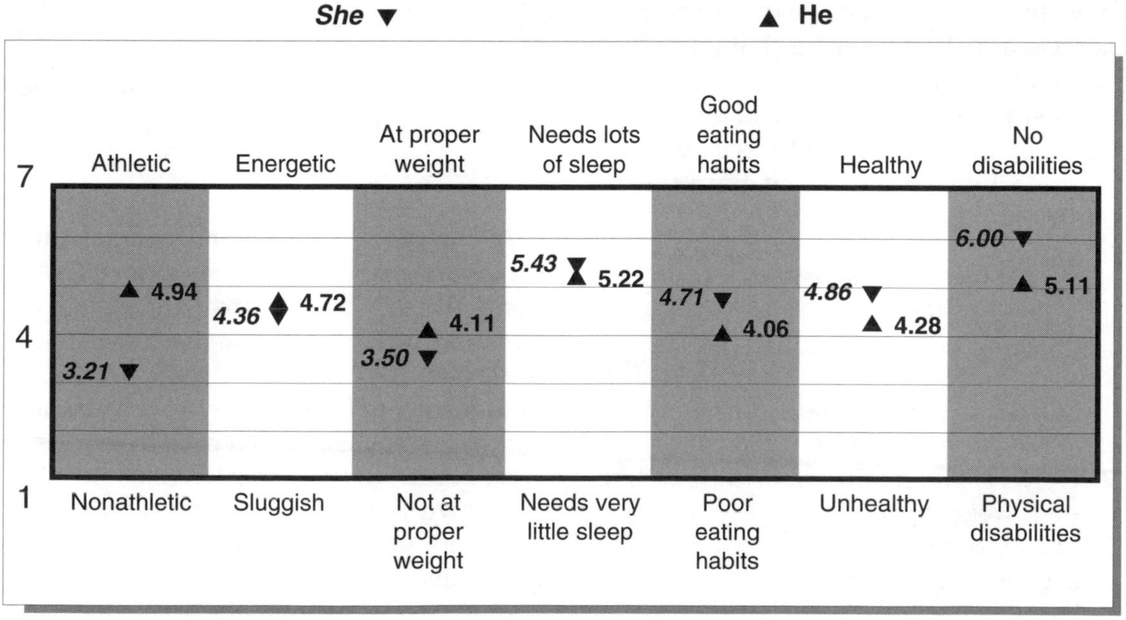

	He	She
3. Fatigue	28%	47%
4. Overeating	33%	33%
5. Proper eating	67%	40%
6. Keeping attractive	28%	20%
7. Adequate sleep	67%	40%

In general givers have more problems than the norm with their physical condition. Fatigue, adequate sleep, keeping fit and getting enough exercise are major concerns. Many put in long hours in sedentary work and do not find time to get adequate physical exercise. Joining a health club would help, but givers will likely do better with workouts at home or walks.

When Joe realized his physical fitness was in jeopardy, he took two steps of action. First he decided to walk to work instead of driving; then he bought some basic home exercise equipment. "Adding four miles of walking and a twenty-minute workout every day has helped me get back in shape," he testified proudly.

Giver husbands (see chart B on page 209) are moderately athletic, but wives admit they are on the nonathletic side. Energy levels tend to be only slightly above the mean, but can be improved with exercise and better eating habits, which givers admit they need.

The survey shows they need more sleep than average—a problem that can be compounded by overwork and burning the candle at both ends.

C. My genuine needs, views or beliefs are:

	He	She
1. I desire to see my mate at the proper weight.	61%	20%
2. I need to overcome my own weight problem.	44%	47%
3. I need to get adequate exercise on a regular basis.	67%	73%
4. I would like to see my spouse get more exercise.	50%	33%
5. I need my mate to be as attractive as possible.	39%	33%
6. I need to improve my eating habits.	61%	47%
7. I am satisfied with how we keep fit, healthy and attractive.	22%	27%

Only a quarter of the giver respondents are satisfied with their fitness. Weight problems are an ongoing concern for themselves and their spouses, as well as the need to improve eating habits. The need for exercise is also of paramount importance. Givers will do better at a specific improvement program if their spouses make the commitment with them.

Category 11: Sexual Relationship

A. I feel we have some problems in our sexual relationship in these areas:

	He	She
1. Frequency	61%	40%
2. Quality	33%	13%
3. Prior affection	50%	33%
4. Nonsexual affection	56%	33%
5. Sexual dissatisfaction	33%	7%
6. Incompatibility	11%	0%
7. Infidelity	0%	0%

In comparison with the norm for all gifts, the givers' responses here show an unusual trend. In every case the answers of the giver wives are much lower than the norm, while the giver husbands' answers are much higher (except for infidelity, to which there was no response). With regard to sex, giver wives seem to live their lives (as in other areas) with greater peace and satisfaction.

Givers view (see chart B on page 211) themselves as able to verbalize love well, communicate adequately about sex and

B. TO WHAT DEGREE, FROM 1 TO 7, ARE YOU ONE WAY OR THE OTHER:

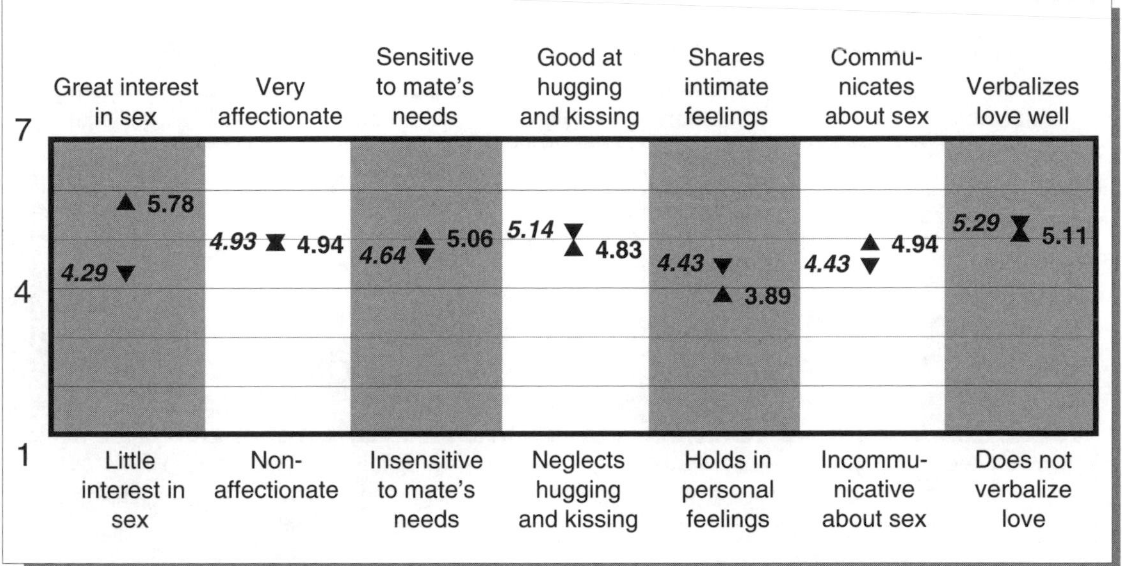

show sufficient affection. Giver wives are a bit better at hugging and kissing and sharing intimate feelings. Giver husbands hold in some of their personal feelings, which may explain in part their greater sexual dissatisfaction. The fact that both see themselves as sensitive to their mates' needs gives a foundation for building a better sexual relationship.

C. MY GENUINE NEEDS, VIEWS OR BELIEFS ARE:

	He	She
1. I need more nonsexual affection from my mate.	39%	40%
2. I need more sexual relations with my mate.	72%	27%
3. I feel I need more hugs and kisses from my spouse.	50%	33%
4. I need to hear more "I love you's" from my partner.	17%	20%
5. I need my husband to better understand my monthly cycle.	0%	7%
6. I feel dissatisfied with our current sexual relationship.	33%	13%
7. I feel satisfied with our current sexual relationship.	56%	47%

In spite of previous negative answers, more than half of the giver husbands express satisfaction with their current marital sexual relationship. But almost three-fourths feel the need for more sexual relations with their mates. Both husbands and wives would welcome more nonsexual affection and hugs and kisses. About half of the giver wives affirm sexual satisfaction.

Category 12: Work and Accomplishments

A. I FEEL WE HAVE SOME PROBLEMS ABOUT WORK AND ACCOMPLISHMENTS IN THESE AREAS:

	He	She
1. Too busy	56%	20%

B. To what degree, from 1 to 7, are you one way or the other:

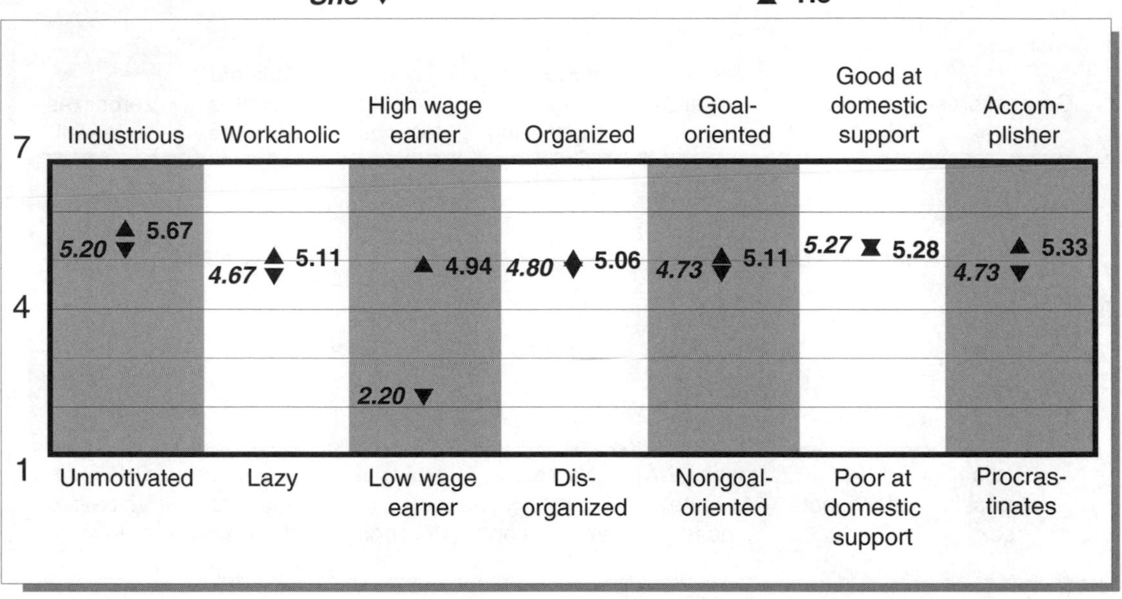

	He	She
2. Career conflicts	22%	0%
3. Overtime work	6%	7%
4. Inadequate income	6%	13%
5. Volunteer work	17%	13%
6. Wife working	6%	7%
7. Priorities	6%	20%

Only twenty percent of giver wives see busyness as a problem. They take time to smell the roses. But 56 percent of giver husbands feel they are too busy. They are more prone to be married to their jobs or neglect family time in preference to business.

JoAnne finally put her foot down. Jeff was becoming an absentee husband and father, using his giver giftedness to build a successful business. "I asked him to hire some part-time help so he could spend more time with us," she said. "I reminded him we could never recapture lost years with our children, and that all of us wanted more time with him, not more money. I'm thankful he listened! He got his priorities back in order."

Inadequate income is seldom a problem for givers since they have strong business abilities and a tendency toward success, which usually translates into more than sufficient income.

Givers (see chart B above) are known for their industriousness. They are reasonably organized, good at goal-setting and great accomplishers. Husbands are more likely to bring in a good income, whether working for themselves or for someone else, and more likely to become workaholics. Wives' scores are much lower on wage-earning, probably because many are content to work part-time or be full-time homemakers. A career-oriented giver wife can command as good an income as her male counterpart. Many are creative entrepreneurs who have started successful home businesses.

C. My genuine needs, views or beliefs are:

	He	She
1. I need my husband to provide our basic expenses.	6%	27%

	He	She
2. I need my wife to be a full-time homemaker.	22%	7%
3. I need to be the sole provider for my family.	22%	0%
4. I need a fulfilling career.	44%	7%
5. I need a challenge to work toward.	50%	20%
6. I get great joy out of my accomplishments.	67%	60%
7. I am satisfied with the way we handle work and accomplishments.	61%	67%

Sixty percent or more of all givers are satisfied with the way they handle work and are happy with their accomplishments. Giver husbands also feel the need for fulfilling careers and enjoy a challenge. Many giver wives do not need fulfilling careers other than that of homemaker. But some do pursue careers, especially after the children are raised.

Glenda, a gifted giver with her own fashion boutique, admits, "I really love running this store and I wouldn't mind opening some others. I know I could do it. But the cost in terms of my time is too much. I still count homemaking as my primary career. Bryan loves to come home to an orderly house and loving wife. I'm there for him when he walks in the door and always will be."

Category 13: Financial Management

A. I FEEL WE HAVE SOME PROBLEMS IN FINANCIAL MATTERS IN THESE AREAS:

	He	She
1. Establishing budget	33%	27%
2. Keeping to budget	22%	20%
3. Living beyond means	22%	20%
4. Credit cards	22%	27%
5. Impulsive buying	22%	20%
6. Money arguments	33%	13%
7. Wife's work role	0%	7%

Giver respondents report fewer than half the problems of other gifts in establishing and keeping a workable budget. They are excellent at handling finances. While they love earning money, they are careful in how they spend it. In fact, most are considered frugal but generous in helping others financially.

Pastor Paul reports, "After I discovered three giver men in our congregation who were excellent in financial skills, I asked them to develop a special ministry to couples in our congregation struggling with financial inability. I assigned each of the givers to such a couple, and he helped them set up a realistic budget and taught them how to live within it. Lives were brought into order, financial responsibility was developed and marriages were literally saved through the ministry of these men."

Givers do not usually live beyond their means, abuse credit cards or fall prey to impulse buying; but their spouses can. This can be the source of money arguments or conflicts.

Not only do givers (see chart B on page 214) keep within the budget, but they are conservative buyers, often bargain-hunters. Bonnie, a seasoned giver with much shopping experience, explained, "I often shop the leader items of the four grocery stores in my neighborhood. It takes a little more time, but with that and the coupons I use, I save about thirty percent on groceries each week. I'm able to use the savings on special missions projects I love to support. My husband thinks it's great."

Givers are good at saving money, feel secure financially and are generous, but like to be anonymous.

Curtis, who owns his own business, claims ardently, "You can't outgive God! Every time I give more to help others or support missionary work, the Lord sends more business. I ask Him where the new

B. To what degree, from 1 to 7, are you one way or the other:

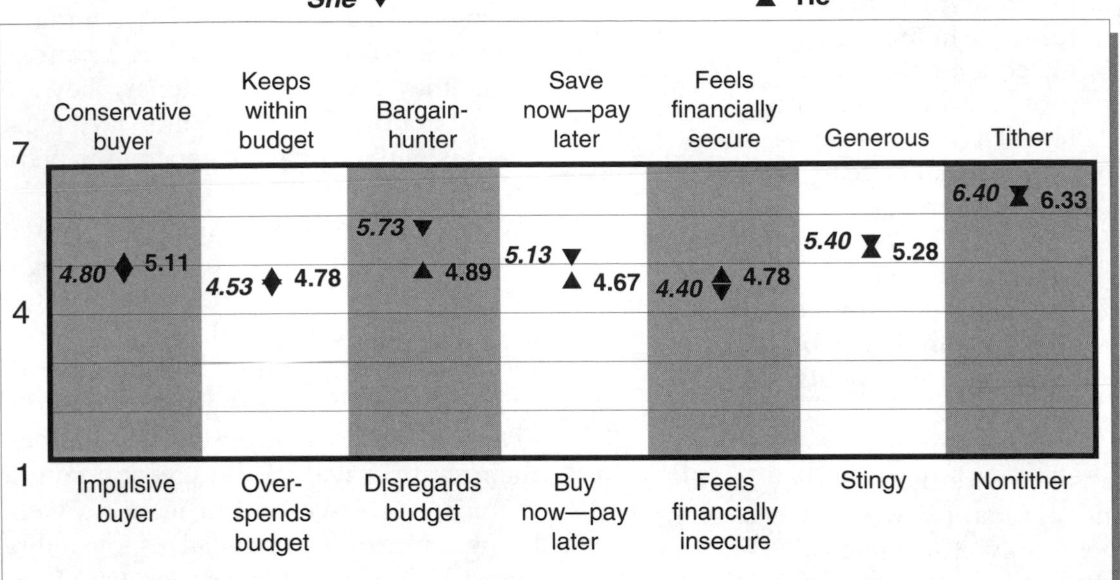

profit should go. I simply see myself as God's errand boy."

One time Curtis noticed a little girl in the congregation who desperately needed braces on her teeth. But her mother was a widow and there was no money for that. Curtis went to the local orthodontist, gave him three thousand dollars and told him to put braces on the little girl's teeth. "If the mother asks who gave the money," he told the orthodontist, "just tell her, 'The Lord has provided.' And if there are additional costs, I will pay them."

Givers are committed tithers. They often give far beyond the tithe as well. As one giver put it, "Tithing is simply not robbing God. The first tenth is His. I don't feel I'm really giving until I go beyond that."

C. My genuine needs, views or beliefs are:

	He	She
1. I feel we need to reduce our debts more effectively.	44%	33%
2. I feel the need to be in charge of our family finances.	17%	13%
3. I believe the husband should handle the family finances.	6%	7%
4. I think the most capable partner should handle the family finances.	61%	80%
5. I need to learn how to handle money more responsibly.	17%	7%
6. I would like to give more to church, missionaries, charity, etc.	28%	87%
7. I am satisfied with how we handle finances.	72%	53%

About half of giver wives and three-fourths of giver husbands are content with how finances are handled. Some still see a need for debt reduction, and more wives than husbands agree that the more capable partner should handle the family finances.

A major desire for giver wives is giving more. The significantly lower score for giver husbands is probably because they are more likely in charge and are already giving generously.

A giver wife may feel thwarted by a husband who does not share her love for giving. Marion says, "My husband and I have several missionary friends I want to help support. He feels all we can afford is our tithe. This was a stress point in our marriage until we worked out a new plan. He has agreed that any money I make on my own, I can give as I like. I work four hours a day now and give half of what I earn to support our friends."

Category 14: Leisure Activities

A. I FEEL WE HAVE SOME PROBLEMS IN HOW WE SPEND OUR FREE TIME IN THESE AREAS:

	He	She
1. Interests	22%	13%
2. Recreational preferences	11%	7%
3. Hobbies	17%	7%
4. Entertainment	33%	13%
5. Vacation preferences	6%	7%
6. Sports	33%	7%
7. TV-watching	44%	53%

Most givers adapt well to their mates' interests, the women even more than the men. Two problem areas identified by some giver husbands are different preferences in entertainment and sports.

Like all other gifts, givers identify too much television-watching as a major concern. Even those who complain about it tend to fall into the habit. Last year our church called a TV fast for a month. Many said it helped them see how much time they wasted on TV. They were delighted to discover how many other leisure activities they could enjoy together.

Giver husbands (see chart B below) are more athletic than their female counterparts, but both like walking. Not only is that good for their health, but it promotes togetherness and conversation.

B. TO WHAT DEGREE, FROM 1 TO 7, ARE YOU ONE WAY OR THE OTHER:

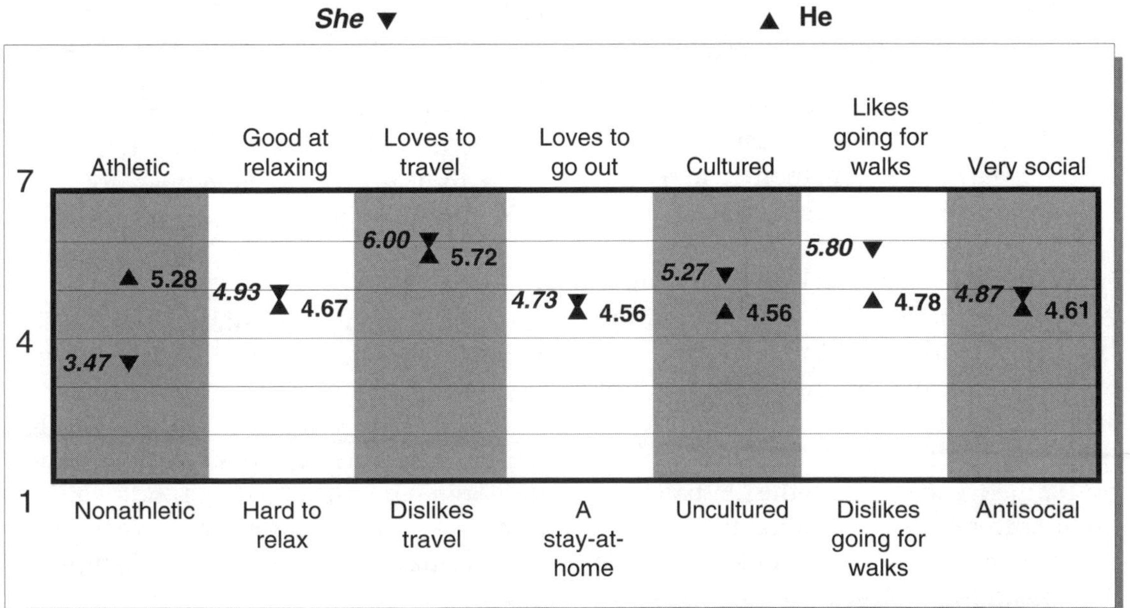

Givers especially love to travel. We believe it is because God calls people most often from this gifting to be evangelists and missionaries. So He gives these folks a love for travel, seeing other countries and getting to know other cultures in their hearts. Even if givers are not called to the mission field, they often take interest in and support those who are.

C. My genuine needs, views or beliefs are:

	He	She
1. I need my partner to be a recreational companion.	39%	33%
2. I need to do more fun things with my spouse.	67%	40%
3. I need more meaningful vacations.	28%	0%
4. I need to be involved in nonathletic leisure activities.	17%	27%
5. I prefer active group or competitive sports.	17%	20%
6. I prefer individual noncompetitive sports.	17%	40%
7. I am satisfied with how we spend our leisure time.	44%	47%

Almost half are satisfied with how they spend their leisure time, while many would like their partners to join them in more fun things and recreational activities.

Sherrie was frustrated with her husband's lack of interest in doing fun things with her, so she decided to do something about it. "First I bought us season tickets for the football season, then tickets for our local theater, and I signed us up to learn square-dancing. At first he mumbled and complained, except about the football tickets. But after getting involved in the other activities, he found out he enjoyed it. We plan ahead for each season now."

Category 15: Parenting

A. I feel we have (had) some problems in the child-rearing process in these areas:

	He	She
1. Type of discipline	28%	40%
2. Amount of discipline	17%	7%
3. Who disciplines	11%	13%
4. Misconduct determination	33%	20%
5. Love expression	28%	13%
6. Time spent	61%	20%
7. Money given	22%	13%

Differences over the kind of discipline are typical, but givers have fewer differences over the amount or who does it. Giver men score higher than the norm on misconduct determination, the way love is expressed and the amounts of time and money spent on the children. Giver wives tend to be more content in these areas.

A particular danger for giver parents (like Ben at the beginning of this chapter) is giving their children too much. Since giving is a natural joy to them, they are not always aware that they are spoiling their kids. It is wise for givers to ask their spouses to alert them when this begins to happen.

Giver fathers (see chart B on page 217) report more negative scores here than giver mothers. Permissiveness, too little time involvement, spoiling and inconsistent discipline are areas that may need attention.

Giver mothers score high in much affectionate touching and spending lots of time with their children—the two things researchers have said children most often feel expresses love. "That's why I hug my kids lots each day," giver Linda said. "I know how important it is to have my love communicated to them in body language, not just in words."

B. To what degree, from 1 to 7, are you one way or the other:

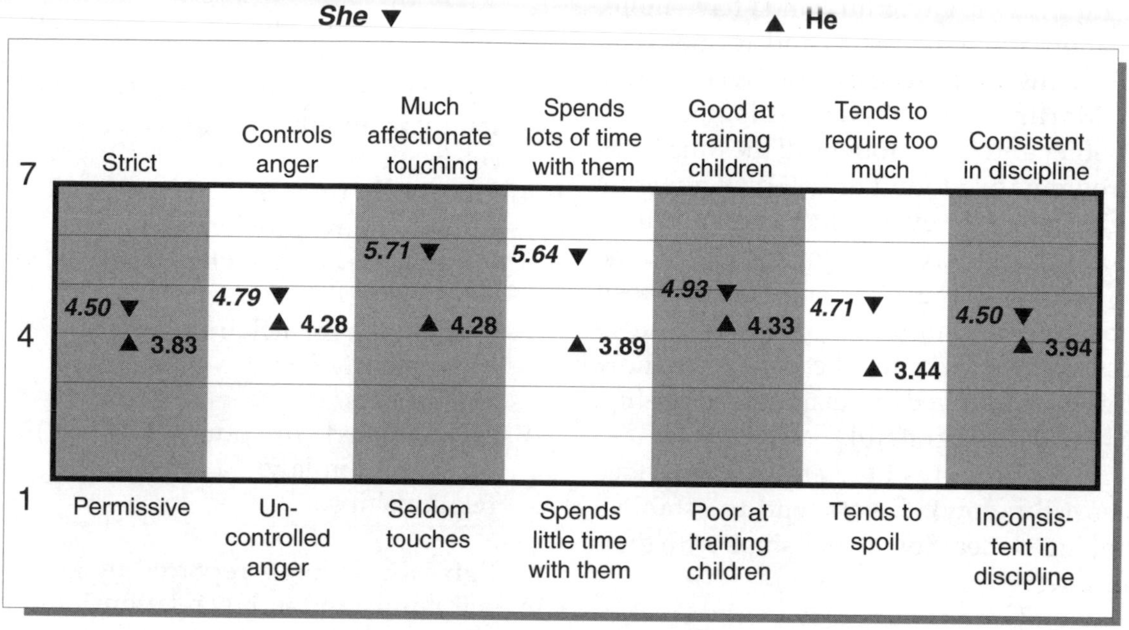

She ▼ ▲ He

7	Strict	Controls anger	Much affectionate touching	Spends lots of time with them	Good at training children	Tends to require too much	Consistent in discipline
She ▼	4.50	4.79	5.71	5.64	4.93	4.71	4.50
He ▲	3.83	4.28	4.28	3.89	4.33	3.44	3.94
1	Permissive	Uncontrolled anger	Seldom touches	Spends little time with them	Poor at training children	Tends to spoil	Inconsistent in discipline

C. My genuine needs, views or beliefs are:

	He	She
1. We need to provide better spiritual guidance for our children.	44%	40%
2. We need to give our children more love and affection.	56%	20%
3. I would like my spouse to help more with the children.	6%	0%
4. I need to be more affirming of our children.	44%	20%
5. I feel we need to agree more on discipline.	11%	20%
6. I feel we need more quality family time and activities.	61%	27%
7. I am satisfied with our parenting styles and skills.	28%	40%

Giver fathers are aware they need to spend more time with their children and give them more love, affection and affirmation. Giver mothers score lower since they already fulfill these important parental responsibilities.

Both recognize the need to provide better spiritual guidance. Givers tend to pray regularly for their children, but Christ-centered devotions, family times and instruction in faith will help shape the children's spiritual lives more adequately.

Category 16: In-Laws and Family

A. I feel we have some problems with our families and in-laws in these areas:

	He	She
1. Interference	17%	7%
2. Their expectations	11%	7%
3. Their visits	11%	0%
4. Comparisons	22%	0%
5. Borrowing money	17%	7%
6. Former abuse	11%	7%
7. Dysfunction affect	44%	13%

Giver wives report few or no problems with in-laws. Giver husbands have more, namely in comparisons and former dysfunctions that affect the marital relationship.

Martin, a quiet giver, explained, "My mother and father fought all the time I was growing up. I found myself picking fights with my wife even when she had done nothing wrong. Our pastor encouraged me to get counseling in this area, and I've been able to work through the forgiveness necessary to set me free. I can't believe how this has improved our marital relationship. My wife is so grateful."

Overall scores here are excellent (see chart B below). Givers tend to establish balanced, healthy relationships with their in-laws.

C. My genuine needs, views or beliefs are:

	He	She
1. I need my spouse to put me before his or her family.	44%	13%
2. I need to see or talk to my parent(s) regularly.	6%	20%
3. I need to include my family in holiday celebrations.	39%	33%
4. I need help in overcoming in-law problems.	6%	0%
5. I need to be accepted by my in-laws.	11%	7%
6. I need to be financially free from my family and in-laws.	39%	7%
7. I am satisfied with our family and in-law relationships.	67%	73%

High satisfaction is reported by givers in their family and in-law relationships.

Category 17: Social Relationships

A. I feel we have some problems in social relationships in these areas:

	He	She
1. Friends' demands	11%	7%

B. To what degree, from 1 to 7, are you one way or the other:

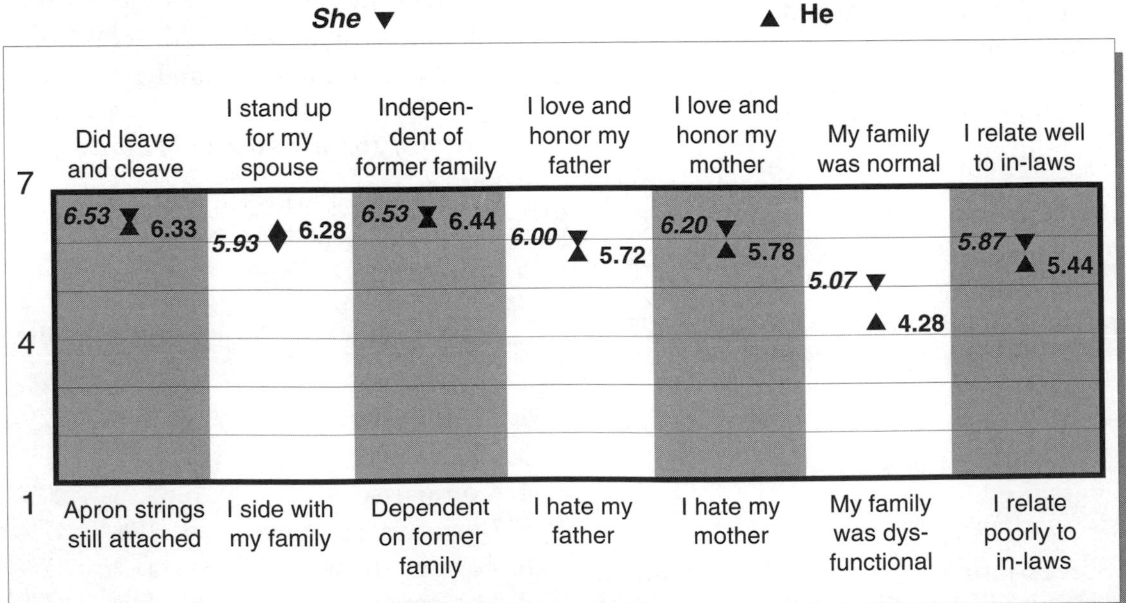

B. To what degree, from 1 to 7, are you one way or the other:

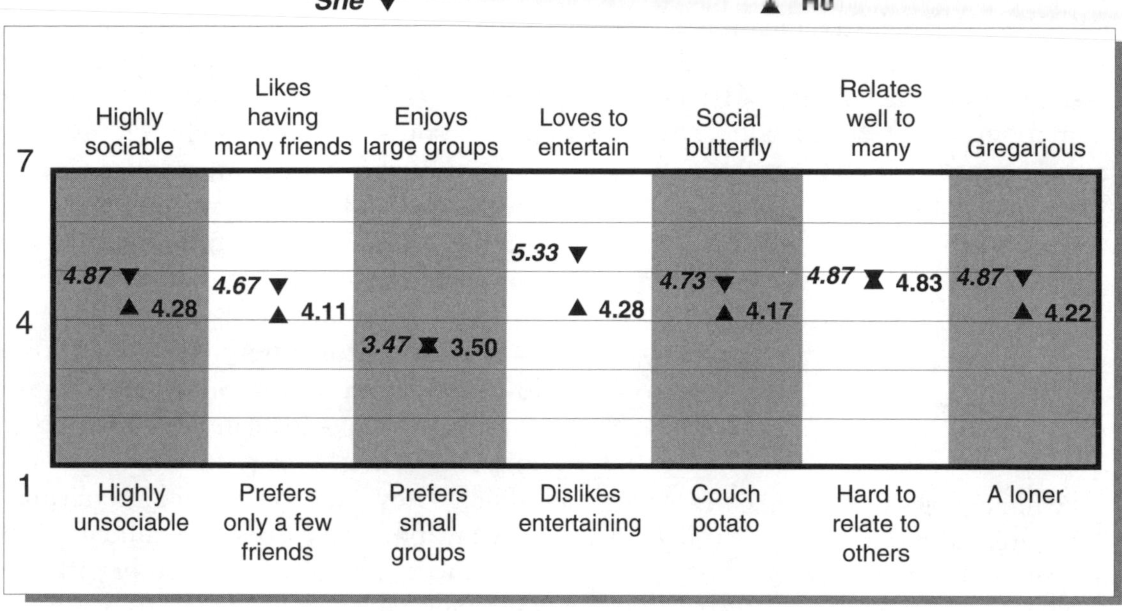

	He	She
2. Time for friends	56%	33%
3. Unsocial partner	17%	0%
4. Too social partner	6%	13%
5. Wrong friendships	0%	0%
6. Negative influence	0%	0%
7. Overinvolvement	0%	0%

In most cases givers' problems with social relationships are fewer than the norm, with the exception of the concern of giver husbands for having enough time for friends. Leon discovered that the only way to have enough time was to eliminate some of his overtime work. "Betty and I agreed this was important for me to do," he says, "in order to maintain the friendships we already have. It has been worth it."

Givers (see chart B above) are average socially. They prefer small groups to large ones or getting together with just one other couple or family at a time.

Marianne admits she likes to entertain friends at home. "But I prefer to have just a couple or two at a time," she explains. "I've always felt a bit overwhelmed with big groups. I tend to clam up in them. When there are just a few, I am able to interact with them comfortably."

C. My genuine needs, views or beliefs are:

	He	She
1. I need to have many friends.	6%	20%
2. I especially love to entertain in our home.	44%	47%
3. I need a good deal of private time.	22%	27%
4. I need our home to be a haven of rest.	56%	27%
5. I need to be involved in social groups.	6%	7%
6. I think we need to change some friendships.	0%	0%
7. I am satisfied with our social life.	78%	73%

Three-fourths of the giver respondents are satisfied with their social lives. Entertaining at home is an activity that enables their giver characteristics to go into action. Half of the giver men also mention the need to have home a place of retreat and rest.

Givers do not need a lot of friends but want to maintain the friendships they have. They are loyal to them and will stick by them no matter what.

Category 18: Religious Orientation

A. I FEEL WE HAVE SOME PROBLEMS IN OUR SPIRITUAL LIFE AND ORIENTATION IN THESE AREAS:

	He	She
1. Affiliation disagreement	0%	0%
2. Church attendance	0%	0%
3. Different backgrounds	11%	0%
4. Theological differences	11%	0%
5. Commitment level	22%	20%
6. Irregular attendance	0%	0%
7. Hypocritical behavior	11%	7%

Givers tend to have faith that runs quiet and deep. They live their faith and feel free to share it. They tend to get along spiritually with their mates, even despite some different beliefs. They are usually drawn to intercessory prayer, especially praying for the needs of others and for the salvation of souls. They enjoy church involvement and are faithful in attendance. As one giver says, "If the church doors are open, I'm there. Not because I feel I ought to be, but because I love being there with God's people."

Excellent scores here (see chart B below)! Faith and commitment are strong in givers. They love to be involved in prayer ministry, evangelism, witnessing and missions. They not only give generously to support the work of the ministry but like (more than any of the other gifts) to take their vacation time to go in person to assist evangelists or missionaries. They also like to help young people gain experience in these areas. It is not unusual for a giver to mentor someone, even paying that person's way through Bible school.

B. TO WHAT DEGREE, FROM 1 TO 7, ARE YOU ONE WAY OR THE OTHER:

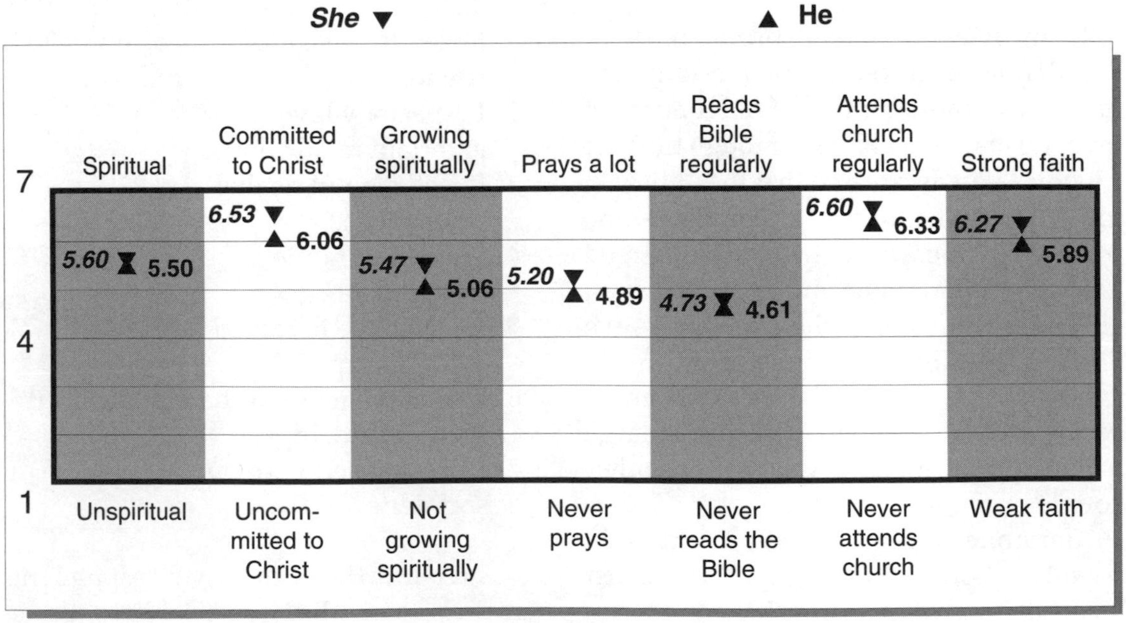

C. My genuine needs, views or beliefs are:

	He	She
1. I need to attend church regularly.	78%	73%
2. I need my partner to pray with me daily.	44%	47%
3. I greatly desire to see my spouse grow spiritually.	67%	73%
4. I believe we need to have regular family devotions.	56%	80%
5. I need my spouse to give spiritual leadership.	11%	73%
6. I need to be able to live my faith, not just talk about it.	67%	73%
7. I am satisfied with our religious orientation and practice.	61%	53%

Scores here are positive and high, except the response of giver husbands on needing their wives to give spiritual leadership. Naturally they want to do it themselves.

I have already said that I have observed these characteristics at work in and through Don. With his strong secondary gift of giving, he walks his talk, sees that we are in church regularly, leads our church's mission program and prods me on, when I need it, to spiritual growth.

Category 19: Maturity

A. I feel we have some problems in maturity in these areas:

	He	She
1. Inexperience	0%	0%
2. Irresponsibility	0%	0%
3. Blame game	6%	7%
4. Stress coping	33%	27%
5. Criticism	6%	13%
6. Infidelity	0%	0%
7. Dishonesty	0%	0%

Givers tend to mature well. They take life and responsibility seriously. They try

B. To what degree, from 1 to 7, are you one way or the other:

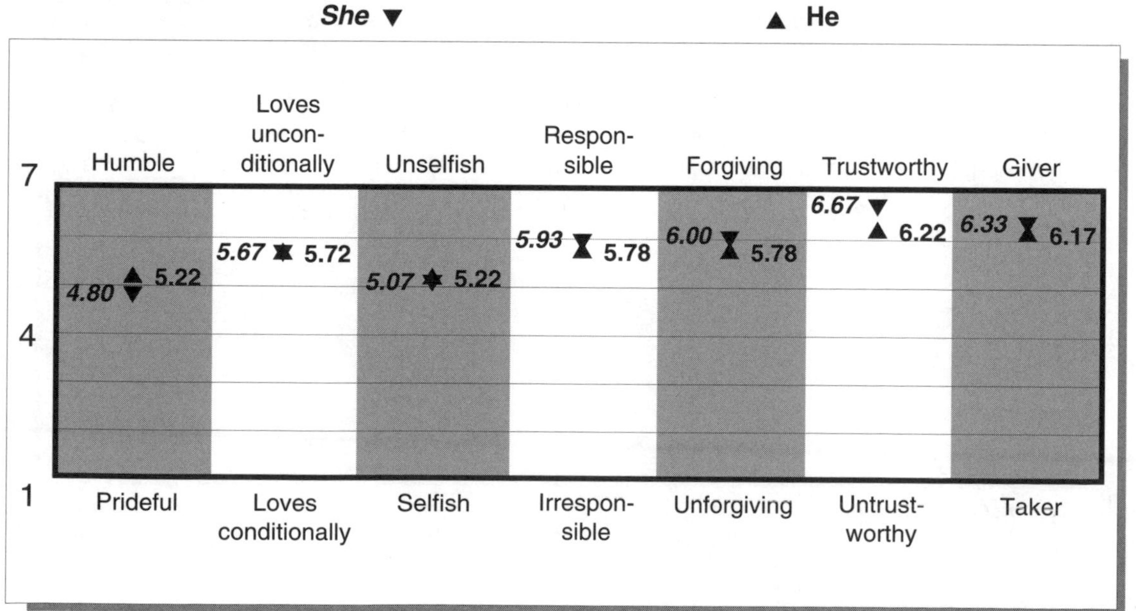

hard to get along with and are generally accepting of their partners. Coping with life's stresses is the biggest concern here, and they usually do better than most.

Once again, excellent scores (see chart B on page 221). No wonder givers make wonderful mates!

C. My genuine needs, views or beliefs are:

	He	She
1. I need to be able to trust my mate.	50%	67%
2. I need my spouse to be dependable.	50%	60%
3. I need to be quick to forgive and, hopefully, be forgiving quickly.	67%	87%
4. We need to learn from and grow through every experience.	61%	67%
5. I need my mate to be able to handle responsibility well.	50%	40%
6. I need my mate to love me unconditionally.	50%	73%
7. I feel that we are a reasonably mature couple.	89%	93%

Not only do givers see themselves as reasonably mature, but they *are*. They also expect their mates to develop and exhibit the same positive qualities.

Category 20: Dysfunctionality

A. I feel we have some problems in the following areas that produce dysfunction:

	He	She
1. Alcohol abuse	0%	0%
2. Drug abuse	0%	0%
3. Physical abuse	0%	0%
4. Sexual abuse	0%	0%
5. Verbal abuse	17%	13%
6. Emotional abuse	17%	13%
7. Unresolved abuse	6%	7%

B. To what degree, from 1 to 7, are you one way or the other:

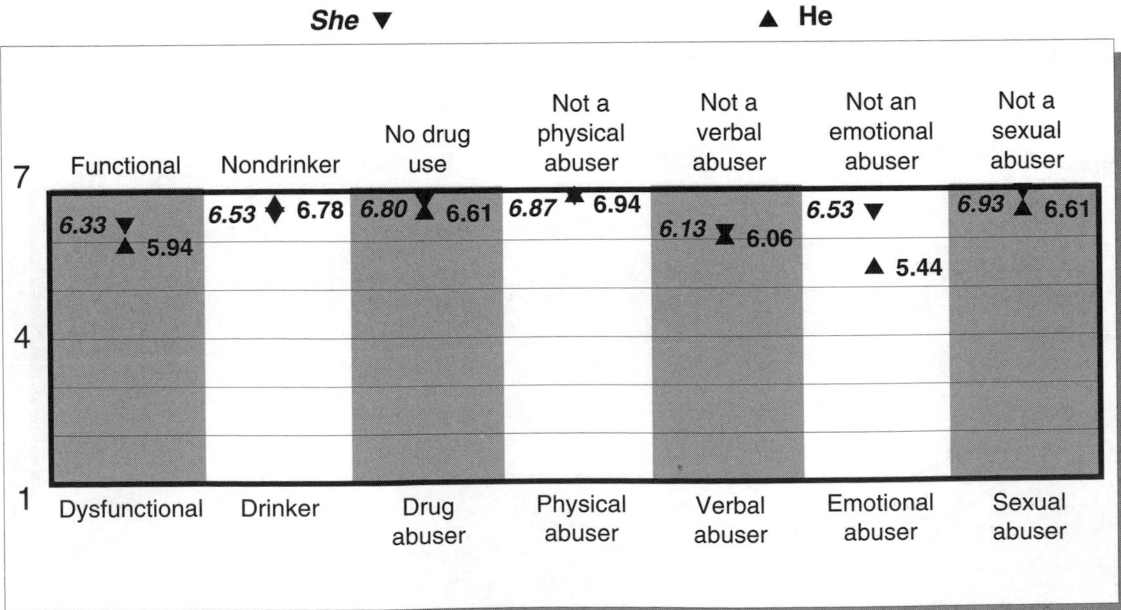

No substance or sexual abuse is reported by our giver respondents. The amount of verbal and emotional abuse is small. With good abilities to resolve abuse from the past, givers report only small amounts of unresolved abuse—less than half reported by the norm for all gifts.

Extremely high scores here (see chart B on page 222) verify how free givers are from the dysfunctions that can easily ruin a marriage.

C. My genuine needs, views or beliefs are:

	He	She
1. I need our marriage to be free of alcohol use and abuse.	22%	53%
2. I need our marriage to be free of drug use and abuse.	33%	53%
3. I need my spouse to treat me more kindly.	17%	20%
4. I need my mate to give me positive emotional support.	39%	40%
5. One or both of us need to get help for abuse in childhood.	6%	7%
6. One or both of us need to get help for dysfunctional behavior.	11%	13%
7. I believe there is no dysfunctional behavior in our marriage.	67%	73%

With two-thirds or more givers reporting no dysfunctional behavior, dysfunction is not a common problem. The main area that needs attention is the need for more emotional support from their mates. Affirmation and encouragement go a long way to build up *any* marriage.

Living with an Administrator Spouse

12

One of the things we have learned about administrators is that they do not do well in any kind of team leadership. They have strong convictions about the way they lead. Each has his own style and two leaders will clash. Administrators prefer specific areas in which they are solely in charge to what they view as a no-man's-land of dual leadership.

One of the rare couples we know who share the motivational gift of administration is a young pastor and his wife, Duncan and Judy. Both were raised on farms and loved gardening, so in their first pastorate they decided to plant a vegetable garden in the backyard.

"The rows should go north and south," Duncan declared.

"Oh, no," Judy blurted out. "We always planted east to west."

"The tall vegetables need to go over here on the south side to help shade the other crops," Duncan claimed.

"You've got to be kidding!" exclaimed Judy. "Anyone knows it's best to plant the corn and beans on the north so the smaller plants get enough sunshine."

They spent the next hour arguing over where each vegetable should go.

"We were getting nowhere," Judy reports. "We were both so sure we were right. I don't think we would ever have gotten our garden planted if God had not given Duncan some special wisdom. He got a stick and drew a line right down the middle of the plot, and gave me the right side while he took the left. Our rows went in different directions and we followed the methods we'd been used to. And you know what? We each had a beautiful, productive garden."

Five Major Problem Areas

First we will look at the five most significant problem areas of the administrator gift that influence the problems experienced in each of the twenty categories of our survey.

1. Bossiness

Administrators love to tell others what to do. This can include spouses, who may not always appreciate it. The spouses' degree of receptivity may have to do with the way things are said. "I can handle it if my administrator husband asks me to do something for him," one woman said, "but when he *tells* me to do something, I dig in my heels."

As administrators write out their "to do" lists, they think, *To whom can I delegate this task?* It is easy to see the spouse as the logical candidate.

Sometimes administrators can become overbearing, dominating or controlling. This is especially a problem for administrator husbands, whose jobs may enable them to be strongly in charge. But a take-charge attitude carried over into the marital relationship can cause the wife to feel resistant and resentful, used or even abused. A wise administrator husband does well to remember the apostle Paul's admonitions to the early Christians to submit to one another in love and not to lord it over others.

2. Doing Too Much

Administrators love to be involved. A full schedule is comfortable, a too-full schedule endurable. They tend to overextend with work or extracurricular activities, neglecting spouse and family. It is important for administrators to keep their priorities in order: God, spouse, family, job, ministry. The problem is, they are often asked by those who recognize their leadership abilities to take on additional responsibility. Too much can tip the scale. Administrators must learn when to say no.

3. Neglecting Routine Work

Routine work bores administrators, who would rather delegate it to others if possible. An administrator spouse may prefer hiring the boy next door to mow the lawn. Weeds can overtake the flowerbeds because the administrator is out doing "more important" volunteer work at church. He or she may have meant to clean out the garage for so long that it is almost impossible to get the car in anymore!

Inside the house, the administrator cannot imagine why anyone would dust twice a week when once a month will do! After all, the dust just settles back down again anyway. The dishes get washed and the family eats on them again. A load of dirty clothes goes through the washer and a week later appears in the laundry basket again. The kitchen floor gets scrubbed and everyone in the family tracks dirt over it again.

So both house and yard can get looking run-down, and impromptu company can present a problem. A smart administrator spouse keeps on top of these chores or delegates enough of them to family members to be relieved of part of the load. If the budget allows, a part-time housekeeper or landscape service may be a wise investment.

4. Forgetfulness

With their busy schedules and wide areas of interest, administrators have a lot on their minds. There may be a point at which they go on overload and forget what they need to remember, so they develop lists of things to do. If something does not get on their lists, it may not get done.

Many administrators are addicted to appointment calendars, which they live by. Once I left my Day-Timer at our cabin. A few evenings later I was out shopping with Don when I suddenly remembered I had a speaking engagement that very night. We zoomed over to the church, only to find a substitute speaker halfway through her presentation. Since then I do not let my Day-Timer out of my sight!

5. Procrastination

Why do today what can be put off till tomorrow? This seems to be a slogan for administrators, who tend to procrastinate. It is easy for them to do what they love or what presents an enjoyable challenge. But the tasks that seem to be time-wasters, boring or just plain uninteresting get put off—and off.

My downfall is filing. How I would love a server secretary to do it all for me and keep it wondrously up-to-date! I made another New Year's resolution this year—the sixteenth!—to catch up on my filing. I bought another secondhand four-drawer file cabinet, two hundred file folders (many of them in color) and four sets of stacking trays to use as sorting slots. They are still empty while my seventeen boxes of things to file are still full!

The Twenty Problem Categories of the Administrator Gift

Let's take a look at the twenty categories of problem areas for administrator spouses indicated by our marriage survey.

Category 1: Communication

A. I FEEL WE HAVE SOME PROBLEMS IN COMMUNICATION IN THESE AREAS:

	He	She
1. Misunderstandings	42%	37%
2. Free to share	46%	47%
3. Listening	61%	70%
4. Conversation	40%	27%
5. Correction	40%	27%
6. Body language	26%	20%
7. Ridicule	42%	40%

Administrators are good communicators, although a third report some misunderstandings with spouses. Sometimes they are guilty of not listening to their mates. They tend to have one-track minds, tuning out the world around them. If I am reading and Don says something to me, I may be so engrossed that I do not hear him, or hear only the last part of his comment. It helps if he gets my attention first.

Administrators are sometimes reluctant to share all their thoughts and feelings with their mates. John, a high school principal, says he is able to be more candid about his feelings with his staff than with his wife. "I married a compassion gift," he explains. "She is so sensitive and gets her feelings hurt so easily that I have to be careful what I tell her."

Administrators like to talk. If married to one of the server gifts—a server, giver or compassion person—they may overwhelm them with their need to converse. If married to one of the speaking gifts—a perceiver, teacher, exhorter or another administrator—they may compete over who gets to do most of the talking. Since Don is an exhorter, we sometimes have to take turns to get out all we want to say to the other.

Giving too much correction is a tendency for about a third of administrators. They need to take care not to correct their spouses, especially in public.

While administrator spouses do not normally use ridicule or sarcasm in their work or ministries, at home they can give into it when irritated or angry. They usually repent of it later.

Definitely good communicators, administrators (see chart B on page 227) nevertheless try not to dominate conversations. They also want to hear what their spouses have to say. When administrator men say they may talk too little to their wives, it may be because they have talked a lot at work and are content to rest from it at home. Also, they do not care for chit-chat,

B. TO WHAT DEGREE, FROM 1 TO 7, ARE YOU ONE WAY OR THE OTHER:

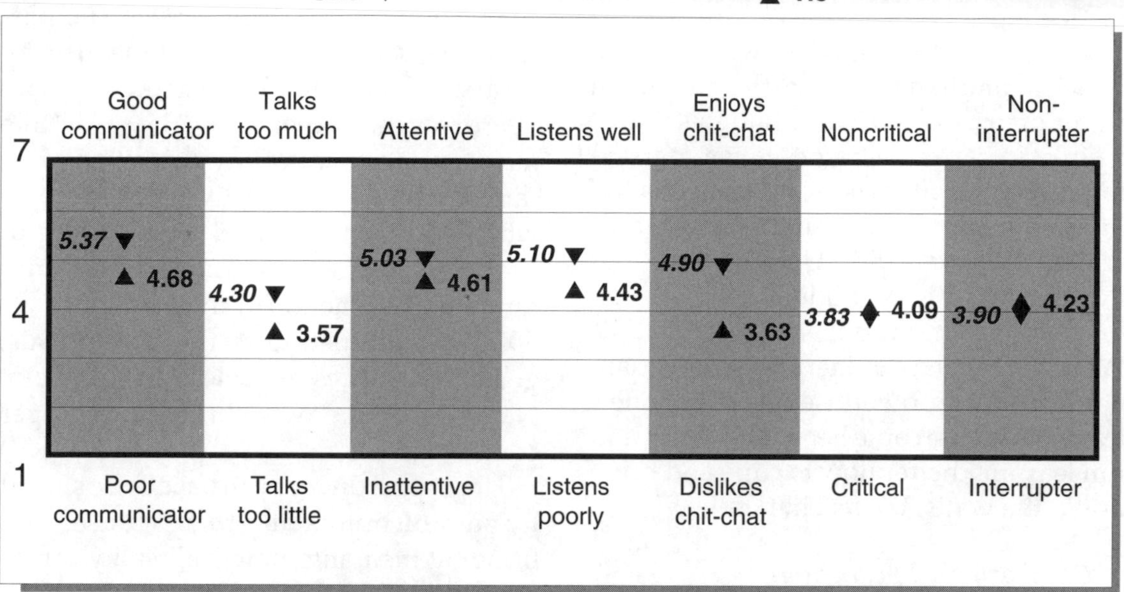

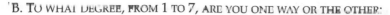

while their female counterparts may enjoy it to some degree.

The "critical" scores reflect the administrators' analytical mode—difficult to turn off. They do not mean to be critical but are constantly evaluating, comparing, processing. It is a feature that makes them good at leadership but irritating at times to their mates.

While the interrupting tendency is not strong, administrator spouses lapse into it sometimes. It can be a special problem if the mate is an exhorter (as in our case). In extreme cases we have seen both spouses talking at each other at the same time. How they hear what the other is saying, we have never figured out!

C. MY GENUINE NEEDS, VIEWS OR BELIEFS ARE:

	He	She
1. I need more conversation with my mate.	35%	53%
2. I need my partner to listen to me more attentively.	40%	57%
3. I need more quiet time without conversation.	25%	13%
4. I feel we need to share more intimately our thoughts and feelings.	46%	70%
5. I get hurt easily by my mate's unkind remarks.	30%	40%
6. I need more of my partner's undivided attention.	23%	40%
7. I am satisfied with our communication and conversation.	28%	40%

Women administrators desire more conversation with their mates, more intimate sharing of thoughts and feelings, and being listened to more attentively. Administrator Briana says her problem is not inadequate communication with her teacher husband, but a lack of intimate communication. "He does very well talking about his work, our children or abstract ideas," she says. "But he doesn't open up his heart to me very often. I long to know what he really feels deep inside. I wish he could relate better to my feelings."

Administrators can deal with spousal criticism or unkindness like the proverbial water off a duck's back, although some of it sinks in. Administrator Oliver, married to perceiver Anton, says, "I felt I was living in a negative atmosphere of Anton's critical remarks. I didn't let it stop me, but I discovered I was building a wall of callousness around me that was unhealthy. We both realized our marriage was in danger and got into counseling. Now she's learning to overcome her critical spirit and I'm learning better how to cope and bring down the walls. We feel hopeful."

Category 2: Expectations

A. I FEEL WE HAVE SOME PROBLEMS IN WHAT WE EXPECT OF EACH OTHER IN THESE AREAS:

	He	She
1. Lifestyle	23%	17%
2. Priorities	54%	40%
3. Ideals/goals	32%	13%
4. Holidays	11%	17%
5. Hopes/dreams	32%	23%
6. Conduct	23%	10%
7. Homework	46%	53%

Administrators generally have a live-and-let-live perspective on relationships, but in their marriages they like to be directly or indirectly in control. Administrator husbands usually take charge and it works reasonably well, especially with more submissive wives. Administrator wives tend to control more subtly. More dominant husbands recognize and resent or resist it.

Priorities are important to administrator spouses. They set them, consciously or unconsciously, and expect their mates to agree. Adam admits that he, like most administrators, lives with a daily planner and lists of things to do—prioritized, of course. Evelyn, his disorganized compassion wife, sets priorities spontaneously by whatever seems important at the moment. "We drive each other crazy," he says. "She makes mincemeat of my priorities, yet I can't stop making them. I've learned to live with modifications, and she's trying to keep at least my most important priority for the day at the top of the list."

Most administrators find that ideals, goals and values are seldom a problem. Neither are holiday celebrations or proper conduct.

Hopes and dreams can usually be shared by administrators and their spouses, but bringing them into practical reality can be more of a challenge. Don and I have dreamed of building our retirement home on our summer home property. As I write it is half-finished. He prefers a simpler design, I opt for the unique. He picks a material or an appliance by how workable it is. I have to research a product thoroughly and weigh the pros and cons before I can make up my mind. We will get the house finished, but the process is an education for us both!

The biggest problem in expectations is who should do what around the house. Administrators do not like routine housework, home maintenance or yardwork, doing it only because they have to. While administrator Trena lived in the Philippines, she was able to have a full-time cook, housemaid and two nannies for her children. "It was like heaven," she exclaims. "I made lists of things for them to do and it all got done!"

Hearing this, I felt jealous and told Don I would love to have some maids, too. He punctured my balloon with, "You already have plenty of maids—your Mobile Maid dishwasher, your automatic oven, your

B. To what degree, from 1 to 7, are you one way or the other:

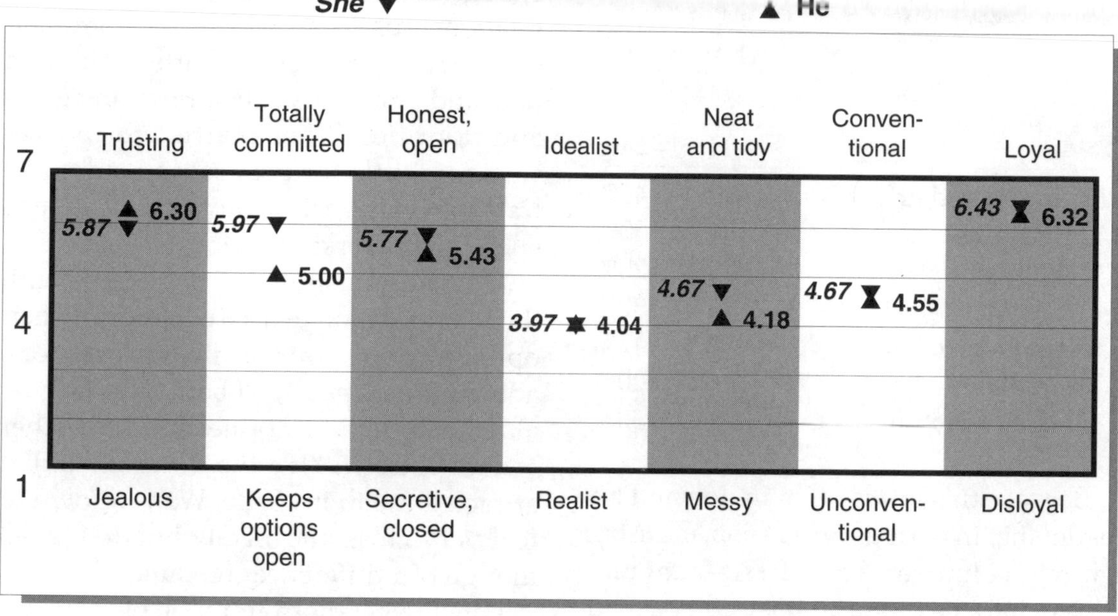

frost-free freezer, your clothes washer and dryer . . ." and he went on and on.

Good qualities (see chart B above) like being trusting, committed, honest, open and loyal are natural to administrator spouses. Balanced between realism and idealism, they can demonstrate either in a particular situation. They are slightly on the conventional side but allow for those who are more unconventional. They do not believe everyone needs to be alike.

Their scores slightly on the neat and tidy side refer to areas of house or office that are in full view. Don't ask to look in drawers or closets or that off-limits catch-all room! Administrators are notorious stackers; almost anyplace will do. They mean to get around to filing the stuff away, but other priorities tend to put that effort off, sometimes indefinitely.

C. My genuine needs, views or beliefs are:

	He	She
1. I need to be more sure of my partner's motives.	16%	17%
2. I need a mate who is dependable.	35%	53%
3. I feel we need to work more at setting joint priorities.	53%	40%
4. I need to be more confident in how my mate handles stress.	39%	27%
5. I need my spouse to be totally honest with me.	39%	47%
6. I need to have former family customs part of my life.	2%	13%
7. I feel our expectations are realistic and workable.	70%	90%

A high percentage of administrator respondents report that their own expectations and the expectations of their mates are realistic and workable. They expect and need their mates to be honest and dependable. Some also feel the need to work more at joint priorities.

Category 3: Marital Cohesion

A. I FEEL WE HAVE SOME PROBLEMS IN GETTING ALONG WITH EACH OTHER IN THESE AREAS:

	He	She
1. Time together	39%	43%
2. Give and take	30%	33%
3. Feeling one	25%	20%
4. Closeness	32%	37%
5. Goals/priorities	42%	47%
6. Loneliness	16%	20%
7. Love/affection	35%	50%

Because this gift is often in demand for leadership in various areas—job, ministry, church, volunteer work, PTA—activities can cut into the time administrators would otherwise spend with their spouses. As one wise administrator wife put it, "I had to learn to draw the line, to put time with my husband and kids before volunteer work. I like to help out, but not at the sacrifice of my family."

Most administrators are adaptable enough for give-and-take in their marital relationships. They love input from their spouses on almost every matter, collecting data and perspectives before setting goals and priorities. When married to spouses who care little for goal-setting, administrators may have difficulty getting them to spend time working on it.

Most administrators feel oneness with their mates. Good marital cohesion, in their opinion, grows out of diversity. As one administrator put it, "If both of us are just alike, one of us is not needed." Another acknowledged, "It's the differences that attracted me to my wife. We've grown to feel very close and firmly bonded, even though our differences remain."

Loneliness is not a common problem for most administrators since they tend to be people-oriented. They interact constantly with others, including their spouses. The administrator will draw even the most aloof or reclusive spouse into a more active relationship.

B. TO WHAT DEGREE, FROM 1 TO 7, ARE YOU ONE WAY OR THE OTHER:

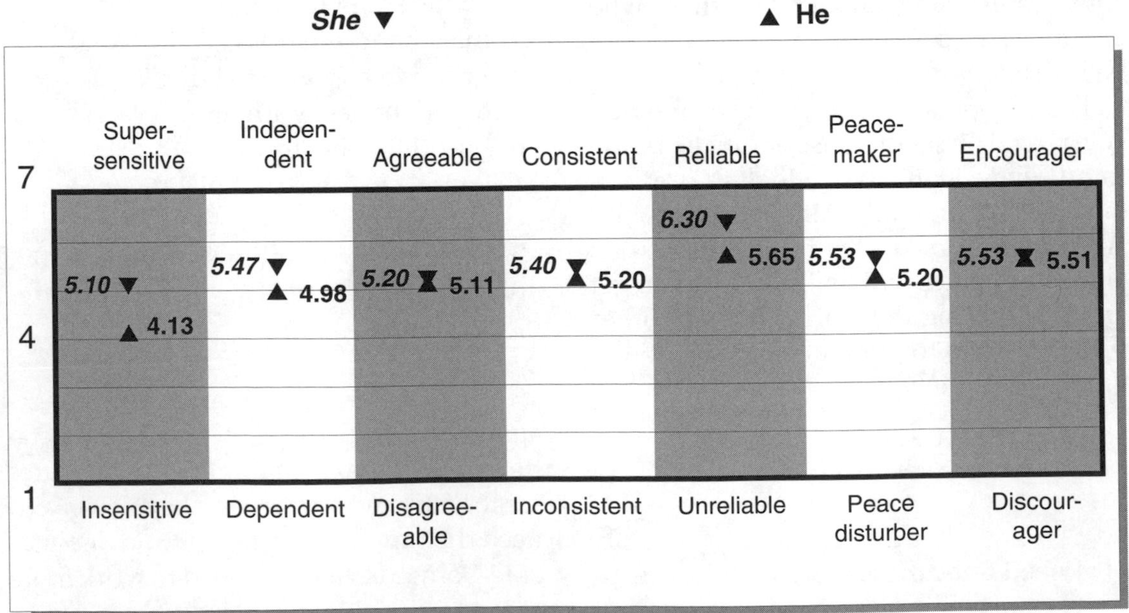

Almost everyone would like more romantic love and affection. While almost half the administrator respondents desire this, they are also the ones with the capacity to plan for more of it in their marital relationships. They can schedule romantic events into their daily calendars with the greatest of ease. Jim did that for Amy and found he had a more responsive wife than he had thought possible.

With mostly 5-plus scores (see chart B on page 230), it is easy to see that administrator spouses have qualities that make for good marital cohesion. It is a matter of putting into practice what they are capable of doing. Every mate can use some encouraging. Ian found that Bethany blossomed in her love for him the more he affirmed her. "I need to be more sensitive to her needs and practice the Golden Rule right here in my marriage," he explains.

C. My genuine needs, views or beliefs are:

	He	She
1. I need to be able to confide more in my mate.	32%	33%
2. I feel there needs to be more unity in our relationship.	26%	23%
3. I need to feel more secure in our marriage.	11%	13%
4. I am afraid to share some of my feelings with my partner.	35%	47%
5. I need my mate to be more sensitive to my needs.	26%	50%
6. I do not consider divorce ever to be an option.	84%	87%
7. I am satisfied with our marital interaction and closeness.	47%	57%

About half of the administer respondents say they are satisfied with their marital interaction and closeness, and a vast majority believe divorce will never be an option. Half of the administrator wives need their mates to be more sensitive to their needs, and admit they are afraid to share some feelings. Honesty and openness can help overcome these problems.

Feelings are not necessarily either good or bad, but ones that are detrimental to the relationship can be resolved. Sometimes a person just needs to hear the helpmate say, "I hear what you are saying and am glad to be able to talk with you about your feelings." Sometimes the expressed feelings may be a surface manifestation of even deeper feelings that may never be revealed until the previous ones are acknowledged and dealt with kindly.

Category 4: Roles and Responsibilities

A. I feel we have some problems in our marriage roles and responsibilities in these areas:

	He	She
1. Authority	21%	27%
2. Submission	23%	10%
3. Responsibilities	35%	43%
4. Decision-making	32%	30%
5. Roles	16%	13%
6. Feeling overworked	32%	53%
7. Home management	32%	53%

Administrators respect authority and feel comfortable within its framework, whether they *are* the authority or under it. They do not like unclear authority. When I was the editor of *Aglow* magazine, I was the authority. When I came home I was under Don's authority. I was secure in either position.

Administrator wives have little problem with marital submission as long as their husbands do not lord it over them. Wholehearted submission requires trust and respect. Submission forcibly extracted is tyranny; genuine submission is given gladly.

Administrators have definite ideas about sharing responsibilities in a marriage. Our administrator son, Dave, married administrator Scotti. They had been president and vice-president of their university's student body organization and had learned a bit about working together before they wed. They admit they have faced challenges because both like being the leader and delegating responsibilities. "We have a very good relationship now," Dave says, "but we have to keep working on it. We both share cooking, cleaning and other home responsibilities since we both have full-time jobs. We try to define the specifics and make most of our decisions together. Sometimes we take turns being the leader. It works for us."

Administrators enjoy making decisions and may do so without the involvement of their spouses. This can cause conflict and resentment by spouses who like to participate in the decision-making process. Others are happy to leave it up to the administrator mate. The main thing is agreeing on how it is to be done.

Administrators can fit fine into traditional roles. They can also be creative in how their roles are defined. Charles wanted to see if he could make it as a full-time free-lance writer. "I talked it over with Claudia," he said, "and she was willing to take a full-time job for a couple of years and let me stay home and ply my trade. I did most of the housework during that time. My administrative gifting helped me juggle it all and find I could make a good living that way. Then Claudia was able to stay home, and we started our family as she entered the traditional role and I was back to being the sole breadwinner."

Administrators (see chart B below) tend to feel overworked because they get over-involved. They may slip into overtime work without noticing it.

Domestic responsibilities, as we have already noted, are low on the administrator's list of favorite things. Most wish they

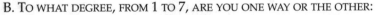

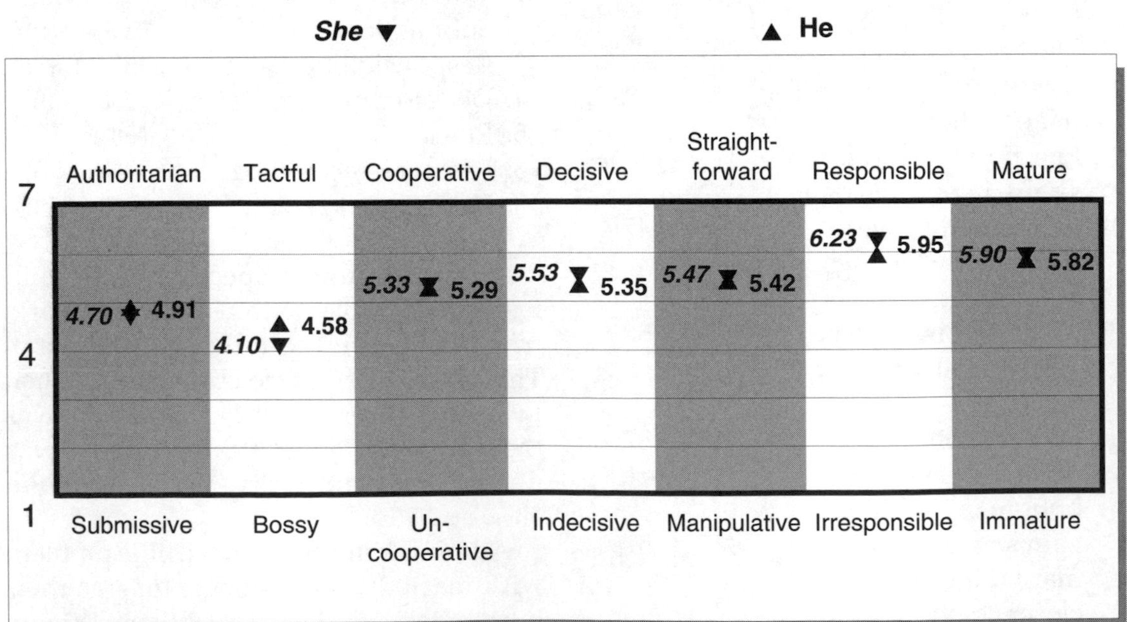

had someone to delegate those tasks to. Those who can afford it often arrange it.

Administrators see themselves as mature and responsible. They usually are, except in possible areas of procrastination. "As an administrator," Glenda says, "I believe firmly in not doing anything I can get someone else to do. I find my 'honey do this' list gets rather long sometimes and Ben digs his heels in and barks, 'Do it yourself!' Then I know I've overdone it."

Good scores on being cooperative, decisive and straightforward show that administrator spouses can relate well to their spouses and handle effective teamwork.

C. My genuine needs, views or beliefs are:

	He	She
1. I need my role clarified more.	4%	7%
2. I need more freedom to discuss ideas and options.	26%	10%
3. I need to use some of my capabilities more.	30%	30%
4. I need to receive more respect from my partner.	26%	20%
5. I need more domestic help and support from my spouse.	11%	47%
6. I would like to help more in planning together.	21%	13%
7. I am satisfied with the roles and responsibilities we have established.	49%	40%

Roles are clear for administrators, except for the expectation and hope of administrator wives for more domestic help from their mates. They need to speak up more about this.

Administrators have many capabilities and the need to use them. The amazing businesswoman-home manager of Proverbs 31:10–31 must have been an administrator gift! Some women get exhausted just reading about her and need to be reminded that she did not do everything in one day. A husband of any gifting would be wise to see that his administrator wife has some opportunity to use her leadership capabilities. She will feel more fulfilled and be more content as a wife.

Category 5: Conflict Resolution

A. I feel we have some problems in how we deal with conflicts in these areas:

	He	She
1. Anger management	53%	47%
2. Who's right	39%	43%
3. Final decisions	21%	10%
4. Silent treatment	44%	37%
5. Ultimatums	18%	7%
6. Personal attacks	56%	47%
7. Blame game	30%	40%

Almost half of the administrator respondents admitted some anger management problems in their marital relationships. Anger is not the problem, but how the anger is used or stuffed. Administrators communicate well enough that they do not usually follow the stuffing route, which causes the anger to fester and eventually blow. Most try to understand why the angry feelings surfaced and take steps of action to deal with them properly.

Like all the speaking gifts, administrators like to be right and defend their positions. Since they also like to see the overall picture, however, they usually listen to their mates' points of view and are willing to adjust their own, if necessary.

B. To what degree, from 1 to 7, are you one way or the other:

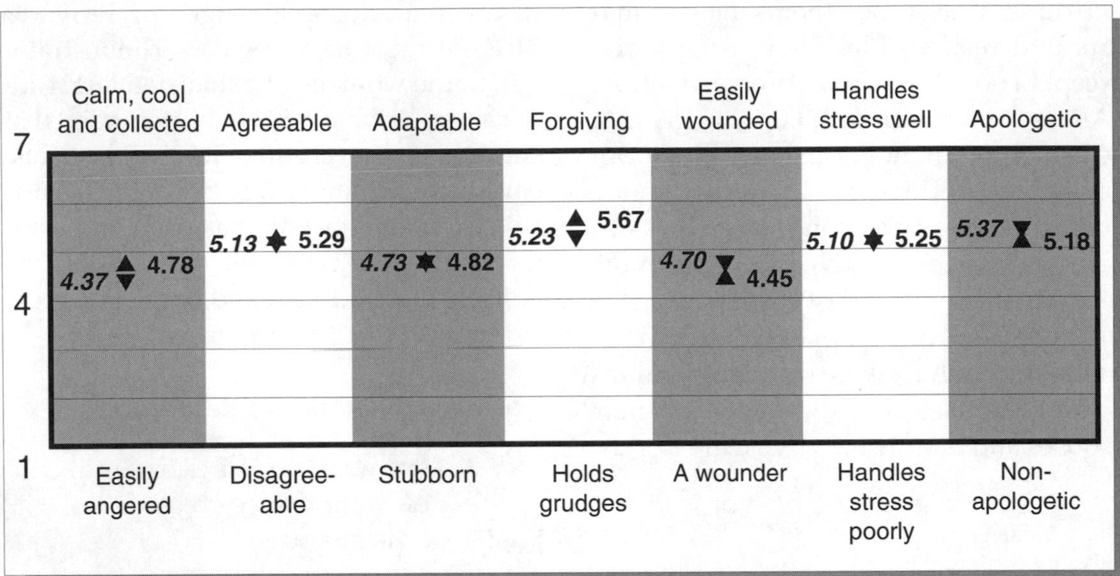

Final decision-making is not much of a problem, perhaps because an administrator husband may already be the final decision-maker and an administrator wife is happy to submit this task to her husband, providing she has had some input.

About forty percent of the administrators admit that the silent treatment is a tool they or their spouses resort to. Women are more likely to do this than men, and server gifts more than speaking gifts. Administrators can usually be effective in breaking through the wall of silence and insisting on working toward resolution.

Most administrator spouses have learned that ultimatums do not work well. If they resort to personal attack, they will soon be sorry for it and apologize. They can regress into personal attack or blame, but most are willing to take responsibility.

Administrator spouses (see chart B above) are usually cool, calm and collected. They tend to look objectively at life in general and situations in particular. As one husband put it, "It takes a lot to ruffle my feathers. That applies to my marital relationship as well."

Administrators handle stress well, which is good since leadership carries much potential for stress. They are good at looking at the whole picture and finding ways to relieve stress. Most have learned the value of forgiveness and are quick to apologize to their mates in order to restore a right relationship.

C. My genuine needs, views or beliefs are:

	He	She
1. I need to gain control over my temper.	46%	30%
2. I need my spouse to gain control over his or her temper.	33%	20%
3. I need to have my point of view heard more often.	14%	17%
4. I feel a strong need to avoid arguments and conflicts.	37%	20%
5. I need my mate to forgive me more quickly.	26%	23%

	He	She
6. I think we need better ground rules for resolving conflicts.	46%	27%
7. I am satisfied with the way we resolve conflicts.	30%	60%

Twice as many administrator wives as husbands are satisfied with the way personal conflicts are resolved. About half of the husbands admit more need to gain control over their tempers and recognize that better ground rules should be established for resolving conflicts. "Every time my wife and I have a fight," Henry said, "I think there must be a better way to solve this conflict." Then he found a good book on the subject and is seriously working on it. Sound advice for all administrators.

Category 6: Personality Issues

A. I FEEL WE HAVE SOME PROBLEMS IN PERSONALITY CONFLICTS AND ISSUES IN THESE AREAS:

	He	She
1. Being right	46%	30%
2. Pride	19%	33%
3. Understanding	40%	27%
4. Change attempts	39%	40%
5. Methodologies	28%	30%
6. Habits	25%	20%
7. Forgetfulness	35%	40%

Being right is a little more important to administrator husbands than wives. They are more used to being in charge at work, which often transfers to home. Administrator spouses can get prideful over their organizational abilities. They need to realize these are gifts from God, not something for which they can take credit.

Women administrators make more effort to understand their spouses. They are more likely to read books on marriage and make conscious efforts to understand their loved ones more fully.

Administrators admit more attempts than the norm to change their mates. Arvid, the CEO of a large company, told us he had tried for years to make his wife into the "typical" executive wife. "She'd try," he explains, "but she just couldn't do it. Then when I found out that she was a compassion gift, I understood why. I did a lot of apologizing to her and have freed her to be the lovely, caring and spontaneous person that she is."

Administrators plan ahead, set goals, make lists of things to do and delegate everything they can. These methods, if the administrator is married to a perceiver or teacher, can work well. Servers are opposites in many ways but can complement administrator spouses. But compassion mates can drive them up the wall with their why-plan-ahead-I've-got-enough-to-handle-right-now lifestyle!

Administrator respondents listed fewer bothersome habits than the norm. Nevertheless, their tendency to stack things, meaning to put them away later, can irritate server and giver spouses and others who like uncluttered surroundings.

Administrators tend to have so much on their minds that if they do not write something down, they are likely to forget it. Sometimes after we have turned the lights out, Don will say, "By the way, will you call the plumber tomorrow to fix the sink, take one of our books over to Steve's, tell Linda we can't come over until Saturday and get some of our order forms duplicated?" I know very well that by morning I will be lucky to remember two of the four items! So on go the lights and I grab my notepad and pen.

The very high scores (see chart B on page 236) reflect the administrators' natural respect for authority. They will not dishonor or violate it. They are also consider-

B. To what degree, from 1 to 7, are you one way or the other:

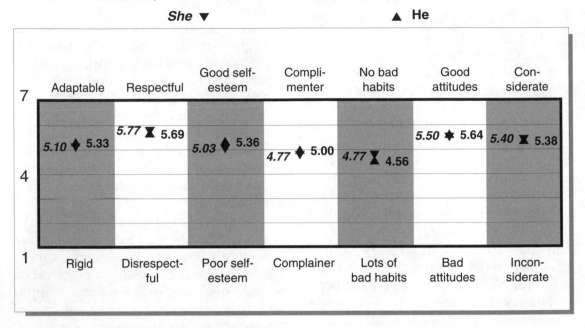

She ▼ ▲ He

	Adaptable / Rigid	Respectful / Disrespectful	Good self-esteem / Poor self-esteem	Complimenter / Complainer	No bad habits / Lots of bad habits	Good attitudes / Bad attitudes	Considerate / Inconsiderate
She	5.10	5.77	5.03	4.77	4.77	5.50	5.40
He	5.33	5.69	5.36	5.00	4.56	5.64	5.38

ate, taking into account the feelings and needs of others. They are good at identifying these in their mates and adaptable enough to allow room for differences.

Administrators tend to have good self-esteem. They usually like who they are and are not prone to have personality problems. They also have good attitudes. Lillian says of her administrator husband, "Cecil is such a positive person. He likes himself and he likes me just the way I am. He compliments me a lot and builds up my self-esteem all the time."

C. My genuine needs, views or beliefs are:

	He	She
1. I wish my partner complimented me more.	14%	40%
2. I need more encouragement from my mate.	35%	47%
3. I need to be accepted and appreciated for who I am.	46%	33%
4. I need to retain my unique identity.	23%	13%
5. My partner needs to understand my gifts.	25%	20%
6. I need more admiration and respect from my partner.	19%	17%
7. We do not seem to have any personality conflicts.	37%	40%

While administrators are good complimenters, some wish their spouses would reciprocate more with appreciation and encouragement. Often administrators seem so confident that their spouses do not realize they need building up as well, especially if they are in high-stress jobs. Bob, who manages a large real estate firm, confides, "I can take lots of guff and stress at work every day if I know my wife will be there for me when I come home to unwind. She listens intently as I share the problems and challenges of the day. Just one word of encouragement from her and I feel renewed and ready to tackle the next day."

Category 7: Emotional Responses

A. I FEEL WE HAVE SOME PROBLEMS IN THE WAYS WE RESPOND TO EACH OTHER EMOTIONALLY IN THESE AREAS:

	He	She
1. Hurt feelings	51%	47%
2. Carrying offenses	30%	20%
3. Unforgiveness	18%	3%
4. Insensitiveness	32%	23%
5. Feeling unloved	18%	27%
6. Moodiness	37%	47%
7. Anger	54%	37%

While almost half of the respondents to our survey indicated problems with hurt feelings, administrator women scored slightly lower than the norm and administrator men slightly higher. Administrator women are more objective than most women and can remain more detached from and resilient to spousal offenses. All administrators try to resolve offenses quickly. They want nothing to get in the way of productivity. As one husband said, "Why waste time carrying around offenses? Besides, they're heavy."

Forgiveness, the antidote to anger, is also administered quickly by administrator spouses. Many administrators (myself included) have learned that unforgiveness is dangerous to our emotional, physical and spiritual health. Forgiveness is a choice, and the quicker we make it, the better.

Administrators are observant and reasonably sensitive to their spouses. They are not good, however, at reading between the lines. Tim told us, "If Wilma says everything is O.K., I take her literally. If she tells me later that she really wasn't O.K. and that I should have sensed it, I tell her she needs to understand I believe exactly what she says."

Administrators are motivated primarily by facts, not feelings. They know by the empirical evidence that they are loved and do not necessarily need to be told again and again. One busy administrator wife says, "If my husband gets sarcastic or speaks unkindly to me, I do wonder if he really loves me as much as he says he does. I look hopefully for signs that he is sorry, but underneath I know he loves me. Maybe he's just had a bad day."

Scores on moodiness are surprisingly high, showing that even the cool and collected administrator spouse slips into bad moods from time to time. The scores may also reflect the moodiness of the administrator's spouse.

More administrator husbands than wives have a problem with anger. Liking to be in control, the husband may have a problem when he thinks his wife is too independent or is resisting his expectations. His ability to be objective and maintain a broad perspective can help him work through anger.

Gordon says he is working at learning to express anger more appropriately. "I don't get angry at Mona very often," he says, "but when I do it's usually when she does something negative that reminds me of my mother. Through counseling I've worked through some of the maternal resentments I've had, and it's defused my reactions. My anger is definitely more under control."

The rational nature (see chart B on page 238) of the administrator husband, along with his male reserve, makes him less emotional than his female counterpart. Most husbands say they never cry and that they are less demonstrative and sympathetic than administrator wives. But both are caring and able to express love verbally.

Frank, a devoted administrator, says his marriage is improving every year. "Like a good piece of cheese," he says proudly, "marriage gets better with age. Angie and I love each other more deeply than ever,

B. To what degree, from 1 to 7, are you one way or the other:

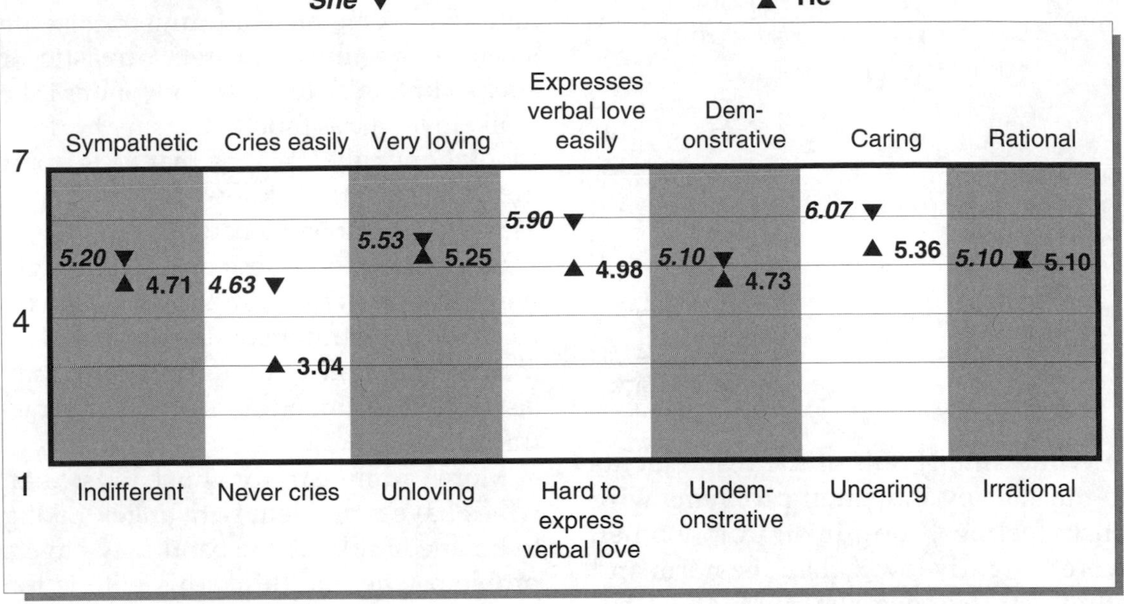

and I'm able to express love to her more spontaneously now."

C. My genuine needs, views or beliefs are:

	He	She
1. My feelings tend to rule my life.	11%	13%
2. My mate needs to understand my moods more.	18%	17%
3. I need to hear more "I love you's" from my partner.	25%	20%
4. I need to be able to express both positive and negative feelings.	40%	60%
5. I feel my spouse takes everything too personally.	40%	17%
6. I often feel put down by my partner.	23%	17%
7. I am satisfied with our emotional responses to each other.	35%	47%

More administrator women than men are satisfied with their emotional interaction with their mates. Two-thirds of the men recognize room for improvement.

Respondents scored the highest on needing to express both positive and negative feelings. Cathy says, "I need to be honest about my negative feelings, but my husband seems to get upset and take what I say too personally. Then I hold back."

Category 8: Intellectual Capacity

A. I feel we have some problems relating to intellectual interests and capacities in these areas:

	He	She
1. Different interests	39%	23%
2. Reading	18%	13%
3. Continuing education	12%	3%
4. Know-it-all attitude	21%	27%
5. Correcting grammar	12%	17%
6. Children's education	4%	3%
7. Being accurate	23%	33%

Administrators are known for their wide range of interests. They tend to embrace the interests of their spouses. Some of the problem areas indicated here may suggest the respondents' concern that their mates do not share their interests.

Administrators are avid readers, preferring nonfiction but enjoying a good novel now and then, especially if it is educational. They usually read extensively in the areas of their special interests. Cheryl says her husband reads at least an hour a day in his field of rest home management. "Ray heard an education expert say that if a person reads that much each day in their field, in ten years or so he or she will become an expert in that field. It's working for Ray. He gets calls from all over the nation for advice, and there's no end to job offers."

Administrators continue to learn all their lives. Their only regret is that there is not enough time to read and study all they would like. Most mates recognize their administrator spouses' need to learn, and are often willing to sacrifice so that night courses or even back-to-college episodes can be scheduled.

Some know-it-all attitudes can pop up, so spouses of administrators are wise to nip these in the bud. They realize, living with an administrator, that their mates know a lot but definitely not everything. "Sue knows how to pop my balloon when I need it," Mark says.

It can irritate the spouse if the administrator persists in correcting grammar. But if the spouse sees it as a benefit, it can be a blessing. George, a server married to Esther, an administrator, says he has benefited from her ability to correct his grammar. "I was raised in a home where grammar was sloppy," he said. "At first Esther's correction bothered me, but when I realized she was helping me in a way that was giving me promotions at work, I thanked her for it."

Administrators work well with their spouses regarding their children's education. They also appreciate accuracy and are apt to correct their mates—not as persistently as the teacher gifts, but a close second. This is irritating to the exhorter spouse, who feels it is the *point* that is important; or to the compassion spouse, who does not fancy facts but relationships; or to the server spouse, who feels that what you do is more important than what you say.

Administrators (see chart B on page 240) are intellectual, articulate, opinionated and analytical. Peggy, who administers a staff of forty people, says she finds these qualities helpful in her job. "But in my marriage," she adds, "I've had to learn to soft-pedal my opinions and words. The most difficult trait to try to adapt is being analytical. It's like there's an 'on' switch inside of me and it's always there, functioning whether I want it to or not. My wonderful husband, Richard, is a classic server gift who puts up with me patiently. But sometimes he says, 'Peggy, you don't have to analyze everything to death.' He's a good balance for me."

Pride can surface occasionally, but it is balanced for the most part with humility. Administrators can get too serious at times, but they can have fun-loving natures.

C. My genuine needs, views or beliefs are:

	He	She
1. I need adequate time for reading or study.	58%	53%
2. I am easily sidetracked by new interests.	42%	23%
3. I need to question things before I can accept them.	44%	43%
4. I need my mate to listen to my opinions more.	16%	23%

B. TO WHAT DEGREE, FROM 1 TO 7, ARE YOU ONE WAY OR THE OTHER:

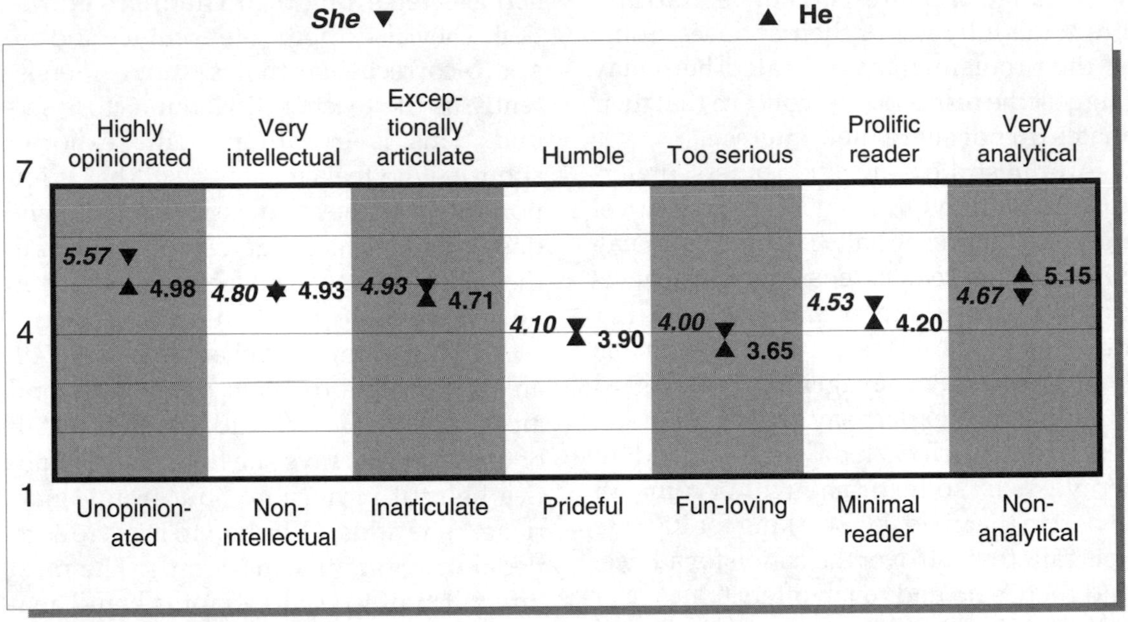

She ▼ ▲ He

Scale 7	Highly opinionated	Very intellectual	Exceptionally articulate	Humble	Too serious	Prolific reader	Very analytical
She ▼	5.57	4.80	4.93	4.10	4.00	4.53	4.67
He ▲	4.98	4.93	4.71	3.90	3.65	4.20	5.15
Scale 1	Unopinionated	Non-intellectual	Inarticulate	Prideful	Fun-loving	Minimal reader	Non-analytical

	He	She
5. I realize I need to be less dogmatic.	18%	30%
6. I find I constantly analyze what my partner says and does.	16%	20%
7. I am satisfied with how we handle intellectual matters.	49%	70%

Most administrators are satisfied with their handling of intellectual matters. The big concern is for adequate time for reading and learning. "Time has a way of filling itself up," Malcolm affirms, "so I've learned to schedule time for reading just as I schedule time for devotions each day. Even if I can get a half-hour in, I feel better about my use of time that day."

Getting sidetracked seems to be more of a problem for administrator husbands, but both admit needing to question things before accepting them. When Don and I discuss a matter, even when he wishes I would stop questioning him, it enables me to process it and then receive it wholeheartedly.

Category 9: Volitional Issues

A. I FEEL WE HAVE SOME PROBLEMS IN THE USE OF THE WILL IN THESE AREAS:

	He	She
1. Decisions and choices	28%	33%
2. Practical decisions	18%	13%
3. Stubbornness	42%	37%
4. Agreements	18%	10%
5. Right actions	5%	10%
6. Judgmentalism	30%	43%
7. Rebelliousness	11%	17%

Administrators usually make decisions well, but not quickly. They feel they must look at all the facts and get the whole perspective first. Their decisions are usually good and fair.

If we are going on vacation, Don figures the best course is a straight line. I like to look at the possible alternate routes as well and evaluate their interest value. Maybe there is a more scenic route or a better motel with a pool or a friend who lives along the way we can stop and visit. I study maps, check with AAA, examine the facts and read all I can. Meanwhile Don is tapping his fingers, thinking, "Why does it take her so long to decide?"

Because of the good communication and thorough research of the administrator, ultimate decisions are usually practical and comfortable for both spouses.

Administrators can be stubborn, although only about a third of them admit it. They are especially stubborn when they have researched a matter thoroughly and reached a conclusion they are convinced is best. But if their spouses introduce new information that changes the basis for the decision, they will adapt accordingly. Since administrators are willing to discuss almost anything for any length of time, they will eventually come into agreement with their spouses.

Being and doing what is right is very important to administrators. They often investigate many avenues in search of the "best" or "most correct" course of action. But they also want to be sure this is right in the sight of the mate.

The administrator's tendency to analyze, compare and evaluate sets him or her up to become judgmental. It is not so much an attitude problem as an occupational hazard of their highly analytical gifting. "My wife is a very kind administrator gift," Rob reports. "She would never be judgmental about someone, even me, on purpose. Sometimes her words sound judgmental, but it's more that she is weighing the facts, and the logical conclusion raises a standard that is not necessarily met."

Rebelliousness is not usually in the heart of the administrator. But the strength of his or her desire to be right may *look* like rebelliousness, especially if the mate is one of the more strong-willed ones: perceiver, teacher, exhorter or another administrator.

Next to the perceiver gift, the administrator gift is the most strong-willed, decisive, outspoken and strong in convictions (see chart B below). Imagine these gifts

B. To what degree, from 1 to 7, are you one way or the other:

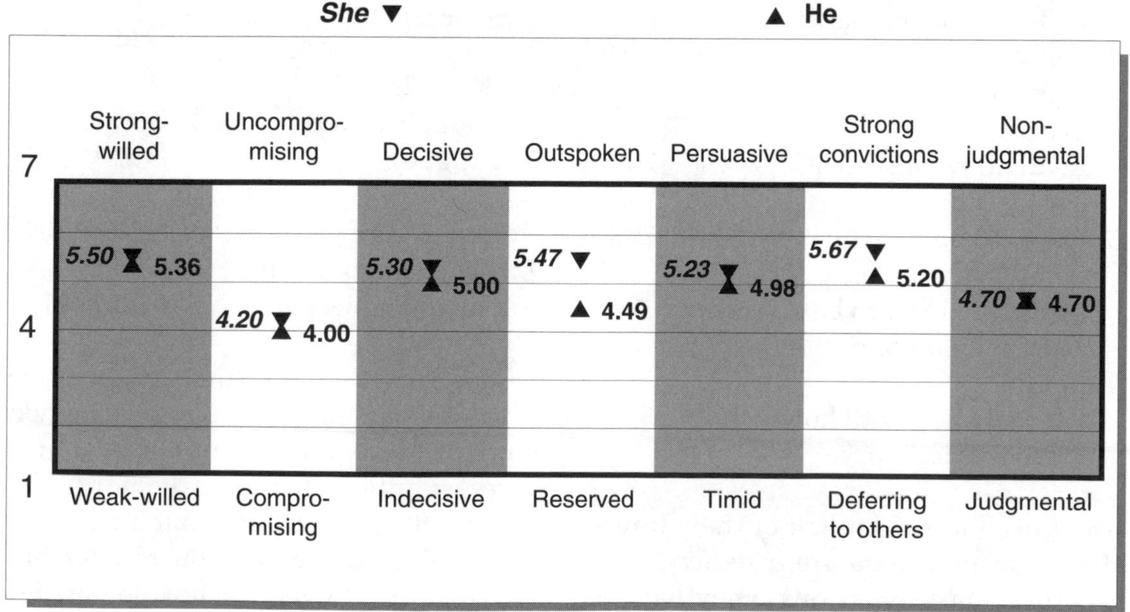

married to each other! Sparks fly during the battle of the wills.

Philip was drawn to Alicia because she had a mind of her own, but he was unprepared for the full impact of her perceiver gift until after they were married. Neither was she aware of all the ramifications of Philip's administrator gifting.

"At first we got along fairly well," Philip wrote us, "because we were so eager to please each other. But when the proverbial honeymoon was over, the battle began. It wasn't so much that we clashed over major issues; it was the day-to-day matters where we locked horns. After we read your book *Discover Your God-Given Gifts*, we began to understand the clash of our wills and took steps to deal with it realistically and sensibly. We still clash but we know how to handle it now."

C. MY GENUINE NEEDS, VIEWS OR BELIEFS ARE:

	He	She
1. I have a definite inner need to be right.	32%	43%
2. I have a strong need to be a decision-maker.	51%	63%
3. I need my mate to make most of the decisions.	5%	0%
4. I will do what is right even if it hurts.	44%	70%
5. I need to operate by definite principles.	47%	70%
6. I need my mate to be more tolerant of my opinions.	26%	17%
7. I am satisfied with how we make decisions.	53%	57%

Slightly more than half of the administrator respondents are satisfied with how they make decisions. They have a strong need to be the decision-maker and do not want to be left out of the process or turn the responsibility totally over to their mates.

Administrator wives are even more emphatic than their male counterparts about operating by definite principles and doing what is right even if it hurts. I have always strongly believed, for instance, that my word is my word.

Once when I was having a garage sale, a woman asked if she could buy a doll I had marked at eight dollars. I agreed. Then she asked me to hold it for her while she looked around some more. Another woman saw the doll and offered fifty dollars for it. I explained that I had promised another woman she could buy it for eight. "I'll give you a hundred dollars for it," she said. Then I realized that this was a Shirley Temple doll! But I had given my word to the first woman. When she returned, I sold it to her for eight dollars.

Category 10: Physical Conditions

A. I FEEL WE HAVE SOME PROBLEMS IN THE PHYSICAL REALM IN THESE AREAS:

	He	She
1. Being fit	49%	63%
2. Enough exercise	53%	73%
3. Fatigue	33%	53%
4. Overeating	37%	40%
5. Proper eating	42%	50%
6. Keeping attractive	19%	20%
7. Adequate sleep	42%	47%

Like everyone else, administrators have problems keeping physically fit. The two main problem areas for administrator wives, significantly above the norm, are keeping fit and getting enough exercise. They tend to get so busy in their leadership roles that they forget to schedule time for exercise, which is the only way they will fit it in.

The two main problem areas for administrator men, also significantly above the norm, are eating properly and getting adequate sleep. Because they tend to get overinvolved, they are more likely to resort to junk food or skipping meals and burning the midnight oil to get done what the day could not accomplish.

Matt, the CEO of a manufacturing company, admits he is guilty on both counts. "Sometimes I can't get home in time for supper, so I grab a burger and fries or order in a pizza. My doctor has warned me that this habit is taking a toll, and I'm trying to change. He's also told me I can't go on forever on six hours of sleep, so I've scheduled bedtime two hours earlier."

Most administrators (see chart B below) tend to be reasonably healthy. They are only moderately athletic, so a scheduled plan of exercise is necessary to motivate them to do it regularly. Many report weight problems, probably due to lack of exercise and poor eating habits.

Warren told us, "I used to feel I didn't have time to walk or jog, and the pounds began to add up. My wife and I decided to schedule a half-hour walk each morning, and not only have we both returned to our proper weights, but I have more energy and alertness for my day's work. I get more done in less time. What an excellent investment in good health the walking has been!"

C. My genuine needs, views or beliefs are:

	He	She
1. I desire to see my mate at the proper weight.	53%	47%
2. I need to overcome my own weight problem.	44%	53%
3. I need to get adequate exercise on a regular basis.	75%	77%
4. I would like to see my spouse get more exercise.	58%	40%

B. To what degree, from 1 to 7, are you one way or the other:

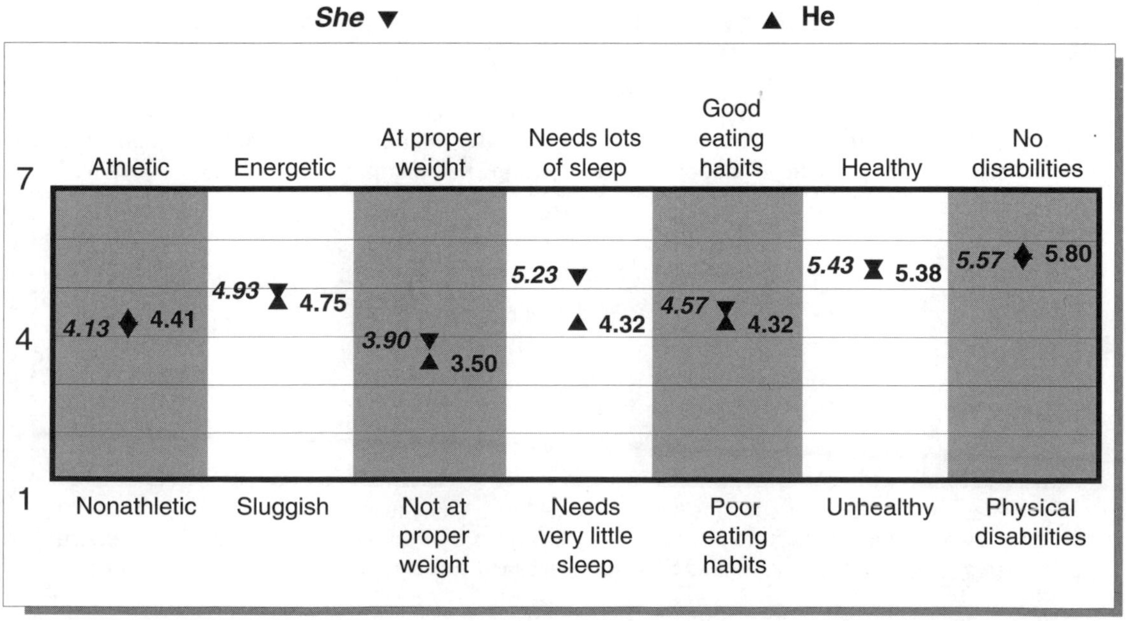

She ▼ ▲ He

7	Athletic	Energetic	At proper weight	Needs lots of sleep	Good eating habits	Healthy	No disabilities
She	4.13	4.93	3.90	5.23	4.57	5.43	5.57
He	4.41	4.75	3.50	4.32	4.32	5.38	5.80
1	Nonathletic	Sluggish	Not at proper weight	Needs very little sleep	Poor eating habits	Unhealthy	Physical disabilities

	He	She
5. I need my mate to be as attractive as possible.	35%	40%
6. I need to improve my eating habits.	53%	47%
7. I am satisfied with how we keep fit, healthy and attractive.	26%	20%

About half of the respondents admit weight problems and the need to improve their eating habits. Three-fourths say they need to get adequate, regular exercise. Only a quarter claim to be satisfied with how they keep fit and healthy.

Our son Dave and his wife, Scotti, both administrator gifts, have done well in this area during their eight years of marriage. Both have executive-type jobs but make health a priority. They exercise daily indoors or out, as weather permits. Their weekends run the gamut from river-rafting to cross-country skiing. Both cook healthy food with high emphasis on whole grains, fruits and vegetables. They have been an inspiration to Don and me!

Category 11: Sexual Relationship

A. I feel we have some problems in our sexual relationship in these areas:

	He	She
1. Frequency	46%	37%
2. Quality	28%	27%
3. Prior affection	18%	50%
4. Nonsexual affection	23%	43%
5. Sexual dissatisfaction	7%	17%
6. Incompatibility	5%	0%
7. Infidelity	2%	3%

Administrator respondents' scores are fairly close to the norm for all gifts. Frequency of sexual relations is slightly less of a problem, as are several other items. Wise administrators and their spouses block time for romance and sex into their busy schedules.

Administrator wives (see chart B below) are more demonstrative, affectionate and communicative about sex than administra-

B. To what degree, from 1 to 7, are you one way or the other:

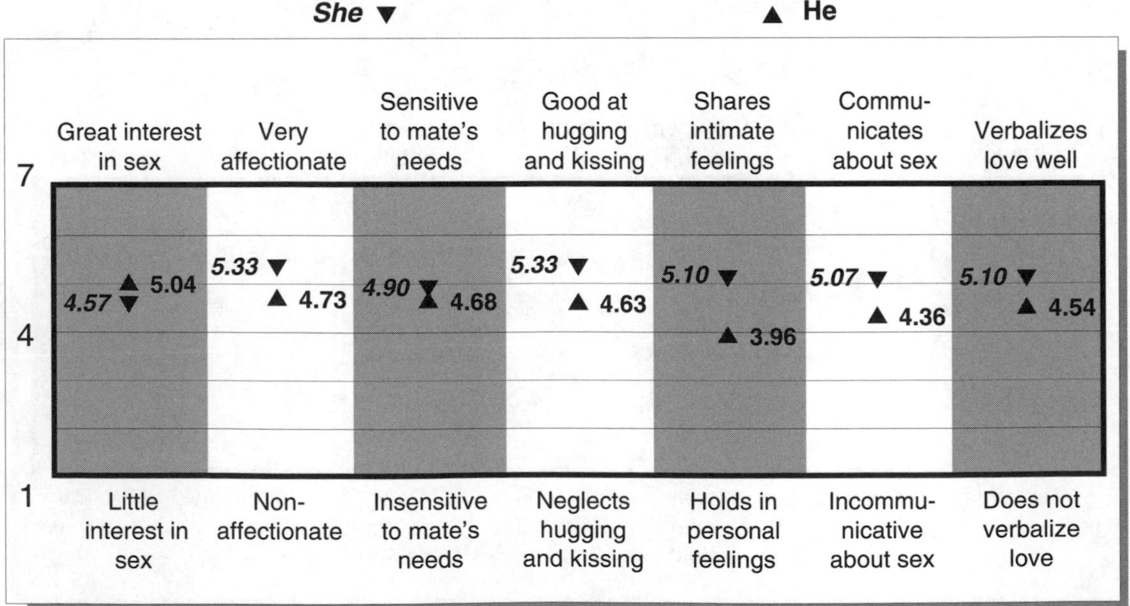

tor husbands, although both score reasonably well in these areas. Husbands need to learn how to share intimate feelings better.

C. My genuine needs, views or beliefs are:

	He	She
1. I need more nonsexual affection from my mate.	19%	57%
2. I need more sexual relations with my mate.	39%	13%
3. I feel I need more hugs and kisses from my spouse.	28%	33%
4. I need to hear more "I love you's" from my partner.	23%	23%
5. I need my husband to better understand my monthly cycle.	0%	20%
6. I feel dissatisfied with our current sexual relationship.	21%	17%
7. I feel satisfied with our current sexual relationship.	56%	67%

A good percentage are satisfied with their sexual relationship, but more than half of all administrator wives express the need for more nonsexual affection. One administrator wife realized her husband did not understand this need, so she got him a good book on the subject and flagged the appropriate pages. She found he responded once he knew what she needed.

Category 12: Work and Accomplishments

A. I feel we have some problems regarding work and accomplishments in these areas:

	He	She
1. Too busy	35%	50%
2. Career conflicts	12%	30%
3. Overtime work	23%	13%
4. Inadequate income	46%	40%
5. Volunteer work	9%	13%
6. Wife working	11%	3%
7. Priorities	18%	7%

Administrators can easily become married to their jobs. They enjoy a challenge and throw themselves wholeheartedly into whatever they do. If their jobs enable them to utilize their God-given gifting, it is easy to become overinvolved.

Career conflicts are experienced more by administrator wives who work outside the home. As one explained to us, "I work the same forty hours a week at my job as my husband does, but I have more work to do at home. But he is learning to pitch in and do his share."

They score higher in the belief that their income is inadequate. Administrators are more often overqualified for what they do and realize their potential for earning more. Their income satisfaction level may not be as easily met. They establish priorities easily, but husbands admit a little more difficulty keeping priorities in order.

Administrators (see chart B on page 246) live by setting goals. It helps them keep their focus and avoid distractions. They are industrious without necessarily becoming workaholics. They are great accomplishers. While they are organized in handling their responsibilities, however, they are not organized in handling details or routine things, preferring to delegate. My greatest dream (as I have already hinted) is to have a full-time maid/secretary!

While administrator wives have the potential for earning good wages, scores are lower here because some respondents are currently homemakers or working only part-time.

B. To what degree, from 1 to 7, are you one way or the other:

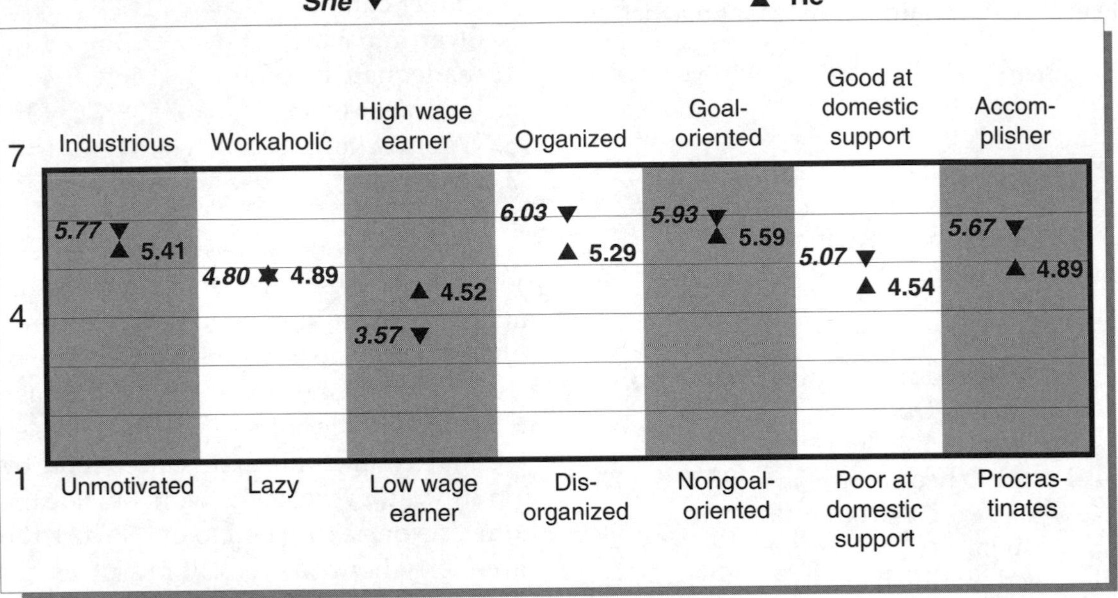

C. My genuine needs, views or beliefs are:

	He	She
1. I need my husband to provide our basic expenses.	0%	50%
2. I need my wife to be a full-time homemaker.	21%	0%
3. I need to be the sole provider for my family.	16%	0%
4. I need a fulfilling career.	61%	20%
5. I need a challenge to work toward.	68%	50%
6. I get great joy out of my accomplishments.	81%	87%
7. I am satisfied with the way we handle work and accomplishments.	56%	70%

Most are satisfied with work and accomplishments. Administrators need a challenge to work toward. Don often tells me he is the only challenge I need. That may be true. Mostly he is the delight of my life! But my career opportunities over the years have all offered challenges—being a director of Christian education, writing Sunday school curriculum, developing the *Aglow* magazine and TV talk show, and now writing books. I have loved it!

Category 13: Financial Management

A. I feel we have some problems in financial matters in these areas:

	He	She
1. Establishing budget	46%	47%
2. Keeping to budget	58%	53%
3. Living beyond means	35%	33%
4. Credit cards	25%	13%
5. Impulsive buying	30%	40%
6. Money arguments	26%	17%
7. Wife's work role	4%	3%

Like most gifts, administrators have some problems establishing and keeping to a budget, although administrator husbands scored lower than the norm. They also scored lower in living beyond their means and impulsive buying. Women scored higher on the latter. Administrator wives tend to think, *As long as I'm here and it's something we can use, why not buy it now? I might not be back here for a while.* This is rationalization and needs reining in. Don and I have agreed that I am not to buy any item over $25 without consulting him first.

Jennifer, a usually well-disciplined administrator, says, "I actually don't mind working with Jerry to set up our budget. It's just that I get so busy I forget to refer to it. So he brings me back in line when I need it."

Administrators (see chart B below) are above average in handling money well. They like to see the overall financial picture, even making graphs or pie charts and setting goals. "Now that I'm computer-literate," says Byron, "I do monthly printouts so my wife and I can go over our budget and evaluate how we're doing."

Note the bargain-hunting scores. I always thought my love of garage and rummage sales came from being born at the tail-end of the Depression, but other administrators say they, too, love to scrounge around for good items at fantastic prices.

Administrators are reasonable savers, mostly generous and strong tithers. The only low score reflects slight feelings of financial insecurity by some administrator husbands, yet most are more than adequate providers. It is more likely feeling than reality.

C. My genuine needs, views or beliefs are:

	He	She
1. I feel we need to reduce our debts more effectively.	58%	40%
2. I feel the need to be in charge of our family finances.	28%	23%
3. I believe the husband should handle the family finances.	26%	37%
4. I think the most capable partner should handle the family finances.	56%	67%

B. To what degree, from 1 to 7, are you one way or the other:

7 (top) / 1 (bottom)	She ▼	He ▲
Conservative buyer / Impulsive buyer	4.97	4.73
Keeps within budget / Over-spends budget	4.73	4.45
Bargain-hunter / Disregards budget	5.70	4.86
Save now—pay later / Buy now—pay later	4.73	4.68
Feels financially secure / Feels financially insecure	4.60	3.95
Generous / Stingy	5.17	4.88
Tither / Nontither	6.50	5.41

	He	She
5. I need to learn how to handle money more responsibly.	26%	13%
6. I would like to give more to church, missionaries, charity, etc.	58%	43%
7. I am satisfied with how we handle finances.	40%	50%

While a good percentage of administrator spouses are satisfied with how they handle finances, quite a few feel the need for more effective debt reduction. They tend to worry about expenses compared to income, taking financial responsibility seriously.

For a while Marshall did some moonlighting to make sure expenses were covered. "One day I realized this was not wise," he explained. "We had expanded our standard of living too much. So I had a heart-to-heart talk with my family and we readjusted our lifestyle to fit one salary. We found there were lots of things we really didn't need. We get along fine now."

Category 14: Leisure Activities

A. I FEEL WE HAVE SOME PROBLEMS IN HOW WE SPEND OUR FREE TIME IN THESE AREAS:

	He	She
1. Interests	32%	30%
2. Recreational preferences	16%	17%
3. Hobbies	32%	33%
4. Entertainment	30%	20%
5. Vacation preferences	16%	10%
6. Sports	25%	13%
7. TV-watching	35%	37%

Administrators have more differences with their mates than the norm on interests, hobbies and entertainment preferences. Scores are mostly around thirty percent, however, which means more than two-thirds do not see these as problem areas.

Administrators allow naturally for differences. Vance, a builder-developer, says, "Lucille and I enjoy movies and plays, but if I suggest going to a football game, she suggests I take our son instead. We love traveling together, but she's a seashore person and I'm a mountain man. So we take turns picking a vacation spot. My hobby's woodcarving and she restores old dolls. But at least we can pursue these together in our basement workshop."

Too much TV-watching is less of a problem than the norm. Mostly administrators are too involved in life to waste time. They are more likely to pick and choose when they want to escape into TV-land.

Administrator wives score a little higher here (see chart B on page 249) but both are definitely on the social side. Relationships are essential to administrators. They relate well to people of all kinds and ages, including children. Reasonably athletic, they also enjoy long walks and talks. They have a greater-than-average appreciation for the arts, often taking advantage of cultural opportunities.

About average at relaxing, most administrators tell us they can relax better if they get out of town. Don and I are grateful to have a cabin to escape to, only 45 minutes away but like a different world, and the only place we are free from the constant ringing of the phone.

C. MY GENUINE NEEDS, VIEWS OR BELIEFS ARE:

	He	She
1. I need my partner to be a recreational companion.	47%	43%
2. I need to do more fun things with my spouse.	65%	70%
3. I need more meaningful vacations.	39%	37%

B. To what degree, from 1 to 7, are you one way or the other:

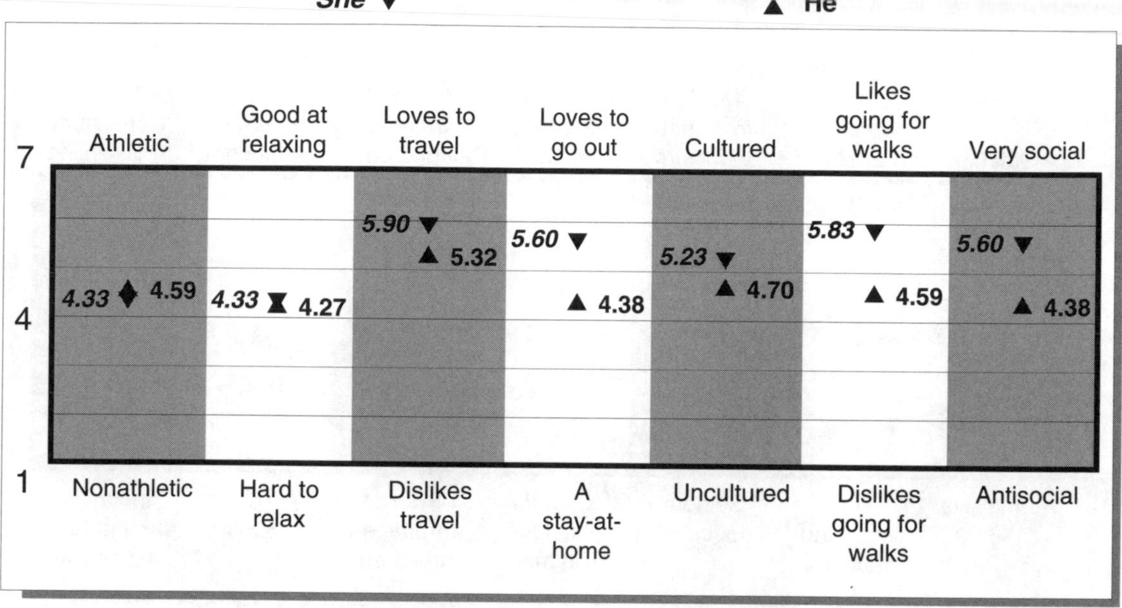

	He	She
4. I need to be involved in nonathletic leisure activities.	25%	20%
5. I prefer active group or competitive sports.	42%	17%
6. I prefer individual noncompetitive sports.	16%	33%
7. I am satisfied with how we spend our leisure time.	30%	43%

Leisure time is important for rest and refreshment. One administrator pastor neglected a weekly day of rest for so long that he experienced burnout. His wise board insisted that he take a month off and promise to take his day of rest from then on.

Administrator spouses express a strong need for their spouses to be recreational companions, and especially to do more fun things together. If necessary they should schedule these in their daily planners. R&R is essential for balance in any marital relationship.

Category 15: Parenting

A. I feel we have (had) some problems in the child-rearing process in these areas:

	He	She
1. Type of discipline	21%	33%
2. Amount of discipline	21%	27%
3. Who disciplines	16%	20%
4. Misconduct determination	19%	27%
5. Love expression	16%	7%
6. Time spent	33%	17%
7. Money given	19%	17%

Administrator spouses are usually good at parenting. What they do not know, they are likely to research until they feel confident. They believe strongly in lines of authority in the family and the children's responsibility to be obedient to the father as head of the household and to the mother as second-in-command. Administrators are methodical and fair about discipline, and they follow through!

B. To what degree, from 1 to 7, are you one way or the other:

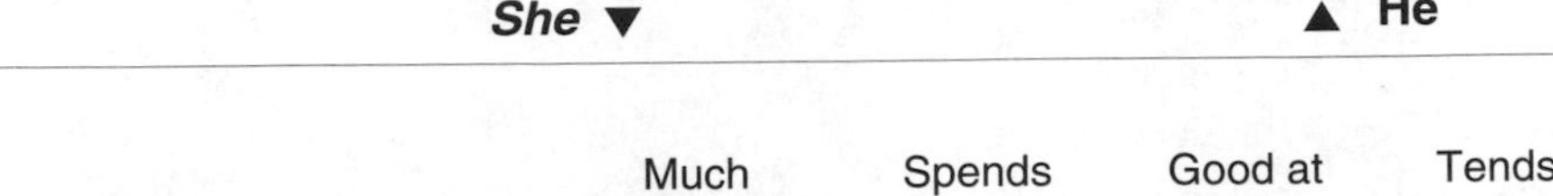

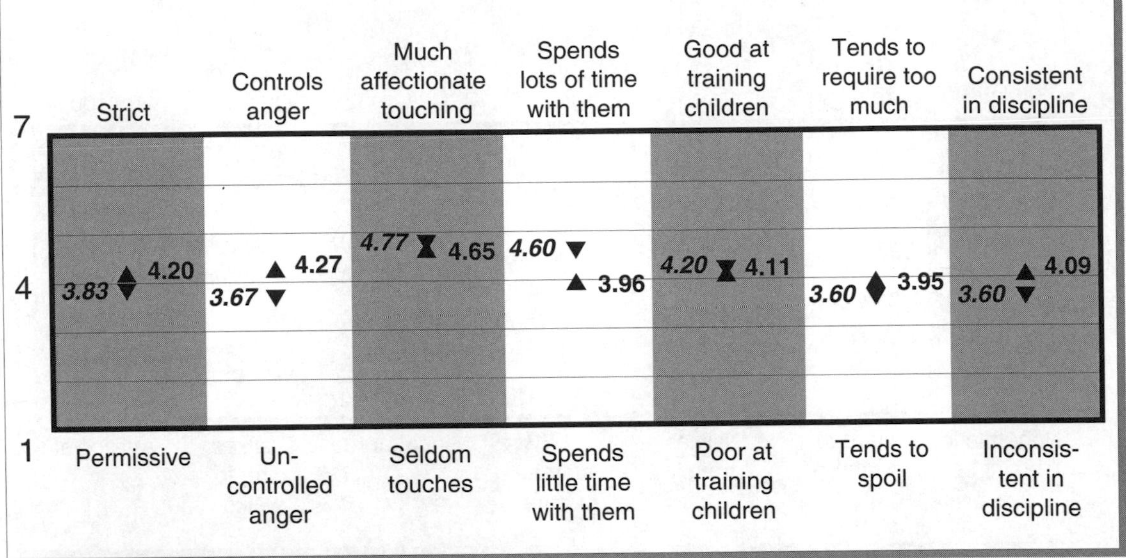

Administrator wives do even better than administrator husbands in expressing love to their children and spending quality time with them.

The respondents scored near the middle here (see chart B above), balanced in how they handle child-rearing. Scores in affectionate touch and time spent with the children were higher, except for some husbands who realized they need to spend more quality time with their children.

C. My genuine needs, views or beliefs are:

	He	She
1. We need to provide better spiritual guidance for our children.	42%	37%
2. We need to give our children more love and affection.	26%	17%
3. I'd like my spouse to help more with the children.	2%	33%
4. I need to be more affirming of our children.	32%	33%
5. I feel we need to agree more on discipline.	11%	13%
6. I feel we need more quality family time and activities.	42%	30%
7. I am satisfied with our parenting styles and skills.	37%	53%

While half of the administrator wives are satisfied with their parenting skills, only a third of the husbands are. Busyness may account for part of this, as indicated by their expressed need for more quality family time and providing better spiritual guidance.

Category 16: In-Laws and Family

A. I feel we have some problems with our families and in-laws in these areas:

	He	She
1. Interference	12%	10%

B. To what degree, from 1 to 7, are you one way or the other:

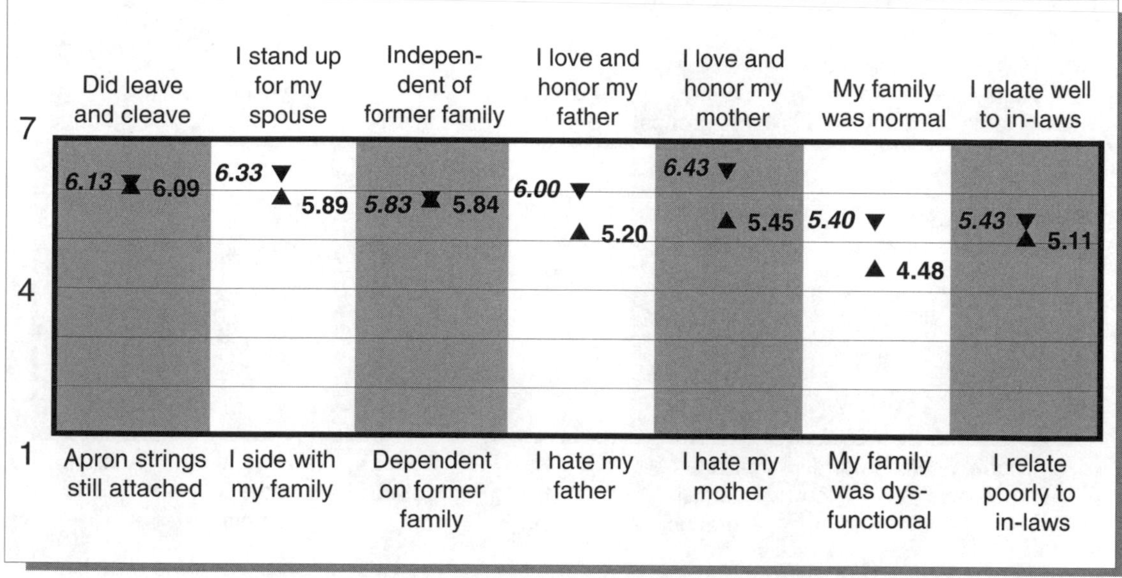

	He	She
2. Their expectations	12%	7%
3. Their visits	2%	0%
4. Comparisons	9%	17%
5. Borrowing money	5%	3%
6. Former abuse	14%	13%
7. Dysfunction affect	23%	30%

Problems are minimal here. With administrators' keen sense of responsibility to their primary families, they do not usually allow extended family interference.

Administrators (see chart B above) have very high scores on in-law relationships. They are able to cut the apron strings appropriately, yet love and honor their parents.

C. My genuine needs, views or beliefs are:

	He	She
1. I need my spouse to put me before his or her family.	30%	50%
2. I need to see or talk to my parent(s) regularly.	19%	43%
3. I need to include my family in holiday celebrations.	23%	40%
4. I need help in overcoming in-law problems.	5%	13%
5. I need to be accepted by my in-laws.	12%	13%
6. I need to be financially free from my family and my in-laws.	18%	13%
7. I am satisfied with our family and in-law relationships.	67%	80%

Most administrators are satisfied with their extended family relationships. Administrator women feel the need more than administrator men to relate to their parents and include them in birthday and holiday celebrations. Both handle this wisely and well.

B. To what degree, from 1 to 7, are you one way or the other:

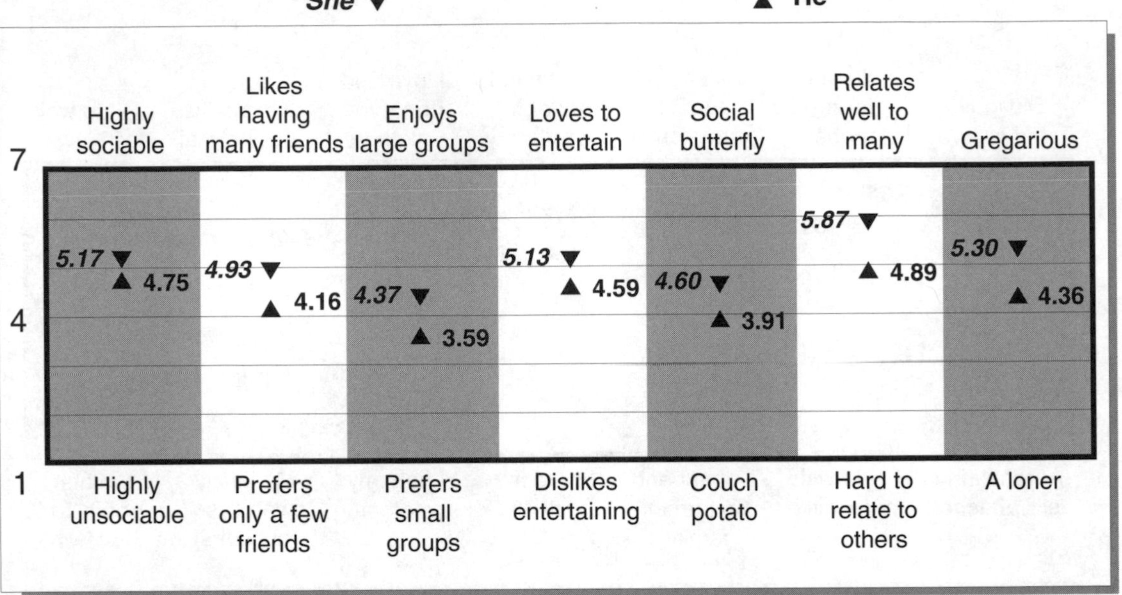

Category 17: Social Relationships

A. I feel we have some problems in social relationships in these areas:

	He	She
1. Friends' demands	5%	7%
2. Time for friends	35%	43%
3. Unsocial partner	14%	13%
4. Too social partner	7%	7%
5. Wrong friendships	0%	0%
6. Negative influence	5%	0%
7. Overinvolvement	5%	7%

Responses here are average, some even less of a problem. Having enough time for friends is the major problem (as it is for the other gifts). Many administrators say they usually get together enough with current friends but have former friends they long to see.

Lloyd, who has a large accounting business, says, "We often go out for dinner spontaneously with friends after church. My work causes us to get together socially with our friends there. But we have friends from former churches and from high school and college days we seldom see unless we deliberately schedule a time. So now we've worked out a plan. Every spring vacation is time for a reunion with our closest high school friends. Each Christmas season we schedule a special open house for our college friends. The second Saturday of each month we plan dinner, either in or out, with two to four of our former church friends. With planning we do it. Without planning, time slips by and we regret it."

Administrator spouses (see chart B above) are gregarious, highly sociable and like having many friends. They like to entertain, relate well to many kinds of people and enjoy groups. Administrator husbands prefer their groups somewhat smaller and admit that sometimes they enjoy being couch potatoes—but not all the time. Administrator wives tend to think, *The more the merrier,* and feel better if their social calendars are reasonably full.

C. My genuine needs, views or beliefs are:

	He	She
1. I need to have many friends.	14%	27%
2. I especially love to entertain in our home.	25%	47%
3. I need a good deal of private time.	40%	30%
4. I need our home to be a haven of rest.	61%	57%
5. I need to be involved in social groups.	23%	47%
6. I think we need to change some friendships.	7%	3%
7. I am satisfied with our social life.	46%	63%

A good percentage of these respondents are satisfied with their social lives. The scores underline the fact that administrator wives are generally more sociable than their male counterparts, but both need times when their homes are truly havens of rest.

Category 18: Religious Orientation

A. I feel we have some problems in our spiritual life and orientation in these areas:

	He	She
1. Affiliation disagreement	2%	3%
2. Church attendance	4%	0%
3. Different backgrounds	7%	0%
4. Theological differences	2%	0%
5. Commitment level	14%	17%
6. Irregular attendance	12%	3%
7. Hypocritical behavior	7%	10%

Administrators usually have a solid belief system. They have probably examined the basis of their faith thoroughly. While they are open to look at various theological perspectives, they tend to hold firmly to their own. They give their spouses room for differences of belief as long as these differences are not foundational.

Administrators have high scores here (see chart B below). They see themselves as spiritual and growing spiritually. Their faith is strong and their commitment to

B. To what degree, from 1 to 7, are you one way or the other:

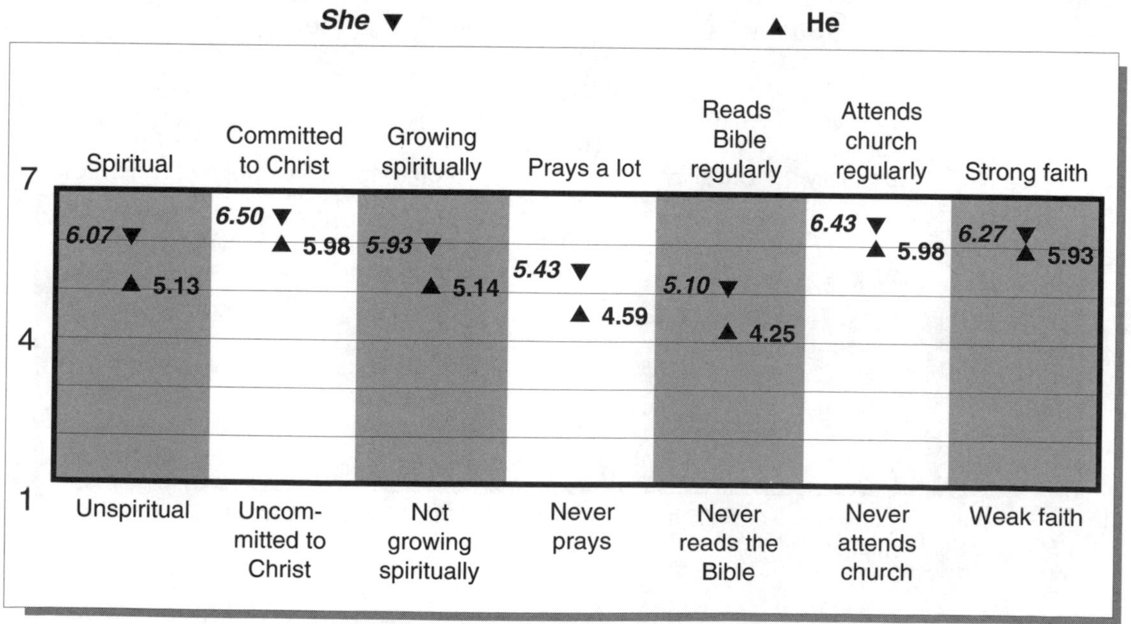

Christ unwavering. Church attendance is regular unless they are truly unable to get there. Because Fred's sales territory covers the entire Northwest, he says, "it means that at least once a month I have to be out of town. I really dislike missing church. But wherever I am, I find a local body of believers to worship with."

Administrator wives pray and read the Bible more than administrator husbands. Because wives tend to have more time to do so? Just a conjecture.

C. My genuine needs, views or beliefs are:

	He	She
1. I need to attend church regularly.	67%	73%
2. I need my partner to pray with me daily.	30%	57%
3. I greatly desire to see my spouse grow spiritually.	56%	73%
4. I believe we need to have regular family devotions.	49%	70%
5. I need my spouse to give spiritual leadership.	5%	70%
6. I need to be able to live my faith, not just talk about it.	58%	67%
7. I am satisfied with our religious orientation and practice.	54%	63%

Most administrators report satisfaction with their spiritual lives. They are concerned about living their faith, and most want to be involved in ministry in their churches, more than just attend services. They like having their mates involved in that ministry, too. While I have enjoyed all the ministries the Lord has given me, my favorite has been team-teaching with Don these past 21 years.

An administrator wife greatly desires to have her husband's spiritual leadership in the family and in family devotions. But if he will not, she will, not wanting a spiritual vacuum to be left.

B. To what degree, from 1 to 7, are you one way or the other:

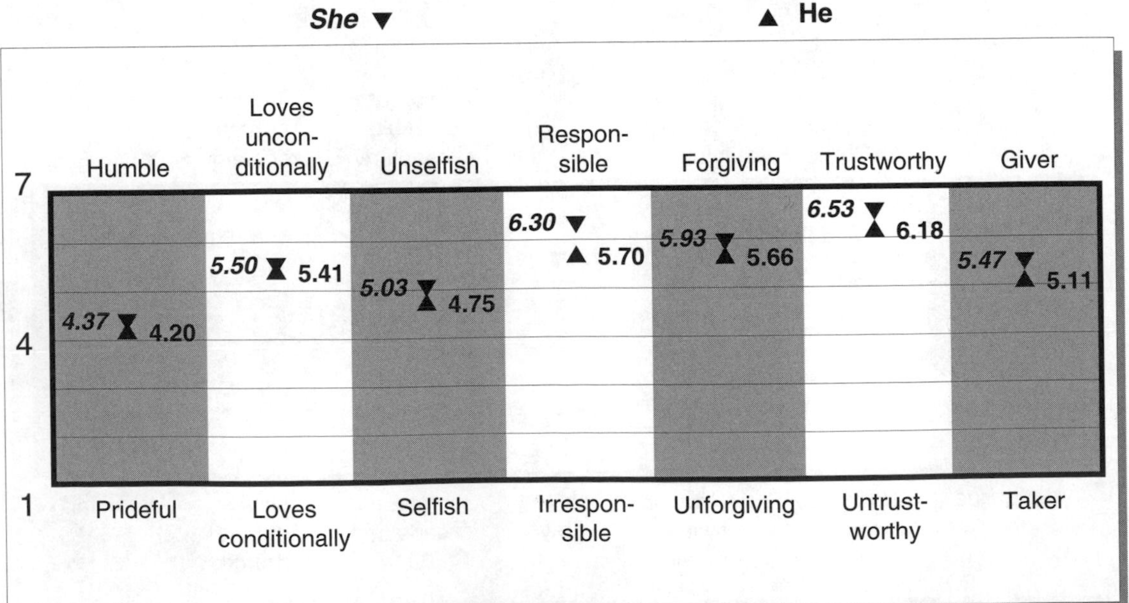

Category 19: Maturity

A. I FEEL WE HAVE SOME PROBLEMS IN MATURITY IN THESE AREAS:

	He	She
1. Inexperience	4%	10%
2. Irresponsibility	12%	7%
3. Blame game	16%	17%
4. Stress coping	28%	40%
5. Criticism	25%	10%
6. Infidelity	0%	0%
7. Dishonesty	2%	3%

Administrators tend to take their marriage responsibilities seriously and do their best to be responsible and mature. Coping with stress, the major problem here, nevertheless ranks lower than the norm. Administrator mates seem to have some natural abilities for dealing with stress.

Strong character traits (see chart B on page 254) for administrators are responsibility and trustworthiness. Their mates can count on them. Administrators are also unselfish, quick to forgive and love unconditionally. They tend to be givers rather than takers.

C. MY GENUINE NEEDS, VIEWS OR BELIEFS ARE:

	He	She
1. I need to be able to trust my mate.	46%	67%
2. I need my spouse to be dependable.	46%	70%
3. I need to be quick to forgive and, hopefully, be forgiving quickly.	67%	63%
4. We need to learn from and grow through every experience.	67%	80%
5. I need my mate to be able to handle responsibility well.	49%	73%
6. I need my mate to love me unconditionally.	53%	67%
7. I feel that we are a reasonably mature couple.	81%	97%

Administrators score themselves very highly in being part of "a reasonably mature couple." They usually are. The qualities they try to demonstrate they hope to see in their mates as well, and they will give positive encouragement to that end.

They look at life comprehensively, weighing all in light of learning and growing through every experience. They tend to view even negative experiences with God's long-range plan in mind. They want to leave something of value to the world from their lives and ministries.

Category 20: Dysfunctionality

A. I FEEL WE HAVE SOME PROBLEMS IN THE FOLLOWING AREAS THAT PRODUCE DYSFUNCTION:

	He	She
1. Alcohol abuse	2%	0%
2. Drug abuse	0%	0%
3. Physical abuse	0%	0%
4. Sexual abuse	2%	0%
5. Verbal abuse	19%	13%
6. Emotional abuse	16%	10%
7. Unresolved abuse	16%	20%

The responses here basically fit the norm for all gifts. Administrator men score a bit higher than administrator women in the areas of verbal and emotional abuse. Most will repent of it quickly when it is brought to their attention.

Administrator spouses (see chart B on page 256) seldom tend to be abusive or dysfunctional.

B. To what degree, from 1 to 7, are you one way or the other:

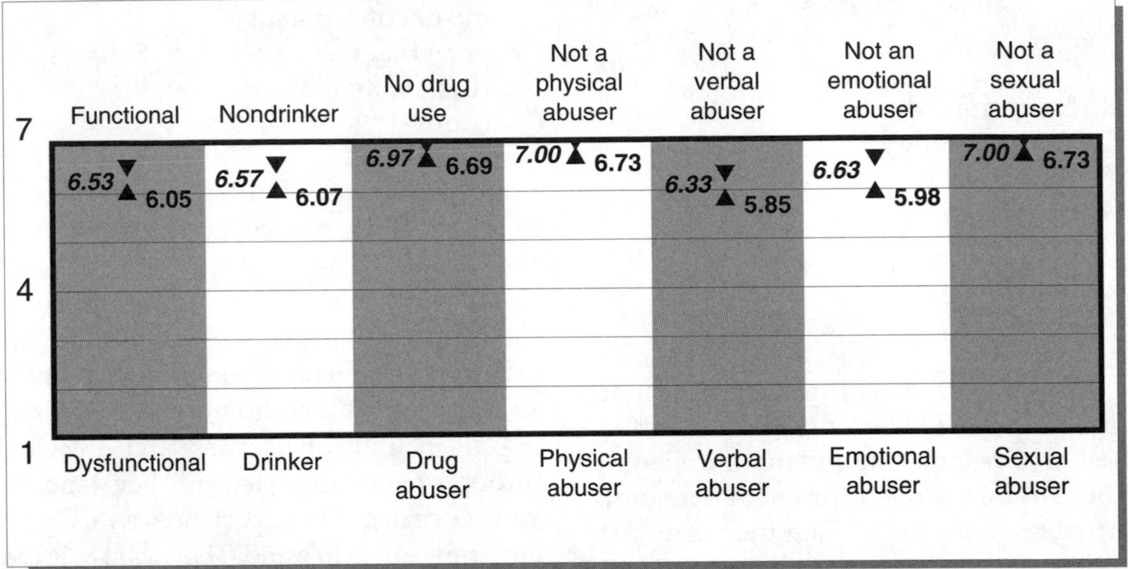

C. My genuine needs, views or beliefs are:

	He	She
1. I need our marriage to be free of alcohol use and abuse.	32%	30%
2. I need our marriage to be free of drug use and abuse.	44%	40%
3. I need my spouse to treat me more kindly.	18%	20%
4. I need my mate to give me positive emotional support.	46%	53%
5. One or both of us need to get help for abuse in childhood.	11%	13%
6. One or both of us need to get help for dysfunctional behavior.	12%	10%
7. I believe there is no dysfunctional behavior in our marriage.	58%	70%

The majority of administrator spouses believe there is no dysfunctional behavior in their marital relationships. About half, on the other hand, could use more positive emotional support.

Living with a Compassion Spouse

It is difficult for compassion people to make decisions. They will ponder the possible consequences, delay as long as they can and transfer the responsibility, if possible, to others.

One young man in our church with a compassion gift married a young woman with the same gift. Decision-making became double trouble.

On the way home from work one afternoon, an hour earlier than usual, Chuck was excited about surprising Sue by taking her out for dinner. They did not do it often, and usually only on special occasions. Married only a year with a tight budget, they had to be frugal. But with both of them having a compassion gift, they were content living on love.

"Sue!" Chuck called as he walked in the front door. "I've got a surprise for you."

"Chuck, what are you doing home early?" she asked as she appeared from the kitchen. "I was just trying to decide what to have for dinner."

"That's the surprise," Chuck announced. "The boss let me come home early. I'm taking you out for dinner."

"What's the occasion? Did I forget something?"

"No, nothing special. It's just that *you're* special and it's been a while since we've gone out for dinner."

"But can we afford it?"

"I just want to spend some special time with the special person in my life. We can have macaroni and cheese tomorrow night."

"You're wonderful," Sue cooed, giving Chuck a big hug and a squeeze.

"So, where would you like to go?"

"Oh, I don't care. You decide."

"No, you pick the place."

"I'd feel better if you did."

"I had to make the choice last time. It's your turn."

"Anyplace is O.K. with me."

"Just pick one, then."

"I don't want to!"

"Well, I don't either."

By this time they were getting angry. Dinner out was aborted. But the conversation helped them realize they needed help in decision-making, and they sought counsel from the pastor.

Five Major Problem Areas

First we will look at the five most significant problems areas of the compassion gift, which in turn influence the problems experienced in each of the twenty categories of our survey.

1. Indecisiveness

Compassion spouses prefer their mates to be the decision-makers. They will help with the process, if asked, but will defer the final decision, if possible. They do not want to be responsible for making bad decisions or decisions that hurt someone's feelings. They would rather go with the flow, adjust to the situation or blend in. They prefer a chameleon role. They are natural followers, not leaders.

Compassion husbands must learn a measure of leadership for their families, however, and develop decision-making abilities. Wise counsel from a pastor or elder can help immensely.

2. Compromise

Because compassion spouses want to get along with everyone, especially their spouses, they are quick to adjust or accommodate. They compromise easily. There are some areas in which they will not budge, but usually they are content to give in to their spouses' desires.

They are peacemakers, sometimes to the extreme of peace at any price. This is why some endure abuse without complaint, often blaming themselves for not being better partners. A harmonious relationship takes precedence over everything. I have counseled many compassion wives who are surprised to learn that God does not expect them to put up with ongoing abuse. And they fear that, as one woman put it, "My husband might leave me if I complain or resist his abuse."

3. Slowness

Compassion people are the slowest of all the gifts. They take their time. *Hurry* is not in their vocabulary. They are nearly always late. They wish clocks did not exist. Their idea of paradise is a tropical island without time constrictions. If two people with compassion gifts are married to each other, they understand one another and go with the flow. A compassion gift married to one of the other six motivational gifts, however, will likely frustrate the spouse with a seeming lack of concern for punctuality.

Although the problem of slowness and disregard for time may never be fully resolved, a couple can work out ways of mitigating the effect. As one husband discovered, "If I tell my compassion wife we must leave fifteen minutes before we actually have to, she's always 'on time'!"

4. Supersensitivity

Compassion people, of all the gifts, are the most easily wounded. They are supersensitive and easily offended. They tend to be strongly subjective, taking things personally and often fearing to do something wrong or disappoint their mates. They cry easily, sometimes not even knowing why. A spouse's reprimand may ruin the day. If spoken to firmly, they may harbor hurt for the rest of the day. If put down by their mates, they may grow angry but they seldom express the anger outwardly. They are stuffers of negative feelings and must learn to express those feelings appropriately. They need lots of expressions of love daily, through words and physical touch. They heal quickly in this kind of loving atmosphere.

5. Illogic and Emotion

Compassion people are more dependent than all the gifts on their feelings and emotions. God has made them this way and they need to be accepted for the loving, caring people they are. But they tend at times to be illogical. Unless the spouse can enter their feeling world, understanding will be difficult. Compassion spouses can be told not to do something, yet wind up doing it "just because I felt like it." Compassion wives especially can be emotional and illogical. A husband can give his compassion wife a dozen reasons why she should break off an unhealthy friendship, but she will give a dozen reasons why she needs to continue to reach out to her dysfunctional friend.

Sometimes compassion mates are unrealistic about life, responsibilities or relationships. Reason does not always compute. They can also drift into fantasy when real life becomes too painful. Denial is easy for those with a compassion gift. They are also the most prone to escape life's hard realities (especially physical and emotional abuse) through the avenue of drugs or alcohol.

A word of wisdom for the spouse of a compassion gift: Handle with care, lots of it!

The Twenty Problem Categories of the Compassion Gift

Let's take a look at the twenty categories of problem areas for compassion spouses indicated by our marriage survey.

Category 1: Communication

A. I FEEL WE HAVE SOME PROBLEMS IN COMMUNICATION IN THESE AREAS:

	He	She
1. Misunderstandings	38%	43%
2. Free to share	50%	54%
3. Listening	50%	61%
4. Conversation	27%	57%
5. Correction	50%	41%
6. Body language	19%	28%
7. Ridicule	38%	37%

In general compassion people indicate more problems in communication than the norm. One area is misunderstanding. Often the compassion spouse takes things the wrong way. Brenda admits she is prone to read negative overtones into her husband's remarks. "When he says, 'We're out of milk,'" she explains, "I hear, 'You've let us run out of milk again.' I tend to take everything personally. I'm trying to overcome this, but it's difficult."

Compassion spouses tend to fear what others will think about what they say. If they have been rebuffed by their spouses when they have been brave enough to open up and share their feelings honestly, they will start to "turtle."

Tony, a compassion man married to a perceiver, confessed, "I tend to pull in and hide my feelings a lot. Gloria has such a sharp tongue that I've found it safer not to tell her always what I'm feeling. But we're getting some good counseling now and we're both learning to change."

Compassion spouses listen well. They are genuinely interested in what their mates have to say and will even stop what they are doing to listen attentively. They tend to feel rejected if their mates ignore what *they* say.

Compassion spouses require some spousal communication from the heart.

B. To what degree, from 1 to 7, are you one way or the other:

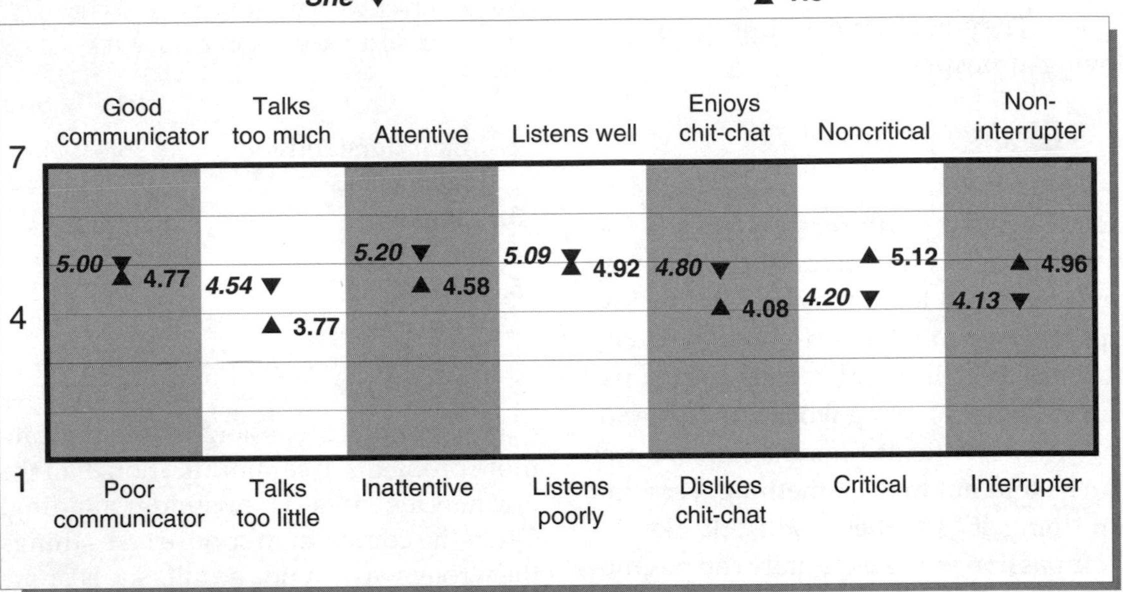

"Frank can tell me all the details of his day at work," Lisa says, "but that's not enough for me. I need to hear how he feels about what happened as well. I need him to be interested in how I feel, too."

Giving correction is not a habit of compassion spouses, but they do have difficulty taking correction from their mates, which they tend to interpret as criticism. One man said that even if he points out a misspelled word in a letter his compassion wife has written, she gets tears in her eyes.

Compassion people are usually good at reading and expressing all kinds of nonverbal communication. They can hardly hide what they feel. "Sometimes I chuckle at my wife," Ian says. "She tries to cover up what she's feeling, but her eyes, her facial expression and her body language reveal it all. She easily reads my body language as well."

Compassion people try hard to be kind, considerate and careful with their words. "I've watched my husband stop in the middle of a sentence to pick a word carefully so as not to offend me," Yvonne told us. "Larry is so considerate. He never ridicules me or makes sarcastic remarks. But if I do, I really hurt his feelings."

Compassion husbands (see chart B above) claim they talk too little while their female counterparts lean toward talking too much. Wives enjoy chit-chat more, even if it is insignificant. They feel there is value in the warm interaction. Robin, a compassionate missionary at home and abroad, loves to get people together in small groups so they can get to know each other better. "It's the interaction in the conversation that builds relationships," she says.

C. My genuine needs, views or beliefs are:

	He	She
1. I need more conversation with my mate.	46%	67%
2. I need my partner to listen to me more attentively.	23%	70%
3. I need more quiet time without conversation.	19%	15%

	He	She
4. I feel we need to share more intimately our thoughts and feelings.	35%	65%
5. I get hurt easily by my mate's unkind remarks.	42%	54%
6. I need more of my partner's undivided attention.	27%	54%
7. I am satisfied with our communication and conversation.	42%	20%

Most compassion mates, especially wives, are starved for meaningful communication with their spouses. "I would love it if Mike would just sit and talk with me when he gets home from work," Sheila said longingly. "He feels he can't 'waste' the time because there's always so much to do. Even when he makes the effort, I feel he's only half there."

Compassion gifts married to one another (the gift most likely to marry the same gift) will find the greatest opportunity for intensive as well as extensive conversation. If married to exhorters or administrators, they may fare almost as well.

Compassion people are the most easily wounded of all. They are tenderhearted, softspoken and exceedingly kind. They wish other people were that way, too. It is especially difficult for a compassion person to be married to a perceiver gift, unless the perceiver is mature and gentle. We have counseled many couples with this combination and found the stress on the compassion partner so overwhelming that he or she may want to escape the relationship.

Toby put it this way: "My wife is biting and devouring me. I love her but not what her mouth does to me. She constantly criticizes and ridicules me in public. If she doesn't change, I want out." We spent many counseling sessions with Toby and his wife, with good results. Coming to understand one another's motivational gifts enabled them to accept their differences, develop more positive ways of communication and rebuild the love that had been destroyed.

Category 2: Expectations

A. I FEEL WE HAVE SOME PROBLEMS IN WHAT WE EXPECT OF EACH OTHER IN THESE AREAS:

	He	She
1. Lifestyle	19%	37%
2. Priorities	42%	57%
3. Ideals/goals	12%	33%
4. Holidays	12%	26%
5. Hopes/dreams	8%	26%
6. Conduct	12%	33%
7. Homework	38%	50%

Because compassion spouses operate on the feeling level more than any other gift, they can hold unrealistic expectations of their mates. Compassion women are often attracted to men with opposite characteristics, yet expect these men to be as sensitive, caring and kind as they are. "At first I projected impossible expectations onto my teacher husband," Lois admitted. "I set myself up for disappointment. Now that I understand how differently we're gifted, my expectations have become realistic and our marital problems have diminished greatly."

Top priority for compassion spouses is a loving and peaceful relationship. Anything less than this is considered a failure. They will work hard to achieve it and experience great disappointment if their mates are not as concerned about it as they are.

Compassion people are idealists rather than realists, sometimes to the extreme. They would like a perfect world in which everyone loves everyone else—a world without war, hatred, sin, even death. They

B. To what degree, from 1 to 7, are you one way or the other:

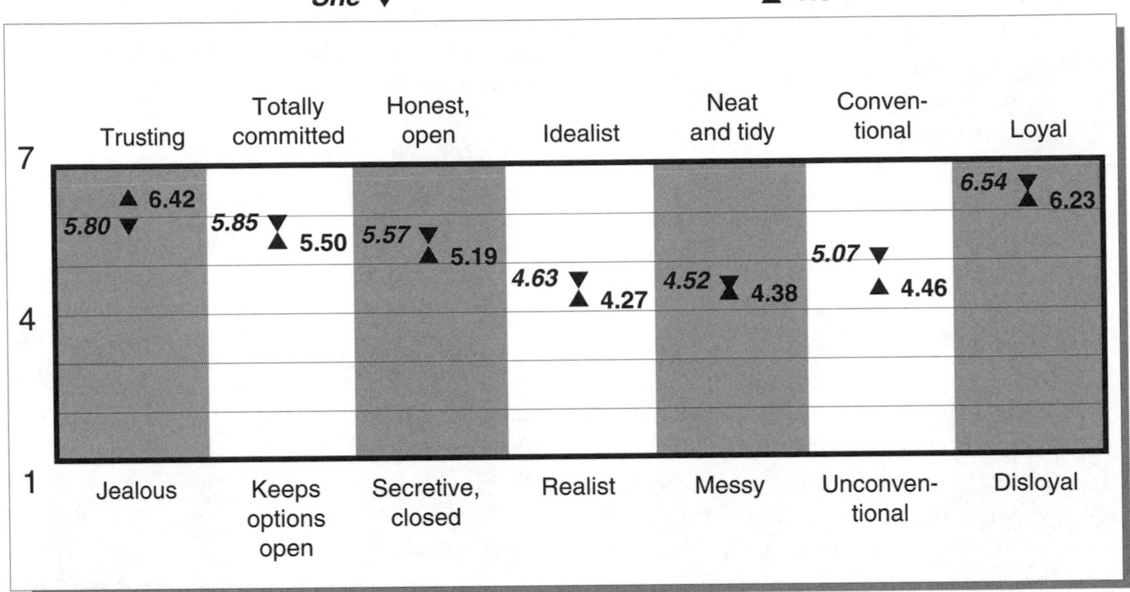

tend to have the highest ideals for their marriages and must adjust these to reality or they will live with disappointment. Daydreaming is a habit often developed during childhood that may still be there in adulthood. These dreams need to become more realistic.

Compassion wives are more concerned about the specifics of holiday celebrations. They are more likely to want extended family together and to develop special family customs.

Compassion wives are a bit more opinionated about what is proper and acceptable conduct than wives with other gifts, and also than compassion husbands, who score at the norm.

Compassion gifts are fairly good at helping with housework, although they are sidetracked easily and their pace can be slower than some. Rene, who does childcare at home, says, "I really like to have my home neat and orderly, but with three extra children to care for, it seems like a never-ending job. Blowing noses and listening to the children takes precedence over dusting and putting away toys, so sometimes Alan gives me a hand when he gets home."

Trusting and *trustworthy* describe a compassion person (see chart B above). Even when someone proves untrustworthy, the compassion person will offer another chance, and another. This tends to apply to the marriage as well. Some might call this naïve, but compassion people see it as expecting the best eventually to develop in their mates. Compassion people are committed strongly to their marriages; loyalty is a way of life.

Compassion mates are seldom the ones to initiate divorce, sticking by their spouses even to the extreme of staying in an abusive relationship. Tamera kept thinking her husband would stop beating her, and his tirades began to make her think she was somehow at fault. "I kept trying to be a better wife so he'd stop the abuse," she shared with us. "I became reclusive, depressed and hardly able to function. My parents finally had to rescue me from the situation that was destroying me."

C. My genuine needs, views or beliefs are:

	He	She
1. I need to be more sure of my partner's motives.	15%	20%
2. I need a mate who is dependable.	31%	41%
3. I feel we need to work more at setting joint priorities.	31%	57%
4. I need to be more confident in how my mate handles stress.	38%	35%
5. I need my spouse to be totally honest with me.	38%	37%
6. I need to have former family customs a part of my life.	15%	15%
7. I feel our expectations are realistic and workable.	92%	54%

Almost all compassion husbands feel their expectations are realistic and workable, while little more than half of the compassion wives feel that way. About a third express the need for their spouses to handle stress better and to be more honest with them. They want dependability in their mates, along with better work in setting joint priorities.

Category 3: Marital Cohesion

A. I feel we have some problems getting along with each other in these areas:

	He	She
1. Time together	46%	65%
2. Give and take	15%	39%
3. Feeling one	27%	50%
4. Closeness	19%	46%
5. Goals/priorities	42%	54%
6. Loneliness	12%	41%
7. Love/affection	38%	48%

Compassion people love spending time with their spouses, although 65 percent of the women respondents report not enough time for this. They feel the need more keenly than the men, who scored 46 percent.

More than twice as many compassion wives as husbands identify problems with the give and take of marriage. It is likely that compassion spouses are more into the giving part than mates of other giftings.

Compassion spouses long for unity and closeness; and compassion wives—who get their strong "feeling" inclinations not only from their giftedness but also from their womanhood—sense the lack of it more. Because of their openness and transparency, compassion spouses can feel vulnerable. Yet they are willing to be that way, especially if their mates are willing, too.

"When I first married Duane," said Irene, "I could see he was having a more difficult time being open with me about his feelings. But as I encouraged him to share his innermost thoughts and feelings, he did so. Now we feel very close to each other."

While some goals and priorities between compassion spouses and their mates differ, they can find common meeting ground. Compassion people live for the *now.* They do not take interest in long-range goals. As one compassion wife put it, "Why plan ahead for five years, or one year, or even one month? I have enough of a challenge just living my life each day!"

Compassion people must have other people in their lives. Relationships are everything. Compassion wives do not like being home alone and may experience loneliness. Betsy attests to this: "Barney did not want me to work outside the home, so I agreed to it. But I felt isolated and longed to be with others. So I joined a women's Bible study, volunteered at the children's orthopedic hospital, found a jogging buddy and got involved in a local

B. To what degree, from 1 to 7, are you one way or the other:

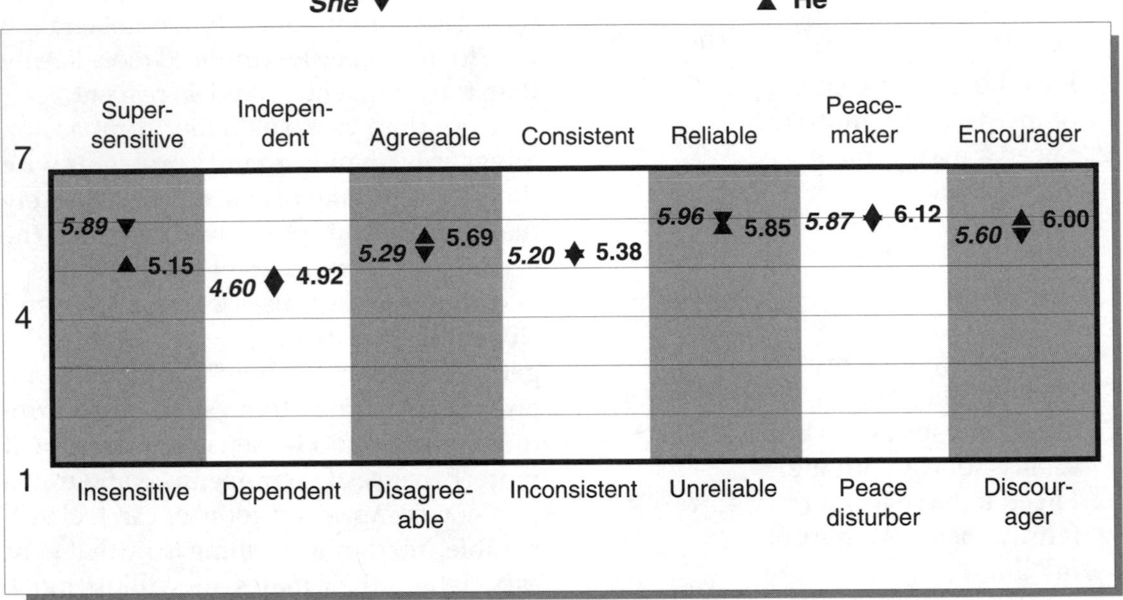

artists group." Compassion husbands who have jobs and people around them every day do not share this problem.

Compassion people are incurable romantics. A husband brings his wife flowers even on nonoccasions. He may whisk her away to a romantic rendezvous or even send a singing telegram. A compassion wife makes wonderful candlelight dinners, puts love notes in her husband's lunch box and whispers sweet nothings in his ear. She wishes her noncompassion-gift husband would do the same!

Compassion spouses (see chart B above) are indeed sensitive—even supersensitive, with all its ramifications. On the positive side they are caring and careful and able to read between the lines. On the negative side they get their feelings hurt easily and can be perceived as needing kid-gloves treatment.

They are reliable, usually doing what they say they will, even if it takes a while. They are agreeable to the point of giving in too much, and consistent to the point of being predictable. They are determined peacemakers, sometime trying to mend relationships that do not want mending or putting their noses into other people's business. Always they like to encourage their mates and ensure peace in the relationship.

C. My genuine needs, views or beliefs are:

	He	She
1. I need to be able to confide more in my mate.	23%	35%
2. I feel there needs to be more unity in our relationship.	19%	41%
3. I need to feel more secure in our marriage.	12%	15%
4. I am afraid to share some of my feelings with my partner.	35%	33%
5. I need my mate to be more sensitive to my needs.	27%	54%
6. I do not consider divorce ever to be an option.	88%	67%

	He	She
7. I am satisfied with our marital interaction and closeness.	73%	39%

Almost twice as many compassion men as women are satisfied with their marital interaction and closeness. Compassion wives, perhaps wanting perfection in their marriages, are less willing to settle for a mediocre relationship. They will do all they can to improve their marriages, whether by management, motivation or manipulation.

"I admit I conspire to make our marriage better," says Paula, "but it is the most important thing in the world to me. I do not consider divorce an option, so I'd better fix what I can and learn to live with the rest. Actually, my husband's a great guy, just rather insensitive to some of my needs and feelings. But he's doing better."

Category 4: Roles and Responsibilities

	He	She
1. Authority	23%	41%
2. Submission	4%	30%
3. Responsibilities	27%	46%
4. Decision-making	15%	37%
5. Roles	19%	20%
6. Feeling overworked	15%	46%
7. Home management	38%	46%

A. I FEEL WE HAVE SOME PROBLEMS IN OUR MARRIAGE ROLES AND RESPONSIBILITIES IN THESE AREAS:

Compassion wives report more problems than average in the authority structure of their marriages. Even though they tend to be compliant, they may feel their husbands do not listen to their viewpoints adequately. Compassion wives have more difficulty fully understanding submission. They can have submissive hearts but still be concerned about specific expectations of submission from their husbands.

Compassion spouses tend to be cooperative, so sharing responsibilities is not often much of a problem. But they do like to have their responsibilities defined clearly.

Compassion wives prefer their mates to make the decisions. They are prone to *let* things happen rather than *make* things happen.

"I'm a classic compassion gift and my husband is a giver/compassion combination," Laurel explains. "We both tend to procrastinate at making decisions and we miss out sometimes because of it. Like when the church announced that those who would like electrical and water hookups at summer camp should contact the church office. After yo-yoing about whether we should or not, we finally called the office a week later, only to find all the hookups taken."

Traditional roles are acceptable for most compassion spouses, although husbands can have difficulties fulfilling some of the head-of-household responsibilities. Al explains that, being married to an administrator wife, he has often been content to let her take the lead. "She seems so much more capable in decision-making and goal-setting," he says, "that I'm really happy to let her do it. But she wants me to take more leadership, so we're working at it together."

Compassion spouses are not prone to overachieve or overwork. They do what is necessary but put great stock in rest, recreation and time with the family.

Compassion wives have strong nesting instincts and the desire to take good care of their homes. They also tend to be artistic and creative about it. Penny says there was not much money for decorating their first home. "So I'd sit in my mom's attic and ponder what I could use to give my home a personal touch. I found a tattered fake fur coat and made luxurious covers for the sofa pillows. Old curtains became our bed-

B. To what degree, from 1 to 7, are you one way or the other:

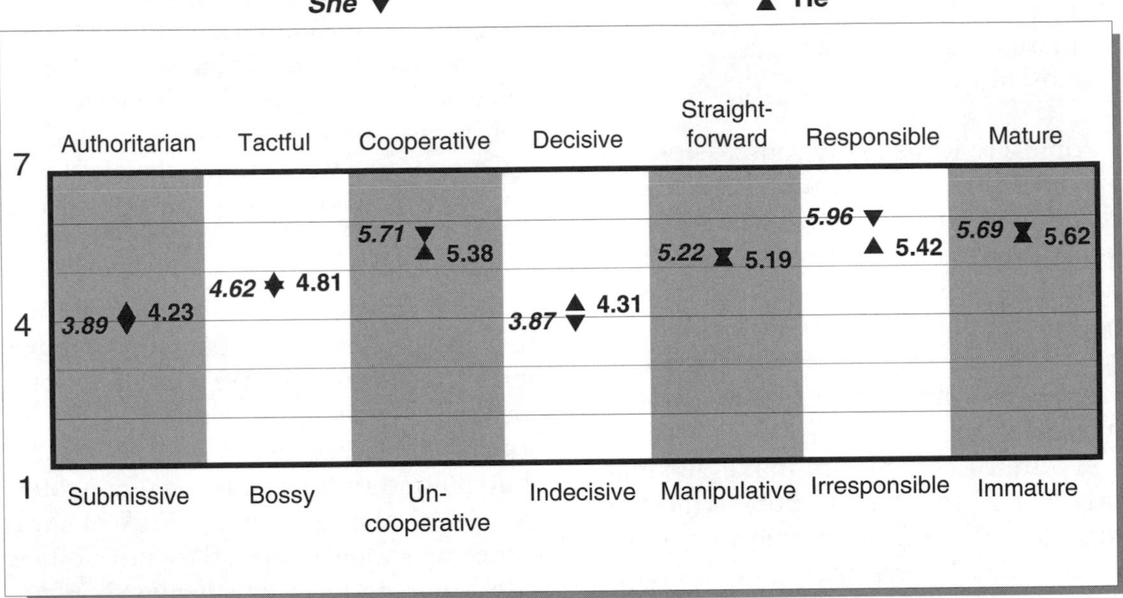

spread. Old picture frames got painted bright colors to match our decor, and a bird-cage houses my favorite ivy plant."

Compassion wives (see chart B above) are comfortably submissive. Compassion husbands score only slightly on the authoritarian side. Both are tactful and want to cooperate. They score themselves high on being straightforward, but they can also be manipulative.

While they see themselves as responsible and mature (and they try to be), their mates may not give them the same scores. One candid compassion husband says, "I tend to fly by the seat of my pants. My perceiver wife hates that. I wish I could be more responsible."

C. My genuine needs, views or beliefs are:

	He	She
1. I need my role clarified more.	12%	13%
2. I need more freedom to discuss ideas and options.	12%	13%
3. I need to use some of my capabilities more.	31%	37%
4. I need to receive more respect from my partner.	27%	24%
5. I need more domestic help and support from my spouse.	4%	35%
6. I would like to help more in planning together.	15%	26%
7. I am satisfied with the roles and responsibilities we have established.	77%	46%

Most compassion spouses are satisfied with their roles and responsibilities—husbands more than wives, who feel the need for more domestic help. "My husband is talented in not seeing what he could do to help around the house," Sabrina complained. "He ignores the socks he drops on the floor, lets the newspapers pile up by his favorite chair and doesn't even offer to help me with the dishes."

Category 5: Conflict Resolution

A. I FEEL WE HAVE SOME PROBLEMS IN HOW WE DEAL WITH CONFLICTS IN THESE AREAS:

	He	She
1. Anger management	42%	48%
2. Who's right	27%	41%
3. Final decisions	19%	24%
4. Silent treatment	54%	52%
5. Ultimatums	8%	22%
6. Personal attacks	27%	39%
7. Blame game	23%	37%

Compassion spouses tend to believe that even *feeling* anger (and other negative emotions) is bad. They like to think that if they are just "good" enough, they will not feel anger. They tend to deny or stuff it, so anger can build inside like a pressure-cooker. If it blows, they cannot imagine where it came from. If they hold it in, anger can cause depression, mental problems, even physical ailments.

Compassion people need to recognize anger when they feel it, then deal with it appropriately. The key is forgiveness. Forgiveness does not mean condoning improper behavior or giving in to hurtful circumstances. They need to learn how to tell their spouses, "What you just did [or said] hurt me very much, and I feel angry about it." Then they can choose to forgive the spouse, whether the spouse is sorry or not. Compassion people need to know that when they are obedient to Jesus and forgive, the feelings will eventually follow.

Most compassion spouses do not feel it is worth arguing over who is right. They are more apt to defer to their spouses than defend their real or supposed rightness. As Jonathan says, "A harmonious relationship with my wife is more important to me than defending a position."

Because they are lovers, not fighters, they often retreat and build a wall of silence around themselves rather than face something unpleasant. The other side of the coin: Consciously or subconsciously they can use the silent treatment as a weapon to punish their mates for hurt or unkindness. It is a passive way of getting even. A wise compassion spouse discovers that talking through a problem is more effective in bringing resolution than long-term simmering, which can do more harm to themselves than to their mates.

Threats or ultimatums are not weapons of choice for compassion spouses. Turtling or tears are more common, along with subtle manipulation.

Compassion mates are more likely to be the recipients than the perpetrators of personal attack. They may feel their partners are to blame but will not necessarily speak it out. Because compassion people focus on building good relationships, it is hard for them to believe they are at fault for breakdowns in their marriages.

Compassion people (see chart B on page 268) are the most easily wounded of all motivational gifts. Their extremely sensitive natures make them the most vulnerable to hurt. More than sixty percent of the people who come to us for counseling are compassion people, wisely seeking (and, if they are willing to become forgivers, receiving) help.

Note that the responses indicate they try to be forgiving, apologetic and agreeable. They want to get along, especially with the love of their lives. They do not do particularly well at handling stress, and wish they did not have to.

C. MY GENUINE NEEDS, VIEWS OR BELIEFS ARE:

	He	She
1. I need to gain control over my temper.	27%	39%

B. To what degree, from 1 to 7, are you one way or the other:

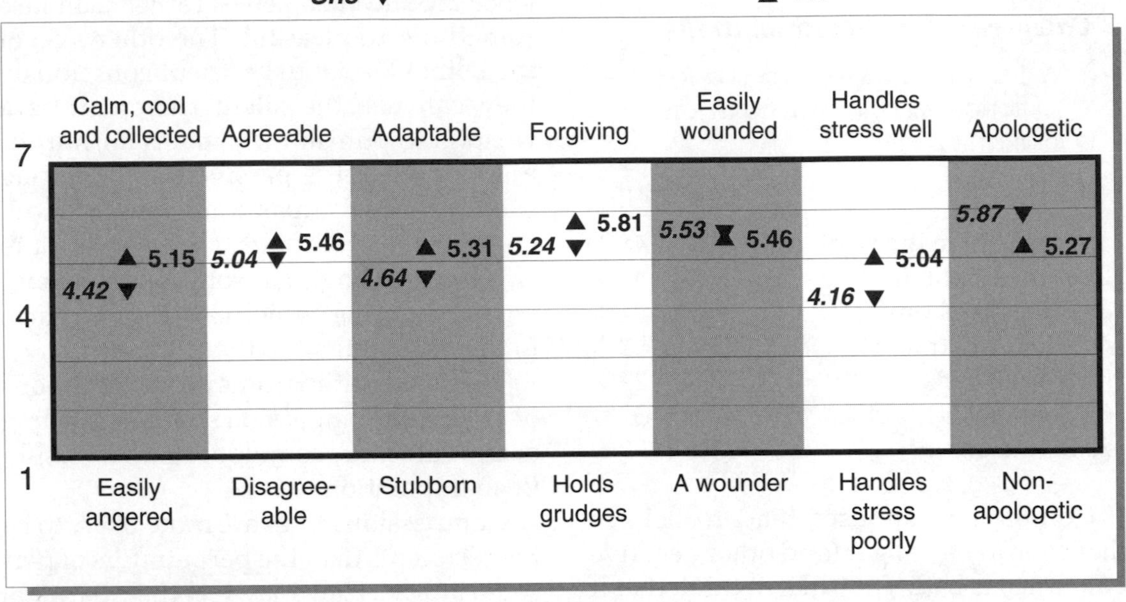

	He	She
2. I need my spouse to gain control over his or her temper.	27%	37%
3. I need to have my point of view heard more often.	15%	26%
4. I feel a strong need to avoid arguments and conflicts.	50%	50%
5. I need my mate to forgive me more quickly.	27%	17%
6. I think we need better ground rules for resolving conflicts.	19%	48%
7. I am satisfied with the way we resolve conflicts.	62%	28%

While more than half of the compassion husbands are satisfied with the way they resolve conflicts, only about a quarter of the compassion wives are. Many compassion wives come to Don and me for marriage counseling because the conflict they face is more than they can handle. In one extreme case a woman's husband had broken her jaw twice in angry tirades. When the dentist wired her jaw back together the second time, he warned her that if it was broken a third time, it would probably be beyond repair. But her husband took no responsibility for his actions, always claiming it was her fault for making him so angry. When he refused to change or get counseling, she decided to separate from him.

Note that half of the compassion husbands and wives feel a strong need to avoid arguments and conflicts. This avoidance mentality can lead to "packing up and going home to Mama." A wise mother of a compassion daughter told her on the night before the wedding, "Honey, I love you with all my heart and expect you to have a good marriage. But even good marriages sometimes have conflicts. So stay and face them. You cannot come home."

Category 6: Personality Issues

A. I FEEL WE HAVE SOME PROBLEMS IN PERSONALITY CONFLICTS AND ISSUES IN THESE AREAS:

	He	She
1. Being right	42%	35%
2. Pride	27%	37%
3. Understanding	27%	61%
4. Change attempts	23%	48%
5. Methodologies	27%	33%
6. Habits	27%	37%
7. Forgetfulness	50%	48%

Pride is not a major problem for compassion people. They tend toward genuine humility or even thinking too little of themselves.

Understanding their spouses, however, can be a major problem. Unique among the seven gifts in being so motivated by emotions, they have difficulties relating to spouses motivated by intellect, and even more to spouses (such as perceivers) motivated by the will.

Henry, a classic compassion gift, has found his teacher wife puzzling. "I wish she could relate to me better," he says. "I'd love to have her cuddle up to me after dinner and we'd watch a good TV movie together. Instead she wants to cuddle up to a good book. I whisper sweet nothings in her ear and she says I'm embarrassing her. I just don't get it!"

Compassion wives are the ones most likely to try to change their spouses and most frustrated when it does not work. Their method is subtle and manipulative.

Compassion people often do something because it *feels* good or right, not necessarily because it *is*. Their methods may seem illogical, especially to mates who score low in compassion. They are motivated by love, caring and the longing to foster good relationships, especially in their primary one—marriage.

Perhaps their most bothersome habit is being late. Sometimes the compassion person seems to have one forward speed: slow. Mary Beth says, "I mean to be on time, but sometimes things just get in the way—distractions, you know." Her husband, James, agrees: "Three out of four Sundays Mary Beth makes us late for church. She never allows enough time to get ready. So last year I decided to change that, and the kids and I drove off and left her. For about two months she was ready on time, and then she started being late again. Whenever that happens we take off again without her, and she's back on schedule for a while."

About half of the compassion respondents (a little higher than the norm) say forgetfulness is a problem. They do better remembering details about people and worse remembering details about things.

Highest scores (see chart B on page 270) here are for respect and consideration. Compassion persons really care about what others feel and think. Their attitudes are good. In fact, they feel shame when bad attitudes surface. They also try to adapt themselves to their mates. Since their opinions tend to be pliable, they often adjust them to their spouses'.

Self-esteem is a problem area, more so for compassion wives than husbands. The opposite admonition of the apostle Paul in Romans 12:3—warning against pride and thinking of ourselves more highly than we ought—could be directed to compassion people, who tend to think of themselves *less* highly than they ought. This is especially true of those who experienced abuse or a difficult childhood.

I worked for months with a lovely compassion wife who was sure her husband would be better off without her. Through prayer ministry she discovered she had

B. To what degree, from 1 to 7, are you one way or the other:

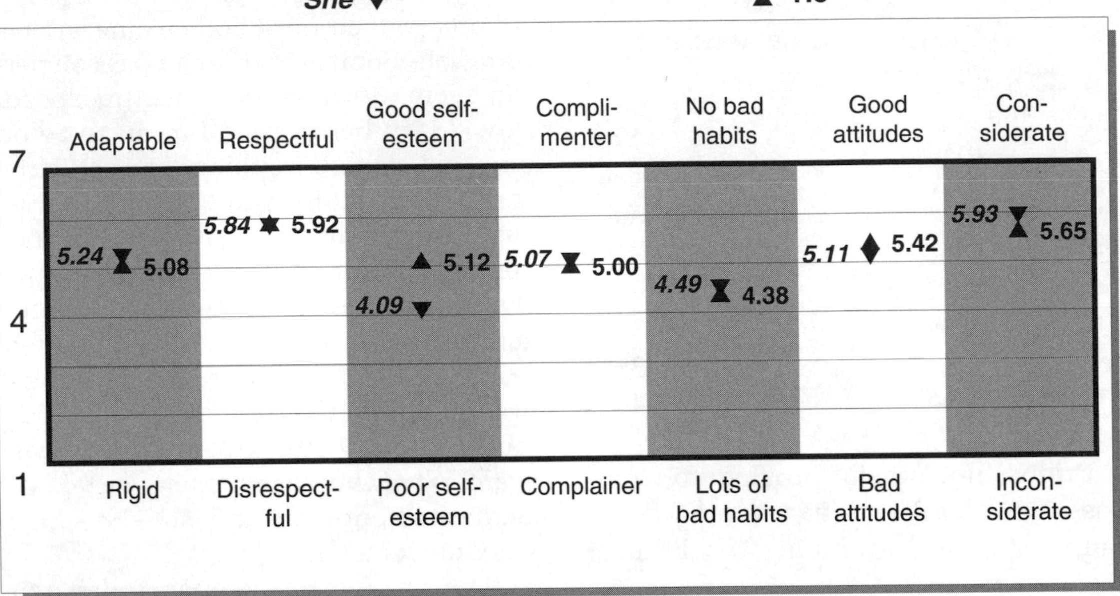

believed and buried years of disparaging remarks from her insensitive father. Jesus healed those painful memories and helped her know how precious she was. What a wonderful transformation as she began to love and accept herself and feel worthy of the love her husband had for her!

I like to encourage all compassion people who suffer from low self-esteem to get help from a pastor, counselor, even a friend.

C. My genuine needs, views or beliefs are:

	He	She
1. I wish my partner complimented me more.	23%	50%
2. I need more encouragement from my mate.	23%	57%
3. I need to be accepted and appreciated for who I am.	35%	41%
4. I need to retain my unique identity.	19%	26%
5. My partner needs to understand my gifts.	23%	35%
6. I need more admiration and respect from my partner.	27%	33%
7. We do not seem to have any personality conflicts.	42%	24%

The needs here are greater for compassion wives. Three-fourths of them experience some personality conflicts with their spouses. Their greatest marital needs are to be accepted, to be complimented more and to receive more encouragement from their mates.

Stacey, married to a server gift, felt she was being starved emotionally. "I longed to hear words of love and caring from Bill, but he seemed to take me for granted. When we took a seminar on the motivational gifts, it changed our lives. He realized what I needed. And even though it is a bit awkward for his gifting to be more verbal, he made the effort because he loved me. It has enhanced our relationship tremendously."

Category 7: Emotional Responses

A. I FEEL WE HAVE SOME PROBLEMS IN THE WAYS WE RESPOND TO EACH OTHER EMOTIONALLY IN THESE AREAS:

	He	She
1. Hurt feelings	46%	70%
2. Carrying offenses	15%	41%
3. Unforgiveness	4%	17%
4. Insensitiveness	23%	30%
5. Feeling unloved	19%	52%
6. Moodiness	38%	57%
7. Anger	35%	52%

Because compassion people more than any other gift operate from the emotions, they tend to have more problems in this area. They are what we might describe as thin-skinned or the most vulnerable to having their feelings hurt. Almost seventy percent of the compassion wives report this as a problem.

Sometimes the hurt is imagined. More often it is real. "Dan is a good husband," Becky admits. "He seldom does anything to hurt me deliberately. But when he is in a cross mood, I tend to wonder what I've done wrong. If he ignores something I've said, I feel he doesn't care. I know I'm too sensitive, and I'm trying to overcome these reactions and be more self-affirming."

Sometimes compassion husbands and wives do not let their mates know they are carrying an offense. The best antidote, of course, is to talk about it and bring resolution. Most compassion spouses forgive quickly, wanting the relationship to be restored.

Compassion people are the most sensitive of all but they complain easily of their mates' insensitivity.

Compassion wives need lots of affirmation of love from their husbands in order to feel loved. One told us, "I know Gerry loves me, but if he goes for days without telling me, I begin to feel insecure. When I bug him about it, he always affirms his love and can't seem to understand why I wonder about it."

Compassion people, especially women, are prone to moodiness to the degree that they allow their emotions to rule. Sometimes they do not know why a mood is there because they have suppressed the cause. "At times I used to feel depressed even to the point of crying," Angela told us. "When Bob asked me what was wrong, I'd tell him I didn't know. Then I'd cry some more. It wasn't until I got some counseling help that I discovered I'd suppressed anger all my life. As I began to face it and work through it, the moods diminished and finally disappeared."

Compassion people usually stuff anger. Because they tend to feel guilty about negative feelings, they ignore them and sleep on them, and the feelings become buried in their subconscious. But even if the conscious mind no longer remembers anger, it is there producing negative effects. A natural downward progression takes place. First the person experiences moodiness, unexplained sadness, self-pity and poor self-esteem. This can develop into feelings of worthlessness, self-hatred, depression and the beginning of psychosomatic or degenerative disease. At the deepest level he or she can experience mental or physical disease, deep depression and self-destruction or suicidal tendencies. (See p. 348, item 29.)

I counseled a compassion wife who had an adoring husband and three lovely children, yet had attempted suicide three times in one month. Outwardly there was no reason for it. But as we sought the Lord's help, it came out that the bottom line was unresolved anger from her childhood, due (once again) to abuse. With a combination of deliverance prayer, facing anger, forgiving and letting Jesus heal her

B. To what degree, from 1 to 7, are you one way or the other:

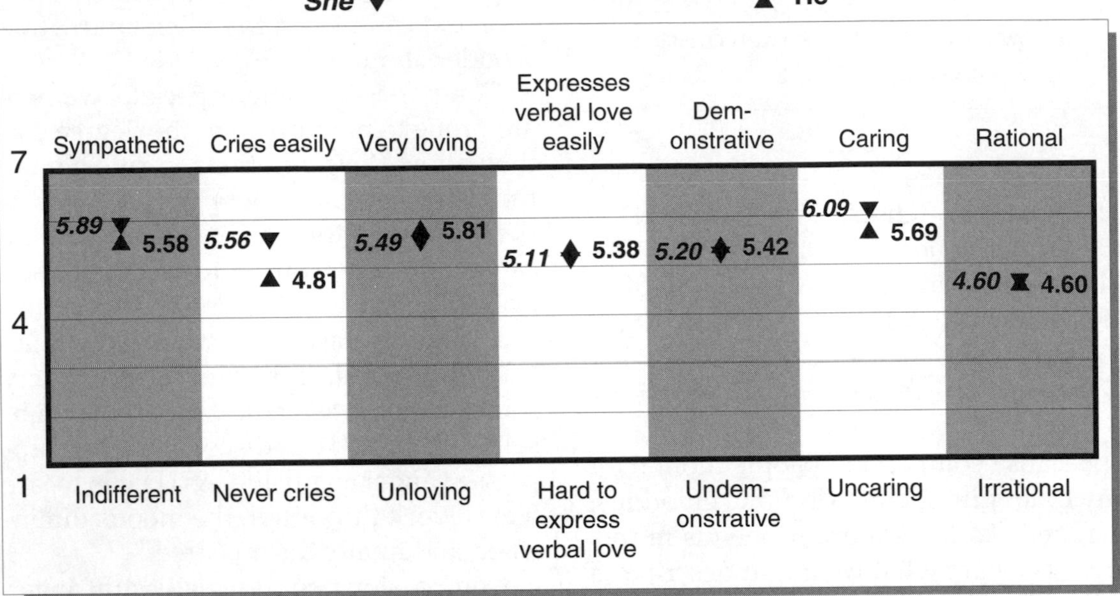

hurts, she was freed in just two sessions of counseling.

If an award could be given for the greatest ability to love, it would go to compassion people. They not only share their own love naturally and beautifully, but radiate God's love to others spontaneously and effervescently. No wonder their scores are high here (see chart B above)—not only for being loving but for being able to express love verbally.

They are also demonstrative, caring and sympathetic. If their spouses are laid up, they have great bedside manner, showering love and care. They identify easily with what others are going through. A compassion husband may even experience a measure of his wife's labor pains.

They cry more easily than any other gift. One compassion husband we met in New Zealand shared with us how embarrassed he was to cry over something sad when his wife did not. We told him not to worry; Jesus wept, and God has gifted compassion people so that it is normal for them to cry easily. It shows the depth of their caring.

C. My genuine needs, views or beliefs are:

	He	She
1. My feelings tend to rule my life.	23%	43%
2. My mate needs to understand my moods more.	15%	33%
3. I need to hear more "I love you's" from my partner.	19%	39%
4. I need to be able to express both positive and negative feelings.	46%	43%
5. I feel my spouse takes everything too personally.	19%	17%
6. I often feel put down by my partner.	35%	33%
7. I am satisfied with our emotional responses to each other.	54%	20%

While half of the husbands are satisfied with the emotional responses in their marital relationships, only twenty percent of the wives are. Most of them recognize that feelings tend to rule their lives, but they do not always know how to cope with this. "I used to feel that my husband and I were on different wavelengths," Melanie wrote. "We approached everything from a different perspective. When I found your book, it was like a revelation to both of us. He's a teacher/exhorter combination and I'm 100 percent compassion. Now we understand and accept each other. It's so good to know it's O.K. to be different."

Compassion wives need to hear "I love you" regularly. (Most wives can say, "Amen!" to that. Husbands take note.) Spouses can also help their compassion mates by encouraging them to be open and honest with their feelings—especially the negative ones they tend to hide. They need help in learning to deal with the negative. A loving, accepting atmosphere will help them do this.

Category 8: Intellectual Capacity

A. I FEEL WE HAVE SOME PROBLEMS RELATING TO INTELLECTUAL INTERESTS AND CAPACITIES IN THESE AREAS:

	He	She
1. Different interests	15%	33%
2. Reading	15%	28%
3. Continuing education	4%	11%
4. Know-it-all attitude	15%	20%
5. Correcting grammar	12%	11%
6. Children's education	8%	13%
7. Being accurate	8%	17%

Compassion spouses usually accept the fact that they will have interests different from their spouses'. "My administrator husband volunteers in our church's Christian education department," says Sally, a shy compassion person. "He loves planning and coordinating. My interest is in animals, so I volunteer at our local animal shelter. We each love what we do; there's no point in trying to cross over into the other's sphere of interest."

Compassion wives love romance books, biographies of people like Helen Keller who have blessed society and animal stories—happy endings preferred. Compassion husbands like mysteries, science fiction and novels with moral truth. Both are content to read in their own fields of interest and let their mates pursue their own preferences.

Compassion people see education as a means to an end, not something to pursue in itself. A compassion wife may study nursing in order to assume a caring-type job or ministry. But she may prefer to skip the education and do hospital volunteer work instead. She sees a college degree not as a badge of success but as a doorway of opportunity to put love into practical action in a field requiring a degree.

Compassion spouses are usually the first to admit they do not know it all. Facts and figures are not their cup of tea, unless these relate to relationships or the practical demonstration of care for animals or other human beings. Being accurate and factual or correcting grammar is a lower priority than being loving or kind.

While compassion parents value the education of their children, they are usually content for them to do their best without pushing for high grades. If a spouse pushes a child beyond what he or she can handle well, the compassion mate may object and point out other values than education that are equally important.

Notice that scores here (see chart B on page 274) are mostly near the middle. While compassion mates have opinions on many matters, they do not push their spouses to agree. They are not particularly analytical, yet can analyze if necessary. They speak well enough but are not known for a large

B. To what degree, from 1 to 7, are you one way or the other:

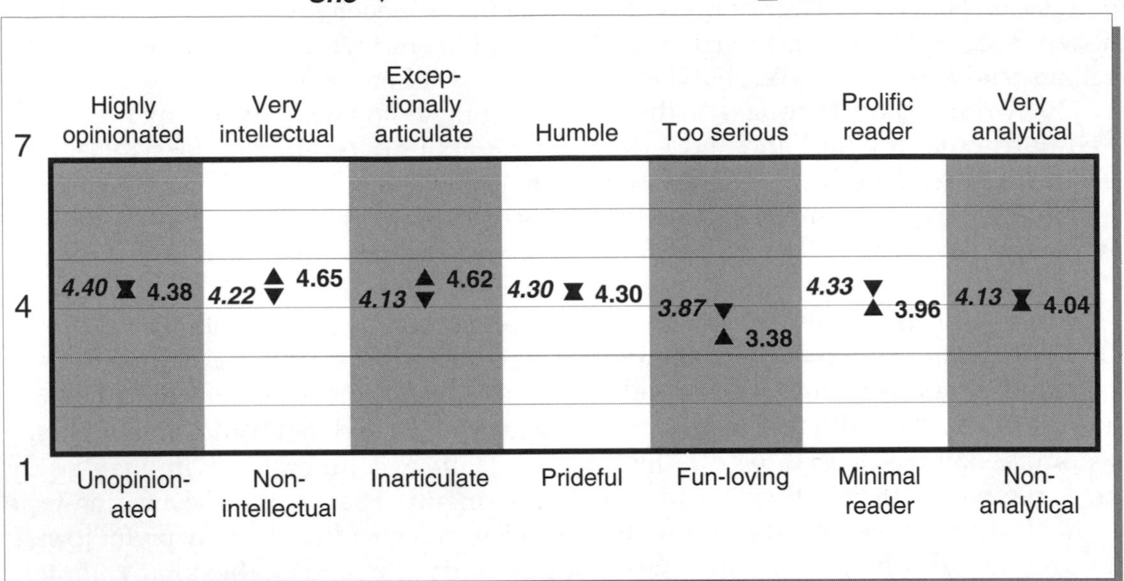

vocabulary or wanting to speak in front of groups. Their humility is genuine.

While life for compassion spouses has its serious side, they tend to be spontaneously fun-loving. Marlene believes having fun together is one of the most important building blocks in a marriage. "Sometimes I have to make Dennis take off his shoes and socks and race with me through the sand," she says. "Otherwise he'd sit on a log and watch the rest of life go by."

C. My genuine needs, views or beliefs are:

	He	She
1. I need adequate time for reading or study.	42%	54%
2. I am easily sidetracked by new interests.	42%	43%
3. I need to question things before I can accept them.	23%	43%
4. I need my mate to listen to my opinions more.	8%	30%
5. I realize I need to be less dogmatic.	19%	4%
6. I find I constantly analyze what my partner says and does.	4%	24%
7. I am satisfied with how we handle intellectual matters.	69%	46%

Half or more of the compassion respondents are satisfied with how they handle intellectual matters, especially if there are not too many of them. They like private time to read their favorite books and magazines, yet enjoy having their spouses in the same room. They may take a little longer understanding something their spouses explain to them and want the right to raise questions, even if they seem "dumb."

Their ability to get sidetracked explains part of their problem being late. If someone calls or comes by, they are likely to drop everything to listen. They may stop to smell some new roses or pet the neighbor's dog and miss the bus.

Joan says she has so many interests in

crafts that she wishes she could pursue them all. "I love counted cross-stitch and have started three so far. But they're not finished yet because I began taking a watercolor class, and it takes a lot of time. My neighbor showed me how to make fantastically beautiful Christmas tree balls, and I need to get busy with that since I want to give them for gifts this year."

Category 9: Volitional Issues

A. I FEEL WE HAVE SOME PROBLEMS IN THE USE OF THE WILL IN THESE AREAS:

	He	She
1. Decisions and choices	27%	39%
2. Practical decisions	8%	24%
3. Stubbornness	27%	37%
4. Agreements	8%	24%
5. Right actions	8%	22%
6. Judgmentalism	31%	35%
7. Rebelliousness	19%	13%

Compassion spouses are not fond of making decisions, often leaving that responsibility up to their spouses or working with them to arrive at conclusions. Since compassion people are adaptable, they can usually live with the decisions that are made.

Stubbornness is not a typical characteristic. They tend to cooperate and are willing to fit in with their spouses' plans.

Sometimes a compassion spouse will compromise rather than stand up for rights. A wife shared that a member of her compassion husband's car pool shirks his share of driving with weak excuses, "so Edgar winds up driving much more than he should. When I ask him why he doesn't put his foot down, his compassion perspective comes through with, 'Oh well, I don't mind, and besides, he has so many problems already. I don't want to add to them by putting pressure on him.'"

Compassion spouses are not prone to be judgmental but they can be sometimes, especially if their spouses are not being "nice." But they are more likely to hold the judgment in rather than speak it out. It bothers them if their spouses are judg-

B. TO WHAT DEGREE, FROM 1 TO 7, ARE YOU ONE WAY OR THE OTHER:

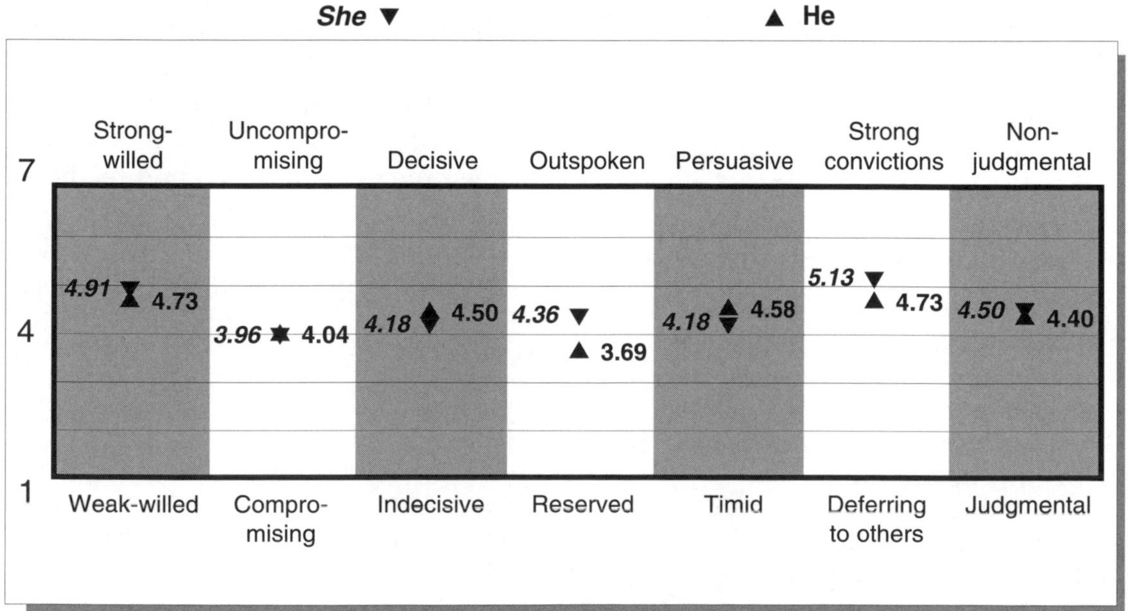

mental toward them or others. Disagreements may arise over this, as well as over hurt feelings.

Rebelliousness is not a compassion tendency unless a spouse is running from God or does not get his or her way. One server wife told us how difficult it was when her compassion husband did not get a promotion he wanted. "He pouted for days," she said. "And when he could see that nothing would change, he stopped doing his best at his job. It was six months before he repented of his rebellious heart and made things right."

While scores (see chart B on page 275) are higher than the midpoint for strength of will, they are lower than for the other gifts. Strength of will is an area that can get compassion mates in trouble. They tend to compromise, seeing it not so much as a negative characteristic but as a way of adapting to others so that they will feel accepted and included.

"Ted is adamantly against drinking alcohol," Tina says. "He can give you fifty reasons why it is harmful, yet when he gets together with his college buddies, he drinks with them. We've had many arguments over this, but he always excuses it as something he needs to do in order to be accepted by them."

Compassion spouses are not outspoken and tend to be timid and reserved. But when championing a special cause like saving the whales or providing for refugees, they are likely to have strong convictions and become persuasive.

C. My genuine needs, views or beliefs are:

	He	She
1. I have a definite inner need to be right.	23%	30%
2. I have a strong need to be a decision-maker.	35%	20%
3. I need my mate to make most of the decisions.	4%	17%
4. I will do what is right even if it hurts.	46%	48%
5. I need to operate by definite principles.	35%	54%
6. I need my mate to be more tolerant of my opinions.	15%	28%
7. I am satisfied with how we make decisions.	77%	43%

About half of the wives and three-fourths of the husbands are satisfied with how they make decisions with their mates. Remember, they tend to defer to their spouses for this task. Note the fairly low scores on needing to be decision-makers.

Many want to operate by definite principles, but they are not as likely as other gifts to have these predetermined. They tend to size up the immediate situation and select principles or guidelines they feel fit. They are willing to be flexible, especially if it helps someone or gives someone another chance.

"When I had an alcohol problem," Arnie recalls, "Shirley tried to lay down the law with me, but then she'd feel sorry for me because I was trying to overcome it. I am grateful because it was her love for me that enabled me to get into AA and really get help."

Half say they will do what is right even if it hurts; the other half have problems in this area. To many, what is right is relative. As one compassion wife says, "If a clerk charges me too little for an item, I want to take it back and pay the difference. My husband says that's dumb, and got really upset with me once when I did it. So now I'm caught in a gray area. I want to be honest, but if it causes a breach with my husband, it's not worth it."

Category 10: Physical Conditions

A. I FEEL WE HAVE SOME PROBLEMS IN THE PHYSICAL REALM IN THESE AREAS:

	He	She
1. Being fit	73%	72%
2. Enough exercise	77%	85%
3. Fatigue	42%	67%
4. Overeating	62%	52%
5. Proper eating	58%	52%
6. Keeping attractive	35%	30%
7. Adequate sleep	38%	59%

In general compassion people are in worse shape physically than the other gifts. More than seventy percent say they have problems keeping fit, and even more say they do not get enough exercise. Fatigue is also a problem. "I mean to start an exercise program," Ginny says, "but I just never get around to it. One of these days I'm going to get organized enough to do it."

Overeating and not eating right are problems. Craig admits he is a junk food addict. "I have a hard time with self-discipline in both exercising and eating right. Instead of having my wife pack a healthy lunch, I'd rather grab a burger with some of the other guys at work. June and I argue about this and I know she's right. One of these days I'm going to change."

Getting adequate sleep is less of a problem for compassion husbands than wives, many of whom say they need more of it.

Note that compassion wives (see chart B below) are less athletic and less energetic than their male counterparts. There may be a correlation between the two since many doctors say exercise is essential to well-being and fitness, and that it diminishes the desire to overeat. While compassion wives score better in good eating habits, it still only approaches the average. Many confess they are not at their proper weight.

Emily says, "I thank God for my exhorter husband, who sees to it that I exercise with him daily, and he limits me to two desserts a week. Otherwise I'd be eligible for the Mrs. Porky contest for sure! I was not well-disciplined in these areas before

B. TO WHAT DEGREE, FROM 1 TO 7, ARE YOU ONE WAY OR THE OTHER:

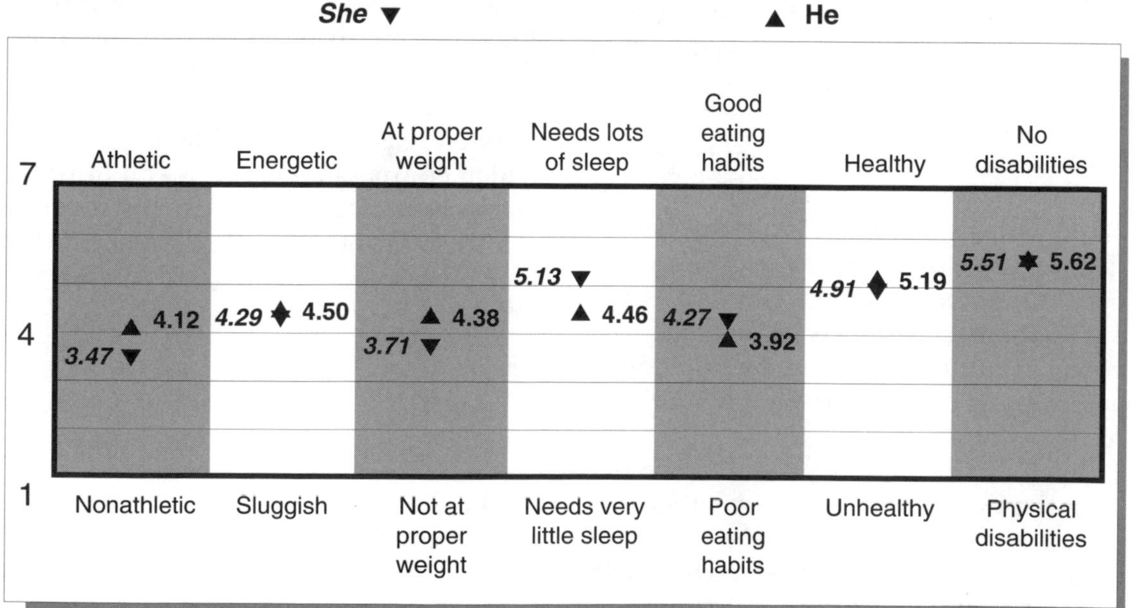

Gordon and I were married, but he motivates me lovingly to keep at it. I have more energy than ever before."

C. My genuine needs, views or beliefs are:

	He	She
1. I desire to see my mate at the proper weight.	65%	46%
2. I need to overcome my own weight problem.	62%	61%
3. I need to get adequate exercise on a regular basis.	81%	85%
4. I would like to see my spouse get more exercise.	58%	52%
5. I need my mate to be as attractive as possible.	35%	22%
6. I need to improve my eating habits.	69%	67%
7. I am satisfied with how we keep fit, healthy and attractive.	8%	11%

Note the extremely low scores by compassion spouses on satisfaction with how they keep fit and healthy—the lowest scoring of all the seven gifts. The other scores reflect their dissatisfaction and recognition of the need for serious joint work on physical fitness.

Elizabeth shares that she and her husband, both compassion gifts, had a losing battle with health and nutrition for the first five years of their marriage. "Bob and I both brought bad eating habits with us into our relationship," she says. "We both loved gooey, creamy things and found endless occasions to reward ourselves with them. Neither of us was used to exercising. We justified our increasingly rounding bodies with the excuse that we were jollier that way. But it was a cover-up. We were miserable but didn't know how to cope with it. Bless our parents! In their love for us, they got together and gave us a membership in a local fitness club and paid our way to join Weight-Watchers. After three years we both look great and we'll never go back to our old ways again."

Category 11: Sexual Relationship

A. I feel we have some problems in our sexual relationship in these areas:

	He	She
1. Frequency	35%	54%
2. Quality	19%	43%
3. Prior affection	23%	50%
4. Nonsexual affection	27%	46%
5. Sexual dissatisfaction	12%	24%
6. Incompatibility	4%	15%
7. Infidelity	0%	4%

Scores here are fairly close to the norm, except compassion wives indicate more problems than compassion husbands with the frequency and quality of sexual relations, prior and nonsexual affection, general sexual dissatisfaction and incompatibility. Being so loving by nature, they are good at affection, but many compassion women do not feel their noncompassion husbands reciprocate well. The more a compassion gift receives love and affection, the more he or she spontaneously gives it back.

Two areas (see chart B on page 279) in which compassion spouses can improve are communicating more about sex and sharing more of their intimate feelings. But they are good at hugging and kissing and expressing affection.

C. My genuine needs, views or beliefs are:

	He	She
1. I need more nonsexual affection from my mate.	19%	50%
2. I need more sexual relations with my mate.	38%	26%

B. To what degree, from 1 to 7, are you one way or the other:

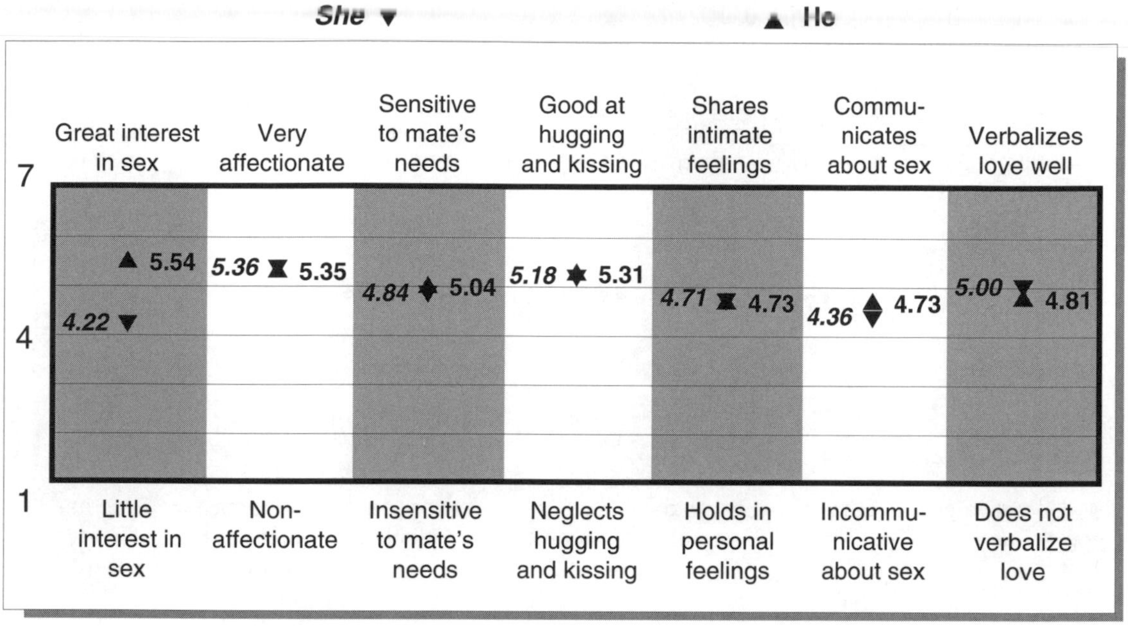

She ▼ ▲ He

7	4	1
Great interest in sex	▲ 5.54 / 4.22 ▼	Little interest in sex
Very affectionate	5.36 / 5.35	Non-affectionate
Sensitive to mate's needs	4.84 / 5.04	Insensitive to mate's needs
Good at hugging and kissing	5.18 / 5.31	Neglects hugging and kissing
Shares intimate feelings	4.71 / 4.73	Holds in personal feelings
Commu-nicates about sex	4.36 / 4.73	Incommu-nicative about sex
Verbalizes love well	5.00 / 4.81	Does not verbalize love

	He	She
3. I feel I need more hugs and kisses from my spouse.	35%	46%
4. I need to hear more "I love you's" from my partner.	19%	37%
5. I need my husband to better understand my monthly cycle.	0%	24%
6. I feel dissatisfied with our current sexual relationship.	19%	26%
7. I feel satisfied with our current sexual relationship.	65%	39%

While about two-thirds of the compassion husbands reported satisfaction with their current sexual relationship, only 39 percent of compassion wives felt satisfied, and the rest either expressed dissatisfaction or chose not to commit themselves to an answer. The key to a compassion person's heart is kindness, tenderness and lots of nonsexual affection.

Category 12: Work and Accomplishments

A. I feel we have some problems about work and accomplishments in these areas:

	He	She
1. Too busy	38%	46%
2. Career conflicts	19%	35%
3. Overtime work	19%	24%
4. Inadequate income	58%	48%
5. Volunteer work	8%	17%
6. Wife working	8%	15%
7. Priorities	12%	24%

Scores are typical except for two areas. First, compassion wives report more problems than normal with career conflicts. Part of this is the compassion wife's strong desire to be an at-home mom during child-rearing years, yet loving the idea of a career, especially if it is creative. Judy said this was a dilemma at first for her and Wayne. "Then we came up with the idea of my doing childcare in our home. It was

B. To what degree, from 1 to 7, are you one way or the other:

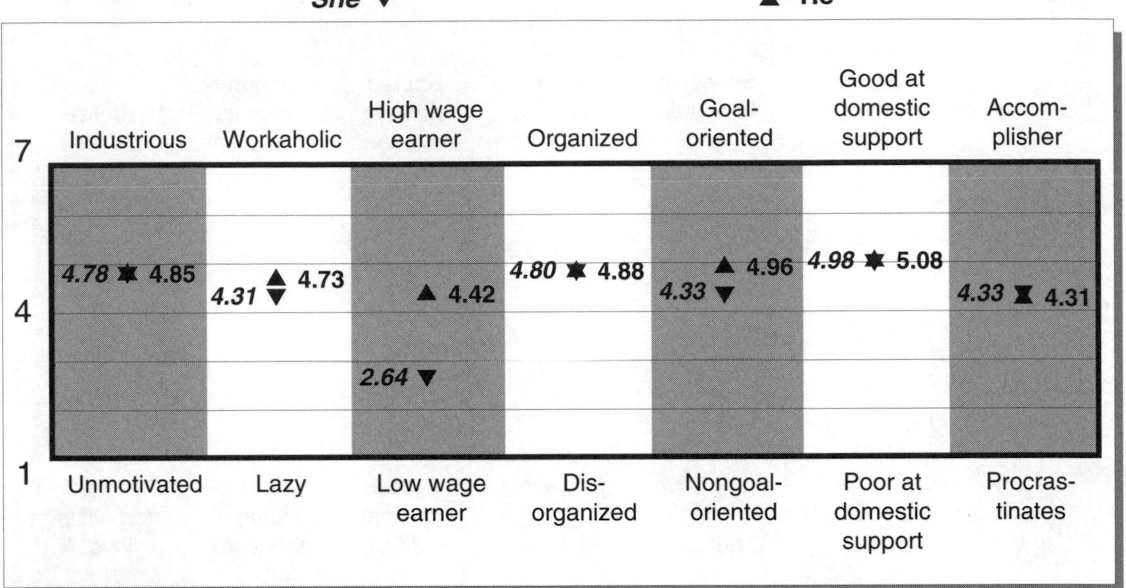

wonderful! I loved working with other children as well as our own. Now our kids are in high school and I have a full-time creative office job that I love."

The other distinctive problem area is having inadequate income. Part of this may be because compassion people tend to choose careers that do not pay as well but offer greater rewards in helping and blessing others. "I'd rather have my life count in helping other people," Gary says emphatically. "I chose to become a male nurse because it gives me endless opportunities to show love and genuine care to people. I gripe about my salary sometimes, but I wouldn't trade jobs with anyone."

Because of their laid-back approach to life, compassion people (see chart B above) tend to be only moderately industrious, not too organized and, while accomplishers in some areas, procrastinators in others. "I'm married to an administrator who is so organized I can hardly stand it," Betsy told us. "He lives by his daily planner and tried to get me to do so, too. Half the time I can't find it and the other half I forget to refer to it. I do best just living one day at a time."

C. My genuine needs, views or beliefs are:

	He	She
1. I need my husband to provide our basic expenses.	0%	52%
2. I need my wife to be a full-time homemaker.	19%	0%
3. I need to be the sole provider for my family.	8%	0%
4. I need a fulfilling career.	38%	15%
5. I need a challenge to work toward.	31%	22%
6. I get great joy out of my accomplishments.	46%	57%
7. I am satisfied with the way we handle work and accomplishments.	58%	57%

Slightly more than half say they are satisfied with the way they and their spouses handle work and accomplishments. Almost that many say they get great joy out of their accomplishments. These accomplishments may not be business productivity, honors or financial success. Rather, compassion people regard making a difference in other people's lives, relieving some suffering in the world, being able to love and care for people or animals.

One young wife, Lisa, told us how pleased she was that she and others had worked together to pressure cosmetic companies to stop animal testing. Josiah said it makes his day if he can get even one resident in the nursing home to smile.

Category 13: Financial Management

A. I FEEL WE HAVE SOME PROBLEMS IN FINANCIAL MATTERS IN THESE AREAS:

	He	She
1. Establishing budget	46%	57%
2. Keeping to budget	42%	43%
3. Living beyond means	15%	35%
4. Credit cards	15%	26%
5. Impulsive buying	19%	39%
6. Money arguments	8%	37%
7. Wife's work role	4%	9%

Most compassion people are careful in money matters. They do not like to be in debt or become financially dependent on others. For them, establishing a budget is a challenge (as it is for half of all couples). But once they do, they are good at keeping to it.

They do not usually try to live beyond their means. Many compassion husbands need their wives to work at least part of the time in order to make ends meet. "Even though my wife has a part-time job she can do at home," Jerry says, "we try to keep it to no more than twenty hours a week. There are lots of things we could buy if she worked more, or if I carried an extra job. But we have learned to be satisfied with less, and it keeps our life uncomplicated."

Money arguments and impulsive buying are more problematic for compassion wives than husbands. "At one point I had to quit going shopping except for groceries," Elaine says. "I kept bringing things home I thought we needed and we really didn't. My wise giver husband has trained me to be nonimpulsive in this area."

Compassion spouses (see chart B on page 282) are generous, to others as well as to their mates. "At Christmas I always wind up giving my husband more than he does me," Wilma says. "But it's O.K. because I make most of his presents, so I don't spend any more than he does."

Like givers, compassion spouses are great bargain-hunters, especially the wives. "I love stretching our budget," Lucy explains. "I shop the grocery ads and clip coupons and even do some rebating when it's worthwhile. I love garage sales and always feel good when I make a special find at a really great price."

Even with their careful spending, compassion spouses often feel financially insecure and work toward greater fiscal soundness. Most are dedicated tithers and give to caring-type ministries.

C. MY GENUINE NEEDS, VIEWS OR BELIEFS ARE:

	He	She
1. I feel we need to reduce our debts more effectively.	31%	57%
2. I feel the need to be in charge of our family finances.	19%	15%
3. I believe the husband should handle the family finances.	15%	37%
4. I think the most capable partner should handle the family finances.	58%	50%
5. I need to learn how to handle money more responsibly.	23%	28%

B. TO WHAT DEGREE, FROM 1 TO 7, ARE YOU ONE WAY OR THE OTHER:

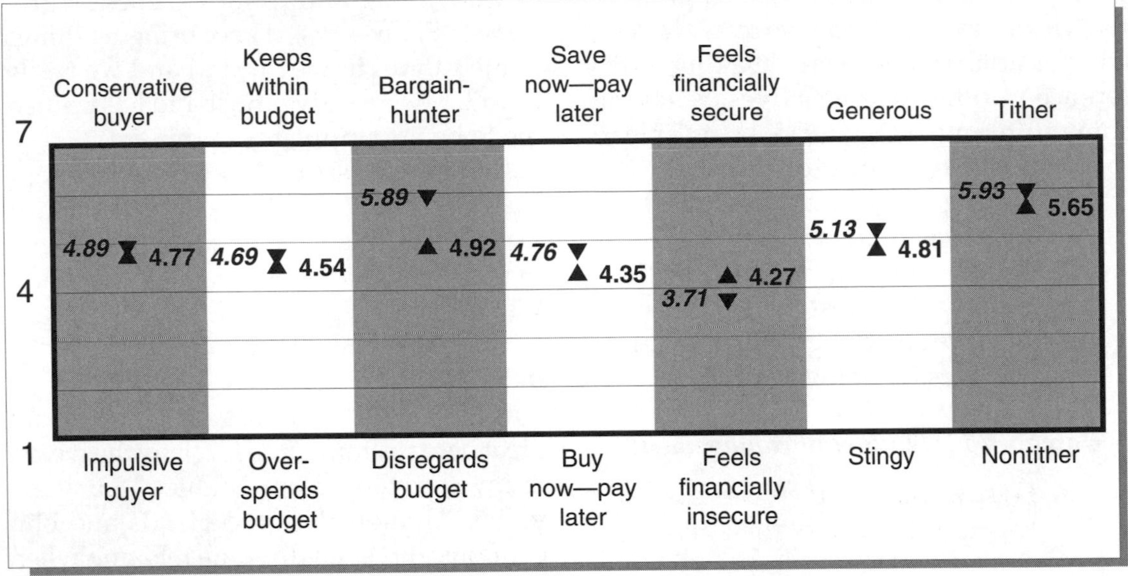

	He	She
6. I would like to give more to church, missionaries, charity, etc.	58%	67%
7. I am satisfied with how we handle finances.	42%	43%

About forty percent of all compassion spouses are satisfied with how they handle finances. Most would like more finances to handle! More than half would like to give more to church and charity. They also believe the most capable partner should handle the family finances.

Category 14: Leisure Activities

A. I FEEL WE HAVE SOME PROBLEMS IN HOW WE SPEND OUR FREE TIME IN THESE AREAS:

	He	She
1. Interests	23%	35%
2. Recreational preferences	12%	22%
3. Hobbies	19%	26%
4. Entertainment	8%	28%
5. Vacation preferences	8%	15%
6. Sports	15%	30%
7. TV-watching	59%	65%

In general compassion husbands are more content with leisure activities than compassion wives, who seem more concerned about differences in interests, hobbies, sports and recreational preferences. "My teacher husband's idea of a perfect vacation is to retreat to a cabin in the woods with a stack of books," Miriam says. "My idea is to spend a week at church camp where we can have wonderful fellowship with our friends."

Compassion people are interested in the arts and are often musically or artistically inclined. They would like their spouses to share in their creativity, but this is not always possible. One husband who recognized his compassion wife's artistic ability encouraged her to develop it through classes and tutoring. "Now she has her own art shows," he says. "I'm very proud of her. But best of all she feels fulfilled and happy."

TV-watching is seen as a real time-stealer by most compassion people, who would rather invest that time in relationships.

While scoring in the average range in being "cultured," compassion people (see chart B below) are known for their interest in cultural pursuits like art museums, plays and the symphony. They are definitely on the social side, love to travel and even go for walks, providing there is someone to accompany them.

C. My genuine needs, views or beliefs are:

	He	She
1. I need my partner to be a recreational companion.	23%	41%
2. I need to do more fun things with my spouse.	54%	80%
3. I need more meaningful vacations.	31%	48%
4. I need to be involved in nonathletic leisure activities.	15%	43%
5. I prefer active group or competitive sports.	27%	9%
6. I prefer individual noncompetitive sports.	23%	54%
7. I am satisfied with how we spend our leisure time.	46%	35%

Doing more fun things is a major need for compassion spouses. They love life and having fun. They can motivate less sociable spouses to enjoy life more. While some compassion husbands like competitive sports, hardly any of the compassion wives do. Both tend to be cooperators rather than competitors.

Category 15: Parenting

A. I feel we have (had) some problems in the child-rearing process in these areas:

	He	She
1. Type of discipline	12%	46%

B. To what degree, from 1 to 7, are you one way or the other:

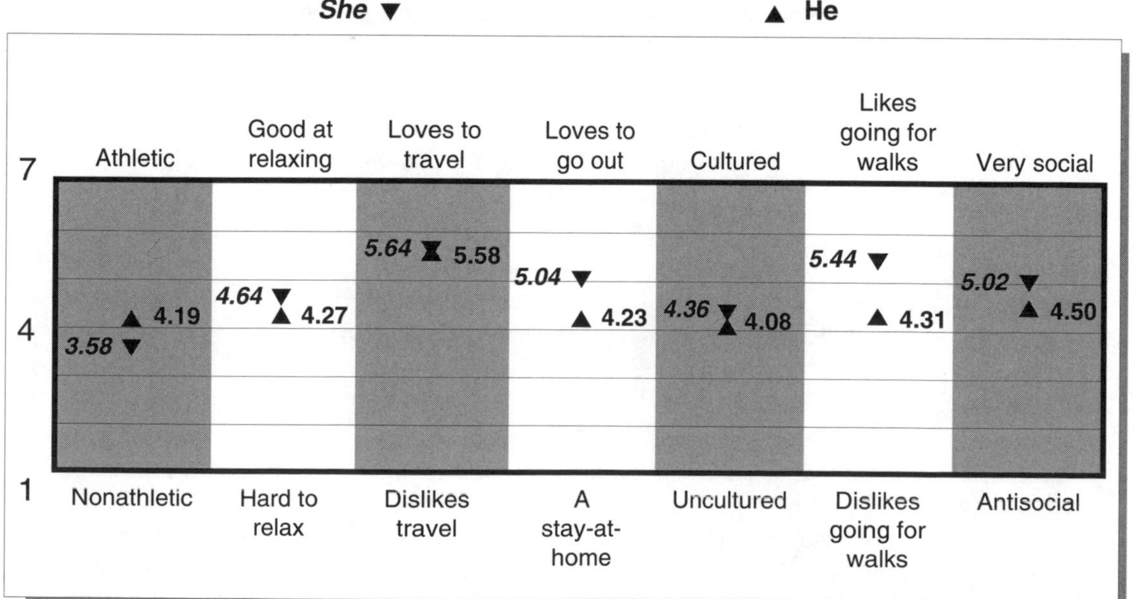

	He	She
2. Amount of discipline	15%	43%
3. Who disciplines	15%	28%
4. Misconduct determination	19%	35%
5. Love expression	8%	26%
6. Time spent	23%	41%
7. Money given	19%	35%

Compassion people love children—having them, raising them, enjoying them. The one area that gives them problems is discipline. They do not like to do it and wish children would behave automatically. Compassion people often leave it to their spouses to handle (or not handle) discipline.

Chuck and Vivian, both compassion gifts, have five children. They described their home as a zoo and came to realize that the kids were out of hand. So they sought counsel from their pastor, who sent them through a child-rearing course and taught them personally how to discipline their children more effectively. "They learned well," the pastor recounts. "Within a year their household had come into order, and after five years they were doing so well that they began adopting hard-to-adopt children."

Compassion wives (see chart B below) are natural at giving the two things children most often identify as love—quality time and much affectionate touch. But they tend to be permissive, inconsistent in discipline and to spoil their children.

Many compassion moms I have counseled are frustrated with their undisciplined children. When I first recommend the scriptural rod, they are horrified. Then I explain the procedure and the reasoning (as we share in our book *Discover Your Children's Gifts)* and they give it a try. They come back amazed at how it works, and how their children come to respect and love them even more.

C. My genuine needs, views or beliefs are:

	He	She
1. We need to provide better spiritual guidance for our children.	27%	61%

B. To what degree, from 1 to 7, are you one way or the other:

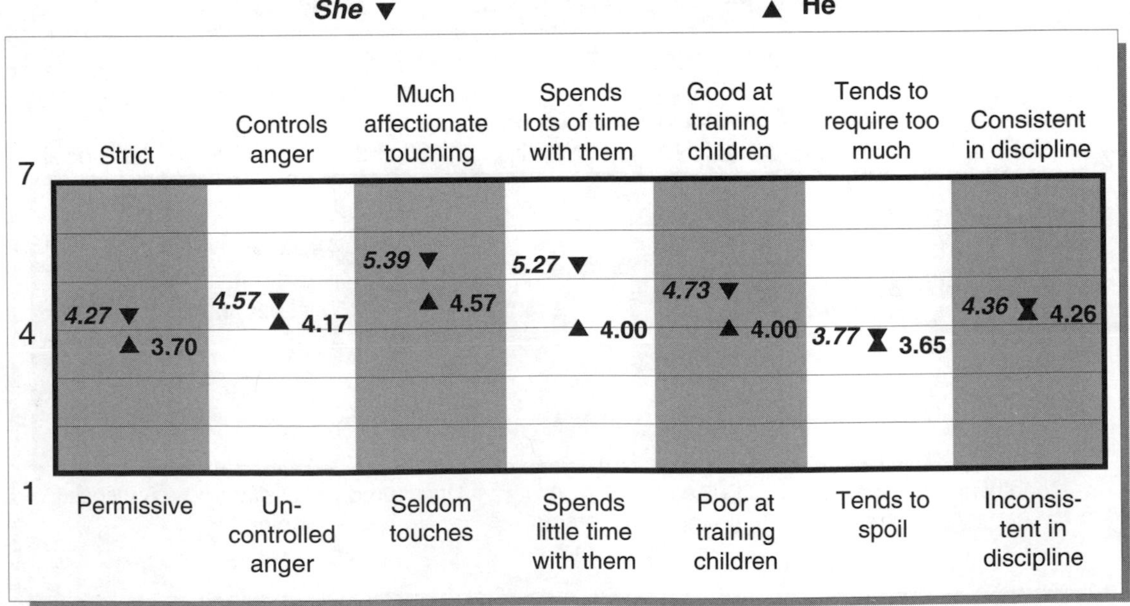

	He	She
2. We need to give our children more love and affection.	12%	30%
3. I would like my spouse to help more with the children.	4%	39%
4. I need to be more affirming of our children.	8%	30%
5. I feel we need to agree more on discipline.	4%	28%
6. I feel we need more quality family time and activities.	46%	59%
7. I am satisfied with our parenting styles and skills.	58%	33%

While compassion husbands indicate more satisfaction with their parenting styles and skills, compassion wives may be more accurate in their more modest evaluations. Both recognize the need for more quality family time and activities. Compassion wives are more aware of the need to provide better spiritual guidance for their children and to agree more on discipline. The latter is a necessity if there is to be any consistency and success.

Compassion wives are more likely to see the need for more positive affirmation of the children and often want more help from their spouses with the children. Lorene says, "My perceiver husband is great in leading devotions with our children, but he seems to be blind in giving me other kinds of help with them. But when I point it out, he's willing to help."

Category 16: In-Laws and Family

A. I FEEL WE HAVE SOME PROBLEMS WITH OUR FAMILIES AND IN-LAWS IN THESE AREAS:

	He	She
1. Interference	27%	17%
2. Their expectations	15%	24%
3. Their visits	4%	7%
4. Comparisons	0%	15%
5. Borrowing money	15%	20%
6. Former abuse	8%	28%
7. Dysfunction affect	27%	41%

Compassion husbands report a few problems with in-law interference. Do the in-laws think their compassion sons-in-law are not motivated adequately? Some are not. Compassion wives are more likely to complain of in-laws who compare them adversely with others.

Both score above the norm with problems about borrowing money from family, probably because they wish they did not have to ask for financial help.

Some indicate that childhood abuse is still affecting adult behavior. Remember that compassion children tend to perceive as abuse some things that others would not. A strict father might seem hurtful to a compassion child, whereas other children of the same father might see him as firm and fair. But if abuse, real or imagined, is affecting a compassion person's adult life, it is wise to get counseling.

Compassion respondents score well here (see chart B on page 286). They appear able to leave and cleave and develop a new family unit. They honor father and mother except when there was actual abuse. One woman shared that she used to feel guilty for avoiding any contact with her father. "My husband insists that I never see my father alone. I love my father and have forgiven him for the sexual abuse, but I will never be able to trust him again with myself or my children. My husband is right to protect us. Dad is not a safe person to be around."

While scores indicate that many compassion spouses feel their families were not

B. To what degree, from 1 to 7, are you one way or the other:

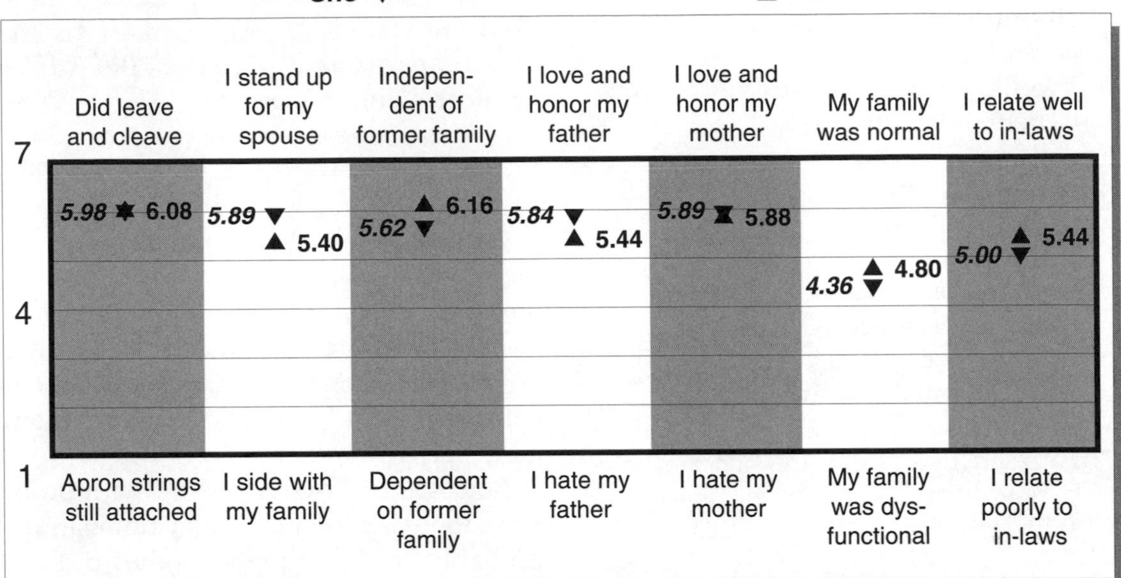

free from dysfunction, they find they can relate well presently to them and to in-laws.

C. My genuine needs, views or beliefs are:

	He	She
1. I need my spouse to put me before his/her family.	27%	26%
2. I need to see or talk to my parent(s) regularly.	15%	33%
3. I need to include my family in holiday celebrations.	38%	43%
4. I need help in overcoming in-law problems.	4%	13%
5. I need to be accepted by my in-laws.	19%	22%
6. I need to be financially free from my family and my in-laws.	23%	24%
7. I am satisfied with our family & in-law relationships.	54%	59%

More than half of the compassion spouses are satisfied with their extended families and in-law relationships. The rest are likely to try to improve these relationships and tolerate imperfect ones. Kathy sought my advice about attending her husband's family get-togethers. "I always feel on the outside," she complained. But as we talked and prayed, she realized she had judged various members of his family in her heart. She released those judgments, and actually found that from then on, she felt accepted by everyone!

Both compassion husbands and wives enjoy including extended family and in-laws in birthday and holiday celebrations. As one compassion husband said, "It helps me feel my roots, and to feel more a part of my wife's family as well."

Category 17: Social Relationships

A. I feel we have some problems in social relationships in these areas:

	He	She
1. Friends' demands	8%	15%
2. Time for friends	31%	37%

	He	She
3. Unsocial partner	15%	15%
4. Too social partner	12%	7%
5. Wrong friendships	0%	9%
6. Negative influence	0%	13%
7. Overinvolvement	12%	9%

Of all the gifts, compassion people are the most likely to make time for friends. While some say they would like even more time, most do well at keeping in touch. One compassion wife said, "A friend is a friend for life. I wouldn't think of not getting together occasionally. If they are too far away, I write or phone."

Compassion spouses can pick up friends who hold a degree of negative influence over them. Sam admits he has had to drop some of his old friends. "I loved getting together with some of my buddies from high school, but my wife felt I was compromising my newfound faith. She was right. We've made new friends at church that we enjoy together now."

Compassion respondents (see chart B below) see themselves as fairly balanced in their sociability. Note that they tend to prefer small groups of friends rather than large ones. "We can relate to people better and more personally that way," our compassion daughter, Linda, says.

While they like a variety of friends, they are not as gregarious as administrators or exhorters. They love to entertain, often having a friend or two over for dinner or going somewhere together or just getting together at home. Some could be called social butterflies while others are more balanced.

C. My genuine needs, views or beliefs are:

	He	She
1. I need to have many friends.	23%	30%
2. I especially love to entertain in our home.	31%	39%
3. I need a good deal of private time.	31%	28%
4. I need our home to be a haven of rest.	65%	59%

B. To what degree, from 1 to 7, are you one way or the other:

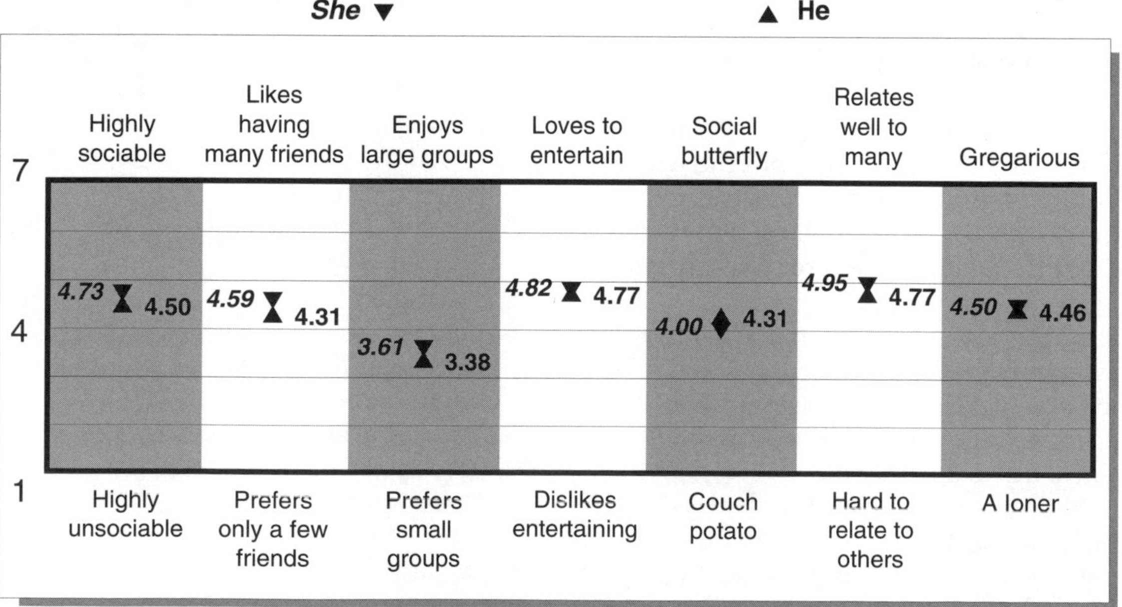

	He	She
5. I need to be involved in social groups.	19%	28%
6. I think we need to change some friendships.	8%	4%
7. I am satisfied with our social life.	73%	54%

Most compassion spouses are satisfied with their social lives, though some would enjoy more socializing. Few feel the need to change any friendships. Many enjoy opening their homes to friends, but they also need home to be a retreat from the world, a place to be alone with spouse or family.

Category 18: Religious Orientation

A. I FEEL WE HAVE SOME PROBLEMS IN OUR SPIRITUAL LIFE AND ORIENTATION IN THESE AREAS:

	He	She
1. Affiliation disagreement	4%	7%
2. Church attendance	4%	4%
3. Different backgrounds	8%	11%
4. Theological differences	8%	9%
5. Commitment level	19%	30%
6. Irregular attendance	4%	9%
7. Hypocritical behavior	12%	13%

Most compassion spouses say their commitment to God is steady, but the walking out of their faith can vacillate from time to time. "I love the Lord with all my heart," Douglas says, "but I struggle sometimes with my commitment to regular church attendance. If I'm really tired on a Sunday morning, I've been known to sleep in. I tell my wife we'll go to evening service instead. I can see that my spirit is willing but sometimes my flesh is weak."

Sharon says her most difficult commitment is regular prayer and Bible study. "I make time for it about four or five days a week. I don't know where the time goes the other days. Our pastor gave us a daily Bible reading schedule, and that's helping me stay on track."

Theological differences with spouses are not usually a problem since compassion people tend to accept the personal beliefs of others.

Compassion respondents (see chart B on page 289) see themselves as spiritual, committed to Christ and growing spiritually. They are keenly sensitive to spiritual matters and want to keep close to God. "I talk with Him all the time," Gayle says. "I'm a mom on the go and don't always have time to draw apart to pray, so I pray as I drive, clean house and shower."

Compassion gifts, along with perceivers and givers, tend to be intercessors. If they know someone is sick or hurting, they will pray faithfully. Their prayers in a group are deep and heartfelt. Others who hear them often wish they could pray so beautifully. Many recognize their ministry in prayer and will volunteer for an organized prayer chain, prayer counseling or active involvement in a prayer group.

C. MY GENUINE NEEDS, VIEWS OR BELIEFS ARE:

	He	She
1. I need to attend church regularly.	58%	72%
2. I need my partner to pray with me daily.	46%	63%
3. I greatly desire to see my spouse grow spiritually.	58%	78%
4. I believe we need to have regular family devotions.	62%	72%
5. I need my spouse to give spiritual leadership.	4%	72%
6. I need to be able to live my faith, not just talk about it.	58%	80%

B. TO WHAT DEGREE, FROM 1 TO 7, ARE YOU ONE WAY OR THE OTHER:

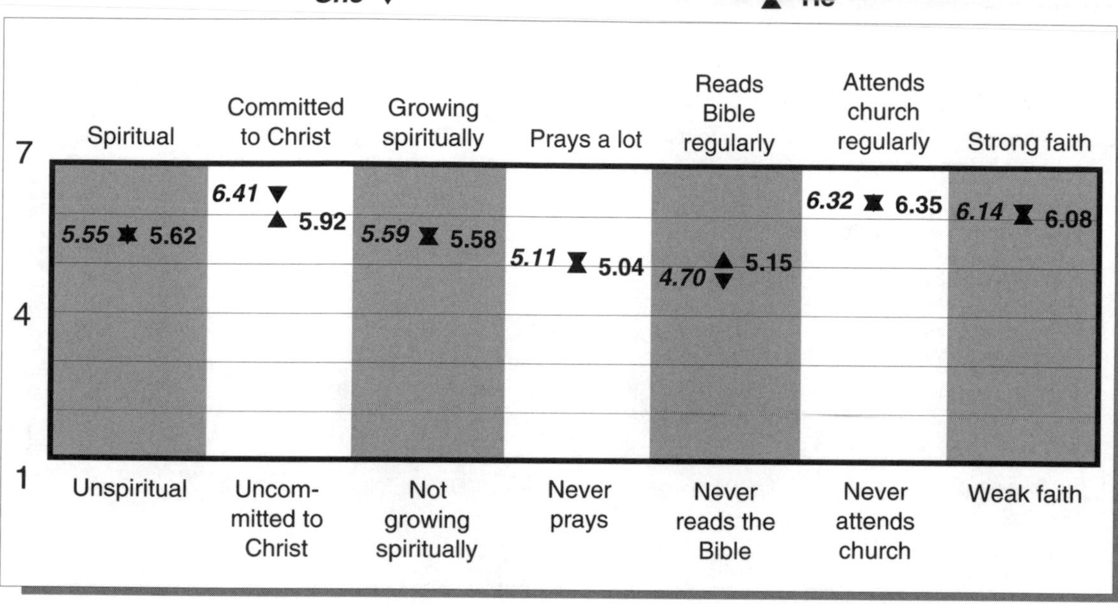

	He	She
7. I am satisfied with our religious orientation and practice.	58%	37%

More compassion husbands than wives are satisfied with their spirituality. Wives seem more concerned about living their faith and not just talking about it. They also want their spouses to give spiritual leadership. Both desire to see ongoing spiritual growth in themselves as well as their mates.

Because compassion people love to pray, they also love to pray with their spouses. "We try to spend time in prayer at the first of each day," Nadine says. "It helps us keep focused on what's really important. When Fred's out of town, I miss this."

Category 19: Maturity

A. I FEEL WE HAVE SOME PROBLEMS IN MATURITY IN THESE AREAS:

	He	She
1. Inexperience	8%	2%
2. Irresponsibility	12%	20%
3. Blame game	23%	24%
4. Stress coping	38%	57%
5. Criticism	15%	20%
6. Infidelity	4%	2%
7. Dishonesty	8%	11%

Scores for coping with stress are higher than the norm. Problem avoidance is the strategy of choice, although in many cases it is not possible. Ignoring stress does not work well either. Compassion spouses have to learn to face what is causing the stress.

"I get headaches when Rich gets mad at me," Cindy admitted. "I know it's because I don't want anything wrong with our relationship. In his everything-works-together-for-good exhorter approach, he says if we work our problem through, we'll both be stronger. I know he's right and I'm getting better at it."

The blame game can also be resorted to by compassion spouses, especially if they

B. To what degree, from 1 to 7, are you one way or the other:

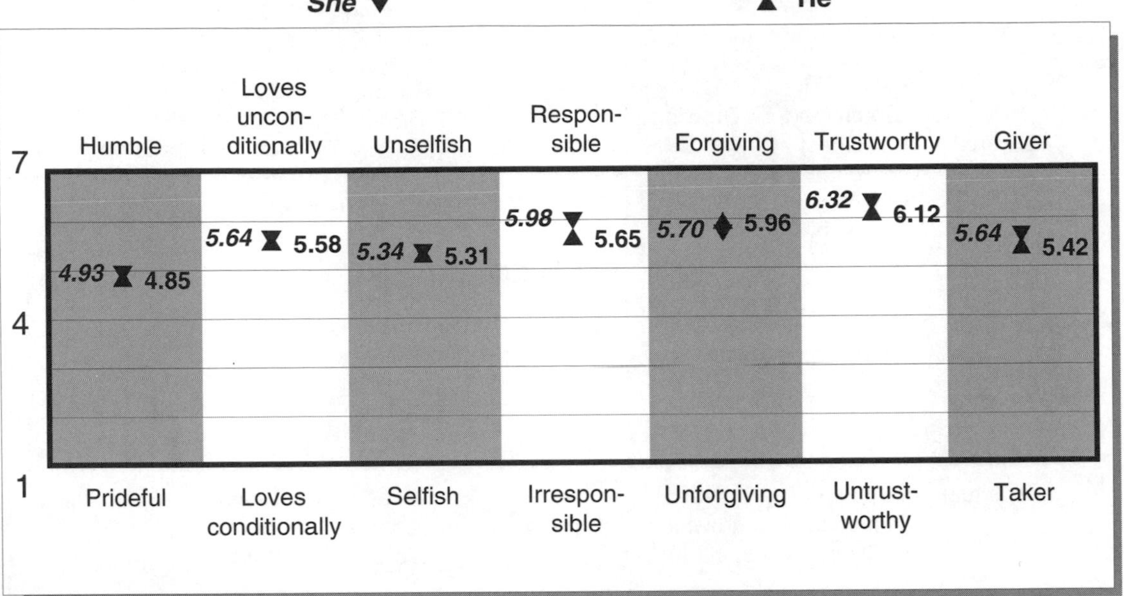

do not want to take responsibility for something. But once they blame a spouse, they usually feel bad about what they have done or left undone and will apologize to him or her.

Highest scores here (see chart B above) are for trustworthiness. What compassion people promise, they make every effort to do. They also tend to trust others—sometimes too much or too often. Our daughter, Linda, says, "I like to take people at their word. If they say they will do something, I assume they will. Sometimes I get disappointed, but I will give them another chance, and another. I know I let people take advantage of me sometimes, but I like to expect the best in people."

Compassion spouses love unconditionally most of the time. They often forgive. They tend to be givers rather than takers and are unselfish, deferring to their mates and allowing them to have the best, the nicest or the most beneficial.

While humility is the lowest score in this section, we can safely infer that these compassion respondents were humble even in their answers, for humility comes easily to them.

C. My genuine needs, views or beliefs are:

	He	She
1. I need to be able to trust my mate.	42%	50%
2. I need my spouse to be dependable.	38%	52%
3. I need to be quick to forgive and, hopefully, be forgiving quickly.	54%	70%
4. We need to learn from and grow through every experience.	58%	67%
5. I need my mate to be able to handle responsibility well.	23%	52%
6. I need my mate to love me unconditionally.	54%	57%
7. I feel that we are a reasonably mature couple.	88%	78%

Most see themselves as part of a reasonably mature couple. They certainly want to be. The main aspect of their lives that can keep them from the measure of maturity they desire is their tendency to be ruled by their emotions. One compassion husband admitted some time ago that every so often, when things got really stressful at work, he felt like quitting his job and pursuing a hermit's life. "I know it's not realistic," he said. "I have a wife and family to support." He is doing much better now.

Given the high scores on most of the items above, it is easy to see that compassion spouses care deeply about their marital relationships and want their mates to be equally trustworthy, dependable, loving and forgiving. Most also see the importance of viewing every experience as an opportunity to learn and grow. They will press on.

Category 20: Dysfunctionality

A. I FEEL WE HAVE SOME PROBLEMS IN THE FOLLOWING AREAS THAT PRODUCE DYSFUNCTION:

	He	She
1. Alcohol abuse	4%	4%
2. Drug abuse	4%	4%
3. Physical abuse	0%	4%
4. Sexual abuse	0%	4%
5. Verbal abuse	12%	22%
6. Emotional abuse	15%	22%
7. Unresolved abuse	15%	30%

Abuse scores for compassion spouses are higher than the norm, especially in physical and sexual abuse experienced by compassion wives in childhood. From what Don and I have observed through much counseling, females with a compassion gifting become victims of abuse more easily and are less likely to report it.

One told us that her father controlled her by saying if she told her mother about the sexual abuse, it would cause a breakup of the family that would be all her fault. It was not until she was fifteen that she came to realize she would *not* be at fault for telling, and that it was her father's fault for abusing her. She did tell and there were dire consequences, about which she had mixed feelings for years. She is free now.

Compassion women are more easily wounded by verbal and emotional abuse than other women, and also more than compassion men. It is important that they resolve hurts of any kind and get healing so they can move on. Loving Christian counseling is of tremendous value for them.

Compassion spouses are more likely than the other gifts to abuse alcohol or drugs. These can represent an avenue of escape from problems or hurt in their lives or marriages. One woman said, "When my husband starting having extramarital affairs, I couldn't face it. So before he'd come home from work, I'd have enough to drink so I wouldn't have to deal with the hurt and anger. It only prolonged the problem and set me up for a serious problem of my own. I thank God for parents who did an intervention and got me going to proper counseling."

Compassion people (see chart B on page 292) are seldom abusers of other people but are the most likely to become victims of abuse and to tolerate it longer than they should. A friend who is now married to a wonderful man admits that her first husband tormented her. "He wanted out of the marriage, but didn't want the stigma of initiating a divorce because of his profession. He took advantage of unhealed abuse from my childhood and played twisted mind games until I wound up in a mental insti-

B. To what degree, from 1 to 7, are you one way or the other:

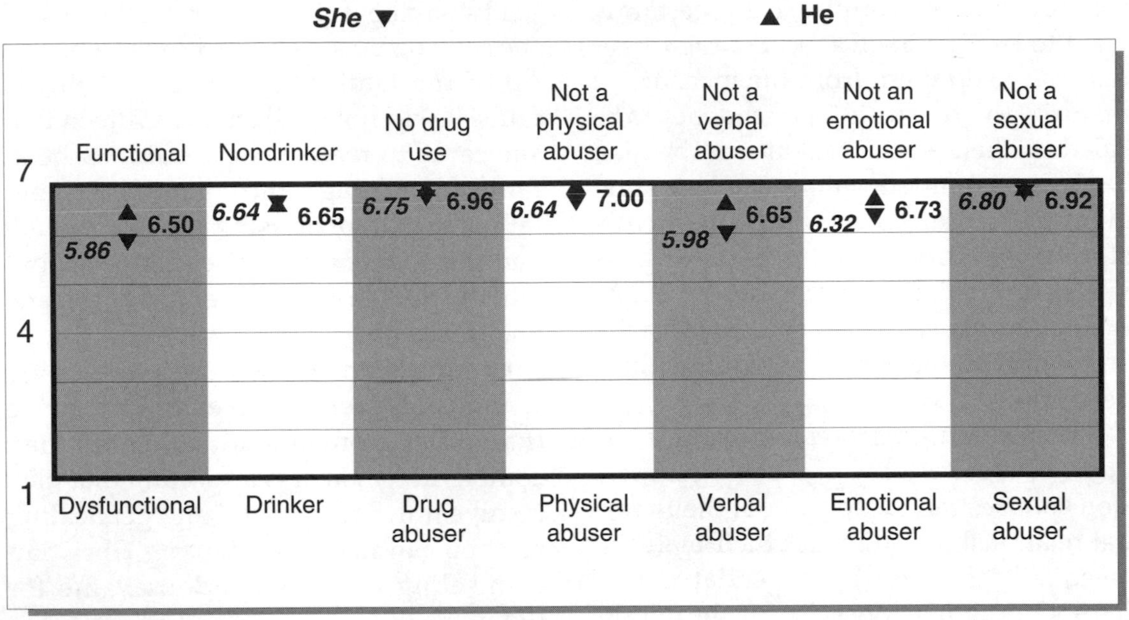

She ▼ ▲ He

	Functional / Dysfunctional	Nondrinker / Drinker	No drug use / Drug abuser	Not a physical abuser / Physical abuser	Not a verbal abuser / Verbal abuser	Not an emotional abuser / Emotional abuser	Not a sexual abuser / Sexual abuser
She ▼	*5.86*	*6.64*	*6.75*	*6.64*	*5.98*	*6.32*	*6.80*
He ▲	6.50	6.65	6.96	7.00	6.65	6.73	6.92

tution, at which point he could justify the divorce."

Those willing to respond to our survey reported little use of alcohol or drugs. In a cross-section sampling of society, more problems in these areas would show up.

C. My genuine needs, views or beliefs are:

	He	She
1. I need our marriage to be free of alcohol use and abuse.	31%	43%
2. I need our marriage to be free of drug use and abuse.	38%	48%
3. I need my spouse to treat me more kindly.	12%	24%
4. I need my mate to give me positive emotional support.	46%	57%
5. One or both of us need to get help for abuse in childhood.	8%	22%
6. One or both of us need to get help for dysfunctional behavior.	8%	28%
7. I believe there is no dysfunctional behavior in our marriage.	81%	46%

Note that four-fifths of compassion men believe there is no dysfunctional behavior in their marriages, while only about half the compassion women believe this. Compassion wives recognize more readily their need for getting help for former abuse and present dysfunctional behavior. Women in general are more likely to admit the need and get help; men tend to deny such needs and resist counseling.

Both see the need for positive emotional support from their mates—a genuine need for every marriage to stay healthy.

PART

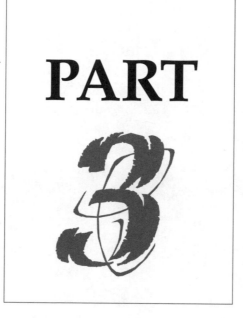

How to Enrich Your Marriage

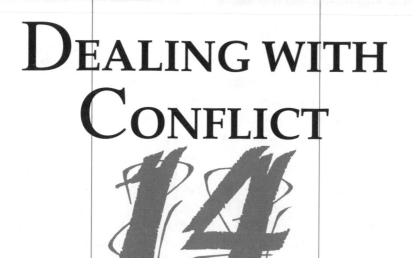

Dealing with Conflict

14

Is the old saying true that opposites attract? How likely is it that opposite gifting attracted you to the person you married (or intend to marry)? What if two persons with the same gift marry? What problems would crop up in either of these cases?

Yes, opposite gifts usually attract in marriage. One spouse frequently has a speaking-type gift and the other a serving-type gift. Or a perceiver is attracted to a compassion person, a teacher to an exhorter, a server to an administrator—in all cases, seemingly opposite gifts.

About 95 percent of the time people choose mates with motivational gifts different from their own. You may find this true for yourself.

If You Married the Same Gift

About five percent of the time people marry someone with the same gift. If both are mature for their ages, their similarities can be an asset; if they are immature, their problem areas will be amplified.

Of the small percentage that marry the same gift, about half are compassion gifts. This is because they can identify with and understand one another's feelings so well. On the positive side they are loving and kind with each other; on the negative side they tend to be so indecisive that decisions and accomplishments are scarce. Income levels can be low and finances tight. But they will be the first to admit, "We're living on love." And at least when they are late to an event, they are late together!

Some exhorters are also attracted to each other. Exhorter couples we have known have done well together, perhaps because of their adaptability and positive outlook on life. Mark and Barbara have a counseling ministry that utilizes their exhorter giftedness to the fullest extent and benefits counselees tremendously. "The only problem we have," says Barbara, "is our temptation to give each other advice!"

The other five gifts seldom marry the same gift, although there are exceptions. A couple in our former home group are teacher gifts who met at the University of Washington, where they were both working for doctorates in physics. They have the most intellectual marital relationship of any couple we have ever known. Their idea of a fun night out is attending a lecture by a visiting research scientist. It works for them.

The most difficult pairing is that of two perceivers. Because they have such strong wills, the relationship is almost guaranteed to be peppered with drastic differences of opinion and ongoing struggles over who is really in control.

If You Married an Opposite

Most likely you have married (or intend to marry) a person with one of the six giftings other than your own. Within these possibilities are many areas for potential conflict and problems. If you can identify these and understand the likely problems, you will get a handle on the situation. You may find that just gaining understanding releases you to accept your spouse's gifting as is. Or it may give you both the opportunity to discuss why your gifting is causing problems and what you can do to improve the situation. Perhaps one of you will discover some polluting in your gifting that needs to be repented of and changed. Increased awareness of your gifting may enable you to give and take with greater ease, be more willing to be flexible or, in some cases, compromise for the sake of the other.

Don often shares how important it is to give place to a spouse's gifting. It is a matter of showing love and caring. If you are married to a compassion wife who loves fresh flowers, and you with your gifting think they are a waste of money, give her some now and then anyhow. Or if you are married to a perceiver husband who loves some peace and quiet, and you are an exhorter who loves to talk, do not fill every void with words. Let him have his spaces.

There are potential advantages in every one of the 49 possible marital combinations. No matter who your mate is, the two of you have wonderful opportunities to do things together you would never have had apart.

Don and I have had the privilege of traveling around the world (we did that literally once) teaching seminars. As an administrator/teacher I love to meet people and teach. As an exhorter/giver Don also loves teaching and meeting people. By meshing our giftedness into a joint ministry, we get to do what we love and in the process have greater quality time together, which we both enjoy greatly. We thank God for gifting us as He did and then bringing us together. He is truly the best matchmaker of all. But that is another story!

Improve Your Relationship

Use the chart on page 302 to help you gain insight into your mate's or potential mate's personality. Be sure you have taken the motivational gifts test in chapter 3. Review the problem areas from the five problem characteristics of your primary gift—and possibly your secondary gift, if it was close.

Here are some more typical problem areas of each gift:

Perceivers are often strong-willed, judgmental, blunt, opinionated, intolerant, too idealistic, critical, prideful, domineering, controlling, pushy, unforgiving, loners and plagued with poor self-image.

Servers are often easily embarrassed, overly shy, perfectionists, critical, interfering and overly dependent on appreciation.

Teachers are often prideful, intolerant, legalistic, dogmatic, opinionated, unfriendly, aloof and prone to transmit know-it-all attitudes.

Exhorters are often opinionated, interruptive, compromising, overly talkative, pushy, stretchers of the truth and prone to give unsolicited advice.

Givers are often stingy, overly focused on money, overly frugal, tempted to steal, manipulative, overworkers, overly generous and prone to give without their mates' approval.

Administrators are often bossy, domineering, insensitive, callous, procrastinating, forgetful, messy, overzealous, overextended and neglectful of routine work.

Compassion persons are often easily wounded, overemotional, compromising, indecisive, undependable, late, unrealistic, illogical and overly empathetic.

Possible Problems and Advantages

We offer the following examples of gift-related potential problems and advantages sometimes found in each of the 49 possible marital combinations. In every case the man's gift is listed first and the woman's second, except with identical gifts, in which case the positions are interchangeable.

Take special note of examples fitting your marital gift combinations for other hints of possible conflict.

1. *Perceiver* (husband and wife)
   Potential problem: They have conflicts over who is right.
   Potential advantage: Both have strict standards.

2. *Perceiver* (husband)—*Server* (wife)
   Potential problem: He is bossy; treats her like a servant.
   Potential advantage: He is honest and loyal to her.

3. *Perceiver* (husband)—*Teacher* (wife)
   Potential problem: He is threatened by her opinions.
   Potential advantage: Both love to study the Word.

4. *Perceiver* (husband)—*Exhorter* (wife)
   Potential problem: He is irritated over her talkativeness.
   Potential advantage: Her gregariousness modifies his reclusiveness.

5. *Perceiver* (husband)—*Giver* (wife)
   Potential problem: He controls her ability to give.
   Potential advantage: They have joint intercessory prayer power.

6. *Perceiver* (husband)—*Administrator* (wife)
   Potential problem: He intimidates and squelches her leadership potential.
   Potential advantage: Her practical, organized approach balances his idealism.

7. *Perceiver* (husband)—*Compassion* (wife)
   Potential problem: He has the tendency to hurt her feelings.
   Potential advantage: Both are sensitive to the needs of others.

8. *Server* (husband)—*Perceiver* (wife)
   Potential problem: He tends to feel overwhelmed by her strong personality.
   Potential advantage: Both are perfectionists in their own way.

9. *Server* (husband and wife)
   Potential problem: Both try to outdo each other at serving; becoming competitive.

Potential advantage: They work exceptionally well together as a team.

10. *Server* (husband)—*Teacher* (wife)
Potential problem: He resents her lack of practical helpfulness.
Potential advantage: Opposite traits of doing (husband) and thinking (wife) balance each other.

11. *Server* (husband)—*Exhorter* (wife)
Potential problem: His interest in things conflicts with her interest in people.
Potential advantage: She helps draw him into social activities he would otherwise miss.

12. *Server* (husband)—*Giver* (wife)
Potential problem: Their need to do and feel appreciated makes both partners insecure.
Potential advantage: They are helpful to each other and everyone around them.

13. *Server* (husband)—*Administrator* (wife)
Potential problem: He feels threatened by her leadership ability.
Potential advantage: He is able to carry out effectively projects she initiates.

14. *Server* (husband)—*Compassion* (wife)
Potential problem: His high energy level conflicts with her slowness and tardiness.
Potential advantage: Both are gentle in spirit.

15. *Teacher* (husband)—*Perceiver* (wife)
Potential problem: He is frustrated over her emotional mood swings.
Potential advantage: Both are highly analytical.

16. *Teacher* (husband)—*Server* (wife)
Potential problem: His intellectual emphasis makes her feel inferior.
Potential advantage: She is glad to care for routine responsibilities while he reads or studies.

17. *Teacher* (husband and wife)
Potential problem: Differences of opinion readily become arguments.
Potential advantage: Both love to read books.

18. *Teacher* (husband)—*Exhorter* (wife)
Potential problem: They have disagreements over how truth is arrived at.
Potential advantage: Both love to talk.

19. *Teacher* (husband)—*Giver* (wife)
Potential problem: He is threatened by her better business ability.
Potential advantage: She helps him be more practical and down-to-earth.

20. *Teacher* (husband)—*Administrator* (wife)
Potential problem: He gets upset with her procrastination and clutter.
Potential advantage: Both enjoy learning.

21. *Teacher* (husband)—*Compassion* (wife)
Potential problem: He is frustrated with her illogical or irrational behavior.
Potential advantage: She compensates for his shyness in social situations.

22. *Exhorter* (husband)—*Perceiver* (wife)
Potential problem: He feels her perceptions are personal criticisms of him.
Potential advantage: He encourages her to have broader social relationships.

23. *Exhorter* (husband)—*Server* (wife)
Potential problem: His talkativeness overwhelms her, causing further reserve.
Potential advantage: She enjoys hosting his many friends.

24. *Exhorter* (husband)—*Teacher* (wife)
Potential problem: He is frustrated by her disinterest in social relationships.
Potential advantage: He helps her be more life- and people-related.

25. *Exhorter* (husband and wife)
Potential problem: They are competitive in talking.
Potential advantage: They encourage one another constantly.

26. *Exhorter* (husband)—*Giver* (wife)
Potential problem: He resents her overemphasis on money.
Potential advantage: Both enjoy many friends.

27. *Exhorter* (husband)—*Administrator* (wife)
Potential problem: He gets upset with her procrastination.
Potential advantage: Both love being around lots of people.

28. *Exhorter* (husband)—*Compassion* (wife)
Potential problem: He is frustrated over her indecisiveness.
Potential advantage: Both are great counselors.

29. *Giver* (husband)—*Perceiver* (wife)
Potential problem: He resents her telling him whom not to trust in business relationships.
Potential advantage: Both are very honest.

30. *Giver* (husband)—*Server* (wife)
Potential problem: She is upset when he gives away things without consulting her.
Potential advantage: Both are easy-going.

31. *Giver* (husband)—*Teacher* (wife)
Potential problem: His focus on business conflicts with her interest in education.
Potential advantage: Both operate diligently.

32. *Giver* (husband)—*Exhorter* (wife)
Potential problem: He feels she wastes too much time on the phone and socializing.
Potential advantage: He is a good provider, freeing her to help others with their problems.

33. *Giver* (husband and wife)
Potential problem: Their frugality can turn into stinginess.
Potential advantage: Both enjoy offering help as well as gifts to others.

34. *Giver* (husband)—*Administrator* (wife)
Potential problem: He resents her telling him what to do, especially regarding business matters.
Potential advantage: They can work together in business, but only if she submits to his authority.

35. *Giver* (husband)—*Compassion* (wife)
Potential problem: He is frustrated over her lack of industriousness and punctuality.
Potential advantage: Both enjoy building interpersonal relationships.

36. *Administrator* (husband)—*Perceiver* (wife)
Potential problem: He gets upset when she judges his actions or decisions.
Potential advantage: Both enjoy competition.

37. *Administrator* (husband)—*Server* (wife)
Potential problem: He takes her for granted, forgetting to express appreciation.
Potential advantage: She is glad to carry out his directions.

38. *Administrator* (husband)—*Teacher* (wife)

Potential problem: He resents her focus on reading and learning instead of on him.
Potential advantage: Both are achievers.

39. *Administrator* (husband)—*Exhorter* (wife)
Potential problem: He saves everything; she throws away items with no more practical use.
Potential advantage: They make a great teaching team with complementary styles.

40. *Administrator* (husband)—*Giver* (wife)
Potential problem: His bossiness offends her, especially in monetary matters.
Potential advantage: She supports his projects.

41. *Administrator* (husband and wife)
Potential problem: Organizational ideas conflict.
Potential advantage: Harmonious relationship if individual areas of authority are clearly defined.

42. *Administrator* (husband)—*Compassion* (wife)
Potential problem: He is perplexed by her emotional reactions.
Potential advantage: He helps keep her relatively organized and on schedule.

43. *Compassion* (husband)—*Perceiver* (wife)
Potential problem: He often feels she dominates him.
Potential advantage: He can soften her somewhat abrasive personality.

44. *Compassion* (husband)—*Server* (wife)
Potential problem: They let others take advantage of them too often.
Potential advantage: They do not criticize each other.

45. *Compassion* (husband)—*Teacher* (wife)
Potential problem: Communication is difficult because of feeling/thinking differences.
Potential advantage: Both enjoy the arts.

46. *Compassion* (husband)—*Exhorter* (wife)
Potential problem: He feels threatened by her decision-making abilities.
Potential advantage: They are very loving to each other.

47. *Compassion* (husband)—*Giver* (wife)
Potential problem: His casual handling of finances conflicts with her superior financial ability.
Potential advantage: They are very helpful to each other.

48. *Compassion* (husband)—*Administrator* (wife)
Potential problem: He feels pressured by her organizational abilities.
Potential advantage: He helps her to balance personal relationships with an achievement orientation.

49. *Compassion* (husband and wife)
Potential problem: Both are indecisive and lack motivation.
Potential advantage: Both have tremendous capacity to show love to one another.

Now list your actual or potential problems on the chart on page 302. Then have your spouse do the same. You can both work on the *Our Problems* section. List conflicts you experience presently and ones that could develop between you. Look over your responses together. Discuss them with an openness to new insights. Pray about them and ask the Lord to give you fresh revelation and practical solutions.

After listing problems, jot down possible ideas, steps of action and potential solutions. Consider how the increased understanding of your respective gifts can overcome problems and conflicts. Discuss needed changes in attitudes or actions. Pray further, asking the Lord to guide you as you seek solutions, making some commitments to action. Forgive one another. Cancel unreasonable expectations. Dissolve any judgments. Hug a lot. Be ready to start with a clean slate. Remember, *you cannot change anyone else, but you can change yourself, your viewpoints, your attitudes and your actions.*

Finally, look again at the list of 49 combinations on pages 297–300 and see what potential advantages your partnership might yield. Add others you already recognize. Appreciate and cultivate the dynamic possibilities of your gifts in your relationship.

Giftedness in Marriage Problems and Possible Solutions

His Gifts

(primary gift)

(secondary gift)

Her Gifts

(primary gift)

(secondary gift)

His Problems

Possible Solutions

Her Problems

Possible Solutions

Our Problems

Possible Solutions

Our Advantages

Surveying Your Own Situation

15

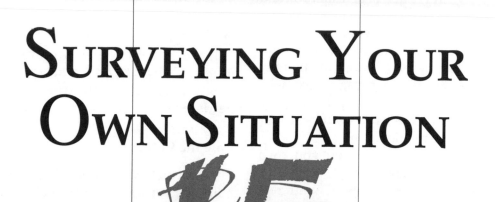

Now it is time to survey your own situation. You have learned a lot about your own gifting and your mate's gifting. You have examined the results of our marriage survey in chapters 7–13 and have an understanding of how different gifts operate in a marriage relationship. Though spouses may be gifted similarly, each couple is unique, with secondary giftings that may have a strong effect on their lives if the scores are close, and a measure of effect even if the scores are not close.

Even the configuration of all the other gifts in a person's scoring helps make that person unique. Jody, for instance, scored 74 in giver, 55 in server, 51 in compassion, 48 in exhorter, 39 in perceiver, 35 in teacher and 27 in administrator. Givers can be extroverts or introverts depending on the configuration of the other gifts. Jody is the quiet type because her second and third gifts, though quite a bit lower than her primary gift, are serving gifts that like to work more behind the scenes.

Jody's husband, Robert, scored highest in giver as well—79 points. But his secondary gifts, though quite a bit lower than his first, are 61 in perceiver, 59 in exhorter, 56 in administrator, 50 in teacher, 43 in server and 39 in compassion. His four higher secondary gifts are all speaking gifts. So Robert is a extroverted giver, a successful businessman and part-time evangelist with a powerful ministry. Jody is happy to back him up any way she can, but does not feel comfortable speaking in front of large groups herself.

You and your spouse will find that your own special gifting and relationship to each other are unique.

Your Own Marriage Survey

Be candid in the survey on pages 305–26. Do not be afraid to admit your problem areas. Your mate is probably already aware of them. This survey will become a valuable tool as you take time to go over it together to evaluate what it means to your relationship. Remember, it is O.K. to be different, even drastically so. God has created you and then brought you together in marriage, and He has a special plan for your life.

The survey covers the same twenty subject categories of the previous chapters in three sub-categories of seven items each:

1. Possible problems or conflicts in your marriage relationship
2. Personal estimations about your own traits and tendencies
3. Personal assessments of your real and/or felt needs

Section A

The first kind of question is multiple choice. Indicate what you feel are problem or conflict areas in your marriage by checking either the *minor problem* box or the *major problem* box. If you have no problems in the area, move on to the next one. See section A in the sample on the next page.

Section B

In the second section evaluate yourself in light of the two opposite traits or tendencies. Husbands, draw a square around the number that best describes you. Wives, draw a circle around the number that best describes you. See section B in the sample on the next page.

Section C

In the third section check only the boxes located beneath *He* or *She* that match statements reflecting your true views and needs. See section C on the sample.

Rate the Categories

After you have completed your personal marriage survey, fill in the chart on page 326 to rate each of the twenty categories that hold major or minor problems for you and your spouse. This overview will help you determine which areas need your attention the most. Obviously an area you both check as a major problem would take precedence over an area you both check as minor. Below the twenty categories on the chart is a place for noting where you would like to start working, and determining some possible actions or goals. It will help get you off to a good start.

We believe that just knowing your mate's gifts and traits will eliminate many problem areas you have had previously. Other areas will need prayerful consideration and dedicated action.

Category 1: Communication

A. *I feel we have some problems in communication in these areas:*

He: Minor Problems	He: Major Problems		She: Minor Problems	She: Major Problems
☒	☐	1. Frequent misunderstandings	☒	☐
☐	☒	2. Not feeling free to share what we really feel	☐	☒
☒	☐	3. Not listening well to what the other says	☐	☒
☒	☐	4. Not enough meaningful conversation	☒	☐
☐	☐	5. Giving too much correction to what is said or done	☐	☐
☐	☐	6. Negative nonverbal communication (body language, etc.)	☒	☐
☒	☐	7. Ridicule, sarcasm or unkind words	☐	☐

B. *To what degree, from 1 to 7, are you one way or the other?*

Husband: *Mark a ☐ around the number that best describes you.*
Wife: *Mark a ◯ around the number that best describes you.*

1.	Poor communicator	1	2	3	[4]	5	(6)	7	Good communicator
2.	Talks too little	1	2	[3]	4	5	6	(7)	Talks too much
3.	Inattentive	1	2	3	[4]	(5)	6	7	Attentive
4.	Listens poorly	1	2	[3]	4	(5)	6	7	Listens well
5.	Dislikes chit-chat	1	[2]	3	4	5	(6)	7	Enjoys chit-chat
6.	Critical	1	2	3	4	[(5)]	6	7	Noncritical
7.	Interrupter	1	2	3	4	[5]	6	(7)	Noninterrupter

C. *My genuine needs, views or beliefs are:*

He: True		She: True
☒	1. I need more conversation with my mate.	☐
☐	2. I need my partner to listen to me more attentively.	☒
☒	3. I need more quiet time without conversation.	☐
☐	4. I feel we need to share more intimately our thoughts and feelings.	☐
☐	5. I get hurt easily by my mate's unkind remarks.	☐
☐	6. I need more of my partner's undivided attention.	☒
☒	7. I am satisfied with our communication and conversation.	☐

Category 1: Communication

A. *I feel we have some problems in communication in these areas:*

He: Minor Problems	He: Major Problems		She: Minor Problems	She: Major Problems
☐	☐	1. Frequent misunderstandings	☐	☐
☐	☐	2. Not feeling free to share what we really feel	☐	☐
☐	☐	3. Not listening well to what the other says	☐	☐
☐	☐	4. Not enough meaningful conversation	☐	☐
☐	☐	5. Giving too much correction to what is said or done	☐	☐
☐	☐	6. Negative nonverbal communication (body language, etc.)	☐	☐
☐	☐	7. Ridicule, sarcasm or unkind words	☐	☐

B. *To what degree, from 1 to 7, are you one way or the other?*

Husband: *Mark a* ☐ *around the number that best describes you.*
Wife: *Mark a* ◯ *around the number that best describes you.*

1.	Poor communicator	1 2 3 4 5 6 7	Good communicator
2.	Talks too little	1 2 3 4 5 6 7	Talks too much
3.	Inattentive	1 2 3 4 5 6 7	Attentive
4.	Listens poorly	1 2 3 4 5 6 7	Listens well
5.	Dislikes chit-chat	1 2 3 4 5 6 7	Enjoys chit-chat
6.	Critical	1 2 3 4 5 6 7	Noncritical
7.	Interrupter	1 2 3 4 5 6 7	Noninterrupter

C. *My genuine needs, views or beliefs are:*

He: True		She: True
☐	1. I need more conversation with my mate.	☐
☐	2. I need my partner to listen to me more attentively.	☐
☐	3. I need more quiet time without conversation.	☐
☐	4. I feel we need to share more intimately our thoughts and feelings.	☐
☐	5. I get hurt easily by my mate's unkind remarks.	☐
☐	6. I need more of my partner's undivided attention.	☐
☐	7. I am satisfied with our communication and conversation.	☐

Category 2: Expectations

A. *I feel we have some problems in what we expect of each other in these areas:*

He: Minor Problems	He: Major Problems		She: Minor Problems	She: Major Problems
☐	☐	1. Our general lifestyle	☐	☐
☐	☐	2. The establishing of priorities	☐	☐
☐	☐	3. Ideals and goals and values	☐	☐
☐	☐	4. How the holidays are celebrated in our home	☐	☐
☐	☐	5. Our hopes and dreams	☐	☐
☐	☐	6. What is proper and acceptable conduct	☐	☐
☐	☐	7. What should be *shared* work at home	☐	☐

B. *To what degree, from 1 to 7, are you one way or the other?*

Husband: *Mark a* ☐ *around the number that best describes you.*
Wife: *Mark a* ◯ *around the number that best describes you.*

1.	Jealous	1	2	3	4	5	6	7	Trusting
2.	Keeps options open	1	2	3	4	5	6	7	Totally committed
3.	Secretive, closed	1	2	3	4	5	6	7	Honest, open
4.	Realist	1	2	3	4	5	6	7	Idealist
5.	Messy	1	2	3	4	5	6	7	Neat and tidy
6.	Unconventional	1	2	3	4	5	6	7	Conventional
7.	Disloyal	1	2	3	4	5	6	7	Loyal

C. *My genuine needs, views or beliefs are:*

He: True		She: True
☐	1. I need to be more sure of my partner's motives.	☐
☐	2. I need a mate who is dependable.	☐
☐	3. I feel we need to work more at setting joint priorities.	☐
☐	4. I need to be more confident in how my mate handles stress.	☐
☐	5. I need my spouse to be totally honest with me.	☐
☐	6. I need to have former family customs a part of my life.	☐
☐	7. I feel our expectations are realistic and workable.	☐

Category 3: Marital Cohesion

A. *I feel we have some problems in getting along with each other in these areas:*

He: Minor Problems	He: Major Problems		She: Minor Problems	She: Major Problems
☐	☐	1. Spending enough time together	☐	☐
☐	☐	2. The give and take in marriage	☐	☐
☐	☐	3. Feeling truly one	☐	☐
☐	☐	4. Feeling really close to each other	☐	☐
☐	☐	5. In setting goals and priorities together	☐	☐
☐	☐	6. Feeling lonely	☐	☐
☐	☐	7. Lack of romantic love and affection	☐	☐

B. *To what degree, from 1 to 7, are you one way or the other?*

Husband: *Mark a* ☐ *around the number that best describes you.*
Wife: *Mark a* ◯ *around the number that best describes you.*

1.	Insensitive	1	2	3	4	5	6	7	Super sensitive
2.	Dependent	1	2	3	4	5	6	7	Independent
3.	Disagreeable	1	2	3	4	5	6	7	Agreeable
4.	Inconsistent	1	2	3	4	5	6	7	Consistent
5.	Unreliable	1	2	3	4	5	6	7	Reliable
6.	Peace disturber	1	2	3	4	5	6	7	Peacemaker
7.	Discourager	1	2	3	4	5	6	7	Encourager

C. *My genuine needs, views or beliefs are:*

He: True		She: True
☐	1. I need to be able to confide more in my mate.	☐
☐	2. I feel there needs to be more unity in our relationship.	☐
☐	3. I need to feel more secure in our marriage.	☐
☐	4. I am afraid to share some of my feelings with my partner.	☐
☐	5. I need my mate to be more sensitive to my needs.	☐
☐	6. I do not consider divorce ever to be an option.	☐
☐	7. I am satisfied with our marital interaction and closeness.	☐

Category 4: Roles and Responsibilities

A. *I feel we have some problems in our marriage roles and responsibilities in these areas:*

He: Minor Problems	He: Major Problems		She: Minor Problems	She: Major Problems
☐	☐	1. The authority structure in our marriage	☐	☐
☐	☐	2. What marital submission really means	☐	☐
☐	☐	3. How responsibilities should be shared	☐	☐
☐	☐	4. How decisions are made	☐	☐
☐	☐	5. Traditional male / female roles in marriage	☐	☐
☐	☐	6. Feeling overworked	☐	☐
☐	☐	7. Household and yard responsibility and management	☐	☐

B. *To what degree, from 1 to 7, are you one way or the other?*

Husband: *Mark a ☐ around the number that best describes you.*
Wife: *Mark a ◯ around the number that best describes you.*

1.	Submissive	1	2	3	4	5	6	7	Authoritarian
2.	Bossy	1	2	3	4	5	6	7	Tactful
3.	Uncooperative	1	2	3	4	5	6	7	Cooperative
4.	Indecisive	1	2	3	4	5	6	7	Decisive
5.	Manipulative	1	2	3	4	5	6	7	Straightforward
6.	Irresponsible	1	2	3	4	5	6	7	Responsible
7.	Immature	1	2	3	4	5	6	7	Mature

C. *My genuine needs, views or beliefs are:*

He: True		She: True
☐	1. I need my role clarified more.	☐
☐	2. I need more freedom to discuss ideas and options.	☐
☐	3. I need to use some of my capabilities more.	☐
☐	4. I need to receive more respect from my partner.	☐
☐	5. I need more domestic help and support from my spouse.	☐
☐	6. I would like to help more in planning together.	☐
☐	7. I am satisfied with the roles and responsibilities we have established.	☐

Category 5: Conflict Resolution

A. *I feel we have some problems in how we deal with conflicts in these areas:*

He: Minor Problems	He: Major Problems		She: Minor Problems	She: Major Problems
☐	☐	1. Anger management	☐	☐
☐	☐	2. Over who's right	☐	☐
☐	☐	3. Over who makes the final decisions	☐	☐
☐	☐	4. Clamming up and the silent treatment	☐	☐
☐	☐	5. The use of threats or ultimatums	☐	☐
☐	☐	6. Discussion of problems develops into personal attacks.	☐	☐
☐	☐	7. We regress into the blame game.	☐	☐

B. *To what degree, from 1 to 7, are you one way or the other?*

Husband: *Mark a* ☐ *around the number that best describes you.*
Wife: *Mark a* ◯ *around the number that best describes you.*

1. Easily angered	1	2	3	4	5	6	7	Calm, cool and collected
2. Disagreeable	1	2	3	4	5	6	7	Agreeable
3. Stubborn	1	2	3	4	5	6	7	Adaptable
4. Holds grudges	1	2	3	4	5	6	7	Forgiving
5. A wounder	1	2	3	4	5	6	7	Easily wounded
6. Handles stress poorly	1	2	3	4	5	6	7	Handles stress well
7. Nonapologetic	1	2	3	4	5	6	7	Apologetic

C. *My genuine needs, views or beliefs are:*

He: True		She: True
☐	1. I need to gain control over my temper.	☐
☐	2. I need my spouse to gain control over his / her temper.	☐
☐	3. I need to have my point of view heard more often.	☐
☐	4. I feel a strong need to avoid arguments and conflicts.	☐
☐	5. I need my mate to forgive me more quickly.	☐
☐	6. I think we need better ground rules for resolving conflicts.	☐
☐	7. I am satisfied with the way we resolve conflicts.	☐

Category 6: Personality Issues

A. *I feel we have some problems in personality conflicts and issues in these areas:*

He: Minor Problems	He: Major Problems		She: Minor Problems	She: Major Problems
☐	☐	1. My partner always wants to be right	☐	☐
☐	☐	2. The problem of pride	☐	☐
☐	☐	3. Understanding each other	☐	☐
☐	☐	4. Trying to change one another	☐	☐
☐	☐	5. Methods of doing things	☐	☐
☐	☐	6. Bothersome habits	☐	☐
☐	☐	7. Forgetfulness	☐	☐

B. *To what degree, from 1 to 7, are you one way or the other?*

Husband: *Mark a ☐ around the number that best describes you.*
Wife: *Mark a ◯ around the number that best describes you.*

1.	Rigid	1	2	3	4	5	6	7	Adaptable
2.	Disrespectful	1	2	3	4	5	6	7	Respectful
3.	Poor self-esteem	1	2	3	4	5	6	7	Good self-esteem
4.	Complainer	1	2	3	4	5	6	7	Complimenter
5.	Lots of bad habits	1	2	3	4	5	6	7	No bad habits
6.	Bad attitudes	1	2	3	4	5	6	7	Good attitudes
7.	Inconsiderate	1	2	3	4	5	6	7	Considerate

C. *My genuine needs, views or beliefs are:*

He: True		She: True
☐	1. I wish my partner complimented me more.	☐
☐	2. I need more encouragement from my mate.	☐
☐	3. I need to be accepted and appreciated for who I am.	☐
☐	4. I need to retain my unique identity.	☐
☐	5. My partner needs to understand my gifts.	☐
☐	6. I need more admiration and respect from my partner.	☐
☐	7. We do not seem to have any personality conflicts.	☐

Category 7: Emotional Responses

A. *I feel we have some problems in the ways we respond to each other emotionally in these areas:*

He: Minor Problems	He: Major Problems		She: Minor Problems	She: Major Problems
☐	☐	1. Hurt feelings	☐	☐
☐	☐	2. Carrying offenses too long	☐	☐
☐	☐	3. Unwillingness to forgive	☐	☐
☐	☐	4. Insensitiveness	☐	☐
☐	☐	5. Not feeling loved	☐	☐
☐	☐	6. Moodiness	☐	☐
☐	☐	7. Expressing anger inappropriately	☐	☐

B. *To what degree, from 1 to 7, are you one way or the other?*

Husband: *Mark a* ☐ *around the number that best describes you.*
Wife: *Mark a* ◯ *around the number that best describes you.*

1.	Indifferent	1	2	3	4	5	6	7	Sympathetic
2.	Never cries	1	2	3	4	5	6	7	Cries easily
3.	Unloving	1	2	3	4	5	6	7	Very loving
4.	Hard to express verbal love	1	2	3	4	5	6	7	Expresses verbal love easily
5.	Undemonstrative	1	2	3	4	5	6	7	Demonstrative
6.	Uncaring	1	2	3	4	5	6	7	Caring
7.	Irrational	1	2	3	4	5	6	7	Rational

C. *My genuine needs, views or beliefs are:*

He: True		She: True
☐	1. My feelings tend to rule my life.	☐
☐	2. My mate needs to understand my moods more.	☐
☐	3. I need to hear more "I love you's" from my partner.	☐
☐	4. I need to be able to express both positive and negative feelings.	☐
☐	5. I feel my spouse takes everything too personally.	☐
☐	6. I often feel put down by my partner.	☐
☐	7. I am satisfied with our emotional responses to each other.	☐

Category 8: Intellectual Capacity

A. *I feel we have some problems regarding intellectual interests and capacities in these areas:*

He: Minor Problems	He: Major Problems		She: Minor Problems	She: Major Problems
☐	☐	1. Differences of interest	☐	☐
☐	☐	2. What we read or study	☐	☐
☐	☐	3. Continuing education (formal and / or informal)	☐	☐
☐	☐	4. Know-it-all attitudes	☐	☐
☐	☐	5. Correction of grammar	☐	☐
☐	☐	6. Education of our children	☐	☐
☐	☐	7. Being accurate and/or factual	☐	☐

B. *To what degree, from 1 to 7, are you one way or the other?*

Husband: *Mark a ☐ around the number that best describes you.*
Wife: *Mark a ◯ around the number that best describes you.*

1. Unopinionated	1	2	3	4	5	6	7	Highly opinionated
2. Nonintellectual	1	2	3	4	5	6	7	Very intellectual
3. Inarticulate	1	2	3	4	5	6	7	Exceptionally articulate
4. Prideful	1	2	3	4	5	6	7	Humble
5. Fun-loving	1	2	3	4	5	6	7	Too serious
6. Minimal reader	1	2	3	4	5	6	7	Prolific reader
7. Nonanalytical	1	2	3	4	5	6	7	Very analytical

C. *My genuine needs, views or beliefs are:*

He: True		She: True
☐	1. I need adequate time for reading or study.	☐
☐	2. I am easily sidetracked by new interests.	☐
☐	3. I need to question things before I can accept them.	☐
☐	4. I need my mate to listen to my opinions more.	☐
☐	5. I realize I need to be less dogmatic.	☐
☐	6. I find I constantly analyze what my partner says and does.	☐
☐	7. I am satisfied with how we handle intellectual matters.	☐

Category 9: Volitional Issues

A. *I feel we have some problems in the use of the will in these areas:*

He: Minor Problems	He: Major Problems		She: Minor Problems	She: Major Problems
☐	☐	1. Making good decisions and choices	☐	☐
☐	☐	2. Making decisions we both can live with	☐	☐
☐	☐	3. Stubbornness	☐	☐
☐	☐	4. Inability to come into agreement	☐	☐
☐	☐	5. Doing what is right	☐	☐
☐	☐	6. Judgmentalism	☐	☐
☐	☐	7. Rebelliousness	☐	☐

B. *To what degree, from 1 to 7, are you one way or the other?*

Husband: *Mark a ☐ around the number that best describes you.*
Wife: *Mark a ◯ around the number that best describes you.*

1.	Weak willed	1	2	3	4	5	6	7	Strong-willed
2.	Compromising	1	2	3	4	5	6	7	Uncompromising
3.	Indecisive	1	2	3	4	5	6	7	Decisive
4.	Reserved	1	2	3	4	5	6	7	Outspoken
5.	Timid	1	2	3	4	5	6	7	Persuasive
6.	Deferring to others	1	2	3	4	5	6	7	Strong convictions
7.	Judgmental	1	2	3	4	5	6	7	Nonjudgmental

C. *My genuine needs, views or beliefs are:*

He: True		She: True
☐	1. I have a definite inner need to be right.	☐
☐	2. I have a strong need to be a decision-maker.	☐
☐	3. I need my mate to make most of the decisions.	☐
☐	4. I will do what is right even if it hurts.	☐
☐	5. I need to operate by definite principles.	☐
☐	6. I need my mate to be more tolerant of my opinions.	☐
☐	7. I am satisfied with how we make decisions.	☐

Category 10: Physical Conditions

A. *I feel we have some problems in the physical realm in these areas:*

He: Minor Problems	He: Major Problems		She: Minor Problems	She: Major Problems
☐	☐	1. Being physically fit	☐	☐
☐	☐	2. Getting enough exercise	☐	☐
☐	☐	3. Coping with fatigue	☐	☐
☐	☐	4. Overeating	☐	☐
☐	☐	5. Eating the right foods for good health	☐	☐
☐	☐	6. Keeping attractive	☐	☐
☐	☐	7. Amount of sleep needed	☐	☐

B. *To what degree, from 1 to 7, are you one way or the other?*

Husband: *Mark a* ☐ *around the number that best describes you.*
Wife: *Mark a* ◯ *around the number that best describes you.*

1. Nonathletic	1	2	3	4	5	6	7	Athletic
2. Sluggish	1	2	3	4	5	6	7	Energetic
3. Not at proper weight	1	2	3	4	5	6	7	At proper weight
4. Needs very little sleep	1	2	3	4	5	6	7	Needs lots of sleep
5. Poor eating habits	1	2	3	4	5	6	7	Good eating habits
6. Unhealthy	1	2	3	4	5	6	7	Healthy
7. Physical disabilities	1	2	3	4	5	6	7	No disabilities

C. *My genuine needs, views or beliefs are:*

He True		She True
☐	1. I desire to see my mate at the proper weight.	☐
☐	2. I need to overcome my own weight problem.	☐
☐	3. I need to get adequate exercise on a regular basis.	☐
☐	4. I would like to see my spouse get more exercise.	☐
☐	5. I need my mate to be as attractive as possible.	☐
☐	6. I need to improve my eating habits.	☐
☐	7. I am satisfied with how we keep fit, healthy and attractive.	☐

Category 11: Sexual Relationship

A. *I feel we have some problems in our sexual relationship in these areas:*

He: Minor Problems	He: Major Problems		She: Minor Problems	She: Major Problems
☐	☐	1. Frequency of sexual relations	☐	☐
☐	☐	2. Quality of sexual relations	☐	☐
☐	☐	3. Amount of affection needed prior to sex	☐	☐
☐	☐	4. Inadequate affection in nonsexual times	☐	☐
☐	☐	5. General dissatisfaction with our sexual relations	☐	☐
☐	☐	6. Sexual incompatibility	☐	☐
☐	☐	7. Infidelity	☐	☐

B. *To what degree, from 1 to 7, are you one way or the other?*

Husband: *Mark a ☐ around the number that best describes you.*
Wife: *Mark a ◯ around the number that best describes you.*

1. Little interest in sex	1	2	3	4	5	6	7	Great interest in sex
2. Nonaffectionate	1	2	3	4	5	6	7	Very affectionate
3. Insensitive to mate's needs	1	2	3	4	5	6	7	Sensitive to mate's needs
4. Neglects hugging and kissing	1	2	3	4	5	6	7	Good at hugging and kissing
5. Holds in personal feelings	1	2	3	4	5	6	7	Shares intimate feelings
6. Incommunicative about sex	1	2	3	4	5	6	7	Communicates about sex
7. Doesn't verbalize love	1	2	3	4	5	6	7	Verbalizes love well

C. *My genuine needs, views or beliefs are:*

He: True		She: True
☐	1. I need more nonsexual affection from my mate.	☐
☐	2. I need more sexual relations with my mate.	☐
☐	3. I feel I need more hugs and kisses from my spouse.	☐
☐	4. I need to hear more "I love you's" from my partner.	☐
☐	5. I need my husband to better understand my monthly cycle.	☐
☐	6. I feel dissatisfied with our current sexual relationship.	☐
☐	7. I feel satisfied with our current sexual relationship.	☐

Category 12: Work and Accomplishments

A. *I feel we have some problems regarding work and accomplishments in these areas:*

He: Minor Problems	He: Major Problems		She: Minor Problems	She: Major Problems
☐	☐	1. Both of us are too busy	☐	☐
☐	☐	2. Our careers / jobs cause conflicts	☐	☐
☐	☐	3. Amount of overtime work	☐	☐
☐	☐	4. Income not enough to live on	☐	☐
☐	☐	5. Amount of volunteer work	☐	☐
☐	☐	6. Wife working outside of the home	☐	☐
☐	☐	7. Priorities out of order	☐	☐

B. *To what degree, from 1 to 7, are you one way or the other?*

Husband: *Mark a ☐ around the number that best describes you.*
Wife: *Mark a ◯ around the number that best describes you.*

1. Unmotivated	1	2	3	4	5	6	7	Industrious
2. Lazy	1	2	3	4	5	6	7	Workaholic
3. Low wage earner	1	2	3	4	5	6	7	High wage earner
4. Disorganized	1	2	3	4	5	6	7	Organized
5. Nongoal-oriented	1	2	3	4	5	6	7	Goal-oriented
6. Poor at domestic support	1	2	3	4	5	6	7	Good at domestic support
7. Procrastinates	1	2	3	4	5	6	7	Accomplisher

C. *My genuine needs, views or beliefs are:*

He: True		She: True
☐	1. I need my husband to provide our basic expenses.	☐
☐	2. I need my wife to be a full-time homemaker.	☐
☐	3. I need to be the sole provider for my family.	☐
☐	4. I need a fulfilling career.	☐
☐	5. I need a challenge to work toward.	☐
☐	6. I get great joy out of my accomplishments.	☐
☐	7. I'm satisfied with the way we handle work and accomplishments.	☐

Category 13: Financial Management

A. *I feel we have some problems in financial matters in these areas:*

He: Minor Problems	He: Major Problems		She: Minor Problems	She: Major Problems
☐	☐	1. Establishing a proper and workable budget	☐	☐
☐	☐	2. Keeping to our budget	☐	☐
☐	☐	3. Living beyond our means	☐	☐
☐	☐	4. Too much on our credit cards	☐	☐
☐	☐	5. Impulsive buying by one or both of us	☐	☐
☐	☐	6. Arguing over money spent or amount to spend	☐	☐
☐	☐	7. Disagreement over wife working outside the home	☐	☐

B. *To what degree, from 1 to 7, are you one way or the other?*

Husband: *Mark a ☐ around the number that best describes you.*
Wife: *Mark a ◯ around the number that best describes you.*

1. Impulsive buyer	1	2	3	4	5	6	7	Conservative buyer
2. Overspends budget	1	2	3	4	5	6	7	Keeps within budget
3. Disregards budget	1	2	3	4	5	6	7	Bargain-hunter
4. Buy now—pay later	1	2	3	4	5	6	7	Save now—pay later
5. Feels financially insecure	1	2	3	4	5	6	7	Feels financially secure
6. Stingy	1	2	3	4	5	6	7	Generous
7. Nontither	1	2	3	4	5	6	7	Tither

C. *My genuine needs, views or beliefs are:*

He: True		She: True
☐	1. I feel we need to reduce our debts more effectively.	☐
☐	2. I feel the need to be in charge of our family finances.	☐
☐	3. I believe the husband should handle the family finances.	☐
☐	4. I think the most capable partner should handle the family finances.	☐
☐	5. I need to learn how to handle money more responsibly.	☐
☐	6. I would like to give more to church, missionaries, charity, etc.	☐
☐	7. I am satisfied with how we handle finances.	☐

Category 14: Leisure Activities

A. *I feel we have some problems in how we spend our free time in these areas:*

He: Minor Problems	He: Major Problems		She: Minor Problems	She: Major Problems
☐	☐	1. We have drastically different interests.	☐	☐
☐	☐	2. We have incompatible recreational preferences.	☐	☐
☐	☐	3. Our hobbies take us in different directions.	☐	☐
☐	☐	4. Our preferences in entertainment conflict.	☐	☐
☐	☐	5. We disagree on vacation plans.	☐	☐
☐	☐	6. We don't enjoy the same sports.	☐	☐
☐	☐	7. Too much TV-watching	☐	☐

B. *To what degree, from 1 to 7, are you one way or the other?*

Husband: *Mark a ☐ around the number that best describes you.*
Wife: *Mark a ◯ around the number that best describes you.*

1. Nonathletic	1	2	3	4	5	6	7	Athletic
2. Hard to relax	1	2	3	4	5	6	7	Good at relaxing
3. Dislikes travel	1	2	3	4	5	6	7	Loves to travel
4. A stay-at-home	1	2	3	4	5	6	7	Loves to go out
5. Uncultured	1	2	3	4	5	6	7	Cultured
6. Dislikes going for walks	1	2	3	4	5	6	7	Likes going for walks
7. Antisocial	1	2	3	4	5	6	7	Very social

C. *My genuine needs, views or beliefs are:*

He: True		She: True
☐	1. I need my partner to be a recreational companion.	☐
☐	2. I need to do more fun things with my spouse.	☐
☐	3. I need more meaningful vacations.	☐
☐	4. I need to be involved in nonathletic leisure activities.	☐
☐	5. I prefer active group or competive sports.	☐
☐	6. I prefer individual noncompetitive sports.	☐
☐	7. I am satisfied with how we spend our leisure time.	☐

Category 15: Parenting

Check one: ☐ *No children: this section does not apply. Skip.*
☐ *Children are grown: answer as you recall.*
☐ *Children are ages:*

A. *I feel we have (had) some problems in the child-rearing process in these areas:*

He: Minor Problems	He: Major Problems		She: Minor Problems	She: Major Problems
☐	☐	1. The type of discipline and training	☐	☐
☐	☐	2. The amount of discipline	☐	☐
☐	☐	3. Who does the disciplining	☐	☐
☐	☐	4. The misconduct that requires discipline	☐	☐
☐	☐	5. The way love is expressed to our children	☐	☐
☐	☐	6. The amount of time spent with our children	☐	☐
☐	☐	7. The amont of money given to or spent on our children	☐	☐

B. *To what degree, from 1 to 7, are you one way or the other?*

Husband: *Mark a* ☐ *around the number that best describes you.*
Wife: *Mark a* ◯ *around the number that best describes you.*

1.	Permissive	1	2	3	4	5	6	7	Strict
2.	Uncontrolled anger	1	2	3	4	5	6	7	Controls anger
3.	Seldom touches	1	2	3	4	5	6	7	Much affectionate touching
4.	Spends little time with them	1	2	3	4	5	6	7	Spends lots of time with them
5.	Poor at training children	1	2	3	4	5	6	7	Good at training children
6.	Tends to spoil	1	2	3	4	5	6	7	Tends to require too much
7.	Inconsistent in discipline	1	2	3	4	5	6	7	Consistent in discipline

C. *My genuine needs, views or beliefs are:*

He: True		She: True
☐	1. We need to provide better spiritual guidance for our children.	☐
☐	2. We need to give our children more love and affection.	☐
☐	3. I would like my spouse to help more with the children.	☐
☐	4. I need to be more affirming of our children.	☐
☐	5. I feel we need to agree more on discipline.	☐
☐	6. I feel we need more quality family time and activities.	☐
☐	7. I am satisfied with our parenting styles and skills.	☐

Category 16: In-Laws and Family

A. *I feel we have some problems with our families and in-laws in these areas:*

He: Minor Problems	He: Major Problems		She: Minor Problems	She: Major Problems
☐	☐	1. Their interference in our lives	☐	☐
☐	☐	2. Unreasonable expectations of us	☐	☐
☐	☐	3. Too many visits (or, staying too long)	☐	☐
☐	☐	4. My spouse compares me with his / her parent	☐	☐
☐	☐	5. Borrowing money from family	☐	☐
☐	☐	6. Childhood abuse still affects his / her behavior	☐	☐
☐	☐	7. Dysfunction in former family negatively affecting us now	☐	☐

B. *To what degree, from 1 to 7, are you one way or the other?*

Husband: *Mark a ☐ around the number that best describes you.*
Wife: *Mark a ◯ around the number that best describes you.*

1. Apron strings still attached	1	2	3	4	5	6	7	Did leave and cleave
2. I side with my family	1	2	3	4	5	6	7	I stand up for my spouse
3. Dependent on former family	1	2	3	4	5	6	7	Independent of former family
4. I hate my father	1	2	3	4	5	6	7	I love and honor my father
5. I hate my mother	1	2	3	4	5	6	7	I love and honor my mother
6. My family was dysfunctional	1	2	3	4	5	6	7	My family was normal
7. I relate poorly to in-laws	1	2	3	4	5	6	7	I relate well to in-laws

C. *My genuine needs, views or beliefs are:*

He: True		She: True
☐	1. I need my spouse to put me before his or her family.	☐
☐	2. I need to see or talk to my parent(s) regularly.	☐
☐	3. I need to include my family in holiday celebrations.	☐
☐	4. I need help in overcoming in-law problems.	☐
☐	5. I need to be accepted by my in-laws.	☐
☐	6. I need to be financially free from my family and my in-laws.	☐
☐	7. I am satisfied with our family and in-law relationships.	☐

Category 17: Social Relationships

A. *I feel we have some problems in social relationships in these areas:*

He: Minor Problems	He: Major Problems		She: Minor Problems	She: Major Problems
☐	☐	1. Friends who demand too much of our time	☐	☐
☐	☐	2. Having enough time for friends	☐	☐
☐	☐	3. Partner refuses to be social	☐	☐
☐	☐	4. Partner is too social	☐	☐
☐	☐	5. Wrong type of friends	☐	☐
☐	☐	6. Friends who negatively influence my spouse	☐	☐
☐	☐	7. Too much club / group involvement	☐	☐

B. *To what degree, from 1 to 7, are you one way or the other?*

Husband: *Mark a ☐ around the number that best describes you.*
Wife: *Mark a ◯ around the number that best describes you.*

1. Highly unsociable	1	2	3	4	5	6	7	Highly sociable
2. Prefers only a few friends	1	2	3	4	5	6	7	Likes having many friends
3. Prefers small groups	1	2	3	4	5	6	7	Enjoys large groups
4. Dislikes entertaining	1	2	3	4	5	6	7	Loves to entertain
5. Couch potato	1	2	3	4	5	6	7	Social butterfly
6. Hard to relate to others	1	2	3	4	5	6	7	Relates well to many
7. A loner	1	2	3	4	5	6	7	Gregarious

C. *My genuine needs, views or beliefs are:*

He: True		She: True
☐	1. I need to have many friends.	☐
☐	2. I especially love to entertain in our home.	☐
☐	3. I need a good deal of private time.	☐
☐	4. I need our home to be a haven of rest.	☐
☐	5. I need to be involved in social groups.	☐
☐	6. I think we need to change some friendships.	☐
☐	7. I am satisfied with our social life.	☐

Category 18: Religious Orientation

A. *I feel we have some problems in our spiritual lives and orientation in these areas:*

He: Minor Problems	He: Major Problems		She: Minor Problems	She: Major Problems
☐	☐	1. Can't agree on religious affiliation	☐	☐
☐	☐	2. Spouse won't go to church	☐	☐
☐	☐	3. Different religious backgrounds	☐	☐
☐	☐	4. Theological differences	☐	☐
☐	☐	5. Level of commitment to God	☐	☐
☐	☐	6. Irregular church attendance	☐	☐
☐	☐	7. Hypocritical behavior	☐	☐

B. *To what degree, from 1 to 7, are you one way or the other?*

Husband: *Mark a* ☐ *around the number that best describes you.*
Wife: *Mark a* ◯ *around the number that best describes you.*

1. Unspiritual	1	2	3	4	5	6	7	Spiritual
2. Uncommitted to Christ	1	2	3	4	5	6	7	Committed to Christ
3. Not growing spiritually	1	2	3	4	5	6	7	Growing spiritually
4. Never prays	1	2	3	4	5	6	7	Prays a lot
5. Never reads the Bible	1	2	3	4	5	6	7	Reads Bible regularly
6. Never attends church	1	2	3	4	5	6	7	Attends church regularly
7. Weak faith	1	2	3	4	5	6	7	Strong faith

C. *My genuine needs, views or beliefs are:*

He: True		She: True
☐	1. I need to attend church regularly.	☐
☐	2. I need my partner to pray with me daily.	☐
☐	3. I greatly desire to see my spouse grow spiritually.	☐
☐	4. I believe we need to have regular family devotions.	☐
☐	5. I need my spouse to give spiritual leadership.	☐
☐	6. I need to be able to live my faith, not just talk about it.	☐
☐	7. I am satisfied with our religious orientation and practice.	☐

Category 19: Maturity

A. *I feel we have some problems in maturity in these areas:*

He: Minor Problems	He: Major Problems		She: Minor Problems	She: Major Problems
☐	☐	1. Being young and inexperienced	☐	☐
☐	☐	2. Irresponsibility	☐	☐
☐	☐	3. We resort to the blame game.	☐	☐
☐	☐	4. Coping with life's stresses	☐	☐
☐	☐	5. Continuous criticism	☐	☐
☐	☐	6. Infidelity	☐	☐
☐	☐	7. Dishonesty	☐	☐

B. *To what degree, from 1 to 7, are you one way or the other?*

Husband: *Mark a* ☐ *around the number that best describes you.*
Wife: *Mark a* ◯ *around the number that best describes you.*

1.	Prideful	1	2	3	4	5	6	7	Humble
2.	Loves conditionally	1	2	3	4	5	6	7	Loves unconditionally
3.	Selfish	1	2	3	4	5	6	7	Unselfish
4.	Irresponsible	1	2	3	4	5	6	7	Responsible
5.	Unforgiving	1	2	3	4	5	6	7	Forgiving
6.	Untrustworthy	1	2	3	4	5	6	7	Trustworthy
7.	Taker	1	2	3	4	5	6	7	Giver

C. *My genuine needs, views or beliefs are:*

He True		She True
☐	1. I need to be able to trust my mate.	☐
☐	2. I need my spouse to be dependable.	☐
☐	3. I need to be quick to forgive and, I hope, be forgiven quickly.	☐
☐	4. We need to learn from and grow through every experience.	☐
☐	5. I need my mate to be able to handle responsibility well.	☐
☐	6. I need my mate to love me unconditionally.	☐
☐	7. I feel that we are a reasonably mature couple.	☐

Category 20: Dysfunctionality

A. *I feel we have some problems in the following areas that produce dysfunction:*

He: Minor Problems	He: Major Problems		She: Minor Problems	She: Major Problems
☐	☐	1. Alcohol abuse	☐	☐
☐	☐	2. Drug abuse	☐	☐
☐	☐	3. Physical abuse	☐	☐
☐	☐	4. Sexual abuse	☐	☐
☐	☐	5. Verbal (mental) abuse	☐	☐
☐	☐	6. Emotional abuse	☐	☐
☐	☐	7. Unresolved abuse from the past	☐	☐

B. *To what degree, from 1 to 7, are you one way or the other?*

Husband: *Mark a ☐ around the number that best describes you.*
Wife: *Mark a ◯ around the number that best describes you.*

1.	Dysfunctional	1	2	3	4	5	6	7	Functional
2.	Drinker	1	2	3	4	5	6	7	Nondrinker
3.	Drug abuser	1	2	3	4	5	6	7	No drug use
4.	Physical abuser	1	2	3	4	5	6	7	Not a physical abuser
5.	Verbal abuser	1	2	3	4	5	6	7	Not a verbal abuser
6.	Emotional abuser	1	2	3	4	5	6	7	Not an emotional abuser
7.	Sexual abuser	1	2	3	4	5	6	7	Not a sexual abuser

C. *My genuine needs, views or beliefs are:*

He: True		She: True
☐	1. I need our marriage to be free of alcohol use and abuse.	☐
☐	2. I need our marriage to be free of drug use and abuse.	☐
☐	3. I need my spouse to treat me more kindly.	☐
☐	4. I need my mate to give me positive emotional support.	☐
☐	5. One or both of us need to get help for abuse in childhood.	☐
☐	6. One or both of us need to get help for dysfunctional behavior.	☐
☐	7. I believe there is no dysfunctional behavior in our marriage.	☐

He: Minor Problems	He: Major Problems	She: Minor Problems	She: Major Problems	
☐	☐	☐	☐	1. Communication and conversation
☐	☐	☐	☐	2. Expectations of each other
☐	☐	☐	☐	3. Marital cohesion, building love and unity
☐	☐	☐	☐	4. Roles, authority and responsibility
☐	☐	☐	☐	5. Conflict resolution and handling differences
☐	☐	☐	☐	6. Personality conflicts and attitudes
☐	☐	☐	☐	7. Emotional responses and issues
☐	☐	☐	☐	8. Intellectual capacity and interests
☐	☐	☐	☐	9. Volitional (will) issues and choices
☐	☐	☐	☐	10. Physical conditions, exercise and attractiveness
☐	☐	☐	☐	11. Sexual relations and affection fulfillment
☐	☐	☐	☐	12. Work, career and accomplishments
☐	☐	☐	☐	13. Financial earning, management and responsibility
☐	☐	☐	☐	14. Leisure activities and recreational companionship
☐	☐	☐	☐	15. Parenting and family commitment
☐	☐	☐	☐	16. In-laws and extended family relationships
☐	☐	☐	☐	17. Social relationships and friendships
☐	☐	☐	☐	18. Religious beliefs, orientation and spirituality
☐	☐	☐	☐	19. Maturity and proper adult behavior
☐	☐	☐	☐	20. Dysfunctionality, substance abuse, and abusiveness

Our Major Problem Areas

____

____

____

____

Our Proposed Steps of Action

____

____

____

____

The ABCs of Christian Marriage

16

Your marriage is the most important relationship you will ever have. Marriage was God's plan from the beginning. God said it is not good for man to be alone, so he created Eve. Adam's response was *Wow!*

It was indeed a good idea. Not that marriage is free from problems. But problems can be good for us. They make us grow, and grow up. If we run from our problems, we remain immature and will probably need a few more laps around the mountain until we learn our lesson and offer the proper response.

Marriage merits our intense effort to learn how to have a good one. Take advantage of church-sponsored marriage classes and seminars. Read good books on the subject. Talk to those who have successful marriages. Seek wisdom from your parents, pastor, a marriage counselor and others you admire who have insights to share.

God wants every marriage to be strong, blessed and secure. A good marriage produces rich soil for happy family life and well-adjusted, loving children. Someone has said that the best gift you can give your child is to consistently love your spouse. A good marriage and a happy family are the best building blocks of society, and you pass on all the benefits to your children, your grandchildren and even beyond.

Some marriages have few problems; others have many. Whatever you face in your marriage relationship, there is hope and help. God gives us abundant grace to handle anything, if we ask. Marriage is work. But it is also a joy. Any marriage can be happy if both parties are willing to put serious effort into it.

We have a choice to handle our marriage relationship God's way or our way. God's way brings blessing and happiness. It requires self-sacrifice and determined commitment, but the results are of value beyond measure. To have a successful marriage we must put God's laws and principles into action. They work whether or not we are aware of them. When we violate one we put another in motion—the principle of sowing and reaping (Galatians 6:7). Going our way gets us into trouble as, knowingly or unknowingly, we break God's commandments.

Marriage is the best training ground for righteousness. While it is true that Christ's righteousness is imparted to us "legally" by His grace, we have the opportunity to *demonstrate* it in this most intimate of relationships. Give it all you've got! Guard it carefully and prayerfully. Cherish it. Expect to be blessed through it.

We would like to share with you some helpful pointers to help you make your marriage all it can be.

A. Affirm Who You and Your Spouse Are in Christ

The most important thing you can do is to come into a personal relationship with Jesus Christ. This brings you into the Kingdom of God, but that is only the beginning. Your whole life is a growth process of letting Christ be formed in you. You and your spouse have the ongoing opportunity to affirm and encourage one another in spiritual growth. You have a tremendous inheritance in the Lord! Consider Paul's prayer:

> I pray also that the eyes of your heart may be enlightened in order that you may know the hope to which he has called you, the riches of his glorious inheritance in the saints.
>
> Ephesians 1:18, NIV

You may not feel like a saint, but you are. You and your spouse have been made the righteousness of God in Christ. Encourage each other to see yourselves as forgiven, justified and made righteous because of Jesus' death on the cross. Affirm your ability to do all things through Christ who strengthens you, to forgive because God has forgiven you and to be more than conquerors through Jesus residing in your hearts.

B. Build a Foundation of Love and Trust

The foundation of marriage is love and trust. If you do not feel loved, you cannot love and accept yourself and others. But God loved you first. And as you draw on His love, you can love and accept yourself—not in a self-centered way, but seeing yourself as someone for whom Christ died, to provide not only eternal life but the ability to love and be loved.

The most beautiful expression of love is found in 1 Corinthians:

> Love is patient, love is kind. It does not envy, it does not boast, it is not proud. It is not rude, it is not self-seeking, it is not easily angered, it keeps no record of wrongs. Love does not delight in evil but rejoices with the truth. It always protects, always trusts, always hopes, always perseveres. Love never fails.
>
> 1 Corinthians 13:4–8, NIV

As you continue to receive Jesus' love, let His love flow out to your spouse. Express your love often to each other in specific ways: in what you say, in what you do or do not do, in your attitudes, in smiles and hugs and other expressions of affection, in quality time spent together. As your love flows back and forth, trust grows, building a foundation that cannot be shaken.

C. Communicate Openly and Often

Open and honest communication is essential for marital cohesion. Communication can be a major problem between spouses or an ongoing source of blessing.

Remember your courtship days—how you could hardly wait to get together and talk, how you hung on every word the other said? Recapture some of that. Take time each day to talk with each other. Share your deepest thoughts and feelings, your ideas, your hopes and dreams.

Listening is the other side of the coin. Pay careful attention to what your spouse says. Be interested. Let each other know you really hear what has been said.

Don and I have at least three times a day when we share with each other. (We enjoy spontaneous times as well.) One is before he takes off for the church office, while we eat breakfast or enjoy a long cup of coffee. It is a time to plan the day, to let the other know what we will be doing, to find out what we can do for each other. The second time is late afternoon before I start dinner—a time to catch up on the events of the day. The third regular time is after we turn out the lights. It is a time for hugging, mulling over things and ideas, sharing how much we love and appreciate each other.

D. Determine Responsibility Clearly

Each couple has their own set of responsibilities. Be sure you and your spouse are clear about yours. Neglecting a responsibility because it was not clearly defined can lead to unjust blame and hurt feelings.

If the wife is employed outside the home, it is only fair that the husband do his fair share of domestic chores. Who does the laundry at your house? How often? Do you take turns at cooking and cleanup, or does one cook and the other do the dishes? What about grocery shopping? Would it go better if both of you did it together? (Don and I split the list and meet at the checkout counter.) How are cleaning jobs designated? (Don does the bathrooms and I do the kitchen. He usually vacuums the rec room and I do the living and dining rooms.)

If the wife is a full-time homemaker content with 95 percent of the household responsibilities, fine. But if you are that homemaker and you secretly wish your husband helped out more often, don't stew about it. Let him know. Work out a plan.

If you have children at home, define responsibilities regarding them, too. Who helps them with their homework, if needed? Who supervises the baths? Does one spouse especially love to read the bedtime story, or do you take turns? Find out what works for you.

E. Expect the Best of Each Other

We go into marriage with great expectations of our mates, only to discover they are not so perfect after all. Sometimes we carry into marriage what we have learned to expect of the opposite sex. Sometimes our spouses tend to become what we expect them to be.

Paula told us her father always disappointed her mother in some way. So when she married John, she expected him to disappoint her, too. At first he did not, and she told him how that amazed her. But with the atmosphere of expectation still there, he began to fulfill it.

"I began to realize that subconsciously I was doing things to disappoint her," John says, "because her expectation of disappointment was drawing it out of me. I would disappoint her if I *didn't* disappoint her! It was only when we got this out in the open that we got free of it. She deliberately canceled her negative expectations and asked the Lord to replace them with positive expectations. It made a tremendous difference in our relationship."

Don't say, "I figured you'd be late," or, "I knew you'd make a mess of things." Negative expectations only reinforce negative behavior. Instead, develop positive expectations. Affirm your faith in your spouse's abilities. Give encouragement when it is needed.

Wives, according to the apostle Paul, expect and need love to feel secure. But husbands expect and need their wives' respect in order to feel secure and loved:

> Let each man of you (without exception) love his wife as [being in a sense] his very own self; and let the wife see that she respects and reverences her husband—that she notices him, regards him, honors him, prefers him, venerates and esteems him; and that she defers to him, praises him, and loves and admires him exceedingly.
>
> Ephesians 5:33

F. Forgive Frequently and Completely

God allows imperfect people to marry imperfect people in an imperfect world. When your spouse blows it, be ready to forgive. When your mate makes a mistake, allow for a correction. If your loved one is being difficult to live with, address the situation but be quick to minister forgiveness, too.

Forgiveness cancels out a debt that, if unresolved, will hang like a cloud over your lives and further hamper your relationship. How often we learn our best lessons in life from our mistakes! What if God did not extend forgiveness to us? We would soon wonder what the good is in trying, and we would give up. In the same way, we must not overburden our spouses with our judgments or use unforgiveness to manipulate them into doing what we want them to do.

Jesus taught a lot on forgiveness.

> Then Peter came up to Him and said, Lord, how many times may my brother sin against me, and I forgive him and let it go? As many as up to seven times? Jesus answered him, I tell you, not up to seven times, but seventy times seven!
>
> Matthew 18:21–22

Seventy times seven is 490 times—even in a day. If we divide that into the number of minutes in a day, it means we have to be willing to forgive every three minutes—or, if we want our eight hours of sleep, every two minutes! Is Jesus asking us to be that specific? Probably not, but He *is* asking us to conduct a lifestyle of forgiveness. Can you be willing to forgive your mate constantly? It is the only way to stay free.

G. Give Generously and Wholeheartedly

Marriage is a wonderful place to give of yourself. The scriptural admonition to give and it will be given unto you applies not only to finances but to relationships. You can give of your time, energy, love, laughter, encouragement, abilities and appreciation. Be lavish. Pour into your mate's life all the good things you possibly can. Blessing cannot help but follow.

Jenny was discouraged because her husband of two years began to close off his life. He did not talk with her as he had before. He would clam up, go for a walk or disappear behind the newspaper or TV. He seemed increasingly sad and morose.

"He wouldn't or couldn't tell me what the problem was," she says. "He refused to get help. So I decided to start pouring into his life everything I could to bless him, whether he responded or not. I gave him lots of extra hugs and squeezes. I'd rub his back and tell him how much I loved him. I'd give him space to do his withdrawing but pepper it with smiles and adoration. I cooked his favorite meals and served lots of affirmation of how wonderful I thought he was. Suddenly it broke. He had been dealing inwardly with feelings of unworthiness. Drenched by my wholehearted love, he began to see that his negative feelings were not from God but from the enemy, bent on destroying his sense of self-worth, and he stood against them. I got my husband back."

H. Handle Finances Wisely

Finances are one of the major potential stress areas in marriage that must be faced realistically and practically. Unfortunately our culture touts getting ahead financially and having things—a nice house, a new car, stylish clothes, getting ahead of the Joneses. If you and your mate sense these influences tainting your marriage, take time to pray about it and seek the Lord's will for you in the area of finances. The apostle Paul found the key:

> . . . For I have learned to be content whatever the circumstances. I know what it is to be in need, and I know what it is to have plenty. I have learned the secret of being content in any and every situation, whether well fed or hungry, whether living in plenty or in want.
>
> Philippians 4:11–12, NIV

There is nothing wrong with having nice things, but there is if those things take on too much importance or put a family into serious debt. The best plan is to consider your money, income and assets as belonging to the Lord. He has made you a steward over everything, and He is the One who can best direct your use of those resources. Tithing is simply returning to the Lord what is already His; anything less is actually robbing Him, and consequently robbing yourself of a blessing. You cannot afford *not* to tithe!

Planning a budget together will help you both to know where the money goes and what is left over for extras. Probably one of you is better gifted to handle the finances, but some couples prefer doing it together. Find out what works for you.

I. Invest in Quality Time with Each Other

Time has a way of filling itself up. It is easy to find yourself out of time for each other after responsibilities take their chunk out of your schedule. If necessary, schedule time for yourselves. Why not have a night out every week or two? Do something you especially enjoy—buy tickets to your local theatre production, the symphony or a sports event. How about one of those two-for-the-price-of-one dinners? Or a movie, ice-skating or a special speaker at a neighboring church? Do what you both enjoy.

In addition to doing fun things together, make time just to enjoy one another's company. Walk to a park and swing together, take a picnic to the beach, sip lemonade on your patio, watch a sunset, soak in the neighbor's hot tub, turn off the TV and give each other a good backrub. Talk, really talk—not superficially, but intimately. Share your feelings.

Some of my most precious times with Don have been at our little cabin, sitting around the fireplace reading good books or walking through the woods or strolling down the beach or sitting on a log watching the ships go by. We love being with our family and friends, but nothing can compare with our special times alone together.

J. Judge Not

How tempted we human beings are to judge others, especially our mates! But that prerogative belongs alone to God:

> "Do not judge, or you too will be judged. For in the same way you judge others, you will be judged, and with the measure you use, it will be measured to you. Why do you look at the speck of sawdust in your brother's eye and pay no attention to the plank in your own eye?"
>
> Matthew 7:1–3, NIV

Your job is to love your spouse. Let God take care of the judging. It is the job of the Holy Spirit to convict your partner of sin or mistakes. Don't get in His way.

Often we cannot see the whole picture. Seldom do we know the real reason for behavior we do not like. And whose yardstick do we use, anyway? My own sinful nature, imperfections, lack of perspective and a lifelong coloring of opinion disqualifies me to judge or condemn anyone. Jesus said of the woman taken in adultery, "If any one of you is without sin, let him be the first to throw a stone at her" (John 8:7, NIV). Our friend Marguerite gave us a smooth stone with the words *First stone* painted on it. "A reminder," she said, "that we'd better hold onto it!"

K. Keep Physically Fit

About eighty percent of the respondents to our marriage survey report problems with physical fitness. Only twenty percent are satisfied with how they keep physically fit. And 75 percent say they do not get enough exercise. Many say that they need a plan in order to get adequate exercise—joining a fitness club, buying some home exercise equipment, following an exercise video or jogging or walking regularly. How is your fitness status? Do you need to set a plan and follow it? Many doctors say that even walking twenty minutes a day or every other day does wonders for our systems.

About half of our survey respondents confess they are not at their proper weight—which for most means being overweight. Another major problem! An exercise plan will help. Cutting back on fattening foods does wonders. Diets work only while you follow them faithfully, but about 95 percent of dieters gain the weight right back, and usually more. Find a sensible plan that works for you and follow it.

Don and I were surprised at how many people say they do not get enough sleep—48 percent. Burning the candle at both ends seems a big problem. Is this a problem for you? Your mate? Find out where you can cut out some nonessentials and hit the hay earlier. Maybe you do not need to stay up to watch the late evening news. Or cut your TV-watching in half and read a little before going to bed. Promise yourself not to take on any more committees or projects and phase out on some you are involved in now. You have only one body; take good care of it.

L. Love Unconditionally

It is easy to love a mate who loves you. That is probably why you fell in love and got married in the first place. But when the honeymoon is over and bumps in your relationship begin to show up, the test of true love is at hand.

People need unconditional love—not for what they do or do not do, but just because they are. Spouses need to know that nothing can separate them from the love of their mates, just as nothing can separate us from the love of God:

> I am convinced that neither death nor life, neither angels nor demons, neither the present nor the future, nor any powers, neither height nor depth, nor anything else in all creation, will be able to separate us from the love of God that is in Christ Jesus our Lord.
>
> Romans 8:38–39, NIV

It is not because our own love can be as perfectly unconditional as God's, but because Christ lives in us, that we can draw on His perfect love and extend it to our spouses. Do not try to manipulate or control your mate by threatening to withdraw love if certain performance levels are not attained. Keep your marriage vow to love. Put no conditions on it.

M. Make Your Careers Count

Every couple is a two-career couple. Being a stay-at-home homemaker is a career in itself, as is full-time mothering. If some women go to college just to get their MRS degree, more power to them! It is a wonderful investment of a woman's life.

Other women desire an additional career. Some careers fit easily into home life. When our boys were small, I could write twenty hours a week at the dining room table while they played at my feet or napped. It is even more common now with home computers and the increasing frequency of working for a company in the home office (literally!). Teaching music, tutoring, editorial services, freelance photography, childcare, utilizing artistic talent, telephone marketing, selling products like Avon—all are careers that can be handled out of the home.

Other careers require working outside the home. My friend Ethel went back to finish college after her kids were in their teens and now loves her full-time nursing career. It makes use of her giftedness and she feels fulfilled. Some women juggle home and career responsibilities successfully throughout their married lives with no detriment to their children's sense of security and love. It is an individual matter, but one that needs to be made in agreement with the husband.

Whatever career you follow, be sure it is one that uses your God-given gifting. Both of our previous books feature a chart—for those considering a career change or who want to know where they are likely to be successful—evaluating 180 of the most common careers in light of the seven categories of gifts. Whatever you do, do it as unto Christ.

N. Nurture a Positive Home Atmosphere

Negatives beget negatives and positives beget positives. Once again the apostle Paul has excellent advice:

> Finally, brothers, whatever is true, whatever is noble, whatever is right, whatever is pure, whatever is lovely, whatever is admirable—if anything is excellent or praiseworthy—think about such things.
>
> Philippians 4:8, NIV

Don and I like to offer twelve suggestions (detailed in chapter 19 of *Discover Your God-Given Gifts*) to help couples make their home atmosphere positive and pleasant:

1. Set the example.
2. Watch your words.
3. Check attitudes.
4. Lavish love.
5. Listen attentively.
6. Learn to apologize.
7. Forgive frequently.
8. Observe body language.
9. Let music ring.
10. Express thankfulness.
11. Make room for differences.
12. Teach the Word.

If you do these things, your home cannot help but have a positive atmosphere—one conducive to spiritual growth and in which everyone is loved and accepted.

Are you doing all you can to enable your spouse to grow closer to the Lord? Are your children secure in love that flows freely and consistently? Do friends remark about the peace they sense in your home?

When an ambassador is sent to another country, the furnishings of the embassy, even its architecture, reflect the culture of the sending country. A visitor from that country will feel right at home in the embassy. So it is with us. We are citizens of God's Kingdom and ambassadors in the world. Your home should reflect the nature of the Kingdom of which you are part. Even non-Christians should be able to sense that your residence is different.

O. Open Up Your Heart

I did a computer search once on the word *heart* in the Bible and found 980 references. It was almost overwhelming, but I studied every reference and began to see that the biblical expression of *heart* always refers to that inner part of us called the soul. Sometimes part of the soul is indicated—the mind or the will or the emotions. But mostly *heart* refers to the whole soul—the part of your tripartite being that lives inside your body.

It is your soul (or heart) that is being transformed day by day into the likeness of Christ, who dwells in your spirit. You are not yet perfect but you are being perfected. You are loved by Father God just the way you are, but He is not finished with you yet. What better place to be transparent and honest than with the mate God has given you!

If you are having a difficult time in an area of your life, open up and share it with your mate. Pray together about it. Give him or her an opportunity to encourage and help you. If you are having problems in the area of the will, let your spouse stand with you in asking God to help you make right choices. If there is fear or guilt or pain in the area of the emotions, let your spouse minister God's love or healing to you. If there is confusion or wrong thinking in the area of the mind, let your partner bring the clarity of the Word to help you.

What a privilege you both have to minister to each other in this way!

P. Pray with and for Each Other Consistently

It is important for both of you to pray for each other privately, as the Lord leads. No person is more important for you to support in prayer than your spouse.

Prayer *with* your spouse is important, too. Yet Don and I are amazed at how many Christian couples do not pray together regularly. Some do not pray at all. The problem may be lethargy. As one husband told us, "I just forget to get around to it." Some do not believe prayer does any good or that God really hears and answers prayer. This problem is unbelief. Sometimes couples are so busy there is no time left for prayer. This problem is misplaced priorities.

Prayer makes a huge difference in a marital relationship. Husbands and wives each have their spheres of interests, ideas, beliefs, desires and expectations. Where these circles overlap, harmony prevails (see figure on page 335). But conflicts can emerge from the nonoverlapping areas. Here is where prayer really helps. If you and your spouse seek the Lord in these areas, you will discover God's will that encompasses your lives together. In some cases the husband is right, in other cases the wife. More often God has a plan different from your plans, but one that works well for both of you. You are not likely to discover it until you commit the situation to Him.

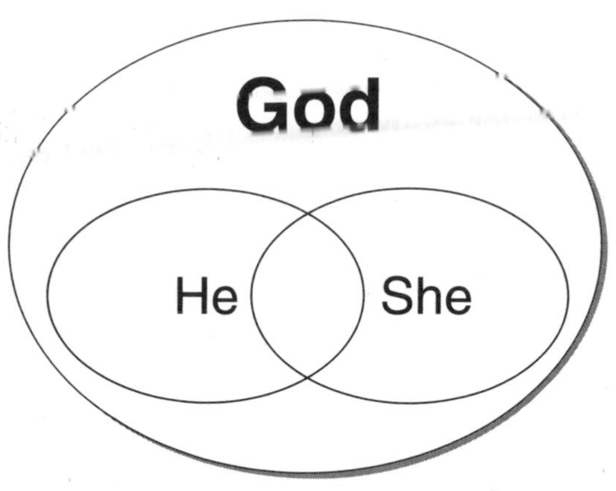

Q. Quote What God Says about Marriage

Husband and wife come to marriage equipped with separate ideas about what marriage should be like. Where these ideas coincide (like the circles in the figure above), the husband and wife do well. Where ideas differ, the couple can see stress in their relationship.

It is important for both partners to search the Word of God to see what *He* says about marriage, and then to agree with it. For instance:

> "At the beginning of creation God 'made them male and female.' 'For this reason a man will leave his father and mother and be united to his wife, and the two will become one flesh.' So they are no longer two, but one. Therefore what God has joined together, let man not separate."
>
> Mark 10:6–9, NIV

> He who finds a wife finds what is good and receives favor from the LORD.
>
> Proverbs 18:22, NIV

> Marriage should be honored by all, and the marriage bed kept pure, for God will judge the adulterer and all the sexually immoral.
>
> Hebrews 13:4, NIV

R. Reach Out to Others

While your relationship with one another is of primary importance, you are not to hide your light under a bushel. Look for ways you can reach out and help others.

One way is to practice hospitality. Have another couple or family over for dinner or dessert. It is amazing how having a meal together produces bonding and gives you an influence in their lives, even to speak into their lives good things that will help and encourage them.

Another way is to become part of a home group or cell group (whatever your church calls it). It is impossible to relate personally to hundreds of people, but you can get to know the people in a smaller group well. It is a safe place to open up and share your heart.

Another way is mentoring. Perhaps you have been the beneficiary of mentoring in the past. If so, you know what a blessing it is. Usually the mentoring couple are older in years or Christian experience or both. They discover a younger couple who need encouragement and take them under their wings—spending time with them, teaching them, being an example, building them up spiritually and in their ability to love one another. It involves a commitment of time and interest and love, and the mentors themselves get blessed in the process.

Another way is to build a relationship with a couple who do not yet know Christ personally, and through that loving relationship earn the right to share the Gospel. It is a wonderful way to win others to Christ.

S. Share Your Feelings Honestly

There are different levels of sharing in marriage. You share a home, car(s), bank account, bills, perhaps children. Then there is the level of ideas. You talk about them, analyze them, agree with some of them and agree to disagree about others. But a deeper level still is sharing your feelings with each other.

Feelings express who you are. Some feelings are best not shared outside the one relationship where you should find safety and security. As you open up to your spouse in this way, be sure to guard each other's safety. Never put your mate down because some feeling seems dumb or unnecessary to you. Remember, feelings just are. If your mate has taken ownership of them and been willing to be transparent, accept those feelings.

Sometimes such honest sharing will bring something to the surface that needs to be dealt with. One wife realized she was developing a pattern of lying to her husband. The Holy Spirit began to convict her of it. Finally she opened up to her husband, who received her confession lovingly and asked her if she knew why she was doing it.

"Yes," she said. "I've become afraid of your anger. It makes me feel as I did when I was little and my father got angry with me about something I did or didn't do."

She went on to explain that when she forgot to do something her husband had asked her to do, she had been lying and saying she had done it so she would not have to face his possible angry reaction. Then she would go ahead and do whatever it was she had forgotten, to cover up the situation.

Her husband had no idea she was so afraid of him, and took the revelation of her feelings as an opportunity to change his own behavior so she would not have to fear him in the future. He also prayed with her that she would be set free from the conditioned responses from her childhood—and she was. She returned to truthfulness and their relationship deepened in love and trust.

T. Thank Each Other

How easy it is for a couple to take one another for granted! She may begin to think, *He's supposed to be the breadwinner; why should I thank him for that?* He may begin to think, *Of course she's supposed to cook the meals and wash my clothes; isn't that the wife's responsibility?*

Giving thanks is a way you can express appreciation for even those routine, thankless jobs. Having an attitude of gratitude is encouraged in God's Word:

> At all times and for everything giving thanks in the name of our Lord Jesus Christ to God the Father.
>
> Ephesians 5:20

> Be joyful always; pray continually; give thanks in all circumstances, for this is God's will for you in Christ Jesus.
>
> 1 Thessalonians 5:16–18, NIV

A thankful heart will spill over naturally into your spouse's life. How often do you express appreciation to him or her? It can be for specific acts like fixing the toaster or mending a shirt. It can come easily when your spouse gives you a present or does something obviously special for you. But how about giving thanks on nonoccasions: "Thanks for your faithfulness to the Lord, to me and to our children" or "I want you to know how much your hugs mean to me. Thanks for being so affectionate." Do you express thanks when she brings you a cup of coffee or when he runs to the store for you? Be spontaneously abundant in giving thanks to your loved one. It is God's will for you.

U. Understand Each Other's God-Given Gifts

Years ago I was complaining to the Lord about how often He was having me teach about the motivational gifts. I wanted to do other subjects as well. Then I heard His voice: *I want My people to know their gifts.*

The words penetrated my heart. It was a commission. I did not even need to hear the rest of His words; they were burned into my spirit: *I want you to do everything you possibly can to make their gifts known to them.*

For 21 years Don and I have attempted to fulfill that commission, and in the process we have known joy unspeakable. Hundreds of couples have told us how understanding the motivational gifts has saved their marriages. Many more have told us how the knowledge of their gifting has enriched their relationships, given them a sense of direction or opened the door to joint ministry.

We pray that this book will bless you as individuals and as a couple. If you have gained even a little more understanding of one another in light of your giftedness, our work on this book has been worthwhile. And we pray that you will have ongoing revelation of the wonder of God's endowment in your lives and the greatness of His plan in bringing the two of you together to fulfill His purposes—not only in your own lives, but through all the lives you will continue to influence.

V. Value Each Other Intensely

How much is a person worth? Someone has said that if you were the only one on earth, Jesus would have come to die for your sins. God values each person infinitely. You should, too. Above all, value your spouse—the person God created especially for you, to be your companion and helpmate, your lover and encourager, your best friend and confidant.

True, you can see your mate's problems and weaknesses, faults and failures, tendencies and tantrums. But what about your own? It is no surprise that there are no perfect people, and therefore no perfect couples. But couples are in the process of being perfected as they allow Christ to be truly Lord of their lives. In the crucible of our less-than-perfect status, the perfecting process goes on. Meanwhile, accept your joint imperfections and look with joy at the person inside who is of infinite value:

> Are not two little sparrows sold for a penny? And yet not one of them will fall to the ground without your Father's leave and notice. But even the very hairs of your head are all numbered. Fear not, then; you are of more value than many sparrows.
>
> Matthew 10:29–31

You are not only husband and wife; you are brother and sister in Christ. You share the same heavenly Father. Jesus is your elder Brother. As you treat each other as beloved members of the family of God, you bring delight to Father God. Perhaps Solomon says it most beautifully in the alphabetical acrostic of Proverbs 31:10–31, and most specifically verse 10:

> A capable, intelligent and virtuous woman, who is he who can find her? She is far more precious than jewels, and her value is far above rubies or pearls.

W. Work Together to Resolve Conflicts

Here are some practical steps to take in resolving conflicts:

1. *Pray before you act or react.* Seek God's wisdom. James promises that

> If any of you lacks wisdom, he should ask God, who gives generously to all without finding fault, and it will be given to him.
>
> James 1:5, NIV

Admit to God that you do not know how to solve the conflict and that you need His help to know what to think, feel and do. Ask Him to help you have the right attitude, the grace to forgive and the wisdom to do what He wants you to, to restore unity.

2. *Look at the facts about your mate and the situation.* Is the action typical of your mate or an exception to the rule? Is it possible there has been a misunderstanding or false assumption? Was hurt intended or did you take something the wrong way? It is best, according to Matthew 18:15, to address your mate about it as soon as possible. Ask, "Did you really mean what you said a few minutes ago?" Or, "Do I understand correctly what you said to me? Was it that . . . ?" Or, "I need to tell you that what you just said hurt my feelings." This gives your mate the chance to clear up a possible misunderstanding or to say, "I'm sorry."

3. *Seek godly counsel if you need it.* Often someone you trust can be objective about the situation and give good advice.

> The way of a fool is right in his own eyes,
> but he who listens to counsel is wise.
>
> Proverbs 12:15

4. *Resolve your own emotions.* If you are feeling angry or resentful, admit that to the Lord. Choose to forgive your mate. Make a decision to confront the situation from a perspective of humility. Do not blame or condemn. Own up to your part of the conflict and ask forgiveness. Allow an opportunity for your mate to do the same.

X. Explain Expectations to Each Other

Marriage partners are not mindreaders. If you have expectations of your mate, explain them and allow for open discussion. Your expectations may not be realistic or workable. Sometimes they are so colored by your past experience that you only *assume* they are realistic. My husband's mother was a server gift who waited on him hand and foot. Don assumed I would do that, too. But with server as my lowest gift, I preferred delegating tasks to him! Soon he realized I was not going to fulfill these particular expectations. We discussed it and came to agreement on what he could expect of me. It took some pressure off of our relationship.

Have you discussed your expectations of one another? Why not take some time to do so? Seek to understand why you have the expectations you do. What factors from your growing-up years have influenced what you expect in husband and wife roles? Find out if either of you has been trying to fulfill the other's expectations and getting frustrated in the process. This is a good time to develop your definitions of marital roles and responsibilities.

Y. Yearn to Be All You Can Be Together

God has a special plan for your life together with your spouse:

> "For I know the plans I have for you," declares the LORD, "plans to prosper you and not to harm you, plans to give you hope and a future."
>
> Jeremiah 29:11, NIV

> You made all the delicate, inner parts of my body, and knit them together in my mother's womb. Thank you for making me so wonderfully complex! It is amazing to think about. Your workmanship is marvelous—and how well I know it. You were there while I was being formed in utter seclusion! You saw me before I was born and scheduled each day of my life before I began to breathe. Every day was recorded in your Book!
>
> Psalm 139:13–16, TLB

Your highest purpose in life is to know God, discover the plans He has for you and cooperate with Him in fulfilling them. God's plans for you and your spouse individually coincide in many ways, and include His plans for you as a couple. As you yearn to be all He wants you to be and seek His guidance, He will be there for you, as He promised:

> Lean on, trust and be confident in the Lord with all your heart and mind, and do not rely on your own insight or understanding. In all your ways know, recognize and acknowledge Him, and He will direct and make straight and plain your paths.
>
> Proverbs 3:5–6

Z. Zero In on Christian Values

Our world is getting darker. Although the United States was established on Christian values, secularism now reigns. But in this darkness the light of the Lord shining through dedicated Christians glows brighter and brighter, because our value system contrasts sharply with that of unbelievers.

John announced Jesus as the light of the world. Peter explains that we have been "called . . . out of darkness into his wonderful light" (1 Peter 2:9, NIV). Paul warned the Ephesians about the darkness of the world in contrast to the light by which Christians are to live:

> For you were once darkness, but now you are light in the Lord. Live as children of light (for the fruit of the light consists in all goodness, righteousness and truth) and find out what pleases the Lord. Have nothing to do with the fruitless deeds of darkness, but rather expose them.
>
> Ephesians 5:8–11, NIV

Uphold and live by the Christian values in your daily lives. Many a life has been changed by observing the godly character of a Christian couple or family. Continue to do as Jesus exhorts you:

> "You are the light of the world. . . . Let your light shine before men, that they may see your good deeds and praise your Father in heaven."
>
> Matthew 5:14, 16, NIV

THE ABCs OF CHRISTIAN MARRIAGE

Affirm who you and your spouse are in Christ.

Build a foundation of love and trust.

Communicate openly and often.

Determine responsibility clearly.

Expect the best of each other.

Forgive frequently and completely.

Give generously and wholeheartedly.

Handle finances wisely.

Invest in quality time with each other.

Judge not.

Keep physically fit.

Love unconditionally.

Make your careers count.

Nuture a positive home atmosphere.

Open up your heart.

Pray with and for each other consistently.

Quote what God says about marriage.

Reach out to others.

Share your feelings honestly.

Thank each other.

Understand each other's God-given gifts.

Value each other intensely.

Work together to resolve conflicts.

Xplain expectations to each other.

Yearn to be all you can be together.

Zero in on Christian values.

Note: This is available on parchment-type paper suitable for framing in 9 x 12 inch size. See "Additional Material Available," page 349.

APPENDIX A

Thirteen-Week Study Guide

This study plan is designed to help you teach or discuss the material in this book. Organized as a thirteen-week study, it may be lengthened or shortened to fit any time frame. Assign the chapters and questions in advance of the discussion time.

First Week: Read Chapters 1–2

Chapter 1: A Bird's-Eye View of the God-Given Gifts

1. What nine gifts are mentioned in 1 Corinthians 12:7–10? Define each one.
2. What are the functions of the five gifts listed in Ephesians 4:11–13?
3. How do the seven gifts found in Romans 12:6–8 shape our personalities?
4. What is the difference between a classic gift and a combination gift?
5. When do we receive our motivational gifts? What is the evidence?
6. How should parents respond to a child's gifting? When can it be discovered?
7. How do your gifts influence your personality?
8. In what ways are different basic needs met by the seven motivational gifts?
9. How do the seven gifts relate to different parts of the body?
10. What is the difference between the speaking gifts and the serving gifts?
11. In what sense can we function in all seven areas of the motivational gifts?

Chapter 2: Yes, Men and Women Are Different, But . . .

12. What is involved in leaving a family to get married?
13. What are some important spiritual foundations in marriage?
14. Describe some basic differences between husbands and wives.
15. What differences in husband and wife roles are pointed out in Ephesians 5?

16. What statistical and physical differences in men and women can you describe?
17. How is intimacy to be more than just sexual?

Second Week: Read Chapters 3–4

Chapter 3: Test Yourself and Your Mate

1. Do the twenty characteristics part of the test.
2. Evaluate your scores along with your spouse's scores.
3. What have you learned about yourself? Your mate?
4. Now do the five negative scores for each gift.
5. In what areas do you need to improve?
6. What steps can you take to begin this process?

Chapter 4: Combination Gifts and Mates

7. Do you have a close secondary gift? How does it influence your primary gift?
8. Score yourself on the combination gift scales.
9. What have you learned about how your gifts are modified by each other?
10. Describe some ways you have seen these gifts in action in your life.
11. Describe how you have seen these gifts in action in your spouse's life.

Third Week: Read Chapters 5–6

Chapter 5: Your Three-Part Nature and the Gifts

1. Describe the relationship among your body, soul and spirit.
2. How is your soul three in nature? What is the function of each part?
3. Why do opposite gifts often face the greatest challenges being married to each other?
4. In what ways are gifts in the "triangular arrangement" still quite opposite?
5. Why is it easiest to relate to and understand the gifts "next door"?
6. How is the giver gift unique?
7. Fill in the diagrams on page 50. What does this show about you and your mate?

Chapter 6: Introduction to the Seven Spouses

8. What do you think were Bob's main problems?
9. Why do you think Alice was so hurt by Bob's actions?
10. Describe the A, B and C categories and how they differ.

Fourth Week: Read Chapter 7

Chapter 7: Living with a Perceiver Spouse

1. Why was it essential for Amy to become an intercessor?
2. Describe the five major problem areas of the perceiver spouse.
3. How do you think these problems can affect a marriage negatively?
4. As you read through the twenty categories of gifts, what are the strengths you see in the perceiver spouse?
5. What are the weaknesses you see in the perceiver spouse?
6. What advice would you give to a perceiver son who is about to marry?
7. What advice would you give to a perceiver daughter who is about to marry?
8. What counsel would you give to a husband seeking to understand his perceiver wife?

9. What counsel would you give to a wife seeking to understand her perceiver husband?

Fifth Week: Read Chapter 8

Chapter 8: Living with a Server Spouse

1. Why is it important that server spouses feel appreciated?
2. Describe the five major problem areas of the server spouse.
3. How do you think these problems can affect a marriage negatively?
4. As you read through the twenty categories of gifts, what are the strengths you see in the server spouse?
5. What are the weaknesses you see in the server spouse?
6. What advice would you give to a server son who is about to marry?
7. What advice would you give to a server daughter who is about to marry?
8. What counsel would you give to a husband seeking to understand his server wife?
9. What counsel would you give to a wife seeking to understand her server husband?

Sixth Week: Read Chapter 9

Chapter 9: Living with a Teacher Spouse

1. What suggestions would you give Von to help him learn to be a bit more romantic?
2. Describe the five major problem areas of the teacher spouse.
3. How do you think these problems can affect a marriage negatively?
4. As you read through the twenty categories of gifts, what are the strengths you see in the teacher spouse?
5. What are the weaknesses you see in the teacher spouse?
6. What advice would you give to a teacher son who is about to marry?
7. What advice would you give to a teacher daughter who is about to marry?
8. What counsel would you give to a husband seeking to understand his teacher wife?
9. What counsel would you give to a wife seeking to understand her teacher husband?

Seventh Week: Read Chapter 10

Chapter 10: Living with an Exhorter Spouse

1. List some ways to express love to a spouse. Indicate which gifts would likely express love in the ways you have listed.
2. Describe the five major problem areas of the exhorter spouse.
3. How do you think these problems can affect a marriage negatively?
4. As you read through the twenty categories of gifts, what are the strengths you see in the exhorter spouse?
5. What are the weaknesses you see in the exhorter spouse?
6. What advice would you give to an exhorter son who is about to marry?
7. What advice would you give to an exhorter daughter who is about to marry?
8. What counsel would you give to a husband seeking to understand his exhorter wife?
9. What counsel would you give to a wife seeking to understand her exhorter husband?

Eighth Week: Read Chapter 11

Chapter 11: Living with a Giver Spouse

1. What ground rules would you suggest to Jean and Leonard about his giving items away?
2. Describe the five major problem areas of the giver spouse.
3. How do you think these problems can affect a marriage negatively?
4. As you read through the twenty categories of gifts, what are the strengths you see in the giver spouse?
5. What are the weaknesses you see in the giver spouse?
6. What advice would you give to a giver son who is about to marry?
7. What advice would you give to a giver daughter who is about to marry?
8. What counsel would you give to a husband seeking to understand his giver wife?
9. What counsel would you give to a wife seeking to understand her giver husband?

Ninth Week: Read Chapter 12

Chapter 12: Living with an Administrator Spouse

1. Since administrators love to lead, how would you suggest they handle leadership when married to each of the other six gifts?
2. Describe the five major problem areas of the administrator spouse.
3. How do you think these problems can affect a marriage negatively?
4. As you read through the twenty categories of gifts, what are the strengths you see in the administrator spouse?
5. What are the weaknesses you see in the administrator spouse?
6. What advice would you give to an administrator son who is about to marry?
7. What advice would you give to an administrator daughter who is about to marry?
8. What counsel would you give to a husband seeking to understand his administrator wife?
9. What counsel would you give to a wife seeking to understand her administrator husband?

Tenth Week: Read Chapter 13

Chapter 13: Living with a Compassion Spouse

1. What counsel would you give Chuck and Sue on how to become better decision-makers?
2. Describe the five major problem areas of the compassion spouse.
3. How do you think these problems can affect a marriage negatively?
4. As you read through the twenty categories of gifts, what are the strengths you see in the compassion spouse?
5. What are the weaknesses you see in the compassion spouse?
6. What advice would you give to a compassion son who is about to marry?
7. What advice would you give to a compassion daughter who is about to marry?
8. What counsel would you give to a husband seeking to understand his compassion wife?
9. What counsel would you give to a wife seeking to understand her compassion husband?

Eleventh Week: Read Chapter 14

Chapter 14: Dealing with Conflict

1. Where are some possible problem areas when you are married to the same gift?
2. Why is it more likely that people marry a somewhat opposite gift?
3. What does it mean to have a polluted gift?
4. What are some of the negative characteristics of each of the seven gifts?
5. Fill out the *Problems and Possible Solutions* chart on page 302.
6. Discuss some possible steps of action you can take right away.
7. What special advantages do you and your spouse have because of your gifts?
8. Share some specific ways your spouse is a blessing to you.

Twelfth Week: Read Chapter 15

Chapter 15: Surveying Your Own Situation

1. Fill out the marriage survey. Have your mate do it, too.
2. Go over your scores and compare them to your spouse's scores.
3. Circle or highlight areas that indicate strong differences that cause or could cause problems in your relationship.
4. Review one category at a time with your mate. (This may be a long-term project. Don't rush through this wonderful opportunity to learn more about each other. Take time to pray together about specific items in each category.)
5. Talk over your major and minor problems in section A. Evaluate why these problems exist. Discuss ways you can overcome them.
6. Look at the traits and tendencies you have both scored in section B. Talk over possible improvements that could enhance your relationship.
7. Discuss your feelings, needs, views and beliefs indicated in section C. Are there any areas of misunderstanding? Are there things you see that you did not know about your spouse? Are there goals you can set to improve your situation?

Thirteenth Week: Read Chapter 16

Chapter 16: The ABCs of Christian Marriage

1. List some of the reasons you married your spouse.
2. Evaluate your present communication skills.
3. How do you deal with forgiveness?
4. What are your financial needs and goals?
5. How can you spend more quality time together?
6. Define your fitness status and propose a plan, if needed.
7. How can you improve your prayer times, together and individually?
8. How well are you expressing appreciation to each other?
9. How can you let your light shine?

APPENDIX B

Additional Material Available

To assist you in testing yourself, your children or others, or in presenting the material in this or other books by Don and Katie Fortune in a teaching or sharing situation, the authors make the following items available:

1. *Adult Questionnaire Scoring Set* (16 pp.). This includes the seven adult testing sheets from *Discover Your God-Given Gifts*, along with a profile sheet for final scoring. Tie-breakers (enabling a person to determine which gift is stronger when scores are close or the same) are also included.

2. *Youth Questionnaire Scoring Set* (16 pp.). Designed for teenagers (grades 7–12) and college-age young adults, this set is based on the material in chapter 6 of *Discover Your Children's Gifts*. It includes the seven scoring sheets for teens, a profile sheet and tie-breakers.

3. *Junior Children's Questionnaire Scoring Set* (16 pp.). Designed for grade-schoolers (grades 4–6), this test should be administered by a parent, teacher or other adult. It is based on the material in chapter 5 of *Discover Your Children's Gifts*. Tie-breakers included.

4. *Primary Children's Questionnaire Scoring Set* (16 pp.). Designed to be completed by parents of primaries (grades 1–3), this testing set is based on material in chapter 4 of *Discover Your Children's Gifts*. Tie-breakers included.

5. *Children's Survey Testing Sheets: Preschool* (16 pp.). This packet includes three sets of scoring sheets from the material in chapter 3 of *Discover Your Children's Gifts*. Use these to help determine the gifts of children from toddler through kindergarten age. The tests can also help determine the gifts of older children and help adults clarify their own scores by comparing the survey characteristics with those from their own childhood.

6. *Objective Questionnaire Testing Set* (16 pp.). Designed to be used for objective (not

teaching) testing situations. The adult questionnaire is arranged randomly so a person taking the test cannot tell how the gifts relate to each characteristic. Tie-breakers, scoring key and decoder sheet included.

7. *Ministry Discovery Set* (16 pp.). This set contains expanded material from chapter 31 of *Discover Your God-Given Gifts* and a listing of ministries most fulfilling for persons with each gift. Selected material from chapter 30, "Living Your Gift," helps the user put gifts into practical action.

8. *Occupational Success Testing Set* (16 pp.). This set contains information from chapter 32, "Careers and Jobs," of *Discover Your God-Given Gifts*, along with a detailed analysis of the 180 most common careers and jobs, showing the degree to which each gift is likely to be successful. Also included is an evaluation of built-in traits that bring joy and satisfaction to persons with each gift.

9. *Secular Objective Questionnaire Testing Set* (16 pp.). This test is arranged randomly and designed to be used in situations where secular adult objective testing is desired. Christian terms and interests have been replaced by generic ones. Tie-breakers, scoring key and decoder sheet included.

10. *Children's Gifts Teaching Tape Set* (6 cassettes). Nine hours of seminar teaching on the book *Discover Your Children's Gifts*, recorded on six 90-minute cassette tapes and packaged in an attractive case. By following the teaching outline in the back of the book, the tapes can be used for teaching others. The following syllabus is recommended for use with the tapes.

11. *Children's Gifts Seminar Syllabus* (48 pp.). This workbook is designed for use in seminars or with the seminar teaching tapes, and covers the subjects discussed in *Discover Your Children's Gifts*. Many charts and practical application ideas included.

12. *Forms & Charts Packet* (32 pp.). This includes enough forms and charts from Part III, "Practical Insights," in *Discover Your Children's Gifts* to keep records for a family of four or five children. In 8 1/2" x 11" size it constitutes a permanent family record, but individual forms or charts can be removed. (It does *not* contain the motivational gifts testing sets.)

13. *The ABCs of Christian Parenting* (parchment). This inspirational reminder, taken from *Discover Your Children's Gifts*, makes a thoughtful gift for new parents or anyone with children. It is available on 9" x 12" parchment-type paper suitable for framing.

14. *Variety Packet, Children* (13 items). This packet contains one each of the above items: all testing and discovery sets, syllabus, tapes, a parchment and the Forms & Charts Packet—everything needed to teach the material from *Discover Your Children's Gifts*.

15. *Discover Your God-Given Gifts* (book, 276 pp.). Here is how to discover the gifts God has built into every person according to Romans 12:6–8. This book, a comprehensive study complete with study guide, is fun as well as revealing. A continuing bestseller, it is used by pastors and educators to help people understand the motivating forces of their lives and get involved in vital ministry.

16. *Motivational Gifts Seminar Tape Set* (6 tapes). This set includes nine hours of seminar teaching on motivational gifts based on the book *Discover Your God-Given Gifts*, recorded on six 90-minute cassette tapes and packaged in an attractive case. The following syllabus is recommended for use with the tapes.

17. *Motivational Gifts Seminar Syllabus* (48 pp.). This attractive workbook is designed for use in motivational gifts seminars or with the seminar teaching tapes above, and

covers the material and subjects in *Discover Your God-Given Gifts.* Testing sheets and tie-breakers for adults included, as well as biblical examples and practical application material.

18. *Video Teaching Tape Sets* (two tapes per set). Each of these two sets contains material from the nationally broadcast Canadian TV program *It's a New Day*, featuring Don and Katie Fortune. Each of the segments, in an interview format, is about 45 minutes long but can be shown in shorter units. Each is informal and lively, including introductory and life-related material, and can be used in teaching a smaller group.

The first set contains five segments on the motivational gifts, covering the adult testing material for all seven gifts from *Discover Your God-Given Gifts.* The second set contains four segments on the book *Discover Your Children's Gifts,* covering the characteristics for all seven types of gifted children. To order specify *Adult Gifts* or *Children's Gifts* teaching videos.

19. *Foreign Language Adult Questionnaire Scoring Sets* (8 pp. each). The adult testing sets have been translated so far into Danish, Finnish, French, German, Indonesian, Japanese, Korean, Polish, Portuguese, Norwegian, Russian, Spanish and Swedish. More translations are in process. Inquire about special permissions for missionaries and those teaching in foreign countries. To order specify the language needed.

20. *Free Information Packet #1.* Information about the procedure for having the authors present a motivational gifts seminar (or other subject) for a group, church, retreat or conference.

21. *Free Information Packet #2.* Information about the authors' books, tapes and materials on various subjects.

22. *Variety Packet, Adult* (11 items). This packet contains one each of the above items 1–9 and 16–17: testing material, syllabus, tapes and everything needed to teach the material from the book *Discover Your God-Given Gifts.*

23. *Discover Your Children's Gifts* (book, 296 pp.). Here is how to discover the gifts God has built into every child according to Romans 12:6–8. This book, a comprehensive study complete with study guide, is enlightening and practical. It is a valuable tool for parents, grandparents, youth workers, teachers, daycare providers, Sunday school teachers, Christian education leaders and anyone involved with children or youth of any age. The book is being used by parents, pastors and educators around the world.

24. *Discover Your Spouse's Gifts* (book, 352 pp.). Here is how the discovery of the motivational gifts of Romans 12:6–8 can enhance a marriage relationship. Based on an extensive marital survey conducted by the Fortunes, the book gives valuable information on how the gifts affect marriage, how to identify problems that stem from not knowing about the motivational gifts and how to overcome those problems and release a couple into the freedom and joy of a God-given, God-gifted marriage.

25. *Survey Your Marriage* (16 pp.). Based on an extensive marriage survey conducted by the Fortunes, this personal copy of the survey will enable you and your spouse to pinpoint the differences you have and the problem areas in your marriage. It will give you insight and understanding that will greatly enhance your marital relationship. It is also an excellent tool for couples' groups or classes and in premarital or marital counseling. The survey is based on the twenty most common categories of problems in marriage.

26. *Marriage Seminar Tape Set* (6 tapes). Nine hours of seminar teaching on the

book *Discover Your Spouse's Gifts*, recorded on six 90-minute cassette tapes and packaged in an attractive case. By following the teaching outline in the back of the book, the tapes can be used for teaching others. The following syllabus is recommended for use with the tapes.

27. *Marriage Seminar Syllabus* (48 pp.). This attractive workbook is designed for use in marriage seminars or with the seminar teaching tapes above, and covers the material and subjects of the book *Discover Your Spouse's Gifts*. Dual motivational gift testing sheets for couples are included, as well as a personal copy of the marriage survey and practical application material. Ideal for teaching couples who want to make their marriages better.

28. *The ABCs of Christian Marriage* (parchment). This inspirational reminder, taken from *Discover Your Spouse's Gifts*, makes a thoughtful gift for engaged couples, newlyweds or any Christian couple. It is available on 9″ x 12″ parchment-type paper suitable for framing.

29. *Dealing with Anger* (tape and book). Katie Fortune shares a life-changing teaching based on Matthew 5:21–26 on how to get free from the negative effects of anger in the heart. Couples and individuals will discover the scriptural key to dealing with anger. Christian counselors will have a tool for helping people with the number-one problem: buried anger.

For orders or a free price list write:

Don and Katie Fortune
Heart to Heart International Ministries
P.O. Box 101
Kingston, WA 98346
For phone inquiries or orders call
(360) 297-8878